RENEWALS 691-4574

DATE DUE

DEC 16			
MAY 18			
NOV 28			
JUL 24			
ILL 1327056 TEX		NOV 11 1995	
NO RENEWALS			
MAR 15			
AUG 5			

Demco, Inc. 38-293

THIRD EDITION

INTERNATIONAL FINANCIAL MANAGEMENT

Rita M. Rodriguez

Director
Export-Import Bank of the United States

Professor of Finance
University of Illinois at Chicago

E. Eugene Carter

Professor and Head
Department of Finance
University of Illinois at Chicago

PRENTICE-HALL, INC., Englewood Cliffs, New Jersey 07632

Library of Congress Cataloging in Publication Data

Rodriguez, Rita M., (date)
    International financial management.

    Includes bibliographies and index.
    1. International finance.   2. International business
enterprises—Finance. I. Carter, E. Eugene. II. Title.
HG3881.R584   1984   658.1'5   83-27073
ISBN 0-13-472969-2

Editorial/production supervision
 and interior design by Margaret Rizzi
Cover design by Wanda Lubelska Design
Manufacturing buyer: Ed O'Dougherty

Printed in the United States of America

10 9 8 7 6 5 4 3 2 1

ISBN   0-13-472969-2

Prentice-Hall International, Inc., *London*
Prentice-Hall of Australia Pty. Limited, *Sydney*
Editora Prentice-Hall do Brasil, Ltda., *Rio de Janeiro*
Prentice-Hall Canada Inc., *Toronto*
Prentice-Hall of India Private Limited, *New Delhi*
Prentice-Hall of Japan, Inc., *Tokyo*
Prentice-Hall of Southeast Asia Pte. Ltd., *Singapore*
Whitehall Books Limited, *Wellington, New Zealand*

To

Jerry and Kay Alajajian

*with the respect and affection
of their granddaughter's parents*

Contents

3   International Monetary Agreements
          and Institutions   *32*

4   Money and Banking in International
          Markets   *61*

5   The Foreign Exchange Market:
          Nature and Relation to the Money
          Market   *88*

14 The Acceptance Criteria for
International Projects   *480*

15 Risk Evaluation in Foreign
Investments   *505*

16 Portfolio Considerations in the
Multinational Capital Budgeting
Process   *566*

Preface

THIS THIRD EDITION of our textbook reflects revisions in line with our own learning over these intervening years. That learning is a function of the colleagues we have known, the students we have faced, and the developments in the field, both economically and academically. Our own tastes as well as academic, industrial, financial and governmental experiences are inevitably reflected here. Thus, we offer materials for people with different tastes, but do assert that this book reflects the balance of items we recommend for a course in international finance within a business school.

The questions and bibliographies accompanying particular chapters are moderately revised for this edition, but have been updated to reflect recent events and publications. The cases are entirely new for this edition, except for the revised exercise known as Chaolandia and the condensed version of the Green Valley Corporation. The exercises at the end of some chapters have been revised. In addition, exercises on a foreign exchange trader's activities and the behavior of an international treasurer are new for this edition. The materials on international taxation are now placed as an extensive appendix to the introductory chapter on the determination of cash flows in international capital budgeting (chapter 13), since we find most instructors cover the tax material at this point. The appendix includes relevant revisions from recent Federal tax changes through 1983. We have retained the extensive risk analysis simulation of Freeport Minerals' Australian venture, although the case itself has been deleted.

In terms of balance, this edition has a reduced emphasis upon the balance of payments and international capital markets, and an expanded discussion of treasury management in the multinational firm. We have responded to market requests by abbreviating the total length of the book. We have integrated Eurocurrency markets, foreign exchange markets, and balance of payments materials within many chapters much more extensively than before.

The introductory chapter presents an outline for the students about this text and offers some historical information about foreign investment by the United States over the last several decades. We also raise some of the broader moral and political issues surrounding the multinational corporation.

In Part One, we focus on the international financial environment. We briefly survey the balance of payments analysis and information about international monetary agreements. Throughout this section, as later, we consider these elements not from their significant economic nature to society nor their historical importance, but from the impact which can be felt upon the corporate officer dealing in an environment heavily influenced by national balance of payments considerations and the various adjustment mechanisms. Similarly, the introduction to the international banking activities of both public and private agencies in chapter 4 continues this perspective. These three chapters lead directly to two chapters on the foreign exchange and money markets. Within chapters 5 and 6, we discuss the mechanics of trading activities in these markets, as well as theories about the determination of spot and forward market relationships, and the movements of spot exchange rates over time. We stress various explanations for market failure which are required for the nonequilibrium assumptions to hold only after developing the equilibrium relationships.

Part Two turns much more sharply to the typical concerns of officers involved in the international operations of a corporation. Standard cash management considerations and activities are discussed in chapter 7, followed by trade financing instrument and analysis discussions in chapter 8. Long- and short-term financing options available in domestic and Euromarkets are discussed in chapter 9. Chapters 10 and 11 summarize external and internal accounting issues; chapter 10 concerns measurements of exposure for reporting purposes and internal management, while chapter 11 looks at the evaluation and control procedures for a foreign operation facing differential inflation and currency receipts compared to the parent. Finally, chapter 12 includes an analysis of how a treasurer might evaluate covering activities with multiple divisions and a centralized financial management.

Part Three turns to the analysis of foreign investment analysis. Chapter 13 reviews the determination of relevant cash flows including taxation, chapter 14 considers the cost of capital, and chapter 15 summarizes measures of risk in the international setting with an extended example. Chapter 16 offers frameworks for coping with intertemporal portfolio budgeting in the multinational firm, with summary appendices addressing both anti-trust and international security portfolio issues. Finally, chapter 17 reviews salient material from the fields of organization design and corporate strategy.

The text is ideally designed for upper-level undergraduates or MBA/MS students who have completed introductory courses in finance and economics. There are exercises, questions, and cases at the end of most chapters, which can be used by the instructor to emphasize different points. Some instructors will want to include all the cases in their courses, perhaps using the chapters only for casual or background reading. Given the detail with which some of these cases may be handled, these cases and exercises can require at least 20 class sessions. Additional cases could be used in the remaining classes in a typical 30-class, one-semester course. Other instructors will prefer to emphasize the text and exercises supplemented by articles. The detail of these chapters and exercises can easily support 20 or more classes. Supplementary articles and notes on various capital markets and other items could complete the one-semester course.

Instructors with a one-quarter course also could use this text, assuming they have only 20 or 25 classes. If all the topics are to be covered, we suggest having students read chapters 2 and 3 and the summary to chapter 4, with the instructor lecturing on various proposals regarding the balance of payments once the students understand the background materials. A single class on the balance of payments for students who are not familiar with the subject might involve reading chapter 2 and the summaries to chapters 3 and 4. The Euromarket materials in chapter 4 and chapters 5 and 6 could be read in total. Depending on the instructor's tastes, two to four of the basic chapters (7–10) in Part Two could be used. The more involved framework offered for controlling the multinational firm in an inflationary environment and for handling exposure to exchange risk presented in chapters 11 and 12 may be deleted or left for optional reading. Chapters 13 and 14 outline the basics of international capital budgeting. The additional material from other disciplines and security/portfolio models in chapters 15, 16, and 17 could be deleted or reviewed in a lecture. Four or five of the simpler cases and the exercises could round out the one-quarter course.

Our approach is to use a simple lecture or case to highlight a problem, then have a chapter and a lecture to suggest various ways of looking at the problem (the theory), and conclude with the application of the theory to the complex real situation presented by another case. Accordingly, the materials in this book can more than fill a one-semester course of 30 or 35 classes. The selection of materials will be at the judgment of the instructor, consistent with the instructor's background and interests, the previous exposure of the students, and their particular needs in the course.

If students have a strong background in international economics, chapters 2 through 4 and chapter 6 can be skipped. For instructors who particularly want to emphasize this topic, additional readings and texts may be assigned with this material used only as background. Similarly, instructors who are not interested in the particular elements of trade credit financing will have their students skip the latter part of chapter 8, whereas other instructors will want to supplement this material with one of the bank booklets on international financial instruments. Students who have been exposed to international business courses will not need to read the last half of chapter 1, which brings in various historical aspects of foreign investment; other instructors will supplement this chapter with readings from the international business area. In some classes, more time can be spent on the various international security portfolio studies and the capital asset pricing model, with the implications of these topics for corporate diversification. With other groups, chapter 6 can be deleted if this topic is not of interest or if the small amount of algebra included here is beyond the level of the students. Finally, some instructors will not find the institutional material on the Euromarkets contained in chapters 4 and 9 of relevance or interest to their students.

Thus, the segmentation of the text in various parts and the inclusion of cases, questions, and exercises provide a range of basic materials. In most courses, this material will provide sufficient coverage for a semester. For those instructors who wish further supplemental materials, the three parts of the text are somewhat self-contained, permitting use of the text as a basic book supplemented by other readings. Our desire has been to present a text that has a sufficient amount of basic material from which many instructors can select topics for their international corporate finance courses.

This textbook reflects our biases and prejudices toward the blending of various disciplines under the umbrella of an international corporate finance framework, and toward the mix of theory, practice, and institutional description. We have benefited from the suggestions on portions of the text from many individuals. Gunter Dufey (University of Michigan), Hai Hong (University of Singapore), and Warren Law (Harvard Business School) commented on the entire first edition manuscript in detail with many useful and insightful suggestions. We thank them on behalf of the readers.

Our appreciation also to Tamir Agmon (Tel Aviv University); Mark Eaker and Edward M. Graham (University of North Carolina); Ian Giddy (Columbia University); Christine Hekman (Duke University); Charles Kindleberger, Donald Lessard, Franco Modigliani, James Paddock, and Richard Robinson (Massachusetts Institute of Technology); Stephen J. Kobrin (New York University); Jon Ingersoll (Yale University); Michael McIntyre (Wayne State University); David A. Ricks (Ohio State University); Rostislov Romanoff (Northern Trust); Henry Schloss (University of Southern California); N. Jackendoff (Temple University); Oscar Holzmann (University of South Carolina); Lemma Senbet (University of Wisconsin-Madison); Dennis Logue (Dartmouth); D.M. Pattille (Northeastern University); L. William Murray (University of San Francisco); Michael Rice (Wake Forest University); and Robert Stobaugh, Raymond Vernon, and William White (Harvard Business School) for reacting to various ideas and chapters in the first and second editions.

All of the cases were authored by Rita M. Rodriguez, and we gratefully acknowledge the assistance or co-authorship of Linda Davis and Ken Adamitis. We are also grateful for the outstanding contribution of our first edition editor, Paul McKenney, who endured the convoluted prose emerging from an immigrant's and a technocrat's collaboration. His efforts sharply improved the text.

Our third edition production editor, Margaret Rizzi, carefully handled mail drops at seven locations in three states, and we thank her for her patience.

We owe a special debt to two Finance editors at Prentice-Hall. Susan Anderson took the risk on the field and our book, signing this book in 1973 while she was still a novice. David Hildebrand carefully handled the second and third editions. Both are talented individuals who have left publishing to pursue other interests, and the field is less enjoyable with their departure.

Any deficiencies in style or substance are the responsibility of the authors.

1

Introduction

DURING RECENT YEARS, the corporate financial manager has become increasingly concerned with the changing international scene. Fluctuating foreign exchange rates, balance of payments difficulties, the growth of "petrodollars," and the debt problems of developing countries have come to be important issues for all U.S. and foreign corporations with international operations. To confront these problems with some hope for resolution requires a knowledge of both the macroeconomic environment in which the firm operates (balance of payments, government policies, credit availability) and the microeconomic environment which relates to the specific decisions that the manager will face (how the firm manages its exposure to foreign exchange risk, how it analyzes its capital budgeting problem, how it accommodates the demands for funds from subsidiaries in different countries). Before we embark on the discussion of specific financial problems, however, it may be useful to introduce briefly the business institution that houses the international decision-makers: the multinational company.

THE MULTINATIONAL FIRM

For many critics, the multinational firm is a global octopus, which at best is spreading knowledge and technological pollution around the world while swallowing assets everywhere and evading all national attempts to control it. Multinationals have been charged with subverting governments (with or without another government's help), adding to the instability of the international financial markets by switching funds between currencies, avoiding taxes everywhere by the use of tax havens, and encouraging apartheid in South Africa and the continuation of low-wage unskilled labor forces in Colombia, among other sins.

In their own defense, the multinationals emphasize their rationalization of resources and the spread of technology. Deemphasizing the impact of their economic power, they also argue that in seeking profits they are doing good in the societies in which they operate by contributing much-needed capital and other resources of the industrialized world to less developed areas. Thus, they are the chronological reverse of many Hawaiian missionaries, whose families today have major fortunes based on pineapple and other commodities. As has often been observed, the missionaries came to do good and did right well.

While there are many definitions of the *multinational firm,* for the purposes of this text the term will mean a company with substantial operations (usually 30% or more of its total activity) carried on outside its own national borders. These activities may be trading or manufacturing. There may be many separate corporations outside the national borders, with the parent functioning as an operating or holding company. Whatever the particular corporate form, the important fact is that the firm must make decisions about project returns which have a sizable impact on the company and are in more than one currency. A $500,000,000 business that occasionally sells a few million dollars worth of goods to a Dutch manufacturer will probably not care much about currency rates. The sale is infrequent; its size is relatively small; and the guilder is a known, freely traded currency. On the other hand, a $10,000,000 firm that has three plants in three different nations and whose business represents sales from all over the globe (such as a small specialty goods manufacturer) will be very interested in currency rates, barriers to trade, and fund repatriation.

The philosophy of business of international firms is a separate study, often called *international business policy,* and is not the subject of this text. Similarly, the reform of the international monetary system and the analysis of why nations trade belong in a course in international economics. However, the impact of judgments in these two areas will affect the field of international corporate finance. Multinationals are often entangled in the web of doing nothing (which supports the status quo) and acting for good or ill (which supports charges of interference in the domestic affairs of one or more nations). Multinationals usually have legal and financial talent beyond the level of the department of inland revenue in a small nation of limited resources. On the other hand, the small nation often has what the multinational wants (a market or a natural resource) and is in a position to demand a suitable price for access to that desired feature. Some of these relationships, and the behavior of various parties involved in these international financial decisions, are explored in this text.

In making public pronouncements, many economists forget that the firm operates within society and not just within an industrial sector. As the noted economist Arthur Okun observed, economists are the only people who have to be reminded that not everything should have a price. Societies set the ground rules for firm behavior. An important issue is whether the markets in which a firm operates are sufficiently competitive for the benefits of firm rivalry to create an efficient allocation of resources, the key benefit of the market economy. A second issue is whether the resulting allocation of resources is desired. The firm may allocate assets efficiently, but is the final distribution equitable? There is nothing sacrosanct about free enterprise per se, nor is it enshrined in the U.S. Constitution, as some social critics frequently remind business executives.

However, one should also bear in mind that the various proposals to reform corporations on the international scene often come from social critics who ignore the benefits of resource allocation. The evils of pollution and materialism may seem less threatening when a booming economy slides into recession; unlimited personal freedom can appear less important if one is out of a job. The median per capita income on Earth is less than $50 per year. Even allowing for comparability of purchasing power and standards, government security systems (political and social), a rural economy for many people, and the like, a conservative doubling of the figure does not give one room for comfort. Many Americans are amazed to learn that *only* 20% of U.S. families have an after-tax income of more than $35,000. Most governments cannot be so oblivious to statistics such as these.

An even narrower view than that of the economists and the social critics comes in the self-serving nonsense sometimes presented by the multinationals themselves. Anxious to assuage public opinion in a particular nation so as to move ahead with the task of making XYZ International more powerful and more profitable, the firm puts forth rhetoric which frequently is based on little knowledge of the actions of various subsidiaries. Limits on information from the field and the whole problem of decentralization mean that headquarters officials rarely know details of activities in other lands and often are only vaguely aware of their lack of knowledge. Further, this ignorance may be deliberate, thus creating the possibility of deniability, which has counterparts in political and military leadership. By design, the top managers can deny they knew anything about the nasty activities of underlings, while they continue to make subordinates aware that it is their job to see that "things are taken care of." This supervisory problem is merely an international extension of the common issues of accounting and managerial control, with the difficulties compounded by distance, culture, and language-related complexities.

This text is primarily concerned with international corporate finance; therefore, many of the above issues will be left to the reader's appraisal of contemporary socioeconomic and political trends and to his or her particular value system. Although most of our examples deal with the position of the U.S. multinational, the issues and problems that we address apply to all multinationals.

A HISTORY OF AGGREGATE
U.S. FOREIGN DIRECT INVESTMENT

Although the data are notoriously bad because of incomplete reporting and odd translation procedures, a tabulation of U.S. foreign direct investment by region and by industry is shown in Exhibits 1.1 and 1.2. In the early part of the century investment was in mining ventures, and most investment was in the Western Hemisphere. More than one-third of the investment was in Mexico, Cuba, and the West Indies, and one-fourth of the investment was associated with utility, agricultural, and railroad projects.

After World War I there was a discernible movement toward manufacturing with aggregate foreign investment in manufacturing rising to 24% of the total by 1929. Together with growth in petroleum and utility projects, the percentage loss was absorbed by railroads and mining ventures. Note that these declines are relative, except for a few nationalizations, reflecting fewer new investments in mining and railroads. Mexico's early relative importance diminished and was offset by greater investments in Central and South America.

During the Great Depression the book value of foreign investments declined from $7.6 billion to $7 billion, reflecting write-offs of assets. In addition, Mexico nationalized all U.S. petroleum investments in 1938. Interestingly enough, the United States was seen as a relatively desirable market in this period, for there was a net investment inflow each year from 1933 to 1939, probably stimulated by economic turmoil and increased probabilities of war in Europe.

In the two decades from 1950 to 1970 there was a 10½% compounded growth in foreign investment in the first half and 9½% in the last half, exceedingly high figures considering the relatively large base. Investment moved sharply to manufacturing and petroleum mining, which together accounted for 69% of all direct investment by 1970.

EXHIBIT 1.1 Sector Distribution of U.S. Foreign Direct Investment, 1914–1970

	Total (in billions)[a]	Manufacturing	Petroleum	Sales	Mining	Utilities	Other
1914	$ 2.7	18%	13%	6%	27%	5%	13% agriculture, 9% railroads, 9% other
1919	3.9	20	15	6	22	4	15% agriculture, 8% railroads, 10% other
1929	7.6	24	17	5	16	13	13% agriculture, 4% railroads, 8% other
1940	7.0	27	19	7	11	23	6% agriculture, 7% other
1950	11.8	32	29	7	9	12	11% other
1960	31.8	35	34	8	9	8	6% other
1970	78.2	41	28	8	8	4	11% other

[a]All figures are book values as of date indicated.

SOURCE: Calculations based on Mira Wilkins, *The Maturing of Multinational Enterprise*, Harvard University Press, 1974, various tables; Cleona Lewis assisted by Karl T. Schlotterbeck, *America's Stake in International Investments*, The Brookings Institution, 1938; U.S. Department of Commerce, *Survey of Current Business*; and other publications, various issues.

EXHIBIT 1.2   Geographic Distribution of U.S. Foreign Direct Investment, 1914–1970[a]

	Europe	Canada	Mexico	Cuba and West Indies	Central and South America	Asia
Total						
1914	22%	23%	22%	11%	16%	5%
1919	18	21	17	15	20	5
1929	18	22	9	14	26	6
1940	20	30	5	10	25	6
1946	14	35		43		7
Manufacturing						
1950	24	50		20		2
1960	34	44		14		3
1970	42	31		14		5

[a]All figures are based on book values as of date indicated.

SOURCE: Calculations based on Mira Wilkins, *The Maturing of Multinational Enterprise*, Harvard University Press, 1974, various tables; Cleona Lewis assisted by Karl T. Schlotterbeck, *America's Stake in International Investments*, The Brookings Institution, 1938; U. S. Department of Commerce, *Survey of Current Business;* and other publications, various issues.

Utilities and mining diminished in importance, and certainly by the late 1970s petroleum had also declined because of Middle East nationalization. Data for manufacturing firms show that Europe became the dominant spot for U.S. investors, reflecting the booming markets after World War II, coupled with a desire of U.S. firms to take advantage of lower tariffs among European Economic Community (EEC) countries for internally manufactured goods after the Common Market emerged.

AN OVERVIEW OF THE TEXT

The following chapters are divided into three major parts. Part One provides a basic understanding of the forces that affect the relative values of currencies in international markets. This section of the text largely corresponds to the information traditionally related in a course on international monetary economics. We will approach this important material from the point of view of the participants in the international markets who have to take the world system as given. Chapter 2 begins with the mechanics of the foremost reporting tool used to assess the international situation of a country—the balance of payments. In Chapter 3, the situation of a given country and the insights derived from the previous chapter are placed within the context of the international monetary system and domestic economic priorities. Chapter 4 discusses the forces that shape rates in the international markets as well as in some specific national markets, emphasizing the Eurocurrency and the international bond markets. Chapter 5 focuses directly on the foreign exchange market. It analyzes how price relationships are established in this market and discusses in detail the behavior of the major actor in the foreign exchange market—the foreign exchange trader. Chapter 6 uses both equilibrium and nonequilibrium approaches to confront the economic forces that lie behind the figures reported in the balance of payments and that affect the international purchasing power of a currency. The objective of these five chapters is not to demonstrate how to forecast foreign exchange rates, but to build a framework for analyzing the forces that produce changes in foreign exchange rates.

Part Two discusses the major problems encountered by the firm in financing large international operations. International cash management involving the money market and the forward exchange market are reviewed in Chapter 7. Their mutual relationships are emphasized in studying the financing alternatives open to the merchandise trader and the manager with business operations in foreign countries. Chapter 8 looks at the problems of financing international trade. Chapters 9 and 10 study the cost of financing foreign operations and the management of the foreign exchange position of the company. Chapter 11 analyzes the impact of inflation and exchange fluctuations on operations and discusses how to measure these effects for management control purposes. An appendix to that chapter reviews accounting practices for different countries and methods to report the impact of inflation. Chapter 12 consolidates the elements developed in the previous five chapters with traditional financial theory on cost of funds and presents an integrated approach to the decision of how to finance the operations of a firm that functions across several national boundaries.

Part Three covers the issues associated with capital budgeting. Chapter 13 suggests the form of analysis for a single project and discusses the types of international project risk. An appendix to the chapter outlines the basic characteristics of international corporate taxation. Chapter 14 introduces the problems of selecting the relevant acceptance criteria for projects. Chapter 15 reviews various theoretical and practical approaches to single-project risk evaluation in the international environment. It provides an extended computer simulation model of a mining project in Australia. Appendices to Chapters 14 and 15, respectively, review discounting procedures and some of the approaches to project risk evaluation. Chapter 16 reviews some of the evidence from international security portfolio studies and outlines how a corporation can employ these concepts in selecting its portfolio of capital budgeting projects when risk is considered. Finally, Chapter 17 offers some insights on the international capital budgeting problem from the perspective of both organizational decision-making and corporate strategy, drawing upon selected literature in these areas.

BIBLIOGRAPHY

Aharoni, Yair, "On the Definition of a Multinational Corporation," *Quarterly Review of Economics and Business,* Autumn 1971, pp. 27–37.

Behrman, Jack N., *National Interests and the Multinational Enterprise.* Englewood Cliffs, N.J.: Prentice-Hall, Inc., 1970.

Blond, David, "The Future Contribution of Multinational Corporations to World Growth: A Positive Approach," *Business Economics,* May 1978, pp. 80–94.

England, George W., "Managers and Their Value Systems: A Five-Country Comparative Study," *Columbia Journal of World Business,* Summer 1978, pp. 35–44.

Ewing, David W., *Freedom Inside the Organization: Bringing Civil Liberties to the Workplace.* New York: E. P. Dutton, 1977.

Fayerweather, John, editor, *Host National Attitudes toward Multinational Corporations.* New York: Praeger, 1982.

Haq, Khadija, ed., *Dialogue for a New Order.* New York: Pergamon Press, 1980.

Jacoby, Neil H., Peter Nehemkis, and Richard Eells, "Naivete: Foreign Payoffs Law," *California Management Review,* Fall 1979, pp. 84–87.

Killick, Tony, ed., *Adjustment and Financing in the Developing World.* Washington, D.C.: International Monetary Fund, 1982.

Phatak, Arvind V., *Managing Multinational Corporations,* Ch. 5. New York: Praeger Publishers, 1974.

Reubens, Edwin P., ed., *The Challenge of the New International Economic Order,* Boulder, Colo.: Westview Press, 1981.

Robinson, Richard D., *International Business Management,* 2d ed. New York: Holt, Rinehart and Winston, 1978.

Schlesinger, Stephen, and Stephen Kinzer, *Bitter Fruit: The Untold Story of the American Coup in Guatemala.* New York: Doubleday and Co., 1982.

Sigmund, Paul E., *Multinationals in Latin America: The Politics of Nationalization.* Madison, Wisc.: University of Wisconsin Press, 1980.

Solomon, Lewis D., *Multinational Corporations and the Emerging World Order.* New York: Kennikat Press, 1978.

Steade, Richard D., "Multinational Corporations and the Changing World Economic Order," *California Management Review,* Winter 1978, pp. 5–12.

Stobaugh, Robert B., "The Multinational Corporation: Measuring the Consequences," *Columbia Journal of World Business,* Jan.–Feb. 1971, pp. 59–64.

Stopford, John M., John H. Dunning, and Klaus O. Haberich, *The World Directory of Multinational Enterprises.* New York: Facts on File, 1980.

Tarleton, Jesse S., "Recommended Courses in International Business for Graduate Business Students," *Journal of Business,* Oct. 1977, pp. 438–447.

Vernon, Raymond, *Sovereignty at Bay: The Multinational Spread of U.S. Enterprises.* New York: Basic Books, 1971.

_____ , *Storm over the Multinationals: The Real Issues.* Cambridge, Mass.: Harvard University Press, 1977.

Vernon, Raymond, and Yair Aharoni, *State-owned Enterprise in the Western Economies.* New York: St. Martin's Press, 1981.

_____ , **and Louis T. Wells, Jr.,** *Manager in the International Economy,* 4th ed. Englewood Cliffs, N.J.: Prentice-Hall, Inc., 1981.

Waldmann, Raymond J., *Regulating International Business through Codes of Conduct.* Washington, D.C.: American Enterprise Institute for Public Policy Research, 1980.

2

International Transactions and the Financial Markets

THE AGGREGATE OF economic flows among countries affects the financial variables, such as interest rates and exchange rates, that are the raw material of financial decisions. Thus, it is useful at this point to outline the major types of international transactions and relate them to the financial markets. We will show how separate transactions can be financed and how the aggregate of these transactions can affect the foreign exchange market—the market in which different currencies are traded.

In our discussion of international transactions we will follow the general outline provided by the statement most commonly used to record the economic flows between one country and the rest of the world—the so-called *balance of payments.*

THE CONCEPT OF BALANCE OF PAYMENTS

The balance of payments catalogs the *flow* of economic transactions between the *residents* of a given country and the residents of other countries during a certain *period of time.*

The balance of payments measures *flows* rather than stocks. That is, in spite of the word "balance" in the term "balance of payments," only *changes* in asset holdings and liabilities, and not the *levels* of these items, are presented in this statement.[1] In this sense, the balance of payments for a country is very similar to a statement of sources and uses of funds for a firm.

As with the traditional statement of sources and uses of funds, the accounting for the balance of payments is based on a double-entry system. The part of a transaction that gives rise to an increase in the external purchasing power of the country is called a *source* of funds and the part of a transaction that gives rise to a decrease in the external purchasing power of the country is called a *use* of funds. It is impossible to talk about any transaction in the balance of payments accounts without discussing both sources and uses of funds. As in any double-entry accounting system, the balance of payments is kept in terms of debits and credits—uses of funds are debits and sources of funds are credits.

A country *increases* its external purchasing power whenever it *decreases* (sells) its tangible or intangible assets (exports goods and services), when it *decreases* its ownership of foreign financial assets (through their sale), or when it *increases* its liabilities to foreigners (as, for example, when a domestic corporation takes out a loan from a foreign source, or a domestic bank accepts a deposit from a foreigner). All of these transactions represent *sources* of external purchasing power—credit entries.

A country *decreases* its external purchasing power whenever it *increases* (buys) tangible or intangible assets (imports goods or services), when it *increases* (buys) holdings of foreign financial assets, or when it *decreases* its previous liabilities to foreigners. All of these transactions represent *uses* of external purchasing power—debit entries.

In the context of the balance of payments, a *resident* of a country is any individual, business firm, government agency, or other institution legally domiciled (but not necessarily a citizen) in the given country. Therefore, the subsidiary (but not a branch) of a German company legally established in the United States would be treated as any other U.S. enterprise for balance of payments purposes. Transactions that affect only the local residents are not recorded in the balance of payments.[2] However, these domestic transactions can lead to conditions that are reflected in the balance of payments. For example, if the monetary authorities of the United States decide to sell part of their Treasury bill portfolio to U.S. residents, this transaction will not enter the

---

[1]The statement measuring the *levels* of foreign assets and liabilities among countries is the *balance of indebtedness* discussed later in this chapter.

[2]The exception occurs when the transaction involves a foreign currency that is exchanged between a country's private resident and the country's monetary authority, or central bank. Even though both parties are residents of the same country, this transaction will be reflected in the balance of payments as offsetting entries in two different accounts: private capital flows and official reserves. These accounts are discussed in the following section.

U.S. balance of payments accounts. However, as a result of the selling of securities, an increase in U.S. interest rates might occur, which could induce, say, the British to purchase U.S. securities. This latter transaction, in contrast to the first one, will be between the residents of two different countries—the United States and England—and it will be registered in the balance of payments accounts.

Finally, the balance of payments can be prepared for any specific *period of time.* Typically, it is prepared monthly, quarterly, and annually. To facilitate comparisons, the monthly and quarterly figures are often presented on an annual rate basis. When analyzing monthly and quarterly figures, one must be careful to consider whether these figures have been adjusted for seasonal fluctuations. The presence of such fluctuations, if not identified, might lead one to confuse a recurrent seasonal pattern with a change in trends in the balance of payments accounts.

ACCOUNTING FOR INTERNATIONAL TRANSACTIONS IN THE BALANCE OF PAYMENTS

The balance of payments statement is traditionally divided into three major groups of accounts: (1) the current accounts, (2) the capital accounts, and (3) the official reserves accounts. We will define these accounts and illustrate them with some transactions. The double-entry system used in the preparation of the balance of payments allows us to see how each transaction is financed and how international transactions usually affect more than one type of account in the balance of payments.

The illustrative transactions presented here are for a country called Lilliput in the year 1900. Lilliput's currency unit is the Lilliput dollar, which we will call the dollar for convenience.

Current Accounts

The *current accounts* record the trade in goods and services and the exchange of gifts among countries.

The *trade in goods* is composed of exports and imports. A country increases its exports when it sells merchandise to foreigners. This is a source of funds and a decrease in real assets. A country increases its imports when it buys merchandise from foreigners. This is a use of funds and an acquisition of real assets.

EXAMPLE 1. A manufacturer in Lilliput exports $5,000 in goods to a customer in Greece. According to the sales terms, this account will be paid in 90 days. In this case two things happen. The merchandise export, a reduction in real assets, provides Lilliput with an increase in external purchasing power—a credit entry. But the exporter is financing the transaction for 90 days—that is, the exporter's accounts receivable have increased by $5,000. She has made a short-term investment abroad. This acquisition of a short-term asset or claim represents a use of the country's external purchasing power—a debit entry. In the Lilliput balance of payments accounts this transaction will appear as shown in the following table:

	Debit	Credit
Increase in short-term claims on foreigners (the account receivable)	$5,000	
Exports		$5,000

The *trade in services* includes interest and dividends, travel expenses, and financial and shipping charges. Interest and dividends received measure the services that the country's capital has rendered abroad. Payments received from tourists measure the services that the country's hotels and shops provided to visitors from other countries. Financial and shipping charges to foreigners measure the fees that the financial community and ship owners charged to foreigners for the special services they rendered. In these cases the nation gave the service of assets it possessed (for example, a hotel) to foreigners. Thus, these transactions are a source of external purchasing power. In contrast to the preceding cases, when the country's residents are the recipients of the services from foreign-owned assets, then the given country loses purchasing power to the rest of the world.

EXAMPLE 2. A Japanese resident visits Lilliput. Upon his arrival, he converts his $2,500 worth of yen into dollars at the airport bank. When the visitor departs he has no dollars left. In this case, Lilliput provided services (such as hotel rooms and meals) to foreigners in the amount of $2,500. In exchange for these services, Lilliput banks now have $2,500 worth of yen. The willingness of Lilliput banks to hold the yen balances—a liability of the Japanese government—provided the required financing for the Japanese tourist. The services that Lilliput provided to the Japanese are clearly a source of purchasing power for Lilliput—a credit entry. However, the accumulation of yen in Lilliput banks is an increase in Lilliput's holdings of foreign financial obligations—a use of purchasing power, and thus a debit entry. In the Lilliput balance of payments this transaction will appear as shown in the following table:

	Debit	Credit
Increase in short-term claims on foreigners (the yen holdings)	$2,500	
Receipts for travel services to foreigners		$2,500

The exchange of gifts among countries is recorded in the *unilateral transfers account*. This account is also labeled *remittances* or *unrequited transfers*. A typical entry in this account is the money that emigrants send home. Another example is a gift that one country makes to another. When a country makes a gift, it can be said that it is acquiring an asset which we may call *goodwill*. As with any other asset acquisition, the gift represents a use of external purchasing power.

EXAMPLE 3.   A Lilliput resident who left his family in Hungary sends a $1,000 check to his wife in Hungary. The gift that the Lilliput resident sent is a unilateral or unrequited transfer. For accounting purposes it can be treated as a purchase of goodwill (wife's devotion?), that reduces Lilliput's purchasing power—a debit entry.[3] However, this gift was made possible by the credit or financing that the Hungarians extended to Lilliput when they accepted a financial obligation (a check) in Lilliput dollars from a Lilliput resident. This latter part of the transaction, an increase in liabilities to foreigners, is a source of external purchasing power—a credit entry. The entry of this transaction in the Lilliput balance of payments will be shown in the table below:

	Debit	Credit
Gifts to foreigners	$1,000	
Increase in short-term liabilities to foreigners (the check)		$1,000

---

[3]If this individual were a temporary foreign worker in Lilliput, we could also think of the debit entry as the importation of the services of foreign labor.

Capital Accounts

The *capital accounts* record the changes in the levels of international financial assets and liabilities. The various classifications within the capital account are based on the original term to maturity of the financial instrument and on the extent of the involvement of the owner of the financial asset in the activities of the security's issuer. Accordingly, the capital accounts are subdivided into *direct investment, portfolio investment,* and *private short-term capital flows.*

Direct investment and *portfolio investment* involve financial instruments that had a maturity of more than 1 year when issued initially. The distinction between direct investment and portfolio investment is made on the basis of the degree of management involvement. Considerable management involvement is presumed to exist in the case of direct investment (usually a minimum of 10% ownership in a firm), but not of portfolio investment.

EXAMPLE 4. A Lilliput resident buys a $3,000 bond newly issued by a German company. The payment is made with a check drawn on a Lilliput bank account. As a result, the Lilliput resident now owns a German bond, and the German company owns Lilliput dollar deposits. Lilliput's acquisition of the German bond (a financial asset) implies a decrease in Lilliput's external purchasing power; the account long-term investments or claims on foreigners must be debited. However, the dollar balances that the German company now owns represent an increase in Lilliput's liabilities to foreigners, which increases Lilliput's foreign purchasing power; the account short-term liabilities to foreigners must be credited. Two possible interpretations are possible here. We can say that the purchase of the German bond was financed with short-term liabilities issued by Lilliput, or we can say that the purchase of short-term dollar instruments by the Germans was financed by their issuing a long-term bond. In the Lilliput balance of payments this transaction will appear as shown in the table that follows:

	Debit	Credit
Increase in long-term claims on foreigners (the German bond)	$3,000	
Increase in short-term liabilities to foreigners (the dollar deposits)		$3,000

Short-term capital movements involve financial paper with an original maturity of less than 1 year. In the previous examples, payment or financing of various transactions was made with either currency or a short-term financial note (except for the alternative interpretation of the financing of Example 4). Payments in Lilliput dollars were called changes in Lilliput's short-term liabilities to foreigners. Payments in foreign currency were called changes in Lilliput's short-term claims on foreigners. These accounts are part of the short-term capital accounts. The given examples produced a net increase in short-term claims on foreigners—a debit—of $7,500, and a net increase in short-term liabilities to foreigners—a credit—of $4,000. A different type of entry in these accounts is presented in the next example.

EXAMPLE 5.   A Swiss bank buys $6,000 worth of Lilliput Treasury bills. It pays by drawing on its dollar account with a Lilliput bank. The sale of Treasury bills to a foreigner is equivalent to Lilliput's borrowing external purchasing power from foreigners, an increase in liabilities to foreigners—a credit entry. However, the purchase is paid by reducing another debt that Lilliput had to foreigners (Lilliput dollars in the hands of foreigners). This reduction in Lilliput's liabilities is a use of funds—a debit entry. In the Lilliput balance of payments the transactions will be entered as shown in the following table:

	Debit	Credit
Decrease in short-term liabilities to foreigners (the dollar account)	$6,000	
Increase in short-term liabilities to foreigners (the Treasury bill)		$6,000

Official Reserve Accounts

Official reserve accounts measure the changes in international reserves owned by the country's monetary authorities, usually the central bank, during the given period. International reserves are composed mainly of gold and convertible foreign exchange. Foreign exchange reserves are financial assets denominated in such currencies as the U.S. dollar, which are freely and easily convertible into other currencies, but not in such currencies as the Indian rupee, because the Indian government does not guarantee the free conversion of its currency into others and not much of an exchange market exists. An increase in any of these financial assets constitutes a use of funds, while a decrease in reserve assets implies a source of funds. In some situations, this fact seems to run against intuitive interpretations, as when we say that an increase in gold holdings is a use of funds (signified by a minus sign or debit in Lilliput's balance of payments). However, an increase in gold holdings *is* a use of funds in the sense that Lilliput might have chosen to purchase an alternative asset such as a bond issued by a foreign government.

In order to be considered part of official reserves, the financial asset must be owned by the monetary authorities. The same asset in private hands is not considered part of official reserves. In addition, the country's own currency cannot be considered part of its reserve assets; a country's currency is a *liability* of its monetary authorities. Changes in these liabilities are reported in the short-term capital account, as illustrated previously.

EXAMPLE 6. An exchange trader is worried about a recent economic forecast anticipating an increased rate of inflation in Lilliput. As a result, she sells $4,700 of Lilliput dollars against marks (she buys marks). The transaction is done with Lilliput's central bank. One reason the central bank may have wanted to be a party to this transaction is to support the exchange rate of the Lilliput dollar—that is, to prevent the possible decline in the value of the Lilliput dollar that could result from the sale of the dollars by the trader. When the central bank purchases the dollars there is a decrease in Lilliput's liabilities to foreigners—a debit entry. The central bank pays for these dollars with marks it maintained as part of the country's foreign exchange reserves. The central bank is financing the support of the exchange rate with its reserves. The decrease in the level of reserves (a financial asset) represents a credit entry. In Lilliput's balance of payments this transaction will appear as indicated in the table below:

	Debit	Credit
Decrease in short-term liabilities to foreigners (the dollars)	$4,700	
Decrease in official exchange reserves (the marks)		$4,700

THE BALANCE OF PAYMENTS STATEMENT

Exhibit 2.1 summarizes the transactions discussed in the examples of this section, together with some additional transactions, in a balance of

EXHIBIT 2.1 Balance of Payments for Lilliput for the Year 1900

(+: Sources of funds; −: Uses of funds)

Current Accounts			
Merchandise account			
Exports	$5,000		
Imports	−4,000		
Balance on merchandise trade		$1,000	
Service account			
Receipts for interest and dividends, travel, and financial charges	2,500		
Payments for interest and dividends, travel, and financial charges	−2,000		
Balance in invisibles (services)		500	
Balance of trade in goods and services			$ 1,500
Unilateral transfers			
Gifts received from foreigners	500		
Gifts to foreigners	−1,000		
Balance in unilateral transfers			−500
Current accounts balance			1,000
Capital Accounts			
Long-term capital flows			
Direct investment			
Lilliput's investment abroad (+: decrease; −: increase)	−4,500		
Foreigners' investment in Lilliput (+: increase; −: decrease)	2,000	−2,500	
Portfolio investment			
Lilliput's claims on foreigners (+: decrease; −: increase)	−3,000		
Lilliput's liabilities to foreigners (+: increase; −: decrease)	5,000	2,000	
Balance on long-term capital			−500
Basic balance			500
Private short-term capital flows			
Lilliput's claims on foreigners (+: decrease; −: increase)	−4,000		
Lilliput's liabilities to foreigners (+: increase; − decrease)	3,800		
Balance on short-term private capital			−200
Overall balance			$ 300
Official Reserves Accounts			
Gold exports less imports (−)			$−5,000
Decrease or increase (−) in foreign exchange			4,700
Balance on official reserves			$ −300

increase in gold holdings is a use of funds (signified by a minus sign or debit in Lilliput's balance of payments). However, an increase in gold holdings *is* a use of funds in the sense that Lilliput might have chosen to purchase an alternative asset such as a bond issued by a foreign government.

In order to be considered part of official reserves, the financial asset must be owned by the monetary authorities. The same asset in private hands is not considered part of official reserves. In addition, the country's own currency cannot be considered part of its reserve assets; a country's currency is a *liability* of its monetary authorities. Changes in these liabilities are reported in the short-term capital account, as illustrated previously.

EXAMPLE 6. An exchange trader is worried about a recent economic forecast anticipating an increased rate of inflation in Lilliput. As a result, she sells $4,700 of Lilliput dollars against marks (she buys marks). The transaction is done with Lilliput's central bank. One reason the central bank may have wanted to be a party to this transaction is to support the exchange rate of the Lilliput dollar—that is, to prevent the possible decline in the value of the Lilliput dollar that could result from the sale of the dollars by the trader. When the central bank purchases the dollars there is a decrease in Lilliput's liabilities to foreigners—a debit entry. The central bank pays for these dollars with marks it maintained as part of the country's foreign exchange reserves. The central bank is financing the support of the exchange rate with its reserves. The decrease in the level of reserves (a financial asset) represents a credit entry. In Lilliput's balance of payments this transaction will appear as indicated in the table below:

	Debit	Credit
Decrease in short-term liabilities to foreigners (the dollars)	$4,700	
Decrease in official exchange reserves (the marks)		$4,700

THE BALANCE OF PAYMENTS STATEMENT

Exhibit 2.1 summarizes the transactions discussed in the examples of this section, together with some additional transactions, in a balance of

EXHIBIT 2.1 Balance of Payments for Lilliput for the Year 1900

(+ : Sources of funds; − : Uses of funds)

Current Accounts			
Merchandise account			
Exports	$5,000		
Imports	− 4,000		
Balance on merchandise trade		$1,000	
Service account			
Receipts for interest and dividends, travel, and financial charges	2,500		
Payments for interest and dividends, travel, and financial charges	− 2,000		
Balance in invisibles (services)		500	
Balance of trade in goods and services			$ 1,500
Unilateral transfers			
Gifts received from foreigners	500		
Gifts to foreigners	− 1,000		
Balance in unilateral transfers			− 500
Current accounts balance			1,000
Capital Accounts			
Long-term capital flows			
Direct investment			
Lilliput's investment abroad (+ : decrease; − : increase)	− 4,500		
Foreigners' investment in Lilliput (+ : increase; − : decrease)	2,000	− 2,500	
Portfolio investment			
Lilliput's claims on foreigners (+ : decrease; − : increase)	− 3,000		
Lilliput's liabilities to foreigners (+ : increase; − : decrease)	5,000	2,000	
Balance on long-term capital			− 500
Basic balance			500
Private short-term capital flows			
Lilliput's claims on foreigners (+ : decrease; − : increase)	− 4,000		
Lilliput's liabilities to foreigners (+ : increase; − decrease)	3,800		
Balance on short-term private capital			− 200
Overall balance			$ 300
Official Reserves Accounts			
Gold exports less imports (−)			$ − 5,000
Decrease or increase (−) in foreign exchange			4,700
Balance on official reserves			$ − 300

18

payments statement for Lilliput.[4] The additional transactions are the following:

1. A foreign car, priced at $4,000 equivalent, is purchased. Payment is made with foreign currency held by the importer in Lilliput.
2. A foreigner's fully-owned subsidiary in Lilliput earns $2,000 in profits after taxes. These profits are kept as part of retained earnings in the subsidiary.
3. A Lilliput resident receives a $500 check in guilders as a gift from a cousin who lives abroad.
4. A Lilliput company purchases 30 percent of a foreign candy store for $4,500. Payment is made in Lilliput dollars.
5. A Lilliput resident sells a $5,000 bond issued by a Lilliput company to a French investor. Payment is made in Lilliput dollars.
6. Lilliput's central bank purchases $5,000 worth of gold to be kept as part of foreign reserves. Payment is made in Lilliput dollars.

Each of the figures shown in a balance of payments represents the total of the transactions affecting the given account during the reporting period. However, these totals are not calculated from entries such as the ones we have discussed. In our examples, we recorded a debit and a credit for each international transaction. In practice, the data reported in the balance of payments are gathered from sources that often are concerned with only a portion of the transactions discussed above. For example, the data presented in the import account are often collected from customs declarations, while the financing of these transactions appears largely among the data for changes in foreign assets and liabilities reported by financial institutions. That is why we often find an additional account in the balance of payments statement—*errors and omissions*.

The accounts in the balance of payments are often presented in a format similar to the one shown in Exhibit 2.1. Entries appear under the three major groupings of accounts discussed in the preceding section: current accounts, capital accounts, and official reserve accounts. The statement often supplies totals for these major groups of accounts, as well as for some of their components. In addition, as one reads from top to bottom, the typical presentation of the balance of payments provides cumulative running subtotals, usually called *balances*.

In Exhibit 2.1 the *trade balance in goods and services* shows a positive balance of $1,500. The sources of external purchasing power exceeded the uses on the trade accounts by $1,500. This balance is

---

[4]This is also the format followed by the International Monetary Fund in its "analytic presentation" of balance of payments figures which appears in *The Balance of Payments Yearbook*.

composed of a positive balance in trade in merchandise of $1,000 and a positive balance in trade in services of $500. When we add the negative balance of $500 in unilateral transfers to the balance of trade in goods and services, we obtain the *balance on the current accounts*. In Lilliput, the current accounts balance is a surplus of $1,000.

In the long-term capital account, Lilliput had a deficit in direct investments. While foreigners invested $2,000 in Lilliput (Lilliput increased its liabilities to foreigners—a source of funds for Lilliput), Lilliput made direct investments in foreign countries in the amount of $4,500 (Lilliput acquired financial assets—a use of funds for Lilliput). Many of these investments involved acquiring whole ventures in other countries. Although in some cases the ownership had to be shared with others, the direct investor retained a substantial share (at least 10%) of the total ownership and, presumably, management.

The deficit in the direct investment accounts of Lilliput was somewhat compensated for by the surplus in the portfolio accounts. Foreigners bought $2,000 more of long-term financial instruments from Lilliput than Lilliput bought from other countries. When the balance in the long-term capital accounts is added to the current accounts balance, the result is called the *basic balance*. Lilliput's basic balance is a positive $500.

In the private short-term capital accounts, foreigners bought $3,800 worth of short-term securities issued by Lilliput, while Lilliput invested $4,000 in short-term securities issued by foreign countries. The sum of the private short-term capital accounts and the basic balance produces another subtotal, often referred to as the *overall balance*. In Lilliput the overall balance produces a surplus of $300—a net source of external purchasing power for Lilliput.

By definition, the net change in official reserves must be equal to the overall balance. Given the double-entry system of accounting in the balance of payments, the net of the accounts included in any balance must equal the net of the remaining accounts. In Lilliput the surplus in the overall balance of $300 equals the increase in official reserves (a debit or minus entry) of $300. Alternatively, we can say that the total of all the entries in the Lilliput balance of payments is 0.

THE BALANCE OF PAYMENTS
AND THE EXCHANGE MARKETS

The discussion of the balance of payments statement for Lilliput makes it clear that the number of possible "balances" in the balance of payments is equal to the number of possible groupings of accounts in that statement. Whenever we segregate a group of accounts and take their total, we have a "balance" in the balance of payments. To say that "the balance of payments is in surplus or deficit" is meaningless, unless one specifies which accounts are being included in the computation of such a balance. A balance of the whole balance of payments must always equal 0.

Balances computed on the basis of certain accounts in the balance of payments provide an indication of how given economic sectors contribute to the economic position of the country in international markets. For example, an analysis of a surplus in the merchandise trade account can show the contribution that net exports of goods from that country make to the country's acquisition of external purchasing power. However, the most common reason for computing "a balance" in the balance of payments is to understand the net market pressures that affect the international value and availability of the currency. Thus, when one talks about "a surplus in the balance of payments," the implication is that there is pressure for the country to accumulate foreign exchange reserves or to have the exchange rate of its currency appreciate, regardless of the accounts included in the computation of such a surplus. If we want to place this special significance on a balance, we must be very careful in selecting the accounts to be included in its computation.

Before trying to associate any balance in the balance of payments with specific pressures in the exchange markets, we must make explicit the relationship between different types of entries in that statement and the exchange market. Earlier, we referred to a *credit* entry in the balance of payments as the part of the transaction that gives rise to an increase in the external purchasing power of the country—a source of funds. This is the same as an *increase in the supply of foreign currency and demand for the home currency.* We referred to a *debit* entry in the balance of payments as the part of the transaction that gives rise to a decrease in the external purchasing power of the country—a use of funds. This is the same as an *increase in the supply of the home currency and demand for foreign currency.*

As an illustration, consider Example 1, in which Lilliput exported $5,000 to Greece, payable in 90 days. We entered this transaction in the Lilliput balance of payments as a credit to the export account and a debit to increases in short-claims on foreigners. If the exports are billed in Lilliput dollars, then the Greek importer must acquire the needed Lilliput dollars in order to pay for the exports. This will be done by selling Greek drachmas to purchase Lilliput dollars. That is, from Lilliput's point of view, there will be an increase in the supply of foreign exchange (Greek drachmas) and demand for the home currency (Lilliput dollars). Had the export sale been billed in Greek drachmas, then the Lilliput exporter would have had to sell the drachmas to purchase the Lilliput dollars probably needed to pay for the costs of her business operations. The result of the export sale (a credit entry) would have been the same, namely, an increase in the supply of foreign currency and in the demand for home currency.

In Example 1, the export sale was financed by the Lilliput exporter's extending credit to the Greek importer—an acquisition of a financial asset by the Lilliput exporter, and thus a debit entry in the balance of payments of Lilliput. Had this been a separate transaction, say denominated in Lilliput dollars, then in order for the Greek issuer of the instrument to settle the Lilliput exporter's claim on him, he would have had to sell drachmas and buy Lilliput dollars upon maturity of the 90-day security. This is the same kind of exchange transaction we described as required for the importer to pay for Lilliput exports. The financing that the exporter extended to the Greek importer essentially postponed the pressures on the exchange market (increase in supply of drachmas and demand for Lilliput dollars) to 90 days later when the account will become payable.

Referring to the major accounts in the balance of payments of Lilliput, we can translate the various entries into changes in supply and demand for foreign currency and Lilliput dollars as shown in the following table:

MARKET FOR GOODS, SERVICES, AND TRANSFERS
(Current Account)

Imports	Exports
Supply Lilliput dollars Demand foreign currency	Demand Lilliput dollars Supply foreign currency

PRIVATE FINANCIAL MARKETS

Lilliput's Purchase of Securities Issued by Foreigners or Foreigners' Sales of Securities Issued by Lilliput	Lilliput's Sale of Securities Issued by Foreigners or Foreigners' Purchases of Securities Issued by Lilliput
Supply Lilliput dollars Demand foreign currency	Demand Lilliput dollars Supply foreign currency

---

For the exchange markets to remain in equilibrium and the exchange rates for the Lilliput dollar to remain constant, the combined effect of transactions in the market for goods and services and the private financial markets must produce the following relationship:

$$\left\{ \begin{matrix} \text{Supply of Lilliput dollars} \\ \text{or} \\ \text{Demand for foreign currency} \end{matrix} \right\} = \left\{ \begin{matrix} \text{Demand for Lilliput dollars} \\ \text{or} \\ \text{Supply of foreign currency} \end{matrix} \right\}$$

If instead of this equality we have an inequality between supply and demand for Lilliput dollars and foreign currency, then forces for change will appear. Governments will have to intervene to bridge the gap between private supply and demand either by affecting their foreign exchange reserves or by imposing controls (such as import quotas) on the private sector. Alternatively, the exchange rate at which market participants are willing to transact will change.

The balance of payments figures report the amount of international flows on a historical basis, after the fact. Thus, when we include the reserves accounts, the supply of exchange equals the demand for exchange, just as "debits equal credits." If we want to use the balance of payments as a tool to measure the pressures in the exchange markets, we must look to the future. It is only in this sense that we can see imbalances between supply and demand for foreign exchange developing at the going exchange rates. Governments may choose to provide the funds needed to reestablish balance at the going exchange rate or, alternatively, they may let the exchange rate fluctuate to bring the forces of supply and demand into balance. International monetary agreements among governments have existed which sanction both approaches to adjusting imbalances in international flows. This will be discussed further in the next chapter.

THE BALANCE OF INDEBTEDNESS

While the *balance of payments* measures the *flows* of economic transactions that take place between the residents of a given country and the rest of the world, the *balance of indebtedness* measures the *levels of assets and liabilities* that the country has in relation to the rest of the world. That is, the changes that occur between the balances of indebtedness drawn at two different points in time are measured by the balance of payments for the period.[5]

In the analysis of the international value of a country's currency thus far, we have emphasized the balance of payments. However, it stands to reason that the balance of payments and the balance of indebtedness statements should be analyzed in conjunction. Although it is true that a business would go bankrupt for lack of liquidity or inability to pay its current debts, it is also true that continual deficits in operations can be sustained for a much longer period when the business has a large equity base.

---

[5]For many countries, a balance of indebtedness is not compiled. For the United States, this statement is published by the U.S. Department of Commerce, Bureau of Economic Analysis, in *Survey of Current Business*. The statement usually appears in one of the monthly issues published in the Fall.

SUMMARY

The balance of payments accounts of a nation are analogous to the double-entry system of sources and uses of funds for a corporation. Thus, the *balance of payments statement* for a nation measures the *flow* of transactions between a country's *residents* and the rest of the world for a particular *period of time*. Sources of funds for the corporation are analogous to increases in the external purchasing power of a country. In the balance of payments they arise from the sale of goods or services (exports), the sale of foreign assets, or an increase in liabilities to foreigners. Uses of funds in the firm's flow of funds statement are analogous to decreases in external purchasing power of a country. These decreases appear in the balance of payments in the forms of purchases of goods or services from other nations (imports), a purchase of foreign assets, or a decrease in liabilities to foreigners.

The *current accounts* show the commerce in goods (exports and imports), the trade in services (dividends, interest, travel, and financial and shipping charges), and unilateral transfers (gifts) among countries. The *capital accounts* involve changes in financial assets and liabilities, and are subdivided into changes in direct investment, portfolio investment, and short-term capital flows. Direct investment (usually more than 10% of the equity of a firm) and portfolio investment involve financial instruments of more than 1-year maturity when issued. Short-term capital movements involve securities with a maturity of 1 year or less when issued (for example, the account receivable due from a customer to whom a resident has exported goods). The *official reserve accounts* measure changes in reserves owned by the nation's monetary authorities during the period, and primarily involve gold and convertible foreign currencies.

The *balance in goods and services* is the net of the goods and services accounts; adding in the balance in unilateral transfers results in the *balance on the current accounts*. The *basic balance* is the balance on current accounts plus the balances in long-term portfolio transactions and direct investment. Adding the balance in private short-term capital accounts provides the same *overall balance* as simply adding the balance on current accounts and the balance on capital accounts. Because of the double-entry system of bookkeeping, the overall balance, by definition, is equal to the change in official reserves, but with the opposite sign. Thus, the total of all sources and uses must be equal to 0.

The manager of the multinational firm is often interested in the balance of payments because the various transactions ultimately affect the exchange markets where currencies are traded. Increases in external purchasing power (sources of funds) are credits in the balance of payments, and are the same as increases in supply of foreign currency and in the demand for the home currency. Similarly, debit entries correspond to decreases in external purchasing power, and are increases in the supply of the home currency and in the demand for foreign currency. For exchange markets to remain in equilibrium, the supply of home currency (or the demand for foreign currency) must equal the demand for home currency (or the supply of foreign currency). Without such equilibrium, the monetary authorities must accommodate the imbalance by changes in the official reserve accounts or the exchange rates, or both.

Although not available in standard published form for all nations, a *balance of indebtedness statement* measures the levels of the various asset and liability accounts at a point in time. The balance of payments is thus the change between two balance of indebtedness statements.

QUESTIONS

1. What do we mean when we talk about a balance of payments statement? What are some possible implications of such a statement? What are its potential uses?

2. A country's assets and liabilities can each be viewed as sources of external purchasing power and uses of external purchasing power. Provide an example of each of the four possible situations and describe why each is a source or use.

3. What does a positive trade balance on goods and services in Lilliput mean?

4. How might a large surplus in Lilliput's balance of payments affect the international value and availability of its currency? What actions might Lilliput take? Explain your answer.

BIBLIOGRAPHY*

The Balance of Payments Statistics of the United States. Report of the Review Committee for Balance of Payments Statistics to the Bureau of the Budget, April 1965, Edward M. Bernstein, Chairman, U.S. Government Printing Office: 1965.

Baldwin, Robert E., "Determinants of the Commodity Structure of U.S. Trade," *American Economic Review*, 1977, pp. 126–146.

Bame, Jack J., "Analyzing U.S. International Transactions," *Columbia Journal of World Business*, Fall 1976, pp. 72–84.

---

*See also the bibliographies to Chapters 3, 4, and 6.

Caves, Richard E., and Ronald W. Jones, *World Trade and Payments*. Boston: Little, Brown and Company, 1973.

Denison, Edward F., and William K. Chung, *How Japan's Economy Grew So Fast*. Washington, D.C.: Brookings Institution, 1976.

Deppler, Michael C., and Duncan M. Ripley, "The World Trade Model: Merchandise Trade," *International Monetary Fund Staff Papers*, Mar. 1978, pp. 147–206.

Gray, H. Peter, and Gail E. Makinen, "Balance of Payments Contributions of Multinational Corporations," *Journal of Business*, July 1967, pp. 339–343.

Heller, H. Robert, *International Monetary Economics*. Englewood Cliffs, N.J.: Prentice-Hall, Inc., 1974.

Kindleberger, Charles P., and Peter H. Lindert, *International Economics*, 6th ed. Homewood, Ill.: Richard D. Irwin, Inc., 1978.

Kravis, Irving B., and Robert E. Lipsey, "Price Behavior in the Light of Balance of Payments Theories," *Journal of International Economics*, May 1978, pp. 193–246.

Kreinin, Mordechai E., "The Effect of Exchange Rate Changes on the Prices and Volume of Foreign Trade," *International Monetary Fund Staff Papers*, July 1977, pp. 297–329.

Meade, J. E., *The Balance of Payments*. London: Oxford University Press, 1952.

Report of the Advisory Committee on the Presentation of Balance of Payments Statistics, Washington, D.C.: U.S. Department of Commerce. *Survey of Current Business*, June 1976, pp. 18–27.

Root, Franklin R., *International Trade and Investment*, 4th ed., Part One. Cincinnati, Ohio: South-Western Publishing Co., 1978.

Spitaller, Erich, "A Model of Inflation and Its Performance in the Seven Main Industrial Countries, 1958–76," *International Monetary Fund Staff Papers*, June 1978, pp. 254–277.

Stern, Robert M., et al., "The Presentation of the U.S. Balance of Payments: A Symposium," *Essays in International Finance*, No. 123. Princeton: Princeton University, Aug. 1977.

Vernon, Raymond, "A Skeptic Looks at the Balance of Payments," *Foreign Policy*, Winter 1971–1972, pp. 52–65.

———, and Louis T. Wells, Jr., *Manager in the International Economy*, 4th ed. Englewood Cliffs, N.J.: Prentice-Hall, Inc., 1981.

Walter, Ingo, and Kaj Areskoug, *International Economics*, 3rd ed. New York: John Wiley, 1981.

EXERCISES ON BALANCE OF PAYMENTS ACCOUNTING*

The transactions between the country of Colchis and the rest of the world (ROW) for last year are given here. Colchis' currency is the

---

*These exercises were prepared by Kenneth Adamitis under the supervision of Professor Rita M. Rodriguez.

mark (M). Perform the following steps to reflect these transactions in Colchis' balance of payments statement:

1. Enter the debits and credits associated with each transaction in the appropriate "T-accounts" provided in Exhibit A.1.
2. Prepare the balance of payments statement for Colchis following the format presented in Exhibit A.2.

TRANSACTIONS

1. **(a)** A company in Colchis imports shoes worth M5,000 from France. To pay for this shipment the importer gets a short-term loan in francs from Société Generale in Paris. The interest on this loan is 5% per annum.

(b) At maturity, 1 year later, the loan is repaid with francs purchased from a bank in Colchis.

2. **(a)** An exporter in Colchis sells M50,000 worth of cars to Yugoslavia. Exports are billed in U.S. dollars. In payment, the exporter accepts M5,000 worth of U.S. dollars in cash and a 1-year bill of exchange denominated in U.S. dollars for the remainder.

(b) The exporter discounts the bill of exchange with Bankers Trust in New York and leaves the dollar proceeds deposited with that bank. (Assume a 5% discount rate.)

3. Mr. Chirac, a resident of Colchis, visits Poland on a vacation. He leaves Colchis with M2,000 and returns with M150. He spent M1,000 on services received while in Poland and the rest on Polish glass and textiles, which Mr. Chirac brings with him.

4. Mr. Fernandez, a citizen of Spain, emigrates to Colchis because of the higher wages paid in this country. He leaves his family in Spain and brings with him M100 worth of pesetas. He exchanges his money into marks at a bank in Colchis.

5. Mr. Fernandez finds a job and sends M200 to his family in Spain. The money is sent in the form of a check drawn on his checking account in marks held with a bank in Colchis.

6. XYZ, a corporation of Colchis, decides to open a subsidiary in Belgium. The total cost is M60,000. Half of the investment is made in the form of cash in marks. The remainder is raised through the sale of bonds issued by the parent company and sold in Switzerland. The bonds are denominated in Swiss francs.

7. XYZ's plant in Belgium makes M2,000 profit during the first quarter of operation. Dividends are declared and remitted to XYZ's headquarters in Colchis in the amount of M500 worth of Belgian francs. The rest is reinvested in the plant.

EXHIBIT A.1 Exercises on Balance of Payments Accounting: T-Accounts for Colchis' Balance of Payments

Merchandise Exports	Merchandise Imports	Service Receipts	Service Payments

Unilateral Transfers	Direct Investment	Long-Term Claims on Foreigners	Long-Term Liabilities to Foreigners

Short-Term Claims on Foreigners	Short-Term Liabilities to Foreigners	Official Reserves

EXHIBIT A.2 Exercises on Balance of Payments Accounting: Balance of Payments for Colchis for the Year 19XX

Current Account

Merchandise account
  Exports
  Imports
  Balance on merchandise trade ——————

Service account
  Receipts
  Payments
  Balance on invisibles (service) ——————

Balance on goods and services ——————

Unilateral transfers
  Gifts received from abroad
  Gifts to foreigners
  Balance on unilateral transfers ——————

Current account balance ——————

Capital Account

Long-term capital flows

Direct investment
  Direct investment in Colchis
    (sale of Colchis' financial assets)
  Direct investment abroad
    (purchase of foreign financial assets)

Portfolio investment
  Colchis' liabilities to foreigners
    (sale of Colchis' financial assets)
  Colchis' claims on foreigners
    (purchase of foreign financial assets)
  Balance on long-term capital ——————

Basic balance ——————

Private capital flows (short-term)
  Colchis' liabilities to foreigners
    (sale of Colchis' financial assets)
  Colchis' claims on foreigners
    (purchase of foreign financial assets)
  Balance on short-term private capital ——————

Overall balance ══════

Official Reserves Account

  Gold exports less imports $(-)$

  Decrease or increase $(-)$
    in foreign exchange

Balance of official reserves ══════

---

8. Due to market conditions, there is considerable pressure for the mark to appreciate against other currencies. In order to maintain the present exchange rate, the Central Bank of Colchis buys M40,000 worth of foreign exchange. Payment is made in marks.

9. As allowed by the bond indenture, XYZ calls at par half the bonds issued earlier to finance the investment in Belgium. To make the necessary payments, XYZ draws on its cash balances in marks held with its leading bank in Colchis.

10. Miss Correa, a cousin of Mr. Fernandez, decides to join him in Colchis. She travels on Iberia, Spain's national airline. The airline ticket, which costs M150, is purchased and paid for at her local travel agency. According to an international agreement, Iberia is paid in marks soon thereafter.

11. The government of Luxembourg issues M50,000 worth of 20-year, 5% coupon bonds denominated in U.S. dollars. Of the total amount, 20% is bought by residents of Colchis. They acquire the U.S. dollars necessary to make the payment at foreign banks located outside Colchis.

12. The Central Bank of Colchis decides to increase its gold reserves. It buys M20,000 worth of gold from South Africa. Half the payment is made in marks. The other half is paid from U.S. dollar balances held by the Central Bank of Colchis.

13. An exporter in Colchis sells M25,000 worth of farm machinery to Colombia. Payment in marks is received upon delivery. The Colombian importer obtains the marks needed to make the payment through a loan from a local bank in Colombia.

14. XYZ's plant in Belgium makes M5,000 in profits and declares M2,500 in dividends. However, new currency restrictions in Belgium prohibit remitting dividends outside the country. Therefore, XYZ uses M2,000 to purchase bonds issued by the government of Belgium from a local resident, and keeps M500 in the form of a 6-month time deposit with a Belgian bank.

15. A U.S. exporter sells M15,000 worth of grain to Colchis. Payment is made in U.S. dollars, bought from a local bank in Colchis.

16. The government of Luxembourg pays the annual interest on its 5% bonds.

17. Bowing to government pressure from Belgium, XYZ Corporation sells half its interest in the Belgian subsidiary to a local resident for M32,000. Payment is received in the form of M30,000 in cash in marks (borrowed from a local bank in Belgium) and M2,000 worth of 5% bonds issued by the government of Belgium.

18. An importer in Colchis pays M2,500 to a shipping line from England for delivery of grain. Payment is in U.S. dollars bought from a bank in London.

19. To reduce the amount of marks held by foreigners, the Central Bank of Colchis sells M10,000 worth of gold to foreign residents.

20. Mr. Fernandez, the immigrant to Colchis, sells his house in Spain in order to pay to have his family join him. Of the M2,500 worth of pesetas realized from the sale, M1,500 are used to pay for passage of the family on Colchis National Airline. The family brings the remainder with them and exchanges it into marks at a local bank in Colchis.

3

International Monetary Agreements and Institutions

THE FINANCIAL OFFICER who operates in international markets must do so within the framework provided by the international monetary system in existence at the time. The nature of the system affects the sources of financing available to business and to the countries in which business operates. This system also specifies the role of governments and other institutions in the determination of exchange rates when these rates are not allowed to be determined freely by market forces.

The international monetary system in modern times has both public and private components. The public part comprises a series of governmental agreements among nations and the functions of international public institutions. The private component in the system is provided by the banking industry. In this chapter we will address the subject of international monetary agreements and institutions. (We will discuss the role of international banking in this monetary system in Chapter 4.) The two appendices to this chapter present a chronology of the major events in the international monetary system during the post–World War II period and some of the institutions that helped to cope with the problems that developed during this period.

WHY INTERNATIONAL MONETARY AGREEMENTS ARE NEEDED

The international transactions and the resulting balance of payments we presented for Lilliput in Chapter 2 illustrate the monetary problems that must be solved at the international level for commerce among countries to occur. Financing must be available so that these international transactions may be conducted smoothly. The need for this financing spans a continuum that runs from the necessity to have enough funds to finance those transactions that must be done on a cash basis—a *liquidity* problem—to the need to have financing available to bridge the gap between demand and supply for currencies when temporary imbalances develop at the current exchange rates—an *adjustment* problem. When the financing of a disequilibrium is not possible or desirable, an alternative mechanism of adjustment must be available that is acceptable to the countries in the system. In addition, the international financial arrangements to cope with these problems must be consistent with a degree of *stability* which limits the amount of uncertainty in international business decisions.

Need for Liquidity

Except for the case of a barter economy in which goods are exchanged for goods, international transactions (as any other commercial transaction) require that a financial instrument acceptable to both parties to the transaction be exchanged to settle payment. In the case of Lilliput, transactions were settled in Lilliput dollars or foreign currency. Many countries have only one option available to settle their international accounts—namely, foreign currency. If the liabilities issued by the country are not acceptable to foreign investors for whatever reason, then some other country's liabilities are needed to settle the payment. For example, if Lilliput's dollars were not acceptable as a means of international payment, then Lilliput would have had to borrow an acceptable currency, say U.S. dollars, to complete any international purchase. Alternatively, it could have drawn on its existing balances in U.S. dollars.

Given that the currencies of most countries are not readily acceptable by financial investors, these countries need alternative avenues to obtain the currencies which are acceptable. Of course, an obvious way to obtain internationally acceptable currencies is to sell the country's goods and services in exchange for such foreign currencies. However, if a country must wait to sell its products to obtain the needed currency before purchasing anything, then international trade would suffer. For countries whose currencies are not accepted as a means of international payment, there must be a certain volume of international funds available to facilitate day-to-day trade without having to wait for offsetting trade transactions to take place. It is to everybody's advantage to have a monetary system that provides sufficient *liquidity* in the system to finance international transactions at a reasonable price. One possibility is to provide certain key currencies with total convertibility into other currencies and a market environment that makes them attractive to investors. Another possibility is to create international paper money. Both approaches require an international agreement among participating countries.

Mutual Acceptance of Adjustment Mechanisms

Another monetary problem that must be solved to conduct international transactions successfully is the settlement of aggregate imbalances between supply and demand for various currencies. One possible solution to this problem is to finance the imbalance. Some imbalances develop because of factors such as seasonal patterns, crop failures, and temporary conditions in the economy. These factors can be expected to be reversed in the relatively near future, at which time funds will be available to repay any financing used to adjust the earlier disequilibrium.

Other imbalances are produced by permanent changes in economic conditions, such as the increase in oil prices enforced by the Organization of Petroleum Exporting Countries (OPEC). In this case, a structural change in the international flows will be required. Eventually, real resources must be transferred from oil-consuming countries to oil-producing countries, or oil-consuming countries must stop consuming that oil. However, financing can smooth this transition until increases in the exports of oil-consuming countries and imports of oil-producing countries materialize. The so-called recycling of petrodollars in recent years has done exactly that.[1] Of course, governments could also try to use other means (such as military power) to reverse the initial source of change in economic power.[2] However, discussion of this type of adjustment in the balance of payments is outside the scope of this book.

In the cases where governments have discretionary powers to manage the imbalance between supply and demand for different currencies, the financing of the imbalance can take the form of changes in the governments' level of exchange reserves and international borrowings. When this alternative is not available or desirable, there are two other options available to settle an international imbalance: changes in exchange rates and adjustments in the domestic economy. Each of these avenues to adjustment produces a different degree of economic

---

[1]See the section titled "Banking and the Financing of Imbalances" in Chapter 4.

[2]One of the explanations often given among the causes of World War II is the Germans' attempt to correct the economic imbalance created by the reparations payments required of them after World War I.

pain and has a different political consequence. From a political point of view, changes in reserves and borrowings are the least painful alternative, at least in the short term. Inducing an inflation or a recession in the domestic economy to adjust an external imbalance is the most painful alternative. (The latter conditions make it difficult for politicians to keep their jobs!)

We can expect individual governments to have preferences about how to settle external imbalances. However, individual governments' choices for bridging the gap between demand and supply for different currencies can be executed only with the cooperation of other countries. To increase international borrowings, a country needs somebody else to lend to it. To depreciate the external value of a currency, another country's currency must appreciate. To decrease imports through a domestic recession, some other country's exports and income must decrease. Unilateral adjustments in international markets are impossible and attempts to pursue them only increase the instability of the system as a whole.[3] Agreements among governments specifying which avenues are acceptable to settle international imbalances are necessary to avoid disruptive situations.

Roots of the Current Monetary System

The monetary system which has existed officially since April 1978 (although de facto it has existed since March 1973) is a hybrid one. Its genealogy begins with the fixed exchange rate regime established by the Bretton Woods Agreement of 1944. In 1971, repeated crises in the exchange markets produced a collapse of the parities then in existence. In December 1971, attempts to retain the existing system with only minor repairs produced the Smithsonian Agreement, a new set of parities with expanded room for fluctuations around these parities. However, these attempts to repair the system failed. By 1973, the governments of the major currencies were ready to let the market decide what the proper exchange rate for their currencies should be, instead of trying to support rates set by international agreements. But the degree to which these governments were willing to allow the market alone to determine the exchange rates varied from country to country. In the meantime, other countries were experimenting with alternative ar-

---

[3]A good example of the deleterious effects that such unilateral moves can have is the "beggar thy neighbor policies" of the 1930s. Countries were engaged in a series of self-destructive retaliatory devaluations of their currencies in an attempt to avoid other countries' taking exports away from them through the devaluation of their own currencies.

Devaluation refers to a general change of parity of one currency versus most other currencies. Devaluation, revaluation, and upvaluation are terms traditionally used with fixed rate currencies, whereas depreciation and appreciation are often used in a floating rate environment. In this text, they will be used interchangeably. Note that some people mistakenly use "revaluation" to mean upvaluation.

rangements. Finally, in 1978, the recognition that each country could choose the exchange rate regime it wished became official.

Next we will examine how the problems of providing liquidity for international transactions and of settling temporary imbalances in the system are solved under existing alternatives.

SOURCES OF LIQUIDITY

As we discussed earlier, any international monetary system needs liquidity to finance transactions in the short term. In a system of fixed exchange rates, liquidity is also needed to provide reserves that can be used by governments to support exchange rates around their fixed parity.

In a system of fixed exchange rates, the exchange rate for each currency is initially fixed in terms of its par value against another currency or a metal. In the Bretton Woods system the parity exchange rate for all currencies in the system was defined in terms of the U.S. dollar, while the value of the U.S. dollar was defined in terms of gold only. Market exchange rates were to be allowed to fluctuate by only a narrow margin of 1% (¾% in practice) around the parities thus defined.

In a fixed-rate system, when the exchange rate of a currency approaches the limits within which it is allowed to fluctuate, the country is expected to intervene in the foreign exchange market by buying or selling the given currency. Purchases of the home currency require international reserves; sales of the home currency result in the acquisition of international reserves. In the Bretton Woods system, with the narrow bands allowed around parity rates, the intervention points where countries gain or lose reserves were reached quickly.

In the Bretton Woods system, reserves were composed of gold, foreign currencies traded internationally (initially only U.S. dollars), and the right to borrow from an institution created by the agreement—the International Monetary Fund (IMF). However, gold is a non-interest-earning asset, and the IMF borrowing privileges are limited in amount and, for the most part, difficult to obtain. Since the U.S. dollar was the only currency fully convertible into other currencies throughout most of the 1950s, it was the main source of international reserves and world liquidity.

In later years, other financial assets have gained importance in their use as an international reserve. Currencies other than the U.S. dollar have gained convertibility; gold holdings have come to represent a larger share of exchange reserves as rising gold prices increased the value of those holdings; and international currencies, such as Special Drawing Rights (SDRs) and European Currency Units (ECUs), have been created and accepted as exchange reserves. (See Exhibit 3.1.) In addition, the need for international liquidity among countries that adhere to a fixed-rate system has been somewhat decreased by allowing for larger margins of fluctuations of their exchange rates around the chosen parities.

Foreign Currency Holdings

As Exhibit 3.1 shows, the vast majority of foreign reserves in the current system are held in the form of foreign exchange—most of them denominated in U.S. dollars. Although several major currencies have become fully convertible since the 1970s, none of them has achieved a status comparable to the U.S. dollar. Several factors account for this outcome. In some cases, governments (including those of Switzerland

EXHIBIT 3.1 Distribution of Outstanding Reserves by World Areas, End of Years 1975–1982

	Gold		Foreign Exchange	IMF Reserve Positions	SDRs	ECUs	Nongold Total
	(millions of ounces)			(billions of U.S. dollars)			
All countries							
1975			160.9	14.8	10.2	—	185.9
1977	1,011.8	166.9	243.0	22.1	9.8	—	274.9
1979	942.6	493.9	283.9	15.5	16.5	42.8	358.7
1980	950.3	560.2	315.4	21.5	15.1	63.6	415.6
1981	949.7	379.9	302.6	24.8	19.1	49.8	396.3
1982	946.8	424.2	283.1	28.1	19.6	41.4	372.2
Group of Ten and Switzerland							
1975			65.0	8.4	7.8	—	81.1
1977	832.5	137.3	104.5	13.9	7.6	—	126.0
1979	740.7	388.1	109.0	9.0	11.1	42.1	171.2
1980	739.6	436.0	118.6	12.1	10.2	63.0	203.9
1981	739.0	295.6	107.6	14.4	12.5	49.4	183.9
1982	739.2	331.1	96.6	17.7	14.3	41.0	169.6
Total oil-importing countries							
1975			109.8	9.6	9.9	—	129.4
1977	976.8	161.1	173.4	15.5	9.4	—	198.3
1979	905.4	474.3	213.3	11.5	15.0	42.8	282.6
1980	909.7	536.2	225.4	16.2	13.4	63.6	318.6
1981	907.5	363.0	212.8	18.0	16.9	49.8	297.5
1982	904.2	405.1	204.4	20.6	17.2	41.4	283.6
Total oil-exporting countries							
1975			51.0	5.1	0.4	—	56.6
1977	35.0	5.8	69.6	6.6	0.4	—	76.6
1979	37.2	19.6	70.6	4.0	1.5	—	76.1
1980	40.6	24.0	90.0	5.3	1.7	—	97.0
1981	42.2	16.9	89.8	6.8	2.2	—	98.8
1982	42.6	19.1	78.7	7.5	2.4	—	88.6

SOURCE: *Bank for International Settlements Annual Report,* various issues.

and Japan) have actively tried to stop their currencies from becoming a major reserve currency because of the possible impact of such a development on the manageability of their domestic money supply. With the one exception of sterling, a money market as broad and deep as the U.S. money market has been lacking. Such a market is necessary for countries' reserves to be maintained in the form of liquid earning assets. Finally, the U.S. dollar continues to be the currency in which a large portion of international trade is denominated.

In addition to the actual holdings of foreign currency, another instrument has been used as a second line of defense. This instrument is the so-called *swap lines of credit* that can be converted quickly into holdings of foreign currency. These lines are arranged on a bilateral basis between central banks and are used mainly to support existing exchange rates.[4] In the swap lines, two countries agree to borrow one another's currency for a specified period of time with offsetting interest payments and protection against revaluations. The proceeds from these swap loans are then used for central bank intervention in the foreign exchange market. Suppose, for example, that the United States and France agree to a swap line of credit in the amount of $100 equal FF500. When the swap line of credit is used, the United States receives FF500 and France receives $100. This provides the U.S. Central Bank operating through the New York Federal Reserve with francs to stabilize the franc–dollar exchange rate. Upon maturity of the swap, the United States repays FF500 to France and receives $100 in exchange.

Gold Holdings

As we mentioned earlier, the Bretton Woods Agreement included gold holdings among reserves that countries could maintain to support the exchange rate parity of their currencies. For this purpose the price

---

[4]The Bank for International Settlements (BIS), in conjunction with the IMF, provided the forum for the negotiation of many of these policies. The BIS was created after World War I to facilitate the transfer of funds among countries whose currencies were not then convertible into one another in Europe. Since free convertibility was established for most of these currencies in the late 1950s, the major function of the BIS was to provide a forum for the monetary authorities of various countries to meet and to exchange ideas. Charles Coombs described the BIS in graphic terms, noting that some people considered Basel, where the BIS is located, a Swiss Philadelphia. The BIS was a converted hotel with rooms made into small offices. It was located near the Bahnhofplatz, with a small doorway between a pastry shop and a jeweler's shop. No agreements were ever signed and no memoranda of understanding were ever initialed at the BIS. However, the press learned to seek out bankers coming from BIS meetings where new agreements were discussed. As a U.K. banker told reporters outside the offices, after being asked whether he thought a new 1968 agreement would stop the gold rush, "Yes, I think this will do the trick; I am sure it will." Later he remarked that the major duty of every central banker was to "learn how to exude confidence without positively lying." [*The Arena of International Finance* (New York: Wiley Interscience, 1976), p. 166.] The U.S. Federal Reserve System owns around 10% of the BIS's equity, but has never filled the two seats reserved for it on the board of directors.

of gold was fixed at US$35 per ounce. In 1944, this price appeared high for a reserve item that did not earn any interest. However, at this price, the U.S. gold holdings at the time were more than twice the amount needed to guarantee the convertibility of the U.S. dollar into gold. As attacks on the fixed dollar price of gold mounted, a two-tier system was established in 1968. In this system governments continued to trade among themselves at $35 per ounce, while leaving the market price to fluctuate according to the whims of speculators. Finally, in August 1971, after continued attacks on the U.S. dollar, the United States unilaterally terminated the convertibility of the U.S. dollar into gold and let the price of gold be determined by market forces only.

Exhibit 3.1 shows that although the holdings of ounces of gold did not change drastically throughout the period, the contribution of this gold to aggregate reserves measured in U.S. dollars increased enormously to more than half of aggregate reserves in 1982. This increase in the role of gold parallels the increases in gold prices from the official fixed rate of $42.22 per ounce in 1971, after the United States terminated the convertibility of the U.S. dollar into gold and devalued the U.S. dollar. From a low of $100 in 1976, the market price of gold reached a peak of $875 per ounce in January 1980. Exhibit 3.1 shows that these gold holdings are concentrated in the Group of Ten[5] plus Switzerland, which together account for about 80% of the official holdings of gold. Other countries, including the oil-exporting countries, maintain most of their reserves in the form of foreign exchange.

Credit from the IMF

The resources of the IMF consist of money received from member countries' quotas. These resources constitute a pool from which participant countries can draw during short-term balance of payments difficulties. Until 1976, a country's quota in the IMF had to be deposited 25% in gold and 75% in its own currency. Since 1976, the portion of the quota that used to be contributed in the form of gold is now subscribed to either in currencies acceptable to the IMF or in Special Drawing Rights, which are described subsequently.

Member countries have an absolute claim on the IMF, up to the amount of the gold or exchange reserve subscription—that is, they can draw this amount from the IMF at any time. This is called the *gold or reserve tranche position* and is counted among the countries' reserves. Beyond this point, a country can draw upon its *credit tranche*—the ad-

---

[5]For the country composition of the Group of Ten, see the appendix to this chapter, "Some International Associations."

ditional credit the IMF can grant.[6] Approval from the IMF is necessary for a country to draw on its credit tranche. This approval is usually accompanied by restrictions that become increasingly tight as the drawings on this credit rise. Thus, this additional credit is used more often to finance temporary disequilibriums in the balance of payments than to provide temporary liquidity.

Special Drawing Rights (SDRs)

Even in the early 1980s, U.S. dollars represented more than 75% of the world's exchange reserves maintained in the form of foreign exchange. U.S. dollars are liabilities of the United States. To rely on this currency as the major source of liquidity to the system implies relying on continued U.S. acquisitions of foreign assets. [If increases in liabilities are a credit (a plus), then somewhere else in the U.S. balance of payments there must be a debit (a minus).] As long as there was an ever increasing number of financial investors who wanted to invest in securities denominated in U.S. dollars, this problem was only one of equity. Some countries argued that this role of the U.S. dollar gave economic advantages to the United States, which could acquire real and financial assets around the world and pay with the special U.S. liabilities. However, as the level of U.S. dollars abroad continued to increase, investors became increasingly suspicious of the ability of the U.S. dollar to maintain its exchange rate. Whenever these doubts became significant, investors sold U.S. dollars in the market and bought other currencies. When these transactions reached a very high volume in a very short period of time, exchange crises were produced. Thus, to the problem of possible inequity in using the U.S. dollar as the main source of liquidity, the problem of instability in the exchange markets was also added. A response to this problem was the creation of the Special Drawing Right (SDR).

The machinery of the creation of SDRs was activated on August 6, 1969, when the required majority of IMF members became participants in the SDR system. SDRs are international paper money created and distributed by the IMF in the quantities and at the times dictated by special agreements among member countries. As of 1981, this paper money was used only in transactions among governments and between the IMF and these governments. The private sector's use of the SDR was restricted to its role as a unit of account. Settlement of transactions

---

[6]The credit tranche is the amount of drawings beyond the gold tranche that would bring the Fund's total holdings of that currency to 200% of quota. Temporary increases of the credit tranche to 400% of quota have been allowed in the past, usually while waiting for overall increases in quota contributions, as in 1983.

denominated in SDRs was still done in terms of traditional currencies. The first allocation of SDRs was made in January 1970, with the creation of $3.5 billion for that year. By the end of 1981, a total of $22.7 billion (SDR21.5) worth of SDRs had been allocated by the IMF representing approximately 5% of total nongold reserves in that year (see Exhibit 3.1).

Allocations of SDRs are made for *basic periods,* usually 5 years in duration, and they are allocated to IMF members on the basis of IMF quotas at a uniform rate throughout the basic period. The amount of SDRs must be approved by a majority of the IMF participating countries with 85% of the weighted voting power of the Fund. When a participating member receives an allocation of SDRs, it is not required to deposit an equivalent amount of its own currency, as it must when drawing on its IMF borrowing rights. SDRs are a permanent addition to the stock of international liquidity.

SDRs were initially expressed in terms of a fixed amount of gold that was equivalent to the gold content of the U.S. dollar. After the value of the dollar was severed from gold in 1971 and was allowed to float in the exchange markets in 1973, the value of the SDR was redefined. First, in June 1974, the SDR was redefined in terms of sixteen currencies. Then, effective January 1981, the definition was simplified to include only five of the major currencies. The new definition specifies the *amount* of each of the currencies to be included in the computation of the dollar value of the SDR. The specific daily SDR exchange rate is the product of these amounts and the market exchange rates for the corresponding currencies.[7] This latter simplification was expected to expand the marketability of SDR-denominated instruments by appealing to private investors who can use SDRs as a unit of ac-

---

[7]As an illustration of the computation of the SDR spot exchange rate, the valuation of the SDR on January 16, 1981, at noon, would have been calculated as follows:

Currency	Currency Amount (1)	Market Exchange Rate (2)	U.S. Dollar Equivalent (3)	Effective Weight of Each Currency (4)
U.S. dollar	0.5400	1.00000	0.540000	42.69%
German mark	0.4600	2.01720	0.228039	18.03
Pound sterling	0.0710	0.41675	0.170365	13.47
French franc	0.7400	4.65970	0.158809	12.55
Japanese yen	34.0000	202.67000	0.167760	13.26
	U.S. dollar value of SDR1		1.264973	100.00%
	SDR value of US$1		0.790531	

SOURCE: International Monetary Fund, *IMF Survey,* Jan. 26, 1981, p. 18.

In this calculation the currency amounts are those fixed at the end of 1980 for a period of 5 years. The market exchange rates, and thus the effective weights shown in column 4, change daily.

count.[8] To the same end, it was planned that should the IMF need to raise funds in the financial markets, it would be done in the form of SDR-denominated financial paper.

European Currency Units (ECUs)

The European Currency Unit (ECU) was created by the European Monetary Cooperation Fund (FECOM) as part of an attempt to achieve a more integrated monetary system in the EEC. Each of the nine participating EEC countries (Greece will participate in 1986) contributes 20% of its gold and dollar reserves in a 3-month swap, receiving ECU reserves. Although the stabilizing aspects of this unit are to be discussed later, the unit itself has become a market basket measure for commercial transactions. The nature of the required interventions of one currency against another (or indeed, against all other eight currencies) assures commercial interests about minimum and maximum fluctuations in the currency with respect to others. In 1983 the mark accounted for about one-third of the value of the ECU; the French franc, the English pound, and the Dutch guilder each accounted for 10%–18%, and the balance was spread among the Danish krone, the Irish pound, the Italian lira, the Belgian franc, and the Luxembourg franc. Since FECOM does not have the status of a central bank and does not intervene against EEC currencies or against non-EEC currencies, the ECU is not a "super currency," although that is the ultimate goal of many of the EEC bankers. Although divergent national economic policies and other issues complicate this trend, the ECU is more widely used for regular commercial activity than its EEC predecessor, the European Unit of Account.

ALTERNATIVE ADJUSTMENT MECHANISMS

In a system of freely floating exchange rates, there are no imbalances between demand and supply for various currencies. Instead, we observe changes in exchange rates. In a system of fixed exchange rates, the imbalances require a government decision. In a hybrid system (such as the present one), both outcomes occur.

We now discuss how the adjustment mechanism operates under

---

[8]The use of the SDR as a unit of account in the private sector is discussed in Chapter 9, with the instruments available in international finance.

alternative arrangements within the context of the most important systems that have evolved during the post–World War II period.

Fixed Rates with Narrow Bands:
The Bretton Woods System

In a fixed exchange rate system a country with a deficit in its balance of payments loses foreign reserves; a country with a surplus in its international accounts accumulates foreign reserves. However, if the imbalance in payments persists over a longer period of time, this short-term method of adjustment becomes ineffective. It is certainly not available to the deficit country (which might run out of reserves) and it is very undesirable to the surplus country (which accumulates an excessive amount of low-return assets). At this point the system offers two avenues to correct a persistent disequilibrium in the balance of payments. In the case of a deficit, a country can choose either to deflate the domestic economy or to devalue its currency. In the case of a balance of payments surplus, a country can choose either to inflate the domestic economy or to upvalue its currency. However, these measures have proven hard to implement.

Economic policies designed to correct a balance of payments disequilibrium encounter problems when the measures required to improve the balance of payments differ from the measures that domestic objectives would indicate. For example, it is easier to conceive of a deliberate deflation of the economy when the balance of payments deficit which suggests such a policy is accompanied by an overheated economy than when the economy is in a recession. As to changes in foreign exchange parities, governments have historically been reluctant to take such steps. For surplus countries, an upvaluation of their currencies exposes their governments to the wrath of the export industry and of labor in general. For deficit countries, a devaluation increases the domestic cost of living and is considered a loss of international economic power.

Another difficulty with these adjustment mechanisms is that they are biased against deficit countries. Surplus countries are under less pressure to correct their imbalances than are deficit countries. The accumulation of reserves in the surplus countries can fail to induce any sense of urgency in the need to correct the imbalance, for excessive reserves have only an opportunity cost. While deficit countries have to ask for the collaboration of the banking system and the IMF to continue borrowing from them, the system can exert little pressure on a surplus country that chooses neither to adjust its domestic economy nor to upvalue its currency. When the surplus country refuses to carry its part of the adjustment burden, the total adjustment process has to be carried by the deficit country alone, making the required deflation or devaluation in that country larger than if the adjustment process had been shared by the surplus country.

Of course, the major advantage of a fixed-rate system (which can be expected to counteract the problems in the adjustment mechanism just described) is the stability in exchange rates provided by the system. However, even this stability can be threatened when the refusal of countries to carry out the needed adjustments transpires in the form of exchange crises in which private speculators bet against countries' ability to maintain existing rates.

Fixed Rates with Wider Bands: The Smithsonian Agreement and Its Aftermath

By 1971 the failures of the Bretton Woods system were most apparent in the form of recurring crises in the exchange markets. Finally, in August of that year, the United States unilaterally suspended the U.S. dollar convertibility into gold and allowed the value of its dollar to float in the exchange markets. To resolve this situation, the Group of Ten nations agreed on December 18, 1971, to a new set of parity rates and new conditions.

In addition to the new set of rates, currencies were to be allowed to fluctuate over a band wider than in the past (2¼% on either side of the central rate) without requiring government intervention. This was expected to reduce the magnitude of the adjustment problem requiring government intervention. Speculators would be discouraged by the wider possible fluctuations of the exchange rates, and the exchange rate fluctuations themselves would accomplish part of the needed adjustment.

In mid-March 1973, after repeated exchange crises earlier in the year and a couple of weeks when the values of all the major currencies were allowed to fluctuate according to market forces, the foreign exchange market opened again with a new set of rules. While European currencies were to try to maintain parity among their currencies, as a group they would be allowed to fluctuate in value with regard to the U.S. dollar. Managed floating exchange rates had arrived.

Fixed Rates among a Few and Floating Rates against the Others

The members of the European Economic Community (EEC or Common Market) agreed early in 1972 to keep their currencies fluctuating against one another within a band narrower than the one allowed under the Smithsonian Agreement.[9] When the agreement of the European monetary union was reached in 1972, the EEC countries, together with the United Kingdom and Denmark (who were scheduled to join the EEC in 1973), agreed to allow their currencies to fluctuate only a maximum of 2¼% among themselves. However, the group as a whole could fluctuate against other currencies within the larger band provided by the Smithsonian Agreement. This created what was called a "snake within a tunnel." The snake was the narrower band allowed among the EEC currencies; the tunnel was the wider band allowed by the Smithsonian Agreement. The snake was to be allowed to move freely outside the tunnel in 1973. As we mentioned previously, the snake survived in 1973, but the tunnel disappeared.

The European monetary union tried to provide a measure of stability for exchange rates of participating currencies. In a world where major currencies moved toward greater flexibility in exchange rates, the objectives of the monetary union met with only limited success. As domestic economic pressures in the participating countries mounted, many of the initial members abandoned (at least temporarily) attempts to fix the parity of their exchange rate. Some of these episodes were short-lived and a change in parity was enough for the given currency to reenter the snake. Other countries (including France) never returned to the system in its initial form.

The sharp fall in the value of the dollar during 1978 further bolstered the desire for exchange stability among European currencies. Germany and France led the efforts to create a new European Monetary System (EMS), which began operating in 1979. The new version of the European union was a more comprehensive package than the one envisaged in 1972. Its major features are: (1) a system of bilateral exchange rates defining central rates and allowing fluctuations only within a 2¼% band around the central rates, as in the snake; (2) establishment of the European Currency Unit (ECU), a cocktail of European currencies with specified weights as the unit of account of the system; (3) establishment of the European Monetary Cooperation Fund (FECOM), with contributions of domestic currencies and international reserves made available to participating countries in the form of credit facilities; and (4) commitment to increased transfers of funds to participating countries with weaker economies. Some referred to the package as the creation of a European IMF cum World Bank.

As we noted earlier in the chapter, FECOM receives 20% of a participating nation's gold and dollar reserves in a 3-month swap for ECU reserves. FECOM can then lend these reserves to nations (in ECU-denominated debt) to help nations intervene in stabilizing their curren-

---

[9]The initial European Common Market included France, West Germany, Italy, Belgium, Luxembourg, and the Netherlands. See the appendix to this chapter, "Some International Associations."

cies relative to other currencies while taking any additional domestic economic steps required by diverging national parities. In addition to the 2¼% guideline, there is an early warning indicator in terms of a currency's composition within the ECU which also requires action on the part of the involved currency's central bankers. For example, a currency might not be at the floor of its 2¼% central rate band against any other currency, but could nevertheless be deteriorating against the group such that its relative weight within the ECU would be shrinking rapidly. Such an event would trigger the early warning. (Italy is subject to a 6% band rather than the 2¼% band, since the lira has historically been volatile in relation to the other currencies.)

In the first years of its existence, the EMS appeared to have met with greater success than its predecessor. However, the EMS also was proving to be a rather flexible version of a fixed exchange rate system with several currency parity realignments taking place. In the seventh realignment of exchange rates in four years, all seven currencies in the EMS changed their parities in 1983, including a 5½% increase in the German mark and 2.5% depreciation of both the French franc and the Italian lira.

Fixed Rates without a Choice: A Revival of Interest in the Gold Standard

In 1980 a combination of factors (including general dissatisfaction with the instability of exchange rates that accompanied the floating rate regime of the 1970s, greater acceptance of monetarist theories of inflation in the implementation of monetary policy, a "back-to-basics" political attitude that supported balanced fiscal budgets and the discipline imposed by market forces, and the election of a United States president who in precampaign speeches supported returning to the gold standard of earlier years) attracted a renewed interest in the gold standard. In 1981 this interest culminated in the appointment of the Gold Commission by the Reagan administration to analyze the possibility and desirability of bringing the international monetary system back to the gold standard system.

Under this system, international settlements of payments imbalances are made exclusively in gold and domestic money supply is tied to the amount of gold the country has. Foreign exchange (key currencies such as the U.S. dollar) is excluded from international reserves. The exchange rate for each currency is fully convertible. In the case of a balance of payments deficit, a gold outflow takes place to finance the external deficit. This produces a contraction in the domestic money supply and a decrease in prices. As a result, imports decrease and exports increase. The opposite forces are at work in the surplus country. After a while the balance of payments equilibrium is restored.

In this adjustment of the balance of payments disequilibrium, the burden of the adjustment is carried by the domestic economy. It is expected that the domestic economy will inflate and deflate in response to changes in the external balance. In addition, the rules of the game prescribe that monetary policy should not be used to offset gold flows. In cases of downward price rigidity, governments are expected to sit quietly while the economy goes through a period of high unemployment to reduce income and adjust a balance of payments deficit. In the case of a balance of payments surplus, governments are expected to tolerate a period of high inflation.

The gold standard was implemented to some extent before World War I and during the interwar period from 1925 to 1931. Its proponents exalt the virtues of leaving the adjustment process to automatic forces instead of in the hands of policymakers. In addition, sole reliance on gold for international payments has the advantage that all currencies are treated similarly. No country has to incur a deficit to provide the world with its currency, and therefore liquidity. This is usually the argument raised in the context of the present situation, in which the U.S. dollar is an international currency. Before 1971, when the role of the U.S. dollar as the world's reserve currency was not contested by any other currency, countries had to have additional dollars to meet the needs of an expanding world trade. This could be accomplished only by deficits in the U.S. balance of payments. Gold advocates point to this fact as a potential source of inflationary pressures on the world which must see its money supply expanded with the product of its sales to the reserve-currency country.

Opponents of the gold standard maintain that the independence from reserve-currency countries' economic policies is gained only at the expense of putting the system at the mercy of natural resources and the politics of the countries that own those resources (the large suppliers of gold are the Soviet Union and South Africa). Gold supplies certainly would not be responsive to the world needs for liquidity. In addition, the discipline imposed by this standard on domestic economies is not politically feasible. Today's governments are held responsible for maintaining full employment and reasonable growth in an environment of price stability.

THE "OFFICIAL" CURRENT SYSTEM

The system of managed floating rates among major currencies accepted in practice since 1973 terminated the exchange rate system as envisaged by the Bretton Woods Conference in 1944. However, it was not until April 1976 that the Board of Governors of the IMF officially approved a series of changes to the system. The changes were agreed to during protracted negotiations among important member countries during 1973–1976. These changes became effective 2 years later, in April 1978, after the official approval of the necessary number of participating countries was obtained. The major features of these amendments were: (1) legalization of the existing regime of floating exchange rates and freedom for each country to peg or to let float the value of its currency, and (2) termination of the system of par values based on gold. The 25% of quota contribution that was previously made in gold is now made in the form of currencies acceptable to the IMF or SDRs, whose value was severed from gold in 1974. One-third of the IMF's gold was sold in the market over a period of 4 years beginning in early 1976. The Fund was required to avoid the management of the price of gold.

Role of the IMF

In this revised system the International Monetary Fund has the responsibility of surveillance over the exchange rate arrangement that each country chooses and it provides guidance to countries on their exchange rate policies.

The major powers of the IMF continue to be in the area of providing temporary financing for countries with balance of payments difficulties. By 1984, the IMF's lending facilities had increased considerably. In addition to the gold tranche (now called *reserve tranche*) and the four credit tranches established by the Bretton Woods Conference, the IMF has three permanent credit facilities: (1) the compensating financing facility (established in 1963 and liberalized in 1975); (2) the buffer stock financing facility (established in 1969); and (3) the extended facility (established in 1974 and expanded in 1983). In addition, the IMF has other temporary credit facilities created in response to the strains produced by oil price increases in recent years. In 1983, the International Monetary Fund increased its lending authority by almost half to $98.9 (SDR 90) billion. In addition, the special emergency fund created by the General Agreements to Borrow was increased from $7.1 billion to $19 (SDR 17) billion. The total U.S. contribution to these programs was $9.1 billion.

A Tally of Systems in Use as of 1982

Exchange rate practices in effect in 1982 ranged from countries with a relatively free floating of their currency value, with very little government intervention, to countries that pegged the value of their currency to a single major currency and intervened in the market to maintain this value. Canada, the United States, and the EMS as a group are among the countries with floating currencies with limited government intervention. Of course, among the currencies participating in the EMS a system of fixed rates exists, except when individual countries temporarily abandon the agreement.

However, most countries (ninety-three nations) still pursued a policy of fixed exchange rates as of December 1982. Floating on a continued basis has been practiced by only some of the most developed economies. Among the countries with fixed rates, the pegging technique is not as homogeneous as it was before December 1971. In December 1982, thirty-eight countries retained a peg to the U.S. dollar, thirteen were pegged to the French franc, and five were pegged to other single currencies. A growing number of countries (thirty-eight) chose to peg the value of their currencies to a basket of other currencies specially selected or to the SDR. However, even among countries pegging the value of their currencies, there has been a greater willingness to reassess the exchange rate policy and to change the parity value if necessary.

Other arrangements in existence in 1982 included three countries which adjusted their exchange rates following a set of indicators, the eight countries in the cooperative agreement of the EMS, and more than thirty countries which either let the value of their currencies float or followed a mix of the above systems.[10]

SUMMARY

International business requires a financial instrument that is acceptable to both parties in order to settle payment. Either international paper money currency and/or a major currency that is freely convertible into other currencies is necessary to provide the *liquidity* needed by international commercial transactions. A second problem requiring international institutions and arrangements is the development of imbalances which need *adjustments* between supply of and demand for a given currency. The imbalance may arise from a number of factors, including shocks to the system (for example, OPEC), seasonal needs of an economy, or a temporary situation in a nation. The imbalance may be solved by financing through changes in a government's reserves and borrowings, changes in the exchange parities, or adjustments in the home economy. In any of these cases, no single nation can act alone, for the

---

[10]*IMF Survey*, January 24, 1983, p. 21.

other nations must agree (or at least tolerate) a government's action in order to avoid nullifying the action. Hence, some agreement or forum for discussion is required.

The current system can be traced to March 1973, when the fixed-rate system created at Bretton Woods in 1944 was fundamentally scrapped. Today, most countries peg their currencies to a key currency, but the developed countries tend to float their currencies against other developed countries' currencies, with various levels of governmental involvement in the management of the floating. The major sources of liquidity in the system are the holding of gold and foreign currencies, primarily U.S. dollars. The increase in the importance of gold holdings is caused mostly by the increase in the price of that metal. In addition, international paper money has been created. Since 1969, over $21.5 billion of Special Drawing Rights (SDRs) have been issued and allocated by the International Monetary Fund (IMF). SDRs today are a weighted combination of five major international currencies. European Currency Units (ECUs) are a weighted mixture of nine currencies of the European Economic Community.

The fixed exchange rate system of Bretton Woods failed in large part because the adjustment mechanism did not function properly. Countries with undervalued currencies had little pressure to appreciate their currencies; countries with overvalued currencies were required to carry the complete burden of the needed adjustment when forced to devalue their currencies and to adjust their domestic economies. As these failures mounted, they eventually transpired in the form of crises in the foreign exchange markets as speculators began to bet against the ability of the various governments involved to maintain the existing exchange parities.

Many of the European countries have attempted to reduce the fluctuations in their own currencies against other European currencies, and the European Monetary System is the latest arrangement to this end. Intra-European accounting and payments are handled largely through the ECU, an index with fixed weights of various European currencies. The European Monetary Cooperation Fund further provides domestic and international currency reserves to member nations suffering temporary balance of payments difficulties.

The IMF was created by the Bretton Woods Agreement, and provides various credit reserves to nations when those nations want financing beyond their own supplies of gold and convertible foreign currency. However, the IMF does set conditions for the borrowings. The currently approved articles of agreement of the IMF permit countries to fix or float their own currencies, sever exchange parities from the gold standard, and provide a vastly expanded credit system.

QUESTIONS

1. What changes would you make in the present international monetary system? Why?

2. What changes in the present international monetary system do you consider likely to occur in the near future? Why?

3. What role will the U.S. dollar play in international financial markets in the future? Why?

APPENDIX

SOME INTERNATIONAL ASSOCIATIONS

International Monetary Fund (IMF). Institution created in 1944 to supervise the monetary system established at Bretton Woods. The Fund also provides credit to finance balance of payments problems of member countries. Membership at the end of 1983 included 146 countries. Most communist countries are not represented at the IMF.

International Bank for Reconstruction and Development (IBRD or World Bank). Institution created together with the IMF. Its purpose is to provide credit to governments for development purposes. Membership is similar to the IMF's.

European Economic Community (EEC or Common Market)—The Original Six. France, Germany, Italy, the Netherlands, Belgium, and Luxembourg.

Enlarged Common Market—The Nine. The original six plus the United Kingdom, Ireland, and Denmark.

Group of Ten. The ten major industrial countries (the six less Luxembourg plus the United Kingdom, the United States, Sweden, Canada, and Japan) which agreed in October 1962 to stand ready to lend their currencies to the IMF under the General Arrangements to Borrow (GAB). Switzerland has also joined the GAB making the Group of Ten actually eleven. Meetings of the Group of Ten finance ministers and central governors (and those of their deputies) have engineered the main changes in the world's monetary system in the 1960s and 1970s. Central bank governors of these countries hold regular monthly meetings at the Bank for International Settlements (BIS) in Basel. Representatives from the IMF, the Organization for Economic Cooperation and Development (OECD), BIS, and the European Economic Community (EEC) may also attend these meetings.

Bank for International Settlements (BIS).   Organization which operates as the central bank for the central bankers of the Group of Ten.

Interim Committee or Group of Twenty.   Group of finance ministers within the IMF. The United States, Japan, Germany, France, and the United Kingdom plus 15 members elected by the remaining members of the IMF. These same 20 countries form the joint World Bank/IMF Development Committee.

OPEC.   Organization of Petroleum Exporting Countries. Group formed by major oil-producing countries. Its major function has been to provide a forum where a common oil pricing policy can be established and enforced through a cartel.

OECD.   Organization for Economic Cooperation and Development. Established in 1961 as successor to the Organization for European Economic Cooperation. Group of 23 developed nations: the Group of Ten plus Austria, Denmark, Luxembourg, Norway, Switzerland, Finland, Greece, Iceland, Ireland, Portugal, Spain, Turkey, and Australia. (Yugoslavia is an associate.)

APPENDIX

IMPORTANT DATES IN THE WORLD MONETARY SYSTEM[1]

1944   Conference at Bretton Woods, New Hampshire, establishes a fixed exchange rate based on the U.S. dollar. The International Monetary Fund (IMF) and the International Bank for Reconstruction and Development (IBRD), the World Bank, are created.

1948   The U.S. President signs bill appropriating funds for the European Recovery Plan—the Marshall Plan.

1949   Exchange rates of major European countries and many non-European countries devalue. U.S. gold stock peaks at $24.6 billion.

---

[1]For a very detailed chronology of the monetary events during part of this period, see Robert Solomon, *The International Monetary System, 1945–1976.* (New York: Harper & Row, Publishers), 1976.

1950   U.S. balance of payments on a liquidity basis swings into deficit and stays in deficit for a protracted period with only a few exceptions. European Payments Union (EPU) is created by recipients of the European Recovery Plan—the Marshall Plan.

1958   The European Economic Community (EEC) is established. Most European countries restore convertibility of their currencies for nonresidents. EPU is eliminated.

1960   Run on gold pushes price to $40 an ounce and forces central banks to intervene in London market to hold down price. London gold pool is established by central banks of major countries to support price of gold.

1961   German mark and guilder upvalue. Organization for Economic Cooperation and Development (OECD) comes into existence.

1962   French begin turning in dollars for U.S. gold. Policy continues through 1966 and costs United States $3 billion in gold.

1963   United States levies interest equalization tax on foreign borrowing in this country.

1965   United States imposes "voluntary" controls on the export of dollars.

1967   British pound devalues touching off world money crisis that lasts into 1968.

1968   United States adopts mandatory controls on direct investment.

Run on gold in March brings central banks to Washington and leads to elimination of the London gold pool and the creation of a two-price gold market.

1969   French franc devalues in August.

German mark upvalues in October after floating in exchange markets for a very brief period.

1970   Special Drawing Rights (SDRs) are used as supplement to gold and dollars in reserves of nations. The value of one SDR equals one U.S. dollar initially.

U.S. balance of payments deficit reaches record $10 billion.

1971   Massive inflows of money in early May force Germany to float the mark and Switzerland to upvalue the franc.

U.S. gold stock falls below $10 billion for first time since World War II.

United States runs international trade deficit in first half for first time in twentieth century.

U.S. payments deficit in first half is at a $23 billion annual rate.

On August 15 the U.S. dollar is floated, convertibility of the U.S. dollar into gold is eliminated, and an import surcharge is imposed in the United States.

On December 17, in the Smithsonian Agreement, central rates are fixed and the U.S. dollar is devalued. Also, a wider margin of 2¼% on either side of the central rate is established. The United States agrees to eliminate the import surcharge but the convertibility of U.S. dollars into gold is not reinstated.

1972   In May the original Common Market countries, the United Kingdom, and Denmark jointly agree to a narrow range of exchange rate flexibility of 1⅛% among themselves while maintaining the currencies within the 2¼% band on either side of the par value vis-à-vis the U.S. dollar.

On June 23 the pound is floated after a brief speculative period when British international reserves are at record highs. The United Kingdom is joined by Denmark in withdrawing from the monetary agreement with the European countries. Denmark rejoins the agreement later in the year.

1973   In order to protect the domestic economy from international monetary problems, the Swiss franc is floated on January 23.

On February 12, renewed speculation on the dollar leads the United States to devalue the U.S. dollar again. The lira and the yen are floated. Italy leaves the European monetary union.

In March renewed attacks on the U.S. dollar lead governments to close their exchange markets for two weeks. Finally, it is decided to keep the currencies participating in the European monetary agreement, the snake, within 2¼% fluctuation from one another, but to float against the U.S. dollar. Sweden becomes an associate member of the snake.

During the summer, attacks on the dollar are renewed. Prices of major currencies move up relative to the U.S. dollar. However, no official parity changes are made and during the last quarter of the year the pressures on the dollar recede. When the oil-producing nations establish an embargo on oil exports to developed countries, the United States is perceived to be in a more self-reliant position than the other developed countries. After the embargo is suspended, oil prices more than quadruple within a short period of time.

1974   In January the three programs controlling capital outflows from the United States are eliminated. This leads to massive U.S. lending to foreigners.

The French franc withdraws from the European joint-float program.

The oil-producing countries maintain a large portion of their increased reserves in the form of deposits with banks. Recycling these petrodollars to countries with deficits in their balance of payments appears as a new problem for the international monetary system.

In the first half of the year several bank failures with large losses in foreign exchange bring fears to international financial markets. Credit worthiness of institutions is questioned.

On June 28 the IMF redefines the value of SDRs. The new value is based on the weighted value of 16 major currencies instead of reflecting only the value of the U.S. dollar.

1975   Negotiations toward an agreement on a new international monetary system continue unsuccessfully. In practice, major currencies operate on a managed-float basis and the IMF votes to abolish the "official price" of gold.

In July the French franc rejoins the European joint-float program.

The balance of payments surpluses of the oil-producing countries are reduced to almost half of the surplus amount of the preceding year as these countries step up imports from developed countries. The current accounts of developed countries improve considerably as a result.

In November, at Ramboillet, France, heads of six major countries acknowledge the need for a compromise system which allows for currencies to float while pursuing economic goals of growth and price stability.

1976   In Jamaica the decisions to accept a system in which currencies are allowed to float and to stop pegging the price of gold are ratified. A Trust Fund is established to manage the proceeds from sales of IMF gold to be distributed to developing countries.

In March the French franc abandons the European joint-float agreement and its value is allowed to float in the exchange markets.

In April the Board of Governors of the IMF officially accepts the proposals for amendments to the Fund's articles of agreement.

1978   On April 1 the amendments to the IMF's articles of agreement come into force as the acceptance from the necessary number of participating countries is obtained.

On July 7 the heads of state of the nine countries in the European Common Market agree to work toward closer monetary cooperation. A monetary union where parities are maintained within narrow margins ("at least as strict as the snake") is proposed. Also, plans for a European monetary fund financed with a portion of the reserves of the participating countries is envisaged.

In spite of improvements in the balance of trade and current accounts of the United States, the dollar falls sharply throughout the year, particularly against the German mark, the Swiss franc, and the yen.

On November 1 the United States announces measures to defend the dollar. The package includes increased swap lines, drawings from the IMF, sales of SDRs and gold, and bond issues in the Euro-markets. The dollar recovers.

1979   On March 13, EMS starts. It includes Belgium, Denmark, West Germany, France, Luxembourg, the Netherlands, Italy and Ireland. It replaces the European "snake."

During the Nov. '78–Jan. '79 quarter, total gross market intervention by the major central banks reached a record $33.1 billion. Also U.S. intervention in the foreign exchange markets amounted to a record $6,860.6 million equivalent.

On October 10, the U.S. Federal Reserve announces a new anti-inflationary program based on monetary policy controlling monetary aggregates instead of interest rates.

On October 23, the United Kingdom removes all exchange restrictions.

The trade deficit of the non-oil developing countries reaches a record $73.6 billion.

1980   Gold prices in world markets rise dramatically to unprecedented levels.

In May the Fund completes its four-year program to sell 25 million ounces of gold through public auctions, with profits being made available to developing members of the Fund.

In June, a Common Fund, for the stabilization of commodity prices is agreed upon. Agreement will become operational once it has been ratified by 90 countries providing 2/3 of the fund's projected assets. Proposed size of Common Fund is $750 million.

Switzerland lifts all remaining exchange rate restriction on Swiss franc (deposits by nonresidents).

In the financial year 1979–1980, the Fund's total volume of financial activity reached a record level of SDR9.7 billion; about SDR 5.6 billion was on account of developing countries.

The Fund decides to simplify, as of January 1, 1981, the currency baskets that determine the value of and the interest rate on the SDR. The unified basket will be composed of the currencies of the five members having the largest exports of goods and services during the period 1975–1979: U.S. dollar, German mark, French franc, Japanese yen, and pound sterling.

Trade deficit of the non-oil developing countries reaches record $102 billion.

1981   In January, Greece becomes the tenth member of the European Community.

Finance Ministers of the European Common Market approve the establishment of an ECU6 billion facility to provide balance of payments financing to member countries. The funds are to be raised through the international capital markets, with the European Community guaranteeing the loans.

Adjustments are made in the central rates of the European Monetary System in order to relieve downward pressure on the French franc and reduce tension in the foreign exchange markets.

Japan's trade surplus with members of the European Community grows to a record $10.3 billion in 1981 (compared with $8.8 billion in 1980).

1982   On February 22, the currencies of Belgium, Denmark, and Luxembourg are devalued against the other currencies in the European Monetary System (EMS). This realignment is the fifth one since the EMS came into existence in 1979. The United States intervenes in the exchange markets after the realignment.

In July, a new OECD agreement on export credits enters into force. The agreement raises the minimum allowable long-term rate on government-supported export loans.

In August, Mexico closes its exchange markets, unable to meet payments due on foreign debt.

In December, the IMF agrees to the use of Fund's resources totalling SDR3.6 billion by the Government of Mexico; this total represents 450% of Mexico's quota in the Fund.

Drawings by Fund's member countries reach a record level of SDR7.4 billion. An increase of 10% from the record level of SDR6.8 billion in 1981.

1983 On January 10, the Group of Ten decides to raise their aggregate credit commitments under the General Arrangements to Borrow (GAB) from SDR6.4 billion to SDR17 billion in order to meet increased demand for IMF's financing to developing countries facing debt-repayment difficulties.

In February, the Interim Committee of the Board of Governors of the IMF agrees to increase the Fund's quotas from about SDR61.03 billion to SDR90 billion.

In February, the World Bank approves the establishment of a Special Action Program to help developing countries to maintain the momentum of development in spite of world financial problems.

On March 7, the Fund approves the use of resources by the Government of Brazil totalling the equivalent of SDR4.96 billion, which represents approximately 500% of Brazil's quota in the Fund.

BIBLIOGRAPHY

Aliber, Robert Z., *The Political Economy of Monetary Reform.* Montclair, N.J.: Allenheld, Osman and Company, 1977.

Balassa, Bela, "European Monetary Arrangements: Problem Areas and Policy Options," *European Economic Review,* Aug. 1977, pp. 265–81.

"A Bank for All Seasons: A Survey of the World Bank," *Economist* (Survey), Sept. 4, 1982, pp. 1–55.

Bauer, P. T., "Against the New Economic Order," *Commentary,* Apr. 1977, pp. 25–31.

Beveridge, W. A., "Fiscal Content of Financial Programs Supported by Standby Arrangements in the Upper Credit Tranches 1969–78," *International Monetary Fund Staff Papers,* June 1980, pp. 205–249.

Bigman, David, and Teizo Taya, eds., *The Functioning of Floating Exchange Rates: Theory, Evidence, and Policy Implications.* Cambridge, Mass.: Harper, Row and Company, 1980.

Bilson, John F. O., "The Monetary Approach to the Exchange Rate: Some Empirical Evidence," *International Monetary Fund Staff Papers,* Mar. 1978, pp. 48–75.

———, "Recent Developments in Monetary Models of Exchange Rate Determination," *International Monetary Fund Staff Papers,* June 1979, pp. 201–223.

Blejer, Mario I., and Leonardo Leiderman, "A Monetary Approach to the Crawling-Peg System: Theory and Evidence," *Journal of Political Economy,* Feb. 1981, pp. 132–151.

Bond, Marian E., "Exchange Rates, Inflation, and Vicious Circle," *International Monetary Fund Staff Papers,* Dec. 1980, pp. 679–711.

Brittain, Bruce, "Tests of Theories of Exchange Rate Determination," *Journal of Finance,* May 1977, pp. 519–29.

Burns, Arthur F., "The Need for Order in International Finance," *Columbia Journal of World Business,* Spring 1977, pp. 5–12.

Caldwell, J. Alexander, "Gold: The Fundamentals behind the Frenzy," *Euromoney,* Feb. 1980, pp. 110–120.

Caves, Richard E., and Lawrence B. Krause, eds., *Britain's Economic Performance.* Washington, D. C.: Brookings Institution, 1980.

Cline, William R., *International Monetary Reform and the Developing Countries.* Washington, D.C.: Brookings Institution, 1976.

Coats, Warren L., Jr., "The SDR as a Means of Payment," *International Monetary Fund Staff Papers,* Sept. 1982, pp. 422–36.

Coombs, Charles A., *The Arena of International Finance.* New York: Wiley Interscience, 1976.

Cooper, Richard N., et al., *The International Monetary System under Flexible Exchange Rates.* Cambridge, Mass.: Harper & Row, 1982.

Corden, W. M., *Inflation, Exchange Rates, and the World Economy: Lectures on International Monetary Economics.* Chicago: University of Chicago Press, 1977.

Crockett, Andrew, "Determinants of Exchange Rate Movements: A Review," *Finance and Development,* Mar. 1981, pp. 33–37.

Dam, Kenneth W., *The Rules of the Game.* Chicago: University of Chicago Press, 1982.

Day, William H. D., "Flexible Exchange Rates: A Case for Official Intervention," *International Monetary Fund Staff Papers,* July 1977, pp. 330–43.

DeGrauwe, Paul, "The Interaction of Monetary Policies in a Group of European Countries," *Journal of International Economics,* Aug. 1975, pp. 207–28.

deVries, Tom, "An Agenda for Monetary Reform," *Essays in International Finance,* No. 95. Princeton, N.J.: Princeton University, Sept. 1972.

Dreyer, Jacob S., Gottfried Haberler, and Thomas D. Willett, eds., *The International Monetary System: A Time of Turbulence.* Washington, D.C.: American Enterprise Institute for Public Policy Research, 1982.

Driskill, Robert A., "Exchange Rate Dynamics: An Empirical Investigation," *Journal of Political Economy,* Apr. 1981, pp. 357–71.

——— , "Exchange Rate Dynamics, Portfolio Balance, and Relative Prices," *American Economic Review,* Sept. 1980, pp. 776–83.

Frenkel, Jacob A., "The Purchasing Power Parity: Doctrinal Perspective and Evidence from the 1920s," *Journal of International Economics,* May 1978, pp. 169–92.

Frenkel, Jacob A., and Harry G. Johnson, eds., *The Monetary Approach to the Balance of Payments.* Toronto: University of Toronto Press, 1976.

Friedman, Milton, and Robert V. Roosa, "Free versus Fixed Exchange Rates: A Debate," *Journal of Portfolio Management,* Spring 1977, pp. 68–73.

Gailliot, Henry J., "Purchasing Power Parity as an Explanation of Long-Term Changes in Exchange Rates," *Journal of Money, Credit, and Banking,* Aug. 1970, pp. 348–57.

Heller, Robert H., and Mohsin S. Khan, "The Demand for International Reserves under Fixed and Floating Exchange Rates," *International Monetary Fund Staff Papers*, Dec. 1978, pp. 623–49.

Hodgson, John S., and Patricia Phelps, "The Distributed Impact of Price-Level Variation on Floating Exchange Rates," *Review of Economics and Statistics*, Feb. 1975, pp. 58–64.

Holden, Paul, Merle Holden, and Esther C. Suss, "The Determinants of Exchange Rate Flexibility: An Empirical Investigation," *Review of Economics and Statistics*, Aug. 1979, pp. 327–33.

International Monetary Fund, *The Monetary Approach to the Balance of Payments: A Collection of Research Papers by Members of the Staff of the International Monetary Fund*. Washington, D.C.: International Monetary Fund, 1977.

Johnson, Harry G., *The Problem of International Monetary Reform*. London: Athlone Press, 1974.

_____ , "The Monetary Approach to the Balance of Payments Theory and Policy: Explanation and Policy Implications," *Economica*, Aug. 1977, pp. 217–29.

_____ , "The Monetary Approach to the Balance of Payments: A Nontechnical Guide," *Journal of International Economics*, Aug. 1977, pp. 251–68.

Keran, Michael, and Stephen Zeldes, "Effects of Monetary Disturbances on Exchange Rates, Inflation, and Interest Rates," *Economic Review*, Federal Reserve Bank of San Francisco, Spring 1980, pp. 7–29.

Kindleberger, Charles P., *Europe and the Dollar*. Cambridge, Mass.: M.I.T. Press, 1966.

_____ , and Peter H. Lindert, *International Economics*, 6th ed. Homewood, Ill.: Richard D. Irwin, Inc., 1978.

Kortweg, Pieter, "Exchange Rate Policy, Monetary Policy, and Real Exchange Rate Variability," *Essays in International Finance*, No. 140. Princeton, N.J.: Princeton University, 1980.

Kouri, P. J. K., and J. B. deMacedo, "Exchange Rates and the International Adjustment Process," *Brookings Papers on Economic Activity*, No. 1, 1978.

Krause, Lawrence B., and Walter S. Salant, eds., *Worldwide Inflation: Theory and Recent Experience*. Washington, D.C.: Brookings Institution, 1977.

Krueger, Anne O., *Exchange-Rate Determination*, Cambridge: Cambridge University Press, 1983.

Krugman, Paul, "New Theories of Trade Among Industrial Countries," *Journal of Finance*, May 1983, pp. 343–48.

Lipschitz, Leslie, and V. Sundaraarajan, "The Optimal Basket in a World of Generalized Floating," *International Monetary Fund Staff Papers*, Mar. 1980, pp. 80–100.

Magee, Stephen P., and Ramesh K. S. Rao, "Vehicle and Nonvehicle Currencies in International Trade," *American Economic Review*, May 1980, pp. 368–73.

Mayer, Helmut, "The Eurocurrency Market and the Autonomy of U.S. Monetary Policy," *Columbia Journal of World Business*, Fall 1979, pp. 32–37.

McKinnon, Ronald I., "Dollar Stabilization and American Monetary Policy," *American Economic Review*, May 1980, pp. 382–87.

────── , *Money in International Exchange: The Convertible Currency System.* New York: Oxford University Press, 1979.

Nowzad, Bahram, *The IMF and Its Critics.* Essays in International Finance series, No. 146. Princeton, New Jersey: Princeton University, Department of Economics, 1982.

Officer, Lawrence H., "The Purchasing Power Parity Theory of Exchange Rates: A Review Article," *International Monetary Fund Staff Papers*, Mar. 1976, pp. 1–60.

Parkin, Michael, "A Monetarist Analysis of the Generation and Transmission of World Inflation: 1958–1971," *American Economic Review*, Feb. 1977, pp. 164–71.

Root, Franklin R., *International Trade and Investment*, 4th ed. Cincinnati, Ohio: South-Western Publishing Co., 1978.

Salant, Walter S., "International Transmission of Inflation," in Lawrence B. Drause and Walter S. Salant, eds., *Worldwide Inflation.* Washington, D.C.: Brookings Institution, 1977, pp. 167–243.

────── , "A Supranational Approach to the Analysis of Worldwide Inflation," in Lawrence B. Drause and Walter S. Salant, eds., *Worldwide Inflation.* Washington, D.C.: Brookings Institution, 1977, pp. 633–56.

Schadler, S., "Sources of Exchange Rate Variability: Theory and Empirical Evidence," *International Monetary Fund Staff Papers*, July 1977, pp. 253–96.

Solomon, Robert, *The International Monetary System.* New York: Harper & Row, 1982.

Sumner, M. T., and G. Zis, eds., *European Monetary Union: Progress and Prospect*, New York: St. Martin's Press, 1982.

Swoboda, Alexander K., "Monetary Approaches to Worldwide Inflation," in Lawrence B. Krause and Walter S. Salant, eds., *Worldwide Inflation.* Washington, D.C.: Brookings Institution, 1977, pp. 633–56.

Triffin, Robert, *Our International Monetary System: Yesterday, Today, and Tomorrow.* New York: Random House, Inc., 1968.

Vaubel, Roland, "Why the EMS May Have to Be Dismantled," *Euromoney*, Jan. 1980, pp. 78–86.

von Furstenberg, George M., "Internationally Managed Moneys," *Journal of Finance*, May 1983, pp. 54–58.

Whitman, Marina V. N., "Global Monetarism and the Monetary Approach to the Balance of Payments," *Brookings Papers on Economic Activity*, No. 3, 1975, pp. 491–536.

────── , "Global Monetarism: Theory, Policy, and Critique," *Journal of Portfolio Management*, Spring 1977, pp. 7–18.

Willett, Thomas D., *International Liquidity Issues.* Washington, D.C.: American Enterprise Institute for Public Policy Research, 1980.

────── , "U.S. Monetary Policy and World Liquidity," *Journal of Finance*, May, 1983, pp. 43–47.

Yeager, Leland B., et al., *Experiences with Stopping Inflation.* Washington, D.C.: American Enterprise Institute for Public Policy Research, 1981.

4

Money and Banking in International Markets

THE INTERNATIONAL BANKING structure is the private component of the international monetary system. Given the general parameters provided by the international agreements and institutions discussed in the previous chapter, the banking industry provides liquidity (money) to the system and helps finance imbalances that develop among countries. In this discussion we will address each function separately. We will also see how there are two parallel banking systems at the international level for each major currency: the traditional one and the so-called Eurocurrency system.

THE INTERNATIONAL TRANSFER OF FUNDS

Financial officers do not usually cross countries' borders with suitcases packed with paper or metal money.[1] With the exception of the smuggler, international capital transactions generally are not realized through paper or metal money. Instead, most international payments are settled by drawing on deposits with a bank. Thus, banks are the main conduit for the international transfer of funds and the principal

---

[1]This is not to say that some colorful examples of the suitcase version do not exist. The Swiss Alps have witnessed many of these transfers.

private institution providing liquidity to the international monetary system.

Although they are closely interlinked, there are two different banking systems through which the international transfer of funds can be accomplished. One system is the traditional *correspondent banking system*, in which the banks maintain deposits in the home currency of the country in which they are located and are subject to local banking regulations affecting deposits. In the other system, banks' deposits can be denominated in any currency (regardless of the country in which the banks are located), but these deposits are not subject to local regulations affecting the cost and nature of deposits.[2] This is the so-called *Eurocurrency market* in which Eurodollars, Eurosterling, and other Eurocurrencies are traded.

Given the factors that differentiate domestic from Eurocurrency deposits, we can see that the term "Eurocurrency" is a misnomer. One should talk instead of currencies outside the control of domestic banking regulations, or *external currencies*. Although the bulk of these external transactions initially took place in Europe, a sizable amount of the market is now transacted in other parts of the world, particularly Asia, the Middle East, and the Caribbean. Since 1981, Eurocurrencies (including Eurodollars) are also traded in the United States in the *international banking facilities* approved that year by the Federal Reserve. These facilities are exempt from reserve requirements and interest rate ceilings imposed on domestic banks' deposits; that is, they are not subject to the banking regulations on deposits applicable to regular domestic banks. However, these international banking facilities must restrict their business in the United States to the traditional Eurocurrency transactions, which exclude loans to U.S. companies for domestic purposes.

As an illustration of how payments can be settled internationally under the alternative banking systems, we will use an example. Assume that U.S. Corporation imports cars for a total of US$1 million equivalent. The exporter is the ABC Corporation in England. U.S. Corporation's bank in the United States is Chase Manhattan and ABC Corporation's bank in England is Barclays.

Transfer of Funds
in the Traditional Banking System

The car sale used in the illustration is likely to be billed in either sterling (the currency of the seller) or U.S. dollars (the currency of the

---

[2]This difference in regulatory environment also explains the differences observed between interest rates paid on domestic and Eurocurrency deposits denominated in the same currency and with comparable maturity. See the section titled "Eurocurrency Financing" in Chapter 9.

buyer). Of course, any currency can be chosen for the transaction, as long as both parties agree to it.

If the sale is invoiced in sterling, then U.S. Corporation will probably have to convert U.S. dollars, its home currency, into sterling. This conversion is done with its bank, Chase Manhattan. As Exhibit 4.1 shows, U.S. Corporation's dollar payment in the exchange transaction represents a reduction in dollar deposits at Chase. In order for Chase to deliver sterling to U.S. Corporation, it has to draw on its sterling balances. These sterling balances are, in fact, deposits that Chase maintains with a British bank—Chase's correspondent bank in England— say, Barclays. At Barclays (which we have assumed to be ABC's bank also), there will be a change in the ownership of £1 million sterling deposits from Chase to ABC Corporation, assuming an exchange rate of $1.00/£.

If the trade transaction is denominated in U.S. dollars and if ABC Corporation is still interested in converting the dollar proceeds into sterling, then the exchange transaction will take place at Barclays, ABC's bank in England. ABC will present to Barclays a check for US$1

EXHIBIT 4.1   International Transfer of Funds: The Traditional Banking System

---

*Transaction: U.S. Corporation imports $1 million equivalent of cars
from ABC Corporation in England.
Exchange rate: $1.00/£*

A. SALE IS BILLED IN STERLING.

1. U.S. Corp. purchases £ against $ at Chase.	2. ABC deposits £ check drawn on Chase account with Barclays.

Chase U.S.		Barclays U.K.
£ Balance (Barclays) −1,000,000	$ Deposit (U.S. Corp.) −1,000,000	£ Deposit (Chase) −1,000,000 £ Deposit (ABC) +1,000,000

B. SALE IS BILLED IN U.S. DOLLARS.

1. U.S. Corp. draws check on Chase.	2. ABC purchases £ against $ at Barclays.

Chase U.S.	Barclays U.K.	
$ Deposit (U.S. Corp.) −1,000,000 $ Deposit (ABC) +1,000,000	$ Balance (Chase) +1,000,000	£ Deposit (ABC) +1,000,000

3. Barclays deposits $ check drawn on Chase.

Chase U.S.
$ Deposit (ABC) −1,000,000 $ Deposit (Barclays) +1,000,000

million drawn on Chase Manhattan. At the assumed exchange rate, ABC receives in exchange £1 million in deposits with Barclays. At Barclays there is an increase in sterling deposits (ABC's account) and an increase in U.S. dollar balances, which are maintained with Chase. At Chase, there is only a change in ownership of dollar deposits from U.S. Corporation, to ABC Corporation, and to Barclays.

In this example, one of the trading parties must enter a foreign exchange transaction regardless of the currency in which the export sale is billed. If the sale is denominated in sterling, the U.S. buyer has to make the foreign exchange transaction. If the sale is billed in dollars, it is the British exporter who must complete the foreign exchange transaction. Of course, this does not have to be the case in every transaction. In our example the U.S. importer may have already had balances in sterling, or the British exporter may have been willing to hold dollar balances in payment for the export sale. However, given that the revenues of the buyer (U.S. Corporation) are likely to be denominated in U.S. dollars, and that the costs of the seller (ABC Corporation) are likely to be denominated in sterling, the exchange transaction will be necessary more often than not.

After the described transaction, the importer and exporter satisfy the needed international transfer of funds. However, the commercial banks may now have a problem. If we assume that both Chase and Barclays initially had exactly the amount of foreign exchange they wished to hold, then after the settlement of the import payment one of the banks has an amount of foreign exchange different from what it wishes to have. Depending on the currency of the sale, Chase or Barclays will have to sell dollars and buy sterling to revert their exposure to exchange risk to the initial position.

Transfer of Funds in the Eurocurrency System

To illustrate how the Eurocurrency markets function in the international transfer of funds in the example, we need to assume only that when the export sale is billed in U.S. dollars, ABC Corporation chooses to maintain the *dollar balances* with Barclays, instead of Chase. The decision of ABC Corporation to transfer a dollar deposit from Chase in the United States (the bank on which the dollar funds were drawn) to a bank outside the banking regulations of the United States amounts to the creation of a *Eurodollar deposit*—that is, a U.S. dollar-denominated financial instrument that can be traded outside the regulations on banking deposits in the United States. We should note that in this transaction, no foreign exchange conversion is necessary (up to this point), although a Eurodollar deposit is created.

Transaction 1 in Exhibit 4.2 shows the initial creation of the Eurodollar deposit in our example. Barclays has acquired a dollar deposit without having to comply with U.S. regulations on bank deposits. We can expect Barclays to want to invest the dollar proceeds obtained with the deposit as soon as possible. This will usually mean extending a loan.

Assume that shortly after Barclays receives the deposit from ABC Corporation, it also receives an application for a 7-day Eurodollar loan from XYZ Corporation. XYZ Corporation would like to have the Eurodollar funds transferred to Switzerland, where it eventually intends to use the funds. In Switzerland, XYZ Corporation conducts its banking business with the Union Bank of Switzerland.

When Barclays extends a Eurodollar loan in the amount of $1 million to the XYZ Corporation (transaction 2), funds are initially made available to the XYZ Corporation in the form of dollar deposits with Barclays; that is, Barclays increases both its dollar loans and its dollar deposits by $1 million.[3] This raises the total Eurodollar liabilities of non-U.S. banks to $2 million—$1 million deposited by ABC and $1 million deposited by XYZ. Eurodollars, once they come into existence, can reproduce themselves. The pattern followed in this reproduction is the same as the one described for domestic expansion of deposits in most money and banking texts: Any time a bank acquires a new deposit, it can make a loan which creates another deposit.

Next, Barclays must transfer its dollar balances to the account of XYZ Corporation with the Union Bank of Switzerland. Accordingly, Barclays sends a telex to Chase Manhattan requesting that its deposit with Chase be transferred to Union Bank of Switzerland for the Swiss bank's account with XYZ Corporation (transaction 3). After this transaction, the amount of Eurodollar deposits is still $2 million. However, the Union Bank has now acquired Eurodollar balances which are not subject to U.S. regulations on dollar deposits, and which Union Bank will want to invest as soon as possible—that is, make a loan. Note that Union Bank is now in a situation similar to the one in which Barclays was after transaction 1, when the first Eurodollar deposit was created.

However, while these dollar deposits outside the controls of the U.S. Federal Reserve system are being created and transferred, a link with Chase is maintained. Throughout the two transactions Chase had the same amount of deposits. The only change at Chase was in the name of the owner of that deposit from ABC Corporation, to Barclays, to Union Bank of Switzerland. At the same time, however, ABC Corporation thinks it has a Eurodollar deposit with Barclays, and XYZ Cor-

---

[3]Since at this stage there is not a transfer of funds, Chase is not affected by the transaction.

EXHIBIT 4.2 International Transfer of Funds: The Eurocurrency System

TRANSACTIONS	CHANGES IN BALANCE SHEETS OF BANKS			
Exchange rates: $1 = £1 = SwF1 = FF1	Chase Manhattan	Barclays	Union Bank of Switzerland	Credit Lyonnais
A. Eurodollar Creation				
1. ABC Corp. transfers deposit from Chase to Barclays.	Deposit (ABC) −1,000,000 Deposit (Barclays) +1,000,000	$ Balance (Chase) +1,000,000 $ Deposit (ABC) +1,000,000		
2. Barclays makes Eurodollar loan to XYZ Corp.		$ Loan (XYZ) +1,000,000 $ Deposit (XYZ) +1,000,000		
3. XYZ Corp.'s dollars are transferred from Barclays to Union Bank of Switzerland.	Deposit (Barclays) −1,000,000 Deposit (Union Bk) +1,000,000	$ Balance (Chase) −1,000,000 $ Deposit (XYZ) −1,000,000	$ Balance (Chase) +1,000,000 $ Deposit (XYZ) +1,000,000	
4. Union Bank places (lends) its dollar deposit with Credit Lyonnais.	Deposit (Union Bk) −1,000,000 Deposit (Cr Lyon) +1,000,000		$ Balance (Chase) −1,000,000 $ Balance (Cr Lyon) +1,000,000	$ Balance (Chase) +1,000,000 $ Deposit (Union Bk) +1,000,000

Total Eurodollar deposits outstanding: $3,000,000

EXHIBIT 4.2 *(Continued)*

CHANGES IN BALANCE SHEETS OF BANKS

TRANSACTIONS	Chase Manhattan	Barclays	Union Bank of Switzerland	Credit Lyonnais
Exchange rates: $1 = £1 = SwF1 = FF1				
B. Eurodollar Contraction				
5. XYZ Corp. exchanges Eurodollar deposit into Swiss francs.			$ Deposit (XYZ) −1,000,000 SwF Deposit (XYZ) +1,000,000	
6. Union Bank brings its exchange position to zero. (After XYZ converted its dollar deposit into Swiss francs, Union Bank had an asset in dollars and a liability in francs.)			$ Balance (Cr Lyon) −1,000,000 SwF Balance (Cr Lyon) +1,000,000	$ Deposit (Union Bk) −1,000,000 SwF Deposit (Union Bk) +1,000,000
7. Credit Lyonnais brings its exchange position to zero.	SwF Balance (Cr Lyon) −1,000,000 Deposit (Cr Lyon) −1,000,000			$ Balance (Chase) −1,000,000 SwF Deposit (Chase) −1,000,000

Total Eurodollar deposits outstanding: $1,000,000

poration thinks it has a Eurodollar loan from Barclays and a Eurodollar deposit with the Union Bank of Switzerland.

What would happen if, when Union Bank of Switzerland is notified of the impending receipt of a Eurodollar deposit, it requests that the deposit be transferred to Union Bank's account with Credit Lyonnais in Paris? That is, suppose Union Bank of Switzerland wants to place a dollar-denominated deposit with Credit Lyonnais—an interbank loan. Then, Chase Manhattan will transfer the Union Bank of Switzerland dollar deposit to the account of Credit Lyonnais (transaction 4). This creates an additional Eurodollar deposit in the amount of $1 million (the Eurodeposit in Credit Lyonnais). The total of Eurodollar deposits outstanding in the system is now $3 million: $1 million ABC's deposit with Barclays, plus $1 million XYZ's deposit with Union Bank, plus $1 million Union Bank's deposit with Credit Lyonnais. One more round of the traditional multiple creation of deposits has taken place.

Now assume that Credit Lyonnais wishes to have an overnight deposit with Chase. That is, Credit Lyonnais prefers to maintain the dollars obtained from Union Bank's deposit placed with a U.S. bank, instead of placed in the Eurodollar system with another Eurobank. We do not have one more round of increases in Eurodeposits. The deposit with Chase is a domestic U.S. dollar deposit, not a Eurodollar deposit. However, at Chase there is no increase in total deposits, merely one more transfer of the ownership of the initial $1 million dollar deposit.

The example described here illustrates two of the main features that characterize the Eurocurrency markets: (1) In most transfers of Eurocurrency there is a direct link to a bank in the home country of that currency; and (2) Eurocurrency deposits can multiply every time that a Eurobank relends the funds obtained from a Eurodeposit to another Eurobank, but not if these funds are maintained in the home country of the currency. We will consider these two characteristics in greater detail and then raise the question of whether this multiple expansion process can be reversed.

Link to a Bank in the Home Country of the Currency. In the illustrative example, every time that an *interbank transaction* in Eurodollars took place, Chase Manhattan in the United States was involved. Had anyone in the chain decided to use, say, Citibank rather than Chase Manhattan as the recipient of the deposit, then Chase Manhattan would have moved out of the chain of transactions, but a deposit would still have been maintained with an American bank (Citibank). Every time that an interbank transfer of funds takes place in the Eurodollar market, an American bank must be involved. The convoluted nature of the transaction may also involve many other foreign banks, as in the case of Union Bank of Switzerland and Credit Lyonnais in the example.

There are certain transactions in the Euromarkets for which an interbank transfer of funds may not be necessary. For example, if the XYZ Corporation had chosen to maintain its borrowed funds with Barclays instead of transferring them to the Union Bank in the example, then Chase would not have been involved. However, the period during which an American bank is not involved is bound to be short-lived. Even if XYZ Corporation keeps its deposits with the lending bank, Barclays, as soon as XYZ begins to draw on these deposits to make payments, the banks in which the recipients of the dollars keep their deposits are not all likely to maintain their funds with Barclays. As soon as one of these other banks prefers to invest the dollar funds obtained with a bank other than Barclays, Barclays will have to transfer the ownership of its dollar deposits with Chase to the bank indicated. This can be done only through Chase.

Although an American bank is involved in most Eurodollar transactions, the total amount of deposits in the United States is not affected.

Multiple Expansion of Eurodeposits. From the point of view of each individual bank in our example, the particular bank has not been adding to Eurodollar accounts, but only relending the dollars, which for them is simply investing the deposits they receive. However, the aggregate effect is to expand the Eurodollars beyond the original amount.

In this example, in which the banks did not maintain any reserves against their deposits, the potential expansion of Eurodollars is infinite. Each bank that receives a $1 million Eurodollar deposit can lend $1 million, which can then become a new Eurodollar deposit in another bank. If the banks maintain certain reserves against their Eurodeposits, say 10%, then the theoretical limit for the expansion of Eurodollar deposits in the example would be $10 million. As explained in any introductory text in money and banking, the multiplier for the initial deposit is the reciprocal of the reserve requirement. With a 10% reserve requirement, this implies a multiplier of 10 ($1 \div 0.10 = 10$).

Note that the credit creation process refers to *new* dollar-denominated monies—deposits—created and traded outside the banking regulations of the United States. A nondeposit liability denominated in dollars that is traded outside the United States is not part of the Eurodollar market in most definitions. The investor in the dollar financial instrument cannot use that instrument to create more of the same instrument, as was done with the Eurodollar deposits above. The nondeposit liability is traded in a fashion similar to the exchange of General Motors shares among non-American owners.

We should also notice that the example shows Eurobanks in a rather atypical position, in which they act as passive recipients of Eurodeposits and look for a use for Eurofunds only after they receive a deposit, not unlike the behavior of domestic banks in the old-fashioned banking tradition before the days of liability management and active raising of funds in the money market. However, in practice, Eurobanks are more like funds brokers than old-fashioned commercial banks. Interbank lending and borrowing is a very large and active part of the Eurocurrency market. Also, Euroloans are actively solicited before a source of Eurocurrency funds has been found.

Can the Multiple Expansion of Eurodeposits Be Reversed? Typically, there are no legal reserves against Eurocurrency deposits. Thus, it would appear that Eurocurrency deposits could expand to infinity. However, there is a built-in check to this expansion. Most corporations obtaining a Euroloan do so with the purpose of spending the proceeds and not simply to maintain the loan proceeds indefinitely as a deposit in a Eurobank. As expenditures are made, a foreign exchange transaction will often be required to convert the borrowed funds into local currency. This exchange transaction will not only eliminate possibilities for further expansion of Eurodeposits, but it will also alter the exposure to the risk of exchange rate fluctuations in the banks involved. If banks choose to eliminate this risk, the volume of outstanding Eurocurrency deposits will contract.

In the example, the multiple expansion of Eurodollars stopped when one of the recipients of the Eurodeposits, Credit Lyonnais, preferred to make an interbank loan to a U.S. bank instead of a Eurobank. To start the Eurodeposit multiple expansion again, all that is needed is for Credit Lyonnais to transfer its deposit from Chase to a Eurobank, say, by making a Euroloan in which the proceeds are deposited with another bank, say, Westdeutsche Bank. To reverse the process of multiple expansion of Eurodeposits, somebody in the chain of transactions must choose to convert the proceeds received in dollars into another currency.

In section B of Exhibit 4.2 we can see the impact of XYZ Corporation converting the proceeds of the Eurodollar loan into local currency, Swiss francs. If the XYZ Corporation wants the loan to pay a liability denominated in Swiss francs, then the dollar proceeds must be exchanged into Swiss francs before payment can be made. In the example, the foreign exchange transaction is made with the Union Bank of Switzerland (transaction 5). This transaction immediately reduces the amount of outstanding Eurodollar deposits by $1 million.

The exchange transaction by the XYZ Corporation also leaves the Union Bank with a dollar asset (the balances with Credit Lyonnais) and a Swiss franc liability (the XYZ deposit). To eliminate the exposure to the risk of a dollar depreciation against the Swiss franc, Union Bank must convert the dollar asset into Swiss francs (transaction 6). If the exchange transaction is made with Credit Lyonnais, the exchange risk is transferred to Credit Lyonnais, which sees its dollar deposit converted into a Swiss franc deposit. This exchange transaction reduces the amount of outstanding Eurodollar deposits by another $1 million. Total outstanding deposits have contracted to $1 million, the original Eurodollar deposit by ABC Corporation. This is the same result that would have occurred if Union Bank had not lent its Eurodollar balances before XYZ's exchange transaction. That is, the conversion of a Eurodollar deposit into nondollars stops the process of multiple creation of Eurodollars. In addition, if the institution with which the deposit was held had already proceeded to lend the Eurodollars, the exchange transaction would also have contracted the volume of Eurodollar deposits outstanding, assuming the institution did not want to increase its exposure to exchange risk.

For Credit Lyonnais to eliminate the exchange risk created by Union Bank's exchange transaction, it has to convert its dollar balance held with Chase into Swiss francs. [For the sake of simplicity we assume that this exchange transaction is done with Chase, which maintains Swiss franc balances with Credit Lyonnais (transaction 7).] This conversion of dollars into Swiss francs not only eliminates the initial deposit at Chase, but also terminates the deposit-creation chain started by the transfer of a dollar deposit from a U.S. bank to a Eurobank. The net results, after all the transactions in our example, are: (1) creation of $1 million Eurodeposit, ABC's deposit with Barclays; (2) creation of $1 million Euroloan, Barclay's loan to XYZ; and (3) $1 million equivalent reduction in balances in foreign currency at a U.S. bank, Chase.[4]

If the initial trade transaction had been denominated in sterling, the Eurocurrency market would have been used if the exporter, ABC Corporation, had chosen to hold its sterling deposits outside England, say, in the Union Bank of Switzerland. In this case a similar multiple creation of Eurodeposits in sterling could have taken place. However, if one of the Euroloan borrowers chose to exchange the sterling proceeds into another currency, say Swiss francs, the multiple expansion of Eurodeposits would have been reversed, assuming the banks involved did not want to be exposed to the risk of a change in exchange rate between sterling and the Swiss franc. At Barclays, ABC's home

---

[4]If the XYZ Corporation had wanted to use the loan proceeds in the United States, the effects would have been similar, except for the loss of reserves by Chase. If XYZ maintained an account with Chase, the ownership of the Chase deposit would have been transferred from Barclays to XYZ. The Eurodollar deposits outstanding after this would also be $1 million—the initial Eurodollar deposit.

bank in England, the end result would be a reduction in foreign balances denominated in Swiss francs.

It is important to note the contributing factor that stopped the expansion of Eurodeposits and worked to contract the size of outstanding Eurodeposits in this example. We assumed that these commercial banks do not take foreign exchange risks in their lending operations. In the lending operation the currency of the loans and the deposits used to finance these loans are the same. If this relationship is altered, banks take steps to restore the zero exchange position. This is the process that eliminated the Eurodollar deposit at Credit Lyonnais in the example, and it is a fair description of the lending operation of international banks. This is in contrast to the foreign exchange operations in which banks do take exchange risks.

Obviously, the potential multiple creation of Eurodollars has a great impact on the total size of the Eurodollar market. Similarly, the market as a whole is of great relevance in analyzing countries' balance of payments and money supplies. Students of this topic have concluded that the multiplier effect of Eurodollars, in practice, is generally closer to 1 rather than the infinite multiplier theoretically possible under the current situation of no required reserves.[5]

BANKING AND THE INTERNATIONAL
ADJUSTMENT PROCESS

As imbalances develop between the international supply of and demand for the currencies of different countries, the banking system performs two different functions to adjust the imbalance: (1) The banking system can be the conduit through which pressures for changes in rates in the foreign exchange market are brought to bear; and (2) The banking system can finance the imbalances by serving as an intermediary between surplus countries and deficit countries.

Banking and Exchange Rate Adjustment

The previous examples began with the transaction in which U.S. Corporation imports cars from ABC Corporation in England. We noted that at the end of the chain of transactions, a bank always had an ac-

---

[5]For example, see John Hewson and Eisuke Sakakibara, *The Eurocurrency Markets and Their Implications* (Lexington, Mass.: D.C. Heath, 1975), and Jane Sneddon Little, *Euro-Dollars: The Money Market Gypsies* (New York: Harper & Row, 1975.)

count of balances in foreign currencies different from what it had initially, regardless of the banking system used. Attempts to restore the initial position in foreign currencies can be expected to put pressure on current exchange rates.

One way to summarize the pressures on the exchange market created by the examples we have presented here is to distinguish among the following four types of transactions that we have discussed:

1. trade transaction billed in dollars and exporter wants to hold domestic sterling
2. trade transaction billed in sterling and exporter wants to hold domestic sterling
3. trade transaction billed in dollars and exporter wants to hold Eurodollars
4. trade transaction billed in sterling and exporter wants to hold Eurosterling

Traditional Banking System. Exhibit 4.1 shows that when the sale is billed in sterling, Chase sees its balances in sterling reduced. To counteract this, Chase will want to purchase sterling against dollars. If the sale is billed in dollars, Barclays ends with more dollar balances than it had initially. To restore the earlier balance, it will want to sell dollars against sterling. In practice, whether Chase purchases sterling against dollars or Barclays sells dollars against sterling, the effect is the same—namely, an increase in supply of dollars and in demand for sterling. In a free market, this translates into a pressure for an appreciation of sterling against the dollar.

If the exporter wants to hold domestic sterling, the pressures for a depreciation of the dollar against sterling are felt immediately and no other pressure on the exchange market is involved later. The currency in which the trade transaction is denominated, dollar or sterling, affects only which particular bank will see its balances in foreign currency altered—a U.S. bank or a British bank.

Eurocurrency System. When the sale is denominated in dollars and ABC Corporation transfers dollar balances from a deposit with a U.S. bank to a dollar deposit with a bank outside the United States, the final impact on Chase is similar to the one just described—a loss in balances in foreign currency. However, in the traditional correspondent banking system, Chase lost sterling (the currency of the exporter) and this happened as soon as the import payment took place. In the Euro–banking system, Chase loses Swiss francs (the currency into which one of the Euroloan recipients, XYZ Corporation, chose to convert the dollar proceeds) and this happens several transactions after the import payment. In both cases, if Chase wants to replenish the level of foreign

currency balances, it will have to purchase the foreign currency by selling dollars and this produces a pressure for a depreciation of the U.S.
dollar. However, the Eurocurrency system helped to delay this effect
and in our example even changed the currency against which the dollar
depreciating force appeared from sterling, originally, to the Swiss
franc.

When the sale is denominated in sterling, even if ABC Corporation chooses to hold its sterling deposits outside England—a Eurosterling deposit—Chase's loss of balances in sterling occurs as soon as the
importer settles the payment. If Chase wants to replenish the sterling
balances, it will sell dollars to purchase sterling and the downward
pressure on the exchange rate of the dollar against sterling will occur
immediately. If the Eurosterling is eventually used to make a loan to a
party interested in spending Swiss francs, pressures in the market for
an appreciation of the Swiss franc against sterling will appear. If we
combine the earlier depreciation of the dollar against sterling with the
final appreciation of the Swiss franc against sterling, the net forces in
the market are for an appreciation of the Swiss franc against the dollar,
the same as when the Eurodollar (instead of the Eurosterling system)
was involved.

If the exporter wishes to hold the proceeds of the sale in the form
of a Eurodeposit, this is equivalent to a British resident wanting to
make a financial investment in a foreign currency—that is, a capital outflow from England. This creates a downward pressure on sterling.
Thus, sterling shows an upward pressure because of the export sale
and a downward pressure because of the capital outflow. The two effects cancel one another and leaves us with the downward pressure on
the dollar because of the U.S. import transaction. The currency against
which the dollar depreciation force is felt eventually will depend on
the currency in which the Euroloan recipient chooses to spend the loan
proceeds (whether Eurodollars or Eurosterling), Swiss francs in our
example.

If the recipient of the Euroloan chooses to spend the proceeds in
dollars, this will balance the initial downward pressure on the dollar
and the U.S. import transaction is effectively being financed by foreign
investment in the United States. A similar outcome would have taken
place if the exporter had extended financing to the importer. For example, suppose the terms of sale had called for payment after 90 days.
At the end of the 90 days, the forces described above will be set in mo-
tion. Similarly, the foreign investors in the Eurocurrency example may
change their mind about holding dollars for investment purposes after
the investment is made (even before it matures), and the pressures in
the exchange markets described above will appear then.

Other Factors. We should note that if the exchange transaction of a private bank is done with a central bank, the pressures on the exchange rate of the currencies involved may not be seen in the market. If the central bank holds the balances acquired in the exchange transaction with the private bank, the central bank would be doing so for policy reasons—that is, to support current exchange rates.[6]

We note also that in this presentation, the banks' participation in the exchange markets was limited to adjustment of their foreign exchange holdings back to the initial level. However, it is easy to see that a bank's assessment of the desired level of holdings of any currency is influenced by its anticipation of future developments in the exchange markets. When these anticipations change, a bank would want to change the level of different currencies held. Although a large portion of bank holdings of foreign currency is for transaction purposes, another large portion is for investment purposes and the level of this second portion will change with the bank's forecast for that currency. In this way the banks can affect the exchange markets actively, in the same way as any other investor can do so.

Banking and the Financing of Imbalances

In the description of Eurocurrency banking, we saw the typical banking behavior in which the funds received from a deposit with the bank are lent to another party. This is the normal behavior for a financial intermediary whose major assets are loans and whose major liabilities are deposits in the domestic market and the Eurocurrency system.

In doing what is normal for a financial intermediary, banks perform another major function in the adjustment of international imbalances. This is accomplished when banks accept deposits from countries with a surplus of foreign exchange (say, because of a trade surplus) and lend the proceeds to countries with a deficit in foreign exchange (for example, countries wishing to purchase in foreign countries amounts larger than their sales to foreigners would allow at the present time). Of course, if the exporting country made a loan directly to the importer, the work of the financial intermediary would not be necessary. However, the financial preferences of exporters usually do not coincide with the financing terms needed by the importer.

---

[6]Actually, if the central bank chooses to maintain its Eurocurrency deposits with a Eurobank, the whole cycle of Eurocurrency expansion could be started again as a new Eurocurrency deposit is created. Because of the possible multiple creation of credit, most central banks restrain themselves from depositing reserves in the Euromarkets. Instead, these reserves are invested in the domestic money market (for example, in U.S. government securities).

During 1973–1982 banks performed this international financial intermediation on a large scale in the so-called *recycling of petrodollars*. In this situation, the oil-exporting countries (OPEC) had a trade surplus. This trade surplus translated into the accumulation of foreign currencies, since many of these countries could not find enough goods and services to purchase abroad (at least in the short term).

One possible use for the funds accumulated by OPEC countries was to extend loans to oil-importing countries. However, most OPEC countries were willing to make these loans to only a few selected countries, such as the United States, and usually with a rather short-term maturity. This was done not because they intend to use the funds to purchase goods upon maturity of the loan, but because they would rather maintain their financial investments in liquid instruments, and short-term maturity instruments are usually liquid ones. These terms were not what was needed by the deficit countries. The oil-importing countries preferred financing in their own currencies and medium- to long-term maturities. On the other hand, commercial bank deposits denominated in the few currencies in which oil-exporting countries preferred to hold their investments met the financial terms desired by the OPEC nations.

The intermediation process took place when the banks transformed the funds received from OPEC countries (in a selected few currencies and for relatively short maturities) into loans to oil-importing countries. These loans often were in the same currencies as the ones in which the deposits were received; however, the maturities were considerably longer than the maturities of the deposits. That is, in this intermediation process banks assumed the credit risk of the importing countries, but they stayed away from the currency risk associated with lending in a currency different from the one in which deposits were received.

The magnitude of this intermediation process increased every time that OPEC countries increased oil prices. In Exhibit 4.3 we can see how the levels of external claims (loans) and external deposits (liabilities) of banks in the major countries changed through the period 1973–1982. These banks are the ones that report data on external loans and liabilities to the Bank for International Settlements (BIS). They are located in the Group of Ten countries, plus Switzerland, Austria, Denmark, and Ireland.

The position of OPEC countries as major depositors is seen in the net borrowed position these banks had with that area. The level of this net borrowed position increased substantially from 1973 to 1974, the year of the first large oil price increase. Through 1977, the net borrowed position remained more or less constant, and in 1978 it declined.

However, with the new price increases in 1979 and 1980, the net deposits from OPEC in these banks again increased substantially.

The "Group of Ten countries plus other's" has been another net contributor of funds to this banking group. Among these, Switzerland, the United States, and the United Kingdom have been the main contributors to the increase in deposits of these banks.

The other country areas listed in Exhibit 4.3 were net recipients of loans from these banks. In all of them the amount of net loans increased with the increases in oil prices. However, the group for which this increase in aggregate loans was the largest is the non-oil-developing countries. In 1973 the total amount of net loans from the banks to "non-oil developing countries" was $4.5 billion—an amount not very different from the amount of loans to Eastern European countries in that year or to "other developed countries" in 1974. However, by 1982, the net loan position to the non-oil-developing countries had increased to $145.9 billion, in contrast to $36.9 billion for Eastern Europe and $62.7 billion for "other developed countries."

After the first oil price shock at the end of 1973, many countries worried whether this intermediation process was going to be possible. Such worries prompted many economists to try to create some supranational financial institutions that could help in this recycling process. However, long before any of the politicians could begin to agree on the terms for the creation of this kind of "superbank," the behavior of the private banking system was rendering these discussions irrelevant. The recycling process was proceeding smoothly without any government intervention. The willingness of commercial banks to assume the credit risk involved in loans to all these developing countries, and to several developed ones, was solving the recycling problem.

However, by the time of the second and third major price increases in 1979 and 1980, the amount of credit risk in the private banking system had begun to preoccupy more than one central bank. The question of what would happen if one of the large borrowers (such as Brazil) defaulted on a large debt began to be raised often. Such a default could affect the viability of some of the major private banks in some countries, and the implications for the banking system of the country could be severe.

There is only one option for countries to pay back their external debts without refinancing—namely, to sell goods and services to other countries. In the first round of oil price increases, economists underestimated the amount of goods and services that the OPEC countries would be able to import in the near future. However, by 1979 it was thought that new increases in imports of these countries would take longer than in 1973, given the amount of goods and services already

EXHIBIT 4.3 External Positions of Banks Reporting to BIS, End of Year, 1973–1982 (billions of U.S. dollars)

	1973	1974	1975	1976	1977	1978	1979	1980	1981	1982
Banks' claims on Group of Ten plus others[a]					349.9	466.9	587.7	704.0	819.9	893.8
Banks' liabilities to Group of Ten plus others[a]					408.5	533.5	685.7	823.7	948.4	1,026.7
Banks' net position against Group of Ten plus others[a]					−58.6	−66.6	−98.0	−119.7	−128.5	−132.9
Banks' claims on offshore banks[b]					98.9	123.5	155.6	187.5	237.5	268.4
Banks' liabilities to offshore banks[b]					71.5	96.9	139.2	164.6	219.5	249.6
Banks' net position against offshore banks[b]					+27.4	+26.6	+16.4	+22.9	+18.0	+18.8
Banks' claims on other developed countries	23.0	30.5	40.5	53.0	55.5	63.9	72.4	85.6	98.9	112.0
Banks' liabilities to other developed countries	27.0	27.5	33.0	34.5	28.1	38.1	46.1	50.1	51.1	49.3
Banks' net position against other developed countries	−4.0	+3.0	+7.5	+18.5	+27.4	+25.8	+26.3	+35.5	+47.8	+62.7
Banks' claims on Eastern Europe	9.5	13.0	21.5	27.5	38.3	47.5	55.9	59.8	60.8	53.3
Banks' liabilities to Eastern Europe	4.5	6.0	6.5	7.5	8.4	10.6	15.4	15.6	14.8	16.4
Banks' net position against Eastern Europe	+5.0	+7.0	+15.0	+20.0	+29.9	+36.9	+40.5	+44.2	+46.0	+36.9

EXHIBIT 4.3 *(Continued)*

	1973	1974	1975	1976	1977	1978	1979	1980	1981	1982
Banks' claims on OPEC countries[c]	6.5	9.0	14.0	23.5	39.1	56.4	64.1	70.0	72.0	78.6
Banks' liabilities to OPEC countries[c]	16.0	42.5	50.0	62.5	77.9	82.5	120.3	159.7	156.8	135.2
Banks' net position against OPEC countries[c]	−9.5	−33.5	−36.0	−39.0	−38.8	−26.1	−56.2	−89.7	−84.8	−56.6
Banks' claims on non-oil developing countries	32.0	47.0	62.0	78.5	98.7	120.8	157.1	195.0	230.1	246.9
Banks' liabilities to non-oil developing countries	27.5	31.5	35.5	47.0	62.0	76.6	89.6	92.7	98.3	101.0
Banks' net position against non-oil developing countries	+4.5	+15.5	+26.5	+31.5	+36.7	+44.2	+67.5	+102.3	+131.8	+145.9
Banks' total external claims[d]					689.7	893.1	1,110.7	1,323.1	1,542.0	1,686.7
Banks' total external liabilities[d]					672.0	856.3	1,119.3	1,334.6	1,523.0	1,620.4
Banks' net external position[d]					+17.7	+36.8	−8.6	−11.5	+19.0	+66.3

[a]Group of Ten countries plus Switzerland, Austria, Denmark, and Ireland. Also included are the offshore branches of U.S. banks in the Bahamas, Cayman Islands, Panama, Hong Kong, and Singapore.

[b]Bahamas, Barbados, Bermuda, Cayman Islands, Hong Kong, Lebanon.

[c]Liberia, Netherlands Antilles, Panama, Singapore, Vanuatu (formerly New Hebrides) and other British West Indies. Includes, in addition, Bahrain, Brunei, Oman, Trinidad and Tobago.

[d]Including international institutions other than the BIS.

SOURCE: *Bank of International Settlements Annual Report*, various issues.

imported into these countries. In addition, developed countries—the other outlet for exports from developing countries—found themselves with weak economies, partially as a result of the oil price increases.

As a consequence of these worries, the participation of banks in the recycling process in the first half of 1980 was somewhat hesitant. However, as the figures in Exhibit 4.3 show, this hesitancy was overcome rather quickly. At the national policy level the only change was a better control system of the aggregate amount of these loans by a bank to any given country. However, only a few countries outside the United States had control on the consolidated position of a bank and all its branches and affiliates worldwide. The others had data only on the position of the bank within the national boundaries.

By late 1982, the strains on the international banking system from the recyling and lending to developing countries were serious. To the protracted major reschedulings of debt for Poland and Argentina, in August of that year Mexico's inability to meet its debt obligations was added. Brazil's problems were to follow in early 1983. The total lending was staggering. Aggregate loans by the ten largest U.S. banks to Brazil, Mexico, Poland, and Argentina were about 1.5 times their collected equity in 1982.

Countries typically do not default and/or repudiate their debts, for the long-run consequences in terms of future borrowing, International Monetary Fund support and assistance, general economic development and the like are serious. Cuba did default after Fidel Castro came to power, and he has reputedly told other revolutionaries not to make the mistake he made. In recent years, only North Korea has defaulted on some of its loans. However, countries do reschedule their debts, and this became increasingly common by 1982–1983.

As to the rescheduling process proper, one must first recognize that different bank consortia apply in relation to each loan in each nation. Inevitably the bankers in a given situation will themselves have different goals. Some bankers will argue that they have "project loans" (as Chase Manhattan Bank did in the case of its Polish debt). Critics will respond that these so-called project loans were simply created in order that the bank's loans to a single borrower (e.g., the government of Poland) did not exceed U.S. restrictions on the maximum amount of a bank's assets which can be tied to a loan to one party. Other bankers will have short-term loans, and they will have short-term concerns.

Often, of course, the motivation involves various external factors, and the loans themselves may not be that sound. In the case of Poland, for example, about 20% of the loans were from West German banks, and the loans were usually guaranteed by the West German government which was interested in furthering trade relations.

Small banks are often able to hold the others hostage, because cross-default clauses in most loans mean that a single lender can bring the entire house of cards (i.e., the whole range of loans) down. These small banks hope to be bought out by their larger associates (as happened in the case of Turkish rescheduling in the late 1970s). Ultimately, they can often be coerced into acquiescing in any rescheduling by the promise of participation in future opportunities.

The basic rule in reschedulings is that the banks hold together, often under the aegis of the International Monetary Fund which can enforce various types of fiscal and monetary discipline on the government involved. A second general rule is that there is no rescheduling of interest payments, although Nicaragua did obtain such a rescheduling in the early 1980s. Many times, of course, the new loans are made in order to allow the debtor country to recoup the interest payments it has just made. Also, typically, trade-related debt is expected to be maintained current and not included in the rescheduling process.

SUMMARY

Within the framework of the international agreements and institutions described previously, the private banking system operates to facilitate transactions in international trade by providing liquidity and financing. In the traditional role, banks in different countries offset customers' demands for currencies by trading deposits. A French customer drawing on his franc deposit with a local bank to pay for his sports car bought in Italy starts the transaction. Assuming the Italian exporter does not want to hold francs, she deposits the check in lira with her bank. The Italian bank then receives an addition to its franc balances kept on account with the French bank when it turns in the check for payment. The French bank has transferred the franc ownership out of the country. Had the export been billed in lira, a comparable transfer of ownership of lira balances in the Italian bank from the French customer's bank's account to the Italian exporter's account would have occurred, with the French bank charging its customer for the comparable amount in francs.

In the Eurocurrency example of this situation (analogous to domestic money *creation* in the banking system), the typical case would involve the Italian exporter billing in francs, but choosing to leave the francs on deposit with her Italian local bank. The Italian bank now has Eurofrancs—francs available for lending outside the regulations of the French banking authorities. When the bank loans the francs, the loan customer may well deposit the francs in a U.S. bank, which can in turn relend the francs to another customer. In this manner, the multiple expansion of Eurocurrencies takes place. Once a customer brings the money back to the French banking system, however, the expansion halts. Empirically, researchers have found that the theoretically infinite expansion of deposits in the Euromarkets in the absence of reserve requirements does not occur, as the multiplier is closer to 1.

Eurocurrencies appeared after World War II and tended to involve dollars traded in the European banking system. In fact, the term refers to any currency outside the control of the issuer of the currency's monetary authority. Eurodollars now trade also in the international banking facilities in the United States where American banks make dollar loans at times to American customers for nondomestic activities. These deposits are not subject to the Federal Reserve requirements, just as comparable loans or deposits to the same customer for the same activity in the same currency when made by Barclays Bank or Citibank-U.K. would not be subject to Federal Reserve requirements.

Contraction of the deposits can occur when the banks involved want to alter their exposure to foreign exchange risk. Thus, if the Italian bank did not wish to hold an expanded balance in francs, its movement to offset the franc deposit by conversion to lira would nullify the example suggested. In general, banks seem to be willing to accept credit risk in customers but unwilling to accept currency risk in their lending activities; deposits in one currency are typically matched with loans in the same currency with interest rates set for comparable maturity. When the banks do offset deposits with exchange transactions or enter transactions to offset older deposit balances, the pressures can build on the exchange rates as a direct result of the bank's activity in the exchange markets. Should the local bank deal with its own central bank rather than in the exchange markets, then there can be a buffer in the effect on the exchange market should the central bank not enter the exchange market but hold the foreign currency balances itself.

The first OPEC price increase saw purchases by the OPEC nations of goods from the developed countries, some of which led to deposits in the private banks. Other deposits from the OPEC nations permitted the private banks themselves to "recycle" some of the OPEC surpluses by longer-term loans to the non-oil-exporting countries. Hence, the international banks were especially valuable in transforming the OPEC nations' mushrooming surpluses, typically deposited in short-term maturities, into longer-term loans in the same currency to the developing economies that were most severely hurt by the oil price increase. When the price increases in 1979 and 1980 were again cushioned by the private banking system absorbing the credit risk through loans to the poorer nations, the process did not work as smoothly as before and banks themselves became increasingly vulnerable to defaults by the poorer nations on their OPEC-induced debts.

BIBLIOGRAPHY

Abrams, Richard K., and Donald V. Kimball, "U.S. Investment in Foreign Equity Markets," *Economic Review*, Apr. 1981, pp. 17–31.

Adler, Michael, and Bernard Dumas, "The Exposure of Long-Term Foreign Currency Bonds," *Journal of Financial and Quantitative Analysis*, Nov. 1980, pp. 973–86.

Aliber, Robert Z., "Monetary Aspects of Offshore Markets," *Columbia Journal of World Business*, Fall 1979, pp. 8–16.

———, "The Integration of the Offshore and Domestic Banking System," *Journal of Monetary Economics*, Oct. 1980, pp. 509–26.

Bank for International Settlements, *Annual Report*, annual issues.

Coats, Warren L. Jr., "The Weekend Eurodollar Game," *Journal of Finance*, June 1981, pp. 649–60.

———, "The Crash of 198?," *Economist*, Oct. 16, 1982, pp. 23–26.

Davis, Robert, "Effects of the Eurodollar Market on National Monetary Policies," *Columbia Journal of World Business*, Fall 1979, pp. 46–53.

Dufey, Gunter, and Ian H. Giddy, "Innovation in the International Financial Markets," *Journal of International Business Studies*, Fall 1981, pp. 33–51.

———, *The International Money Market*. Englewood Cliffs, N.J.: Prentice-Hall, Inc., 1978.

Einzig, Paul, and Brian Quinn, *The Eurodollar System*. New York: St. Martin's Press, 1977.

Feder, Gershon, and Richard E. Just, "An Analysis of Credit Terms in the Eurodollar Market," *European Economic Review*, May 1977, pp. 221–43.

Feder, Gershon, and Knud Ross, "Risk Assessment and Risk Premiums in the Eurodollar Market," *Journal of Finance*, June 1982, pp. 679–91.

Freedman, Charles, "A Model of the Eurodollar Market," *Journal of Monetary Economics*, Apr. 1977, pp. 139–61.

Friedman, Milton, "The Eurodollar Market: Some First Principles," *The Morgan Guaranty Survey*, Oct. 1969, pp. 1–11.

Giddy, Ian H., "Why Eurodollars Grow," *Columbia Journal of World Business*, Fall 1979, pp. 54–60.

Gurwin, Larry, "Death of a Banker," *Institutional Investor*, October 1982, pp. 258–75.

Hewson, John, and Eisuke Sakakibara, *The Eurocurrency Markets and Their Implications*. Lexington, Mass.: D.C. Heath, 1975.

Hogan, W. P., and I. F. Pearch, *The Incredible Eurodollar*. London: George Allan and Unwin, 1982.

Johnston, R. B., *Theories of the Growth of the Eurocurrency Market: A Review of the Eurocurrency Deposit Multiplier*. Basle, Switzerland: Bank for International Settlements Monetary and Economic Department, 1981.

Klopstock, Fred H., "Money Creation in the Eurodollar Market: A Note on Professor Friedman's Views," *Monthly Review*, Jan. 1970, pp. 12–15.

Lees, Francis A., and Maximo Eng, "Developing Country Access to the International Capital Markets," *Columbia Journal of World Business*, Fall 1979, pp. 71–84.

Little, Jane Sneddon, *Eurodollars: The Money Market Gypsies*. New York: Harper and Row, Inc., 1975.

——— , "The Impact of the Eurodollar Market on the Effectiveness of Monetary Policy in the United States and Abroad," *New England Economic Review*, Mar.–Apr., 1975, pp. 3–19.

——— , "Liquidity Creation by Eurobanks: A Range of Possibilities." *Columbia Journal of World Business*, Fall 1979, pp. 38–45.

Lomas, David F., and Peter G. Gutman, *The Euromarkets and International Financial Policies*. New York: Wiley, 1981.

Makin, John H., and Dennis E. Logue, eds., *Eurocurrencies and the International Monetary System*. Washington, D.C.: American Enterprise Institute for Public Policy Research, 1976.

Mayer, Helmut W., "Some Theoretical Problems Relating to the Eurodollar Market," *Essays in International Finance*, No. 79. Princeton, N.J.: Princeton University Press, 1970.

McKinnon, Ronald I., "The Eurocurrency Market," *Essays in International Finance*, No. 125, Princeton, N.J.: Princeton University Press, 1977.

Mikesell, Raymond F., "The Eurodollar Market and the Foreign Demand for Liquid Dollar Assets," *Journal of Money, Credit, and Banking*, Aug. 1972, pp. 643–83.

——— , and J. Herbert Furth, *Foreign Dollar Balances and the International Role of the Dollar*. New York: Columbia University Press, 1974.

Putman, Bluford H., "Controlling the Euromarkets: A Policy Perspective," *Columbia Journal of World Business*, Fall 1979, pp. 25–31.

Quinn, Brian Scott, "The International Bond Market for the U.S. Investor," *Columbia Journal of World Business*, Fall 1979, pp. 85–90.

Riehl, Heinz, and Rita M. Rodriguez, *Foreign Exchange and Money Markets*. New York: McGraw-Hill Book Company, 1983.

Robichek, Alexander A., and Mark R. Eaker, "Debt Denomination and Exchange Risk in International Capital Markets," *Financial Management*, Autumn 1976, pp. 11–18.

Salomon Brothers, *United States Multinational Banking*. New York, 1976.

Sampson, Anthony, *The Money Lenders*. London: Hodder and Stoughton, 1982.

"Samurai Bonds: Noh Big Drama," *Economist*, Oct. 2, 1982, pp. 89ff.

Sterling, J. F. Jr., "A New Look at International Lending by American Banks," *Columbia Journal of World Business*, Fall 1979, pp. 61–70.

"The Swaps that Unlock Credit," *Business Week*, Aug. 2, 1982, p. 58.

Wallhich, Henry C., "Why the Euromarket Needs Restraint," *Columbia Journal of World Business*, Fall 1979, pp. 17–24.

EXERCISES ON THE INTERNATIONAL TRANSFER OF FUNDS*

Given here are several international financial transactions that affect the Eurodollar market. Assume that banks do not maintain any reserves against Eurodeposits and that the exchange rates are US$1 = DM1 = ¥1. Do the following:

1. For each transaction show the changes that the transaction produces in the balance sheet statements of the banks affected. "T-accounts" representing balance sheets for each bank are presented in Exhibit B.1.
2. After each transaction, show the cumulative amount of Eurodollar and domestic dollar deposits in the system.

TRANSACTIONS

1. A U.S. corporation, Carrod Corporation, imports calculators valued at $1 million from Japan. Carrod pays the Japanese exporter with dollars drawn on Carrod's account wih Continental Bank in Chicago. The exporter deposits the dollar proceeds with the Mitsui Bank in Japan.

2. Eto, Inc., borrows $1 million from Mitsui Bank to pay for radio parts imported from Germany. Eto pays the German exporter, Heilbrun, Inc., with the proceeds from the loan.

3. Heilbrun, Inc., deposits the dollars received with Dresdner Bank in Germany.

4. Dresdner Bank places (lends) $1 million with Barclays Bank in London.

5. Barclays lends $1 million to the Biscuit Company of London.

6. Pending a dollar disbursement in the near future, the Biscuit Company deposits the dollar proceeds from the loan with Continental Bank in Chicago.

7. Heilbrun exchanges its dollar deposits into German marks at the Dresdner Bank.

8. Panic! All banks in the financial system close their exchange positions to eliminate exchange risks. (Assume that each bank does the exchange transaction with the same bank in which the currency sold was held in deposit.)

---

*These exercises were prepared by Michele Dichter under the supervision of Professor Rita M. Rodriguez.

EXHIBIT B.1 Exercises on the International Transfer of Funds: *Balance Sheets for Participating Banks*

	Continental	Mitsui	Dresdner	Barclays
(1)				
(2)				
(3)				
(4)				
(5)				
(6)				

EXHIBIT B.1 *(Continued).*

Continental	Mitsui	Dresdner	Barclays
(7)			
(8)a.			
b.			
c.			
d.			
e.			

5

The Foreign Exchange Market: Nature and Relation to the Money Market

THE FOREIGN EXCHANGE market is the place where money denominated in one currency is bought and sold with money denominated in another currency. In the trade transaction of Chapter 4, in which a U.S. company imported goods from a British company, U.S. dollars were converted into sterling. This conversion from one currency into another is typical of the transactions that take place in the foreign exchange market. Most of these transactions are realized through changes in the ownership of bank deposits.[1] In that example, the settlement of the trade transaction eventually involved a change in ownership of dollar deposits at Chase and sterling deposits at Barclays. The exchange market serves to interconnect the markets for deposits in different currencies—the money markets in those currencies.

In this chapter we will discuss some of the institutional aspects of the foreign exchange market, including the mechanics of foreign exchange quotations. Then, we will discuss the nature of the relationship between the exchange market and the money markets for different currencies.[2]

---

[1]Only a small percentage of the foreign exchange market involves an exchange of actual currencies in circulation. Most of these cases are accounted for by travellers who find it difficult to have their personal checks (regardless of the currency and bank on which they are drawn) accepted in foreign countries where the traveller is not well known.

[2]For a detailed explanation of the foreign exchange market, see Heinz Riehl and Rita M. Rodriguez, *Foreign Exchange and Money Markets* (New York: McGraw-Hill, 1983).

INSTITUTIONS IN THE FOREIGN EXCHANGE MARKET

Currencies may be bought and sold in the *spot exchange market* for immediate delivery (in practice, 2 days later), and in the *forward exchange market* for delivery at some specified date in the future. The exchange rates at which these currencies are bought and sold are the *spot rate* and the *forward rates* for delivery on given dates. In addition, currencies can be bought and sold in the currency *futures market*. (This market is discussed in the appendix to this chapter.)

As an example of how the spot and forward exchange markets work, assume that an exchange trader offers the following exchange rates:

Spot rate	$2.40/£
30-day forward rate	$2.41/£

Suppose we perform the following transactions: (1) Buy sterling against dollars (sell dollars) for spot delivery; and (2) Sell sterling against dollars (buy dollars) for delivery 30 days later. Assume that both transactions are for £100,000. The cash flows today (day 1) and 30 days later (day 31) for the two currencies will be as indicated in the following table:

		CURRENCIES*	
Date	Transaction	$	£
Day 1	Buy sterling against dollars spot	− 240,000	+ 100,000
	Sell sterling against dollars for delivery in 30 days	ncf	ncf
Day 31	Sell sterling against dollars as per contract on day 1	+ 241,000	− 100,000

*(+: Cash inflow; −: Cash outflow; ncf: No cash flow)

That is, the exchange rates and the amounts of each currency were all determined when the transactions were closed on day 1.[3] But the cash flows take place only on the delivery date, or *value date:* the *spot*

---

[3]Throughout this text we will assume that delivery on a spot transaction takes place immediately after the contract is closed (instead of the usual 2 days taken for delivery) to simplify the presentation.

date (here assumed to be on day 1 immediately after the transaction is closed) and the *forward value date* specified in the forward transaction (day 31 in this example). Once a forward transaction has been closed at a given rate, the cash flows at delivery time will take place at that rate. Rarely will the exchange rate on a forward transaction be the same as the spot rate on the day of delivery.[4]

The foreign exchange market is similar to the over-the-counter market in securities. There is no centralized meeting place (except for a few places in Europe and the futures market of the International Monetary Market of the Chicago Mercantile Exchange) and no fixed opening and closing time. The trading in foreign exchange is done over the telephone or through the telex. The currencies and the extent of participation of each currency in this market depend on local regulations that vary from country to country. Of the more than 100 member countries of the International Monetary Fund, only a few have established full convertibility of their currencies for all transactions. The currencies with restricted convertibility play a very small role in the foreign exchange market.

The major participants in the foreign exchange market are large commercial banks that actually "make the market." In the United States, about a dozen banks in New York and another dozen banks located in other U.S. cities have foreign exchange traders who maintain a position in twelve or fifteen major currencies and, to a lesser extent, in other currencies. These banks operate in the foreign exchange market at two levels. At the retail level, they deal with their customers— corporations, exporters, and so forth. At the wholesale level, banks maintain an interbank market. Contact in this market in the United States is usually made through a foreign exchange broker who receives a small commission. In this country there are about six of these brokers. By preserving the anonymity of the seller and the buyer of a currency until the deal is concluded, the broker provides a fuller market than if the banks were to contact other banks directly. However, when dealing with institutions in other countries, banks usually deal directly with each other without the intermediation of brokers.

The other important participants in the foreign exchange market are the various countries' central banks. These institutions frequently intervene in the market to maintain the exchange rates of their currencies within a desired range and to smooth fluctuations within that range. The extent of this intervention depends largely on the exchange

---

[4]Theories that consider the forward rate at one point in time to be an unbiased predictor of the spot rate expected on delivery date will be discussed in Chapter 6. However, even in these theories the forward rate is only a predictor, which is not necessarily accurate.

rate regime followed by the given country's central bank—fixed rates, freely floating rates, and so on.

The other participants in the foreign exchange market are nonfinancial businesses and individuals who deal in the market through commercial banks.

MECHANICS OF FOREIGN EXCHANGE QUOTATIONS

Meaning of Foreign Exchange Quotes

A *foreign exchange quotation* is the price of a currency expressed in terms of another currency. Quotations in the foreign exchange market are generally made in terms of local currency (the local unit of account) per unit of foreign currency. Thus, in the United States, exchange rates are quoted in American terms of dollars per foreign monetary unit (for example, $0.20/FF) and in France the quotations are made in terms of French francs per unit of foreign exchange (for example, FF5.00/$). The major exception to this practice is the United Kingdom, where foreign exchange prices are quoted in terms of foreign monetary units per pound sterling (for example, $2.20/£ and FF11.00/£).

Foreign exchange quotations are usually difficult to understand for those who do not exchange currencies frequently. To overcome this difficulty, it is useful to make clear which currency in the quotation plays the role of the unit of account and which currency is the unit for which the price is being quoted. Following U.S. practice, a quote can be made clearer by placing the currency used as the unit of account before the quoted price and the unit of the currency being priced after the quote.[5] Thus, in the United States we see prices for various articles quoted as follows: $10,000/car, $0.70/head of lettuce, and so on. In the same manner, we can express a quote for the German mark, in American dollar terms, as follows:

$$\$0.50/DM$$

where the unit of account (the local currency) is the U.S. dollar and the unit of currency being priced (the foreign currency) is the mark.

---

[5]This practice is not observed in many countries where the position of the two currencies in a quotation is reversed—that is, where the unit of account or local currency appears after the quoted number.

A foreign exchange quote involves statements about two curren-cies simultaneously. A change in the price of one currency implies a change in the price of the other currency that appears in the quote. For example, if the price of the mark against the dollar moves from $0.50/DM to $0.53/DM, we can say that the mark has appreciated relative to the dollar by $0.03. This is the same as saying that the dollar has de-preciated relative to the mark. When the quoted number increases, this implies an appreciation in the value of the currency used as the item purchased or sold (mark) and a depreciation for the currency used as the unit of account (dollar). In this example, if we wish to translate the quote of $0.50/DM from American terms to German terms, we need only take the reciprocal of 0.50. This gives us the *reciprocal rate*.

$$\text{If} \qquad \frac{\$}{DM} = 0.50 \qquad \text{then} \qquad \frac{DM}{\$} = \frac{1}{0.50} = \frac{DM2.00}{\$}$$

Thus, we have the following quotes: $0.50/DM in American terms and the reciprocal DM2.00/$ in German terms.

Having understood how the terms in which a quote is given can be changed by taking the reciprocal of the given quote, we can extend this concept to more than two currencies. The exchange rate between two given currencies can be obtained from the rates of these two cur-rencies in terms of a third currency. The resulting rate is called the *cross rate*. For example, suppose an American trader gave the following quotations in New York:

$$\$0.50/DM \qquad \text{and} \qquad \$1.80/£$$

From these quotes we can obtain DM/£ and £/DM as follows:

$$\frac{DM}{£} = \frac{DM}{\$} \times \frac{\$}{£} \qquad \text{and} \qquad \frac{£}{DM} = \frac{£}{\$} \times \frac{\$}{DM}$$

Thus,

$$\frac{DM}{£} = \frac{1}{0.50} \times 1.80 = DM3.6000/£$$

and

$$\frac{£}{DM} = \frac{1}{1.80} \times 0.50 = £0.2778/DM$$

Thus, DM3.6000/£ and £0.2778/DM are the cross rates computed from the given direct quotes of $/DM and $/£. As one would expect, 3.6000 is the reciprocal of 0.2778, and vice versa.

Comparing Quotes from Different Traders

The computation of reciprocal rates and cross rates facilitates the comparison of quotes given by different sources when the quotes are expressed in different terms. As an example, consider the following quotes given by two traders, in their respective local terms:

New York	Frankfurt
$0.51/DM	DM2.00/$

To be able to compare the two quotes directly, we must first express them in the same terms, say, DM/$. This requires the computation of the reciprocal rate of $/DM in New York. The DM/$ rate for the two traders are as follows:

New York	Frankfurt
DM1.96/$ ($=1 \div 0.51$)	DM2.00/$ (as originally given)

If we want to *buy* dollars against marks, we would prefer to do this with the trader in *New York;* if we want to *sell* dollars against marks, we would prefer to do this in *Frankfurt.*

A discrepancy in quotes between two traders offers an opportunity for somebody to profit by buying one currency against another from one trader at a price and reversing the transaction with the other trader at a higher price. The nature of such a transaction is called *arbitrage.* For individuals with access to those rates, there is no risk whatsoever in this arbitrage transaction because all the relevant rates are known in advance. Moreover, there is no investment required because the purchase of each currency is financed with the sale of the other currency. The individual who performs these transactions is the *arbitrageur.* In the DM/$ example, the arbitrageur will want to do the following:

In New York	In Frankfurt
Buy $s	Sell $s
Sell DMs	Buy DMs

If we want to make the comparisons in terms of $/DM, we have the following:

New York	Frankfurt
$0.51/DM (as originally given)	$0.50/DM (= 1 ÷ 2.00)

We reach the same conclusion as when the quotes were expressed in terms of DM/$. Both for individuals interested in doing one specific transaction (such as buying dollars against marks) and for arbitrageurs (who are willing to buy and sell each currency simultaneously), the quotes offer the following incentives: Buy DMs against dollars from the trader in Frankfurt and sell DMs against dollars to the trader in New York.

The transactions triggered by the difference between the quotes from two traders will put pressures on the market for a change in the quotes. In the example, the transactions in Frankfurt will tend to increase the price of DMs against dollars (decrease the price of dollars against DMs). In New York, the tendency will be for a decrease in the price of DMs against dollars (increase in the price of dollars against DMs). These trends will continue until the exchange rates between the mark and the dollar are approximately the same for the two traders in the two cities. The pervasiveness of these pressures is such that, given modern means of communication, large discrepancies among the quotes offered by different traders for the same currencies rarely occur in the market, and when they occur they disappear promptly.

We can see how the market pressures to equalize quotes develop when we have more than two currencies. In such cases, cross rates as well as reciprocal rates must be compared. For example, consider the quotes given in the following table:

New York	Zurich
$0.60/SwF	SwF1.67/$
$0.51/DM	SwF0.87/DM

In this case, there are three quotes to be compared for the two traders: $/SwF, $/DM, and SwF/DM. The comparison of $/SwF requires only the computation of the reciprocal of the SwF/$ quoted by the trader in Zurich. However, the comparison of $/DM requires the computation of a cross rate from the Zurich quotes for SwF/$ and SwF/DM offered by the trader; the comparison of SwF/DM for the New York trader requires the computation of a cross rate between the quotes for $/SwF and \$/DM. Further, one could add three more relationships by considering the reciprocals of the previous relationships: DM/\$, SwF/\$, and DM/SwF. These three relationships for the two traders produce the quotes given in the following table:

	New York	Zurich
\$/SwF	\$0.60/SwF	\$0.60/SwF[a]
\$/DM	\$0.51/DM	\$0.52/DM[b]
SwF/DM	SwF0.85/DM[c]	SwF0.87/DM

[a]In Zurich SwF1.67/\$ yields

$$\$/SwF = \frac{1}{1.67} = \$0.60/SwF$$

[b]In Zurich

$$\$/SwF = \$0.60/SwF \quad \text{(from footnote a)}$$

and we know

$$SwF/DM = SwF0.87/DM$$

Then

$$DM/SwF = \frac{1}{0.87} = DM1.15/SwF$$

and

$$\$/DM = \frac{\$/SwF}{DM/SwF} = \frac{0.60}{1.15} = \$0.5217/DM$$

[c]In New York

$$\$0.51/DM = DM1.96/\$$$

and

$$\$0.60/SwF = SwF1.67/\$$$

Then

$$SwF/DM = \frac{SwF/\$}{DM/\$} = \frac{1.67}{1.96} = SwF0.85/DM$$

From the table, we observe the following:

1. There is no arbitrage incentive between the Swiss franc and the dollar.
2. The DM against the dollar is higher for the Zurich trader than for the New York trader.
3. The DM commands a higher price in terms of Swiss francs with the Zurich trader than with the New York trader.

Therefore, there are two arbitrage opportunities:

1. Buy DMs against dollars in New York and sell DMs against dollars in Zurich.
2. Buy DMs against SwFs in New York and sell DMs against SwFs in Zurich.

The quotes also give incentives in the same directions to individuals interested only in executing a specific transaction. For example, anybody interested in buying marks against francs would rather do this through the trader in New York than through the trader in Zurich.

The pressures generated on the market by these transactions will tend to eliminate the discrepancies between the quotes given by two traders. For example, large purchases of marks against francs from the trader in New York will tend to increase the quote of the mark against the franc from that trader; the opposite transaction with the trader in Zurich will make that trader want to decrease the initial quote of the mark against the franc. The trends will continue until the quotes are about the same for both traders.

Relationship between Forward and Spot Rates

As we mentioned earlier, the foreign exchange market provides exchange rate quotes at any point in time for spot delivery and for delivery on different forward value dates. The relationship between each of these forward rates and the spot rate at that time can be quantified. It is usually expressed in the form of a percentage per annum *premium* or *discount* of the forward rate over the spot rate.

A foreign currency is at a *forward discount* against a given currency when the forward price of the foreign currency is lower than its spot price. The opposite is true in the case of a *forward premium*. For example, if the spot rate of the French franc is $0.20 per French franc, then the quote of US$0.19 for 3-month French francs shows a discount in the forward rate of the French franc against the U.S. dollar. That is, a unit of French francs buys fewer dollars for delivery in 3 months than for immediate delivery. This quote also shows that the U.S. dollar is at a forward premium against the French franc. One U.S. dollar buys more French francs for delivery in 3 months than for immediate delivery.

The percentage per annum (p.a.) discount $(-)$ or premium $(+)$ in a forward quote in relation to the spot rate is computed by the following formula:

$$\text{Forward premium (Discount)} = \frac{(\text{Forward rate} - \text{Spot rate})}{\text{Spot rate}} \times \frac{12}{\text{Number of months forward}}$$

For example, assume that the following rates prevail in the market for sterling:

Spot rate $1.80/£

3-month forward rate $1.79/£

Then, the forward discount of sterling against the dollar is determined as follows:

$$\frac{1.79 - 1.80}{1.80} \times \frac{12}{3} = -0.022 = -2.2\% \text{ p.a.}$$

The first term of the equation converts the difference between the forward rate and the spot rate into a percentage of the spot rate, and the second term annualizes this percentage. As will be shown later, this annualization process facilitates comparing the premium or discount on the forward rate with interest rates that are traditionally expressed on a per annum basis.

Bid and Offer in Foreign Exchange Quotes

A foreign exchange trader will usually quote two numbers: the price at which he or she is buying and the price at which he or she is selling a given currency. The first price is the *bid price* and the second price is the *offer* or *ask price*. In either case, the currency for which the bid or offer price is given is the unit of the item priced. In the *bid* quote $0.50/DM the trader is willing to *buy marks* at the price of $0.50 per mark. However, this is tantamount to being willing to *sell dollars* at the price of $0.50 per mark. Implicitly, the quote also establishes the offer price for the currency used as the unit of account. Similarly, the trader's *offer* price per *mark* implicitly quotes the rate (per mark) at which *dollars* would be *bought*.

In transactions among traders, usually only the last digits of the bid and offer rates are quoted; the rest is understood. These last digits are called *points*. For example, the quotation of the spot dollar-lira rate might be 1250/1260. Given that lira quotes are usually specified with six decimal places, this means that the trader is willing to

Buy liras at $0.001250 per lira

and   Sell liras at $0.001260 per lira

which is the same as being willing to

Sell U.S. dollars at $0.001250 per lira

and   Buy U.S. dollars at $0.001260 per lira

A foreign exchange dealer who receives a call asking for a quote is under a general moral obligation to quote and to deal at the rate quoted. He or she need not deal for unlimited amounts, but if the dealer is asked the price at which he or she will buy a given currency and then offers to transact only a small amount, it is clear that the dealer prefers to be at the other end of the transaction—in this case, to sell that currency. A good dealer will provide a prompt response (to avoid giving the caller the opportunity to shop around) and narrow spreads. Otherwise, it is obvious on which side of the transaction he or she wishes to be. Quotations are stated both to buy and to sell. Given the narrow spreads, a dealer will very often sell when a buy is preferred, and vice versa.

The quotations for forward rates can be made in two ways. They can be made in terms of the amount of local currency at which the quoter will buy and sell a unit of foreign currency, as described previously. This is called the *outright rate* and it is used by traders in quoting to customers. The forward rates can also be quoted in terms of points of discount and/or premium from spot, called the *swap rate*, which is used in interbank quotations. The outright rate is the spot rate adjusted by the swap rate. To find the outright foward rates when the premiums or discounts on quotes of forward rates are given in terms of *points* (swap rate), the points are *added* to the spot price if the foreign currency is trading at a forward *premium;* the points are *subtracted* from the spot price if the foreign currency is trading at a forward *discount.* The resulting number is the outright forward rate.

It is usually well known to traders whether the quotes in points represent a premium or a discount from the spot rate, and it is not customary to refer specifically to the quote as a premium or a discount. However, this can be readily determined in a mechanical fashion. If the first forward quote (the bid or buying figure) is smaller than the second forward quote (the offer or selling figure), then there is a premium—that is, the swap rates are added to the spot rate. Conversely, if the first quote is larger than the second, then it is a discount.[6] This procedure assures that the buy price is lower than the sell price, and the trader profits from the spread between the two prices. For example, when asked for spot, 1-, 3-, and 6-month quotes on the French franc, a trader based in the United States might quote the following:

.2186/9   2/3   6/5   11/10

In outright terms these quotes would be expressed as indicated in the following table:

---

[6]A 5/5 quote would require further specification as to whether it is a premium or a discount.

Maturity	Bid	Offer
Spot	.2186	.2189
1-month	.2188	.2192
3-month	.2180	.2184
6-month	.2175	.2179

Notice that the 1-month forward franc is at a premium against the dollar, whereas the 3- and 6-month forwards are at discounts.

The remaining discussion in this book will ignore the existence of bid and ask prices. Instead, there will be only one rate, which can be treated as the *midrate* between bid and ask prices.

RELATIONSHIP BETWEEN FOREIGN EXCHANGE MARKETS AND MONEY MARKETS

In a competitive market, the amount of financial return is directly linked to the amount of financial risk in the investment. Transactions in which there is no financial risk are not expected to produce any financial return. If we borrow funds through a given financial instrument and invest the proceeds immediately thereafter in another financial instrument with the same risk and maturity, the combined operation offers no risk; but there also should be no net return. The interest rate on the borrowings and the investment should be the same (except for the usual spread between bid and offer rates). For example, if a bank borrows 30-day dollars in the interbank market and invests the proceeds in a 30-day dollar placement with another bank of comparable credit standing, we would not expect to see any net return. If a net return were possible from this transaction, then profits would be possible without risk and without needing any investment—that is, there would be profits to be made by arbitrageurs. As soon as a number of these arbitrage transactions took place, there would be a trend toward an increase in the borrowing rate and a decrease in the investment rate. This trend would continue until the two rates were approximately the same and there were no profits to be made from arbitrage between the two rates.

The exchange market gives us access to money (deposits) in any currency traded in the exchange markets. Therefore, this market should also be subject to the principle that financial return is proportional to the amount of financial risk in the investment. If we borrow funds in one currency and invest the proceeds in another currency, there should not be any return if there is no financial risk. However, in such a transaction there *is* a financial risk—namely, the risk that the currency in which the investment is made may depreciate against the currency of the borrowings before maturity of the operation. For example, if a bank borrows 30-day marks in the interbank market at 13% and invests the proceeds in a 30-day dollar placement with another bank of comparable credit standing at 15%, the bank's risk is that the dollar may depreciate against the mark before the two transactions mature. Such a depreciation of the dollar could convert the initial 2% interest gain into a net loss. In contrast to the earlier transaction in which both borrowings and investment were made in dollars, this is not a riskless operation because we are dealing with two currencies. At the end there may be a financial gain or loss, depending on the fluctuations in the spot exchange rate.

If we want to make the operation of borrowing in one currency and investing in another one a riskless transaction, we must find a way to lock in from the beginning an exchange rate at which the currency of the investment can be exchanged into the currency of the borrowing upon maturity. This can be done in the forward exchange market. Today, we can lock in a rate at which we can convert dollars into marks 30 days hence. The rate at which we will make that exchange transaction on day 31 is today's 30-day forward rate. This forward transaction will eliminate the risk created from borrowing in marks and investing in dollars. The forward transaction converts the whole operation into a riskless one so that there should not be any financial return associated with it.

In our example, there was a net interest gain from borrowing marks at 13% and investing in dollars at 15%. If the return on the total transaction (including the forward transaction) must be close to 0, then we can assert what the forward rate must be relative to the spot rate at which the marks are initially converted into dollars. The forward rate of the dollar against the mark must be at a 2% per annum discount relative to the spot rate. That is, the forward discount on the dollar (premium on the mark) must equal the interest differential between the two currencies in favor of the dollar. In such a case, it is said that *interest rate parity* exists. In this condition, it is not possible to realize any profits from borrowing in one currency and investing in another one without undertaking some risk.

If a net return were possible from borrowing in one currency and investing in another with a *cover* in the forward market, there would be an incentive for *covered-interest arbitrage* to take place. To see what happens when the relationship between the forward premium (discount) and the interest rate differential is not maintained (that is, when interest rate parity does not hold), consider the following situation:

Spot rate	$0.4800/DM
30-day forward rate	$0.4812/DM
30-day interest rates	
DM	13% p.a.
US$	15% p.a.

To compute the per annum percentage premium (discount) of the 30-day mark against the dollar, we can use the formula presented previously:

$$\text{Forward premium (Discount)} = \frac{\text{Forward rate} - \text{Spot rate}}{\text{Spot rate}} \times \frac{12}{\text{Number of months forward}}$$

$$= \frac{0.4812 - 0.4800}{0.4800} \times \frac{12}{1}$$

$$= 0.03 = 3\% \text{ per annum}$$

That is, the premium of the forward mark against the dollar, 3%, is larger than the interest differential of 2% in favor of the dollar. Thus, there is an incentive to profit from covered-interest arbitrage. In this example, the arbitrageur could realize 1% profit by performing the transactions described in the following table:[7]

Borrow $s	− 15%
Convert $s into DMs spot	
Invest DMs	+ 13
Sell DMs forward against $s at a premium for DMs	+ 3
Net profit	+ 1%

[7]If by mistake, the arbitrageur tried to do the transactions in the opposite direction, there would be a 1% loss instead of a gain, as shown here:

Borrow DMs	− 13%
Convert DMs into $s spot	
Invest $s	+ 15
Sell $s forward against DMs at a discount for $s	− 3
Net loss	− 1%

The cash flows associated with this interest arbitrage are presented in Exhibit 5.1. With $100,000 initially, the net profit of $86 for 30 days represents a net profit of 1% per annum ($86/100,000 \times 12$ months $= 0.01$). The principal amount on which the arbitrageur can earn this 1% is limited only by the amount he or she can borrow at the current rate. As the amounts involved in this interest arbitrage increase, the following pressures will develop in the exchange markets:

1. The *spot* rate of the mark against the dollar will tend to *appreciate* as marks are bought against dollars.

2. The *forward* rate of the mark against the dollar will tend to *depreciate* as marks are sold against dollars.

This will tend to *decrease the initial forward premium* of the mark against the dollar. In the money markets, the following pressures will develop:

1. The interest rate for the dollar will tend to *increase* as dollars are borrowed.

2. The interest rate for the DM will tend to *decrease* as more funds are available to invest in DMs.

These pressures will tend to *increase the initial interest differential* between the mark and the dollar.

As these tendencies continue over time, the returns on a covered basis on the top currencies will move toward each other. When they

EXHIBIT 5.1 Cash Flows in a Covered-Interest Arbitrage Operation

Date	Transaction	CURRENCIES*	
		$	DM
Day 1	Borrow $s at 15% p.a. for 30 days	+100,000	
	Sell $s against DMs spot	−100,000	+208,333
	Invest DMs at 13% for 30 days		−208,333
	Sell DMs against $s for delivery in 30 days	ncf	ncf
	Net cash flows	0	0
Day 31	DM208,333 investment matures		
	Interest $= 0.13 \times 208,333 \times \frac{1}{12}$		
	$\quad = 2,257$		+210,590
	$100,000 borrowing matures		
	Interest $= 0.15 \times 100,000 \times \frac{1}{12}$		
	$\quad = 1,250$	−101,250	
	Deliver on forward contract from day 1	+101,336	−210,590
	Net cash flows	+86	0

*(+: Cash inflow; −: Cash outflow; ncf: No cash flow)

meet, the discount on the forward rate of the currency with the higher interest rate will equal the interest differential in its favor. Also, the swap rate expressed as a percentage of the spot rate will equal the interest differential. For example, if we assume that all the necessary adjustments produced by interest arbitrage are done through changes in the forward rate (that is, the interest rates and the spot rate remain constant), then we can calculate what the new forward rate in our example will be. It must be a 2% premium on the mark against the dollar; the swap rate must be 2% of the spot rate.

$$\text{Swap rate for 12 months} = +2\% \text{ (Spot rate)}$$
$$= +2\% \text{ (0.4800)}$$
$$= +0.0096$$
$$\text{Swap rate for 30 days} = 0.0096 \div 12 = 0.0008$$

Then

$$\text{New forward rate} = \text{Spot rate} + \text{Swap rate}$$
$$= 0.4800 + 0.0008$$
$$= 0.4808 \quad \text{or} \quad \$0.4808/\text{DM}$$

Alternatively, we have:

$$\begin{aligned}\text{Forward premium} \atop \text{on mark} \quad &= +2\%\\[6pt]
&= \frac{\text{New forward rate} - \text{Spot rate}}{\text{Spot rate}} \times \frac{12}{\text{Number of months forward}}\\[6pt]
&= \frac{X - 0.4800}{0.4800} \times \frac{12}{1}\end{aligned}$$

$$\begin{aligned}\text{New forward rate} &= +2\%(\text{Spot rate})\left(\frac{\text{Number of months forward}}{12}\right) + \text{Spot rate}\\[6pt]
&= +2\%(0.4800)\left(\frac{1}{12}\right) + 0.4800\\[6pt]
&= 0.4808 \quad \text{or} \quad \$0.4808/\text{DM}\end{aligned}$$

This shows the roots of the term *swap transaction* used often among exchange dealers. When a covered–interest rate transaction takes place, we do in the forward market the opposite of what we do in the spot market. For example, if in the spot market we sell marks against dollars to generate dollar proceeds, then the cover in the forward market involves a purchase of marks against dollars. Buys equal sells for each currency. There is just a temporary "swap" of one currency into another—marks into dollars, in this case. The rate for this swap is the swap rate—the difference between the forward and the spot rates. Swap transactions will be discussed in detail later in Chapter 7.

In general, when there is an opportunity for covered-interest arbitrage, there is an incentive to invest in the currency with the higher interest to the point where the discount of that currency in the forward market is less than the interest differential. If the discount in the forward market of the currency with the higher interest rate becomes larger than the interest differential, then it pays to invest in the currency with the lower interest and take advantage of the excessive forward premium on this currency.

Covered-interest arbitrage does not involve any risk. From day 1, we know all the relevant interest rates and exchange rates, although some of the cash flows do not take place until later in the future. Furthermore, this arbitrage does not require any investment; the funds to begin the arbitrage are borrowed. Anybody with access to borrowed funds and investment outlets at those rates can profit from covered-interest arbitrage. Given modern information systems and the large number of major banks that have access to these markets, opportunities to profit from covered-interest arbitrage are rarely seen in the market, and when they do appear they disappear promptly.

However, interest rate parity holds among currencies only when we deal in *net interest rates accessible* to banks—that is, rates net of costs associated with taxes, exchange controls, reserve requirements, and so on. Thus, interest rate parity can best be observed when examining Eurorates among banks of comparable credit standing. Except for the Eurocurrency interbank market, financial markets are usually *not* completely free and strict interest rate parity does *not* hold. In these cases the forward discounts and premiums reflect not only interest differentials, but other factors as well. This is particularly true in periods of heavy speculation about a future change in the spot rate.

Empirical evidence of the validity of the interest rate parity relationship can be seen in Exhibit 5.2 for the mark and the Swiss franc against the dollar. The exhibit compares the interest rate obtained on those currencies on a covered basis (nominal rate plus forward premium or discount against the dollar) with the rate on Eurodollars. The difference between these two rates is plotted by the line labeled *differential,* which hovers around 0 for both currencies. That is, there was not much incentive for covered-interest arbitrage. The nonzero differences can often be explained by discrepancies in the exact time of the day when the data were compiled. The relationship holds only for the time period during which quotes are valid—often no longer than while

EXHIBIT 5.2 Incentive for Covered-Interest Arbitrage on 3-Month Funds between Dollars and Swiss Francs and between Dollars and Marks 1979–1982

(Averages for Week Ending Wednesday)

Differential: (+) favors borrowing francs or marks and investing in dollars   (−) favors borrowing dollars and investing in francs or marks

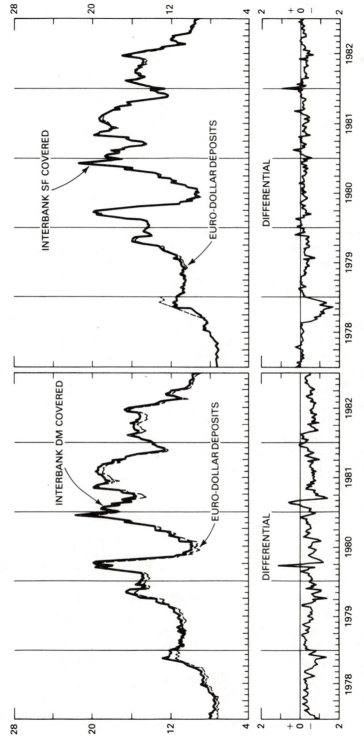

1 PERCENT ON DIFFERENTIAL SCALE = 2 PERCENT ON RATE SCALE DIFFERENTIAL

SOURCE: U.S. Board of Governors, Federal Reserve System, *Selected Interest and Exchange Rates*, Chart 8, various issues.

you hold the telephone line. Once the line has been disconnected, a trader is free to change his or her quotes in any or all the rates involved in interest rate parity. Although the relationship will again hold at the revised rates, this will not be seen if the data are gathered from transactions closed at slightly different times (as, for example, if the spot rate is collected from a transaction closed at 4:07 P.M. and the forward rate is collected from a transaction closed at 4:09 P.M.).[8]

SUMMARY

Trading in currencies occurs in the foreign exchange market either for immediate exchange (the *spot market*) or for exchange in the future (the *forward market*). The market is a worldwide network of traders who typically operate from commercial banks. These traders deal at the retail level with customers (such as corporations) and they also deal in the interbank market among themselves. Major banks deal in a dozen or so major currencies. Central banks also operate in the foreign exchange market in order to adjust the value of the nations' currencies.

Spot quotations are given in terms of the amount of local currency required to buy one unit of a foreign currency (although the United Kingdom provides an exception to this practice). Such a standard quotation is a *direct quotation*. The quotient of two foreign currencies in terms of the local currency (the *cross rate*) also can be used to find the price of a foreign currency in terms of the other.

Forward quotations can be made at the *outright rate*, which is done in the same terms as the direct price quotation for spot transactions. Among dealers, quotations are usually at bid/ask premiums or discounts from the spot rate, called the *swap rates*. The forward premium or discount of a currency is computed as follows:

$$\frac{(\text{Forward rate} - \text{Spot rate})}{\text{Spot rate}} \times \frac{12}{\text{Number of months forward}}$$

Exchange rates in the forward market largely reflect interest rate differentials. *Arbitrageurs* operate to equilibrate the rates for a currency in various parts of the world by buying and selling the same currency for the same maturity at different places. *Covered-interest arbitrage* is the process by which the forward exchange rates are brought into equilibrium with differing interest rates in various countries.

---

[8]See Jacob A. Frenkel and Richard M. Levich, "Transaction Costs and Interest Arbitrage: Tranquil versus Turbulent Periods," *Journal of Political Economy*, December, 1977, pp. 1209–26.

Through this type of arbitrage, the final returns in a given period for all currencies from the combination of interest plus premium or discount in the forward market are approximately the same. This outcome is also known as *interest rate parity* and exists generally in the Eurocurrency interbank market. Most other financial markets are not completely free in operation, and hence they will deviate in outcome from the predications of strict interest rate parity.

APPENDIX

CURRENCY FUTURES MARKET

The futures market in the Chicago Mercantile Exchange presents an alternative to the forward exchange market.* The International Monetary Market (IMM) of this Exchange deals in eight currencies: Swiss francs, German marks, French francs, British pounds, Dutch guilders, Canadian dollars, Mexican pesos, and Japanese yen. It is unrealistic for the average individual to walk into a bank and ask the bank's exchange trader to purchase £10,000 for delivery in 3 months. However, the IMM of the Chicago Mercantile Exchange is a possible option.

Conceptually, trading in futures is similar to trading in the forward exchange market. The major characteristic that distinguishes the futures market from the forward exchange market is that a *margin* or security deposit must be maintained with a broker as a guarantee of ability to fulfill a contract in the IMM. This margin is a security designed to cover any initial loss due to adverse price movements. For each currency, the Exchange establishes an *initial margin* and a *maintenance margin* per contract in that currency. The size of a contract for each currency is determined by the Exchange. The original margin is approximately 2½% of the value of the contract. If the initial margin for a sterling contract is $1,500 and the maintenance margin is $1,000, then the individual buying or selling sterling contracts initially deposits $1,500 per contract with a broker as margin. If this individual's equity in a contract declines to below $1,000, this person will receive a *margin call* from his or her broker requesting an addition of $500 to the margin account. If the contract is liquidated at that point, the additional margin becomes a realized loss. Conversely, gains in the price of the contract can become realized gains. These adjustments are completed daily and margin calls must be settled on a daily basis. This situation is

---

*Similar markets also exist in some cities in Europe.

in contrast to the transactions with banks' exchange traders where there are no margin requirements and where the gain or loss in a forward exchange contract is not settled until maturity.

The gains or losses that a speculator in the IMM may suffer in a given day are also limited by the Exchange, which establishes limits on the amount that the prices of specific contracts can fluctuate on a daily basis. In the case of large changes in prices, the Exchange provides a procedure for larger limits for 2 days, and for 1 day of trading without limits before the normal limits are reinstated. For example, the contract size for the British pound is £25,000 and the normal limit of price fluctuation in a given day is $0.05/£—that is, $1,250. After two successive days on which the contract loses or gains $1,250 per day, the maximum price change allowed on the third day is increased to 150% of the normal limit, to $1,875. If at the end of the third day the closing price has changed to the allowed limit, then the allowed price change on the fourth day is increased to 200% of the normal limit, to $2,500. Finally, on the fifth day of sustained maximum price changes, the price of a contract is allowed to float without any limits before normal limits are set again on the sixth day.

As implied in the preceding discussion, the amounts traded in the futures market are multiples of the Exchange's contract size in each currency. Fractions of a contract are not traded. The futures market also establishes specific dates of delivery. All contracts are for delivery on the third Wednesday of March, June, September, or December. Tailor-made contracts of a given amount for specific dates of delivery are not possible in the IMM. As a matter of fact, currencies are treated by the Exchange as any other commodity (for example, pork bellies), where actual delivery of the contracted merchandise takes place in only a very small percentage of the transactions—less than 3%. Most transactions are settled before maturity.

Transactions in the futures market require payment of a commission to the broker. The size of commissions is negotiated between the customer and the broker. Brokers discourage small transactions by imposing relatively high commissions.

In addition to the individuals who are forced to operate through the IMM because of lack of an alternative in commercial banks, large businesses have also found it advantageous to transact through the IMM on some occasions. Such situations arise particularly when the IMM is very active relative to the banks, and its spreads between bid and offer prices become narrower than the banks' market. Generally, there is a considerable amount of arbitrage between the IMM and the banks' market. However, large multinationals still consider the size of their transactions too large for the IMM to handle without destabilizing the market. Although the IMM is a very active market with more than half the outstanding contracts often changing hands on a daily basis, its size is still relatively small.

Foreign currency *options* (as opposed to futures) are traded in a variety of currencies in both the United States and Europe. On the Philadelphia Stock Exchange, for example, contracts for half the size of the corresponding futures contracts on the Chicago Board–Options Exchange are traded with up to 9 months maturity in marks, sterling, yen, Swiss francs, and Canadian dollars. In contrast to futures, options can be exercised at any time during the contract life and require a deposit subject to normal margin requirements. The futures contract must be exercised and the purchaser must continually make up the margin balance; hence, a wrong price move could result in the speculator losing far more than the original investment, as he cannot simply walk away from the futures contract as he can from an option contract.*

BIBLIOGRAPHY

Aliber, Robert Z., ed., *The International Market for Foreign Exchange.* New York: Praeger, 1969.

Babbel, David F., "The Rise and Decline of Foreign Currency Options," *Euromoney*, Sept. 1980, pp. 141–49.

Coninx, Raymond G. F., *Foreign Exchange Today.* New York: John Wiley and Sons, 1979.

"Currency Options: W. C. Fields Had a Phrase for It," *Economist*, Oct. 30, 1982, pp. 76ff.

Dalal, Ardeshir J., "Decision Rules for an Investor in Forward Exchange Markets," *Journal of International Economics*, Sept. 1979, pp. 539–58.

Dillon, Laura White, "The Do's and Don'ts of Foreign Exchange Trading," *Institutional Investor*, Jan. 1980, pp. 161–64.

Einzig, Paul, *A Textbook on Foreign Exchange.* London: Macmillan, 1966.

————, *The Dynamic Theory of Foreign Exchange*, 2d ed. London: Macmillan, 1967.

Feiger, George, and Bertand Jacquillat, "Currency Option Bonds, Puts and Calls on Spot Exchange, and the Hedging of Contingent Foreign Earnings," *Journal of Finance*, Dec. 1979, pp. 1129–39.

Frenkel, Jacob A. and Richard M. Levich, "Transaction Costs and Interest Arbitrage: Tranquil versus Turbulent Periods," *Journal of Political Economy*, Dec. 1977, pp. 1209–26.

---

*See "Currency Options: W. C. Fields Had a Phrase for It," *The Economist*, October 30, 1982, p. 76f. Question: What was W. C.'s phrase?

Giddy, Ian H., "Research on the Foreign Exchange Market," *Columbia Journal of World Business,* Winter 1979, pp. 4–6.

Gupta, Sanjeev, "A Note on the Efficiency of Black Markets in Foreign Currencies," *Journal of Finance,* June 1981, pp. 705–10.

International Monetary Market of the Chicago Mercantile Exchange, *The Futures Market in Foreign Currencies.* Chicago: The Chicago Mercantile Exchange, undated.

————, *Trading in International Currency Futures.* Chicago: The Chicago Mercantile Exchange, undated.

————, *Understanding Futures in Foreign Exchange.* Chicago: The Chicago Mercantile Exchange, undated.

Kolb, Robert W., Gerald D. Gay, and James V. Jordan, "Managing Foreign Interest Rate Risk," *Journal of Futures Markets,* Summer 1982, pp. 151–58.

McFarland, James W., R. Richardson Pettit, and Sam K. Sung, "The Distribution of Foreign Exchange Price Changes: Trading Day Effects and Risk Measurement," *Journal of Finance,* June 1982, pp. 693–714.

Riehl, Heinz, and Rita M. Rodriguez, *Foreign Exchange and Money Markets.* New York: McGraw-Hill Book Company, 1983.

Walker, Townsend, *A Guide for Using the Foreign Exchange Market.* New York: Ronald Press, 1981.

EXERCISES ON FOREIGN EXCHANGE MECHANICS*

1. Assume that the buying rate for U.S. dollars spot in Frankfurt is DM1.8550.

    (a) What would you expect the price of the German mark to be in the United States?

    (b) If the German mark were quoted in New York at $0.5360, how would the market react?

2. If the French franc is selling for Hfl0.4699 in Amsterdam and the Dutch guilder for FF2.1280 in Paris, how should the market react and why?

3. The buying rate for Swiss francs spot in New York is $0.5900. Ms. Enrico is going to buy francs in Zurich at SwF1.6760/$ and sell them in New York. How much profit will she make per Swiss franc?

4. Assume that the Japanese yen spot was quoted at $0.004710 in New York at the same time the Italian lira was quoted at $0.001030.

---

*These exercises were prepared by Kenneth Adamitis under the supervision of Professor Rita M. Rodriguez.

(a) What would you expect the price of yen to be in Italy?

(b) If the price of yen were quoted in Rome at Lit4.1680/¥, how could you make a profit?

5. About the same time that the German mark spot was quoted at $0.5360 in New York, the price of the pound sterling was quoted at $2.4420.

(a) What would you expect the price of the pound to be in Germany?

(b) If the pound were quoted in Frankfurt at DM4.5000/£, what would you do to profit from the situation?

6. Assume the Belgian franc spot was quoted at FF0.1435 in Paris while the Canadian dollar was quoted at FF3.7037.

(a) What would you expect the price of the Belgian franc to be in Canada?

(b) If the price of the Canadian dollar quoted in Antwerp were BF25.6500, how could you make a profit?

7. On October 24, 1980, the German mark was quoted at $0.5360/DM and the French franc was quoted at $0.2328/FF in Chicago. If at the same time Paris was quoting FF2.3000/DM and FF4.2955/$, what are the incentives for arbitrage?

8. About the same time when Amsterdam is quoting Hfl2.0185/$ and Hfl0.00228/Lit, New York is quoting $0.00113/Lit and $0.4900/Hfl. What are the incentives for arbitrage?

9. About the same time when the Swiss franc was quoted at DM1.1132/SwF and the French franc DM0.4343/FF in Frankfurt, Zurich was quoting SwF0.8950/DM and SwF0.3901/FF. What are the opportunities for arbitrage?

10. You have called your foreign exchange trader in New York and asked for quotations on the Belgian franc spot, 1-month, 3-month, and 6-month. The trader has responded with the following:

$0.033400/17   73/89   142/124   257/221

(a) What are the outright rates implied by this quote in terms of dollars per Belgian franc?

(b) If you wished to buy spot Belgian francs, how much would you pay in dollars?

(c) If you wanted to purchase spot U.S. dollars, how much would you have to pay in Belgian francs?

(d) What is the per annum premium or discount of the Belgian franc against the dollar in the 1-, 3-, and 6-month forward rates? (Assume that you are buying Belgian francs.)

11. Your foreign exchange trader in the United States has quoted the following rates for the Swiss franc spot, 1-month, 3-month, and 6-month:

$0.5965/72   50/61   127/133   242/247

(a) What are the outright rates in terms of dollars per Swiss franc?
(b) If you wished to buy 3-month Swiss francs, how much would you pay in dollars?
(c) If you wanted to buy 6-month dollars, what would be the price in terms of Swiss francs?
(d) What is the per annum premium or discount of the Swiss franc against the U.S. dollar in the 1-, 3-, and 6-month forward rates? (Assume that you are buying Swiss francs.)

12. The following rates are quoted by your foreign exchange trader in the United States on the pound sterling spot, 1-month, 3-month, and 6-month:

$2.4480/93   63/54   147/135   190/173

(a) What are the outright rates in terms of dollars per pound sterling?
(b) How much would you have to pay in dollars to buy 1-month pounds?
(c) What is the price of 6-month dollars if you were to pay in pounds sterling?
(d) What is the per annum premium or discount of sterling against the U.S. dollar in the 1-, 3-, and 6-month forward rates? (Assume that you are selling pounds sterling.)

13. The spot Danish krone is selling for $0.17400 and the 3-month forward is selling for $0.17440. The 3-month interbank rate for the U.S. dollar is 11.60% and for the Danish krone is 11.25%.

(a) Are the forward rates and interest rates in equilibrium? Why?
(b) If not, what would you do to take advantage of the situation?
(c) If a large number of individuals take similar actions, what rate trends will appear in the market?

14. The Finnish markka is selling for spot at $0.2695 and 3-month at $0.2705.

   (a) What is the forward per annum premium or discount of the markka against the dollar?

   (b) If the 3-month interbank rate for the U.S. dollar is 9.75% and for the markka is 8.75%, is there equilibrium between the exchange and money markets? Why?

   (c) How would you profit from this situation?

   (d) What rate trends would appear in the market if a large number of people took these actions?

15. In Frankfurt the spot French franc is selling for DM0.4343 and the 3-month forward is selling for DM0.4300. The 3-month interbank rate for the German mark is 5.75% and for the French franc is 9.00%.

   (a) Are the exchange and money markets in equilibrium? Why?

   (b) Is there any way to take advantage of the situation? If so, how?

   (c) What rate trends would appear in the market if a large number of people took similar actions?

6

Exchange Rate and Interest Rate Determination Theories

THE THEORIES EXPLAINING the determination of exchange rates and interest rates are intimately related. These theories can be classified into two major groups, depending on their time horizon. One set of theories portrays the relationships that should obtain on average over the long term. The rates determined by these theories represent equilibrium points toward which the market will tend to move. The other set of theories has a shorter-term horizon. They are based on the analysis of the relationships between supply and demand, given that resource immobilities limit the participation of each sector in the market over the short term.

This classification of the theories according to their time horizon is somewhat unconventional. In practice, there is a tendency for different people to believe one set of theories over the other. Thus, academicians tend to emphasize the validity of equilibrium theories and practitioners tend to rely on short-term relationships between supply and demand. In our view, the difference between the two sets of theories is only one of degree. Here we will present first the general equilibrium theories and then contrast them with those derived from the partial analysis of supply and demand forces.

GENERAL EQUILIBRIUM THEORIES

In an economy based on money, not barter, the general equilibrium theories emphasize the role of money and treat it just as one more asset—an asset whose value is determined as the reciprocal of the price level.[1] When we compare price levels of two different countries, the theory becomes the *purchasing power parity theory* of exchange rate determination. When we analyze the problems in terms of *expected* changes in price levels, the theory determines the interest rate for each currency and the exchange rates among currencies.

Purchasing Power Parity

The value of a currency in one country is determined by the amount of goods and services that can be purchased with a unit of the currency. This is called the *purchasing power of the currency* (the reciprocal of the price level). If there is more than one currency, then the exchange rate between two currencies must provide the same purchasing power for each currency; this condition is called *purchasing power parity*. If the exchange rate is such that purchasing power parity does not exist between the two currencies, then the exchange rate between the two currencies will adjust until purchasing power parity prevails.[2]

At its simplest level this theory says that commodity prices, after adjustments for transportation and other costs, should be the same in different countries. If this were not the case, there would be incentives to purchase the commodity in the country where its price is the lowest and sell it in the country where its price is the highest until the proper price relationship were established. At this level the theory is almost a tautology and it is devoid of much insight into what determines exchange rates. The more interesting interpretation of this theory of determination of exchange rates is based on *general price levels*, not commodity prices.

If an exchange rate is such that one currency has a higher pur-

---

[1]The appendix to this chapter discusses these theories in algebraic terms. A collection of articles on this approach is contained in Jacob A. Frenkel and Harry G. Johnson eds., *The Monetary Aprroach to the Balance of Payments* (Toronto: University of Toronto Press, 1976). A good review is presented in Marina V.N. Whitman, "Global Monetarism and the Monetary Approach to the Balance of Payments," *Brookings Papers on Economic Activity*, No. 3, 1975, pp. 491–536.

[2]This theory is more or less implicit in the writings of some of the classical economists such as Ricardo and Mill. However, the name of the theory and its applications to practical situations is first associated to Gustav Cassel, "Abnormal Deviations in International Exchanges," *Economic Journal*, Vol. 28, December 1918, pp. 413–15. An excellent review of the theory is contained in Lawrence H. Officer, "The Purchasing-Power-Parity Theory of Exchange Rates: A Review Article, *International Monetary Fund Staff Papers*, March 1976, pp. 1–60.

chasing power in one country than in another, then the demand for money and expenditures in each country will change, affecting the level of imports and exports and, eventually, the exchange rate. To see these forces in action, we can assume that the exchange rate of the dollar against the mark shows the dollar to be undervalued relative to the mark based on the relative purchasing power (PP) of the two currencies. As an example assume that the market exchange rate is DM/$ = 1.90. However,

$$PP_{DM} = \frac{1}{\text{Price level in Germany}} = \frac{1}{0.50} = 2.00$$

and

$$PP_{\$} = \frac{1}{\text{Price level in United States}} = \frac{1}{1.00} = 1.00$$

Thus,

$$\text{Purchasing power parity} = \frac{PP_{DM}}{PP_{\$}} = \frac{2.00}{1.00} = DM2.00/\$$$

Given certain levels of income and prices, individuals in each country will decide how much of their income to spend in goods and services and how much to maintain in cash balances (hoarding). The exchange rate of DM1.90/$, in face of the purchasing power parity rate of DM2.00/$, is equivalent to increasing mark prices of goods relative to the dollar prices of those goods. If the money supplies in each currency are assumed to be constant, then an increase in mark prices will result in increased demand for liquid funds in marks and decreased expenditures in goods sold by Germany. A decrease in dollar prices results in a decrease in the demand for liquid funds in dollars and an increase in expenditures in goods and services denominated in dollars. This change in expenditure patterns represents an increase in exports from the United States and a decrease in exports from Germany.

In a system of floating exchange rates, this sequence of events will produce an appreciation of the dollar against the mark, which would tend to correct the initial undervaluation of the dollar and to restore purchasing power parity between the two currencies. In a system of fixed exchange rates there will be a loss of official exchange reserves in Germany and an increase in official reserves in the United States. In Germany the level of exchange reserves (plus borrowing power) maintained by the country imposes a physical limit to the deficit. In the United States the monetary authorities would have to hold increasing levels of foreign exchange in order to absorb the excess liquidity in the economy. The limit to this process is the country's willingness to exchange real resources (exports of goods and services) for financial assets.[3]

In both systems of exchange rates, fixed and floating, the adjustment mechanism in this theory works through changes in expenditures in response to changes in real money balances. Prices of goods remain constant so the increased receipts in the exporting country represent real increases in money balances. These increases are then available to become expenditures in goods and services in the domestic market and abroad. The change in expenditures abroad produces the change in exchange rates.

This version of purchasing power parity, in which actual price levels are the base for comparisons, is known as *absolute purchasing power parity*. An alternative formulation, known as *relative purchasing power parity*, is based on *changes* in price levels. In this version of the theory changes in exchange rates are determined by the relative movements in price levels.

There are a number of recognized factors that will prevent purchasing power parity in one or both of its presentations from determining exchange rates. These factors include the following: (1) government intervention, either directly in the exchange markets or indirectly through trade restrictions; (2) speculation in the exchange market; (3) long-term flows that continue in spite of the disequilibrium between purchasing power parity and exchange rates; and (4) structural changes in the economies involved. However, the theory considers these departures to prevail only during the short term. Over longer periods of time, purchasing power parity will tend to dominate the changes in exchange rates, according to this theory.

The major problem with the applicability of this theory is in the specification of the relevant price level indices to be used in the computation of the purchasing power parity. Questions pertaining to what is an appropriate sample and the relative weights that should be allocated to each commodity in the sample are the subject of considerable debate. For example, should the sample represent all goods and services, or only those that are traded? Should the weights given to each item be those of the importing country, the exporting country, or a third country? A discussion of the technical problems involved in the calculation of price indices is beyond the scope of this book. Suffice it to say that the problem is complex and that definite answers are not available.

The tendency for exchange rates to compensate for changes in relative prices over long periods of time (such as a decade) is generally accepted. However, supporting research has often been based on

---

[3]The effectiveness of this mechanism rests on the inability of monetary policy to counteract the changes in money supply produced by an increase in imports or exports. This inability makes domestic money supply an *endogenous* variable in a system of fixed exchange rates.

wholesale price indices, which are heavily weighted by traded goods, instead of an index more representative of the general price level. This becomes a test of the strength of commodity arbitrage instead of the validity of purchasing power parity, which is based on the relative value of money expressed in terms of general price levels.

The conditions in which purchasing power parity can be considered to have the heaviest weights in determining exchange rates involve large monetary disturbances such as very high inflation. In these cases, the response of individuals to changes in values of real and monetary assets can be expected to be strong and the predictions of purchasing power parity for exchange rate can be realized. Outside these extreme monetary conditions, purchasing power parity has been found to be a very poor predictor of exchange rates in the short term.[4]

Market Expectations and Rate Determination

The return that an investor obtains in a fixed-rate security depends on the nominal rate of return and the rate of inflation between the period when the investment is made and when it is liquidated. The return of an exchange position depends on the fluctuations in the exchange rate between the time when the position is created and when it is closed. From these facts, these theories postulate that a knowing investor would take into account the expected rate of inflation and the expected fluctuations in the exchange rate before either investing in a fixed-rate security or engaging in an exchange position. Furthermore, because both interest rates and exchange rates represent prices for money, the investor's expectations about future inflation rates, interest rates, and exchange rates are closely related.

Interest Rate Determination.   At the heart of the monetary theory of interest rate determination is the investor who is considered to contemplate investments in real assets as an alternative to investments in financial assets. Investments in real assets do not require a forecast of future inflation rates. Prices of real assets are expected to change to incorporate the effects of actual inflation. However, investments in financial assets with a fixed interest rate require an assessment of expected inflation. The monetary return obtained from these investments remains fixed, regardless of the actual inflation rate. A compensation for

---

[4]For the applicability of the theory over the long term, see Henry J. Gaillot, "Purchasing Power Parity as an Explanation of Long-Term Changes in Exchange Rates," *Journal of Money, Credit and Banking*, Vol. 2, August 1970, pp. 348–57. Gaillot bases his study on averages for periods of several years and prices are measured by wholesale price indices. For the problems over the short term, see Paul Krugman, "Purchasing Power Parity and Exchange Rates," *Journal of International Economics*, August 1978, pp. 397–407.

the depreciation in monetary value produced by inflation can be obtained only to the extent that the nominal rate of return incorporates an allowance for expected inflation. For an investor to be indifferent between investing in a real asset or a financial asset with a fixed rate of interest, the allowance made for inflation in the nominal rate of return in the financial asset must approximate the inflation rate expected by the investor.

If the nominal rate of interest incorporates an allowance for inflation below the rate expected by investors, then investors will borrow funds at that rate and invest the proceeds in real assets whose prices are expected to increase together with the higher rate of inflation. If many individuals did this, the increased borrowings would increase the level of nominal interest rates to the point where there was no more incentive to continue this operation. At that point the nominal rate would incorporate the rate of inflation expected by the investor. On the other hand, if the nominal interest rate incorporates an allowance for inflation higher than the one expected, there would be an incentive for selling real assets to invest the proceeds in financial assets. This would tend to reduce the level of the nominal interest rate to the point where there was no more incentive to continue this operation. Again, the nominal rate would incorporate the expected inflation rate—not more, not less.

To induce the investor to postpone consumption and instead use the funds to make an investment, it is necessary to pay a compensation. In the absence of inflation, this compensation is called the *real rate* of return paid to the investor. Thus, the observed nominal interest rate for maturity i can be defined as

$$\text{Nominal interest rate}_i = \text{Real rate} + \text{Expected inflation}_i$$

The real rate has been estimated at 3% to 4% per annum, and the theory assumes it to remain fairly constant through time, regardless of the currency or country involved. With a constant real rate and a given observed nominal interest rate, we can derive the inflation rate expected by the market. For example, with an annual nominal interest rate of 16% for 6-month Treasury bills and an assumed annual real rate of 3%, this theory leads us to conclude that the market is expecting an annual rate of inflation of 13% over the following 6 months.

In this expectation theory, the relationship between short-term rates and long-term rates is established in a fashion similar to that used to determine nominal interest rates. In equilibrium, a given long-term rate must incorporate the short-term rates expected to prevail in the future. For example, the observed 3-month rate must be equal to the observed 1-month rate plus the 2-month rate expected to hold 1 month from today. If the 1-month rate is 16% per annum and the 3-month rate is 18% per annum, then we can derive the 2-month rate implicit in these rates as follows:

$$(1 + 0.18)\left(\frac{3}{12}\right) = \left(1 + 0.16\right)\left(\frac{1}{12}\right) + (1 + X)\left(\frac{2}{12}\right)$$
$$X = 0.1898 = 18.98\%$$

In equilibrium an investor would be indifferent between investing in a 3-month bill at 18%, or in a 1-month bill at 16% followed by an investment in a 2-month bill at the expected rate of 18.98%. If this were not the case, there would be an incentive for borrowing for one maturity and investing for another one. The borrowings would tend to increase the interest rate for that maturity and the investment would tend to depress the interest rate for that maturity. This process would continue until investors and borrowers were indifferent between alternative maturities.

As described here, this theory postulates that the observed nominal rate is the sum of the real rate plus the inflation rate expected between now and the maturity date. If this is correct, then when we compare two nominal interest rates for two different maturities we can see the market's estimate for the rate of inflation between the two periods of time in the future.

Relationship among Interest Rates in Different Currencies. If the interest rate in each currency for maturity i is determined through the process described previously, then we have the following:

Currency X_i = Real rate + Expected inflation in X_i

Currency Y_i = Real rate + Expected inflation in Y_i

$$\bullet$$
$$\bullet$$
$$\bullet$$

Currency Z_i = Real rate + Expected inflation in Z_i

If the real rate in each currency is similar, then the differences between observed nominal rates represent differences between the inflation rates expected in each currency.

We can complement the above theory by taking into account the interest rate parity that exists among currencies which are freely traded. Interest rate parity makes a currency's forward premium (or discount) against another currency equal to the interest rate differential between the two currencies for the given maturity. Using a theory based on expectations, we previously concluded that the difference between observed nominal rates represents the difference in expected inflation rates. If this theory is true, then we can also say that the forward premium (or discount) between two currencies represents the difference between the inflation rates expected in the two given currencies.

We should note, however, that in reaching the last conclusion, we have combined two theorems which require market participants to assume different amounts of risk. Interest rate parity requires the participation of arbitrageurs who do not incur any risk. From the beginning of the transaction to arbitrage interest rates, the arbitrageur knows exactly the interest rates in the currency borrowed and the currency invested as well as the relevant spot rate and forward rate at which the two necessary exchange transactions are made. This arbitrage operation does not require any expectations about future rate developments. On the other hand, in order to arbitrage returns between financial assets and real assets, or between two different maturities of a financial asset, the arbitrageur must accept uncertainty as to the eventual inflation rate in that market. To arbitrage between a financial investment in one currency and an investment in another currency, the arbitrageur has uncertainty as to the eventual exchange rate in two different markets.

The empirical validation of the interest rate parity requires only a comparison of observed nominal interest rates and forward rates at one point in time. On the other hand, the verification of the expectation theory requires an understanding of how expectations are formed as well as the comparison of rates at two different points in time. Interest rate parity can hold without having to accept the validity of the expectation theory of interest rate determination.

Exchange Rate Determination. If market participants constantly contrast the option of holding an exchange position in a given currency with the option of covering it, then in equilibrium the returns for the two options should be similar. If an exchange position remains open, its return is equal to the interest rate earned in the currency plus the percentage change in the spot rate during the holding period. If the position is covered, the return is equal to the interest rate in the currency plus the forward premium or discount on that currency. If an investor is indifferent between the two options, it must be because the expected change in the spot rate is comparable to the known forward premium or discount. This implies that the forward rate is an estimate of the spot rate expected to prevail in the future.

Given the existence of interest rate parity, then the forward premium or discount is equal to the difference between the nominal interest rates in the two currencies. Since the nominal rates, according to the theory, are determined by the respective expected inflation rates, then we can infer that a currency's forward rate is determined by the inflation expected in that country relative to inflation rates in the other countries. If this is so, future spot rates are determined by the differential between expected inflation rates in different countries.

Implications of Efficient Markets.

If we assume that markets are efficient in the sense that all the available information is acted upon and incorporated rationally in the rates, then the theory has the following additional implications for the meaning of observed rates:

1. Nominal interest rates contain unbiased estimates of inflation rates expected in the future.
2. Long-term rates contain unbiased estimates of short-term rates expected in the future.
3. Forward rates are unbiased estimates of spot rates expected in the future.

THEORIES OF PARTIAL EQUILIBRIUM OF SUPPLY AND DEMAND

In a free market, the observed price is the price which clears the market—that is, the price at which quantity supplied equals quantity demanded. Interest rates and exchanges rates determined according to the equilibrium theories presented in the preceding section are rates or prices which clear the market. However, not all observed rates represent long-term equilibrium rates. To the extent that there are imperfections in the market whereby resources do not flow freely and quickly in search of the highest return available in the market, the observed rates or prices will not conform to those postulated under the long-term equilibrium theories. If market conditions are such that nonequilibrium rates occur more often than equilibrium ones, then observed rates may be understood better by analyzing the forces of supply and demand of funds in each economic sector, than by assuming a free flow of funds among these sectors.

Within the domestic economy, the *flow of funds accounts* offer data on the sources and uses of funds for each economic sector (including the foreign sector) and the relationships among these sectors through financial markets. The *balance of payments* offers further details on the various sectors involved in the transactions between the given country and the rest of the world—the foreign sector contained in the flow of funds accounts. The information gained about the behavior of each sector in the past, together with the situation expected in the future, establishes the total amount of supply and demand for funds in the domestic market and the exchange markets. The prices at which the quantity of funds demanded equals the quantity of funds supplied in the various domestic financial markets determines domestic interest rates, both short-term and long-term. The price at which the quantity of funds demanded equals the quantity of funds supplied in the foreign exchange markets determines the foreign exchange rate.

Interest Rates and Domestic Flow of Funds

The three major economic sectors affecting the domestic flow of funds are the household sector, the business sector, and the government sector. For the system as a whole, the household sector is a net provider of funds, while the business and government sectors are net users of funds. Between these net users and net providers of funds we find the financial institutions and the various financial markets. The foreign sector is also part of the domestic financial markets. However, since this sector plays a relatively larger role in the determination of exchange rates than in the determination of interest rates, it will be discussed together with the balance of payments accounts.

Household Sector.   The major source of funds for this sector is income and its major use of funds is consumption. The difference between consumption and income produces consumers' savings.

Consumers' savings take two major forms: real assets (housing and consumers' durables) and financial assets. Because of the cost of housing, this purchase is usually made with the aid of a mortgage; and because the mortgage payment absorbs a significant portion of a consumer's income over a long period of time, consumers' purchases of houses are highly sensitive to the level of interest rates. During periods of high interest rates, consumers use their savings much less to purchase houses than during periods of low interest rates. The funds diverted from purchasing houses often find a channel in financial assets that offer a higher return during these periods.

Consumers also must choose the form in which financial assets will be maintained. The first choice involves whether to invest these funds in short-term or long-term instruments. Traditionally, consumers have shown a preference for keeping the largest share of their financial assets in the form of short-term investments—particularly demand and savings deposits. Related to the maturity choice, but independent of it, is the consumer's choice of whether to invest in marketable instruments (such as Treasury bills or stocks) or in the nonmarketable instruments issued by financial intermediaries (such as bank deposits or insurance premiums). Traditionally, financial institutions have attracted a larger share of consumers' savings than direct market investments.

Financial Intermediaries. The financial intermediaries that attract consumers' savings can be classified into two major groups: contractual-type and deposit-type institutions. Because of the diversity of financial institutions around the world, we will refer here only to the institutions in the United States.

The contractual-type financial institutions are insurance companies and pension funds. These institutions offer specific products, such as insurance money during times of adversity and income during retirement. Although some insurance premiums have a savings feature, by and large the considerations involved in the purchase of insurance involve the ability of the individual to overcome the financial consequences of events such as fire or death in the family. Contributions to a pension fund trade off consumption today against consumption during retirement—essentially a savings process. However, in the case of the United States this analysis includes also the different tax treatment of income spent in consumption today as compared to income held for consumption during retirement. While income consumed today is taxed as ordinary income today, the income deposited in a pension fund is not taxed until the time when the pension benefits are distributed— when the individual is likely to be in a lower tax bracket. The level of income also affects the decision to deposit funds with an insurance company or a pension fund. Income increases the ability to buy the services provided by insurance companies and pension funds; however, it also decreases the need for some of them. For example, with a higher income it is easier to withstand the loss of a house through fire.

While the decision to invest funds in a contractual-type financial institution seems heavily determined by considerations of a social and institutional nature, the decision to invest in a specific deposit-type institution is determined more by expected financial return. The deposit-type institutions are commercial banks and the various types of savings banks created to facilitate mortgage financing for their depositors—savings and loan associations, mutual banks, and savings banks. The ability of these institutions to compete on the basis of interest rates paid to depositors in the past was heavily regulated by government through interest rate ceilings. During periods of high interest rates, these ceilings meant that consumers diverted their savings from deposits in financial institutions to market instruments—particularly Treasury bills and money market funds more recently—in the so-called process of *disintermediation*. However, this type of regulation was practically terminated by the Depositary Institutions and Monetary Control Act of 1980.

The nature of the liabilities of financial institutions determines, to a large extent, the ability to invest in different assets. Institutions with access to contractual savings have a larger certainty over the future inflow of funds than deposit-type institutions. The contractual-type institutions can also plan the disbursements associated with their liabilities with relative certainty based on actuarial methods. By contrast, the deposit-type institutions find the short-term interest rates they must pay on their deposits to be highly volatile in a deregulated market. The greater certainty contractual-type institutions have about the future cash flows translates into an ability and willingness to invest a relatively large proportion of their portfolio in long-term assets. Thus, insurance companies and pension funds provide a ready-made pool of funds available for investment in the bond market and the stock market. In spite of possible short-term returns, the cash flows of the liabilities of these institutions are such that many analysts consider these institutions to have a natural preference for long-term investments—a preference that would require the payment of a premium in the form of higher short-term interest rates to attract the investments of these institutions to this segment of the market.

Among the deposit-type institutions, commercial banks have been much more successful than the savings-type institutions in matching the rate structure of their assets with the rate volatility of their short-term liabilities. The main tool used by commercial banks to achieve this objective has been the floating-rate loan. Although loans may have an average maturity of 5 years and deposits have an average maturity of only 90 days, the interest rate on floating-rate loans fluctuates with the rates paid on the much shorter-term deposits. The savings-type institutions created to help their depositors in the mortgage market have found themselves with a very unbalanced balance sheet which impedes their competing during periods of high interest rates. A large proportion of the assets of these institutions is composed of household mortgages with a fixed interest rate and an average maturity of 7 or 8 years. However, on the liability side, they have deposits with very short maturities—3 to 6 months. During periods of high interest rates in market instruments, these institutions have lost substantial amounts of deposits. Although interest rate ceilings have been eliminated, the long-term portfolio of mortgages with fixed rates has made it impossible for these institutions to compete for new deposits at much higher rates. As a consequence, the supply of funds to the mortgage market during these periods has also been severely restricted.

Business Sector. The demand for funds by this sector originates with the need to finance investments in plant and equipment, and in working capital. Part of these financing needs are met from internally generated funds (profits). However, the remaining portion of funds must be obtained from outside this sector, from financial institutions or direct market issues.

It is often conceded that the business sector responds to the changes in the costs of funds with different degrees of lags. The lag is largest for investments in plant and equipment that have a long gestation period and are hard to interrupt or accelerate in the middle of their construction. The lag in response is shorter for investments in working capital; however, the cost of reversing marketing policies (such as reducing the number of days in the terms of sales on credit) can be high. As a result, business is often reluctant to change these policies in response to what may be perceived as short-term fluctuations in the cost of funds. In addition, the nature of the business cycle is such that the demand for investments in working capital may be highest when the contribution from internal sources is lowest. For example, during the early stages of a recession, payment terms slow down and inventories accumulate while profits decrease.

The business sector (particularly large corporations) can be more sensitive to the cost of funds when choosing among alternative sources of funds. For short-term financing, commercial banks and the commercial paper market compete to provide funds to the business sector. In the longer-term sector, insurance companies and pension funds compete to purchase bonds issued by the corporate sector; in addition, the bond market is an alternative to longer-term loans from commercial banks or private placements of funds from insurance companies or pension funds. Finally, the corporate sector can trade off the rates of obtaining short-term funds against the rates charged for obtaining long-term funds. However, the business sector is generally bound by considerations of appropriate ratios for liquidity purposes and maintaining a presence in the different financial markets.

Government Sector.   The government participates in the financial markets at the federal, state, and municipal levels. Among these, the federal government is the most important one. The degree of the participation of this sector in the financial markets is determined by the size of the government surplus or deficit. Government income is determined by taxation; government expenditure is determined by laws that entitle individuals and organizations to be compensated according to certain rules (entitlement programs) and by other expenditures approved in the current budget.

Traditionally, the participation of the government in the financial markets has been countercyclical. As an economic expansion advances and income increases, so do government revenues from taxation. At this time the need for government expenditures in many programs also decreases, particularly unemployment compensation. Thus, during economic expansions, governments often decrease the amount of funds raised in the capital markets. However, as the economy enters a downswing, government revenues decrease together with national income. At the same time, the need for government expenditures often increases. The combination of the two factors increases the amount of funds the government must obtain from the financial markets during recessionary periods.

In the post–World War II period there has been a trend for increased government deficits. Although the government surplus or deficit has exhibited a cyclical behavior in counterphase with the economic cycle, the underlying trend has been one of growing deficits and growing demands for funds from the capital markets. For many analysts, this has meant a growing tendency for higher interest rates. These analysts argue that, with a given pool of funds available in the financial markets, and government financing not being interest-sensitive, the larger share of market funds taken by government can mean only higher interest rates. At higher interest rates, it is economic to finance a smaller proportion of private investment. This is the so-called "crowding-out argument" against large government deficits—government crowds out the private sector. However, we must note that for this argument to be completely true, savings in the form of financial assets must not increase in response to the higher interest rates, assumed to be triggered by the larger government deficits.

Interest Rate Determination and Policy. The picture that emerges from this description of the financial behavior of the various sectors is one where, although interest rates are important, other considerations also play an important role.

The supply of funds in the market depends first on the total volume of savings, and then on how much of these savings take the form of investments in financial assets. This decision is considered to be sensitive to interest rate levels because of the effect of mortgage rates on investments in real assets. However, the disposition of funds among different types of financial assets is less influenced by changes in interest rates. The portion of savings allocated to insurance companies and pension funds is based on long-term considerations and institutional factors such as current taxation. In addition, households do have a definite preference for short-term investments and for the liquidity offered by fixed-rate deposits.

The pattern of savings at a given point in time determines the financial institutions that will be the recipients of these funds and, therefore, the users of funds that are likely to be favored, other things constant. For example, a larger amount of funds invested in pension funds is likely to imply a larger amount of funds available to the corporate bond market. A larger amount of funds deposited with savings and loan associations implies a larger amount of funds available to the mortgage market.

On the demand side for funds, the government is seen as being insensitive to the cost of funds. The business sector is seen as sensitive, but taking into account many other considerations.

At any point in time, one could estimate the amount of funds that the household sector would provide and the institutions that would receive these funds. Coupling this information about supply of funds in the capital market (segregated by the type of instrument in which each institution specializes) with the demand for funds one anticipates from the government sector and the business sector one can estimate the interest rate at which the amount of funds supplied in the market will equal the amount demanded. A very large inequality between the amount of funds expected to be supplied at current interest rates and demanded would produce a large change in interest rates. This adjustment in interest rates, in turn, would modify the amounts of funds supplied and demanded; however, this response would be subject to the restrictions which bind each sector.

If we take the demand and supply of funds in the financial markets as given, then the impact of monetary policy on interest rates is predictable. An increase in the growth rate of money supply will increase the supply of funds and tend to decrease interest rates; a decrease in the growth of money supply will decrease the amount of funds available in the market and tend to increase interest rates. In order for these conclusions to be valid, it is important that the initial assumptions hold—that is, that the private supply and demand of funds in the market remain constant. To the extent that changes in money supply affect expectations about future inflation, this assumption cannot be maintained. If an increase in the growth of the money supply increases the rate of inflation expected in the future, then a smaller amount of funds will be supplied by investors at that rate and, as a result, interest rates will increase instead of decreasing. But, until such a change in expectations takes place, the increase in money supply may succeed in lowering the level of interest rates. On the other hand, if a decrease in the growth of money supply fails to convince investors that the inflation rate will decrease (because other factors seem to indicate otherwise), this monetary policy will not succeed in decreasing interest rates. In this approach to the determination of interest rates, it will be necessary to specify not only the given monetary policy—expansion or contraction of money supply—but also the impact of this policy on investors' expectations about the inflation rate in the future. It is the net of both forces that determines the impact of monetary policy on interest rates.

Exchange Rates and International Flow of Funds

The flow of funds in the exchange markets occurs as the result of purchases of goods, services, and financial assets in a country different from where the good, service, or financial asset was produced. As we discussed earlier, because each country has a different national currency, these international transactions eventually produce an exchange transaction and affect exchange rates. (These exchange transactions also affect the flow of funds within each domestic market and their respective interest rates. In the preceding discussion of interest rate determination, these foreign transactions were included within each of the domestic sectors discussed there.)

The supply and demand of funds in the exchange markets can be explained in terms of types of transaction in the balance of payments. The two major groups of transactions are those included in the current account and in the capital account of the balance of payments.

The Current Account. This account includes trade in goods and services and international gifts or unilateral transfers.

To explain the long-term behavior of the trade accounts, economists analyze relative labor productivity, the availability of different factors of production, and the state of technology in each country. A country that is relatively well endowed to produce a given product will tend to be a net exporter of that product. However, over the short term, cyclical fluctuations in relative prices of traded goods and relative national incomes of the trading partners are the more immediate determinants of international trade.

Given the cost structure for domestic production of a given good, world prices will determine whether the country can produce the good profitably and export it or whether the country would be wiser to import the good from a country with a lower cost structure. The responsiveness of quantity produced to changes in prices is called *supply price elasticity*. The price elasticity of supply is limited by available capacity in the short term. If capacity is being used fully, the country would not be able to increase the volume of its exports in response to price increases. If the price increase is perceived as permanent, more productive capacity will eventually be brought on line, but this takes time. Over the short term, the price elasticity of supply tends to be low.

The impact of prices on demand depends on the nature of the goods involved. By and large, when prices go down, the quantity demanded tends to increase. However, some commodities are indispensable and the quantity demanded of them is relatively independent of the prevalent price. In other cases, a decline in price produces a large response in the quantity demanded, which may be proportionally more or less than the decrease in price. The difference in responsiveness of quantity purchased to changes in the price is called *demand price elasticity*.[5]

The impact of national income on trade derives from the impact of income on national consumption and investment. When national income goes up, both consumption and investment increase, with some consumption and investment channeled to foreign markets via imports.

Other things constant, when the trade partners of a country are in an expansionary phase of their business cycle, while the given country is experiencing a slowdown in its economy, the country's balance of trade is likely to improve. Its exports will increase in response to the higher demand from abroad and its imports will decrease as national income declines. The magnitude of the response of the trade accounts to change in income levels can be measured in terms of *income elasticity*.[6]

Prices and incomes often change simultaneously. Econometric models in which trade flows are explained in terms of several variables try to capture this reality. Unfortunately, the parameters estimated by these models, although good in explaining historical data, are limited in their forecasting capabilities. The parameters appear to change through time.

Exhibit 6.1 summarizes the types of income and price elasticities

---

[5]More specifically, import price elasticity is measured by the percentage change in imports associated with a given percentage change in prices:

$$\eta_p = \frac{\Delta Q}{Q} \div \frac{\Delta P}{P} = \frac{\Delta Q}{\Delta P} \times \frac{P}{Q}$$

where η_p = Price elasticity $\eta_p < 1$: Inelastic demand

            Q = Quantity $\eta_p = 1$: Unitary elasticity of demand

            P = Price $\eta_p > 1$: Elastic demand

The levels of P and Q (in contrast to changes) are usually measured at the midpoint between the initial and the final levels.

[6]More specifically, income elasticity is measured by the percentage change in imports associated with a given percentage change in national income. This is equivalent to the ratio of the marginal propensity to import to the average propensity:

$$\eta_Y = \frac{\Delta M}{M} \div \frac{\Delta Y}{Y} = \frac{\Delta M}{\Delta Y} \times \frac{Y}{M} = \frac{\Delta M}{\Delta Y} \div \frac{M}{Y} = \frac{\text{MPM}}{\text{APM}}$$

where η_Y = Income elasticity

           Y = National income

         M = Imports

     MPM = Marginal propensity to import

     APM = Average propensity to import

The levels of Y and M (in contrast to their changes) are usually measured at the midpoint between the initial and the final levels.

EXHIBIT 6.1   Characteristic Demand Elasticities of Major Types of Goods

	DEMAND ELASTICITY	
	Price	Income
Food	Low	Low
Industrial supplies (raw materials)	Low	High
Manufactured goods		
Highly specialized	Low	High
Not specialized	High	High

that tend to characterize the demand for three major groups of traded goods: food, industrial supplies, and manufactured goods. At one end, the demand for food can be considered to have both low price and low income elasticities. The demand for industrial supplies appears to be better explained as highly dependent on income changes. The demand for manufactured goods is usually considered to be both price and income elastic. It is here where conflicting results between the analysis of changes in prices and changes in income can easily occur. An increase in domestic prices tends to decrease export demand; however, if a foreign country is expanding at a high rate, this will tend to reverse this effect. The actual result will depend on the relative strength of these two opposing forces. Manufactured goods are also more highly differentiated than commodities. Copper of certain quality has an identifiable world price, but a piece of machinery is not so easily identified and priced.

Relative prices and incomes affect the trade in services as well as the trade in real goods. This is particularly the case for travel and transportation expenditures. The flows of funds associated with interest and dividends payments are determined, of course, by investments made in the past. Large investments in foreign assets should produce relatively high investment income in the future. Finally, countries with a sophisticated financial center are net earners of fee income, while the other countries show a net payment in this category.

The other transactions included in the current account are called unilateral transfers. These are gifts given by individuals and governments to foreigners. Countries that are net importers of people (such as the United States) have a net payment in this account. Countries that are net exporters of people (Spain, for example) are net receivers of this type of funds. Finally, government gifts or grants are a function of the foreign policy of each country.

The Capital Account.   International capital flows are traditionally divided between long-term and short-term flows, depending on whether the original maturity is more or less than 1 year. In addition, there are the flows associated with the change in official exchange reserves, which are discussed in the following section.

The first classification in long-term capital flows is between government and private flows. Government long-term flows do not include the change in short-term loans among governments (to be discussed in the next section). The motivation behind long-term government loans is similar to that behind government grants. Some of these loans are for development projects, others are associated with defense, and others simply reflect government foreign policy. All of these loans carry interest, but not all have a fixed repayment schedule.

Private long-term investments are classified into two groups, depending on whether management of operations is involved. For practical purposes, managerial involvement is considered to exist whenever the investment accounts for more than 10% of the ownership of the entity. In this case, the capital flow is called *direct investment*. With less than 10% of the ownership, the capital flow is classified as a *portfolio investment*.

The general motivation for international investment is a higher anticipated rate of return in the foreign country than in the home country. A mature country tends to increase its investment abroad as its own stock of capital grows and its rate of return falls relative to other countries. In the case of direct investment, factors such as availability of cheaper labor or raw material, or economies of scale affect the measurement of this relative return. Also, since the return on foreign securities has to be measured in terms of local currency, the exchange risk of the currencies involved plays an important role. Foreign stocks and bonds are usually exposed to exchange risk. A devaluation in the foreign currency relative to the local currency will reduce return to the investor. In cases of devaluation-prone currencies, the nominal yield on the investment has to be high enough to compensate for the potential devaluation.

Among short-term capital flows, we can see that most trade transactions are associated with a short-term capital movement. An exporter who sells merchandise may get paid immediately, in which case demand deposits owned by the country increase. If the sale is invoiced and paid for in local currency, the acquisition of the deposit represents a reduction in liabilities to foreigners. If the payment takes place in a foreign currency, the exporter has acquired a financial claim on foreigners. When credit is extended to the importer either directly by the exporter or through a local commercial bank, the country of the exporter increases its financial claims on foreigners, regardless of the currency in which the sale is denominated.

In the same manner, when merchandise is imported, a capital transaction also takes place. The importing country may either pay with foreign financial assets that it has accumulated earlier or it may receive credit from the exporter. Either a decrease in claims on foreigners or an increase in liabilities to foreigners will take place to finance the imports.

As we previously discussed in detail, capital flows initially associated with trade financing inevitably affect financial markets. Eventually, a financial investor will have to make a decision whether to hold a financial instrument (often denominated in a foreign currency). The decision will depend on the return expected from this investment.

The return on a financial investment in a foreign country depends on the interest rate received and on the intervening fluctuation in the exchange rate. Thus, we can think of short-term international capital flows in search of profit as responding to each of the following:

1. Higher interest rates (assuming exchange rates will remain constant or not change enough to compensate for the interest rate differential)
2. Expectation of appreciation in a given currency (assuming the cost of receiving a lower interest rate in that currency will be more than compensated by the subsequent appreciation)

These explanations of international capital flows are in sharp contrast to those given by the expectation theory presented earlier. Here it is possible for interest rate differentials to persist and to induce capital flows without the exchange rate fluctuating in response. In this situation it is possible for a central bank to manipulate interest rates in order to affect international capital flows and the exchange rates. Under the expectation theory, an interest rate differential represented the market's forecast for future exchange fluctuations and attempts by the central bank to alter interest rates in order to influence international capital flows would be of little use.

Short-term capital movements are the hardest to measure. Particularly in periods of heavy foreign exchange speculation, many of these flows end up in the all-encompassing category "errors and omissions" or "statistical discrepancy." In the sections on the balance of payments discussed earlier, the analysis was simplified since the nature of the flow was properly identified. For example, once the level of exports was identified, it was explained in terms of several economic variables. In the case of short-term capital movements, however, the analysis is more difficult. The nature of the capital flow must be derived from the attending circumstances. That is, capital flows in response to trade and capital flows initiated by other considerations are not properly segregated. The problem is not a trivial one since the impact on the future of the country's balance of payments and on its foreign exchange rate is completely dependent on the nature of the short-term capital flow.

Exchange Rate Determination and Policy. Having analyzed the economic forces behind the fluctuations in the major accounts in the balance of payments, we now consider the problem of assessing the impact of actual and expected developments in these accounts on the exchange rate. One approach is to determine the balance in the balance of payments. A surplus would indicate pressures for the upvaluation of that currency, while a deficit would indicate pressures for the devaluation of that currency.

The double-entry system of accounting used in the preparation of the balance of payments implies that, by definition, *debits equal credits*. In this sense, the balance of payments always balances. It is only when we segregate a group of accounts and take their balance that we can talk about "a balance" in the balance of payments. A reading of the pressures on the exchange rate of a currency can be obtained by separating the accounts in the balance of payments of the currency's home country into two groups: (1) those whose changes are induced by economic relationships external to the balance of payments (for example, relative domestic prices and incomes); and (2) those that change mainly as a result of changes in the first group of accounts. The surplus or deficit balance in the first group can be considered a measure of the pressures on the exchange rate of that currency.

In the economic literature, the first group of accounts, which is affected by the economic relationships regardless of other items in the balance of payments, is called *autonomous*. The second group of accounts, which changes only in order to finance other items in the balance of payments, is called *compensating* or *accommodating*. Economists often refer to an imaginary line that separates the two groups of accounts. The accounts "above the line" comprise the autonomous accounts, whose balance determines whether the balance of payments is in surplus or deficit. The accounts "below the line" present the accounts that show how the balance of payments surplus or deficit was financed.

Examples of *autonomous* receipts are all normal commercial exports, gifts, and capital movements that take place because of private enterprise's search for higher profitability. Examples of *accommodating* receipts are the sale of gold or foreign exchange by the central bank in order to finance imports into the country at the current exchange rate or a loan to the government by an international agency for the explicit purpose of bridging the gap between international payments and receipts of the country.

In a fixed-rate system the historical balance of payments can give a direct indication of the pressures that are mounting on the exchange rate while governments attempt to maintain the current rate. This reading can be particularly clear in the case of countries in which the private sector is not allowed to hold assets denominated in foreign currency and where foreigners are not interested in investing in the financial assets issued by that country. Under these conditions, we can say that the overall balance in the balance of payments represents a rather accurate measure of the autonomous transactions of that country and the pressures on the currency's exchange rate. In such cases, a surplus in the autonomous account is accompanied by an increase in foreign reserves or a decrease in official liabilities in the compensating accounts. This puts an upward pressure on the external value of the home currency. A deficit in the autonomous accounts is associated with a decrease in foreign reserves or an increase in liabilities to foreigners. This tends to put a downward pressure on the external value of the home currency. A country cannot endure continuous deficits in its balance of payments without eventually having to devalue its currency. The balance of payments figures we have examined report the amount of flows on a historical basis, after the fact. On this basis one can say that all capital flows reported for private parties reflect autonomous transactions. In the absence of controls from the government, the purchases and sales of securities reported in the balance of payments indicate responses to interest rate differentials and anticipations about the exchange markets. In this sense, only the capital flows reported for official authorities can be treated as financing transactions—they filled the gap left by private transactors operating in response to market forces.

Thus, if we want to think of autonomous transactions as a barometer of the pressures in the exchange market, we must look into the future and ask the following two additional questions:

1. How much of future imbalances in the goods and services market will the financial markets want to finance at current interest and exchange rates?
2. How much of the outstanding financial assets will financial markets want to continue holding?

The answers to these questions will provide an estimate of the gap between supply and demand for the various currencies which official agencies will be called to fill if the current rates are to be maintained. If the answers indicate that no disequilibrium in the exchange markets will occur or that official agencies can be expected to fill the gap left by financial markets, then rates will remain constant. Otherwise, rates will have to change or controls will have to be imposed. To the extent that official agencies are called upon to fill this gap, an assessment must be made of how long these authorities will want, or will be able, to continue in that role. Their ability to continue holding the current rate will depend heavily on the amount of reserves accumulated and in the potential borrowing they can make from private sources, as well as from international institutions, such as the IMF (see Exhibit 6.2). Even when this ability exists, the final decision also de-

EXHIBIT 6.2 Permanent Financial Facilities of the International Monetary Fund and Their Conditionality[a]

Type of Facility and Condition for Its Use	Percent of Quota Available	Cumulative Percent of Quota Available
Gold Tranche	25	25
Balance of payments need is sufficient.		
First Credit Tranche	25	50
Requires a program representing reasonable efforts to overcome balance of payments difficulties; performance criteria and installments are not used.		
Higher Credit Tranches	75	125
Requires a program giving substantial justification of the member's efforts to overcome balance of payments difficulties; resources are normally provided in the form of stand-by arrangements which include performance criteria and drawings in installments.		
Extended Facility	140[c]	190[b]
Requires a medium-term program for up to 3 years to overcome structural balance of payments maladjustments; detailed statement of policies and measures for first and subsequent 12-month periods; resources are provided in the form of extended arrangements which include performance criteria and drawings in installments.		
Compensatory Financing Facility	100	290
Available when temporary export shortfall exists for reasons beyond the member's control; member cooperates with the Fund in an effort to find appropriate solutions for any balance of payments difficulties.		
Buffer Stock Financing Facility	50	315
Available when an international buffer stock accepted as suitable by the Fund exists; the member is expected to cooperate with the Fund as in the case of compensatory financing.		
Enlarged Access Policy		
Provides supplementary financing in conjunction with the use of the Fund's ordinary reserves to members facing serious payments imbalances which are large in relation to their quotas.		

[a]Members are not expected, and may not qualify, to use all the available facilities at the same time. In addition, use of the maximum available resources under a particular facility—namely, tranche policies—is usually made in a period of years, not in 1 year.

[b]The combined use of the extended facility and the regular credit tranches may not be above 165% of quota. Adding the use of the gold tranche raises the maximum to 190% of quota.

[c]Normally, not more than 50% of quota in any 12-month period.

SOURCE: *IMF Survey, Supplement on the Fund,* July 5, 1982, p. 198.

pends on the willingness of the government to accept the political consequences of a currency devaluation or upvaluation.

In an open exchange market, despite the government exchange reserves and willingness to defend an exchange rate, private capital flows may deplete exchange reserves and force a devaluation. In a system of freely floating exchange rates, government intervention in the exchange markets would be kept to a minimum and exchange rates would be determined by the free interaction of the various international operations.

SUMMARY

This chapter has presented material dealing with the general equilibrium theories of exchange rate and interest rate determination as well as partial equilibrium analyses of short-run determinants of exchange rates and interest rates. *Purchasing power parity* relates to the law of one price and implies that the same market basket of goods purchased with different currencies should cost the same regardless of the currency. That is, the exchange rate between two currencies should ensure that the bundle of commodities purchased in either currency should cost the same. Goods arbitrage and a floating exchange rate system should support this purchasing power parity outcome in terms of predicted levels of the exchange rates. *Absolute purchasing power parity* relates to actual price levels. When one acknowledges various non-traded goods and other impediments to arbitrage, then one may suggest that absolute purchasing power parity will not hold in the world, but that changes in price levels in different countries will result in proportionate changes in the exchange rates from the initial conditions; this is the theory of *relative purchasing power parity*. Many factors can prevent the occurrence of relative purchasing power parity, but adherents argue that these factors disturb the results only in the short run; they believe some form of purchasing power parity must exist in the long run.

Interest rate parity suggests that the real interest rate is constant across currencies (that is, money has a common cost regardless of its denomination) and that nominal interest rates reflect inflationary expectations. Hence, different nominal interests rates for the same period and riskiness but in different currencies reflect different anticipated inflation in the two economies. However, the forward rate premiums or discounts for the currencies should also reflect these nominal interest rate differentials and inflationary expectations, in part because of the action of arbitrageurs. Associated with the theories of interest rate parity and purchasing power parity in most general equilibrium views of the world is the notion of the forward rate as an unbiased predictor of the future spot rate. These ideas are summarized algebraically in the appendix to this chapter.

According to the partial equilibrium explanations of exchange rates, the domestic flow of funds accounts and the balance of payments levels and changes largely determine exchange rates. The three major components within the domestic economy are the household sector, the business sector, and the government sector. The various financial institutions and financial markets facilitate the movement of funds within and among sectors. Various subcomponents of these sectors are

more or less sensitive to the level of interest rates, and the central bank
and national government can influence the level of rates through monetary and fiscal policy.

Within the balance of payments, the operation of various factors
also affects the exchange rate in the short run and the long run. Within
the *current account*, for *trade*, comparative advantage is the principal
factor affecting the *long-term* export/import balance. Whether the advantage comes from comparative labor ratios, capital resources, labor
skills as embedded capital, or some other factor is indeterminant. The
United States seems to export labor-intensive goods, in spite of relatively high costs per hour of labor. Technological gaps and managerial
gaps also have been offered as major explanatory factors for the long-
term trade balance. In the *short term*, changes in relative prices can
explain some variability in the trade balance. Relative prices are, in
turn, a function of wage rates, productivity, and other costs in a fixed
exchange rate world, and they are often measured in a unit cost of production statistic. The price elasticity of supply and demand of each
country's imports and exports is important in predicting the ultimate
effect of a rise in prices vis-à-vis trading partners for a specific nation.
There are different sensitivities in the markets for various goods, and
the final trade balance depends on how the elasticities and the volume
of each good involved net against each other for the partners. Relative
national incomes and different positions in the business cycle also affect the trade balances between nations.

In the *capital accounts*, for *long-term capital account*, we have
direct investment which is determined by long-term considerations
about where the investors want to have marketing and production facilities. In the other long-term capital account, *portfolio investment*,
the major factors are the relative performance of the various stock markets and relative long-term interest rates, and expected exchange rate
developments. Taxation in general and withholding in particular play
a part, for many investors in other lands prefer to have no withholding
applied to their earnings.

The most volatile accounts in recent years have been the *short-
term capital accounts*. These are also the ones subject to most debate
over whether they are autonomous or accommodating. As exports increase, the short-term capital account rises with accounts receivable increases, an accommodation. There are often speculative flows of a massive nature, as the pattern of the U.S. balance of payments during crises
in the exchange markets has shown. These flows can be stabilizing or
not, depending on whether they accentuate a stampede against a currency or dampen it; most of the managed floating in recent years has
sought to ameliorate the effects of these large speculative flows. Fi-

nally, although these comments imply that short-term flows are sometimes accommodating (trade) or autonomous (speculative), they may be autonomous yet derived from a simple desire for access to the U.S. short-term capital markets. Relative interest rates, liquidity, security, and the like may induce foreigners to use the U.S. capital markets for short-term funds. Yet, for balance of payments data collection purposes, we cannot separate funds stimulated by these different motivations.

Using historical data from the balance of payments, students of partial equilibrium analysis will ask about trends regarding imbalances in the various goods and services accounts and maintenance of existing holdings of financial assets given the current exchange and interest rates. To the extent that there is a disequilibrium situation perceived, then the question is one of forecasting the actions of the official agencies and of the participants, together with a forecast of the effectiveness of such activities in moving interest and exchange rates.

APPENDIX

EXCHANGE MARKET AND MONEY MARKET EQUILIBRIUM*

For readers who prefer a mathematical approach, in this appendix we place the concepts of interest rate parity and purchasing power parity in algebraic form, in the context of an exporter's covering decision.

For discussion, we will assume that a U.S. exporter will receive pounds in amount £A at time t†. For simplicity, it may be useful to assume that t equals 1 year. All interest rates are also for the period t. The problem for the exporter is how to make a decision among alternatives I (no covering), II (covering in the forward market), and III (covering in the money market).

---

*Our thanks to Professor Edward M. Graham for comments and suggestions on this appendix. A similar analysis is presented in Ian H. Giddy, "An Integrated Theory of Exchange Rate Equilibrium," *Journal of Financial and Quantitative Analysis*, Dec. 1976, pp. 883–892.

†The problem of financing foreign trade is discussed in detail in Chapter 8. For this appendix, it suffices to assume the existence of a receivable denominated in foreign currency.

DEFINITIONS

r_0 = Spot \$/£ exchange rate *now*

f_0 = Forward \$/£ exchange rate *now*

d = Discount of £ against \$; if positive, the £ is at a premium against the \$

$\tilde{r}_t$ = Spot \$/£ exchange rate at time t, where $\sim$ denotes a random variable which is unknown now

$\tilde{e}$ = Depreciation of £ against the \$ from now to time t

$f_0 = r_0(1 + d)$

$\tilde{r}_t = r_0(1 + \tilde{e})$

i_{US} = U.S. interest rate for time t maturity

i_{UK} = U.K. interest rate for time t maturity

Alternative I: Do Not Cover

At time t the firm receives £A and converts this amount to dollars:

$$\$ \text{ Proceeds}_t = \tilde{r}_t A = r_0(1 + \tilde{e})A \tag{1}$$

Since $\tilde{r}_t$ is uncertain, the exporter will examine the costs of covering.

Alternative II: Cover in the Forward Market

The exporter will sell sterling for dollars in the amount of £A in the forward market. At maturity, the amount received after delivering £A to purchase the dollars at the agreed upon rate will be:

$$\$ \text{ Proceeds}_t = f_0 A = r_0(1 + d)A \tag{2}$$

Since f_0 is known, there is no uncertainty.

The cost of II versus I is the difference:

$$\begin{aligned}
\$ \text{ Cost}_{I-II} &= (\tilde{r}_t A - f_0 A) \\
&= r_0 A[(1 + \tilde{e}) - (1 + d)] \quad \text{from (1) and (2)} \\
&= r_0 A(\tilde{e} - d) \tag{3}
\end{aligned}$$

Alternative III: Cover in the Money Market

The exporter will borrow sterling in the amount of $£A/(1 + i_{UK})$. At this interest rate, upon maturity the exporter will owe the bank $£A$, the amount to be received from the customer at time t. The amount borrowed now will be converted to dollars at r_0 and invested in a U.S. bank at i_{US}. Therefore,

$$\$ \text{ Proceeds}_t = r_0 \left(\frac{A}{1 + i_{UK}} \right) (1 + i_{US}) \qquad (4)$$

Since r_0 and both interest rates are known, there is no uncertainty. The cost of III versus I is the difference:

$$\$ \text{ Cost}_{I-III} = \left[\tilde{r}_t A - r_0 \left(\frac{A}{1 + i_{UK}} \right) (1 + i_{US}) \right] \qquad \text{from (1) and (4)}$$

$$= r_0 (1 + \tilde{e}) A - r_0 \left(\frac{A}{1 + i_{UK}} \right) (1 + i_{US}) \qquad \text{from (1)}$$

$$= r_0 A \left[1 + \tilde{e} - \frac{1 + i_{US}}{1 + i_{UK}} \right] \qquad (5)$$

Interest Rate Parity

If the money market and forward market are in equilibrium, then the cost of covering under II and III should be equal. Therefore,

$$r_0 A (\tilde{e} - d) = r_0 A \left[1 + \tilde{e} - \frac{1 + i_{US}}{1 + i_{UK}} \right] \qquad \text{from (3) and (5)}$$

Simplifying, we get:

$$d = \frac{1 + i_{US}}{1 + i_{UK}} - 1$$

$$= \frac{i_{US} - i_{UK}}{1 + i_{UK}} \qquad (6)$$

Notice in (6) that the discount on sterling under interest rate parity is equal to the differences in the U.S./U.K. interest rate discounted to time 0 at the U.K. interest rate. If interest rates are relatively low, interest rate differentials in the numerator are a good approximation of this fraction as the denominator approaches 1.

Purchasing Power Parity (PPP)

Using $\sim$ for unknown values and Δ for change, we may compute anticipated price levels and the changes in price levels in the U.S. and the U.K. as:

$$\widetilde{\Delta P}_{UK} = \frac{\widetilde{P}_{UK_t} - P_{UK_0}}{P_{UK_0}}$$

$$\widetilde{\Delta P}_{US} = \frac{\widetilde{P}_{US_t} - P_{US_0}}{P_{US_0}}$$

and PPP suggests that

$$\tilde{e} = \frac{1 + \widetilde{\Delta P}_{US}}{1 + \widetilde{\Delta P}_{UK}} - 1$$

$$= \frac{\widetilde{\Delta P}_{US} - \widetilde{\Delta P}_{UK}}{1 + \widetilde{\Delta P}_{UK}} \qquad (7)$$

Inflation is the value (price $\times$ quantity) weighted index of goods and services costs between two periods of time. If the weighted general inflation index coincides with the weighted index of internationally traded goods and services, commodity arbitrage will produce this result. Otherwise, according to PPP theory, the general change in value of money produced by inflation and the resulting monetary adjustments are expected to bring about this result.

Fisher Effect

If the Fisher effect holds, then a nominal country interest rate consists of a real rate and an expected country inflation rate. Interest rates in various countries reflect differential inflation rates.

$$i_{US} = \text{Real rate} + \widetilde{\Delta P}_{US}$$

$$i_{UK} = \text{Real rate} + \widetilde{\Delta P}_{UK}$$

Then, a measure of differential anticipated inflation between two countries may be expressed as:

$$\frac{i_{US} - i_{UK}}{1 + i_{UK}} = \frac{(\text{Real rate} + \widetilde{\Delta P}_{US}) - (\text{Real rate} + \widetilde{\Delta P}_{UK})}{(1 + \text{Real rate} + \widetilde{\Delta P}_{UK})}$$

Simplifying and noting that the real rate is relatively small in the denominator (≈ 0.03), we get:

$$\frac{i_{US} - i_{UK}}{1 + i_{UK}} = \frac{\widetilde{\Delta P}_{US} - \widetilde{\Delta P}_{UK}}{1 + \text{Real rate} + \widetilde{\Delta P}_{UK}} \approx \frac{\widetilde{\Delta P}_{US} - \widetilde{\Delta P}_{UK}}{1 + \widetilde{\Delta P}_{UK}} \tag{8}$$

SUMMARY

Therefore, if interest rate parity, the Fisher effect, and purchasing power parity hold as formulated here, then,

$$\tilde{e} = \frac{i_{US} - i_{UK}}{1 + i_{UK}} \qquad \text{from (7) and (8)} \tag{9}$$

and

$$\tilde{e} = d \qquad \text{from (6) and (9)}$$

So, the expected change in the spot rate of the sterling against the dollar equals the discount in the forward market; thus, the forward rate is an unbiased predictor of the future spot rate.

BIBLIOGRAPHY

Agmon, Tamir, "Inflation and Foreign Exchange Rates under Production and Monetary Uncertainty," *Journal of Financial and Quantitative Analysis*, Nov. 1980, pp. 969–71.

Baldwin, Robert E., "Determinants of Trade and Foreign Investment: Further Evidence," *Review of Economics and Statistics*, Fall 1979, pp. 40–48.

Batra, Raveendra N., and Rama Ramachandran, "Multinational Firms and the Theory of International Trade and Investment," *American Economic Review*, June 1980, pp. 278–90.

Bowers, David A., "A Warning Note on Empirical Research Using Foreign Exchange Rates," *Journal of Financial and Quantitative Analysis*, June 1977, pp. 315–19.

Burt, John, Fred R. Kaen, and Geoffrey G. Booth, "Foreign Exchange Market Efficiency under Flexible Exchange Rates," *Journal of Finance*, Sept. 1977, pp. 1325–30.

Burt, John, Fred R. Kaen, and Geoffrey G. Booth, "Foreign Exchange Market Efficiency under Flexible Exchange Rates: Reply," *Journal of Finance*, June 1979, pp. 791–93.

Calderon-Rossell, Jorge R., and Moshe Ben-Horim, "The Behavior of Foreign Exchange Rates," *Journal of International Business Studies,* Fall 1982, pp. 99–111.

Callier, Philippe, "One-Way Arbitrage, Foreign Exchange, and Securities Markets: A Note," *Journal of Finance,* Dec. 1981, pp. 1177–86.

Caves, Douglas W., and Edgar L. Feige, "Efficient Foreign Exchange Markets and the Monetary Approach to Exchange Rate Determination," *American Economic Review,* Mar. 1980, pp. 120–34.

"The Common Scandal of the Uncommon Market," *Economist,* Sept. 19, 1981, pp. 56–60.

Cornell, Bradford, "Spot Rates, Forward Rates, and Exchange Market Efficiency," *Journal of Financial Economics,* Aug. 1977, pp. 55–66.

Cornell, Bradford, and Marc R. Reinganum, "Forward and Futures Prices: Evidence from the Foreign Exchange Markets," *Journal of Finance,* Dec. 1981, pp. 1035–45.

Craig, Gary A., "A Monetary Approach to the Balance of Trade," *American Economic Review,* June 1981, pp. 460–66.

Cumby, Robert E., and Maurice Obstfeld, "A Note on Exchange Rate Expectations and Nominal Interest Differentials: A Test of the Fisher Hypothesis," *Journal of Finance,* June 1981, pp. 697–703.

Deardorff, Alan V., "The General Validity of the Heckscher-Ohlin Theorem," *American Economic Review,* Sept. 1982, pp. 683–94.

Dornbusch, Rudiger, and Jacob A. Frenkel, eds., *International Economic Policy.* Baltimore: The Johns Hopkins University Press, 1979.

Frenkel, Jacob A., "Efficiency and Volatility of Exchange Rates and Prices in the 1970s," *Columbia Journal of World Business,* Winter 1979, pp. 15–27.

Frenkel, Jacob A., and Harry G. Johnson, eds., *The Monetary Approach to the Balance of Payments.* Toronto: University of Toronto Press, 1976.

———— , "Transaction Costs and Interest Arbitrage: Tranquil versus Turbulent Periods," *Journal of Political Economy,* December 1977, pp. 1209–26.

Frenkel, Jacob A., and Richard M. Levich, "Covered-Interest Arbitrage and Unexploited Profits? Reply," *Journal of Political Economy,* Apr. 1979, pp. 418–22.

Frenkel, Jacob A., and Michael L. Mussa, "The Efficiency of Foreign Exchange Markets and Measures of Turbulence," *American Economic Review,* May 1980, pp. 374–81.

Frenkel, Jacob A., and Carlos A. Rodriguez, "Exchange Rate Dynamics and the Overshooting Hypothesis," *International Monetary Fund Staff Papers,* Mar. 1982, pp. 1–30.

Geweke, J., and E. Feige, "Some Joint Tests of the Efficiency of Markets for Forward Foreign Exchange," *Review of Economics and Statistics,* Oct. 1979, pp. 334–41.

Giddy, Ian H., "An Integrated Theory of Exchange Rate Equilibrium," *Journal of Financial and Quantitative Analysis,* Dec. 1976, pp. 883–92.

Grubel, Herbert G., *International Economics,* rev. ed. Homewood, Illinois: R. D. Irwin and Sons, 1981.

Hansen, Lars P., and Robert J. Hodrick, "Forward Exchange Rates as Optimal

Predictors of Future Spot Rates: An Econometric Analysis," *Journal of Political Economy*, Oct. 1980, pp. 829–53.

Holthausen, D., "Hedging and the Competitive Firm under Price Uncertainty," *American Economic Review*, Dec. 1979, pp. 989–95.

Huang, Roger D., "The Monetary Approach to Exchange Rates in an Efficient Foreign Exchange Market: Tests Based on Volatility," *Journal of Finance*, Mar. 1981, pp. 31–41.

Ibbotson, Roger G., and Aruna S. Ramamurti, "Analysis of International Bond Returns," working paper, Center for Research in Security Prices, University of Chicago, 1981.

Jacobs, Rodney L., "The Effect of Errors in Variables on Tests for a Risk Premium in Forward Exchange Rates," *Journal of Finance*, June 1982, pp. 667–77.

Kohlhagen, Steven W., "The Identification of Destabilizing Foreign Exchange Speculation," *Journal of International Economics*, Sept. 1979, pp. 321–40.

———, "Testing for the Role of Speculation in the Forward Exchange Market: Some Problems if There Are Fisherian Expectations," *Review of Economics and Statistics*, Nov. 1979, pp. 608–10.

Kreicher, Lawrence L., "An International Evaluation of the Fisher Hypothesis Using Rational Expectations," *Southern Economic Journal*, July 1981, pp. 58–67.

Krugman, Paul R., "Purchasing Power Parity and Exchange Rates," *Journal of International Economics*, Aug. 1978, pp. 397–407.

Laulan, Yves, *General Theory of Employment, Interest, and Cheating*. New York: Richardson and Snyder, 1982.

Levi, Maurice D., "Underutilization of Forward Markets or Rational Behavior?" *Journal of Finance*, Sept. 1979, pp. 1013–17.

Levi, Maurice D., and John H. Makin, "Anticipated Inflation and Interest Rates: Further Interpretation of Findings on the Fisher Equation," *American Economic Review*, Dec. 1978, pp. 801–11.

———, "Fisher, Phillips, Friedman, and the Measured Impact of Inflation on Interest," *Journal of Finance*, Mar. 1979, pp. 35–52.

Levich, Richard M., "Are Forward Exchange Rates Unbiased Predictors of Future Spot Rates?" *Columbia Journal of World Business*, Winter 1979, pp. 49–61.

Logue, Dennis E., and Richard James Sweeney, " 'White Noise' in Imperfect Markets: The Case of the Franc/Dollar Exchange Rate," *Journal of Finance*, June 1977, pp. 761–68.

Mansfield, Edwin, Anthony Romeo, and Samuel Wagner, "Foreign Trade and U.S. Research and Development," *Review of Economics and Statistics*, Feb. 1979, pp. 49–57.

Meese, Richard A., and Kenneth J. Singleton, "On Unit Roots and the Empirical Modeling of Exchange Rates," *Journal of Finance*, Sept. 1982, pp. 1029–35.

Miles, Marc A., "The Effects of Devaluation on the Trade Balance and the Balance of Payments: Some New Results," *Journal of Political Economy*, June 1979, pp. 600–20.

———— , "Foreign Exchange Market Efficiency under Flexible Exchange Rates: Comment," *Journal of Finance*, June 1979, pp. 787–89.

Otani, Ichiro, and Siddharth Tiwari, "Capital Controls and Interest Rate Parity: The Japanese Experience, 1978–81," *International Monetary Fund Staff Papers*, Dec. 1981, pp. 793–815.

Pagoulatos, Emilio, and Robert Sorenson, "Domestic Market Structure and International Trade: An Empirical Analysis," *Quarterly Review of Economics*, Sept. 1976, pp. 44–59.

Panton, Don B., and Maurice O. Jay, *Empirical Evidence on International Money Market Currency Futures*, pp. 59–68. Lawrence, Kansas: The University of Kansas Press, 1981.

Riehl, Heinz, and Rita Rodriguez, *Foreign Exchange and Money Markets*. New York: McGraw-Hill Book Company, 1983.

Rogalski, Richard J., and Joseph D. Vinso, "Price Level Variations as Predictors of Flexible Exchange Rates," *Journal of International Business Studies*, Spring/Summer 1977, pp. 71–81.

Salop, Joanne, and Erich Spitaller, "Why Does the Current Account Matter?" *International Monetary Fund Staff Papers*, Mar. 1980, pp. 101–34.

Schadler, Susan, "Sources of Exchange Rate Variability: Theory and Empirical Evidence," *International Monetary Fund Staff Papers*, July 1977, pp. 253–96.

Walter, Ingo, and Kaj Areskoug, *International Economics*, 3d ed. New York: John Wiley and Sons, Inc., 1981.

Westerfield, Janice Moulton, "An Examination of Foreign Exchange Risk under Fixed and Floating Regimes," *Journal of International Economics*, May 1977, pp. 181–200.

CHAPTER

7

International Cash
Management:
Foreign
Exchange
and Interest
Rate Risks

CASH MANAGEMENT INVOLVES finding temporary financing sources to meet business needs and investing funds that are not required by operations in the short term. In the multinational enterprise, both financing and investing of temporary funds involve a diversity of currencies. Thus, in addition to the traditional interest rate risk involved in cash management, we must also manage the associated exchange risk. In managing these risks, the financial officer may choose to cover all financial risks, bear all these risks, or take calculated risks. The selection of a risk policy will be heavily influenced by the manager's perceptions of how rates are determined in the financial markets.

In this chapter we will examine the risks of fluctuations in exchange rates and interest rates associated with cash management in a multicurrency setting. In this presentation we assume that a decision has already been reached as to the risk policy appropriate for the given situation. We will examine the assumptions that could have led the manager to choose this risk posture; however, the emphasis of the discussion will be on showing how to implement the given decision and how to assess its implications. The initial policy as to whether to cover financial risks in cash management should incorporate an analysis of the manager's probabilistic forecast of rates relative to the market's forecasts, as well as the manager's utility function for financial gains and losses. The details of these managerial assessments are outside the scope of this book.

THE NATURE OF INTERNATIONAL CASH MANAGEMENT

The raw materials of cash management are *cash flow* forecasts. Whenever operations generate a negative cash flow—a net *outflow*—a matching source of funds must be found; whenever operations generate a positive cash flow—a net *inflow*—a matching use of funds must be found. The financial manager in a multinational business can meet these cash needs through operations in the money market and through operations in the foreign exchange market. More specifically, the funds manager can make the following transactions in the money market:

1. Borrowings produce an inflow (+) when taken and an outflow (−) upon repayment.
2. Investments produce an outflow (−) when made and an inflow (+) when liquidated.

In the exchange market, the following transactions can be made:

1. Purchase of a currency produces an inflow (+) on delivery date.
2. Sale of a currency produces an outflow (−) on delivery date.

If the manager arranges for financial cash flows to match the flows generated by operations so that the maturity and currency of each cash inflow and outflow are matched one-to-one (for example, a planned outflow in sterling for a given date is matched with a planned inflow in the same currency for the same date), then the returns and costs from cash management can be computed with certainty in advance. In this case, all the relevant rates are locked in from the beginning and we have a so-called *square cash position*. This is the situation we had in the arbitrage transactions discussed in Chapter 5. These transactions did not involve any risk; they were based on square cash positions.

On the other hand, financial risks exist whenever expected net cash flows are allowed to stand without a matching financial cash flow. In such a case, the financial costs or returns from managing the cash needs of the business cannot be determined in advance with certainty. If we allow an expected conversion of one currency into another to stand without arranging for a conversion exchange rate in advance, then a depreciation of the inflow currency would decrease the proceeds in the other currency when the conversion need materializes later. Whenever costs or returns are vulnerable to changes in exchange rates, we say there is an *exchange position*. If we let an expected net outflow in a currency remain without scheduling a financing source, then an increase in interest rates would increase the cost of borrowing funds when the anticipated financing need appears, say, 1 month later. When the costs or returns are vulnerable to changes in interest rates, we say there is an *interest rate position*, and if the interest rate position involves two currencies simultaneously, there is a *swap position*.

Whether a financial manager wants to accept the cash positions generated by business operations (or even create the positions) depends on a decision process in which the manager's expectations about future rates are compared with the market's expectations. In general, the financial manager may follow one of three different strategies:

1. Lock in rates for the transactions needed to meet the business cash needs as soon as these needs are known.
2. Wait until the cash needs materialize and settle them at the rates prevailing then.
3. Alternate between the two previous approaches, depending on the manager's expectations relative to the market's.

In the first strategy the manager covers all financial risks, while in the second the business bears all of these risks. In the third strategy, calculated risks are taken depending on the circumstances.

If the manager believes that the relevant rates are determined by rational expectations in an efficient market, then the third strategy of taking calculated risks would be ruled out in most cases and the selection between the first two strategies would then depend largely on relative transaction costs at the time. On the other hand, if the manager has enough confidence in his or her ability to forecast rates relative to the market, cash management may take an additional dimension in which funds are positioned independently of business needs to profit from the anticipated changes in rates. In an environment where the manager presumes to have judgment superior to the market's, at least on occasion, the manager would act as follows:

1. Square cash positions whenever the manager's expectations (adjusted for risk) imply costs higher, or returns lower, than those implicit in market rates, and when the manager's expectations are similar to those of the market.
2. Leave cash positions open, and even create them, whenever the manager's expectations (adjusted for risk) imply costs lower, or returns higher, than those implicit in market rates.

In this chapter we will analyze situations associated with exchange positions and interest rate positions. However, we will discuss

problems involving exchange risks in greater detail than problems involving interest rate risks. Interest rate risk is usually discussed in corporate finance texts. In addition, the general principles that apply to
managing an exchange position also apply to managing an interest rate
position.

Throughout we will assume that the rates shown in the following
table prevail on day 1:

Market Rates on Day 1		
Exchange Rates		
Spot rate		$0.4500/DM
30-day forward		$0.4510/DM
90-day forward		$0.4542/DM
Interest Rates	$	DM
30-day	16.00	13.25
90-day	16.75	13.00

For the sake of simplicity, we will also assume that the given rates are
available for both buying and selling of currencies and borrowing and
investing of funds. For 30-day funds the interest differential is 2.75%
and for 90-day funds it is 3.75%. These differentials approximate the
forward discounts on the dollar against the mark for both maturities.
There is interest rate parity in the market.

In this presentation we will allow small net cash flow balances in
different currencies to remain after the cash management decision.
These balances in all cases will be associated with the costs of locking
in rates as of today for cash flows to take place in the future. The total
of these balances in each currency for the period as a whole will be
shown as a net exchange position. In practice, these balances also require a financial decision. However, allowing these balances to remain
facilitates the identification of the financing costs associated with the
decisions.

MANAGEMENT OF FOREIGN EXCHANGE RISK

Exposure to exchange risk occurs whenever the amount of expected inflows in one currency is different from the amount of expected outflows
in that currency *for the given period of time.* In that case, there is a *net
exchange position* in that currency. The position in a currency is *long*

if the amount of expected inflows exceeds the amount of expected outflows; the position is *short* if the amount of expected outflows exceeds the amount of expected inflows.

Covering an Exchange Position

Assume that we anticipate that in 90 days we must pay a supplier DM100,000 for goods imported. We plan to meet this payment with an expected net dollar inflow of $45,000 from the collection of receivables forecasted for the same day. At today's spot exchange rate the amounts in the two currencies are equivalent. However, we do not know with certainty what the spot rate will be on day 91. We have an exchange position, long in dollars and short in marks, for day 91. To eliminate the uncertainty created by this exchange position, today we must lock in an effective exchange rate at which this conversion from dollars into marks can be made. We must contract rates at which we can produce the following on day 91: an outflow in dollars, to match the forecast $45,000 inflow; and an inflow in marks, to match the forecast DM100,000 outflow.[1] At that point, the cash flows for day 91 will be squared in both currencies at rates known in advance. We can contract to produce the needed cash flows through the forward exchange market or through the money market. Exhibit 7.1 shows the cash flows for the initial situation and the two alternative solutions available to eliminate the exchange position.

Covering in the Forward Market. We know that on day 91 there will be an inflow in dollars and an outflow in marks. The most direct way to guarantee the exchange rate at which the conversion of dollars into marks will be made is to negotiate a rate for such a conversion in advance. On day 1 this can be done in the forward market by selling dollars against marks for delivery in 90 days at $0.4542/DM. Today's forward transaction does not generate any cash flows on day 1. However, on day 91 there will be an outflow of $45,420 and an inflow of DM100,000 to deliver on the forward transaction.

Although at today's spot exchange rate of $0.4500/DM the $45,000 is equivalent to DM100,000, at the 90-day forward rate of $0.4542 we need $420 more to generate the DM100,000 needed on day 91. This $420 can be seen as the cost, measured relative to today's spot rate, of guaranteeing a conversion rate and eliminating the exchange risk from

---

[1]The exchange risk would be eliminated also if the cover transaction matured on a date other than day 91. However, in that case there would be an exposure to fluctuations in interest rates. *Swap positions* will be discussed later in the chapter.

EXHIBIT 7.1 Covering an Exchange Position

Date	Transaction	CURRENCY*	
		$	DM
	INITIAL SITUATION		
Day 91	Scheduled net cash flows	+45,000	−100,000
	Net exchange positions	+45,000	−100,000
	A. COVER IN THE FORWARD MARKET		
Day 1	Buy DM100,000 against $ for delivery on day 91 at $0.4542	ncf	ncf
Day 91	Scheduled net cash flows	+45,000	−100,000
	Delivery on forward contract from day 1	−45,420	+100,000
	Net cash flows	−420	0
	Net exchange positions	−420	0
	B. COVER IN THE MONEY MARKETS		
Day 1	Borrow $ at 16.75%, 90 days	+45,000	
	Convert $ into DM, spot	−45,000	+100,000
	Invest DM at 13%, 90 days		−100,000
	Net cash flows	0	0
Day 91	Scheduled net cash flows	+45,000	−100,000
	Repayment of borrowings		
	Principal	45,000	
	Interest		
	$0.1675 \times 45{,}000 \times 3/12 =$	1,884	−46,884
	Collection of DM investment		
	Principal	100,000	
	Interest		
	$0.13 \times 100{,}000 \times 3/12 =$	3,250	+103,250
	Net cash flows	−1,884	+3,250
	Net exchange positions	−1,884	+3,250

*(+: Cash inflow; −: Cash outflow; ncf: No cash flow)

the expected cash flows. Since there are no net cash flows on day 1, the net outflow of $420 is also the residual net exchange position for the period as a whole.

Covering in the Money Market. An alternative to guaranteeing a conversion rate from dollars into marks for day 91 is to make the conversion on day 1 at today's spot rate of $0.4500/DM. However, in order to do this we must obtain the dollars on day 1. Since operations will not generate dollars until day 91, in order to have dollars now we have to borrow them at the going rate for 90-day dollars, 16.75%. This provides the dollars necessary to make the conversion into marks. However, the marks are not needed for operations until day 91. We can invest the marks obtained from the spot transaction at the going 90-day rate for marks, 13%. On day 91 the dollar borrowings will be repaid with the dollar inflow scheduled for that day, and the proceeds from

the maturing mark investment will be available to meet the mark outflow initially scheduled for that date.

The bottom line of Exhibit 7.1 shows the net cash flows in dollars
after the borrowing and the investment mature. The $1,884 outflow
represents the interest paid on the dollar borrowings; the DM3,250 inflow represents the interest earned on the mark investment. At the initial spot rate of $0.4500/DM, the mark interest is equivalent to $1,462.
Then, the net cost of eliminating the initial exchange position through
the money market is $422 (equal to $1,462 less $1,884).

Forward Market or Money Market. To eliminate the exchange position created by a net outflow in marks and a net inflow in dollars we
can either accept a discount on the dollar against the mark in the forward market, or accept an interest rate on borrowing dollars that is
higher than the rate obtained from investing in marks. The forward discount on the dollar against the mark, 3.75%, is approximately the same
as the interest differential in favor of the dollar. Both approaches to
covering this exchange position cost about the same—3.75% per annum. (A cost of $420 on $45,000 equals 0.93% for 3 months, or about
3.75% per annum.)

However, if the net rates accessible to the funds manager are different from the ones available to exchange dealers who establish forward rates, then the outcomes from covering in the forward market or
the money market will vary. These differences in net rates accessible
to exchange dealers and the funds manager can arise on two accounts:

1. The presence of exchange controls producing segmented money markets
    (domestic and external)
2. Differences in credit permiums on lending rates charged to different
    borrowers

Government controls apply only to transactions within the country
boundaries (for example, Germany). However, currencies traded outside the country (for example, Euromarks) are not subject to these controls. The subsidiary located in the foreign country has access to its
own domestic market, which traders in the Euromarkets do not have.
This may make a cover using domestic money market rates preferable
to a cover through the forward market. On the other hand, the credit
premiums charged for interbank loans (funds accessible to exchange
traders who quote forward exchange rates) are much smaller than for
industrial companies. Other things constant, this fact tends to favor using forward rates to cover an exchange position, instead of using money
market rates that include a premium for credit risk.

With segmented financial markets, it is worthwhile to obtain information on the cost of covering under the four possible alternatives: (1) domestic money market; (2) Euromoney market; (3) domestic forward market; and (4) forward Euromarkets.

Another consideration to be kept in mind when choosing an approach to covering is the matter of financial reporting. The money market cover will appear directly on the balance sheet as an investment on the asset side and a liability on the liabilities-plus-equity side. The forward transaction will appear only as a footnote. To the extent that the financial officer is concerned about ratios such as the debt-to-equity ratio, financial reporting considerations introduce a bias against using the money market to cover international trade and a bias in favor of using the forward exchange market.

Accepting an Exchange Position

To the extent that the forward exchange rate and interest differentials are unbiased predictors of future spot rates, the cover or hedging decision collapsed the distribution of future spot rates that would affect the value of the exchange position into the average spot rate expected by the market to prevail 90 days later. The distribution of changes in the rate expected by the market to occur in 90 days could be represented by the distribution shown in the following figure:

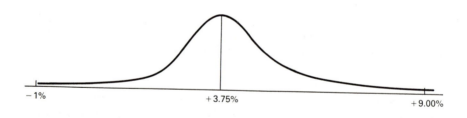

The mean of this distribution, +3.75%, is the cost locked in by the earlier cover transaction. If the forward rate is indeed an unbiased predictor of future spot rates, then our hedging decisions over a long period of time would be locking in the average of spot rate changes during the period.

An alternative solution to the problem presented by this exchange position, short in marks and long in dollars, is to let the exposure stand. Given that the market gives us the choice of locking in a 3.75% premium of the mark against the dollar, the decision not to cover the exposure must be based on our judgment that the appreciation of the mark against the dollar over the 90-day period will be less than 3.75% per annum. That is, our distribution of changes in spot rates in 90 days, when compared with the market's distribution for the same changes in the spot rate, would appear as indicated in the following figure:

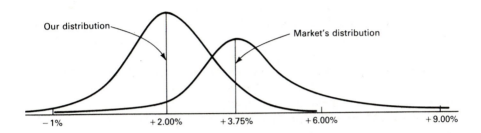

From our point of view, the choices are: (1) lock in with certainty a discount on the dollar (a premium on the mark) of 3.75%; or (2) act according to our expectations and leave the exchange position uncovered, planning to pay (on average) only a 2% premium on the mark against the dollar. Alternatively, we can say that we have the following options: (1) know with certainty that we will need $45,420 to generate DM100,000; or (2) expect to need only $45,220, if the mark appreciates 2% per annum against the dollar. These choices are represented in the next figure.

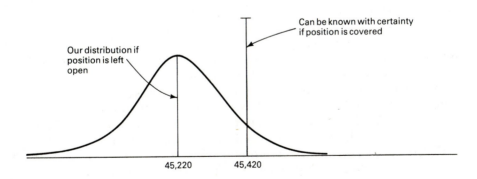

The difficulty in this decision stems from the tradeoff between certainty and lower cost. We can have a higher cost with certainty, or an expected lower cost with uncertainty—that is, an expected lower cost which on day 91 could turn out to be higher than even the 3.75% that we could have locked in on day 1.

Creating an Exchange Position.

This comparison between the future rates expected by the funds manager and the rates expected by the market is one that is made constantly. Even when operations do not generate an exchange position, the funds manager may want to consider creating such a position if his or her expectations are different from those reflected in market rates. Given the distributions of expected changes in the spot rate of the mark against the dollar shown previously, if we wished to take the risk, we would want to create a position short in marks and long in dollars—that is, an outflow in marks and an inflow in dollars for day 91. We can do this in the forward market by selling marks against dollars at $0.4542 (a premium on the mark of $0.0042/DM over the spot rate) or in the money market by borrowing marks and investing the proceeds in dollars at an interest rate differential of 3.75% per annum in favor of the dollar.

Whether this exchange position generates gains or losses depends on the spot rate on day 91. On day 91, we have to buy marks and sell dollars in the spot market either to deliver on the earlier forward contract or to repay the dollar borrowings, depending on the approach used in creating the exchange position. We will have an exchange gain if the spot rate on day 91 is below $0.4542/DM (the rate at which we sold marks against dollars and also the spot rate on day 1 that the market expected to prevail on day 91). If the spot rate on day 91 is higher than $0.4542/DM, then there will be an exchange loss.

Riding an Exchange Position.

The gains or losses associated with an exchange position do not need to be realized upon maturity of the position. Instead, the position can be *rolled over* at that time.

Let us assume that we accepted the original exchange position short in marks and long in dollars. When day 91 arrives, we find that the mark has appreciated against the dollar even more than what the market had anticipated on day 1. On day 1 the market expected a spot rate of $0.4542/DM for day 91; however, the actual spot rate turns out to be $0.4567/DM. At that spot rate the marks outflow requires $45,670, as compared to the $45,420 we could have locked in on day 1 and the $45,220 we had expected to require.

Now we have the following two choices: (1) We can accept the exchange loss of $670 relative to the spot rate of day 1 and close the position; or (2) We can roll over the exchange position in the expectation that the dollar will appreciate against the mark, to compensate at least partially for that exchange loss. If we choose to roll over the exchange position, then we essentially delay the conversion from dollars into marks. However, in the meantime, we must find a source of marks to meet the mark outflow due on day 91. We must also invest the dollar inflow realized on day 91. To maintain the exchange position, the borrowings will be made in marks and the investment of funds will be made in dollars. The exchange position after the rollover is still short in marks and long in dollars, now with value date day 121; however, the amounts involved are larger as interest is added to the position—13.25% on the mark borrowings and 16.00% on the dollar investment. As Exhibit 7.2 shows, the new exchange position is short DM101,104 and long $45,600.

After rolling over the exchange position above, short in marks and long in dollars, at any point in time we have two choices: close the net exchange position or let the position stand open. We would presumably want to leave the position open as long as we expect an appreciation of the mark against the dollar smaller than the appreciation expected by the market, as reflected in the observed rates. At the point when our expectations coincide with the market's expectations, or when we ac-

EXHIBIT 7.2   Rolling Over and Closing an Exchange Position

			CURRENCY*	
Date	Transaction		$	DM
	ROLLING OVER AN EXCHANGE POSITION			
Day 91	Net cash flows scheduled from day 1		+45,000	−100,000
	Borrowing in DM at 13.25%, 30 days			+100,000
	Investment in $ at 16.00%, 30 days		−45,000	
	Net cash flows		0	0
Day 121	Repayment of DM borrowing			
	Principal	100,000		
	Interest			−101,104
	$0.1325 \times 100,000 \times \frac{1}{12} =$	1,104		
	Collection of $ investment			
	Principal	45,000		
	Interest			
	$0.16 \times 45,000 \times \frac{1}{12} =$	600	+45,600	
	Net cash flows		+45,600	−101,104
Net exchange positions			+45,600	−101,104
			+45,600	−101,104
	CLOSING THE EXCHANGE POSITION IN THE FORWARD MARKET			
Day 106	Buy DM101,104 against $ for delivery on day 121 at $0.4550		ncf	ncf
Day 121	Net cash flows scheduled from day 91		+45,600	−101,104
	Delivery on 15-day forward contract from day 106		−46,002	+101,104
	Net cash flows		−402	0
Net exchange positions			−402	0

*(+: Cash inflow; −: Cash outflow; ncf: No cash flow)

tually anticipate an appreciation of the mark larger than the one anticipated by the market, then we will want to close the position.

Now assume that on day 106 (15 days after we rolled over the exchange position for 30 days), we come to the conclusion that the spot
rate anticipated by the market for 15 days later, $0.4550 (that is, the 15-
day forward rate on day 106), is the upper limit we expect the mark to
appreciate against the dollar by that day. So, we decide to close the exchange position now. To close the position requires the same steps as
to cover the exchange position. As we discussed earlier, we can cover
any exchange position through the forward market or through the two
relevant money markets. Assume here that we choose to cover the position in the forward market. The cover will guarantee an exchange rate
at which the outflow in marks expected for day 121 (DM101,104) can
be met with dollars—the currency in which we expect an inflow that
day.

Assume that the market scenario on day 106 is as described in the
following table:

	Market Rates On Day 106	
Exchange Rates		
Spot rate	$0.4520/DM	
15-day forward rate	$0.4550/DM	
	$	DM
15-Day Interest Rates	15.75%	13.50%

We can buy DM101,104 against dollars for delivery on day 121 at
$0.4550/DM. On day 121 these marks require $46,002, which is $402
short of the $45,600 expected dollar inflow on that date (see Exhibit
7.2). However, this cover cost is known with certainty and there is no
risk of a larger exchange loss when day 121 arrives. The $402 exchange
loss locked in is better than the $670 loss that would have been real-
ized if we had closed the position when it was due, and better than the
$420 that it would have cost to close the position on day 1; however, it
is worse than the $220 we had expected it would cost when we left the
position open on day 1.

When we rolled over the position, we hoped that the appreciation
of the mark against the dollar would reverse itself. By day 106 this had
taken place. The spot rate moved from $0.4567/DM on day 91 to
$0.4520/DM on day 106. The spot rate on day 106 is close to the rate
that we had anticipated originally on day 1. However, by waiting until
day 106, we had to pay an exchange cost of $402 (instead of the $220

we expected to pay when we left the position open on day 1). Between day 1 and day 106 the interest differential between the mark and the dollar narrowed from 3.75% to 2.25% (that is, the interest rate on the mark increased and the interest rate on the dollar decreased) and the forward premium on the mark decreased.

When we computed the exchange cost associated with leaving the position open we compared the market rates with the spot rate we expected to prevail upon maturity of the position. If we cover a position before it matures, then we must also take into account changes in interest differentials and forward rates, in addition to changes in the spot rate.

Exchange Risks in Meeting Cash Needs

Exchange risk considerations are also involved when we must borrow funds to meet a temporary business need that requires financing, and when we must invest excess funds temporarily available from operations.

As an example, assume that on day 1 we have a net outflow in marks in the amount of DM100,000. However, we expect to have an inflow in marks of the same amount 90 days later. This situation occurs whenever we must pay production costs (such as labor and raw materials) before collections from sales can be realized. There is a need to generate 90-day funds on day 1 in order to finance operations between day 1 and day 91.

There are two basic alternatives available to meet this financing need: (1) Borrow funds in the local currency which is needed and which will be available to repay the debt (marks); or (2) Borrow funds in a foreign currency and convert the proceeds into marks. Each of these alternatives will generate an inflow in marks on day 1. The maturity of these borrowings should be 90 days, so they can be repaid with the inflow in marks expected on day 91.[2] The cash flows for the initial situation, as well as the alternative solutions, are shown in Exhibit 7.3. If the initial problem called for investing temporary funds, then the cash flows under each situation would be the reverse of those presented in Exhibit 7.3.

Borrow Funds in Local Currency. In this example we could borrow 90-day marks at 13%. The cash flows generated by these borrowings, as

---

[2]The financing need could be met also by borrowing funds with a maturity before or after day 91. However, in that case, we would be exposed to the risk of fluctuation in interest rates. See the section titled "Management of Interest Rate Risk" later in this chapter.

EXHIBIT 7.3 Borrowing Funds with and without an Exchange Position

Date	Transaction	CURRENCY* $	CURRENCY* DM
	INITIAL SITUATION		
Day 1	Scheduled net cash flow		−100,000
Day 91	Scheduled net cash flow		+100,000
Net exchange position			0
	A. BORROW FUNDS IN LOCAL CURRENCY		
Day 1	Scheduled net cash flow		−100,000
	Borrowings in DM at 13%, 90 days		+100,000
	Net cash flow		0
Day 91	Scheduled net cash flow		+100,000
	Repayment of DM borrowings		
	Principal	DM100,000	
	Interest		
	$0.13 \times 100,000 \times 3/12 =$	3,250	−103,250
	Net cash flow		−3,250
Net exchange position			−3,250
	B. BORROW FUNDS IN UNCOVERED FOREIGN CURRENCY		
Day 1	Scheduled net cash flow		−100,000
	Borrowings in $ at 16.75%, 90 days	+45,000	
	Convert $ into DM spot at $0.4500/DM	−45,000	+100,000
	Net cash flows	0	0
Day 91	Scheduled net cash flow		+100,000
	Repayment of $ borrowings		
	Principal	45,000	
	Interest		
	$0.1675 \times 45,000 \times 3/12 =$	1,884	−46,884
	Net cash flows		−46,884	+100,000
Net exchange positions		−46,884	+100,000
	C. BORROW FUNDS IN COVERED FOREIGN CURRENCY		
Day 1	Scheduled net cash flow		−100,000
	Borrowings in $ at 16.75%, 90 days	+45,000	
	Convert $ into DM spot at $0.4500/DM	−45,000	+100,000
	Sell DM100,000 against $ for delivery on day 91 at $0.4542	ncf	ncf
	Net cash flows	0	0
Day 91	Scheduled net cash flow		+100,000
	Repayment of $ borrowings		
	Principal	45,000	
	Interest		
	$0.1675 \times 45,000 \times 3/12 =$	1,884	−46,884
	Delivery on forward contract from day 1		+45,420	−100,000
	Net cash flows		−1,464	0
Net exchange positions		−1,464	0

*(+: Cash inflow; −: Cash outflow; ncf: No cash flow)

shown in panel A of Exhibit 7.3, balance the scheduled cash flows for day 1 and day 91. The DM3,250 net outflow on day 91 represents the interest payment due on that date—that is, the financing cost.

Borrow Funds in Foreign Currency. In principle, we could borrow any currency available to meet the expected outflow in marks on day 1. In this example, the only other currency mentioned is dollars. We can borrow 90-day dollars at 16.75% and convert the proceeds into marks to meet the outflow expected for day 1. At a spot rate of $0.4500/DM, we need to borrow $45,000. The cash flows after the borrowings would be as shown in panel B of Exhibit 7.3.

The borrowings in dollars can balance the scheduled outflow in marks on day 1 after the conversion in the spot market. Thus, on day 1 there is zero net cash flow in both dollars and marks. However, on day 91 there is a net outflow in dollars (the repayment of the borrowings) and a net inflow in marks (the inflow scheduled initially). At the spot rate of $0.4500/DM prevailing on day 1, the marks available from the expected inflow can be converted into $45,000. This would cover the dollar outflow, except for the interest payment of $1,884. However, on day 1 we do not know what the spot rate of the dollar against the mark will be on day 91; it may be above or below $0.4500/DM. If we leave the financing operation as it is now, then we are exposed to the risk of fluctuations in the spot rate between day 1 and day 91, and we have a net exchange position. In the exchange exposure associated with these borrowings we have a short position in dollars and a long position in marks. To make this position acceptable we must expect an appreciation of the mark against the dollar *larger* than the differential of 3.75% per annum over the 3 months, or a spot rate on day 91 higher than $0.4542/DM (the current 90-day forward rate). This is in contrast to the expectations we had to have in the earlier part of this chapter. There the exchange position was short in marks and long in dollars. To make that position acceptable we had to expect an appreciation of the mark against the dollar *smaller* than the one expected by the market.

If we want to eliminate the exchange risk involved in borrowing a currency different from the one that will be available to make the repayment, then today we have to lock in an exchange rate at which the marks can be converted into dollars on day 91. This can be done by selling marks against dollars for delivery in 90 days in the forward exchange market. In our example, this can be done at $0.4542/DM. The cash flows after the borrowings and the forward transaction would be as shown in panel C of Exhibit 7.3. After the forward transaction, we have balanced the cash flows in dollars and marks for both dates, except for a net outflow in dollars on day 91. This net outflow of $1,464 represents the net financing costs. It is composed of the interest cost of $1,884 less the forward premium of $420 on the DM100,000. When we convert the $45,000 borrowed in dollars into marks in the spot market, we obtain DM100,000; however, when we convert the DM100,000 back into dollars at the forward exchange rate, we obtain $45,420, which is more than $45,000.

In bankers' jargon, the funds obtained from borrowing a foreign currency with a forward cover are called *swapped funds*. In this case we "swapped" dollars into marks in the spot market, and marks into dollars in the forward market. The cost of swapped funds is the interest rate on the currency borrowed, plus or minus the swap rate. In our example the cost is 13%, composed of the 16.75% on the borrowed dollars less the discount of 3.75% on the dollar against the mark. This technique is used often by international banks that do not generate funds in a currency in which they make loans (say, pesos); a loan is financed with funds obtained in the Euromarkets and "swapped" into the currency needed for the loan.

Local Currency or Foreign Currency.   We will now compare the financing costs under the alternatives of borrowing marks and borrowing dollars with a forward cover. When we borrowed marks, the interest payment was DM3,250. This interest, paid on a principal of DM100,000 over 3 months, represents a cost of 13% per annum. When we borrowed dollars, the combined cost of interest and forward cover for 3 months was $1,464. This net cost on a principal of $45,000 represents a cost of 13% per annum. The cost of financing the marks needed for 90 days is the same (13% per annum), regardless of whether we use marks or a foreign currency, as long as the foreign currency is covered. There are no risks in either approach. All the rates that affect the financing costs are locked in from day 1, so the cost of the funds under both approaches is the same.

This conclusion will follow most of the time when we use the Eurocurrency markets. These markets are well arbitraged and the interest differential among currencies equals the forward discount on the currency with the higher interest rate (the premium on the currency with the lower interest rate). However, when exchange controls exist in the domestic money market, this indifference between using the two approaches may no longer exist.

Solving Cash Flow and Exchange Position Problems Jointly.   We have seen how to borrow funds from alternative sources and how to cover exchange positions. In each case there were two approaches available to solve the problem. When the two problems occur simultaneously, one of the solutions to each of the problems also solves the other problem. Thus, if we expect a net outflow in marks on day 1 and a net inflow in dollars on day 91, we have two problems. The timing of the inflow and the outflow are 90 days apart and their currencies are different. The timing problem calls for borrowing funds on day 1. The difference in currencies creates an exchange position. If we want to cover the exchange position, we can handle each problem separately within the specific market in which it occurs, or we can handle the two problems jointly.

In separate solutions, the need for marks on day 1 can be met by borrowing 90-day marks at 13%. The exchange position problem can be handled in the forward market by selling dollars against marks for delivery in 90 days at a discount of 3.75% of the dollar against the mark. When day 91 arrives, the scheduled inflow in dollars provides the dollars needed to deliver on the forward transaction, and the marks obtained from the forward transaction can then be used to repay the mark borrowings due on that day. The net cost of obtaining the needed marks on day 1 and covering the exchange position is 16.75%.

In a joint solution, the need for marks on day 1 can be met by borrowing dollars. This approach also eliminates the initial exchange position because the currency of the borrowings (dollars) is the same as the one in which we expect the inflow of funds that will repay the borrowings. Since we need marks on day 1, the borrowed dollars are converted into the needed marks in the spot market. On day 91 the repayment of the dollars can be made with the dollar inflow initially scheduled to take place on that day. The net cost of solving the two problems simultaneously is the same as before—namely, 16.75%. However, in a world where spreads between bid and ask rates exist, the joint solution, using the spot market, usually will cost less.

MANAGEMENT OF INTEREST RATE RISK
IN ONE CURRENCY

In the financing situation discussed in the preceding section we positioned ourselves on day 1 to borrow funds needed on the same date. To the extent that the funds manager operates with a forecast of cash flows to be generated in the future, most cash flows on day 1 do not require financing or investing on that day. However, on day 1 we are uncertain as to the interest rates that will be available to manage those cash flows when they actually occur. We have an *interest rate position*. We may *expect* that the current 90-day interest rate of 13% on marks will continue and that the cost of financing DM100,000 1 month from today for 90 days will be DM3,250. However, we are not *certain* that this will be the case.

Covering an Interest Rate Position

Assume that on day 1 we forecast a net outflow in marks for day 31 and a net inflow for day 91. Today we can see that there is a 60-day financing need in marks to be met between day 31 and day 91. If today we want to lock in the interest rate at which 60-day financing will be obtained on day 31, we have to generate today the same kind of cash flow that we will need on day 31—but with a different maturity. On day 31 we have to borrow funds for 60 days; thus, today (30 days in advance) we borrow funds for 90 days. However, these borrowings leave us with idle funds for 30 days. We can invest these funds at the current 30-day rate. When this investment matures the funds will be available to meet the original financing need from operations scheduled for day 31.

The anticipated borrowings to lock in an interest rate can be done following the same approaches available when the funds are to be used immediately, as we discussed earlier. We can borrow the funds in the local market, or we can borrow the funds in a foreign currency. Exhibit 7.4 shows the transactions and cash flows associated with the original situation and the two alternative solutions. The major difference between the initial situation in Exhibits 7.3 and 7.4 is the date of the scheduled outflow in marks. When the scheduled outflow is on day 1, the borrowings proceeds are used to meet that outflow. When the scheduled outflow is not until day 31, the borrowings proceeds are reinvested for 1 month.

In Exhibit 7.4 the reinvestment of funds for 1 month under each alternative is made in marks, the currency in which the outflow for day 31 is planned. However, it would be possible to invest the funds for 1 month in any currency other than marks. As long as the investment is accompanied by a forward cover from the given currency into marks, the outcome would be the same. For example, the dollar proceeds in panel B of Exhibit 7.4 could be reinvested in 30-day dollars if, in addition, dollars were sold forward against marks for 30-day delivery. In this case, the forward transaction would have locked in an exchange rate at which the dollars could be converted into marks at the end of the investment period. As we showed earlier, the rate of return on 30-day marks (13.25%) would equal the rate of return on dollars (16%), less the 30-day discount on the dollar against the mark (2.75%).

EXHIBIT 7.4 Covering an Interest Rate Position in One Currency

Date	Transaction	CURRENCY* $	CURRENCY* DM
	INITIAL SITUATION		
Day 31	Scheduled net cash flow		− 100,000
Day 91	Scheduled net cash flow		+ 100,000
Net exchange position			0
	A. LOCK IN INTEREST RATE IN LOCAL CURRENCY		
Day 1	Borrow DM at 13%, 90 days		+ 100,000
	Invest DM at 13.25%, 30 days		− 100,000
	Net cash flow		0
Day 31	Scheduled net cash flow		− 100,000
	Collection of DM 30-day investment		
	Principal	100,000	
	Interest		
	0.1325 × 100,000 × ¹⁄₁₂ =	1,104	+ 101,104
	Net cash flow		+ 1,104
Day 91	Scheduled net cash flow		+ 100,000
	Repayment of DM 90-day borrowings		
	Principal	100,000	
	Interest		
	0.13 × 100,000 × ³⁄₁₂ =	3,250	− 103,250
	Net cash flow		− 3,250
Net exchange position			− 2,146
	B. LOCK IN INTEREST RATE IN FOREIGN CURRENCY		
Day 1	Borrow $ at 16.75%, 90 days	+ 45,000	
	Convert $ into DM spot at		
	$0.4500/DM	− 45,000	+ 100,000
	Invest DM at 13.25%, 30 days		− 100,000
	Sell DM100,000 against $ for		
	delivery on day 91 at $0.4542	ncf	ncf
	Net cash flow	0	0
Day 31	Scheduled net cash flow		− 100,000
	Collection of DM 30-day investment		
	(as above)		+ 101,104
	Net cash flow		+ 1,104
Day 91	Scheduled net cash flow		+ 100,000
	Repayment of $ borrowings		
	Principal	45,000	
	Interest		
	0.1675 × 45,000 × ³⁄₁₂ =	1,884	− 46,884
	Delivery on forward contract		
	from day 1		+ 45,420	− 100,000
	Net cash flows	− 1,464	0
Net exchange positions		− 1,464	+ 1,104

*(+: Cash inflow; −: Cash outflow; ncf: No cash flow)

If the rate risk is covered in the mark money market, then the net cost is DM2,146, comprised of a 30-day interest income of DM1,104 and a 90-day interest expense of DM3,250. If the interest rate risk is covered in the dollar money market, there is a 30-day interest income of DM1,104, as before, and a 90-day net interest expense (after forward cover) of $1,464. At the initial spot rate of $0.4500/DM, the interest expense of $1,464 is equivalent to DM3,253, so the net cost of financing is DM2,149—roughly the same as if the financing had been done in marks. This represents 2.14% for 2-month financing, which is equivalent to a cost of 12.84% per annum for 2-month financing, 1 month from today.[3]

Accepting an Interest Rate Position

The interest rates available on day 1 for 30-day and 90-day maturities provide a forecast of what the market expects the 60-day rate to be on day 31. The 90-day rate must be equal to the sum of the 30-day rate plus what the market expects the 60-day rate to be 30 days from today:

$$(1 + 0.13)\left(\frac{3}{12}\right) = (1 + 0.1325)\left(\frac{1}{12}\right) + (1 + X)\left(\frac{2}{12}\right)$$
$$X = 0.1288 = 12.88\%$$

If we want to leave the interest rate position open, we would have to expect the 60-day interest rate on marks, 30 days from today, to be less than 12.88%. The market expectations and ours would appear as shown in the following figure:

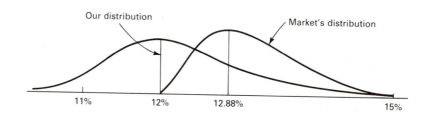

---

[3]Alternatively, we can say that we realize an interest income of 13.25% per annum over 1 month (equal to 1.10% per month) and have an interest expense of 13% per annum over 3 months (equal to 1.08% per month). Interest cost at 1.08% per month equals 3.24% for 3 months. From this we must subtract the interest income of 1.10% per month. Thus, the net cost of the 2-month funds is 2.14%, which is the same as 12.84% per annum.

The market offers us the choice to cover the interest rate position at 12.88% per annum. As we saw in the earlier sections, this was the effective cost of the borrowings when we locked in the 60-day interest rate in advance, on day 1 ignoring small differences. If we do not accept this choice with certainty, it must be because we expect the interest rate on the needed funds to be less than 12.88%. However, we cannot be certain of our expectations. If our expectations are wrong, the actual cost may turn out to be higher than the available 12.88%.

Creating an Interest Rate Position. Whenever our expectations about rates to prevail in the future differ from the rates expected by the market, there is an opportunity to profit. Even if operations do not generate the interest rate position, we can create such a position. Given the rates in our last example, if we expect the 60-day rate that will prevail 30 days from today to be below the 12.88% expected by the market, we can create a cash flow position in which we have an outflow on day 31 and an inflow on day 91—a position similar to the one that we obtained earlier from operations. That is, we must engineer a situation in which we borrow 60-day money, 30 days from today. We can do this by borrowing funds for 30 days and placing the proceeds for 90 days. After 30 days, when the borrowings must be refinanced, we can borrow 60-day marks at a rate lower than 12.88%—if our expectations materialize. The net profit from the operation would be equal to the 13% return for 3 months, less the 13.25% cost for 1 month, less the cost for the remaining 2 months. If we can refinance at only 12.88%, there will not be any interest gain or loss. If the 60-day rate needed for the refinancing turns out to be higher than 12.88%, there will be an interest loss.

Riding an Interest Rate Position. If the market rates on day 31 are those presented in the following table, then our expectations about interest rates on marks back on day 1 would have been proven correct.

Market Rates on Day 31			
Exchange Rates			
Spot rate		$0.4515/DM	
30-day forward rate		$0.4530/DM	
60-day forward rate		$0.4534/DM	
Interest Rates, Per Annum		$	DM
30-day		16.00%	12.00%
60-day		14.00%	11.50%
Implicit 30-day Rates, 30 Days Hence			
Rates		15.00%	11.75%
Differential		3.25%	

On day 1 the market expected the 60-day rate on marks, on day 31, to be 12.88%; we expected it to be lower. The table shows that the 60-day rate on marks on day 31 is actually 11.50%. If we borrow the funds needed for 60 days at this rate we close the interest rate position. We have saved DM220, or 1.32% per annum, on these borrowings by having run the risk of a change in interest rate from day 1 to day 31 (DM100,000 × 1.32% × 2/12). However, these borrowings do not need to be for the same maturity as the length of the business need—namely, 60 days. We could borrow for a longer or a shorter maturity.

The interest rates on marks on day 31 imply a 30-day rate of 11.75% on day 61. There is a downward-sloping yield curve. If we come to the conclusion that the interest rate on the mark will decline, but that the decline will be larger than the one anticipated by the market, then we would want to roll over the interest rate position and borrow the needed funds for only 30 days; this is presented in panel A of Exhibit 7.5. We would do this with the expectation that 30 days from today we would refinance the borrowings at a rate lower than 11.75%.[4]

Now let us assume that on day 46, the market rates shown in the next table prevail:

Market Rates on Day 46		
Exchange Rates		
Spot rate		$0.4480/DM
15-day forward rate		$0.4486/DM
45-day forward rate		$0.4505/DM
Interest Rates, Per Annum	$	DM
15-day	15.50%	12.50%
45-day	17.50%	13.00%
Implicit 30-day Rates, 15 Days Hence		
Rates	18.51%	13.25%
Differential	5.26%	

In Exhibit 7.5 we rolled over the interest rate position on day 31 for 30 more days. After the rollover we have a net outflow in marks on day 61 and a net inflow on day 91. The rates on day 46 show that the market

---

[4]If, on the other hand, we thought that on day 31 the market was overestimating the amount of decline in the mark interest rate, we would instead want to borrow marks with a maturity longer than the period for which they are needed. When operations produce the expected inflow in marks (which otherwise would have been available for repaying a debt maturing on day 91), we could use those funds to reinvest in marks at the higher interest rate we expect to prevail in the mark market at that point. Obviously, our expectations are very different from those held by the market, and if we prove to be wrong there will be a net loss in interest.

EXHIBIT 7.5   Rolling Over and Closing an Interest Rate Position

Date	Transaction	$	DM
		CURRENCY*	
	A. ROLLING OVER AN INTEREST RATE POSITION		
Day 31	Scheduled net cash flow		−100,000
	Borrow DM100,000, 30 days at 12%		+100,000
	Net cash flow		0
Day 61	Repayment of DM borrowings from day 31		
	Principal	100,000	
	Interest		
	$0.12 \times 100,000 \times \frac{1}{12} =$	1,000	−101,000
	Net cash flow		−101,000
Day 91	Scheduled net cash flows		+100,000
	Net cash flow		+100,000
Net exchange position			−1,000
	B. CLOSING AN INTEREST RATE POSITION		
Day 46	Borrow DM100,000, 45 days at 13%		+100,000
	Invest DM100,000, 15 days at 12.50%		−100,000
	Net cash flow		0
Day 61	Repayment of DM borrowings from day 31		−101,000
	Collection of 15-day DM investment from day 46		
	Principal	100,000	
	Interest		
	$0.1250 \times 100,000 \times {}^{0.5}/_{12} =$	520	+100,520
	Net cash flow		−480
Day 91	Scheduled net cash flow		+100,000
	Repayment of 45-day DM borrowings from day 46		
	Principal	100,000	
	Interest		
	$0.13 \times 100,000 \times {}^{1.5}/_{12} =$	1,625	−101,625
	Net cash flow		−1,625
Net exchange position			−2,105

	Effective rates:		
	30 days at 12%		1,000
	45 days at 13%	1,625	
	Less 15 days at 12.50%	−520	1,105
	Effective rate on 60-day marks 12.63%		2,105

*(+: Cash inflow; −: Cash outflow)

expectations have moved further away from ours. We expected to be able to refinance 30-day marks on day 61 at less than 11.75%; the market now expects the 30-day mark rate on day 61 to be 13.25%. If this market move convinces us that our expectations were ill-founded, we will want to close the interest rate position. In panel B of Exhibit 7.5 we do this on day 46 by borrowing funds for 45 days and reinvesting the proceeds for 15 days, until they are needed to repay the 30-day borrowings we made on day 31 when we rolled over the position.

MANAGEMENT OF INTEREST RATE RISK
IN TWO CURRENCIES

In the same manner that we have an interest rate position when we anticipate borrowings needed in 30 days, we also have an interest rate position when we anticipate investing funds to be available in 30 days. If the future financing need and funds availability coincide in date, but not in currency, then, we have a *swap position*.

Covering a Swap Position

Assume that on day 1 we can anticipate the following: (1) an inflow of dollars and an outflow of marks for day 31; and (2) an outflow of dollars and an inflow in marks for day 91. There is no exchange position; for both currencies, inflows equal outflows throughout the period. If the mark appreciates against the dollar between now and day 31, we will have an exchange loss on the exchange conversion scheduled for that day; but we will have an exchange gain on the conversion from marks into dollars scheduled for day 91. This is true throughout the period between today and day 31. However, we are exposed to changes in interest rates and forward rates.

At the point when we make the conversion from dollars into the marks needed on day 31, an exchange position will be created. Assuming the spot conversion on day 31 is settled at the same spot rate as today's ($0.4500/DM), the cash flows on day 31 would be as indicated in the following table:

| Day | Transaction | CURRENCY* | |
		$	DM
Day 31	Scheduled net cash flows	+ 45,000	− 100,000
	Conversion of $ into DM, spot at $0.4500/DM	− 45,000	+ 100,000
	Net cash flows	0	0
Day 91	Scheduled net cash flows	− 45,000	+ 100,000
Net exchange positions		− 45,000	+ 100,000

*(+: Cash inflow; −: Cash outflow)

At that point we would have a net exchange position, short in dollars and long in marks. Losses would occur if the mark depreciates against the dollar, and gains would occur if the mark appreciates against the dollar. To avoid that risk we will want to cover the exchange position. On day 31 this can be done either by selling marks against dollars for delivery in 60 days (on day 91), or by borrowing 60-day dollars and investing the proceeds in 60-day marks. However, today (day 1) we do not know what the forward rate of the mark against the dollar or the interest differential between the two currencies will be on day 31. This is the risk in a swap position. If today we want to lock in a forward rate or an interest differential that will apply 30 days later (on day 31) for 60 days we can do this through the two money markets separately, or through the joint forward exchange market.

Separate Solutions. If we handle the two problems separately, we want to lock in a 60-day borrowing rate for marks needed in 30 days and we want to lock in a 60-day investment rate for dollars to be available in 30 days. The locking in of a rate for marks will follow along the lines discussed in the preceding section. It could be done within the money market, using marks or a foreign currency. Essentially we will borrow 90-day funds today and reinvest the proceeds for 30 days. In a similar fashion, if on day 31 we expect dollars available to be invested for 60 days, today we can borrow dollars for 30 days and reinvest the proceeds for 90 days.

Panel A of Exhibit 7.6 shows the cash flows using only the money market in which each scheduled cash flow takes place. Marks are obtained in advance by borrowing 90-day marks and reinvesting them for 30 days; an investment rate for dollars is locked in by borrowing 30-day dollars and reinvesting them for 90 days. The net exchange position at the end of all transactions is a net outflow of DM2,146 and a net inflow of $1,284. As we explained earlier, the DM2,146 outflow represents the cost of locking in an effective interest rate of 12.84% per annum for the marks needed for 60 days on day 31. In the same manner, we could show that the net inflow of $1,284 represents a rate of 17.12% locked in today for a 60-day dollar investment to be made on day 31. The return of 16.75% for 3 months must equal the return of 16% for 1 month, plus the rate expected for the remaining 2 months:

$$(1 + 0.1675)\left(\frac{3}{12}\right) = (1 + 0.16)\left(\frac{1}{12}\right) + (1 + X)\left(\frac{2}{12}\right)$$
$$X = 0.1712 = 17.12\%$$

Also, a return of $1,284 on an investment of $45,000 for a net period of 2 months equals 2.85% for 2 months, or 17.12% per annum. Effectively, we have locked in an interest differential of +4.2% per annum for 2 months.

Joint Solution. Initially, we do not have an exchange position. We can guarantee that this will continue to be the case if the exchange position is zero not only for all the transactions combined (the initial situation), but also for each transaction date. In the initial situation on day 31 we are short in marks and long in dollars. The opposite is true for day 91. Thus, as of day 1 there is no exchange position. If we want to lock in exchange rates for each separate date, we can do this most sim-

EXHIBIT 7.6 Covering an Interest Rate Position in Two Currencies

		CURRENCY*	
Date	Transaction	$	DM
	INITIAL SITUATION		
Day 31	Scheduled net cash flows	+45,000	−100,000
Day 91	Scheduled net cash flows	−45,000	+100,000
Net exchange positions		0	0
	A. SEPARATE COVERS IN THE MONEY MARKETS		
Day 1	Borrow $ at 16%, 30 days	+45,000	
	Invest $ at 16.75%, 90 days	−45,000	
	Borrow DM at 13%, 90 days		+100,000
	Invest DM at 13.25%, 30 days		−100,000
	Net cash flows	0	0
Day 31	Scheduled net cash flows	+45,000	−100,000
	Repayment of 30-day $ borrowings		
	Principal 45,000		
	Interest		
	$0.16 \times 45,000 \times \frac{1}{12} =$ 600	−45,600	
	Collection of 30-day DM investment		
	Principal 100,000		
	Interest		
	$0.1325 \times 100,000 \times \frac{1}{12} =$ 1,104		+101,104
	Net cash flows	−600	+1,104
Day 91	Scheduled net cash flows	−45,000	+100,000
	Collection of 90-day $ investment		
	Principal 45,000		
	Interest		
	$0.1675 \times 45,000 \times \frac{3}{12} =$ 1,884	+46,884	
	Repayment of 90-day DM borrowings		
	Principal 100,000		
	Interest		
	$0.13 \times 100,000 \times \frac{3}{12} =$ 3,250		−103,250
	Net cash flows	+1,884	−3,250
Net exchange positions		+1,284	−2,146
	B. JOINT COVER IN THE FORWARD MARKET		
Day 1	Buy DM100,000 against $ for delivery on day 31 at $0.4510	ncf	ncf
	Sell DM100,000 against $ for delivery on day 91 at $0.4542	ncf	ncf
Day 31	Scheduled net cash flows	+45,000	−100,000
	Delivery on 30-day forward contract from day 1	−45,100	+100,000
	Net cash flows	−100	0
Day 91	Scheduled net cash flows	−45,000	+100,000
	Delivery on 90-day forward contract from day 1	+45,420	−100,000
	Net cash flows	+420	0
Net exchange positions		+320	0

*(+: Cash inflow; −: Cash outflow; ncf: No cash flow)

ply in the forward market. On day 1, we buy marks against dollars for delivery on day 31 and we sell marks against dollars for delivery on day 91. Now we have locked in exchange rates for each specific transaction date. So, even after all the transactions on day 31 are closed, we are left with no exchange position. At that point the inflow of marks and the outflow of dollars scheduled for day 91 will be matched by the forward contract selling marks against dollars for delivery on that day.

Panel B in Exhibit 7.6 shows the net flows after the two forward transactions as a net inflow of $320, which represents a return of 4.2% per annum. (A return of $320 on $45,000 is 0.7% over an effective period of 2 months, which is equivalent to 4.2% per annum.) The two forward transactions have locked in a positive spread of 4.2%, which is equal to the effective interest differential locked in by the separate solution.

The 4.2% per annum interest differential is also equal to a swap rate of $0.0189/DM per annum, or $0.0030/DM that the market expects to prevail on day 31 for delivery 60 days later. This swap rate is approximately equal to the difference on day 1 between the 90-day forward rate of $0.4542/DM and the 30-day rate of $0.4510/DM.

Accepting a Swap Position

If we expect that 30 days from today the differential on 60-day interest rates will be more than 4.2% per annum in favor of the dollar (which is the same as saying that the 60-day swap rate will be more than $0.0030/DM), then we may wish to leave the swap position open. The distribution of rates expected by the market to prevail 30 days from today, and the rates we expect would be as illustrated in the following figure:

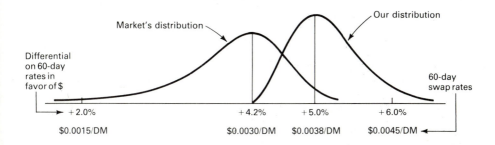

On day 31, after we convert the inflow of dollars into marks to meet the outflow in that currency, we are left with a net exchange position long in marks and short in dollars. To close this exchange position in the forward market we have to sell marks against dollars. If we can sell marks against dollars at a premium on the mark larger than $0.0030/DM, we are better off than if we had closed the swap position at a premium of $0.0030/DM on day 1. On the other hand, if the premium of the 60-day mark turns out to be less than $0.0030/DM, it would have been better to have closed the swap position earlier, on day 1.

It should be clear that the decision of whether to cover a swap position is based on an analysis of expected interest rate differentials or swap rates. Changes in the spot rate are of no consequence in a swap position. In our example, on day 31 we have to sell dollars against marks in the spot market to meet the liquidity requirements of that day. We may realize an exchange gain or loss relative to the spot rate of $0.4500/DM of day 1. However, at the same time that we do this transaction in the spot market we will do the opposite transaction—namely, buy dollars against marks—in the forward market. Whatever gain we realize in the spot transaction because of changes in the spot rate will be equivalent to the exchange loss realized in the forward transaction for the same reason, and vice versa. Changes in the spot rate are inconsequential to the gains or losses associated with a swap position. The important variable that determines the gains or losses in a swap position is the interest rate differential or swap rate. Changes in this differential rate will take place because of changes in interest rates in one or both of the currencies involved.

Creating a Swap Position.   If the expectations of the funds manager about interest rate differentials differ from those reflected by market rates, the funds manager may want to create a swap position to benefit from his or her judgment. With expectations such as the ones described previously, we can engineer transactions that will generate the following cash flows: (1) an inflow of dollars and an outflow in marks for day 31; and (2) an outflow of dollars and an inflow in marks for day 91. We can do this with two forward transactions or with two money market transactions. In the forward market we would sell marks against dollars for delivery on day 31 and buy marks against dollars for delivery on day 91. In the money markets we would borrow marks for 30 days and invest the proceeds for 90 days, and in the dollar money market we would borrow dollars for 90 days and invest the proceeds for 30 days.

Regardless of the approach followed, on day 31 there will be an inflow in dollars and an outflow in marks. The liquidity problem would be solved by converting the dollars into marks. However, we would then be left with the exchange position for day 91, long in marks and short in dollars. If our expectations are correct and the interest differential in favor of the dollar is greater than 4.2%, then we can cover the position by selling marks against dollars for delivery on day 91 at a premium on marks against dollars greater than 4.2%. The amount by which this premium is larger than 4.2% will be the net profit for 2 months, after accounting for the interest expense (or forward discounts) involved in the creation of the swap position. However, if the interest differential in favor of the dollar is less than 4.2%, there will be a loss.

Riding a Swap Position. Whether we let a swap position created by operations stand, or whether we create it in the expectation that we will profit from our judgment, on day 31 in the example we will be left with a net exchange position after settling the liquidity problem. Now we have three choices: (1) Let the exchange position stand and take the exchange risk; (2) Cover the exchange position without creating another swap position; or (3) Cover the exchange position, but roll over the earlier swap position.

If we let the exchange position stand, we will be converting the risk of changes in interest differentials we carried for the first 30 days of the swap position into a risk on changes in the spot rate between marks and dollars for the remaining 60 days. Interest rates would not be relevant to the calculation of eventual profits or losses from this position.

If we cover the exchange position without assuming any other risk, we would have to create an outflow in marks and an inflow in dollars for day 91 to match the cash flows expected in those currencies for that date. We could do this in the forward market or through the money markets. Afterward, we would have a square position: The net cash flows in each currency for every day will be zero, except for the costs involved in covering the exchange position.

In the last alternative, we would cover the exchange position, but retain a swap position. In this approach we would create cash flows in each currency to match those associated with the exchange position; however, the maturities of the cash flows used in the cover would be different from the cash flow maturities in the exchange position. We would eliminate the exchange position, but we would still have a swap position. Since we began the problem with a swap position, we would be rolling over or revising the swap position initially generated or created on day 1.

At any point while we have a swap position we have the choice of continuing with the swap position or closing it. Essentially, we continue comparing our expectations for future interest differentials with the expectations reflected in market rates. Whenever one set of expectations changes, it is time to review the swap position. In our earlier example, as long as we expect the future interest differential in favor of the dollar to be larger than the one anticipated by the market, we will want to maintain the swap position. At the point when this relationship between the two sets of expectations is reversed, we will want to close the swap position.[5]

Closing the swap position essentially means to square the position. We previously had an inflow in dollars and an outflow in marks on day 31, and the opposite flows for day 91. To square the position we would create an outflow in dollars and an inflow in marks for day 31 and the opposite flows for day 91. After these transactions (which can be done either in the forward market or in the two money markets), the cash flows in each currency for each date will be zero, except for the cost or return involved in closing the position at the existing market rates.

Exhibit 7.7 shows the cash flows associated with rolling over the

EXHIBIT 7.7   Rolling Over and Closing a Swap Position

Date	Transaction	CURRENCY* $	DM
	A. ROLLING OVER A SWAP POSITION IN THE FORWARD MARKET		
Day 31	Scheduled cash flows	+45,000	−100,000
	Convert $ into DM spot at $0.4515	−45,150	+100,000
	Sell DM against $ for delivery on day 61 at $0.4530/DM	ncf	ncf
	Net cash flows	−150	0
Day 61	Deliver on 30-day forward contract from day 31	+45,300	−100,000
	Net cash flows	+45,300	−100,000
Day 91	Scheduled net cash flows	−45,000	+100,000
	Net cash flows	−45,000	+100,000
Net exchange positions		+150	0
	B. CLOSING A SWAP POSITION IN THE FORWARD MARKET		
Day 46	Buy DM against $ for delivery on day 61 at $0.4484	ncf	ncf
	Sell DM against $ for delivery on day 91 at $0.4505/DM	ncf	ncf
	Net cash flows	ncf	ncf
Day 61	Deliver on 30-day contract from day 31	+45,300	−100,000
	Deliver on 15-day contract from day 46	−44,840	+100,000
	Net cash flows	+460	0
Day 91	Scheduled net cash flows	−45,000	+100,000
	Deliver on 45-day contract from day 46	+45,050	−100,000
	Net cash flows	+50	0
Net exchange positions		+510	0
	Net return		
	30 days at 4.2% 157.50		
	45 days at 5.4% 303.75		
	15 days at 3.2% 60.00		
	521.25		

*(+: Cash inflow; −: Cash outflow; ncf: No cash flow)

[5]The use of swaps with obviously unmatched maturities, but often with matched long and short positions in total value, has caused many international banks a great deal of trouble. For example, foreign exchange traders in branches (perhaps largely for the thrill of success) have caused large losses to Dai-Ichi Kangyo Bank, Japan's largest commercial bank [$36 million lost from yen/dollar speculation by a Singapore branch trader; see "Singapore Slings—and Arrows," *Economist*, Oct. 2, 1982, p. 90].

initial swap position on day 31 and then closing it on day 46, given the market rates presented earlier.

SUMMARY

Cash flow forecasts of receipts and payments in various currencies for future dates are the basis for international cash management. A *long position* involves inflows greater than outflows in a currency; a *short position* involves outflows greater than inflows. The money market and the forward market are the institutional settings for altering the cash flows generated by operations. An *exchange position* is a situation in which the ultimate costs or returns from cash flows are vulnerable to changes in the exchange rate between currencies over time. Similarly, an *interest rate position,* in which the costs or returns of cash flows in a single currency are subject to changes in the interest rates for various periods in the future, is a concern of a purely domestic corporation's treasurer as a traditional corporate finance issue. If two currencies are involved with future inflows and outflows and if there is a vulnerability to changes in interest rates over time, there is a *swap position*. A firm has a *square position* only when cash flows are matched with respect to both currency and maturity dates.

As the multinational firm carries on its operations, it will generate anticipated cash inflows and outflows in different currencies at particular dates. The managers may either cover or accept these risks regarding exchange and interest rates. In addition, if the managers believe the markets are clearly inefficient, and if the rates implied in the forward rates and interest rate yield curves are different from their own anticipations, then they may actually create exchange and interest rate positions.

In facing foreign exchange risks, a manager may choose to cover using either the forward market (by buying a foreign currency forward to meet a need for that currency at day N, for example) or the money market (by borrowing domestically and lending in the foreign currency for maturity date N). The costs for these strategies may differ, depending on the presence of foreign exchange controls in a country and the credit risk premiums to different borrowers in different countries. Thus, the manager will want to study the money market and forward market costs in both the domestic markets and Euromarkets. In addition, the financial reporting requirements for different covering transactions may vary, and this consideration may play a part in the manager's decision.

The manager who accepts risks rather than covers them is typically expecting lower costs from bearing an acceptable degree of uncertainty versus high costs from transactions that prevent bad outcomes in the foreign exchange position. Given a tolerable level of uncertainty, this anticipated cost savings from taking a risk may cause some managers to create foreign exchange positions, rather than simply to react to the positions created by operations. Regardless of the particular maturity dates of the firm's money market or forward market commitment, the manager can *roll over* the transactions to maintain a position, thus repeatedly adding the losses or gains to the position. Alternatively, when the expectations of the manager are realized and the markets move in the directions anticipated, positions can be *closed out* by reversing transactions, without waiting for the particular maturity dates in the forward contracts or money market instruments. Such early closings can occur when the manager revises expectations to match the market. Short-term cash needs, such as for franc financing for the next 30 days until an inflow of francs on day 30 occurs, can often create a foreign exchange position. In many cases, managers will use *swapped funds*. In the last example, this would be accomplished by borrowing marks, converting to francs, and selling the francs forward against the mark at the time of the borrowing for delivery on day 30.

An *interest rate risk* occurs when the inflows and outflows of a currency do not match; a typical example would be a need to finance an outflow of Swiss francs in 10 days, which will be offset by an inflow of Swiss francs in 30 days. Since the rates today for 10-day and 30-day franc funds imply the rate for 20-day francs commencing 10 days hence, a manager may be in a position to cover this risk or to accept it. Using swapped funds, the manager might use other currencies for funding, locking in exchange rates relative to francs; yet, these other currency borrowings and lendings might still involve accepting or covering the 20-day interest rate risk for 10 days hence. In accepting such a position, when the manager's forecast versus the market is eventually fulfilled or dispelled, the manager can close the position regardless of the particular maturity dates of the instruments. Similarly, positions can be rolled over regardless of the actual operating cash flow needs by simply entering additional transactions that perpetuate an interest rate risk position.

When the firm is vulnerable to changes in *interest rate differentials*, it has a swap position. Separate solutions involve reviewing the rates for each currency for the future periods that are implied in the prevailing money market rates today. A joint solution involves two transactions in the forward market that offset the inflows and outflows in the two currencies for each future date. Given transaction costs, the joint solution typically involves lower total costs than a pair of separate solutions. Again, accepting or creating a swap position depends on the manager's forecast for interest rate differentials for a future period that differ from those implied in the market. As in the previous examples, the manager can roll over positions or close them early, depending on how the expectations and reality coincide over time.

QUESTIONS

1. "As long as the forward rate for the currency is below the spot rate, I should cover my transactions if I have receivables in that currency; the forward discount shows that the currency is likely to devalue." Do you agree with this statement? Why?

2. A French exporter scheduled to receive payment in Italian liras sells the liras on a forward contract, so that she knows the franc value of the receivable. How will she know the cost of this cover? When will she know the cost?

3. A U.S. distributor purchases valves from Norway in the amount of Norwegian kronor 22,850 (approximately $5,000). Payment in Norwegian kronor is due in 3 months. The market scenario is summarized in the accompanying table.

		DAY 90		
	DAY 1	Case A	Case B	Case C
Exchange Rates				
Spot	$0.218850	$0.218850	$0.240735	$0.196965
3-month forward	$0.218140			
Interest Rates				
United States	9.00%	9.00%	9.00%	9.00%
Norway	10.30%	10.30%	10.80%	10.80%

(a) On day 1 what is the premium or discount on the forward Norwegian kronor? What is the interest differential between the United States and Norway? Is there an incentive for interest arbitrage?

(b) If the importer wants to cover its transaction against foreign exchange risks, what alternatives are open?

(c) What is the cost of each alternative? (i) Assume that a 3-month Treasury bill is bought. (ii) Assume that a 1-year bill is bought. (Do not make specific calculations in the latter case.)

(d) Would you advise the importer to cover the foreign exchange transaction? Why or why not?

4. Under what situations would a president of a firm want to monitor the foreign exchange exposure positions of its international treasurer?

What data would a board of directors need to review the performance of the treasurer's activities? Do you believe the boards of most U.S. multinationals have such information? Do you believe they could interpret the information correctly if it were available?

5. A bank wishes to prevent its traders from having net long or short positions in a currency, and so monitors the total future obligations in particular currencies. How could a foreign exchange trader avoid showing swap positions to his superiors in a bank?

BIBLIOGRAPHY

See the references for Chapters 5, 6, and 10.

TREASURERS' PROBLEMS

Market Scenario for Problems 1–5

Exchange Market

Spot rate	DM2.00/$
3-month forward	DM1.97/$

Money Market: Interbank Eurorates

	$	DM
3 months	13%	7%
6 months	12%	6%

---

1. If I borrow marks for 3 months at 7%, and invest in dollars for the same period at 13%, I do not make any profit when I cover the exchange risk. Why?

2. I need dollars for 3 months and I am tempted by the lower interest rates in marks. If I borrow marks for 3 months to meet my financing needs, under what conditions would this be a profitable decision? Under what conditions would this decision generate losses? [*Note:* I expect a dollar inflow in 3 months.]

3. Again, I need dollars for 3 months and I am tempted by the lower interest rates in marks. In addition, I would now like to take advantage of the downward-sloping yield curve and borrow marks for 6 months (instead of 3 months). If I borrow marks for 6 months to meet my dollar financing needs, under what conditions would this be a profitable decision? Under what conditions would this decision generate losses? [*Note:* I still expect the dollar inflow in 3 months.]

4. Refer to question 3. What must I do to cover the exchange position for 3 months? What are the risks after the cover?

5. I am a car dealer in the United States. I import German cars for which I have to pay in marks.

   (a) What are the exchange risks in this operation?

   (b) How can I hedge the exchange risk in the short term? Over the long term? What are the costs of hedging in the short term? In the long term?

6. Ms. Martinez, an exchange trader, is convinced that the Dutch guilder is presently undervalued relative to the U.S. dollar. She wants to profit from her analysis.

Market Scenario for Problem 6	
Exchange Market	
Spot rate	$0.4954
30-day forward rate	0.4976
Spot rate forecasted by Ms. Martinez for day 30	0.4990
Money Market: 1-Month Interbank Rates	
Dollar	11.25%
Guilder	5.95%

   (a) What is the premium or discount of the forward guilder against the dollar?

   (b) Based on interest rate parity, what should the 30-day guilder forward rate be? Why might the actual rate differ? Does it differ in this case?

   (c) What choices does Ms. Martinez have to profit from her forecast of the future value of the guilder?

   (d) What are the costs and gains of each alternative if on day 30 the actual spot rate is:

Case A	Case B	Case C
$0.4954	$0.4990	$0.5010

   (e) What course of action would you advise Ms. Martinez to follow? Why?

7. Hector Blinkowski is convinced that the German mark is presently undervalued relative to the Swiss franc. He would like to profit from his analysis.

Market Scenario for Problem 7

Exchange Market

Spot rate	SwF0.8986
30-day forward rate	0.8951
Spot rate forecasted for day 30 by Mr. Blinkowski	0.8990

Money Market: 1-Month Interbank Rates

Swiss franc	4.33%
German mark	9.00%

(a) What is the premium or discount of the forward German mark against the Swiss franc?

(b) Based on interest rate parity, what should the 30-day mark forward rate be? Why might the actual rate be different? Does it differ in this case?

(c) How can Hector profit from his analysis of the future value of the mark relative to the Swiss franc?

(d) For each of the following possible spot rates on day 30, what would be the profits or losses of the suggested transactions?

Case A	Case B	Case C
SwF0.8930	SwF0.8951	SwF0.8990

(e) What would you advise Hector to do? Why?

8. Based on her research on Britain's economic conditions, Lola Jacobs is sure that the pound is overvalued relative to the U.S. dollar. She would like to profit from her analysis.

Market Scenario for Problem 8

Exchange Market

Spot rate	$2.4480
30-day forward rate	$2.4417
Spot rate forecasted for day 30 by Ms. Jacobs	$2.4375

Money Market: 1-Month Interbank Rates

U.S. dollar	14.00%
Pound sterling	17.81%

(a) What is the premium or discount on the forward pound sterling against the U.S. dollar?

(b) Based on interest rate parity, what should the 30-day dollar forward rate be? Why might this rate differ from the actual rate? Is it different?

(c) In what ways can Lola profit from her analysis?

(d) If the spot rate on day 30 turns out to be one of the following, what would be the potential profits or losses from the suggested transactions?

Case A	Case B	Case C
$2.4480	$2.4417	$2.4375

(e) What would you advise Lola to do?

9. Mr. Plinkus, a trader at one of the major banks in New York, has received information from the economic research department of his bank that interest rates in U.S. dollars are bound to increase by 100 basis points within 1 month (100 basis points equal 1%). He does not think the interest rates on the Canadian dollar will change during the forecast period.

Market Scenario for Problem 9	
Money Market: 1-Year Interbank Rates	
U.S. dollar	13.13%
Canadian dollar	12.56%
Exchange Market	
Spot rate	$0.8560/Can$
1-year forward rate	$0.8610/Can$

(a) What is the premium or discount of the forward Canadian dollar against the U.S. dollar?

(b) What interest rates (on Canadian dollars and on U.S. dollars) and exchange rates (spot and forward) does Mr. Plinkus expect to prevail in 1 month? (Assume flat yield curves in both currencies.) If Mr. Plinkus is bound by the rule "buys equal sells," what opportunities does he have to profit from the information given to him by his economic research department?

(c) Specify the costs or gains of each alternative for each of the following conditions:

(i) The U.S. dollar interest rates increase to 14.13% within 1 month.

(ii) Interest rates remain constant.

(iii) Spot Canadian dollars on day 30 are $0.8550.

(d) What course of action would you advise the trader to follow?

10. Mlle. Prideux, a trader at one of the major banks in Paris, has concluded that interest rates in German marks are going to increase by 100 basis points within 1 month, based on a report from her bank's research department (100 basis points equal 1%). She does not expect the interest rates on the French franc to change within a month.

Market Scenario for Problem 10
Money Market: 1-Year Interbank Rates

French franc	9.50%
German mark	7.50%

Exchange Market

Spot rate	FF2.3024/DM
1-year forward rate	FF2.3484/DM

(a) What is the premium or discount of the German mark against the French franc?

(b) What interest rates (on marks and on francs) and exchange rates (spot and forward) does Mlle. Prideux expect to prevail in 1 month? (Assume flat yield curves in both currencies.) If Mlle. Prideux is bound by the rule "buys equal sells," what opportunities does she have to profit from the information provided by her research department?

(c) Determine the costs or gains of each alternative for each of the following situations:

(i) The interest rate on the mark increases to 8.50% within 1 month.

(ii) Interest rates remain constant.

(iii) Spot marks on day 30 are FF2.3000.

(d) What course of action would you advise the trader to follow?

11. Mr. Pontaro, a trader for a money-center bank in a large midwestern city, believes that various indicators show that interest rates on U.S. dollars will fall by 100 basis points within 1 month (100 basis points

equal 1%). The one major currency whose investments will probably not be affected is the Swiss franc.

Market Scenario for Problem 11

Money Market: 1-Year Interbank Rates

U.S. dollar	13.25%
Swiss franc	5.35%

Exchange Market

Spot rate	$0.5965/SwF
1-year forward rate	$0.6436/SwF

(a) What is the premium or discount of the forward Swiss franc against the U.S. dollar?

(b) What interest rates (on U.S. dollars and on Swiss francs) and exchange rates (spot and forward) does Mr. Pontaro expect to prevail within 1 month? (Assume flat yield curves in both currencies.) If Mr. Pontaro is bound by the rule "buys equal sells," how would he profit from this information in the money market? In the forward market? Which would produce the higher profit if U.S. dollar interest rates fell to 12.25%?

(c) If the spot rate on day 30 is $0.5850/SwF and the dollar short-term interest rate is 12.75%, how much would he lose using the forward market method? The money market method? (Assume interest rate parity holds.)

(d) Which market would you advise Mr. Pontaro to use?

12. A U.S. construction firm purchases timber from a Canadian company for Can$20,000. Payment in Canadian dollars is due in 6 months.

		DAY 181		
	DAY 1	Case A	Case B	Case C
Exchange Rates				
Spot	$0.8560	$0.8560	$0.8750	$0.8425
6-month forward	$0.8614			
Interest Rates				
U.S. dollar	11.76%	11.76%	11.76%	11.76%
Canadian dollar	10.50%	10.50%	11.00%	9.50%

(a) On day 1, is there an incentive for interest arbitrage? Why?

(b) If the U.S. firm wanted to avoid foreign exchange risks, how could it do this using the forward exchange market? The money market?

(c) What is the cost of each alternative for all cases?

(d) Can the transaction be covered by buying a 1-year Treasury bill in the relevant currency? (Do not make specific calculations.)

(e) Would you advise the firm to cover the foreign exchange transaction? Why?

13. A Dutch importer buys wine from a French distributor for FF25,000. He must pay the distributor in 3 months in French francs.

	DAY 1	DAY 90		
		Case A	Case B	Case C
Exchange Rates				
Spot	Hfl0.4699	Hfl0.4699	Hfl0.5010	Hfl0.4250
3-month forward	Hfl0.4671			
Interest Rates				
Dutch guilder (Hfl)	9.45%	9.45%	9.45%	9.45%
French franc (FF)	11.83%	11.83%	10.50%	13.25%

(a) What is the premium or discount on the forward French franc? Is there an incentive for interest arbitrage?

(b) How could the importer cover his transaction against foreign exchange risks using the forward exchange market? The money market?

(c) What is the potential cost of both alternatives in all three cases?

(d) Should the importer cover the foreign exchange transaction? Why or why not?

(e) What are the implications of doing the hedging operation for a maturity of 1 year, instead of 3 months?

14. A Swiss manufacturer exports chocolate to Canada. He will receive Can$15,000 in 3 months.

	DAY 1	DAY 90		
		Case A	Case B	Case C
Exchange Rates				
Spot	SwF1.4350	SwF1.4350	SwF1.4525	SwF1.3975
3-month forward	SwF1.4114			
Interest Rates				
Swiss franc (SwF)	5.35%	5.35%	5.35%	5.35%
Canadian dollar (Can$)	11.93%	11.93%	9.54%	13.42%

(a) Is there an incentive for interest arbitrage on day 1? Why?

(b) If the Swiss exporter is afraid of foreign exchange risks, how could he avoid them using the forward exchange market? The money market?

(c) What is the cost of each alternative for all three cases?

(d) Can the transaction be covered by buying a 1-year Treasury bill in the relevant currency? Why or why not?

(e) If you were the exporter, would you cover the transaction? Why or why not? If you would cover, which method would you use?

15. After conducting a research project required for her international finance class, Jane Barone is convinced that the Dutch guilder is undervalued against the dollar. She has decided to speculate in the International Monetary Market to profit from her forecast.

Contract size:	Hfl125,000
Minimum price fluctuation:	.0001 (1 point) = $12.50/contract
Maximum price fluctuation:	.0100 (100 points) = $1,250/contract
Minimum margin:	Initial $1,200
	Maintenance $ 900
Spot rate:	$0.4954/Hfl

(a) How much cash would Jane need to buy two contracts on Monday? (Ignore brokers' fees.)

(b) If the next day (Tuesday) the price closed at $0.4924, what would happen?

(c) If the price rose 20 points on Tuesday, could Jane gain $3,000 on Wednesday? Why?

(d) If Jane closed her position 104 points above the purchase price, what gain would she realize?

16. Geoff Marke received $5,000 as a gift after completing graduate school and would like to speculate in foreign exchange. After studying those currencies offered in the International Monetary Market, he decided that the Japanese yen was overvalued.

Contract size:	¥12,500,000
Minimum price fluctuation:	.000001 (1 point) = $12.50/contract
Maximum price fluctuation:	.000100 (100 points) = $1,250/contract
Minimum margin:	Initial $1,500
	Maintenance $1,000
Spot rate:	$0.004710/¥

(a) Should Geoff buy a contract to deliver yen or to take delivery of yen in order to speculate based on his research?

(b) How many contracts could Geoff buy with his graduation gift? (Ignore brokers' fees.)

(c) If Geoff bought two contracts and the price rose 50 points the next day, what would happen? (Assume the contracts were in the direction you advised in part a.)

(d) On the day he closed his position the price was 150 points below the original rate. What gain or loss did Geoff realize?

17. A business trip to Mexico has convinced Bill McMahon, a financial analyst, that the Mexican peso is undervalued. He decided to speculate on this belief by buying four contracts for Mexican pesos in the International Monetary Market.

Contract size:	MexPs1,000,000
Minimum price fluctuation:	.00001 (1 point) = $10.00/contract
Maximum price fluctuation:	.00150 (150 points) = $1,500/contract
Minimum margin:	Initial $4,000
	Maintenance $3,000
Spot rate:	$0.04350/MexPs

(a) How much cash did Bill have to pay to buy his contracts? (Ignore brokers' fees.)

(b) If the next day the price closed at $0.04275, would Bill's broker issue a margin call? Why?

(c) If the price rose 150 points on each of the last two days, what is the maximum Bill could gain today?

(d) The price of a contract on the day Bill closed his position was 175 points below the original price. What was the gain or loss Bill realized?

18. A Chicago manufacturing company needs to send cash to its plant in Germany. In 6 months, on December 1, the plant will return the amount, DM500,000. The treasurer is worried about the exchange risk so he has decided to hedge this transaction in the International Monetary Market.

Spot rate on June 1	$0.5360
December futures rate	$0.5400

(a) How would the company hedge this transaction?

(b) If on December 1 the futures rate is $0.5415 and the spot rate is $0.5410, what are the firm's gains or losses?

(c) If on December 1 the futures rate is $0.5350 and the spot rate is $0.5300, what are the firm's gains or losses?

19. An exporter in Peoria will receive ¥ 12,500,000 in 4 months on October 1. Due to the unsettled condition of the U.S. economy, she believes that the exchange risk is very high and so has decided to hedge the transaction in the International Monetary Market.

Spot rate on April 1	$0.004710
October futures rate	$0.004810

(a) How can the exporter hedge this transaction?

(b) If on October 1 the December futures rate is $0.004900 and the spot rate is $0.004875, what is the exporter's gain or loss?

(c) If on October 1 the December futures rate is $0.004650 and the spot rate is $0.004625, what is the exporter's gain or loss?

20. An importer in San Francisco has to pay FF250,000 in 5 months, on June 1, for perfume he received today. He would like to hedge this transaction against exchange risk, but does not have access to a bank's foreign exchange trader. Therefore, he has decided to hedge using the International Monetary Market.

Spot rate on February 1	$0.2328
June futures rate	$0.2342

(a) How can he hedge this transaction?

(b) If on June 1 the futures rate is $0.2370 and the spot rate is $0.2365, what is the importer's gain or loss on this exchange transaction? Did it pay to hedge?

(c) If on June 1 the futures rate is $0.2210 and the spot rate is $0.2200, what is the importer's gain or loss on this exchange transaction?

21. Based on her analysis of economic conditions, Sharon Byrne believes that the interest rate on French francs will drop 1% within the next month. She wants to use this analysis to make money, using the International Monetary Market.

Minimum contract size: FF250,000	
Interest rates:	
U.S. dollar	10%
French franc	9%
Spot rate:	$0.2328
Future rates:	
March	$0.2332
December	$0.2351

(a) How can she profit from this knowledge if she follows the rule "buys equal sells"?

(b) If on day 30 the futures rate for December contracts is $0.2378, the March rate is $0.2339, and the spot rate is $0.2335, what is her gain or loss?

(c) If on day 30 the futures rate for December contracts is $0.2257, the March rate is $0.2219, and the spot rate is $0.2215, what is her gain or loss?

22. Bob Diety, a graduate student at a large midwestern university, is sure that interest rates on the U.S. dollar are going to go up 1% within the next month. To profit from this belief he has decided to buy a contract in Canadian dollars in the International Monetary Market.

Contract size:	Can$100,000
Interest rates:	
U.S. dollar	11.0%
Canadian dollar	12.5%
Spot rate:	$0.8560
Futures rates:	
March	$0.8539
September	$0.8432

(a) What action should Bob take if he follows the rule "buys equal sells"? Why should he follow this rule?

(b) If on day 30 the futures rate for September contracts is $0.8525, for a March contract is $0.8560, and the spot rate is $0.8564, what is his gain or loss?

(c) If on day 30 the futures rate for September contracts is $0.7975, for March contracts is $0.8009, and the spot rate is $0.8012, what is his gain or loss?

(d) If on day 30 the rates are as quoted in part c and the Canadian dollar interest rate is 12.5%, what would the U.S. dollar interest rate be? (Assume interest rate parity holds.)

23. After researching European interest rates for a school project, Jean Barsanti is positive that the Swiss franc interest rate will rise 1.5% within the next month. She decided to use the International Monetary Market to profit from this situation.

Contract size:	SwF125,000
Interest rates:	
U.S. dollar	11.00%
Swiss franc	3.00%
Spot rate:	$0.5965
Futures rates:	
March	$0.6045
December	$0.6442

(a) If she follows the rule "buys equal sells," what should Jean do to profit from her analysis?

(b) If on day 30 the futures rate for December contracts is $0.6585, for March contracts is $0.6249, and the spot rate $0.6215, what is Jean's gain or loss?

(c) If on day 30 the futures rate for December contracts is $0.6220, for March contracts is $0.5902, and the spot rate is $0.5870, what is her gain or loss?

(d) If on day 30 the rates are as quoted in part b and the U.S. dollar interest rate is 8.00%, what would the Swiss franc interest rate be? (Assume interest rate parity holds.)

DOW
CHEMICAL
COMPANY

WILSON GAY, CORPORATE treasurer of Dow Chemical, had spent a whole day discussing the financial practices of Dow with Ms. Adela Mederos, a consultant. It was only at the end of the day, over dinner, when Mr. Gay turned to her and asked, "Frankly, what do you think of our operations? You talk to many financial officers in the multinational companies. What are they doing? How do we compare with them? We are somewhat isolated here in Midland. We think that is good. While we can obtain on the phone information we need—never mind the stream of bankers who are always passing by—we think we are not affected by the recurring fads that a bunch of treasurers and bankers talking to each other all the time in places like New York can create. However, once in a while we get curious as to what other people are doing."

"Well, you are the only treasurer of a major U.S. company I know who brags about speculating and making money in the foreign exchange market," Ms. Mederos responded with a smile of incredulity on her face.

Actually, it had been interest in a recent article about Dow's aggressive practices in the exchange markets that had brought Ms. Mederos to Dow Chemical this time. The subtitle of that article read: "Most companies shudder at the idea of speculating in currencies to make a profit. But Dow Chemical thinks there's more to the currency game than just hedging."[1] Dow's practices ran counter to the thinking of most financial officers in the United States who thought that speculation in exchange markets was not appropriate for industrial companies. Dow's practices also ran against the prescriptions of the many academicians who thought the foreign exchange markets were generally efficient; that is, profits could not be realized consistently by forecasting movements in exchange rates because all the available information was already reflected in the observed exchange rates.

---

[1]Laura White Dillon, "Dow's Controversial Currency Strategy," *Institutional Investor*, July 1979, pp. 159–60.

THE FINANCE FUNCTION AT DOW CHEMICAL

Historical Background

Finance traditionally had played a very important role at Dow Chemical. In an industry where the historical giant, DuPont, had resisted issuing long-term debt or preferred stock until the mid-1970s, and where most companies maintained a ratio of long-term debt to total capital of about 30%, Dow Chemical's comparable ratio of 40%–45% stood out. Beginning with the initial capital when Herbert Dow had to sell company shares from door to door in Midland, Michigan, and continuing with Dow's large foreign expansion in the 1960s and 1970s, external funding and good financial planning were central to the success of Dow Chemical.

From the post–World War II period through the early 1960s, Dow's presence in international markets had been largely in the form of exports from the United States. Management of these international operations was conducted through an international division and their financing was controlled from the corporate treasury department in Midland. Exports grew at a fast pace with the reconstruction of Europe. By 1962, the company decided that further penetration of foreign markets would require increased physical presence of Dow Chemical in foreign countries. So, beginning in 1962, new Dow plants began to appear all over Europe first, and in other areas of the world later. By 1979 foreign sales, excluding exports from the United States, represented half of the $9.2 billion total sales of Dow Chemical.

To accompany the changes in operations, the company was restructured for management purposes in the mid-1960s. The international division was disbanded and the foreign operations were organized into four different geographical areas: Europe/Africa, Latin America, Canada, and the Pacific. In the late 1970s Brazil became an independent area from Latin America. Each of the areas was then endowed with full responsibility for all the business functions, including finance, but excluding research and development.

The decentralization of the finance function took several years to become operational. For some time, financing remained reinforced by the mode chosen to finance the foreign expansion. In 1962, Carl Gerstacker, then chairman of the board, had a position paper prepared in which a weak U.S. dollar was anticipated in coming years. With a sizable investment program envisioned for foreign countries, the implication of this paper were clear: Borrow U.S. dollars as much, and as soon, as possible. As a result, between 1963 and 1968, the treasury in Midland assumed the functions of a pseudo-central bank for Dow Chemical as a whole, administering the dollar funds raised and disbursing them as needed.

Another factor that delayed the decentralization of the finance function was the need to tighten the control over the flow of funds in general and collections in particular. To facilitate this control, Dow acquired in 1963 a 40% interest (later reduced to 29%) in a Dutch bank, Bank Mendes Gans (BMG). The bank was put in charge of collections for exports from the United States, the clearing of intercompany accounts, and collections from European sales. This move helped to control credit and to generate accurate daily balances. The next step was to control the amount of float involved in check clearances through European banks. This required tough negotiations with the other European banks, but soon this aspect of the collection system was also controlled efficiently.

With proper financial controls in place and more and more plants abroad becoming operational, the area concept required the appointment of area treasurers. By 1967, each of the four foreign areas had a treasurer physically located in the area. These treasurers reported administratively to their area presidents and functionally to the corporate treasurer.

Financial Policies

The unifying force in this highly decentralized organization was the budget. Each unit in the company was responsible for preparing specific plans on a monthly basis for 1 year ahead. Subsidiaries' plans were first reviewed and aggregated at the country level and then at the area level. Then they were sent to corporate headquarters. The financial plan followed the same pattern. At each level the financial plan provided information on anticipated levels for short- and long-term debt, marketable securities and time deposits, cash, currency exposures, interest expense and income, and foreign exchange gains or losses. After approval by the treasury department, the financial plan was incorporated into the management plan for the following year. Afterward, corporate treasury monitored planned versus actual figures on a monthly basis. Exhibit C.1 presents the control form used by treasury for this purpose.

The long-term financial philosophy of Dow Chemical had remained fundamentally the same since Mr. Gerstacker's position paper in 1962—a philosophy based on a weak U.S. dollar. Within this overall philosophy (which was not considered to apply constantly in every quarter of every year), the foremost financial objective at Dow Chemical was to minimize financial expenses. The cost was defined to in-

EXHIBIT C.1 The Dow Chemical Company: *Financial Expenses Plan (millions of U.S. dollars)*

	MONTH			YEAR TO DATE		
	1979	1980		1979	1980	
		Plan	Actual		Plan	Actual
Interest income						
Interest expense						
Capitalized interest[a]						
Net interest expense						
Foreign Exchange (Forex)						
Operations[b]						
DBC/Dow finance[c]						
Net Forex						
Total financial expenses						

[a]As per Financial Accounting Standards Board Statement #34 which capitalizes interest cost for capital assets under construction.

[b]Includes gains and losses on translation and transaction exposures.

[c]Translation gains or losses due to consolidation on an equity basis of Dow Banking Corp. in Switzerland and Dow Finance Hong Kong.

clude net interest expense as well as exchange gains or losses. Thus, the overall foreign exchange management policy followed the consequences of the financing choices, instead of dictating these choices. Dow's policies acknowledged that a zero exposure to foreign exchange risk was preferred, other things constant. However, treasury was not willing to pay much in terms of suboptimal financing sources in order to avoid an exchange exposure.

The decisions of whether to hedge exchange transactions related to regular operations were left to the areas. However, "unusual" currency transactions required the approval of corporate treasury, whether hedged or not. At the corporate level, reports containing a combination of translation and transaction exposure figures by currency (adjusted by outstanding forward exchange contracts) were monitored constantly.[2]

Although corporate treasury maintained a close supervision over the financial operations of the areas, financial charges and exchange gains and losses were ultimately the responsibility of the area presidents. Thus, the area president and the area treasurer had the primary responsibility for managing the currency exposure of their area—after all, the decision affected directly the bottom line of the area income statement. However, corporate treasury still could take financial measures to counteract the decision taken by an area. For example, if an

---

[2]*Transaction exposure* is the same as net exchange position, the concept discussed in the preceding chapters. *Translation exposure* is the net of certain assets and liabilities in each currency in the balance sheet. Translation exposure will be discussed in Chapter 10 in this text.

area president borrowed sterling over dollars in the belief that sterling would depreciate in the near future, treasury could counteract this decision if it did not share the views about the future of sterling. In this case, corporate treasury would purchase sterling against dollars in the forward market. From the point of view of the area, the area income statement would show only the effects of the desired sterling borrowings. However, for the corporation as a whole, treasury's operation locked in the cost of sterling at the rate of nominal interest plus the forward premium or discount of sterling.

Prior to 1980 corporate headquarters were neither a profit nor a loss center. Thus, gains or losses in foreign exchange realized by corporate treasury were allocated to the relevant area. Gains were readily accepted by the areas; however, losses were quite another matter and often caused friction between the areas and headquarters. In early 1980, this practice was changed and corporate treasury was allowed to keep the profits and losses generated from its independent decisions. By the end of 1980, these profits amounted to nearly $12 million.

CORPORATE TREASURY
AND THE AREA TREASURERS

In spite of the elaborate procedure to develop financial plans and the statement of general policies to which Dow's management adhered, this fact remained: The plan was no better than the assumptions that went into its preparation. If these assumptions proved to be wrong, so were the financing prescriptions of the plan.

Thus, treasury was prompt to admit that the financial plan represented only a good starting point. It did not believe that treasury or the area treasurers had to adhere to the plan if the financial markets indicated otherwise. Once the financial plan was approved by the corporate management, treasury believed it could go ahead on the basis of the feeling for the market that treasury and the area treasurers had. There was no formal requirement to obtain permission to depart from the anticipated financing strategies as long as treasury approved it. Wilson Gay, in particular, felt he had freedom to follow his best judgment without asking for further approval from senior management. However, treasury maintained continuous communication with the corporate vice-president in charge of finance and with certain members of the finance committee. Thus, major shifts in financing plans and currency exposures were discussed in advance. In addition, treasury reported its results to the finance committee on a monthly basis.

Some Success Stories

The morning the consultant came to Dow in March 1980 provided a good example of the success that the flexibility enjoyed by the treasury department at Dow Chemical had produced. Early in January of the same year, treasury officials had become convinced that the U.S. dollar would firm in the exchange markets in the near future and that the Swiss franc would weaken against the dollar in the coming months. Needless to say, this was not a popular view at the time and even within Dow there were different points of view.

At the corporate level there was a need to raise $300 million in January. The financial plan anticipated that these funds would be obtained from the U.S. commercial paper market. However, given treasury's view of the dollar relative to the Swiss franc, a decision was made to raise part of the needed funds (SwF100 million) in Swiss francs at an average rate of 3.2% for 2 months while the franc was at SwF1.6553/$. Since these Swiss francs were borrowed, the resulting short position had been watched closely from day to day. Finally, on March 11, the day of the visit of the consultant, the position had been closed. Wilson Gay thought that at SwF1.74—that day's spot rate—the franc had reached a "resistance level" beyond which it would not fall. To close the position, Swiss francs were purchased in the forward market at 1.7265 for delivery on March 24, 1980.

The net of the 2-month position had been a total gain of $3 million, composed of a $2.5 million gain in foreign exchange and a $0.5 million savings in interest expense for the funds that were now available through March 24. In the same manner that treasury had departed originally from the financial plan when they thought the exchange markets warranted it, they had closed the position when they thought the market had stabilized again. Although the Swiss franc continued to depreciate in the days immediately following in response to measures announced by the Carter administration, this trend reversed itself so that by late May the franc was at SwF1.63/$.

Taking positions on the Swiss franc was done not only against the U.S. dollar, but also against other currencies. During early February 1979, treasury had borrowed Swiss francs at 1% per annum while the spot rate was at SwF1.69/$. The proceeds were then invested in Canadian dollars at 11% while the spot rate was US$0.8703/Can$. With an interest differential of 10%, corporate treasury thought that shorting the Swiss franc and going long on Canadian dollars offered a fine opportunity. About 2 months later, the position was closed after the Swiss franc had depreciated to SwF1.71/$ and the Canadian dollar had appreciated to US$0.8749/Can$. Thus, an exchange gain was added to the interest gain to generate a total profit in the transaction of about half a million dollars in 2 months.

These positions on the Swiss franc were not without perils. Wilson Gay remembered the experience of late Summer 1979, when treasury had decided to borrow SwF270 million to take advantage of 10%–11% interest differentials against the U.S. dollar. He thought the dollar–Swiss franc exchange rate would stabilize after the dollar depreciations of the earlier part of that summer. So, Swiss francs were borrowed while the spot rate was SwF1.66 in late August. However, in September the dollar came under severe pressure and the Swiss franc appreciated, generating translation losses of up to $2 million *per day*. At the October meeting of the finance committee, some of the members were in favor of taking the losses and closing the position. It took a lot of nerve, but the recommendation of corporate treasury to keep the position open was followed. This was to be rewarded, since the tide in the market finally began to ebb in response to the measures taken by the Federal Reserve in early October. By the time the Swiss franc loan was repaid at the end of November, the dollar had recovered sufficiently to produce a small profit on foreign exchange. The translation loss had not materialized and corporate treasury had taken advantage of 10%–11% savings in interest payments, which represented about $4 million. It had been difficult, but Wilson Gay was certain that if they had taken the loss, the freedom to take such exchange positions in the future would have been curtailed severely.

Taking exchange positions was not confined to the Swiss franc. In March 1978, treasury had decided that the yen was very likely to appreciate and convinced Dow Pacific to take a long position in yen. The Pacific area treasurer decided that the cheapest way to finance a long position in yen was to borrow Hong Kong dollars. Accordingly, Hong Kong dollars were borrowed at 5.42% per annum for 6 months while the spot rate was HK$4.61/$. The proceeds were invested in yen yielding 2.77% per annum and the conversion was done when the yen was at ¥234.5/$. Six months later the interest cost had not only been covered, but the large appreciation of the yen to ¥182.3/$, combined with a small depreciation of the Hong Kong dollar, generated a net gain of about $12 million on a position of $40 million over 6 months.

While the latter transaction appeared to have been done smoothly, its inception was not without problems. The Dow Pacific area management was not nearly as bullish on the outlook for the yen-dollar relationship as was corporate treasury. The area was reluctant to take a major long position in the yen since a mistake would have had a material impact on its profits. It was only after repeated urgings from the corporation (which began in Fall 1977), with the recommendation that the correct long yen position was $40 million, that the Pacific area finally moved. If the Pacific area had not taken the recommended long position by March 1978, corporate treasury would have moved.

The discretionary power enjoyed by corporate treasury in Midland was extended to some degree also to the area treasurers. A good example of this situation occurred in 1979 when the positive feelings that corporate treasury had always had for Mexico were reinforced by the comments made by Dow's president, Paul Oreffice, after a visit to the country. Thus, it was decided to transfer up to $20 million to the treasurer in charge of Latin America to invest in Mexico as best he saw fit. After hesitant beginnings with investments in Mexican commercial paper and partial liquidation of the investments in June with the fears of a Mexican peso devaluation, further encouragement from corporate treasury caused the Latin America treasurer to invest up to $16 million in securities issued by Petroleos Mejicanos for a total yield of 52%. The effects of this investment turned the planned financial expenses for Latin America into profits. For 1979 the plan called for $7.1 million in net financial *expenses*; the actual figures showed a net *profit* of $3.2 million. Wilson Gay reflected on this operation and commented, "Toro (the Latin America treasurer) would not have been so bold to do this on his own, but we gave him the elbow room to operate, and the encouragement to take the risk."

Some Snags in the System

That elbow room for the area treasurers to operate was considered by Wilson Gay to be essential to the proper functioning of the treasury department. Thus, even when treasury would have preferred to transfer excess funds out of a country, a certain portion of those funds was left with the local treasurer. The objective was to maintain sufficient incentive for that person to follow the developments in the local market and possibly to come up with a better alternative. A case in point was Argentina in 1979. Wilson Gay thought that the return of 26% available in the local market at the time was not as interesting as some alternative investments in other currencies, given the local annual rate of inflation of nearly 300% in recent years and a history of severe peso devaluations. However, the treasurer for Argentina was allowed to keep the usual amount of excess funds in the local market so the proper incentives for good performance were maintained.

The corporation's willingness to give freedom to the area management to choose the financing of their operations could also create some problems. For example, the new plant built in Korea in 1977–1979 had its debt portion of the total financing raised in sterling at 8¼% in the

form of export credit guarantees issued by the export agency of the
United Kingdom. This created a short position in sterling to which both
the area and the corporation agreed. Through 1979, the Pacific area
management insisted that sterling was weak and that the short position
on sterling should be maintained. Treasury thought sterling would be
strong in 1979, but the area management's opinion prevailed over treasury's. The result was a $7 million exchange loss as the pound appreci-
ated from $2.03 to $2.22 in 1979. Early in 1980 corporate treasury advised the Pacific area that in order to avoid any further losses on
sterling a forward cover should be taken, and that if the area did not
choose to cover the position, the corporation would. As a result, the Pacific area covered the position in the forward market. The cover operation was limited to no more than $35 million, about 50% of the total
debt in pounds. In March 1980, the forward cover took the form of $8
million at $2.2260 for delivery in June 1980, $9 million at $2.2245 for
delivery between June and July 1980, and $10 million at $2.2300 for
delivery on July 7, 1980.

In spite of the success stories just described, Wilson Gay agreed
that the treasury department did not have perfect forward vision. One
of the most painful mistakes had occurred in 1976 with the Mexican
peso. Treasury had moved $2 million of funds into Mexican pesos just
the week before the peso devalued from MexPs12.50/$ to MexPs20.00/$.
However, that had not been a total disaster since the peso partially recovered and the very high interest rate on Mexican pesos limited the
loss to about $100,000.

Another forecasting error had been made in 1979 with the Canadian dollar. Corporate treasury was holding about $70 million worth of
Canadian dollars. With the appreciation of the U.S. dollar during the
earlier half of the year they had concluded that the Canadian dollar
would not appreciate against the U.S. dollar and had sold the position
in June, generating $1.5 million in exchange losses. With the benefit of
hindsight, it was clear that if they had waited a bit longer they would
have recovered the money lost, for the U.S. dollar did depreciate
against the Canadian dollar in the second half of the year.

Some transactions have a longer gestation period and this was the
case with Dow's long-term Swiss franc bond issues. There had been a
whole series of these issues since 1959 and each one had produced a
major loss on foreign exchange, although this loss was at least partially
offset by the low coupon on the Swiss franc bonds. However, the most
controversial of these borrowings in Swiss francs was arranged in 1974
at 8½% while the Swiss franc was at SwF2.5933/$. The story at the time
had been that the name of Dow Chemical had come to the top of the
queue maintained by the Swiss banks soon after Dow had petitioned to
borrow in the Swiss market. The treasurer for Dow Europe at the time

believed that if they declined to borrow when called, it would affect the credibility of Dow Chemical with the Swiss banks, and certainly it would be a personal embarrassment to the treasurer. Wilson Gay argued that every time they had entered the queue in the past, the same thing had happened—namely, they had been called soon thereafter and informed that Dow was at the head of the queue (long before the expected 6- to 12-month waiting period) and the argument about credibility had been the same. In any case, the area treasurer for Europe had prevailed and Dow borrowed the Swiss francs, SwF60 million. As anticipated, the Swiss franc soon began to strengthen. So Swiss franc bonds issued earlier began to be called as soon as feasible, beginning in spring of the same year. Simultaneously, treasury began to cover the short position in Swiss francs with forward contracts.

It was obvious that the area organization which Dow had created, combined with the freedom of action given to the area management in financial matters, could create situations where differences arose. In one instance Dow Europe was selling Swiss francs forward while corporate treasury was in fact buying Swiss francs forward. Since the areas were judged on a bottom-line basis, their orientation could often be toward the area's financial statements instead of toward the company's consolidated financial statements. As an example, parochial attitudes could arise on intercompany payments. Delaying payments to the corporation could enhance the performance of the country or area operations.

Instances of disagreement between the area and corporate treasury were, however, quite rare. Communication was generally very good, enhanced by frequent (daily or weekly) telephone conversations between Wilson Gay and the area treasurers. These calls, which were almost institutionalized, often generated an agreed-upon course of action, either at the corporate or area level, which may have been missed without the calls. Also, the area presidents visited with the corporate treasurer several times a year to discuss current financial matters, as well as longer-term strategies. In addition, meetings were held at least once a year where all the area treasurers and corporate staff discussed business and financial outlooks.

Dow's track record on financial capabilities seemed to provide the evidence to validate their style of financial management. Still, Ms. Mederos wondered about Wilson Gay's views of exchange markets, Dow's record in this field, and the organizational structure of the firm. To aid in her evaluation, she asked her assistant to compile exchange rate data for many of the transactions she had discussed with Mr. Gay. These data are presented in Exhibits C.1A–C.7A in the appendix to this case.

APPENDIX

MARKET RATES RELEVANT TO DOW'S TRANSACTIONS IN THE CASE

EXHIBIT C.1A Swiss Franc Spot Rates and Forward Rates, January 4 to April 25, 1980

[In Swiss francs per U.S. dollar. Percentage figures show the forward premium or discount (−) of the dollar against the franc.]

Date	Spot	1-Month	3-Months	6-Months	12-Months
January 4	1.5736	1.5605 −9.99%	1.5406 −8.39%	1.5111 −7.94%	1.4686 −6.67%
January 11	1.5830	1.5695 −10.23%	1.5495 −8.46%	1.5206 −7.88%	1.4780 −6.63%
January 18	1.5901	1.5783 −8.91%	1.5570 −8.33%	1.5284 −7.76%	1.4850 −6.61%
January 25	1.6160	1.6036 −9.21%	1.5825 −8.29%	1.5510 −8.04%	1.5020 −7.05%
February 1	1.6320	1.6210 −8.09%	1.5982 −8.28%	1.5684 −7.79%	1.5200 −6.86%
February 8	1.6185	1.6069 −8.60%	1.5830 −8.77%	1.5513 −8.30%	1.4995 −7.35%
February 15	1.6289	1.6145 −10.61%	1.5874 −10.19%	1.5494 −9.76%	1.4849 −8.84%
February 22	1.6615	1.6453 −11.70%	1.6176 −10.57%	1.5785 −9.99%	1.5155 −8.79%
February 29	1.7020	1.6832 −13.25%	1.6560 −10.81%	1.6139 −10.35%	1.5470 −9.11%
March 7	1.7229	1.7034 −13.58%	1.6728 −11.63%	1.6260 −11.25%	1.5580 −9.57%
March 14	1.7541	1.7331 −14.37%	1.7018 −11.93%	1.6565 −11.13%	1.5941 −9.12%
March 21	1.7795	1.7572 −15.04%	1.7255 −12.14%	1.6815 −11.01%	1.6145 −9.27%
March 28	1.8270	1.8070 −13.14%	1.7720 −12.04%	1.7285 −10.78%	1.6620 −9.03%
April 4	1.8700	1.8491 −13.41%	1.8141 −11.96%	1.7721 −10.47%	1.7060 −8.77%
April 11	1.7530	1.7367 −11.16%	1.7044 −11.09%	1.6660 −9.93%	1.6069 −8.33%
April 18	1.7331	1.7244 −6.02%	1.6952 −8.74%	1.6620 −8.20%	1.6050 −7.39%
April 25	1.6920	1.6784 −9.65%	1.6538 −9.03%	1.6221 −8.26%	1.5660 −7.45%

SOURCE: For C.1A–C.7A. Harris Bank, *Weekly Review, International Money Markets and Foreign Exchange Rates*, various issues.

EXHIBIT C.2A Swiss Franc and Canadian Dollar Spot Rates, February 2 to April 20, 1979

Date	Spot SwF/$	Spot $/Can$	Cross Rate SwF/Can$
February 2	1.7135	0.8339	1.4289
February 9	1.6600	0.8366	1.3888
February 16	1.6760	0.8376	1.4038
February 23	1.6650	0.8352	1.3906
March 2	1.6776	0.8433	1.4147
March 9	1.6697	0.8457	1.4121
March 16	1.6822	0.8520	1.4332
March 23	1.6859	0.8563	1.4436
March 30	1.7068	0.8611	1.4697
April 6	1.7144	0.8699	1.4914
April 13	1.7301	0.8735	1.5112
April 20	1.7235	0.8762	1.5101

EXHIBIT C.3A Swiss Franc Spot Rates and Forward Rates, August 3 to November 30, 1979

[*In Swiss francs per U.S. dollar. Percentage figures show the forward premium or discount (−) of the dollar against the franc.*]

Date	Spot	1-Month	3-Month
August 3	1.6584	1.6445 −10.06%	1.6189 −9.53%
August 10	1.6461	1.6319 −10.35%	1.6071 −9.48%
August 17	1.6565	1.6418 −10.65%	1.6158 −9.83%
August 24	1.6565	1.6418 −10.65%	1.6152 −9.97%
August 31	1.6562	1.6431 −9.49%	1.6152 −9.90%
September 7	1.6329	1.6200 −9.48%	1.5916 −10.12%
September 14	1.6360	1.6223 −10.05%	1.5935 −10.39%
September 21	1.5706	1.5563 −10.93%	1.5261 −11.33%
September 28	1.5564	1.5406 −12.18%	1.5132 −11.10%
October 5	1.5803	1.5640 −12.38%	1.5359 −11.24%
October 12	1.6244	1.6064 −13.30%	1.5751 −12.14%
October 19	1.6450	1.6268 −13.28%	1.5958 −11.96%
October 26	1.6669	1.6479 −13.68	1.6159 −12.24%
November 2	1.6410	1.6234 −12.87%	1.5939 −11.48%
November 9	1.6534	1.6367 −12.12%	1.6057 −11.54%
November 16	1.6491	1.6332 −11.57%	1.6026 −11.28%
November 23	1.6499	1.6351 −10.76%	1.6072 −10.35%
November 30	1.5971	1.5840 −9.84%	1.5605 −9.17%

EXHIBIT C.4A Hong Kong Dollar and Japanese Yen Spot Rates, March 3 to September 29, 1978

Date	Spot HK$/US$	Spot ¥/US$	Cross Rate ¥/HK$
March 3	4.5959	237.08	51.59
March 17	4.5998	231.05	50.23
March 31	4.6083	221.24	48.01
April 14	4.6062	219.39	47.63
April 28	4.6232	225.23	48.72
May 12	4.6404	225.68	48.63
May 26	4.6555	225.48	48.43
June 9	4.6555	220.60	47.38
June 23	4.6468	207.47	44.65
July 7	4.6404	202.35	43.61
July 21	4.6555	200.88	43.15
August 4	4.6642	189.57	40.64
August 18	4.7037	189.39	40.26
September 1	4.6970	191.09	40.68
September 15	4.7438	189.83	40.02
September 29	4.7348	188.89	39.89

EXHIBIT C.5A Pound Sterling Spot Rates and Forward Rates, January 1977 to December 1980

[*In U.S. dollars per pound. Percentage figures show forward premium or discount (−) of the pound against the dollar.*]

Date	Spot	1-Month	3-Months	12-Months
1977				
January 7	1.7052	1.6895	1.6634	1.5732
		−11.05%	−9.81%	−7.74%
June 3	1.7177	1.7088	1.6970	1.6472
		−6.22%	−4.82%	−4.10%
December 2	1.8240	1.8247	1.8227	1.8103
		0.46%	−0.29%	−0.75%
1978				
June 2	1.8230	1.8185	1.8097	1.7665
		−2.96%	−2.92%	−3.10%
December 1	1.9345	1.9315	1.9239	1.8960
		−1.86%	−2.19%	−1.99%
1979				
January 5	2.0193	2.0181	2.0144	1.9978
		−0.71%	−0.97%	−1.06%
February 2	1.9795	1.9741	1.9628	1.9275
		−3.27%	−3.37%	−2.63%
March 2	2.0215	2.0178	2.0120	1.9905
		−2.20%	−1.88%	−1.53%
April 6	2.0892	2.0874	2.0857	2.0802
		−1.03%	−0.67%	−0.43%
May 11	2.0448	2.0425	2.0371	2.0223
		−1.35%	−1.51%	−1.10%
June 1	2.0715	2.0688	2.0646	2.0497
		−1.56%	−1.33%	−1.05%
July 6	2.2200	2.2135	2.2030	2.1760
		−3.51%	−3.06%	−1.98%
August 3	2.2690	2.2636	2.2513	2.2175
		−2.86%	−3.12%	−2.27%
September 7	2.2475	2.2440	2.2395	2.2185
		−1.87%	−1.42%	−1.29%

EXHIBIT C.5A *(Continued)*

Date	Spot	1-Month	3-Months	12-Months
1979				
October 5	2.1840	2.1834	2.1794	2.1690
		−0.33%	−0.84%	−0.69%
November 2	2.0675	2.0700	2.0710	2.0660
		1.45%	0.68%	−0.07%
December 7	2.1740	2.1705	2.1600	2.1225
		−1.93%	−2.58%	−2.37%
1980				
January 4	2.2360	2.2326	2.2239	2.1930
		−1.82%	−2.16%	−1.92%
February 1	2.2755	2.2680	2.2575	2.2350
		−3.96%	−3.16%	−1.78%
March 7	2.2265	2.2275	2.2275	2.2205
		0.54%	0.18%	−0.27%
April 4	2.1350	2.1390	2.1415	2.1440
		2.25%	1.22%	0.42%
May 2	2.2560	2.2480	2.2410	2.2210
		−4.26%	−6.00%	−1.55%
June 6	2.3320	2.3160	2.2915	2.2370
		−8.23%	−6.95%	−4.07%
July 6	2.2200	2.2135	2.2030	2.1760
		−3.51%	−3.06%	−1.98%
August 3	2.2690	2.2636	2.2513	2.2175
		−2.86%	−3.12%	−2.27%
September 7	2.2475	2.2440	2.2395	2.2185
		−1.87%	−1.42%	−1.29%
October 7	2.4160	2.4098	2.4003	2.3890
		−3.08%	−2.60%	−1.12%
November 7	2.4105	2.4095	2.4100	2.4075
		−0.50%	−0.08%	−0.12%
December 5	2.3388	2.3506	2.3621	2.3718
		6.05%	3.98%	1.41%

EXHIBIT C.6A Mexican Peso Spot Rates, August 1976 to August 1977

Date	Spot MexPs/$
1976	
August 31	12.500
September 30	19.846
October 31	25.488
November 30	22.073
December 31	19.950
1977	
January 31	22.176
February 28	22.647
March 31	22.687
April 30	22.637
May 31	22.798
June 30	22.995
July 31	22.862
August 31	22.866

EXHIBIT C.7A Canadian Dollar Spot Rates and Forward Rates, January 5 to December 7, 1979

[*In Canadian dollar per U.S. dollar. Percentage figures show the forward premium or discount (−) of the U.S. dollar against the Canadian dollar.*]

	Spot	3-Months
January 5	1.1847	1.1829
		−0.61%
February 2	1.1992	1.2006
		0.47%
March 2	1.1858	1.1864
		0.20%
April 6	1.1496	1.1511
		0.52%
May 11	1.1593	1.1610
		0.59%
June 1	1.1658	1.1680
		0.75%
July 6	1.1592	1.1602
		0.35%
August 3	1.1755	1.1774
		0.65%
September 7	1.1681	1.1664
		−0.58%
October 5	1.1669	1.1641
		−0.96%
November 2	1.1870	1.1840
		−1.01%
December 7	1.1624	1.1617
		−0.24%

IFMG'S
DAILY
TRADING
OPERATIONS

THE INTERNATIONAL FUNDS MANAGEMENT GROUP (IFMG) of Manucraft, Inc. managed the company's funds outside the United States and controlled the company's exposure to exchange risk.[1] The company defined exposure to exchange risk as monetary assets minus liabilities. It was the job of the IFMG to keep the amount of exposure within a range considered acceptable to the company. Any increase in exposure over the accepted limits was hedged immediately. However, within the limits, the IFMG had room to manage the company's exchange position in each currency.

It is difficult to describe how a trader makes decisions in reaction to new information. The following account describes how Mr. Guido Wehrli, the group's manager, conducted his trading operation in mid-1981.

Gathering of Information

Each day the IFMG first checked whether the exposure level in each currency was within the established limits. Exposure figures were recorded in the *daily position sheet*. This sheet listed for each currency the exposure at the beginning of the month plus contributions from operations. Exchange transactions in each currency to date were also recorded on this sheet. The combined total provided a daily running balance of the exchange position in each currency that could be checked against currently allowed limits at any time. When the exposure balance in a currency exceeded the established limit, trading took place to reduce the exposure in that currency, regardless of market conditions or expectations. If the balance was within the established limit, then the second-priority objective of profitability dominated any further decision on the position in that currency. This required an ongoing assessment of the market.

---

[1] A detailed description of the IFMG operations appears in the case "Manucraft, Inc. (A)" presented at the end of Chapter 11.

IFMG's forecast for each currency was founded primarily on an analysis of economic and political forces in each country. The behavior of central banks, in particular, and other traders, in general, was superimposed on this analysis. For example, given a set of economic conditions, whether a central bank appeared to be intervening in the exchange markets influenced the decisions taken by the IFMG. A continuous inflow of information to facilitate these analyses was maintained through the use of a Reuter monitor system and frequent conversations with exchange traders and other market participants. Any piece of new information was considered in reaching a trade or no-trade decision in each currency.

Specific trading transactions were usually associated with given changes in the market. Three major types of changes in the market were analyzed carefully by the IFMG: (1) changes in the direction in which rates were moving; (2) changes in market stability; and (3) changes in cross rate structures.

Reaction to Changes in Market Trends

If a change in market rates occurred, the direction of that movement often determined the next action to be taken. Market movements in the direction anticipated by the IFMG that were also expected to continue led to trading with the tides of the market—that is, purchasing appreciating currencies and selling depreciating ones. If the market move was in the expected direction, but the trend was not expected to continue, the IFMG would try to profit by trading against the market— that is, purchasing depreciating currencies and selling appreciating currencies. Of course, the magnitude of these trading operations was still bound by the existing exposure limits.

When the market moved in a direction opposite to the one anticipated, the IFMG had to determine whether it was a technical market reaction of a nonpermanent nature or a true change in market sentiment. Periods of profit-taking during the day (such as around lunch time when traders reduce their positions before leaving the office) were typical technical reactions. This would not prompt any action by the IFMG, unless it had been awaiting such a temporary reversal in market rates to use to its advantage. However, if it appeared that the unexpected move was not technical, the IFMG usually chose a risk-averse strategy and quickly liquidated previously held positions. This was particularly so in the case of existing large exposures. If the exposure was small and the risk was acceptable, the IFMG could assume a "wait-and-see" attitude and take no immediate action. Exhibit D.1 summarizes the steps in this decision process.

EXHIBIT D.1

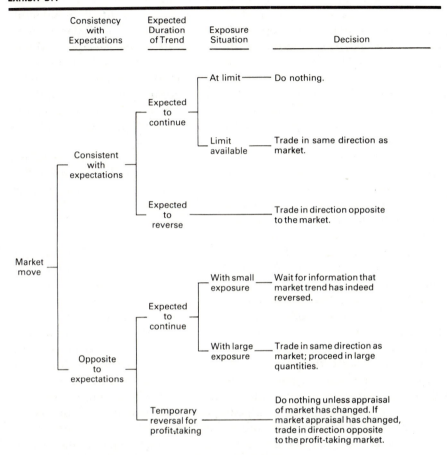

Consistency with Expectations	Expected Duration of Trend	Exposure Situation	Decision

Reaction to Changes in Market Volatility

Changes in the volatility of the market could also cause the IFMG to trade. As market fluctuations increased in magnitude and decreased in predictability, positions that were established in a more stable market often became unacceptable and were closed.

Reaction to Changes in Cross Rates

Not all currencies move in lockstep against the dollar. Some movements are based on the actual strengths and weaknesses of the currencies involved, while other movements are anomalous and can occur only in a thin market. For example, when European currencies appreciated against the U.S. dollar in mid-1980, Mr. Wehrli thought that the German mark was the real strength in this general movement, while the French franc appreciated against the U.S. dollar only to maintain its position relative to the mark within the European Monetary System (EMS). According to Mr. Wehrli, the French franc rates did not represent sustainable rates against the dollar—and would have been corrected promptly within the band permissible by the EMS—if the market in French francs against the U.S. dollar had been larger. This situation was temporary and provided profit-making possibilities to the IFMG.

The analysis of cross rates also influenced the decision of which specific currency to trade when a change in the overall exposure in European currencies was desired. The IFMG tended first to analyze market conditions in terms of the block of European currencies. Then, if a decision to alter this overall exposure was reached, a specific European currency had to be selected to trade against the U.S. dollar.

The following situation illustrates how the selection of the specific currency to trade was handled in mid-June 1981. At this time, concern with exchange losses realized in the first half of the year, as well as the possibility that increasing interest rates in the U.S. dollar could trigger a further strengthening of this currency, suggested that some foreign currency holdings be liquidated. The question, then, was which currency to sell against the dollar—say, German marks or Swiss francs? In making this decision, the IFMG considered the following factors: (1) recent moves in various currencies against the U.S. dollar; (2) the volatility of each currency; and (3) the relevant interest rates.

Since July 1980, the European currencies had been depreciating against the U.S. dollar more often than not. However, by June 1981, Mr. Wehrli thought that the German mark had reached the lowest value in the range now expected by the market. (Exhibit D.2 presents market rates for the preceding year.) During this period, the Swiss franc had depreciated against the dollar less than had the mark. That made it desirable to sell Swiss francs, instead of marks, against dollars. Given Mr. Wehrli's assessment of the mark, he thought that *within the range of rates then expected by the market,* the depreciation potential for the Swiss franc was greater than it was for the mark. However, *if the market's predictions proved to be wrong,* the risk of depreciation against the dollar was larger for the mark than for the franc. That is, if the European currencies as a whole continued to show large depreciations against the dollar, then Mr. Wehrli expected a depreciation in the mark of 5%, as compared to 3% for the Swiss franc, in the coming month. In this case, it would be preferable to sell marks now, instead of Swiss francs.

Another consideration in this decision was the level of interest

EXHIBIT D.2 IFMG's Daily Trading Operations: Exchange Rates and Interest Rates in Selected Currencies, June 1980 to June 1981

| | EXCHANGE RATES | | | | 3-MONTH EURORATES | | | | |
	Pound Sterling	French Franc	German Mark	Swiss Franc	U.S. Dollar	Pound Sterling	French Franc	German Mark	Swiss Franc
1980	(in $/£)	(in foreign currency per U.S. $)			(in percent)				
June 20	2.34	4.11	1.77	1.63	9.25	16.50	12.38	9.19	5.56
July 18	2.37	4.06	1.75	1.61	9.25	15.50	11.88	8.94	5.25
August 15	2.38	4.14	1.79	1.64	10.31	16.25	10.69	8.25	5.19
September 12	2.41	4.14	1.78	1.63	11.81	15.75	12.00	8.62	5.56
October 17	2.42	4.25	1.84	1.66	13.25	15.88	12.00	8.44	5.25
November 14	2.40	4.42	1.92	1.71	15.44	15.50	10.50	9.25	5.38
December 12	2.32	4.63	2.00	1.82	23.75	14.75	11.88	10.38	7.00
1981									
January 16	2.40	4.67	2.02	1.83	18.75	14.38	11.19	8.94	5.56
February 13	2.28	5.08	2.20	2.02	18.06	13.25	10.62	10.38	7.31
March 13	2.22	4.98	2.11	1.93	15.25	13.12	12.25	12.38	8.25
April 17	2.16	5.17	2.19	2.00	15.25	12.31	13.25	12.50	8.88
May 15	2.08	5.54	2.30	2.06	19.62	12.25	18.25	12.81	10.12
June 12	1.95	5.74	2.40	2.08	17.62	12.62	23.12	12.62	10.00

SOURCE: Harris Bank, *Weekly Review, International Money Markets and Foreign Exchange Rates*, various issues.

rates. At the moment, interest rates were lower in Swiss francs than in marks. Regardless of exchange rate movements, the loss of interest income from selling marks was higher than from selling Swiss francs. This thought introduced the related issue of the very high interest rates being foregone in French francs. However, Mr. Wehrli preferred not to speculate on the political uncertainties brought about by the election of the socialist government of François Mitterand in France the previous May.

The final decision between selling marks or Swiss francs required weighing the size of the interest differential between the two currencies against the expected maximum depreciation of each of them against the dollar during the coming month.

Thinking that the rising U.S. interest rates were the primary force behind the depreciation of the European currencies during the past year, Mr. Wehrli pondered the likelihood that U.S. interest rates would continue to increase. At 17.62% in mid-June 1981, U.S. interest rates were well below the peak reached in December 1980. Now the U.S. Congress appeared sure to pass the bill reducing taxes requested by the Reagan administration. In addition, Mr. Volcker, the Chairman of the U.S. Federal Reserve System, had reiterated his intentions to control U.S. inflation, regardless of the level of interest rates. All this pointed to higher interest rates in the U.S. dollar. However, in contrast to Fall 1980, the U.S. economy had now begun to give signs of slowing down, which could keep interest rates from reaching their earlier peak.

Mr. Wehrli was more inclined to believe that the current exchange rates would hold for a while than to expect a further increase in U.S. interest rates with the associated depreciation in the European currencies. However, he assessed the probabilities of a further strengthening of the U.S. dollar to be sufficiently high that he preferred to act as if this were the dominant future scenario. This last analysis dominated the decision and marks, instead of Swiss francs, were sold against the U.S. dollar.

EXERCISE IN TRADING FOREIGN EXCHANGE

Assume you are a foreign exchange trader dealing in the following four currencies:

a. Skandia peso ($)
b. Slovaki rial (SR)
c. Gutchland crown (GC)
d. Latadoran franc (LF)

You begin the trading day with the following general assumptions:

1. The Skandia peso is basically sound. No major drop in its exchange rate is expected.
2. If the crown depreciates past GC1.90/$, Gutchland's central bank is expected to intervene in the market.
3. Sahsma is a developing country to which both Slovaki and Gutchland have lent heavily. The political stability of Sahsma is in doubt and this has made exchange markets skittish for several months. A major political upheaval in Sahsma would produce severe losses in the Slovaki and Gutchland currencies.

Following is a description of events that take place during the day. Exhibit E.1 summarizes the market exchange rate quotes for the relevant currencies at various times throughout the day. Assuming you begin the trading day with the exchange positions you desire, how would you modify these positions (if at all) each time information on a new event is released? [*Note:* All exchange quotes are given in terms of local currency per peso.]

1. At the beginning of trade, the GC had depreciated slightly since the close of trade the previous day, a trend that was expected to continue slowly throughout the day.
2. At 10:00 A.M. an increase in the Latadoran prime interest rate from 7.5% to 8% was announced. This instantly appreciated the LF by 50 basis points.
3. At 12:20 P.M. the Gutchland trade deficit was announced to have been substantially lower than anticipated, reversing the morning's depreciation of the GC. As the GC appreciated against the $, the SR began appreciating as well.
4. At 1:00 P.M. Gutchland employment figures were released, indicating a drop of 0.4% in unemployment, from the previous 8.3%.
5. By 2:00 P.M. some profit-taking began to take place, as the $ appreciated against both the GC and the SR.

EXHIBIT E.1   Exercise in Trading Foreign Exchange: Exchange Rate Quotes throughout the Trading Day

Time	Slovaki Rial (SR)	Gutchland Crown (GC)	Latadoran Franc (LF)
Opening	0.4136/9	1.8915/8	2.2600/3
10:00 A.M.	0.4160/3	1.8950/3	2.2550/4
12:20 P.M.	0.4140/3	1.8910/4	2.2530/4
1:00 P.M.	0.4125/8	1.8890/4	2.2525/9
2:00 P.M.	0.4130/8	1.8900/4	2.2525/9
3:00 P.M.	0.4145/9	1.8940/3	2.2515/9
Close	0.4150/3	1.8970/3	2.2520/3

6. Clicking over the Reuter monitor at 3:00 P.M. came news of widespread rioting in Sahsma's capital city. This fed the general anxiety about the stability of the situation there, although it was unclear what caused this rioting. Despite earlier positive indicators, this touchy area quickly overwhelmed previous optimism about Sahsma and the GC began to depreciate quickly.

7. Finally, near the end of trading, the GC was close to the GC1.90/$ level. This strengthened its position somewhat.

8. A last-minute announcement of annualized inflation figures showed Skandia's inflation rate down 0.5% from the previous month.

8 Financing International Trade

AS WITH ANY other business, international trade requires financing. The exporter needs financing whenever a sale is made in terms other than advance payments. The importer needs financing whenever purchases must be paid in advance of their resale in the domestic market. In addition, international trade often requires the management of the business exposure to fluctuations in exchange rates. Whenever purchases and sales are denominated in different currencies, the merchant's profits are at risk.

Financial officers involved in international trade must identify the financing needs and risks of the operation and then choose a financial strategy. An analysis of this process is presented in the first part of this chapter. Consideration must then be given to a series of documents and financing instruments available to limit the credit risk of the ultimate lender of the funds. A careful selection of the financing vehicle will provide the optimal package to finance international trade. These special documents and financing vehicles are discussed in the latter part of this chapter.

ALTERNATIVE FINANCING STRATEGIES

To illustrate the range of possible financing alternatives, we will use as an example the case of a Mexican business that exports goods to the United States. The exporter has a 3-month contract to deliver goods at a fixed U.S. dollar price. Although the export business is expected to continue indefinitely, the dollar price is fixed for only 3 months. After that period, the export price can be renegotiated to incorporate changes in costs. The export sale is invoiced net 30 days; however, manufacturing costs are paid upon completion of the goods. The initial market rates are as indicated in the accompanying table.

Exchange Rates	
Spot rate	MexPs25.00/$
Interest Rates for 1, 2, and 3 Months	
U.S. dollar	14% p.a.
Mexican peso	51% p.a.

The cash flows for the first 3 months of this business are presented in the initial situation in Exhibit 8.1. There are inflows of $100 on day 31, day 61, and day 91, for a total of $300. There are outflows of MexPs2,000 on day 1, day 31, and day 61, for a total of MexPs6,000. At the initial exchange rate of MexPs25/$, there is a profit of MexPs1,500 for the first 3 months of operations (equal to $300 at MexPs25/$, less MexPs6,000).

The financial officer in this export business has two problems to solve. First, there is a need to finance MexPs2,000 on day 1 for 3 months. Although a dollar inflow will materialize on day 31, there is also a need to finance an additional MexPs2,000 on that date. A similar situation occurs on day 61. Second, there is an exchange position at the end of each month. These produce a total net exchange position for the period of $300 long and MexPs6,000 short.

EXHIBIT 8.1 Financing Export Operations: Alternative Strategies

Date	Transaction	CURRENCIES*	
		MexPs	$
	INITIAL SITUATION		
Day 1	Payment of expenses	−2,000	
	Net cash flow	−2,000	
Day 31	Collection of export receivable		+100
	Payment of expenses	−2,000	
	Net cash flows	−2,000	+100
Day 61	Collection of export receivable		+100
	Payment of expenses	−2,000	
	Net cash flows	−2,000	+100
Day 91	Collection of export receivable		+100
	Net cash flow		+100
Net exchange positions		−6,000	+300

EXHIBIT 8.1 *(Continued)*

Date	Transaction	CURRENCIES*	
		MexPs	$
	A. COVER ALL RISKS		
Day 1	Scheduled net cash flow	−2,000	
	Borrow 1-month $100, at 14%		+100
	Borrow 2-month $100, at 14%		+100
	Borrow 3-month $100, at 14%		+100
	Convert $300 into MexPs spot at MexPs25/$	+7,500	−300
	Invest 1-month MexPs2,000, at 51%	−2,000	
	Invest 2-month MexPs2,000, at 51%	−2,000	
	Net cash flows	+1,500	0
Day 31	Scheduled net cash flows	−2,000	+100
	Repayment of 1-month $100		−101
	Collection of 1-month MexPs2,000	+2,085	
	Net cash flows	+85	−1
Day 61	Scheduled net cash flows	−2,000	+100
	Repayment of 2-month $100		−102
	Collection of 2-month MexPs2,000	+2,170	
	Net cash flows	+170	−2
Day 91	Scheduled net cash flow		+100
	Repayment of 3-month $100		−104
	Net cash flows		−4
	Net exchange positions	+1,755	−7
	B. COVER INTEREST RATE RISK		
	AND BEAR EXCHANGE RISK		
Day 1	Scheduled net cash flow	−2,000	
	Borrow 3-month MexPs6,000, at 51%	+2,000	
	Net cash flows	0	
Day 31	Scheduled net cash flows	−2,000	+100
	Net cash flows	−2,000	+100
Day 61	Scheduled net cash flows	−2,000	+100
	Net cash flows	−2,000	+100
Day 91	Scheduled net cash flow		+100
	Repayment of 3-month MexPs2,000	−2,255	
	Net cash flows	−2,255	+100
	Net exchange positions	−6,255	+300
	C. COVER EXCHANGE RISK AND		
	BEAR INTEREST RATE RISK		
Day 1	Scheduled net cash flows	−2,000	
	Borrow 1-month $300, at 14%		+300
	Convert $ into MexPs spot at MexPs25/$	+7,500	−300
	Invest 1-month MexPs4,000, at 51%	−4,000	
	Net cash flows	+1,500	0
Day 31	Scheduled net cash flows	−2,000	+100
	Repayment of 1-month $300		−303
	Collection of 1-month MexPs4,000	+4,170	
	Net cash flows	+2,170	−203
Day 61	Scheduled net cash flows	−2,000	+100
Day 91	Scheduled net cash flow		+100
	Net exchange positions	+1,670	−3

*(+: Cash inflow; −: Cash flow)

If we finance the MexPs2,000 with 30-day funds, we are exposed to the risk of changes in interest rates between now and the refinancing dates, day 31 and day 61. If we leave the exchange position open, we are exposed to fluctuations in exchange rates between now and the times when dollars are converted into pesos. We have three alternative strategies to deal with these risks while providing the needed financing: (1) cover all risks; (2) cover the interest rate risk, but bear the exchange risk; and, (3) cover the exchange risk, but bear the interest rate risk. The documents that can be used as collateral to facilitate this financing are explained later in this chapter.

Cover All Risks

If we want to eliminate all financial risks, we must balance each of the net cash flows—that is, square the business' cash position. For each date, we want inflows to be equal to outflows in each currency, except for the MexPs1,500 in profits that we want as a net inflow in pesos (the home currency of the exporter).

Since we need to borrow funds to meet peso outflows and we have dollar inflows, we can solve the financing and the exchange position problems simultaneously if we do the borrowings in dollars. However, we must be careful with the total amount and the maturity schedule for this dollar financing. The total amount of borrowings must match the size of dollar exposure, $300. The repayment schedule must match the inflow pattern for the collection of export receivables. Thus, we want to borrow a total of $300: $100 for 1 month, $100 for 2 months, and $100 for 3 months.

The financing need is in pesos. So, we must convert the $300 total borrowings into pesos. However, only MexPs2,000 are needed to meet payments on day 1. The other peso outflows will occur on day 31 and day 61. We can reinvest the pesos to match the maturities of those outflows: MexPs2,000 to mature on day 31, and $2,000 to mature on day 61. The conversion of the $300 into pesos at MexPs25/$ produces MexPs7,500. Then, after meeting the outflow for day 1 and reinvesting MexPs4,000 to meet the outflows in the following 2 months, we are left with a balance of MexPs1,500 on day 1. This is the profit from the export business, as calculated at the current spot rate of MexPs25/$. However, the totals in panel A of Exhibit 8.1 show that we have locked in a total profit of MexPs1,755, less financing costs of $7. The additional profit of MexPs255 represents the 51% interest earned on the MexPs3,000 invested on average over 2 months. The financing cost of $7 is the 14% interest on the average of $200 borrowed over 2 months.

After these transactions, each of the initially scheduled cash flows has a matching cash flow planned at a rate that is known in advance, on day 1. We have met the financing needs of this business and protected profits from the impact of fluctuations in the peso spot rate and changes in the interest rates. However, we have also eliminated the opportunity of profiting from an appreciation of the dollar (the inflow currency) against the peso (the outflow currency) and the possibility of refinancing the MexPs2,000 at a lower interest rate, if rates were to come down.

It should be noticed that in this presentation we borrowed a total of $300, although only $80 (equivalent to MexPs2,000) was needed for financing purposes. The larger amount of borrowings was needed to cover the exchange exposure (including profits). Alternatively, we could cover the exposure in the forward market, instead of in the money market, and borrow a smaller amount of funds. We could borrow $80 for 3 months (the length of the financing need) and sell $100 forward against pesos both for day 31 and for day 61. Alternatively, we could borrow MexPs2,000 for 3 months and sell $100 against pesos each for day 31, day 61, and day 91. In both cases the interest rate is locked in for 3 months, the exchange exposure is covered, and the debt repayment is made with the inflow planned for day 91. However, in many currencies an extensive forward exchange market does not exist. In these markets the approach presented earlier—namely, borrowing enough funds to cover the exposure through the money market—is the only alternative available to reach the stated objectives of financing and covering all financial risks.

Cover Interest Rate Risk and Bear Exchange Risk

We have to generate funds to meet the financing problem on day 1. We can do this by borrowing pesos or dollars. If we borrow MexPs2,000 or $80, and do nothing else, we solve the financing problem; however, we leave a net exchange position open—$300 if we borrow pesos and $220 if we borrow dollars. We would want to do this if we were expecting a devaluation of the peso against the dollar of more than 37% per annum, the interest rate differential.

To guarantee the interest rate on the funds needed, we will borrow, say MexPs2,000 at 51% for 3 months, the length of the financial need. After this operation we know exactly the cost of financing—MexPs255. However, we are still exposed to a fluctuation in the spot rate of the peso against the dollar. Panel B in Exhibit 8.1 shows that after the peso borrowings we have a net exchange position long in dollars, $300, and short in pesos, MexPs6,255. (Had we done the financing with $80, instead of MexPs2,000, the exchange position in dollars would have been $220.) Although we know that dollars will be available on days 31, 61, and 91, we do not know with certainty the exchange rates at which those dollars will be converted into pesos. If the dollar appreciates against the peso by more than 37% per annum, this will prove to be a good solution. Should the dollar appreciate by less than 37% per annum, we would have been better off covering the exchange risk.

Cover Exchange Risk and Bear Interest Rate Risk

To cover the exchange position we need to generate a total outflow of $300 and an inflow of about MexPs6,000. (See the initial situation in Exhibit 8.1.) We can do this in the forward market by selling dollars against pesos, or we can do this in the money markets by borrowing $300 and investing the proceeds in the peso money market. This operation will cover the exchange position regardless of the maturity of the borrowings and investing, or the value date of the forward contract. However, if the maturities of the cover operation do not match the maturities of the scheduled cash flows, we will be left with an interest rate position or swap position.

Panel C of Exhibit 8.1 shows the initial exchange position covered in the money market by borrowing $300 and investing the proceeds in pesos, MexPs7,500; however, both the borrowings of the dollars and the investing of the pesos are done for 1 month. The bottom line shows that the net exchange positions after all transactions are MexPs1,670 (equal to the initial MexPs1,500 in profits, plus the MexPs170 earned in interest) and the $3 paid on the dollar borrowings. However, on day 31, when the investment and borrowings mature, we must find an investment outlet for MexPs2,000 and a financing source for $200. If between day 1 and day 31 the interest rate on the peso increases and the interest rate on the dollar decreases, then we can reinvest the pesos for 30 days (until needed on day 61) and refinance the dollars for the maturities when the dollar inflows are expected (day 61 and day 91) at better rates than those available on day 1. However, if the interest differential between the two currencies decreases, the interest rate position created on day 1 would be less desirable than having squared all the cash flows on that day.

In positioning to take advantage of expected changes in interest rates, we want the borrowings to be for a maturity longer than needed if we expect the interest rate on that currency to increase beyond market expectations; we want a maturity shorter than the length of the need when we expect interest rates in that currency to decrease beyond market expectations. The opposite is true for the investment currency.

To Cover or Not To Cover

In the previous example, we could lock in 30-day interest rates for day 31 and day 61 that were the same as those which prevailed on day 1. We also could lock in a forward exchange rate which produced an exchange gain relative to the current spot rate. Locking in an interest rate did not involve an increase in borrowing costs over the cost of 30-day funds on day 1, and eliminating the exchange risk actually produced profits higher than those computed at the initial spot rate. Although locking in these rates eliminated the possibilities of obtaining better rates later on, the covering decisions appeared to eliminate risks while increasing profits—a painless decision.

Of course, this conclusion is a fallacious one. It is based on the comparison of today's rates for different maturities (such as today's spot rate and the 90-day forward rate) instead of the comparison of today's rates with those expected to prevail in the future (such as today's 90-day forward rate and the spot rate expected to prevail in 90 days). Nonetheless, for the financial officer who must make the covering decision it is easier to explain the reported figures when an exchange gain is locked in than when an exchange loss is locked in. Also, it is easier to justify locking in an interest cost that is the same or lower than current short-term rates than to explain the need to lock in a higher rate. Senior management is usually reluctant to associate exchange losses and higher interest costs with good management practices. Thus, it behooves the financial officer to justify why, say, locking in an exchange loss today may be better than running the risk of realizing a larger loss later.

With respect to foreign exchange risk in particular, the willingness of an importer or exporter to cover the exposure to the risk depends somewhat on whether a system of fixed or floating exchange rates prevails.[1] Under a system of fixed rates, the decision to cover is typically made only when there is a "substantial" probability of loss. Unfortunately, this situation involving a high probability of a devaluation usually coincides with the most severe discounts in the forward

---

[1]The answer to the question of whether firms or individuals face more or less risk under a floating-rate than under a fixed-rate world pivots on questions of the utility of small, frequent changes versus relatively large, infrequent changes. Some evidence for evaluating this issue was found by Janice Moulton Westerfield, who notes that the non-normality of the distribution of changes in exchange rates under both fixed and floating regimes is an important issue, for the changes are more accurately understood in the context of a stable Paretian distribution, with infinite variance (which means that sample estimates of the variance are meaningless). Using several standard statistical indices of risk which may be applied to stable Paretian distributions, she concludes that the floating-rate era has produced far more risk to the firm or individual involved with it. See Janice M. Westerfield, "An Examination of Foreign Exchange Risk Under Fixed and Floating Regimes," *Journal of International Economics*, May, 1977, pp. 181–200.

market. Even assuming this coincidence, the exporter may rationally cover a loss based on a utility function that accepts a lower return with certainty in exchange for a higher expected return in an uncertain world.

In a world of fluctuating exchange rates, however, the situation becomes much more complex. In a system of flexible rates, in contrast to a fixed-rate system, it is likely that there will be fewer large changes in the relative value of currencies during the typical period involved in trade financing. However, under the flexible-rate system there will also be many more changes (although of a smaller amount) over all currencies. Given these complexities, major corporations can certainly be expected to consider their covering decisions with much greater care under the present managed floating exchange rate system than in the past. Various studies of the practices of American multinationals during the 1970s confirm this behavior; however, there have also been changes in the reporting requirements of foreign activities. So, it is not clear whether the greater attention to covering comes from managed floating or from the greater visibility of foreign operations. This issue is discussed further in Chapter 10.

For the handful of currencies whose value is allowed to float freely from time to time, without much government intervention, the issue to cover or not to cover may be simplified somewhat. In efficient markets the forward rate of these currencies would be an unbiased forecast of future spot rates. Businesses that choose to cover systematically all their future payables and receivables in foreign exchange lock in a series of forward exchange rates through time. Over the long term the average of these locked-in forward rates will tend to approximate the average of the spot rates. That is, if the forward rate is an unbiased predictor of the spot, then the policies covering or not covering through time produce approximately the same result. At any time, the exchange rate applicable to a specific transaction will be either the forward rate, if the business chooses to cover it, or the spot rate at the time of the collection of payment, if the business chooses *not* to cover the transaction. However, through time, the average of exchange rates applicable to the overall business will be the same regardless of the covering policy pursued. In this world the only relevant considerations on whether to cover or not to cover are of a technical nature: Transaction costs involved in the spread between bid and ask prices are higher in the forward market than in the spot market.[2]

---

[2]For some historical evidence on this issue see Ian H. Giddy, "Why It Doesn't Pay to Make a Habit of Forward Hedging," *Euromoney*, December 1976, pp. 96–100.

SPECIAL DOCUMENTS USED
IN INTERNATIONAL TRADE

A whole series of documents has been developed to facilitate international trade. Among the most important instruments are the *letter of credit* and the *import or export draft.*

Letters of Credit

Suppose Zebracorp, a U.S. manufacturer of widgets, has agreed with Chao-widgets, a distributor of the product in Chaolandia, to sell a certain quantity of widgets to the firm. Although Zebracorp knows that Chao-widgets wants the product, the firm's credit is not sufficiently well known to Zebracorp. To assure itself of payment, Zebracorp can request that Chao-widgets obtain a letter of credit.

In the most typical use of the *letter of credit* the buyer (Chao-widgets) will go to a local bank acceptable to Zebracorp and ask that bank to issue a letter of credit on Chao-widget's behalf. In this letter the bank will agree to honor the demand for payment resulting from the import transaction described in the document. In exchange, the importer promises to pay the bank the required amount plus fees on mutually accepted terms.

In this example, Chao-widgets, which applied for the letter of credit is the *account party*, and its local bank is the *issuing bank*. Zebracorp is the *beneficiary* of the letter of credit and receives its money from the *paying bank* (also called the *drawee bank*), which is instructed by the issuing bank to make the payment upon presentation of appropriate documents to a specified bank usually called the *accepting bank*. The bank in the importer's country may well operate through its own affiliate in the exporter's country, but often it will deal through one of its *correspondent* banks.

It is easiest to see this financing procedure through a few examples of letters of credit that might occur between firms around the world. In Exhibit 8.2 the exporter and beneficiary, Africa Patterns, Ltd., is informed by Bankers Trust (the issuing bank) that Africa Patterns will be paid an amount not exceeding £800 by the Bank in Manchester (the paying bank) when certain documents are accepted by the Bank in Uganda (the accepting bank), which is Bankers Trust's correspondent bank in Uganda. The account party is the importer, Mainwaring Frocks, Inc. Once the documents are accepted in good order by the Bank in Uganda and the payment is made through the Bank in Man-

EXHIBIT 8.2 Sample of Irrevocable Letter of Credit

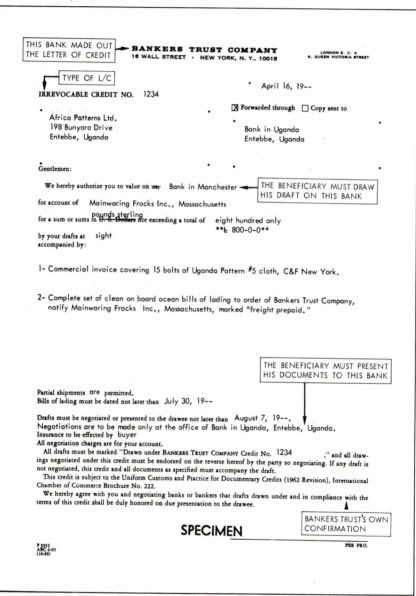

THIS BANK MADE OUT THE LETTER OF CREDIT →

BANKERS TRUST COMPANY
16 WALL STREET · NEW YORK, N. Y., 10015

LONDON E. C. 4
8. QUEEN VICTORIA STREET

TYPE OF L/C

IRREVOCABLE CREDIT NO. 1234

April 16, 19--

☒ Forwarded through ☐ Copy sent to

Africa Patterns Ltd.
198 Bunyoro Drive
Entebbe, Uganda

Bank in Uganda
Entebbe, Uganda

Gentlemen:

We hereby authorize you to value on us, Bank in Manchester ← THE BENEFICIARY MUST DRAW HIS DRAFT ON THIS BANK

for account of   Mainwaring Frocks Inc., Massachusetts

for a sum or sums in ~~U. S. Dollars~~ pounds sterling not exceeding a total of   eight hundred only
£ 800-0-0

by your drafts at   sight
accompanied by:

1- Commercial invoice covering 15 bolts of Uganda Pattern #5 cloth, C&F New York.

2- Complete set of clean on board ocean bills of lading to order of Bankers Trust Company, notify Mainwaring Frocks Inc., Massachusetts, marked "freight prepaid."

THE BENEFICIARY MUST PRESENT HIS DOCUMENTS TO THIS BANK

Partial shipments are permitted.
Bills of lading must be dated not later than July 30, 19--

Drafts must be negotiated or presented to the drawee not later than August 7, 19--.
Negotiations are to be made only at the office of Bank in Uganda, Entebbe, Uganda.
Insurance to be effected by buyer
All negotiation charges are for your account.
  All drafts must be marked "Drawn under BANKERS TRUST COMPANY Credit No. 1234   ," and all draw-ings negotiated under this credit must be endorsed on the reverse hereof by the party so negotiating. If any draft is not negotiated, this credit and all documents as specified must accompany the draft.
  This credit is subject to the Uniform Customs and Practice for Documentary Credits (1962 Revision), International Chamber of Commerce Brochure No. 222.
  We hereby agree with you and negotiating banks or bankers that drafts drawn under and in compliance with the terms of this credit shall be duly honored on due presentation to the drawee.

SPECIMEN

BANKERS TRUST'S OWN CONFIRMATION

F 3352
ABC 6-65
(10-65)

PER PRO.

SOURCE: The American Bankers Association, *Letters of Credit*, Book 2. Washington, D.C., 1968, p. 23.

chester, Bankers Trust will reimburse the Bank in Manchester. Bankers Trust then has the problem of collecting from Mainwaring Frocks. But, the exporter knows that Bankers Trust guarantees that she will be paid upon certification of shipment by various documents as noted in the draft (to be explained). She can be relatively unconcerned about the payment eventually made by Mainwaring Frocks to Bankers Trust.

The bank serves as a *guarantor of payment*, and that is the main value of the letter of credit. The date before which drafts must be negotiated, August 7, 19—, in Exhibit 8.2, gives the beneficiary a firm date until which the credit is guaranteed. The letter of credit can be a useful device when the buyer and seller are not known to each other, when the credit of the buyer is unknown, or when the seller demands quick payment.

The security of the bank involved is of concern to the exporter, of course. Hence, there are several varieties of letters of credit, depending on the relationships among the account party, the issuing bank, and the paying bank.

Confirmed Irrevocable Letters of Credit. If another bank adds its guarantee to the issuing bank's guarantee of payment in the specific letter of credit, this other bank *confirms* the initial letter of credit, which then becomes a *confirmed letter of credit*. Typically, the confirmation would be provided by a bank in the exporter's country—that is, a bank better known to the exporter. If the letter of credit in Exhibit 8.2 were confirmed, the Bank in Uganda would be the most likely bank to issue the confirmation. However, the letter of credit in Exhibit 8.2 is not confirmed and the Bank in Uganda's role is limited to checking and accepting the required documents.

Unconfirmed Irrevocable Letters of Credit. When the local bank rewrites the letter but does not add its name as a confirming bank, it sends an *advice on an irrevocable letter of credit*. In Exhibit 8.3 the Bank in Tokyo is the issuing bank and guarantees the credit of $1,000. Morgan Guaranty, the *advising bank*, will pay Tewig Spice, the beneficiary, upon presentation of the appropriate documents. However, should both the importer/account party (Lantern Trading Company) and the issuing bank (the Bank in Tokyo) fail to pay, Morgan Guaranty would not be responsible for payment.

Revocable Letters of Credit. In some cases neither the issuing bank nor the advising bank guarantees payment. In Exhibit 8.4 the advisory statement at the bottom of the letter indicates that there is no guarantee by either of the banks. However, once the documents are accepted by Irving Trust, showing that Morgan T. Burns, Inc., has

EXHIBIT 8.3 Sample of Advice on Irrevocable Letter of Credit

9-66-6M

FORM 11-4-846

MORGAN GUARANTY TRUST COMPANY
OF NEW YORK
INTERNATIONAL BANKING DIVISION
23 WALL STREET, NEW YORK, N. Y. 10015

February 10, 19--

Tewig Spice Company
568 Mott Street
New York, New York

On all communications please refer to
OUR REFERENCE NUMBER
K-2000

Dear Sirs:

We are instructed to advise you of the establishment by
• Bank in Tokyo
of their IRREVOCABLE Credit No L3-8120
in your favor, for the account of   Lantern Trading Company

for   U. S. $1,000.00 (ONE THOUSAND U. S. DOLLARS)

available upon presentation to us of your drafts at sight on us, accompanied by:

Commercial Invoice.

Full set of on board ocean steamer Bills of Lading to order of Bank in Tokyo, marked
"Notify Lantern Trading Co.,"

evidencing shipment of PLASTIC CHOP STICKS, C. I. F. Tokyo, From New York to Tokyo.

Except as otherwise expressly stated herein, this advice is subject to the Uniform Customs and Practice for Documentary Credits (1962 Revision), International Chamber of Commerce, Brochure No. 222.

Your drafts must indicate that they are drawn under the aforementioned
Advice . . . . , number K-2000   of the
Morgan Guaranty Trust Company of New York   and must be presented
to our Commercial Credits Department, 15 Broad Street, New York, N. Y. 10015 with
specified documents, not later than August 3, 19--   on which date this
advice expires.

▶ **THIS LETTER IS SOLELY AN ADVICE AND CONVEYS NO ENGAGEMENT BY US.**

ADVISING BANK IS NOT
CONFIRMING L/C

Yours very truly,

SPECIMEN
Authorized Signature

Immediately upon receipt please examine this advice, and if its terms are not clear to you or if you need any assistance in respect to your availment of it, we would welcome your communicating with us. Documents should be presented promptly and not later than 3 P.M.

SOURCE: The American Bankers Association, *Letters of Credit*, Book 2. Washington, D.C., 1968, p. 63.

EXHIBIT 8.4   Sample of Advice on Revocable Letter of Credit

Irving Trust Company

ONE WALL STREET
NEW YORK, N.Y. 10015

| TYPE OF L/C | → REVOCABLE ADVICE |

DATE March 1, 19--
REVOCABLE ADVICE
NO. 123456

Morgan T. Burns, Inc.
1421 Elm Road
New York, New York 10012

GENTLEMEN:

WE ARE INFORMED BY { Bank of Finance
London, England }

THAT YOU WILL DRAW ON US AT

SIGHT TO THE EXTENT OF

$10,400.00

FOR ACCOUNT OF   John Brown Ltd., London, England

YOUR DRAFTS MUST BE ACCOMPANIED BY THE FOLLOWING DOCUMENTS (COMPLETE SETS UNLESS OTHERWISE STATED) EVIDENCING SHIPMENT(S) OF:

Pump Parts, F.O.B. Vessel New York, from New York to Southampton

Commercial Invoice

On board ocean bills of lading issued to order of shipper and endorsed
in blank, marked "Notify John Brown Ltd., London, England."

Insurance covered by buyer.

> Description of the engagement of the
> issuing and advising banks to the
> beneficiary.

DRAFTS MUST CLEARLY SPECIFY THE NUMBER OF THIS ADVICE, AND BE PRESENTED AT THIS COMPANY NOT LATER THAN   June 1, 19--

THIS ADVICE IS SUBJECT TO THE UNIFORM CUSTOMS AND PRACTICE FOR DOCUMENTARY CREDITS, 1974 REVISION, INTERNATIONAL CHAMBER OF COMMERCE PUBLICATION 290.

THIS ADVICE, REVOCABLE AT ANY TIME WITHOUT NOTICE, IS FOR YOUR GUIDANCE ONLY IN PREPARING DRAFTS AND DOCUMENTS AND CONVEYS NO ENGAGEMENT OR OBLIGATION ON OUR PART OR ON THE PART OF OUR ABOVE-MENTIONED CORRESPONDENT.

NOTE

YOURS VERY TRULY

DOCUMENTS MUST CONFORM STRICTLY WITH THE TERMS OF THIS
ADVICE. IF YOU ARE UNABLE TO COMPLY WITH ITS TERMS, PLEASE
COMMUNICATE WITH US AND/OR YOUR CUSTOMER PROMPTLY WITH
A VIEW TO HAVING THE CONDITIONS CHANGED.

SPECIMEN

150 70 (8-75) Rev. 8-75

AUTHORIZED SIGNATURE

SOURCE: Irving Trust Company, New York, New York

shipped the goods as ordered by John Brown, Ltd., payment to the extent of $10,400 will be made by Irving Trust, the advising and paying bank. But, Morgan T. Burns, Inc., the beneficiary, has no guarantee that John Brown, Ltd. will not cancel its letter of credit at any time before the documents are presented. The only guarantee the exporter/beneficiary has is that, once the documents are accepted by Irving Trust, he will be paid if the letter of credit has not been canceled.

A summary of the terms and arrangements concerning these three types of letters of credit is shown in Exhibit 8.5. As suggested in the exhibit, letters of credit can have their terms altered at the initiation of the account party, subject to approval of certain other involved parties.

Negotiable Letters of Credit. In some cases the beneficiary of the letter of credit may not find it convenient to present documents to a particular paying bank. In cases when foreign exchange rates quoted by the banks differ, it may be hard for the beneficiary to know before payment date what bank would be most desirable as the paying bank. In these cases the *straight* letter of credit can be replaced by a *negotiable* letter of credit that could be used with any bank willing to act as paying bank. The difference in wording specifies which form is involved, as shown in Exhibit 8.6. In part A, the negotiable letter of credit says specifically that the "Drafts must be negotiated or presented to the drawee not later than. . . ." In contrast, the straight letter of credit in part B does not mention the word "negotiated." In the negotiable letter, the expiration date is the last date the letter of credit can be negotiated. Thus, in A, the expiration date is August 7. In addition, note

EXHIBIT 8.5   Arrangements in Different Letters of Credit

	Revocable Letter of Credit	Unconfirmed Irrevocable Letter of Credit	Confirmed Irrevocable Letter of Credit
Who applies for letter	Account party	Account party	Account party
Who is obligated to pay	None	Issuing bank	Issuing bank and confirming bank
Who applies for amendment	Account party	Account party	Account party
Who approves amendment	Issuing bank	Issuing bank and beneficiary	Issuing bank, beneficiary, and confirming bank
Who reimburses paying bank	Issuing bank	Issuing bank	Issuing bank
Who reimburses issuing bank	Account party	Account party	Account party

SOURCE: The American Bankers Association, *Letters of Credit*, Book 2. Washington, D.C., 1968, pp. 23, 137.

EXHIBIT 8.6 Negotiability Clause in Letters of Credit

(A)

STATEMENT THAT L/C
CAN BE NEGOTIATED

Drafts must be negotiated or presented to the drawee not later than August 7, 19--.
Negotiations are to be made only at the office of Bank in Uganda, Entebbe, Uganda.
Insurance to be effected by buyer
All negotiation charges are for your account.
   All drafts must be marked "Drawn under BANKERS TRUST COMPANY Credit No. 1234   ," and all draw-
ings negotiated under this credit must be endorsed on the reverse hereof by the party so negotiating. If any draft is
not negotiated, this credit and all documents as specified must accompany the draft.
   This credit is subject to the Uniform Customs and Practice for Documentary Credits (1962 Revision), International
Chamber of Commerce Brochure No. 222.
   We hereby agree with you and negotiating banks or bankers that drafts drawn under and in compliance with the
terms of this credit shall be duly honored on due presentation to the drawee.

SPECIMEN

PER PRO.

F 3332
ABC 6-65
(10-65)

(B)

THE ABOVE MENTIONED CORRESPONDENT ENGAGES WITH YOU THAT ALL DRAFTS DRAWN UNDER AND
IN COMPLIANCE WITH THE TERMS OF THIS CREDIT WILL BE DULY HONORED ON DELIVERY OF DOCU-
MENTS AS SPECIFIED IF PRESENTED AT THIS OFFICE ON OR BEFORE February 13, 19--   ; WE CONFIRM
THE CREDIT AND THEREBY UNDERTAKE THAT ALL DRAFTS DRAWN AND PRESENTED AS ABOVE SPECIFIED WILL
BE DULY HONORED BY US.
THIS CREDIT IS SUBJECT TO THE UNIFORM CUSTOMS AND PRACTICE FOR DOCUMENTARY CREDITS (1962 RE-
VISION), INTERNATIONAL CHAMBER OF COMMERCE BROCHURE NO. 222.

YOURS VERY TRULY,

SPECIMEN

ASST TREAS./PER PROCURATION

SOURCE: The American Bankers Association, *Letters of Credit*, Book 2. Washington, D.C.,
1968, pp. 23, 137.

229

that a separate paragraph of A requires that drafts drawn against the letter of credit must be endorsed and marked with reference to Credit No. 1234. This statement is not necessary in B, since the draft can be presented only to the paying bank designated in the letter of credit.

Sight and Time Letters of Credit. In all the examples presented so far, the issuing bank promises to pay a certain amount "at sight" of a draft (to be explained in the following section) and certain other documents. However, if the exporter wishes to extend credit to the importer, the exporter would require only a *time letter of credit.* In such a letter, the issuing bank promises to pay at a specified date *after* the presentation of certain documents. In this way the exporter may provide more lenient credit terms than the bank while retaining the payment guarantee of a major bank.

Transferable Letters of Credit. In a case where a trading house or intermediary does not know in advance the name of the final seller or exporter, the account party (buying importer) will open a *transferable letter of credit* between the firm and the trading house. The trading house can then tell prospective sellers that the buyer has a bank that guarantees payment for the purchase. When the trader finds the seller, the trader will instruct the advising bank to transfer the letter of credit to the seller, letting the seller become the new beneficiary. A transferable letter of credit is created by including a line such as, "This credit is transferable," in the documentation.

Documents Required by Letters of Credit. The various documents described in letters of credit are usually standard commercial forms. Thus, the *commercial invoice* is simply a bill for the goods that have been shipped. It details the banking arrangements and the product shipped, specifies any charges to be paid (such as insurance, freight, and handling), and usually the shipper and ports involved. The *bill of lading* is a control form for the goods, issued by the common carrier transporting the goods. It is usually issued to the exporter or to the bank issuing the letter of credit. This document shows that the merchandise has been received by the carrier, who agrees to deliver it according to special conditions. Possession of this document often establishes the ownership of the merchandise. Thus, it can be used to insure payment before delivery of goods, and it can also be used as collateral against loans. Various insurance policies, consular and customs forms, or invoices may also be required by terms of the letter of credit.

Compliance with governmental regulations may require documents in addition to the standard commercial forms. Among these other documents, the most common ones are the *consular invoice* and the *certificate of origin.* The *consular invoice* is a certification made by the country's consul abroad about the quantity and nature of the merchandise. It is often required for the assessment of import duties and clearance for entry to the given country. The *certificate of origin* is a verification of the origin of the goods. This document, provided by the exporter, may be required to determine appropriate tariffs and even to enforce the embargo on goods proceeding from certain countries.

Commercial attachés of embassies as well as export financing institutions in most countries are well trained to provide interested exporters and importers with information about regulations and restrictions on the movement of various merchandise. For example, in the United States the Department of Commerce oversees movement of merchandise out of the country. Most goods for export are not controlled, but some strategic goods or items with particular legislation may require special licenses. The Government Printing Office distributes copies of the Department's *Export Control Bulletins* and *Control Regulations* which detail these restrictions. Imports to the United States usually involve duty and some require licenses from the Department of the Treasury. Information and forms for these imports are available from the Foreign Assets Control Division of the Federal Reserve Bank of New York.

When there are irregularities in the documents, the paying bank has the choice of asking to have the letter of credit amended, asking the beneficiary to complete the documents in a specified manner, or receiving an indemnification from the beneficiary holding the bank not responsible if the account party later refuses to pay. In this situation the beneficiary has lost most of the benefit conveyed by the letter of credit. However, if the documents are in proper order but do not conform to the facts (for example, description of the color of the merchandise), the paying bank is *not* responsible for this variance. In this case the importer has to refer to the commercial legal code to determine the party responsible for the irregularity.[3]

Documents associated with international trade are complex in

---

[3]The letters of credit shown here all have a clause at the bottom which is typical of U.S.-issued letters of credit. As can be seen in Exhibit 8.4, this phrase reads: "This advice is subject to the Uniform Customs and Practice for Documentary Credits (1974 Revision), International Chamber of Commerce Publication 290." This clause indicates the regulations under which shipment disputes or any arguments between any of the parties are to be settled. They are available from banks, from chambers of commerce, and from other sources. In addition, the *Revised American Foreign Trade Definitions— 1941* specify common terms for adjudication of disputes arising under most U.S. letters of credit if buyer and seller agree to abide by them. (The definitions were adopted on July 30, 1941 by a joint committee representing the Chamber of Commerce of the United States, the National Council of American Importers, Inc., and the National Foreign Trade Council, Inc.)

During the Iranian hostage crisis, some U. S. multinationals asked courts to block payments under letters of credit taken out by those firms in favor of the government of Iran. The argument was that the government had changed so massively that the preconditions of the letter of credit did not apply—that is, the government of the Shah did not exist, and hence the letter of credit was invalid.

number and detail. Based on estimates for one trade year in the United States, the average shipment required 46 documents and a total of 360 copies, at an average shipment cost of about $350. This total amounted to over 8% of the cost of imports and exports. Fortunately, efforts have been made to streamline this process by a reduction in the number of forms and simplification of the remaining forms.[4]

Import/Export Drafts

The final payment in the trade-financing process usually is made after presentation of a *draft*. A *draft* is a written order to pay a specified amount of money, at a specified point in time, to a given person or to the bearer. In this sense, a check you write to someone is one form of a draft. The check orders the commercial bank on which it is drawn to pay a specified amount on sight to the person named in the check, or to the bearer.

The exporter includes a draft together with the documents that the letter of credit specifies. In this case, the draft is a formal version of the account receivable that the exporter possesses as a result of the export sale. The parties involved in a draft are the drawer, the drawee, and the payee. In an export draft, the *drawer* is the exporter who signs the document. The *drawee* is the entity to whom the draft is addressed (the importer or his or her bank), who makes the payment on the document. The *payee* is the importer who ultimately pays for the goods. The payee and the drawee may be the same.

For example, from Exhibit 8.7 one may presume that G. T. Tyler (the drawer) exported goods to an importer who previously arranged a letter of credit with the Bank in Switzerland, the letter of credit's issuing bank for the payee or importer. G. T. Tyler completes the documents required under the Bank in Switzerland's letter of credit and hands them over to Morgan Guaranty (the drawee) with this draft payable to itself (the Tyler Company). However, the draft could have been made payable to a bank or to any other entity. Morgan Guaranty may have confirmed the letter of credit, or it may have been only the agent or the advisor of the letter.

The draft in Exhibit 8.7 is labeled "at sight." As soon as the documents are found to be in good order, the draft is honored by Morgan Guaranty and the Tyler Company has its account credited $1,000. Morgan Guaranty, even if it is only a paying bank, will examine the documents carefully. Should the bank issuing the letter of credit, the Bank

---

[4]Arthur E. Bayalis, "The Documentation Dilemma in International Trade," *Columbia Journal of World Business,* Spring 1976, pp. 15–22.

EXHIBIT 8.7 Sample of Sight Draft

```
┌──────────────────────────────────────────────────────────────┐
│  ┌────────────────────────────────────────────────────────┐  │
│  │  Bank in Switzerland Credit ABZ-6033                   │  │
│  │                                                         │  │
│  │  $  1,000.00 (U.S.)         New York,  September 1,  19 -- │  │
│  │                                                         │  │
│  │   At sight                                Pay to the order of │  │
│  │                                                         │  │
│  │              Ourselves        (A)                       │  │
│  │                                                         │  │
│  │   One thousand and 00/100 - - - - - - - - - - - - - -  Dollars │  │
│  │                                                         │  │
│  │  To:  Morgan Guaranty        G. T. Tyler Company    (B) │  │
│  │     (C)  Trust Company                                  │  │
│  │        New York, N.Y.  SPECIMEN                         │  │
│  └────────────────────────────────────────────────────────┘  │
└──────────────────────────────────────────────────────────────┘
```

SOURCE: The American Bankers Association, *Letters of Credit,* Book 3. Washington, D.C., 1968, p. 77. By permission of the American Bankers Association and Morgan Guaranty Trust Company of New York.

in Switzerland, find any irregularity in the documents after Morgan Guaranty has paid the Tyler Company, then Morgan Guaranty may not be reimbursed—even though it did not confirm or advise on the letter of credit.

Note that the export draft is drawn by the person or company to whom the money is owed. This is in contrast to an import draft, in which the importer (the person who owes the money) is the one who draws the draft. In an import draft the importer is both the drawer and the payee. An import draft is usually made payable to the bank to whom the importer orders itself to pay the given amount at the time specified by the draft. In this case, the draft is a formal version of the account payable the importer has. The bank to whom the draft is payable usually is the same as the drawee, who will then transfer funds from the importer's account to its own account.

Sight and Time Drafts. As explained previously, the draft in Exhibit 8.7 is a *sight draft* and it is paid on presentation when the documents are in good order. An alternative arrangement that the two parties may have agreed upon and confirmed in a letter of credit is a *time draft*. Time drafts will specify payment typically 30, 60, 90, 120, or 180 days *after date* (after the date the draft is drawn) or *after sight* (after the draft has been presented and accepted by the paying bank). The terms of payment are often called the draft's *tenor*. These terms are agreed upon by the importer and the exporter as part of their business arrangements pursuant to the sale of the product. A time draft is a way for the exporter to extend credit to the importer. If a letter of credit is part of the trade transaction, the paying terms in the draft must be the same as those in the letter.

Firms well known to each other often do not find the letter of credit necessary. Instead, the exporter will use a bank as a collection agency, sending a draft drawn according to terms agreed upon by the two parties, together with required documents and a letter of instruction to the bank for collection. Typically, the exporter's local bank will then deal with a bank in the importer's land, arranging for collection of the funds that are due the exporter.[5]

The collecting bank will turn over to the importer the documents certifying title to the goods when the importer pays (if it is a sight draft) or when the importer accepts the draft liability (if it is a time draft). Although the collecting bank can submit the drafts for payment or acceptance on receipt, the bank usually withholds presentation of the drafts until the goods have arrived in the importer's port. As part of the letter of instruction to the local bank, the exporter will specify the fees to be collected (if any), the means and currency for remission of the funds, and so forth.

Documents Required by Drafts.   Drafts are also classified according to the documents that are required to accompany the draft. A *clean draft* does not require any other document. A *documentary draft* requires accompanying documents such as bill of lading, commercial invoices, insurance certificates, and so on.

TRADE FINANCING FROM THIRD PARTIES

Financial institutions often extend credit directly to exporters and importers to finance international trade. Some of this financing is done in the traditional forms of short-term lending. More often, the financing takes the form of the export draft or import draft. These drafts can be refinanced in the credit markets when they become *bankers' acceptances*. In the case when a bank is financing the importer, the ownership of the goods is usually controlled by the bank through a *trust receipt*.

---

[5]There is also a *documented discount note* that may be used. It is essentially a corporate note to which is attached a bank's irrevocable letter guaranteeing payment on the note to any purchaser.

Finally, government agencies in many countries are active in providing financing for the exports from their own countries.

Loans to Importers and Trust Receipts

When the importer pays for the goods some time after they are received, the importer usually signs a *trust receipt* for the goods. Under this arrangement, a bank retains title to the goods, with the importer operating as a trustee. The trust receipt, in fact, converts the goods into a collateral for the funds the importer owes. As the goods are sold, proceeds are remitted to the bank.

If the exporter issued a time draft, the bank pays the exporter when the time draft is due. Part of these funds may have been collected already from the importer under the trust receipt. If a sight draft was used, the exporter is paid when the appropriate documents are presented at sight. In this case, the funds remitted by the importer to the bank under the trust receipt are a repayment for the funds the bank already paid to the exporter on the importer's behalf.

When the exporter insists on a sight draft or the importer prefers this alternative, the importer may borrow directly from a local bank against an import draft, in conjunction with a trust receipt. In this case the loan is supported by the import draft which, in turn, is collateralized by the goods themselves. These import drafts are eligible to be converted into bankers' acceptances (to be explained subsequently).

Direct Loans to Exporters

When the exporter wants immediate payment and the terms of the sale involve a time draft, there are several means for reimbursement. The bank may lend against a set percentage of the drafts outstanding. This process is similar to receivable financing and is based on the credit history of the exporter's customers. In other cases, the exporter may use the drafts as collateral for a bank note. A third method, which is popular when a major exporter can convince the bank to agree, is through bankers' acceptances.

Bankers' Acceptances

Whenever an import draft or an export draft is involved in a trade transaction, the draft has the potential of becoming a *bankers' acceptance*—a draft connected with trade and accepted by a bank.

Suppose the exporter and the importer have agreed to "90-day sight" terms. This arrangement means the the exporter will be paid 90 days after the bank certifies that the documents are in good order. In Exhibit 8.8 the exporter, John Doe and Company, has drawn a 90-day sight time draft against a letter of credit from the Bank in Lima, presumably arranged by the importer of the goods. When Morgan Guaranty, the paying bank, acknowledges the forms as being in good order,

EXHIBIT 8.8 Samples of Time Draft and Bankers' Acceptance

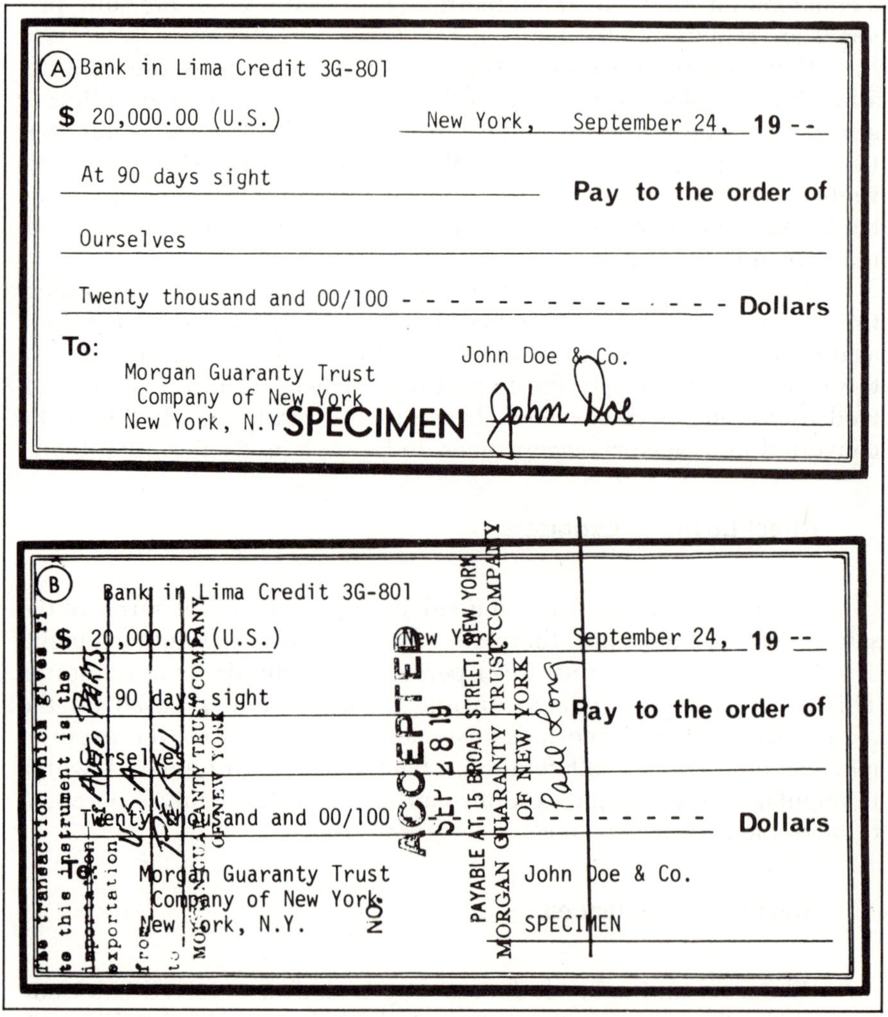

Ⓐ Bank in Lima Credit 3G-801

$ 20,000.00 (U.S.) New York, September 24, 19 --

At 90 days sight Pay to the order of

Ourselves

Twenty thousand and 00/100 ------------------ Dollars

To:

Morgan Guaranty Trust
Company of New York
New York, N.Y.

John Doe & Co.

SPECIMEN

Ⓑ Bank in Lima Credit 3G-801

$ 20,000.00 (U.S.) New York, September 24, 19 --

At 90 days sight Pay to the order of

Ourselves

Twenty thousand and 00/100 ---------- Dollars

To:

Morgan Guaranty Trust
Company of New York
New York, N.Y.

John Doe & Co.

SPECIMEN

ACCEPTED SEP 28 19

PAYABLE AT 15 BROAD STREET, NEW YORK
MORGAN GUARANTY TRUST COMPANY
OF NEW YORK

MORGAN GUARANTY TRUST COMPANY
OF NEW YORK

The transaction which gives rise to this instrument is the importation exportation of ... from ... to ...

SOURCE: The American Bankers Association, *Letters of Credit*, Book 3. Washington, D.C., 1968, p. 35.

it may stamp "ACCEPTED" across the face of the draft, date it, and sign it. This stamp guarantees that Morgan will pay the draft as noted, 90 days from the date of acceptance, or December 28. To accept or guarantee a draft, the accepting bank charges a commission, usually between 1% and 1½% per annum.

With this acceptance in hand, the exporter may sell the draft/ acceptance (now called a *bankers' acceptance*) to an investor at a discount. The investor knows that the bank will pay the face amount at some future date, and the discount represents the going interest rate for bankers' acceptances. Alternatively, the bank may buy the draft/acceptance from the exporter at a discount, repaying itself when the importer's bank remits funds. In many countries the bank may rediscount the acceptance easily with its central bank. Finally, the importer, as the account party to the letter of credit, may have agreed to pay the discount when the beneficiary presents the draft. The beneficiary receives the full face amount and the paying bank receives the discount from the importer. Later, when the bankers' acceptance matures, the bank collects the full amount of the draft (which is what it had paid the beneficiary).

Bankers' acceptances tend to be especially popular in periods of tight money and they have expanded rapidly in total amount in recent years. One reason is that a U.S. bank that sells an export or import acceptance, in contrast to accepting a deposit, is not required to maintain reserves against it if the original maturity of the acceptance is 6 months or less.[6] In mid-1945, over $105 million of U.S. bankers' acceptances were outstanding. By the end of 1982, U.S. bankers' acceptances outstanding had climbed to $79.5 billion. Third-country acceptances, defined as acceptances created to finance the shipment of goods between foreign countries, have dominated the growth of this market in recent years. At the end of 1982 this category of acceptances accounted for 53 percent of the acceptances' market in the United States.

Loans from Governmental Agencies

The Export-Import Bank of the United States (Eximbank), created in 1934, is a major force aiding U.S. exporters. An independent agency of the executive branch, it provides billions of dollars of credit and insurance to help foreigners import U.S. goods. Through the Foreign Credit Insurance Association, a variety of policies are available to ex-

---

[6]See Ralph T. Helfrich, "Trading in Bankers' Acceptances: A View from the Acceptance Desk of the Federal Reserve Bank of New York," *Monthly Review*, Federal Reserve Bank of New York, February 1976, pp. 51-7

porters to protect them against nonpayment by their overseas customers. In many cases Eximbank will participate with commercial banks and/or the exporter in a direct loan to a foreign customer. Eximbank will take the loans of longer maturity, leaving those with shorter maturities to the commercial banks and the exporter.

Other industrial countries have similar financial institutions to encourage the export of their goods. The competition among these institutions to protect the countries' exports can be fierce, particularly when the goods involved are the so-called "big ticket" items that require medium-to long-term financing. In these cases the financial package accompanying the goods can make a big difference to the buyer. The competition in financial terms is such that it is not uncommon to have the government of the exporter's country include direct aid as part of the financial package.

Financing with Barter and Nonconvertible Currencies

Socialist bloc countries and developing countries often resort to special trade arrangements which eliminate the use of their scarce convertible currencies. These arrangements fall into two major categories: barter of goods and settlement in bilateral clearing funds.

Under the *barter of goods* (also called *countertrade*), the importing country must settle at least a portion of the import bill in the form of goods manufactured in the importing country. It is then up to the exporter to find a buyer for these goods. In some well-diversified multinationals, the buyer for the goods received in payment for the export sale can be found within the company's system of subsidiaries. In other cases, brokers who specialize in this kind of transaction can be engaged to find a buyer for the goods, often at a heavy discount.

Countries engaged in trade through barter often make agreements establishing the types and amounts of goods they will barter among themselves. Often these agreements establish that the payment for the traded goods is to be made in terms of special *clearing funds*. For example, suppose such an agreement exists between country A and country B. Then whenever A exports part of the agreed-upon goods to B, it is paid in the form of B's clearing funds. These clearing funds are, in fact, funds denominated in B's currency and available for the settlement of international transactions.

Exporters from a country that does not have such a bilateral agreement with these countries can be paid only with clearing funds on another country—one that does have a bilateral agreement. In our example, if an exporter from a third country sells goods to country A, the exporter may be paid in the form of B's clearing funds. These clearing funds are good to pay for goods purchased from B. If the exporter can use these funds in this manner, that is the end of the transaction. However, if the exporter does not have any need for goods from B, the only way for the exporter to obtain convertible currency is to find somebody who wishes to import goods from B and who is able to pay in convertible currency. The exporter would then sell B's clearing funds to that importer in exchange for convertible currency, usually at a heavy discount. However, the discounts on these clearing funds from various countries are well known in the marketplace.

If we combine these transactions among country A, country B, the exporter, and the importer, we have the following: Country A exported goods to country B and imported goods from the exporter. Both of these transactions were financed with B's clearing funds. Also, the outside exporter and importer did the desired transactions using country B's clearing funds. A diagram of this series of transactions appears in Exhibit 8.9.

EXHIBIT 8.9 Diagram of Transactions Using Bilateral Funds

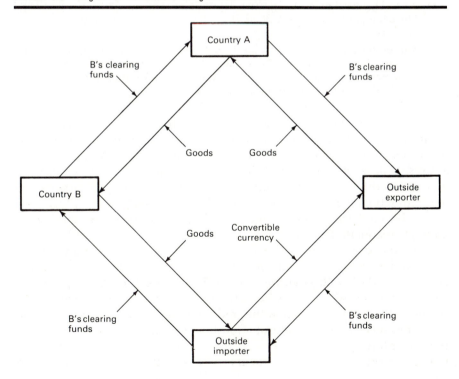

FOREIGN EXCHANGE RISK AND CREDIT RISK:
SOME TRADEOFFS

In the first section of this chapter we considered various financing strategies in a situation in which the exporter arranged for the financing of the export sale (the sale terms called for payment 30 days after delivery) and the exporter bore the initial exchange risk (the Mexican exporter invoiced the sale in U.S. dollars). We then discussed other methods by which international trade can be financed and the credit risk borne by the ultimate lender can be limited. They offer alternatives to the financing arrangements shown in our initial example. We can think about these various alternatives as the answers to two basic questions: (1) How much foreign exchange risk does each party bear? and (2) How much credit risk does each party bear?

In the context of the Mexican exporter example, we can answer these questions in the following manner:

1. The foreign exchange risk is at a maximum to the exporter if he sells in terms of U.S. dollars for payment in the future and does nothing else but wait. The foreign exchange risk is eliminated if the billing is made in Mexican pesos or if a U.S. dollar billing is covered in the financial markets.

2. The credit risk is at a maximum to the exporter when selling on time in an open account, without any collateral. The credit risk is at a minimum if an irrevocable confirmed letter of credit payable upon presentation of a sight draft is required from the importer.

Obviously, the exporter would like to minimize these risks. But so would the importer. In this example the Mexican exporter would minimize the exchange and credit risks if he were paid in Mexican pesos at presentation of a sight draft drawn against an irrevocable confirmed letter of credit. On the other hand, the U.S. importer would rather have the transaction as initially presented—that is, denominated in U.S. dollars to be paid later and on open account. How are these conflicting interests reconciled?

In the discussion of the foreign exchange risks in international trade and how to insure against them, the focus was on the explicit costs associated with covering a cash flow as well as the opportunity gains and losses of the two alternatives of covering or not covering. To the extent that the time when the trade transaction begins and the time when the receipt or payment of a foreign currency occurs are different, there is a foreign exchange risk. If the export sale is denominated in a foreign currency, the exporter bears the risk; if the sale is denominated in the exporter's currency, the importer bears the risk. If this risk is considered high enough to require insurance, somebody is going to have to pay the price for that insurance.

The first section showed how to calculate the cost of covering a cash flow. Whether the exporter bears this cost or whether it is passed on in terms of higher prices or explicit extra charges depends on the bargaining power of each party. An apparent alternative in our earlier example is to bring in a financial intermediary to extend a loan to the U.S. importer in dollars and to pay the Mexican exporter in pesos. Now the exchange risk is shifted from the exporter to a financial institution. However, this action has not necessarily shifted the cost of buying insurance. The financial intermediary has had its foreign exchange position altered as a result of this transaction. It is not difficult to imagine that the costs incurred by the financial institution in changing its foreign exchange position back to the original one will be passed along to the trading parties. If the market is working efficiently, the situation is virtually the same as that of trading under open account, except that now the necessary fees for the financial intermediary are added!

The amount of credit risk incurred by the exporter also has a cost attached to it. Such credit risk can be minimized by bringing in the largest possible number of financial institutions to share the responsibility for payment of the merchandise. However, each of these institutions will testify that payment will be forthcoming only because it receives a fee from the importer as a charge for the letter of credit. This fee effectively increases the price of the merchandise to the importer, therefore minimizing the competitiveness of the exporter's prices.

The solution to the problem of how much credit the exporter will provide to the importer is similar to the evaluation of how much foreign exchange risk each party assumes. To the exporter, the extension of trade credit is similar to the acquisition of a financial asset. The account receivable has an explicit return to the extent that it increases sales and it may be a substitute for lower prices or higher quality goods. However, the account receivable has an opportunity cost that can be measured by the net return that the exporter could make were those funds not used in financing the importer. Notice that this is a *net* return. In order for the exporter to extend this credit, a source of funds must be found, and these funds have a cost attached to them. Thus, another consideration in extending credit to the importer is the cost of money to the exporter, who in this regard is operating as a financial intermediary. Obviously, if the exporter refuses to extend this credit, the problem is only shifted to the importer, who must find a source of funds to finance inventories until sold. This loan also has an interest rate attached to it that can be translated into a higher cost of goods purchased.

It is not always the case that the interests of the exporter and the importer are diametrically opposed. On occasion, the alternatives appear to be somewhat biased. One source of bias may be the difference in credit worthiness between the importer and the exporter. For importers with a very good credit standing it may be better to arrange their own trade financing and to save their bargaining power to extract a better price from the exporter—an area in which the exporter may be more capable of delivering better terms.

Another source of bias in the assessment of financing and insurance costs derives from the fact that most business enterprises consider their local currency as the unit of account. For example, a German person considers the German mark to be the unit of account; an American considers the U.S. dollar to be the unit of account. To the extent that there is some tendency to ignore the opportunity gains from dealing in a currency other than the local one, the German exporter might be very happy to be paid in marks. If the American importer, and even the market, actually thinks that the mark is likely to depreciate by the time that payment is due, the importer will be glad to have the import liability denominated in marks and might even be willing to pay the interest charges for term credit. In cases of different assessments of costs and risks, a compromise is easy to achieve. Given the market facts, the final word will be determined by the bargaining power of each party.

SUMMARY

The need for financing and the associated interest rate and credit risks occur for the international trader as well as for the domestic trader; however, in international trade these problems are accompanied by foreign exchange risk to at least one of the parties. The financial officer in international trade must provide the needed financing and make a choice as to whether to cover all the attendant risks all the time, never to cover them, or to cover them selectively depending on the manager's expectations about market rates relative to the market's expectations.

To finance trade without any financial risk requires obtaining a rate in advance at which the cash flows in each currency, for every date, can be matched. More specifically, covering the rate risk requires obtaining financing for the complete duration of the financing need. Covering the exchange risk involves obtaining a rate at which the conversion of currencies will eventually be made. The financing and the exchange risk problems can be solved simultaneously by denominating the financing in the currency of the expected inflows and borrowing an amount equal to the total inflows. Alternatively, the financing may be done for the required amount and time in any currency, while the exchange risk is covered in the forward market by selling the inflow currency against the outflow currency for the specific dates when the inflows are expected.

Taking selected risks involves financing with a maturity shorter than the length of the financing need, planning to refinance later on, at expected lower interest rates. Exchange risk can be accepted by leaving the exposure open and waiting until later to establish the exchange rate at which the conversion of currencies will be realized. The financial officer must choose whether to take an interest rate risk in one, or both, or none, of the currencies involved, and whether to cover or not to cover the exchange risk.

To facilitate international trade, documents have been developed which serve to reduce the credit risk to the ultimate lender of funds who finances the transaction. Among these, the letter of credit and the import or export draft are the most important ones.

An importer, as the *account party,* may arrange with a bank to issue a *letter of credit* in which the bank guarantees payment, subject to proper certifications of shipment of goods. This letter of credit assures the exporter that there will be reimbursement for goods shipped to the importer. The exporter's local bank may *advise* on or *confirm* the letter of credit, in which case the local bank becomes a coguarantor of the payment. When not confirmed by either the issuing bank or the local bank, letters of credit are *revocable* at the discretion of the account party. However, once the documents and the draft accompanying them are accepted by the paying bank, they cannot be canceled. Letters of credit may be *transferable* (which facilitates the use of a trading intermediary who has found a buyer with credit but who is still seeking a supplier) and may be *negotiable* (which permits the exporter to select the bank for collection at a later time).

Most countries have regulations governing imports and exports of certain products. Additional documents are usually required to show compliance with these regulations. In the United States, the restrictions on exports are noted in the Department of Commerce's *Control Regulations* and *Export Control Bulletins.* Restrictions on imports, in addition to duty collected by the Department of the Treasury, are noted in publications of the Foreign Assets Control Division of the Federal Reserve Bank of New York.

The actual payment in international trade is usually completed by means of a *draft*—that is, a demand for payment by the drawer (the exporter, or beneficiary of the letter of credit) sent to the collecting bank against the issuing bank's letter of credit. The draft may be a *sight draft,* in which case there is immediate payment once the paying bank has acknowledged receipt of the draft and documents required by the letter of credit; or it may be a *time draft,* in which case payment will occur a specified number of days beyond the date of the draft or from sight when the draft is accepted by the bank.

When payment for the imported merchandise is made through a sight draft, the importer usually obtains financing for these goods. A common arrangement is the *trust receipt.* In this arrangement the goods legally belong to the bank (which pays the exporter on the sight draft) and the importer keeps the goods in trust until they are sold. Repayment to the bank is made according to the terms of the trust agreement.

When a time draft is accepted by the bank, it becomes a *bankers' acceptance* and may be negotiated. Hence, the holder of the draft may sell it to the bank or to an investor at a discount, receiving payment immediately. Upon the maturity of the acceptance, the account party pays the holder of the draft the full face amount. In some cases the beneficiary/drawer of the draft will receive the full amount immediately with the account party paying the discount plus the full face amount to the bank at a later date.

In many cases the drafts are used by the exporter and the importer on terms to which they have agreed without the letter of credit of an issuing bank. In these cases the banks usually act as collecting parties, remitting funds to the exporter subject to completion of certain requirements as specified by the importer.

The U.S. Export-Import Bank is an important force for helping U.S. exporters sell their goods to foreign importers. This independent government agency encourages the growth of U.S. exports through a program of guaranteed loans; direct loans to foreign buyers, who may be individuals, firms, or governments; loans to exporters; insurance programs; and other items. Other countries have similar institutions to facilitate the financing of exports of their goods.

Alternative arrangements have evolved to finance trade when the use of convertible currency is restricted. Among these, *barter* (which has existed since ancient times) and *bilateral agreements* for settlement in earmarked clearing funds are often used by socialist countries and many developing countries.

The nature of foreign exchange risk and the financing arrangements between importer and exporter fundamentally depend on the relative bargaining power of the parties when their interests conflict. When financial intermediaries are involved to absolve the participants of some risks, the fees for these intermediaries must be added to the cost of the transaction.

QUESTIONS

1. A U.S. distributor who imports perfumes from France is notified by the French exporter that in the future the exporter does not wish to sell on open account any longer. You are a bank officer who considers the distributor's account a valuable account. What financing arrangements would you offer to the U.S. distributor?

2. A small U.S. manufacturer of specialized heavy equipment has found an export market for his products in Argentina. He now approaches you, an officer in the bank with whom he usually works, to inquire about alternative financial arrangements available. What would you tell him?

3. If there is no change in the spot rate of a currency in a given period, does it make any difference whether one covers a transaction in the forward market or in the money market? Give an example to support your answer.

4. What is the purpose of a letter of credit? What are the major types?

5. How may an exporter use a letter of credit to extend credit to an importer?

6. Who are the parties involved in a draft? Why is a check you write to your department store a draft? Who are the parties in that "draft"?

7. What is meant by a draft's tenor? What are examples of different tenors? Why do these differences exist?

8. Can a banker's acceptance be sold to another party? Since it does not pay interest, why would a person buy it? Who guarantees payment?

9. Edward M. Graham, a United States wholesaler of specialty clothes for men and women, hopes to expand his operations considerably by emphasizing a new line of leisure wear to be marketed through various clothing boutiques. As part of this plan, he has contacted three exporters with a view toward supplying his needs. He considers the products and offerings of each comparable in terms of his business, although each reflects certain national styles and trends.

   Assume the three potential suppliers have offered him various terms. Mary Freed Ltd. of London has suggested that an appropriate financial arrangement would involve a revocable letter of credit since she knows his general reputation. They agree that if Mr. Graham can arrange the letter of credit through a bank, Ms. Freed will draw a time draft payable in sterling 60 days after sight.

Thomas Rodriguez of Spain has an interest in supplying Mr. Graham, but he indicates that he would expect a confirmed irrevocable negotiable letter of credit, with drafts drawn under the letter payable at sight. Credit would be available, he suggests, at a rate of 2% per month, but should not exceed 90 days after shipment.

Finally, Heinz Riehl of Geneva manufactures an Austrian style of après-ski lounging clothes and has indicated that he has long wished to have an American distributor. He suggests that an appropriate method of operation would be for Mr. Graham to deposit funds to the Riehl account in Basel 30 days prior to a shipment, with the deposit equal to 50% of the invoiced value of the goods. After shipment, the balance would be due within 10 days of receipt by Mr. Graham. Mr. Riehl noted that his general impressions of Mr. Graham's business were sufficient to commend the Graham firm as a customer, and he has no need for a letter of credit arrangement.

If you were to help Mr. Graham with this decision, what data would you need? How would you analyze the decision? In addition to any factors you believe are particularly important, consider the following elements and how they would alter the decision. Give an example of how Mr. Graham might favor one supplier over the others depending on the facts surrounding each item noted:

(a) The currency prospects of each of the exporters relative to Mr. Graham's currency, the U.S. dollar

(b) The cost of funds for payable financing by Mr. Graham

(c) The option to accept or to reject the Spanish credit terms as each order is due

(d) The cost of different letters of credit from the banks involved

BIBLIOGRAPHY

Bayalis, Arthur E., "The Documentation Dilemma in International Trade," *Columbia Journal of World Business*, Spring 1976, pp. 15–22.

Bloch, Henry Simon, "Export Financing Emerging as a Major Policy Problem," *Columbia Journal of World Business*, Fall 1976, pp. 85–95.

Feinberg, Richard E., *Subsidizing Success: The Export–Import Bank in the U. S. Economy*, Cambridge: Cambridge University Press, 1982.

The Financing of Exports and Imports. New York: Morgan Guaranty Trust Company, 1973.

Giddy, Ian H., "Why It Doesn't Pay to Make a Habit of Forward Hedging," *Euromoney*, Dec. 1976, pp. 96–100.

Gmur, Charles J., ed., *Trade Financing.* London: Euromoney Publications, 1981.

Greene, James, *Organizing for Exporting.* New York: National Industrial Conference Board Business Policy Study Number 26, 1968.

Harrington, J. A., *Specifics on Commercial Letters of Credit and Bankers' Acceptances.* Jersey City, N.J.: Scott Printing Corporation, 1974.

Helfrich, Ralph T., 'Trading in Bankers' Acceptances: A View from the Acceptance Desk of the Federal Reserve Bank of New York," *Monthly Review,* Federal Reserve Bank of New York, Feb. 1976, pp. 51–57.

Hollis, Stanley E., *Guide to Export Credit Insurance.* New York: Foreign Credit Insurance Association, 1971.

Lehner, Urban C., "How Japan Tries to Shut Out Foreign Goods," *Wall Street Journal,* Sept. 30, 1982, p. 14.

Letters of Credit, Books 2 and 3. Washington, D.C.: The American Bankers Association, 1968.

Overseas Private Investment Corporation, *An Introduction to OPIC.* Washington, D.C., 1973.

Riehl, Heinz, and Rita M. Rodriguez, *Foreign Exchange and Money Markets.* New York: McGraw-Hill Book Company, 1983.

U.S. Government, Department of Commerce, *Control Regulations.* Washington, D.C.: Government Printing Office.

———, *Export Control Bulletins.* Washington, D.C.: Government Printing Office.

Westerfield, Janice Moulton, "An Examination of Foreign Exchange Risk under Fixed and Floating Regimes," *Journal of International Economics,* May 1977, pp. 181–200.

NEW ENGLAND
CHRISTMAS
WREATHS

JOHN MAVERICK, USING the motto "bring the New England Christmas spirit to Japan with a genuine New England Christmas wreath," has succeeded in selling about $90,000 worth of such wreaths in Japan for this Christmas season. However, as of November 1 he has some cash problems which he has asked us to manage for him. He expects the following transactions to take place:

DECEMBER 1:

1. Shipment of the wreaths to Japan is made by air freight. Terms are net 30 days. Sale is invoiced in yen for a total of ¥20.7 million ($90,000 at current spot rate of ¥230/$).
2. Payment for the trees, labor, and freight are due. Total amount due is $44,000.
3. Personal dollar loan taken from the bank to finance promotional expenses, including a trip to Japan, is due. The principal of the 90-day loan is $15,000 and it has a 20% interest rate payable upon maturity.
4. Cash sales in the United States are made for $8,000.

DECEMBER 31:

5. Income taxes are due in the United States for the estimated amount of $19,000.
6. Payment is due for house bought in Caribbean for vacation purposes. Amount due is CarPs481,250.

Mr. Maverick would like to spend a vacation at his new island, and thus wants any remaining profits to be made available in Caribbean pesos. Market rates, as of November 1, are as shown in the accompanying table.

Exchange Rates		
Spot rates		
Caribbean peso	CarPs25.00/$	
Yen	¥230/$	
Forward rates	30-day	60-day
Caribbean peso	CarPs25.84/$	CarPs26.69/$
Yen	¥228.50/$	¥226.94/$
Interest Rates		
Caribbean peso	57.0%	57.0%
Yen	8.5%	8.5%
U.S. dollar	16.5%	16.5%

PRELIMINARY ANALYSIS

The cash flows associated with each of these transactions are as follows:

1. The shipment of wreaths to Japan produces an inflow in yen in the amount of ¥20.7 million on December 30.
2. The payment for trees, labor, and freight is an outflow in dollars in the amount of $44,000 on December 1.
3. The personal loan due on December 1 is a dollar outflow in the amount of $15,750 on that date. (Interest equals $20\% \times \$15,000 \times 3/12$.)
4. Cash sales in the United States are a dollar inflow of $8,000 on December 1.
5. Tax payments are a dollar outflow of $19,000 on December 30.
6. Purchase of the house is an outflow in pesos for CarPs481,250 on December 31.

These cash flows by date and currency are shown as the initial situation in Exhibit F.1. The total cash flows for the period—the initial net exchange positions—show a net outflow in dollars of $70,750, a net outflow in Caribbean pesos of CarPs481,250, and a net inflow in yen of ¥20.7 million. If we express the net cash flows in each currency in terms of dollars using the spot rates for November 1, then net inflows equal net outflows. (¥20.7 million at ¥230/$ equals $90,000; and CarPs481,250 at CarPs25.00/$ equals $19,250. Combined dollar and peso outflows are $90,000, equal to the dollar equivalent of yen inflow.)

John Maverick has a profitable operation. After all expenses are covered, he has profits left to buy a house in the Caribbean for CarPs481,250, equivalent to $19,250 at the initial spot rates. However, he has the following problems that must be managed:

1. On December 1 there is a net cash outflow due in dollars for $51,750. However, the inflows from the sale of wreaths will not be realized until

December 31. Dollar funds are needed on December 1 to finance this cash flow gap of 30 days.

2. On November 1 we are not certain of the interest rate at which funds will be available on December 1, even if lines of credit are available. There is an *interest rate risk.*

3. Although net inflows equal net outflows at December 1 spot rate, this may not be the case if we wait until December 31 to convert the yen inflow realized on that date into dollars and Caribbean pesos. There is a *net exchange position,* long in yen and short in dollars and Caribbean pesos.

If Mr. Maverick has approved lines of credit, the financing problem poses the *risk of interest rate fluctuations* between now and December 1, when the dollar funds are needed. The net exchange positions pose the *risk of exchange rate fluctuations* between now and December 31, when the yen inflow is realized. If we consider the purchase of the island to be approximately equal in value to the profits in the wreath business, then the interest rate risk and the exchange risks make it uncertain whether the CarPs481,250 estimated profit will be realized. Interest rate and exchange rate fluctuations can affect whether profits will be more or less than CarPs481,250. If interest rates increase and/or the yen depreciates, the profits will be less than CarPs481,250. If interest rates decrease and/or the yen appreciates, profits will be more than CarPs481,250. (If we took into account the interaction between changes in interest rates and changes in exchange rates, we could represent the joint distribution of the two risks in a single distribution.)

EXHIBIT F.1　New England Christmas Wreath: Initial Cash Flows

Date	Transaction	CURRENCY*		
		$	¥	CarPs
Dec. 1	Payment for trees, labor, and freight	−44,000		
	Repayment of personal loan			
	Principal　　　　　　　15,000			
	Interest			
	0.20 × 15,000 × 3⁄12 =　　750	−15,750		
	Cash sales	+8,000		
	Net scheduled cash flows	−51,750		
Dec. 31	Payment of income taxes	−19,000		
	Payment for house in Caribbean			−481,250
	Collection of yen receivable		+20,700,000	
	Net scheduled cash flows	−19,000	+20,700,000	−481,250
Net exchange positions		−70,750	+20,700,000	−481,250

*(+: Cash inflow; −: Cash outflow)

THE AP&M
TRADING
COMPANY

The AP&M Trading Company was incorporated in New York in 1948 by Mr. H. Hinson and Mr. R. Kroner, two Polish refugees who arrived in the United States in 1945. From 1948 to 1951 the firm imported $6 to $8 million annually of surplus Japanese silk fabrics left from before the war. During the 1950s and 1960s AP&M became importers of synthetic fabrics, but the yen revaluations of the early 1970s brought that business to an end. By the end of 1983, AP&M had shifted totally to become importers of semi-conductors and had sales of $140 million. AP&M's balance sheet is shown in the accompanying table.

BALANCE SHEET, DECEMBER 31, 1982
(THOUSANDS OF DOLLARS)

Assets		Liabilities & Equity	
Cash	$ 2,240	Accounts payable	$13,820
Accounts receivable	42,640	Acceptances and loans payable	36,620
Inventory	22,540	Accrued taxes	620
Notes receivable	3,060	Accrued expenses	1,320
Total current assets	$70,480	Total current liabilities	$52,380
Long-term investments	510	Notes payable	3,100
Net fixed assets	390	Capital stock	5,460
		Retained earnings	10,440
Total assets	$71,380	Total liabilities and capital	$71,380

At the end of 1983 Mr. Hinson could anticipate growing sales; however, he wondered whether he should change the financing strategy he had followed in his business. The well-recognized overvaluation of the U.S. dollar, particularly against the yen, concerned him.

THE FINANCING SCHEME AT THE TIME

In spite of the changes in the products imported, AP&M's financial arrangements remained substantially the same throughout the years. It commissioned Far Eastern Exporters (Japan) Ltd., a branch of a large

U.S. trading and shipping concern owned by Mr. Hinson's relatives, as AP&M's export agents in Japan. Far Eastern's functions were to handle all dealings with suppliers, shippers, foreign exchange dealers, Japanese banks, and the several official Japanese agencies involved. Mr. K. Yokoma was put in charge of handling the AP&M account. For its services, Far Eastern Exporters charged AP&M 2% of the f.o.b. value of the goods shipped.

Goods bought through Mr. Yokoma were paid in yen; however, prices to AP&M's customers were quoted in dollars based on the f.o.b. price converted at the spot rate on the day of the customer's order. Shipment of the goods ordered from Mr. Yokoma generally took place within 30 days. The ocean voyage, clearing through customs and distribution to the customers, required around 45 days. AP&M's accounts receivable generally were collected within 90 days.

The financing of most of AP&M's operations was done through the mechanisms of *letters of credit* (l/c's) and *trust receipts*. AP&M had lines of credit in the amount of $20 million with New York banks. AP&M could utilize these lines either for l/c's or trust receipts.

Dollar l/c's were opened with AP&M's New York banks who then advised the *negotiating bank* in Japan of the dollar credits in favor of the exporter (Far Eastern Exporters). To receive payment in yen, Mr. Yokoma presented a sight draft (bill of exchange), a bill of lading, a commercial invoice, and a consular invoice (for customs purposes) to the negotiating bank. This bank paid Yokoma in yen the face amount of the draft and forwarded the documents to AP&M's bank. In times of currency fluctuations, AP&M could request that the Japanese bank cable New York immediately, advising of the negotiation of the draft and the equivalent amount in dollars at the day's spot rate. The New York bank credited the dollars to the Japanese bank's account that same day, even prior to the arrival of the documents in New York. Mr. Hinson could opt to instruct his banks to await receipt of the documents. In that case, however, the negotiating bank in Japan converted the dollar l/c's at a rate based on the quotation for contracts 5 days forward. The increase in the dollar cost was borne entirely by AP&M.

Upon receipt of the documents by airmail at the New York bank, some 3 days later, the second phase of the credit was initiated. AP&M was issued a trust receipt under which the New York bank retained title to the imported goods while AP&M was commissioned as the selling agent. Receipts were due in 120 days. The costs to AP&M were 0.25% of the l/c plus cabling charges (approximately $8) for opening the l/c, and 1.25% above prime rate for the 120-day trust receipt loan. The bank could then guarantee the trust receipt loan and discount it in the money market.

THE ALTERNATIVES

A discussion with one of Mr. Hinson's bankers had suggested several financing alternatives. One of these alternatives was the *time l/c* and *bankers' acceptances*. The time l/c instructed the negotiating bank to pay the exporter 120 days (or other specified period of time) following his presentation of a *time draft*. The interest was borne by the exporter, who could simply raise the f.o.b. cost of the goods. AP&M could obtain the bank l/c for 1.25% while Yokoma could have his time draft *accepted* by the Japanese bank and discounted at a rate slightly above the Japanese discount rate. All exchange rate risk, however, was clearly borne by the buyer who might choose to cover in the forward market.

A variation of the time l/c and the bankers' acceptance described above was an instrument instructing the negotiating bank to pay Mr. Yokoma the face value of his time draft immediately. Upon receipt of the documents, the New York bank immediately credited the Japanese bank's account. A 120-day fixed-dollar loan was then automatically credited to AP&M's account. Thus, AP&M avoided the exchange risk during the credit period. The New York bank could then *accept* the time draft by countersigning it and discount it in the money market. The cost to AP&M for the loan was the bankers' acceptance rate plus a 1.5% per annum commission for the bank's accepting the draft. If the time draft had been issued in yen, the U.S. bank would have a yen liability against a dollar asset (the loan to AP&M). In this case the bank would make a charge to AP&M for the additional risk involved.

Mr. Hinson had not investigated the possibility of borrowing yen in Japan to finance the purchases. AP&M had no direct credit relations with banks in Japan.

CHAPTER 9

Financing Operations in the Multinational Enterprise

INTERNATIONAL FINANCIAL MARKETS are available to finance the operations of multinational companies, as well as the operations of one-nation companies which can raise funds in these markets. The largest source of funds in these markets is the Eurocurrency market. Very large sums of money can be obtained through the so-called Euroloans, particularly when they are syndicated among several banks. Eurobonds and foreign bonds are the forms taken by long-term marketable securities in international markets. In addition to the international markets, multinational companies with subsidiaries abroad can tap the financial markets of the countries where they are located, either directly or through bilateral arrangements between entities in the host country and the parent company's country.

In this chapter we will begin with a discussion of how to incorporate the problems of exchange risk in the calculation of the cost of funds, given that the presence of this risk is a distinctive problem of international sources of finance. Then, we proceed to present the characteristics of the major instruments and institutions used to finance operations in international markets and in domestic markets.

THE VALUE OF MONEY
IN INTERNATIONAL FINANCE

In our discussions of international financial markets and cash management we have already addressed the issue of financing the multinational enterprise. The choices for financing included: (1) financing in the currency in which inflows are expected; (2) financing in another currency while covering the exchange exposure in the forward market; and (3) financing in another currency without a forward cover. In the first two choices we did not bear any exchange risk and the forces of covered-interest arbitrage made their costs equal. In the third choice we bore exchange risk, but if efficient markets existed the expected cost of the funds was the same as in the first two alternatives. Over the long term, the costs of the foward premiums or discounts in the second choice would approximate the costs incurred because of fluctuations in the spot rate in the third choice. Of course, if the markets are not efficient, the financial officer would want to try to benefit from her or his superior judgment.

The time horizon of the transactions we have discussed thus far in this text has been very short, usually not more than 1 year. In reality, most of the financing decisions in business have a time horizon larger than this. As we begin to expand the time horizon for the financing decision in international markets, two things happen: (1) The forward exchange market becomes very thin, to the point of almost not existing for practical purposes; and (2) The availability of local-currency financing in most countries is vastly reduced. Under these conditions, some of the financing alternatives described for an efficient market situation may not be available and the financial officer may be forced to bear the exchange risk in financing. The choice among financing alternatives then has to be made in terms of their *net effective cost,* after expected currency revaluations.

Cost of Funds and Inflation

In the computation of the net effective cost of funds we have to take into account the effect of inflation on nominal interest rates and on exchange rates over an extended period of time.

It is well accepted that the interest rates in a given currency have two elements: One is the *real return* that the investor expects; the other is the expected rate of inflation that will erode the value of money received in the future. Given that the repayment of the debt and interest are contracted in advance, if a borrower forecasts a rate of inflation higher than the market's forecast, then the borrower in effect is anticipating payment of a real rate below what the market expects. The lender will be hurt; however, the borrower will benefit. It is this thinking that gives rise to the prescription: "Borrow as much as possible in inflationary situations."[1]

As to the relationship between inflation and the foreign exchange rate, it is true that there is a general tendency for relatively high inflation rates to be followed eventually by a devaluation of the currency in question against other currencies. However, in this general tendency, there are two factors that must be evaluated carefully before translating the effect of the rate of inflation into a net effective rate. One is the phrase, *relative inflation*. To the extent that all the countries are experiencing a similarly large rate of inflation, there is no cause for one particular currency to devalue relative to the other, other things remaining constant. The other factor is derived from the word *eventually*. This eventuality might take a long time to materialize, and it may never materialize if the government can smooth the external implications of the domestic inflation until a turnaround situation arises (for example, other countries catch up with the country's rate of inflation).

If purchasing power parity held all the time (that is, if exchange rates were determined solely by relative inflation rates), then lower interest rates associated with a lower inflation rate would be compensated by the upvaluation of these currencies. This is the assumption behind the usual recommendation that borrowing in a "hard" currency with a low interest does not pay. However, if purchasing power parity

---

[1]Brazil, Finland, France, and Israel, among other countries, have offered a number of bond issues with provisions for adjustment of principal and interest payments by some cost level. Usually these indexed bonds are linked to a general level of prices, although sometimes the adjustment is made to particular cost indices. For example, Finland (from 1952 to 1967) and France (in the late 1950s) issued several series of government bonds that were linked to national wholesale price indices. Other debt issues of various governmental bodies can be linked to particular indices. For example, the Austrian Electric Authority issued bonds in 1953 that were indexed to the cost per kilowatt-hour of electricity. France's railroad authority (SNCF) issued bonds in the 1950s that were indexed to the price of third-class railway tickets. Argentina issued a 1972 bond that was indexed to the price changes in nonagricultural goods. In 1977, a major Swedish bank, Svenska Handelsbanken, issued $23 million of preferred shares whose dividend was linked to Sweden's cost of living but with no adjustment in the redemption price of the shares.

Among the most famous of the commodity bonds was a gold-indexed French bond issued by Valéry Giscard d'Estaing under DeGaulle. Issued in 1973, the 7% coupon bond raised 6.5 billion francs. At the peak price, the face amount of principal which had to be repaid in 1988 was over 100 billion francs; one year's interest payment was almost the face amount of the entire issue.

Indexed bonds are not unknown in the United States. The only issue after World War II was in 1959 by the municipality of Carlsbad, New Mexico. It offered a $3 million conventional issue with a 7% coupon and a 20-year maturity. At the same time, it offered a $4 million issue with a 7% coupon and a 30-year maturity, but with an increase in the coupon as well as the redemption value by the annual percentage rise in the cost of living.

A major reason for the absence of indexed bonds in the United States may well be the prohibition of gold-linked debts as part of the New Deal legislation in 1933. Subsequent Supreme Court action seemed to associate this prohibition wih any linkage of debt repayment to price levels or another commodity. This resolution of Congress was repealed in 1977 by the Helms Amendment. See J. Huston McCulloch, "The Bank on Indexed Bonds, 1933–77," *American Economic Review*, December 1980, pp. 1018–21.

holds only over the long term, if at all, and one repays the borrowings before the upvaluation actually takes place (if it takes place at all), then one will realize a lower cost of funds regardless of the rate of inflation in the local markets.

Cost of Funds and Exchange Fluctuations

In our earlier discussions of cash management we ignored the effects of interest rate compounding on different cash flow patterns. Given that the time horizon was less than 1 year in those discussions, the impact of interest compounding was not very large and could be ignored—as long as interest rate levels were not extraordinarily high. However, to compute the net effective cost of funds borrowed over longer periods of time, we must take into account explicitly the timing and pattern of cash flows.

When only one currency is involved in the analysis, we can see the net present value (NPV) of borrowings as a stream of cash flows. First there are the inflows for the proceeds from the borrowings, and subsequently there are cash outflows for the payment of interest and repayment of principal:

$$\text{NPV} = \text{Borrowings} - \frac{\text{Interest}_1 + \text{Principal repayment}_1}{(1+r)} - \frac{\text{Interest}_2 + \text{Principal repayment}_2}{(1+r)^2} - \ldots - \frac{\text{Interest}_n + \text{Principal repayment}_n}{(1+r)^n}$$

where r is the nominal interest rate on the loan. The timing of principal repayment will have no effect on the NPV to the extent that interest is charged only on the loan balance outstanding. The NPV will be 0.

To compute the cost of borrowing in a foreign currency in terms of the currency available for repayment or any currency used as a numeraire (usually the home currency), another factor must be included in the calculations: the change in relative value between the two currencies. The resulting cash flow stream is as follows:

$$\text{NPV} = \text{Borrowings} - \frac{\text{Interest}_1 + \text{Principal repayment}_1 + \text{Exchange gain (loss)}_1}{(1+r)} - \frac{\text{Interest}_2 + \text{Principal repayment}_2 + \text{Exchange gain (loss)}_2}{(1+r)^2} - \ldots - \frac{\text{Interest}_n + \text{Principal repayment}_n + \text{Exchange gain (loss)}_n}{(1+r)^n}$$

In this case r is unknown and finding its value, while holding $NPV = 0$, will produce the *net effective interest cost*.

Regardless of the size of r, the denominator in the last equation becomes larger with time because its exponent increases by 1 every year. The value of whatever happens in later years tends to be small when discounted by the appropriate factor in the denominator. Therefore, the sooner an appreciation of the borrowed currency takes place, the greater the impact on the effective interest rate r. Whether the loan is a level-principal-repayment loan or a balloon note also affects the impact of the appreciation or depreciation.

As an example, consider a 5-year loan for $1000 at 10%. The accompanying table shows the impact of a 5% appreciation of the currency borrowed on the effective cost of the borrowings, depending on the year in which the appreciation takes place and on the type of the loan (level-principal repayment or 50%-balloon repayment).

	EFFECTIVE INTEREST COST	
Year of Appreciation	Level-Principal Repayment	50% Level-Principal and 50%-Balloon Repayment
1	12.0%	11.6%
2	11.5	11.3
3	11.0	11.0
4	10.6	10.8
5	10.3	10.7

First, we should note that the effective interest cost is higher in *both* types of loans the earlier the appreciation of the borrowed currency occurs in the life of the loan. The later the revaluation takes place, the higher the denominator in the NPV formula, and the smaller the effect of any exchange gain or loss.

If the one-time appreciation occurs in one of the first 2 years, the increase in the effective borrowing cost is larger for the level-repayment loan than for the balloon loan. A larger amount of repayment is made in the earlier years—the years with the smaller denominator in the NPV formula—under the level-repayment loan than under the balloon loan. In later years the amount of repayment decreases for the level-repayment loan and increases for the balloon loan. For example, at the beginning of the fifth year there is $600 still outstanding in the balloon loan, while only $200 of principal remains on the level repayment loan. The 5% loss applied to a larger amount of principal in the balloon loan increases its cost more than the cost of the level-repayment loan when the appreciation occurs in these latter years.

EUROCURRENCY FINANCING

In Chapter 4 we saw how Eurocurrency deposits are created and how international banks can use these funds to make loans. Euroloans are an important source of funds for the multinational enterprise. Because the terms of the loans are so tightly related to the source of the funds to the bank, Eurodeposits, we will discuss first the characteristics of Eurodeposits and Eurorates, and then analyze the typical terms of Euroloans.

Eurodeposits

Most Eurodeposits have a maturity of less than 1 year and are maintained in the form of regular time deposits which may be overnight, call money, or other terms. If earlier withdrawal of deposits is desired, banks usually accommodate the client after the appropriate adjustment in interest rates. Negotiable certificates of deposit are also available, usually for longer (3- to 6-month) maturities.[2] In contrast to the practice in domestic markets, Eurobanks do not maintain demand deposits (checking accounts) for customers. Given the large amounts usually involved, the transfer of funds in the Euromarkets often takes the form of a cablegraphic transfer. Mail is then used to confirm the transactions that have taken place over the telex or cable.

Given the simultaneous existence of a domestic market and a Euromarket in a currency, and the access of many participants to both markets, one would not expect to find any difference in interest rates for comparable instruments in the two markets. However, such differences in rates between the two markets do exist.

One reason for differences between the domestic rate and the Eurorate for a currency is the relative *sovereign risk* or *political risk* of the country where the deposit is held. For example, an investor who wishes to maintain deposits denominated in dollars may prefer to do so outside the political and judicial boundaries of the United States and

---

[2]Negotiable certificates of deposits (CDs) for Eurocurrency were introduced in 1966. The bank allows the holder of a 3- to 12-month or longer deposit to remarket it, should that be desired. Some of these deposits are also formally designated as floating-rate accounts; the interest paid on them will increase or decrease together with the interbank rates. In addition, the London market features "forward forward" CDs, by which a bank commits itself to issue a certificate of deposit in so many months for a certain duration for a particular preset interest rate, usually based on a standard yield curve calculation. Thus, the bank may agree to a 1-year certificate of deposit to be issued in 6 months. If the 6-month rate is 9% and the 18-month rate is 10%, then the 1-year CD to commence in 6 months would have a rate around 10½%, so that the yield on the 9% CD for 6 months and the 10½% CD for months 7 through 18 would average out to the same as the 10% for the spot 18-month CD.

accept a different rate. Thus, after World War II when Eastern European nations and the Soviet Union obtained dollar balances in trade, these were placed on deposit with Soviet banks located in the West, but outside the United States, such as Narodny Bank in London. In the 1980s, Iranians may have developed preferences similar to those attributed to the Communist bloc countries in the 1950s.[3]

However, the major explanation for the difference between the domestic rate and the Euromarket rate for comparable deposits is provided by the main forces behind the growth of the Euromarkets: *domestic regulations on banking* and the presence of *exchange controls*. Some of these regulations affect the cost of deposits in the domestic market, while others limit the availability of domestic funds. In all of these cases the Euromarkets provide the opportunity for bypassing the regulations at a price.

Among the regulations that increase the cost of domestic funds are those requiring that cash reserves be maintained against deposits and that these deposits be insured. These costs in the domestic market are absent from the Euromarkets. Not having to incur these costs in the Euromarkets, banks are willing to pay a higher interest rate to obtain funds—deposits—in that market. In the absence of any other regulation, this factor produces a spread of the Eurodeposit rate over the domestic deposit rate for a given currency and bank.

The major examples of the regulations that limit the availability of funds in the domestic market are ceiling rates payable on domestic deposits and exchange controls. *Interest rate ceilings* on domestic deposits convert the rates on these deposits to a floor for their Eurorate counterparts during periods of high interest rates. *Exchange controls* convert the Euromarkets into an escape valve in which supply and demand for

---

[3]Political risk in terms of sovereignty of branches and parent banks regarding debt repayments has been an issue in various international conflicts in recent times. For example, the British subsidiaries of American banks seized Iranian deposits following President Carter's orders in regard to the seizure of American hostages with the support of the Islamic government of Iran; yet the subsidiaries were legal citizens of the United Kingdom, and both lawyers and international bankers argued that Carter could not enjoin their activities.

To win in U.K. courts, however, the U.S. banks would have had to argue that their foreign deposits were just like U.S. deposits; the argument could be turned around on them by the Federal Reserve in terms of reserve requirements. Part of the U.S.-Iranian settlement voided the issue by placing both the deposits and the Iranian loans from the parent offices in the United States back to the status quo ante, once Iran agreed to pay previous principal and interest obligations with government guarantees. The Iranian government ultimately retired all its debt; given that much of the debt was at low fixed rates or low spreads over the London interbank offered rate (LIBOR), this desire to be free of the U.S. banks on the part of the Islamic government of Iran was welcomed by the U.S. banks which held the low-yielding loans.

In the U.K.-Argentine dispute over the Falkland Islands in 1982, U.K. banks (but *not* their foreign subsidiaries) were enjoined from making additional loans to Argentina, in response to which the Argentine government forbade any repayment of debts to British banks. The question was what would happen with regard to loans for which the British banks were primarily agents. The military conflict and both governments' banking reactions ended quickly, however. See Herman Nickel's article, "The Iran Deal Doesn't Look Bad," *Fortune*, February 23, 1981, pp. 57–59.

the given currency are allowed to determine interest rates outside the scope of domestic exchange controls.[4]

As an illustration of the impact of these factors on the relative cost of Eurofunds and domestic funds, we will consider the case of the United States, where there have not been significant controls on foreign exchange transactions since 1974. Since then, the major determinants of the spread between domestic and Eurodollar rates have been the regulations that affect the relative cost of funds to banks in the markets, and the relative political risk. Exhibit 9.1 shows the resulting relationship for overnight or Federal Funds, and for 90-day deposits in the two markets. In the case of Federal Funds, where reserve requirements are not imposed, the spread between the two markets, although large at times, hovers around 0. For 90-day deposits, which are subject to reserve requirements, the spread is a very narrow (but positive) one in favor of Eurodollars.

Euroloans

Euroloans usually range from a $500,000 base up to $100 million or more, typically in units of $1 million. The usual maturity ranges from 30 days to 5 or 7 years. When the lender is known to the bank, loans of under 12-month maturity are often established very easily. The lender will simply call to request a loan; if the rate and terms quoted by the bank are satisfactory, the loan is immediately accepted. When a parent guarantee is required, as is sometimes the case for a foreign subsidiary requesting a loan, the guarantee can often be based on a telephone conversation. Confirming wires or letters are sent later. Usually, there is no amortization of the loan. Instead, the entire amount is repaid at the maturity date. The loan is also not secured except by the general credit of the firm, although there are often constraints on additional debt incurred by the firm. Some borrowers operate with lines of credit, which are usually given for a period not to exceed 12 months, but which may be renegotiated at the end of the period. A commitment fee of ¼% to ½% may be placed on the unused portion of the line of credit.

The interest rates on Eurocurrency loans are often floating rates, especially for the intermediate and longer maturities (3 years or longer). Thus, although the money availability to the borrower is guaranteed for the medium or long term, the cost of these loans is com-

---

[4]See Heinz Riehl and Rita M. Rodriguez, *Foreign Exchange and Money Markets* (New York, N.Y.: McGraw-Hill, 1983). Also see Gunter Dufey and Ian H. Giddy, *The International Money Market* (Englewood Cliffs, N.J.,: Prentice-Hall, Inc., 1978), Ch. 2.

EXHIBIT 9.1   U.S. Domestic and Eurodollar Rates Compared, 1979–1982

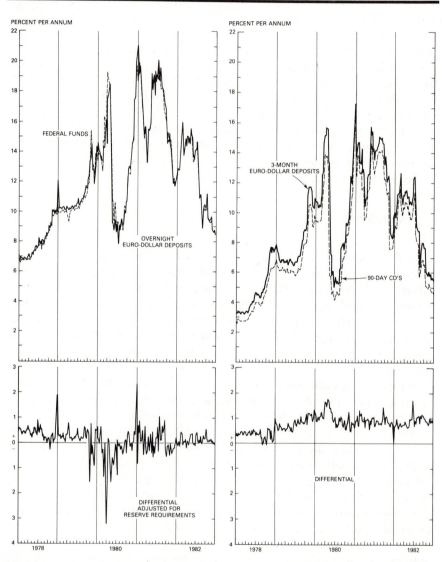

SOURCE: Board of Governors of the Federal Reserve System, *Selected Interest and Exchange Rates,* various issues.

monly determined by short-term rates. The interest rate on Euroloans is usually established at some fixed percentage, called *spread,* over a given interbank lending rate—usually the London interbank offered rate (LIBOR) at which they borrow a substantial part of their funds.[5] This rate is the charge that banks make for loans to each other. Hence, the borrower may find a loan quoted at "1½% over LIBOR, established at 6-month intervals, until maturity." These floating-rate revolving loans (also called "revolvers" or "rollover credits") protect bank profits against increases in the interest rate on Eurocurrency deposits, as long as the terms on the deposits used by the bank to finance the loan are comparable to those of the loan.

Euroloans also can have a multicurrency feature in which the borrower may choose to change the currency denomination of the loan on each rollover date, subject to the availability of the selected currency to the bank. The new interest rate for the next interest period then would be the agreed-upon spread over, say, LIBOR for the selected currency and maturity. An option to change the length of the interest period, say from 3-month to 6-month, for the coming interest period also may be included in these loans. Theoretically, the lending bank would be able to meet any change in the currency or length of interest period by changing the terms of its sources of funds, deposits, when it refinances the initial source. Assuming the bank follows a riskless strategy of matching the terms of its deposits with the terms of its loans, if the bank financed the first interest period of the loan with 3-month dollars (to match the terms requested by the borrower under the loan agreement), then the bank can refinance that deposit with 6-month sterling if the borrower chooses those terms at the end of the first interest period.

The rates for the loans to prime borrowers have ranged from LIBOR + ¾%, for 7- to 8-year maturity, to as little as LIBOR + ⅜% for a 5-year maturity. Nonprime borrowers pay a higher spread of 2% to 3%, depending on maturity and credit worthiness. In addition, there is usually a front-end management fee that ranges between ½% and ¾%. If the loan is not syndicated the bank may waive this fee. In periods of high liquidity in the market, as in 1977 and 1981, the spreads charged to nonprime borrowers tend to approach those charged to prime borrowers and the management fees tend to decline.

Exhibit 9.2 shows the high variability in average terms on Euroloans—base rate, spread, and maturity—in recent years. As market conditions have changed in the Euromarkets, so have the terms on Euroloans. During periods of economic recession in industrial countries, the

---

[5]Euro-CDs are another important source of funds. The Euro-CD rate for prime banks is usually below LIBOR for comparable maturities.

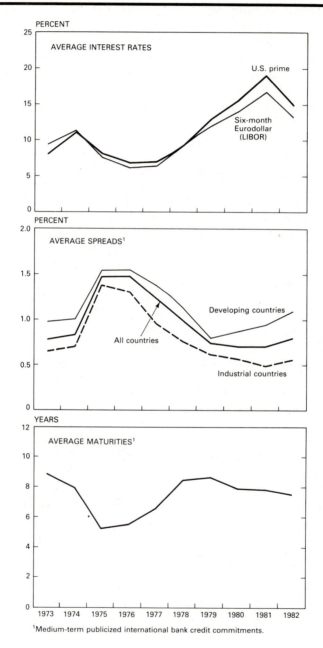

PERCENT

AVERAGE INTEREST RATES

U.S. prime

Six-month Eurodollar (LIBOR)

PERCENT

AVERAGE SPREADS[1]

Developing countries

All countries

Industrial countries

YEARS

AVERAGE MATURITIES[1]

1973 1974 1975 1976 1977 1978 1979 1980 1981 1982

[1]Medium-term publicized international bank credit commitments.

SOURCE: International Monetary Fund, *International Capital Markets: Developments and Prospects*, 1983, p. 6.

decline in demand for loans from those sources has been translated into better terms (lower spreads and longer maturities) for those willing to borrow at those times (primarily developing countries in recent years).

THE INTERNATIONAL BOND MARKET

The Instruments

Companies can issue long-term marketable securities in the international bond market. The distinctive characteristic of this market is that the bonds are sold initially outside the country of the borrower, and often in several countries. These bonds fall into two major categories: foreign bonds and Eurobonds.[6]

Foreign Bonds. A *foreign bond* is an international bond sold by a foreign borrower but denominated in the currency of the country in which it is placed. It is underwritten and sold by a national underwriting syndicate in the lending country. For example, a U.S. company might float a bond issue in the Swiss capital market, underwritten by a Swiss syndicate, and denominated in Swiss francs. The bond issue is sold to investors in the Swiss capital market, where it will be quoted and traded.

Through the mid-1960s, foreign bonds were the dominant form of international bond issues, and foreign bonds issued in the United States accounted for about 60% of the total market. In 1962 foreign bonds issued in the United States amounted to $587 million, while foreign bonds issued in all the European countries combined amounted to $444 million. New York offered a lower interest rate and a more efficient underwriting system than those available elsewhere. However, beginning with 1963, attempts to support the dollar and to limit dollar outflows from the United States translated into regulations that effectively reduced the access to the foreign bond market in the United States. The markets' responses to these regulations were the growth of the Eurobond market and the growth of the foreign bond market in other countries, particularly Switzerland and Germany. In 1972, with the elimination of the regulations designed to support the dollar, the U.S. market opened again to foreign bond issues. However, the market for foreign bond issues in the United States has grown much less than the rest of the international bond market (see Exhibit 9.3) and it has

---

[6]Some portions of this section draw heavily on *The European Market for International Bonds*, prepared by Yoon S. Park under the supervision of Professor Eli Shapiro and distributed by the Intercollegiate Case Clearing House, Boston, Mass. An expanded version of that material appears as Chapter 2 in Yoon S. Park, *The Eurobond Market: Function and Structure* (New York: Praeger Press, 1974.)

EXHIBIT 9.3 New International Bond Issues, 1970–1982 *(millions of U.S. dollars)*

	1970	1971	1972	1973	1974	1975	1976
Eurobonds[a]	$2,996	$3,642	$6,335	$4,193	$2,134	$ 8,567	$14,328
Foreign bonds outside the United States	378	1,538	2,060	2,626	1,432	4,884	7,586
Total international bonds outside the United States	$3,374	$5,180	$8,395	$6,819	$3,566	$13,451	$21,914
Foreign bonds in the United States	$1,216	$1,104	$1,353	$ 960	$3,291	$ 6,462	$10,604
Total	$4,590	$6,284	$9,748	$7,779	$6,857	$19,913	$32,518

[a]Includes European Unit of Account, European Monetary Unit, and multiple-currency option issues.

SOURCE: Morgan Guaranty Trust Company, *World Financial Markets,* New York, various issues.

remained dominated by Canadian entities and international organizations.

In part because of a desire to avoid the Securities and Exchange Commission (SEC) reporting and disclosure requirements, foreign corporations have typically not made offerings of their securities in the U.S. market. American Depositary Receipts, representing issues held by a U.S. bank, are traded in U.S. markets, however. The SEC now permits primary issues of nonconvertible debt by foreign corporations in the U.S. market without the filing of financial statements including sales by product line and geographic region, a disclosure largely resisted by foreign corporations. The firms must have at least $300 million worth of voting securities held by others than management to be "world class" and, hence, eligible for this special permission to sell debt without the full disclosure normally required.

Exhibit 9.4 shows that public institutions (international organizations, governments, and state enterprises) account for the bulk of the foreign bond market outside the United States. These institutions are usually exempt from regulations limiting the access of foreign borrowers to domestic markets. On the other hand, private companies, which are the main target of these regulations, account for less than one-third of the foreign bond market. The participation of each country in this market has been largely determined by the policy of the host government. The Swiss, the German, and the Japanese markets have been the major participants, and their governments have managed the availability of their domestic markets to foreigners to suit domestic monetary policy objectives. Whenever domestic liquidity has been increased by these governments' attempts to support the exchange rates of their currencies against pressures for an upvaluation, the domestic financial markets have been opened more widely to foreigners.

EXHIBIT 9.3 *(Continued)*

	1977	1978	1979	1980	1981	1982
Eurobonds[a]	$17,771	$14,125	$18,726	$23,970	$31,616	$49,839
Foreign bonds outside the United States	8,777	14,359	17,749	14,521	13,817	19,879
Total international bonds outside the United States	$26,548	$28,484	$36,475	$38,491	$45,433	$69,718
Foreign bonds in the United States	$ 7,428	$ 5,795	$ 4,515	$ 3,429	$ 7,552	$ 6,096
Total	$33,976	$34,279	$40,990	$41,920	$52,985	$75,814

[a]Includes European Unit of Account, European Monetary Unit, and multiple-currency option issues.

A more complex version of foreign bonds is the so-called *parallel bonds*. A *parallel bond* is a multinational issue (usually a large issue) comprised of several bonds floated simultaneously among various countries, with each participating country raising funds in its own currency. However, thus far, very few parallel bond issues have been floated.

Eurobonds. The *Eurobond* is an international bond "underwritten by an international syndicate and sold in countries other than the country of the currency in which the issue is denominated."[7] From a minuscule size of $164 million in 1963, the bond market exhibited a phenomenal growth that reached to nearly $50 billion in 1982, as shown in Exhibit 9.5.

The Eurobond market, although centered in Europe, is truly international in the sense that the underwriting syndicates typically comprise investment bankers from a number of countries and the bonds are sold to investors around the world. However, in spite of the cosmopolitan nature of the Eurobond market, a Eurobond is a simple instrument for borrowers and investors to understand. It is denominated in a given currency and issued to the bearer, most often with an annual coupon payment.[8] In addition, there are no major regulations, such as withholding taxes, with which to contend after the bond is issued. The only regulation prevalent in the market pertains to the constraints on new issues in some currencies, such as Euromarks. For these currencies their central banks control the amount of new issues when the local in-

---

[7]Morgan Guaranty Trust Company, *World Financial Markets*, last page of each issue.

[8]Zero-coupon bonds which are sold initially with a deep discount gained great popularity in 1981.

EXHIBIT 9.4 New Foreign Bond Issues Outside the United States, 1966–1982

	1966	1968	1970	1972	1973	1974	1975
Total							
(in millions of dollars)	$378	$1,135	$378	$2,060	$2,626	$1,432	$4,884
By category of borrower							
U.S. companies	6%	12%	15 %	10%	21%	5%	1%
Foreign companies		5	22	17	15	32	28
State enterprises	40	1	4	12	17	40	27
Governments		28	14	9	11	10	16
International organizations	53	54	45	52	36	14	28
	100%	100%	100%	100%	100%	100%	100%
By currency of denomination							
German mark	33%	59%	24 %	24%	14%	18%	22%
Swiss franc	21	21	51	40	58	64	68
Dutch guilder	0		4	2	0[a]	0[a]	4
Japanese yen	0	20	4	15	10	0	1
Other	46		17	20	18	18	5
	100%	100%	100%	100%	100%	100%	100%

[a]Less than 1%.

SOURCE: Morgan Guaranty Trust Company, *World Financial Markets*, New York, various issues.

stitutions are involved (which is usually the case) and when the bonds are placed in the local market.

As we previously described, the impetus for the fast growth of the international bond market was largely provided by the regulations imposed on the international capital flows in the United States. The Interest Equalization Tax (IET) drove foreigners to raise funds outside the United States. The controls on foreign direct investment, initially voluntary but made mandatory in 1968, sent U.S. companies to raise funds in foreign markets for their foreign operations. The growth of the Eurobond market very clearly reflects the impact of these two regulations. Exhibit 9.5 shows the large participation of U.S. companies and non-U.S. companies in the Eurobond market in response to these regulations throughout 1972. In January 1974 the IET and the controls on direct investment were lifted by the U.S. government, and the participation of U.S. companies in this market declined drastically. However, non-U.S. companies have come to represent an increasingly significant portion of the Eurobond market.

State enterprises, which were also subject to the impact of the IET, comprise another significant portion of the Eurobond market.

EXHIBIT 9.4 *(Continued)*

	1976	1977	1978	1979	1980	1981	1982
Total							
(in millions of dollars)	$7,586	$8,777	$14,359	$17,749	$14,521	$13,817	$19,879
By category of borrower							
U.S. companies	0%[a]	1%	2%	1%	2%	4%	10%
Foreign companies	22	16	15	20	22	25	21
State enterprises	32	27	22	19	19	27	27
Governments	17	26	40	43	28	20	18
International organizations	28	31	21	18	29	24	24
	100%	100%	100%	100%	100%	100%	100%
By currency of denomination							
German mark	17%	29%	26%	30%	33%	10%	14%
Swiss franc	71	48	40	55	52	60	56
Dutch guilder	8	3	3	0[a]	2	3	5
Japanese yen	3	18	27	10	7	18	17
Other	2	2	5	4	5	9	8
	100%	100%	100%	100%	100%	100%	100%

[a]Less than 1%.

Governments kept a relatively low profile in the Eurobond market through 1974. However, since then they have become significant issuers of Eurobonds. Entities such as the Mexican and Brazilian governments, the government and the government enterprises of Finland and Sweden, and the provinces of Canada have been particularly large issuers in this market. International organizations have played only a minor role.

The development of the Eurobond market as a substitute for the U.S. domestic market is reflected also in the dominant role that the dollar has played in the Eurobond market. Until 1967 the Eurodollar bond often accounted for as much as 90% of the Eurobond market. After that year the increasing weakness of the dollar made lenders' preferences give a larger role to other currencies such as the German mark. Still, Eurdollar bonds have generally retained between 50% and 80% of the total new issues in the Eurobond market (refer to Exhibit 9.5). The relative participation of each of the major currencies has changed both with the relative strength of these currencies in the exchange markets and the relative liquidity of the Eurobond market in general.

Eurobonds also have proven to be versatile instruments. Their maturities have been tailored to the needs of the borrowers under the

EXHIBIT 9.5   New Eurobond Issues, 1966–1981

	1966	1968	1970	1972	1973	1974	1975
Total							
(in millions of dollars)	$1,142	$3,573	$2,996	$6,335	$4,193	$2,134	$8,567
By category of borrower							
U.S. companies	38%	59%	25%	31%	21%	5%	3%
Foreign companies	33	17	36	20	31	30	34
State enterprises	10	10	20	18	23	25	36
Governments	9	14	12	16	16	23	19
International organizations	9	1	7	6	10	17	7
	100%	100%	100%	100%	100%	100%	100%
By currency of denomination							
U.S. dollar	81%	71%	60%	62%	58%	47%	44%
German mark	13	26	23	18	24	16	27
Dutch guilder	0ᵃ	0ᵃ	13	6	5	18	8
Canadian dollar	6	3	4	0ᵃ	0ᵃ	3	7
European composite units				0ᵃ	2	8	4
Other				14	6	8	4
French franc				0ᵃ	4	0ᵃ	3
	100%	100%	100%	100%	100%	100%	100%

ᵃLess than 1%.

SOURCE: Morgan Guaranty Trust Company, *World Financial Markets*, New York, various issues.

regulations.[9] Also, Eurobonds have appeared with a variety of features designed to make the instrument more desirable to the investor and practical to the borrower. We will now discuss some of these features.

Following the pattern of many direct Eurodollar loans, initially there was an interest in *floating-rate Eurobonds*. These notes or bonds have a medium- to long-term maturity from 5 to 15 years, but the interest rate is based on short-term rates that are adjusted every 3 or 6 months. However, they usually guarantee a minimum rate. Often, floating-rate Eurobonds offer a redemption feature that can be exercised after a certain period of time from the initial offering of the bond. The redemption price may be defined as a discount from par (with the dis-

---

[9]An example of the adaptability of the market in this respect was shown in response to the controls on U.S. foreign direct investment. These controls did not count as capital outflow the repayment of debt with maturity longer than 7 years and repayment of principal after that year. Accordingly, the typical Eurobond had a maturity of more than 7 years and specified a balloon payment at the end of the period for the principal.

EXHIBIT 9.5 *(Continued)*

	1976	1977	1978	1979	1980	1981	1982
Total							
(in millions of dollars)	$14,328	$17,771	$14,125	$18,726	$23,970	$31,616	$49,839
By category of borrower							
U.S. companies	8%	6%	8%	15%	17%	19%	25%
Foreign companies	37	41	32	38	38	41	27
State enterprises	29	27	23	24	24	24	27
Governments	16	17	26	13	13	8	14
International organizations	15	9	11	9	8	8	7
	100%	100%	100%	100%	100%	100%	100%
By currency of denomination							
U.S. dollar	64%	66%	52%	67%	69%	85%	86%
German mark	19	23	37	19	15	4	5
Dutch guilder	4	2	3	3	4	2	1
Canadian dollar	10	4	0[a]	2	1	2	2
European composite units	1	0[a]	1	1	0[a]	1	3
Other	3	5	7	7	11	6	3
French franc	0[a]	0[a]	—	—	—	—	—
	100%	100%	100%	100%	100%	100%	100%

[a]Less than 1%.

count constant or changing with time to maturity) or the redemption price may be at par. Alternatively, the floating-rate bond may be eligible for conversion into a fixed-rate bond with a specified maturity at the option of the holder, or whenever the market interest rate declines to a specified rate *(drop-lock bonds)*. The higher interest rates prevailing since the mid-1970s have given these floating-rate bonds or notes a new impetus.

The instability of exchange rates and the associated exchange risks have prompted the market to develop the option of using various mixes of currencies as the denomination of Eurobonds. The mixes of currencies have been based on two different concepts: (1) maintaining fixed *exchange rates* among the currencies included; and (2) maintaining fixed *quantities* of these currencies. As Exhibit 9.5 shows, these bonds as a group (which appear under the heading "other") have accounted for less than 10% of Eurobonds issued in most years.

Multiple-currency bonds are the most popular version of the *fixed exchange rate* formula for Eurobonds. In their most widely used form,

the bonds entitle the creditor to request payment of the interest and
the principal of the bond in any of the specified currencies, as well as
in the currency of the loan, in accordance with a previously established
fixed exchange rate parity. Thus, the obligation is expressed in various
national currencies at the choice of the *lender,* who loses only if *all* currencies included in the multiple-currency contract depreciate against
the other currencies not included in the contract. If any one currency
in the contract appreciates, the lender gains by that much because payment always can be required in the currency that offers the greatest advantage. From the point of view of the borrower, the obligation appreciates in the same degree as the currency that appreciates the *most.* In
recent years the most common multiple-currency bonds have been
those issued in European units of accounts (EUAs) or European Currency Units (ECUs). Since 1973, the currencies in these bonds are
those participating in the European Monetary System (EMS).[10]

Other attempts to cope with exchange rate instability through the
creation of currency cocktails have been based on the specification of
fixed quantities of the component currencies. Among these are the special drawing right (SDR) and the European composite unit (Eurco).
Since 1981 the SDR is the composite of five currencies, including the
U.S. dollar. The Eurco is based on major European currencies and it
excludes the dollar.

Some Eurobond issues have been convertible into equities and
others have carried warrants. Generally, interest in these features has
declined with the stock market indices, since the value of the convertibility feature or the warrant is related to the conversion price or the
strike price (the price at which the warrant can be exercised to acquire
common stock) compared to the current market price. Firms are reluctant to use convertibles or warrants when the stock is severely de-
pressed, unless the conversion or the strike price is far above market.
Such a spread, of course, lessens the value of the warrant to the bond
purchaser.

A combination of the multiple-currency bond and a convertible
bond is the *dual-currency convertible bond.* As an example, a Japanese
company may issue a dollar convertible bond, in which case the currency of denomination of the bond is the dollar, but the currency of the
shares into which the bond is convertible is the yen. The conversion
rate is expressed in terms of a fixed number of shares. Thus, when the
yen appreciates against the dollar the convertible bond also may appreciate because the dollar value of the yen shares into which the bond is

---

[10]Before 1973, the EUA account involved seventeen currencies. The EUA was succeeded by
the ECU when the European Monetary System was created in 1979. Currently, the ECU account
includes the nine EEC countries excluding Greece, which will join the system (and the ECU) in
1986.

convertible is worth more.[11] The opposite may happen when the yen depreciates against the dollar. If the convertible bond is redeemed as a bond the borrower bears the exchange risk between the dollar and the yen. However, if the conversion feature is exercised by the lender, the borrower is responsible only for the number of shares promised in the conversion rate. Obviously, the value of a convertible bond at any point in time depends on the combined effects of exchange rate fluctuations, the performance of the stock price, and market interest rates.

The Costs

Financial Institutions and Issuing Costs.
Foreign bonds are underwritten in the country of the currency of the bond denomination and the institutions involved in issuing these bonds are those that handle bond issues in the given country. Eurobonds, on the other hand, are underwritten by an international syndicate. The cornerstone of the Eurobond market is the group of thirty to forty financial institutions in Europe and the United States which manage the major share of all new international bonds. Given that the market for institutional investors outside the United States and the United Kingdom is very limited, it is especially important for the investment bankers underwriting Eurobond issues to have experience in preparing an issue for placement with banks and residents in a large number of countries.

The general pattern of a Eurobond syndicate follows the traditional American system—that is, the three-tier structure of the managers, the underwriting group, and the selling group. The investment banks acting as managers select an underwriting group of important concerns with contacts in a number of countries, while the selling group is ordinarily several times larger and has a wider geographical representation. The underwriters of a typical Eurobond issue ordinarily comprise well-known European banking institutions and leading U.S. investment banks, with a total number of participants that usually surpasses the traditional two or three in the United States by a substantial number. The selling group easily can be fifty or more so that the retail market in every country can be reached.

The underwriting costs for Eurobond issues are somewhat higher than for bond flotations in the U.S. domestic market. Whereas the total underwriting cost for an average issue in the United States may be

---

[11]The extent of the appreciation of the bond depends on whether the convertible is selling primarily as a bond or as equity. The closer the selling price is to its equity value, the closer the reflection of the appreciation of the yen in the price of the convertible.

about 2% of issue value, the comparable cost for a Eurobond issued with a maturity of 15 years or more is ordinarily 2.5%, consisting of a 1.5% selling commission, a 0.5% management fee, and a 0.5% underwriting fee. Additional incidental expenses payable by the issuing or borrowing company may run as high as $100,000, with the actual cost partially dependent on the amount of financial advertising. Issues with shorter maturities often cost less.

One difficulty with the European underwriting system is that it usually does not involve a firm commitment on the part of the syndicate members to take precommitted amounts of the issue; rather, they operate on a best-effort basis. This factor means that the lead investment banker has a limited basis for estimating how firm the interest is on the part of the syndicate members prior to the actual issue. Although the European situation typically has a provision relating to loss of commissions if issues are returned to the market during the life of the syndicate (dealing in the so-called *gray market*), this penalty arrangement is difficult to enforce. As a result, syndicates are usually ended promptly, with the lead investment banker and some others bearing the responsibility of stabilizing the market in the bonds after issuance.[12] However, the bonds are traded over-the-counter and the secondary market for them remains relatively narrow.[13]

Unlike the United States, where the underwriters typically must "swallow" the unsold portion of an issue, the underwriters in the European case have the right to raise the coupon or sell the remaining issue at deep discount, to reduce the size of the issue, or simply to cancel it in the event the syndicate does not wish to absorb the balance.

Interest Rates. The interest rates on foreign bonds are directly correlated with the rates prevailing in the given country, adjusted by whatever regulation affects foreign bonds in particular. These regulations have often been modified to cater to government objectives regarding the balance of payments, such as increasing the accessibility to the market when the currency experiences undesirable upward pressures in the exchange markets.

In the Eurobond market, the rates of a one-currency bond are directly related to the long-term rate level in the home country of the currency, the Eurorate for short maturities of that currency, the rates in other currencies, and currency regulations and restrictions. For exam-

---

[12]See Gunter Rischer, "The Role of Underwriters in the Euro-capital Market," *Euromoney*, June 1972, pp. 4–10.

[13]An alternative developed to deal with the problem of decline in price during the early life of the bond is a purchase-fund feature. In this arrangement the borrower agrees to purchase the bonds if the price falls below par during a specified period of time. Because this arrangement is practically forbidden in the U.S. bond market, U.S. institutions tend not to use it even in Eurobond issues.

ple, the Eurodollar bond rate depends on the U.S. long-term rate, the Eurodollar rate (and therefore on U.S. short-term rates), the long-term rate in other currencies, and the regulations in the United States. Thus, given the capital outflow controls in the United States between 1965 and the end of 1973, the U.S. long-term rate actually served as a floor for the Eurodollar bond rate. Lenders could always invest in the United States. However, borrowers were forced to raise the funds used for expansion of foreign operations in the Eurobond market. Depending on the size of this demand for foreign financing, the Eurobond rate could go substantially over the domestic U.S. bond rate. However, long-term rates in other currencies served as a check on how high the Eurodollar bond rate could go.

In spite of the fast growth of the Eurobond market, it is still small compared to the U.S. bond market. As a result, the Eurobond market does not have great depth and breadth. It is not unusual to hear an investment banker advising a customer to decide whether a Eurobond issue would be desirable so that "if a favorable market develops we would be ready," since such a good market can disappear in a period of a couple weeks. Thus, another large determinant of the level of Eurobond rates is the volume of new issues coming to the international market in any one period.

In general, Eurobond interest rates have been rising steadily since 1963, in line with the overall rising interest rate trend in Western Europe and the United States.

Taxation and Finance Subsidiaries. Countries differ in their policies about withholding taxes on dividends and interest payable to residents and nonresidents. Most Western European countries have one withholding tax for residents and nonresidents alike, ranging from 5% to about 40%. Others have withholding tax only on interest paid to nonresidents. Still other nations have no withholding tax. In addition, most nations have tax treaties with other nations which may reduce the withholding tax, and in virtually all cases the holders of the bonds can have credit against their local income taxes for the amount withheld.[14] The difficulty is that many of the Eurobond purchasers have no intention of declaring the income to their local tax authorities; hence, the credit is worthless. Thus, most Eurobond issues have a clause which provides that the borrower will increase the interest payment to offset any future withholding tax on interest to nonresidents should it be legislated.

To avoid the difficulties created by tax withholding, it is not un-

---

[14]For example, under a treaty, Great Britain's withholding on dividends and interest for payments to Americans is reduced from the standard 41.25% to 0. See also the Appendix to Chapter 13 on international taxation.

common to establish a finance subsidiary in a "tax-haven" country or area. This subsidiary then raises the funds needed and redistributes them through the company system. In the United States, a domestic finance subsidiary can meet this objective if certain conditions are met. Section 861 of the Internal Revenue Code establishes that when 80% or more of the gross income of a U.S. corporation is from foreign sources, then there is no withholding required for payment of dividends or interest to nonresidents.[15] Hence, when the financing subsidiary meeting these conditions raises funds in the Eurocurrency market, it can meet a non-U.S. income rule, permitting it to pay the lenders their return without withholding taxes. Delaware is often chosen as the site of incorporation for these finance subsidiaries because of its very low state taxes and few restrictions on the legal ability of a business to change operations. As a domestic subsidiary the gains and losses of the finance subsidiary can be consolidated with the parent company's returns for tax purposes. This is particularly advantageous in cases where the subsidiary generates losses in its initial stages. Also, when foreign taxes are due on the interest the foreign-operation subsidiary pays to the U.S. finance subsidiary, there is a credit against the U.S. tax liability for such tax payments.

Should the proceeds of the funds raised by a domestic finance subsidiary be used in the United States, then the interest paid to it by the (U.S.) operating subsidiaries will be U.S. income, and the payments to the foreign lenders will be subject to U.S. withholding. In this case, overseas finance subsidiaries are desirable. Under Section 482, the IRS ruled that the income of these overseas subsidiaries is *deemed* U.S. source income (hence, payments are subject to U.S. withholding) only if more than 80% of its gross income is from the conduct of a trade or business in the United States. Hence, it is possible that the management may arrange for the interest income to be received by the finance subsidiary, yet not deemed U.S. source income if the activities of the finance subsidiary itself are entirely outside the United States; it is not conducting a trade or business in the United States but merely receiving interest from loans to U.S. firms (the operating subsidiaries). Several countries, such as Luxembourg and Holland, offer incentives to be the site for these financial subsidiaries. For nominal fees, a holding company (which is in effect a finance subsidiary) can be established

---

[15]With the elimination of the Interest Equalization Tax and other capital controls in 1976, the Internal Revenue Service (IRS) has stopped giving rulings guaranteeing that Eurobond issues of U.S. companies under the 80% clause are exempt from withholding taxes. Thus, there is no total assurance that withholding taxes on Eurobond issues of U.S. companies will not be subject to withholding taxes in the future under a separate decision from the IRS.

and be exempt from both local income tax and withholding tax on interest and dividend payments.[16]

FINANCING WITHIN LOCAL CAPITAL MARKETS

To the extent that the foreign subsidiary of a multinational enterprise is treated as a local company, this subsidiary has access to the local capital markets available within the country. The most common form of obtaining funds in these markets is through borrowings from financial institutions, particularly commercial banks. The bond and equity markets in most countries are not developed to the extent that they are in the United States. Also, the subsidiary of a foreign company (in contrast to the parent company) is likely to lack the credit standing to have access to the bond market. To the extent that such market may be available, if the parent company issues the bond, then it would be a foreign bond, as discussed earlier. We will now discuss some of the major characteristics of financial institutions in industrial countries.

Commercial Banks

Commercial banks in Europe and Japan operate differently from the banks in the United States. Whereas national banking (and even branching in some states) is forbidden in the United States, other nations have commercial banks with branches all over the country. In addition, commercial banks in these other countries are allowed to underwrite securities. In the United States, commercial banking and investment banking cannot be performed by the same financial institution. In the European countries and in Japan, commercial banks not only can underwrite securities, but usually they are also active in buying and selling industrial bonds and equities for their own account.

---

[16]Although tax treaties are designed to ease financial commerce between two nations, the Netherlands Antilles-U.S. treaty is the center of much controversy. Both U.S. citizens and foreigners who are not legally entitled to the benefit set up Antilles corporations to own U.S. securities; the U.S. has 10% withholding on dividend and interest payments to residents and citizens, and 30% withholding on payments to foreigners. The treaty with the Netherlands Antilles has no withholding, of course, and many of these individuals neglect to declare the income for U.S. tax purposes. As House Subcommittee hearings indicated, over 15,000 U.S. corporations have Antilles corporations. In general, these financial subsidiaries of the U.S. parents routinely raise capital from foreigners to send to the American parent, avoiding the withholding requirements legally. Unfortunately, if they were forced to withhold to avoid these abuses, most of their issues have clauses that would require the firms to retire the issues should withholding be imposed. Such retirement would, presumably, mean replacing the issue with more expensive (but legal) financing.

The equity holdings, in particular, help to establish a very special relationship between commercial banks and the industrial sector in these countries.

In spite of a relatively large number of banks and branches in the European countries and Japan, the commercial banking business in those countries is highly concentrated in a few banks. In Germany, where there are more than 300 commercial banks with over 5,000 branches, the three largest banks (Deutsche Bank, Dresdner Bank, and Commerzbank) account for about 40% of total commercial bank assets. A similar story can be found in Switzerland, where three banks (Swiss Bank Corporation, Credit Suisse, and the Union Bank of Switzerland) represent a growing 40% of the total assets of Swiss banks. In France the three largest banks (Banque Nationale de Paris, Crédit Lyonnais, and Société Général) are state-owned and account for 75% of total bank assets. In the Netherlands, the Big Two [Algemene Bank Nederland (ABN) and Amsterdam-Rotterdam Bank (AMRO)] now hold more than 50% of all commercial bank assets. In the United Kingdom, the concentration in banking is slightly less, with the largest amount of business being controlled by the ten clearing banks.

In terms of direct loans, commercial banks traditionally have specialized in short-term credits. The most common forms of these credits outside the United States are overdrafts (purposely exceeding a checking deposit balance) against a line of credit, and discounting of trade-related financial paper. However, in spite of the traditional reliance on short-term credits, commercial banks in many countries have begun to play an increasingly significant role in the medium- and long-term funds market. The system in which borrowers maintain compensating balances with commercial banks common in the United States is usually not found in European commercial banks; however, compensating balances are very popular in Japan.

France provides a good example of the form which medium- and long-term credit can take (42% of the average total financial assets acquired in 1976). Most of the medium-term lending of French banks can be rediscounted with Crédit National, one of the public credit institutions. These credits have a maturity of up to 7 years and must be approved both by Crédit National, a government agency, and by the Bank of France. If these institutions do not approve the loan, then the commercial bank cannot rediscount the loan with them. Other things constant, this would make the particular loan less desirable to the commercial bank—the objective of the monetary authorities.

Finally, in analyzing the prevalence of short-term maturities in the loans extended by commercial banks, one must take into account the fact that most of these short-term credits are usually refinanced before or shortly after the loan expires. This process converts short-term loans into de facto long-term credits. This sequence of events is further facilitated in the countries where commercial banks have close ties with the industrial sector through their direct or indirect holdings of equity in these companies.

Nonbank Financial Intermediaries

Commercial banks are not only the largest financial intermediaries in every country, but they also perform a large number of functions. Thus, the role that nonbank financial intermediaries play in the financial markets of these countries is limited. However, the nonbank financial intermediaries play a significant role in the medium- and long-term sectors of the financial markets.

Among the contractual type of nonbank financial institutions, the pension funds are practically nonexistent outside the United States and the United Kingdom. The importance of insurance companies, as measured by the portion of household savings they attract, ranged in 1979 from 80% in the Netherlands to almost nothing in countries such as France, where the government provides insurance compensation for its citizens. The source of funds for this compensation is the annual fiscal budget. In other countries these social services are not provided either by the government or by private institutions. Without pension funds and insurance companies, these countries do not possess a pool of funds for medium- or long-term investment.

The remaining nonbank financial institutions, excluding insurance companies and pension funds, can be further divided between those whose sources of funds are of a long-term nature and those whose sources of funds are mostly short-term deposits. There is a high correlation between the degree of government control over these institutions and their ability to generate long-term sources of funds. In Italy, for example, the institutions that raise funds in the long-term sector of the market are also of a public or semipublic nature. These institutions specialize in three major types of credit: industry and public work, mortgages, and agricultural credit. The main source of funds of these institutions is the bond market which they dominate. The bonds are issued under very attractive terms to the bondholder. Since the institutions are of a semipublic nature, the major criterion in their lending is development of the given economic sector in the country.

Savings banks and specialized banks abound in all these countries. In some countries, savings banks' lending policies can be strictly controlled by the government. In other countries, the savings banks tend to operate more like commercial banks specializing in specific types of credit (such as consumer credit or any other credit demanded by the bulk of the bank's depositors).

CROSS-BORDER
FINANCING IN CONTROLLED
DOMESTIC MARKETS

Whenever governments restrict the access of foreign borrowers (including subsidiaries of foreign companies) to domestic financial markets, a situation of segmented capital markets develops. The major currencies can be provided by the Euromarkets, but usually at a higher rate. For currencies in which a Euromarket does not exist, the currency is usually not available through the normal channels of financial intermediaries and public financial markets. In such cases, the only alternative available to the foreign borrower is to enter into some kind of agreement with an entity with access to the desired domestic currency.

At the core of all these arrangements are the following elements: (1) a subsidiary in a foreign country which needs funds; and (2) a parent company that has excess funds, but is unwilling to transfer the funds directly to the subsidiary in order to minimize exchange risk. When the foreign subsidiary cannot tap the local market for borrowings, the excess funds available to the parent can be used to meet the financing needs of the subsidiary through special arrangements. These arrangements are of three major types: back-to-back loans, parallel loans, and swap agreements.

In the *back-to-back loan* the parent company deposits the excess funds in the home currency with a commercial bank located outside the subsidiary's country. This bank then extends a loan to the subsidiary in the subsidiary's currency.

The *parallel loan* involves two companies, two subsidiaries, and two loans. The parent company lends the excess funds in the home currency and country to the affiliate of a foreign company. This foreign company, which is located in the same country where the subsidiary needing the funds is, then lends the needed currency to that subsidiary.

In the *swap agreement* the parent company exchanges its excess funds for the currency that the subsidiary needs. The exchange is made with another company located where the subsidiary is located. The agreement is that after a specified number of years the transaction will be reversed at the same exchange rate—that is, the parent company will buy back its home currency.

The interest rates on these agreements are related to the interest rates on the respective currencies. In the back-to-back loans and the parallel loans separate interest is paid by each party. In the swap agreement, only the differential in interest is paid to the party contributing the currency with the higher interest rate.

SUMMARY

The multinational manager will make decisions on covering or accepting foreign exchange risks in the short run using the instruments and analyses suggested in previous chapters. For the longer term, there is a general market failure, in the sense that matching money market instruments or forward market covers are typically not available. In this situation, the manager will look at the *net effective interest cost* of a foreign currency debt—that is, the nominal coupon rate adjusted for changes in the foreign exchange rate over time. The key to the net effective interest rate is the eventual reaction in the exchange rate to differential inflation between two economies, as well as to other economic pressures as discussed in Chapter 5.

Eurodeposits are time deposits with a maturity that is typically less than 1 year. They are preferred by some customers in order to avoid sovereign political risk. For example, Eurofranc deposits are free of French banking regulations that might develop with a sharp change in government. In addition to political risks, there are other reasons for rate differences between the Euromarket and the domestic market. These rate differences are a function of domestic regulations (deposit reserves, insurance requirements, or interest rate ceilings, for example) and exchange controls, neither of which are present in the Euromarkets. Hence, the Euromarket often becomes the free market for a currency, with rates reflecting a free market equilibrium.

Euroloans typically are in units of $1 million from a base of about $500,000 up to $100 million. They usually have a maturity from 30 days to 7 years, often with a balloon ("bullet") payment of the entire principal. Euroloans often have a floating rate at a spread over the London interbank offered rate (LIBOR). The borrower may have an option to change the currency in which the loan is denominated at the various rollover points at which the interest rate is reset, based on the rates then prevailing.

A bond sold outside the country of the borrower is an international bond. One type is the *foreign bond,* which is denominated in the currency of the country where it is sold. The bulk of the foreign bond market involves public institutions raising funds in various capital markets around the world. The other type of international bond is the *Eurobond,* which is sold outside the country of the issuer and in countries other than the currency in which it is denominated—for example, a Sony dollar bond sold exclusively in Western Europe. Typically these are bearer bonds with no withholding payments on interest. In large part, this market emerged from U.S. attempts in the 1960s to encourage foreigners and the foreign subsidiaries of U.S. corporations to raise money outside the U.S. capital markets. Variants of the international bond include multiple-currency option bonds, bonds with fixed proportions of currencies weighted in the repayment requirement, and bonds convertible into equity. Rates on international bonds are related to the prevailing domestic rates for the currency of denomination.

In surveying local capital markets, the international manager will see variations in bank and nonbank financial intermediary practices across nations. Outside the United States, banks are often involved in investment banking as well as commercial banking, and are major underwriters of security issues. There is typically more bank concentration in economies other than the United States, and a greater preponderance of short-term loans to customers, even though these loans are often rolled over repeatedly. Nonbank financial intermediaries are important in the medium- to long-term money market. Insurance companies, public and private pension funds, savings banks, and other specialized institutions are typical of these intermediaries. Where there is no Euromarket, back-to-back, parallel, and swap loans are often arranged between a firm with funds available in one market and needs for those funds in a subsidiary in a restricted-access market.

QUESTIONS

1. Explain why the net effective interest cost between two comparably secured loans in different currencies differ for all periods and subperiods over 20 years. How are these results consistent with interest rate parity and purchasing power parity?

2. Suppose a bank offers a loan which permits the floating-rate interest payments to be based on LIBOR for 30-day, 90-day, or 1-year quotes, elected by the borrower as each previous period ends. What information would you use to determine this "submaturity period" for your firm's 5-year Euroloan?

3. What sovereign risk is present in a back-to-back loan? Are these risks present in a parallel loan? What risks are present in the parallel loan situation?

4. How do interest rate ceilings affect different classes of domestic borrowers? Domestic lenders? Which banks would be relatively most hostile to the imposition of a special, short-term 20% increase in domestic reserve requirements on deposits?

5. What are the characteristics of the firm whose treasurer might pay a premium for a multiple-currency option bond?

BIBLIOGRAPHY*

The Banker's Guide to World Financial Centers," *The Banker (London)*. May 1978, pp. 51–140.

Business International Corporation, *Financing Foreign Operations*, current issues, New York.

Dufey, Gunter, and Ian H. Giddy, *The International Money Market*. Englewood Cliffs, N.J.: Prentice-Hall, Inc., 1978.

McCulloch, J. Huston, "The Bank on Indexed Bonds, 1933–77," *American Economic Review*, Dec. 1980, pp. 1018–21.

Nickel, Herman, "The Iran Deal Doesn't Look Bad," *Fortune,* Feb. 23, 1981, pp. 57–59.

Organization for Economic Cooperation and Development, *OECD Financial Statistics*, OECD Publications Center, current issues, Washington, D.C.

Park, Yoon S., *The Eurobond Market: Function and Structure*. New York: Praeger, 1974.

Reynolds, Paul D., *China's International Banking and Financial System*. New York: Praeger, 1982.

Riehl, Heinz, and Rita M. Rodriguez, *Foreign Exchange and Money Markets*, New York: McGraw-Hill, 1983.

Rischer, Gunter, "The Role of Underwriters in the Eurocapital Market," *Euromoney,* June 1972, pp. 4–10.

---

*See also the bibliography to Chapter 4.

MULTINATIONAL BISCUITS, INC.

THE LATEST ACQUISITION by Multinational Biscuits, Inc. (MBI) at the end of 1980 had taken place without a hitch, or so thought Robert Schreiner, president of MBI. With the acquisition of this company in Spain, MBI now had a significant presence in almost every European country.

The acquired Spanish company manufactured biscuits of various kinds that were sold all over Spain. The company had been owned and managed by the founder and his family for the last 40 years. However, the younger generation was not interested in continuing the family business. So, the heirs had agreed to sell the company, on the condition that those family members currently involved in the management of the company would be allowed to retain their positions under the new ownership. (This pattern conformed to many of the acquisitions MBI had made in Europe during the post-War period—namely, family-owned businesses which were small by American standards but which represented a significant factor in the local market. These were also companies in which the owners wanted to increase their financial liquidity.)

Mr. Schreiner had found the conditions and the asking price to be very reasonable, given the history and market position of the company. However, this did not stop him from trying to reduce the price. The Spanish family conceded a little bit—just enough not to embarrass Mr. Schreiner's bargaining approach—and the deal was closed promptly. The amount of the purchase, $5 million, was well within the limits which the Board of Directors of MBI had allowed Mr. Schreiner to purchase this company without further consultations with the Board. So, as soon as the lawyers on both sides prepared the necessary documentation, the ownership of the company was ready to be transferred.

Approximately 1 week before the closing date, Mr. Charles Duval, treasurer of MBI, first heard the particular details of this acquisition. Mr. Schreiner asked him to make sure that $5 million in cash would be available the following week to be transferred into Spain. Some certificates of deposit had to be liquidated and some lines of credit had to be used, but the transfer of $5 million on short notice was done without undue stress. Mr. Duval knew an acquisition in Spain was pending and had prepared for it by keeping MBI's excess funds invested in securities of short-term maturity and by maintaining ample lines of credit with several banks. Thus, transfer of the $5 million dollars was accomplished without much trouble. However, the same could not be said for Mr. Schreiner's second request: that financing be arranged with Spanish banks for the account of the Spanish company. Mr. Schreiner asked Mr. Duval to arrange for the Spanish company to borrow $4 million in pesetas. More specifically, he recommended that, given the expected cash flows of the Spanish company, a 7-year loan with a repayment schedule of 7 approximately-equal annual installments be obtained.

Mr. Schreiner's request for financing of the Spanish company was consistent with the pattern he had followed in the past. He preferred first to purchase a company and only later to worry about the financing. Financing then was carried out in the local markets by the newly acquired company, thus ensuring maintenance of his philosophy of "each tub on its own bottom." Furthermore, he preferred strict financing terms, such as the requested equal installments in the repayment schedule, "to promote financial discipline in the company."

The earlier acquisitions had taken place in major European countries where the local financial markets had been both capable and willing to accommodate the financing necessary for acquisitions according to Mr. Schreiner's preferences. But Spain was different because foreign-owned companies were not allowed to borrow funds in the local market. In addition, Spain had a basic 24% per annum withholding tax on interest payments made by Spanish companies to foreign lenders.

Mr. Duval's first reaction when confronted with the impossibility of borrowing pesetas for the Spanish company was to borrow the needed funds in the Eurodollar market. He was familiar with this market. Also, Mr. Duval had a soft spot for dollar financing: "We are a dollar company, so financing with dollars is a normal thing for us to do." He was very tempted to use this source of funds to accommodate the financing of the Spanish acquisition. But before pursuing this approach, he decided to talk with some banks.

By early 1981 the conversations with the bankers had resulted in the following three different proposals to finance the Spanish subsidiary:

1. A 7-year Eurocurrency loan with a multicurrency option from the London branch of a U.S. commercial bank
2. A 7-year, fixed-rate Dutch guilder loan from a Dutch merchant bank
3. A fixed-rate, 5-year dollar or Swiss franc loan from a Swiss commercial bank

Each of the three alternatives was to be in the form of a loan to the Spanish company with a parent company guarantee. The details of each of the three proposals are presented here.

EUROCURRENCY LOAN FROM LONDON
BRANCH OF U.S. COMMERCIAL BANK

Amount.   US$4 million or its equivalent.

Multicurrency Option.   At the request of the borrower, a floating-rate loan could be denominated in any freely convertible currency or group of currencies, with a minimum of $250,000 in any currency. However, for a currency to be acceptable to the bank, deposits in that currency had to be available to the London branch in the amounts and for the interest period or periods of the loan. If a requested currency such as pesetas were not available, that portion of the loan would be denominated in U.S. dollars.

Final Maturity.   Seven years from date of drawdown. Shorter and longer maturities were also available.

Repayment Schedule.   Seven annual principal repayments beginning 1 year after drawdown or a balloon repayment at the end of the 7 years. In case of annual repayments, the first repayment would be $375,000 followed by five annual installments of $604,166.65 and a final installment of $604,166.75. A similar pattern of annual repayments or a balloon repayment at the end of the loan period were also available for shorter- and longer-maturity loans.

Commitment Fee.   A fee of ½% per annum of the undrawn portion of the loan commencing from the date of signing of the loan. However, if the loan were drawn fairly quickly upon signing (that is, within 30 days or so), this commitment fee would be waived.

Interest Rate.   Both a floating rate and a fixed rate were available. The *floating rate*, with annual repayments, was 1¼% over the London interbank offered rate (LIBOR) for the currency borrowed. Three-month LIBO rates as of the end of February were as follows:

	3-MONTH LIBOR			
U.S. Dollar	German Mark	Pound Sterling	Swiss Franc	Dutch Guilder
16.50	14.62	12.69	8.88	11.50

The spread of the *fixed rate* over LIBOR depended on the maturity chosen and on whether the repayment schedule was based on annual repayments or a balloon repayment at the end of the loan period. The quoted spreads over LIBOR for fixed rates and the LIBOR at the end of February for the two currencies then available on a fixed-rate basis are shown in the following table:

| | INTEREST RATES ON FIXED-RATE LOANS | | | |
| | LIBOR | | SPREAD OVER LIBOR | |
Maturity	$	DM	Annual Repayment	Balloon Repayment
1 year	15⁷⁄₁₆%	11⁷⁄₁₆%	½%	—
2 years	15⅜	11	⅝	—
3 years	15¼	10¾	⅝	—
4 years	15⅛	10½	¾	1 %
5 years	15⅛	10½	¾	1¼
6 years	15	—	1	1½
7 years	15	—	1¼	1½
8 years	—	—	1½	1¾

Interest Period.   In the case of a *floating rate*, MBI could select an interest period of 1, 3, or 6 months, with the choice to be made at the end of every interest period.

Withholding Taxes.   The commercial bank offering this loan believed that recent changes in attitude by the Spanish government had made it possible for a Spanish company to apply to the Spanish Central Bank for relief from the 24% withholding tax and that an exemption of up to 95% was almost automatically granted upon application. If MBI were able to obtain a waiver of 95% of the Spanish withholding tax, the bank was willing to absorb the balance of the withholding tax MBI would have to pay. If MBI could not obtain a waiver of the withholding tax, the bank was willing to work with MBI to determine exactly how much of the withholding tax the bank could absorb.

Documentation.   The documentation would consist of the usual Eurocurrency loan agreement.

Other.   MBI would be dealing directly with the major U.S. bank with which it had a very close relationship. If it became necessary during the life of this loan to reset the terms or to add to this loan for any reason, the bank could be expected to accommodate MBI's needs.

FIXED-RATE DUTCH GUILDER LOAN
FROM DUTCH MERCHANT BANK

Amount. The Dutch guilder equivalent of $4 million.

Currency Options. The loan had to be drawn and denominated in Dutch guilders throughout its entire life.

Final Maturity. Seven years from the date of drawdown.

Repayment Schedule. Seven annual principal repayments beginning 1 year after drawdown. The first repayment would be $375,000, followed by five annual installments of $604,166.65 and a final installment of $604,166.75.

Commitment Fee. No commitment fee as known in the United States. However, there was a flat 1% fee payable on the date of the signing of the loan agreement.

Interest Rate. A fixed rate of approximately 10¾% payable free and clear of all taxation.

Withholding Tax. A waiver of the withholding tax, as in the first option, was believed possible. However, any withholding tax would be charged against MBI.

Documentation. A loan agreement drawn by the Dutch bank subject to Dutch law, accompanied by an outside legal opinion.

Other. The Dutch guilder was a currency in which MBI had a significant exposure through a large investment in the Netherlands. A Dutch guilder financing would provide an automatic hedge in that currency. Since the Netherlands subsidiaries did most of their business in the Netherlands, there would be a natural flow of guilders which could be used to repay this loan.

FIXED-RATE DOLLAR OR SWISS FRANC LOAN
FROM SWISS COMMERCIAL BANK

Amount. The amount would be either US$4 million or its equivalent in Swiss francs.

Currency Option. There was an initial option of drawing and denominating the loan for its entire life in either U.S. dollars or Swiss francs. There was no option to switch currencies during the life of the loan.

Final Maturity. Five years from date of drawdown.

Repayment Schedule. A single repayment of the entire loan at its maturity in 5 years.

Commitment and Other Fees. No commitment or other fees, but immediate drawdown of the loan in full was required.

Interest Rate. Fixed for the full life of the loan at 15½% for a dollar loan and at 6½% for a Swiss franc loan. (This quote had been obtained a week earlier than the date for the LIBO rates presented under the Eurocurrency loan option.)

Withholding Taxes. Spain had a double taxation treaty with Switzerland and the withholding tax was reduced to 5% per annum, subject only to a minimum borrowing period of 5 years. Some additional withholding tax relief could be available but any withholding tax that was assessed would be against MBI's account.

Documentation. No special documentation was anticipated.

Other. The Swiss franc was a currency in which MBI generated earnings that could be used to repay this loan.

Under each alternative, it would be necessary for the Spanish company to apply to the Spanish Central Bank to obtain permission to borrow externally. In that application it would be necessary to detail a final loan proposal stating the amount to be borrowed, the terms of the loan, the interest rate, and other specific loan conditions. The application for the exemption from the withholding tax could be made at the same time. Although no difficulty was anticipated in obtaining the permission for the loan, the exemption from withholding tax was another matter.

Exhibits G.1–G.4 present historical quarterly data on exchange rates, nominal interest rates, and effective interest rates for various currencies.

EXHIBIT G.1 Multinational Biscuits, Inc.: Foreign Exchange Rates, 3-Month Nominal Eurorates, and Effective 3-Month Eurorates, Summary Measures, Quarterly, June 1977 to December 1980[a]

	U.S. Dollar	German Mark	Pound Sterling	Swiss Franc	Dutch Guilder
Exchange Rates to $1					
Mean value	1.00	1.968	0.493	1.830	2.132
Standard deviation	—	0.192	0.053	0.280	0.183
Range	—	1.740	0.418	1.589	1.922
		to 2.355	to 0.582	to 2.489	to 2.488
Nominal Interests					
Mean value	11.04%	5.94%	12.88%	3.34%	7.98%
Standard deviation	4.36%	2.64%	4.25%	2.38%	3.19%
Range	5.75%	3.31%	6.25%	1.25%	2.75%
	to 20.13%	to 10.06%	to 20.00%	to 7.00%	to 14.63%
Effective Interests					
Mean value	11.04	9.31%	19.44%	10.04%	10.32%
Standard deviation	4.36%	18.29%	13.42%	29.93%	18.82%
Range	5.75%	−32.35%	−10.11%	−36.02%	−35.65%
	to 20.13%	to 36.63%	to 40.33%	to 65.92%	to 29.71%

[a]These quotations are nonoverlapping quarterly figures for the period indicated. Interest rates are London interbank quotations. Effective interest rates are nominal rates adjusted for quarterly exchange rate changes ex post.

EXHIBIT G.2 Multinational Biscuits, Inc.: Foreign Exchange Rate Indices, June 1977 to December 1980 (in foreign currency per U.S. dollar, June 1977 = 1.00)

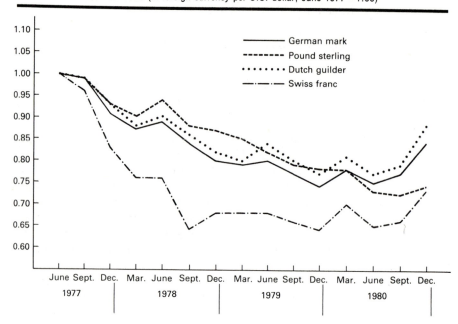

EXHIBIT G.3 Multinational Biscuits, Inc.: Nominal Interest Rates, June 1977 to
December 1980 (annual rates)

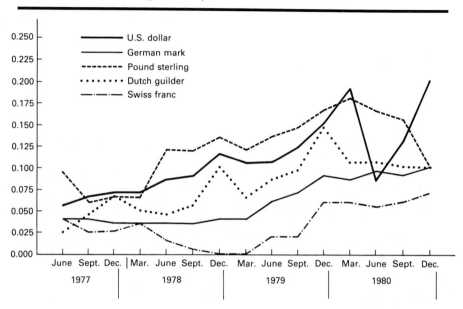

EXHIBIT G.4 Multinational Biscuits, Inc.: Effective Interest Rates, June 1977 to
December 1980 (annual rates)

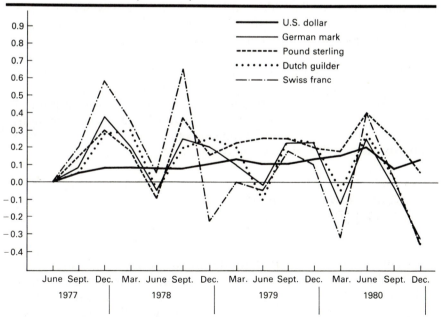

GREEN
VALLEY
CORPORATION

IN THE BEGINNING of March 1977, Len Hamberg, treasurer and vice-president of Green Valley Corporation, was considering how to refinance a recent acquisition done by the company's British subsidiary. Government regulations in the United Kingdom, as well as general unrest in international monetary markets, made the decision particularly complicated. Mr. Hamberg had recently learned about the parallel loan, a new way of financing overseas operations, and he was now in the process of carefully analyzing this alternative.

BACKGROUND

In 1977, Green Valley had sales and manufacturing subsidiaries in five European countries. The oldest and largest of these was Green Valley U.K., Ltd., which was established in 1946 in order to secure the company's participation in the rapidly growing European postwar economy. Green Valley U.K. had originally been constrained in its operations to sales and marketing efforts throughout Western Europe but had subsequently entered into pharmaceutical manufacturing as the European market was deemed large enough to support such local production. The strategy had proven successful and the overseas operations had expanded into four more European countries by 1977, accounting for approximately 20% of total company sales.

THE ACQUISITION OF BEDALES
CHEMICALS, LTD.

In December 1976, David Ballard, the treasurer of Green Valley U.K., Ltd., had been informed by a London merchant banker that a small pharmaceutical company, Bedales Chemicals, Ltd., outside Rhondda in Wales, was for sale. Mr. Ballard decided to visit the company right away and returned 2 days later full of enthusiasm for the potential acquisition. As there were several other companies interested in acquiring Bedales, he immediately contacted Len Hamberg in Warren, Connecticut, and after numerous telephone conversations and telegrams, the executive committee of the U.S. parent decided in early January 1977 to give Mr. Ballard authorization to buy Bedales Chemicals, Ltd., for a maximum price of $6 million in cash.

Meanwhile, in England, Mr. Ballard had been in contact with the London branch of the Gotham National Bank, a major New York bank, in order to discuss the financing of the acquisition. Mr. Ballard had realized the hasty nature of the transaction would not permit a permanent financial arrangement to be worked out until after the acquisition had been made. Furthermore, the European monetary scene was quite unstable in early 1977 and Mr. Ballard did not feel inclined to make any long-term financial commitments on the part of Green Valley U.K., Ltd., without full support from the U.S. parent.

It was thus with some kind of bridge financing in mind that Mr. Ballard approached the London representatives of the Gotham National Bank. Green Valley had been a client of Gotham for many years both in the United States and in the United Kingdom, and Mr. Ballard knew that the bank would do whatever it could to meet his request. An arrangement was soon worked out whereby Gotham would extend a revolving Eurodollar credit line to Green Valley U.K., provided that the obligation would be fully guaranteed by the U.S. parent. The maximum amount of the credit would be $5 million and the interest rate adjusted every 6 months to reflect changes in the Eurodollar market for short-term money. The initial interest rate in January 1977 was to be 6¾%.

As it was a firm policy of Green Valley Corporation to finance all its foreign subsidiaries in local currency as much as possible in order to hedge against any exchange losses, Mr. Ballard had initially requested a credit line denominated in sterling. However, the bankers had explained that it was virtually impossible for them to extend a sterling credit under the current Bank of England credit ceiling restrictions. Credit ceilings, they said, had been on and off in the United Kingdom during most of the 1960s and the present regulations made it impossible for banks to increase their sterling credits above certain limits set by the Bank of England. At present, the minimum lending rate (MLR) for short-term sterling was 12%, but such credit was simply not available to Green Valley under the Bank of England restrictions.

When Mr. Ballard received the authorization to buy Bedales Chemicals he activated the credit line from the Gotham National Bank and proceeded to acquire the company as a wholly-owned subsidiary of Green Valley U.K., Ltd., for £2.5 million in cash. At the current exchange rate of $1.71/£, the acquisition had a value of $4.275 million.

This amount was for plant and net working capital; no long-term debt was acquired as part of the purchase.

THE REFINANCING DECISION

Two weeks after the acquisition, Mr. Ballard was asked to come to the U.S. headquarters of Green Valley in order to discuss the integration of Bedales Chemicals into the company's other U.K. operations. As Mr. Ballard had anticipated, the refinancing question was given high priority.

Len Hamberg, the corporate treasurer, did not like having such a substantial dollar liability in a country that appeared so prone to continuous depreciation especially since he did not have any other sterling liability in addition to the U.K. subsidiary's. Also, the short-term character of the obligation ran contrary to his opinion that long-term assets should be financed with long-term capital. Finally, he considered the credit expensive, especially in light of the fact that he paid only 6¼% on his bank borrowings for Green Valley in the United States.

As soon as Mr. Ballard arrived in Warren, Mr. Hamberg decided to arrange a meeting in order to discuss the refinancing of the Bedales acquisition. Apart from Mr. Ballard and himself, Mr. Hamberg invited Ed Savage, a vice-president from the international department of the Gotham National Bank in New York, and Thomas Rowley, a representative from the New York investment bank Norwich, Stap & Co., whose services Green Valley had used for many years both in the domestic and the international fields.

The following conversation took place during this meeting on February 2, 1977:

Len Hamberg:	Well, as you all know, we have gotten together today to discuss the refinancing of the Bedales acquisition in England. Although I don't really like that revolving credit Dave got for us in London, I understand that this was the only solution considering the rush we were in to get the cash on the table to buy that company. I am also sure that your people at Gotham in London did whatever they could to help us out, Ed. In any case, the deal is all done now and today's problem is rather how to get long-term sterling into our U.K. sub instead of all hot dollars we are sitting on right now. What alternatives do we have, Ed?
Ed Savage:	Thank you, Len. Well, if you want both sterling *and* long-term money I frankly cannot see any alternatives at all. I have already told you about the credit ceilings in London and although we possibly might give

you sterling instead of Eurodollars toward the end of this year, it can certainly never be of any maturity longer than 1 year. The market in sterling is just too tight to enable us to make any longer commitments. Also, if you were to get sterling it would be quite expensive. Today, for example, it would cost at least 12% as compared to the 6¾% you are currently paying on the dollar revolving credit.

Len Hamberg: Twelve percent is certainly no alternative! As a matter of fact, I think that even the 6¾% we are paying right now is too expensive. Can you explain to me, Ed, why you charge 6¾% in London when we pay only 6¼% on our bank borrowings here in the United States? It's the same bank and the same currency, and don't tell me that the credit risk is any larger in the United Kingdom, as we have given you full parent guarantee for the obligation.

Ed Savage: Same bank and same credit risk, I agree, but not the same currency. You see, the money you get here is what we call domestic dollars but the credit in London is in Eurodollars, and that's different although the notes may look the same.

David Ballard: But what if Green Valley Corporation here in the United States borrows the money from Gotham in New York at the lower rates and then just sends it on to us in the United Kingdom?

Ed Savage: You can do that, of course. We could also work out a back-to-back loan, in which you deposit funds with us in New York and we lend dollars to your U.K. subsidiary. But that still leaves you with a dollar liability in the U.K. subsidiary.

Len Hamberg: But let's forget about the currency for a moment and look at the maturity instead. As you all know, I don't like to match up fixed assets with short liabilities. In this particular case I would prefer a maturity of 6 to 8 years; this would permit us to keep our minds off this matter for a while without tying us up for too long which could hurt in case the cost of money should go down significantly. Would there be any way of doing this with bonds, Tom?

Thomas Rowley: Sure, Len, you can do anything with bonds! Seriously speaking, you can always get all the money you want with Eurobonds, but I don't know if that is going to help you because you won't be able to get it in sterling and probably not in the maturity you wanted. The Bank of England would never allow you as a nonresident to sell sterling bonds inside the United Kingdom and as far as I know there is no Eurosterling around. Even your U.K. subsidiary, as a nonresident-controlled foreign corporation, would not be allowed to use the domestic sterling market. If there were Eurosterling available, you would have to obtain it by Green Valley U.S. As to the maturity, 6 to 8 years is what we would call medium-term money and that is pretty hard to find in the Eurobond market today. It would cost around 15% or so, I think.

Len Hamberg: Well, that certainly wasn't encouraging! The revolving credit line we already have in London perhaps isn't that bad after all when you consider that. . . .

Thomas Rowley: Excuse me for interrupting you, Len, but I thought I should mention another way we might consider trying to refinance this deal. What I am thinking of is a so-called parallel loan. This seems to be a particularly attractive alternative in your case as I see that you have a fair amount of excess liquid funds in your balance sheet. In order to arrange one of these transactions we would have to find a U.K. company that has a subsidiary that needs capital here in the United States and that would be willing to lend us the sterling we need in the United Kingdom. In exchange for the sterling loan they give us in the United Kingdom, we would lend a similar amount in dollars for the same maturity to their subsidiary over here and both companies would get the money they need without having any funds cross the Atlantic.

Len Hamberg: That sounds interesting—especially considering that we can make use of some of those liquid funds that we accumulated for a California acquisition that recently fell through. You are, however, working under the assumption that the U.K. company would turn to us to get dollars for their sub here in the United States. What would stop them from just exporting the funds from the United Kingdom or perhaps getting a regular bank loan in New York from Ed's bank?

Thomas Rowley: Well, you see, the British guys are having a tough time in getting funds abroad. To simply export the funds from the United Kingdom is possible but very expensive indeed. They have to acquire so-called investment sterling which according to Bank of England regulations is the only currency they can legally bring out of the country. This investment currency is kept in very limited supply by the authorities and is traded in a special market where it currently commands about a 35% premium to buy—so you understand that they are inclined to try to find other solutions before they go ahead and pay 1.35 pounds just to get one pound to bring abroad!

In order for Ed's bank to lend them the money in the United States, they would like a parent guarantee. The problem is that the U.K. firm needs Bank of England permission to pay on a guarantee, if it becomes necessary. Even then, the U.K. firm has to use that expensive investment sterling, which really makes

	the guarantee an undesirable aspect of borrowing for the U.K. parent.
Len Hamberg:	Tell me, what would the cost be on a loan like this?
Thomas Rowley:	As you would have both a payable and receivable in equal amounts, the only thing that really matters is the spread between the interest rates on these two. I could imagine that the U.S. company would have to pay a little more on its payable than it gets on its receivable, say 2½% as the sterling currently is more expensive than the dollar.
Len Hamberg:	And what would the Bank of England say about this? Wouldn't the foreign sub still have to have a parent guarantee in order to get a dollar loan?
Thomas Rowley:	Not necessarily. You see, included in these loan agreements is always a setoff clause that normally makes parent guarantees superfluous. This clause states that in case of default by either party, principal and interest may be offset against the repayment obligation, or in other words, you can use the payable as security for your receivable. Even if the clause is not written for some regulatory reasons, everyone knows the way the arrangement works.
Len Hamberg:	This really seems to add up to a very interesting alternative, Tom, but would you also say that I could get the maturity I want?
Thomas Rowley:	That's really a question of negotiations. If you find a U.K. company that wants to go along with your terms, you can put together almost any kind of parallel deal you like.
Len Hamberg:	Yes, I realize that what is clearly most important in this kind of a deal is to find the right company in England. I think we know enough about the characteristics of a parallel loan arrangement to realize that it could be a very interesting alternative in refinancing our acquisition of Bedales Chemicals. The next step will have to be to identify the British party in the deal and to negotiate mutually acceptable terms. Do you think that Norwich, Stap & Co. could help us there, Tom?
Thomas Rowley:	We would be delighted to, Len. I'll get in touch with our people in London right away and ask them to start looking for a suitable partner for you. I know that you'd like to get this refinancing done the sooner the better, and I'll get back to you with a memorandum outlining the initial negotiations with the U.K. party.

Four weeks after his meeting with Mr. Ballard and the two bankers from New York, Mr. Hamberg received from Norwich, Stap & Co. the memorandum reproduced in Exhibit H.2. In the meanwhile, Mr.

Hamberg had collected some data on the current state of international financial markets (Exhibit H.1).

Mr. Hamberg had also received a telephone call from Julian DeGray, senior partner of the Warren, Connecticut, accounting firm, DeGray, Erland & Bach. This firm had handled Green Valley's accounting for many years and Mr. Hamberg was often on the phone with Mr. DeGray.

Julian DeGray:	Good morning, Len! I'm calling you about this proposed parallel loan with Abbotsholme Assurance Company. We were just thinking about the consolidation of the statements of your foreign subsidiaries and, to put it frankly, I don't think we ever handled one of these parallel deals before. I talked to a friend of mine at Arthur Andersen yesterday and he said that his clients that had done these transactions—including a major drug company by coincidence—usually netted the two transactions so that neither the receivable nor the payable showed up in the balance sheet. It would of course be nice if we could do that too, especially considering that you want to improve your bond rating in time for that issue you are planning this coming fall.
Len Hamberg:	Yes, I have been thinking about that myself and it would certainly look much better if we could leave the deal outside the books all together. But I suppose that we will have to mention it in a footnote at least?
Julian DeGray:	Look, Len, I think this entire question is important enough to call for an ad hoc meeting. Would it be all right if I bring along one of our whiz-kids and stop by at your office next week?
Len Hamberg:	Sure, Julian, I'd be happy to have you come. In the meantime, I'll bring some of my material together and do my homework! See you then.

Mr. Hamberg then sat down to review carefully the parallel loan proposal in light of the other alternatives and the market data. He thought it was particularly important to estimate the actual cost of the parallel financing as compared to the other alternatives discussed during the meeting in early February. Also, monetary markets were still very unstable and he was not quite sure what the impact of a possible parity change between the dollar and the sterling would be on the parallel loan.

These questions would have to be answered one way or another before the next day when Len Hamberg was to give his final recommendation on the refinancing of the British subsidiary to the executive committee of Green Valley Corporation.

EXHIBIT H.1 Green Valley Corporation: Selected Data on International Financial Markets, 1974–1977 (in percent, end of month)

| | 1974 | 1975 | 1976 | | | 1977 | |
	Dec.	Dec.	Oct.	Nov.	Dec.	Jan.	Feb.
Commercial Bank Deposit Rates							
United States, 3-month	9.25	5.50	5.10	4.70	4.70	4.95	4.85
United Kingdom, 3-month	12.25	10.50	15.13	14.50	14.13	11.94	11.13
Eurodollars, 3-month	10.19	5.81	5.31	5.13	5.00	5.25	5.13
Eurodollars, 6-month	10.19	6.63	5.75	5.31	5.38	5.81	5.63
Commercial Bank Lending Rates to Prime Borrowers							
United States	10.25	7.25	6.50	6.25	6.00	6.25	6.25
United Kingdom	13.00	12.00	15.00	15.00	15.00	14.00	12.50
Eurodollars, 3-month	11.32	6.69	5.94	5.63	5.50	5.75	5.63
Domestic Corporate Bond Yields, Long-term Issues							
United States	9.25	8.55	8.15	7.90	7.35	8.00	8.10
United Kingdom	19.50	14.90	16.91	16.49	15.76	14.64	14.82
Eurodollar Bond Yields, Long-term Issues							
Issued by U.S. companies	9.35	8.52	7.82	7.76	7.39	7.63	7.72
Exchange Rate ($/£)							
Spot		2.021	1.589	1.654	1.701	1.715	1.714
6-months forward		1.975	1.485	1.572	1.622	1.661	1.653

SOURCE: *World Financial Markets*, Morgan Guaranty Trust Company of New York; *Business International Money Report*, various issues.

EXHIBIT H.2   Green Valley Corporation: Memorandum on Parallel Loan Proposal

MEMORANDUM

To: Mr. Len Hamberg, Treasurer and Financial Vice-President, Green Valley Corporation, Warren, Connecticut

From: Thomas Rowley, Partner
Norwich, Stap & Co., New York, New York

Regarding: The partial refinancing of Green Valley U.K., Limited, through a parallel loan transaction.

The London representatives of Norwich, Stap & Co. have been able to identify a U.K. corporation, Abbotsholme Assurance Company Limited, that is willing to participate in a parallel loan transaction with Green Valley Corporation.

Abbotsholme is a U.K. insurance company with total assets of £355 million and total after-tax profits of £9.1 million in 1976. The company established a wholly-owned subsidiary, Abbotsholme U.S. Insurance, Inc., in 1965 in Newark, New Jersey, and their U.S. insurance operations have been growing rapidly since then. The Board of Directors of the Abbotsholme parent organization in the United Kingdom made a policy decision toward the end of 1976 that their U.S. operations should be expanded into the real estate financing area. A few months later, Abbotsholme Properties, Inc., was founded as a wholly-owned subsidiary to Abbotsholme U.S. Insurance, Inc., in order to coordinate this expansion. The U.S. operations of Abbotsholme are already heavily leveraged and the U.S. parent has found it increasingly difficult to transfer equity funds from the United Kingdom to finance the expansion of their U.S. subsidiary without running into restrictive Bank of England regulations.

We approached Abbotsholme in the United Kingdom with our outline for a parallel financing and the corporate treasurer, Alan Weyl, immediately showed a great deal of interest in the proposal. Tentative negotiations have led to the following terms which we feel are very close to the most favorable that Green Valley will be able to obtain:

	Dollar Loan	Sterling Loan
Borrower	Abbotsholme U.S. Insurance, Inc.	Green Valley U.K., Ltd.
Lender	Green Valley Corporation	Abbotsholme Assurance Company, Ltd.
Form	Loan agreement and promissory note	Loan agreement and promissory note
Principal amount[a]	US$6 million	£3.5 million
Maturity[b]	9 years, 360 days	9 years, 360 days
Price and Yield[c]	100% to yield 9½% p.a.	100% to yield 12% p.a.
Sinking Fund	None	None

	Dollar Loan	Sterling Loan
Prepayment	None	None
Default Provisions[d]	Without parent company guarantee but with setoff convenants in case of default.	Without parent company guarantee but with setoff convenants in case of default.
Parity Change Provision[e]	Any time during the life of the agreement when the value of sterling in relation to the dollar decreases by 6% and remains at or below this value for a continuous period of 30 days, the dollar borrower, upon notice, is to reduce the outstanding principal of the dollar loan by paying the dollar lender an amount equal to 6% times the outstanding principal of the dollar loan. (A similar clause existed for the event of dollar depreciation.)	
Bank of England	Abbotsholme Assurance Company, Ltd., has approval for borrowings by Abbotsholme U.S. Insurance, Inc.	Green Valley Corporation will need exchange control approval for sterling borrowings by its U.K. subsidiary.
Fees and Expenses[f]	For the account of Green Valley Corporation.	For the account of Abbotsholme Assurance Company, Ltd.

[a]Abbotsholme is flexible to the amount of the transaction. Green Valley should probably try to borrow as much as Bank of England will allow them. Dollar loan and sterling loan will be of exactly the same amounts at the spot rate of the date of issue.

[b]Abbotsholme insists on minimum maturity of 7 years. Maturity should be kept below 10 years as stamp tax of ½ of 1% is levied by Bank of England on all U.K. debt obligations running 10 years or longer. Renewal options can be negotiated.

[c]Abbotsholme will consider only a fixed interest rate over the life of the obligation and argues that market conditions entitle them to a favorable spread of at least 2½%. Twelve percent on sterling loan equals the minimum lending rate (U.K. equivalent of prime rate) and is the minimum interest rate permitted by Bank of England on the sterling part of a parallel transaction.

[d]Green Valley's security for its dollar receivable is its sterling payable. In case Abbotsholme would default on either interest or principal, Green Valley is entitled to withhold interest as well as total outstanding amount of the sterling payable until such default has been recovered.

[e]Assume sterling is at $1.700 and the loan involes $1,000,000, or £588,235. If sterling depreciates by 6% to $1.598, then the U.S. borrower of pounds has a $940,000 loan. The U.K. borrower of dollars has the same $1,000,000 loan. To restore the balance, the U.K. firm with the larger loan will reduce its loan balance by 6%, for a dollar value of the payment of $60,000.

[f]Total legal fees for arranging Green Valley's part of the transaction will be approximately $10,000. Norwich, Stap & Co. expects to retain a fee equivalent to ¾ of 1% of the principal of the loan.

10

Management of Exposure to Exchange Risk in the Foreign Enterprise

A BRITISH FIRM that sells a product to customers in Italy and invoices in liras is concerned with the value of the lira relative to the pound between the time when the invoice is issued and the receivable is collected. This is the type of exchange risk problem discussed earlier in the context of cash management and international trade.

When the firm expands its operations abroad to include direct investment in a foreign subsidiary (or branch), the problems created by foreign exchange risk become more complicated. At any point in time, the financial officer in this firm is endowed with a set of investment and financing decisions made in the past that result in the firm's having assets, liabilities, and expected cash flows in many currencies. Most of these cash flows (with the major exception of dividends remitted to the parent company) remain in foreign currencies. However, the *value* of the assets and liabilities generating those cash flows can be considered exposed to the risk of fluctuations in exchange rates.

To manage the exposure to exchange risk involved in foreign direct investments we must first define procedures for measuring the magnitude of the exposure. Then we will analyze the avenues available to cover this exposure.

MEASURING EXPOSURE TO EXCHANGE RISK

In trying to determine the value of the firm exposed to fluctuations in exchange rates we encounter three different systems of valuation: (1) the amount of cash flows involved in exchange transactions; (2) the value of the firm as measured according to accounting conventions; and (3) the value of the firm measured in economic terms. These approaches provide three different measures of exposure to exchange risk. These are commonly referred to as: (1) transaction or conversion exposure; (2) translation or accounting exposure; and (3) economic exposure.

Transaction Exposure

This is the exposure to exchange risk that we have discussed thus far in the text. In all the cases we saw earlier, the exposure arose from the prospect of cash flows in different currencies at a specified date in the future—for example, the payment of a supplier in liras to be made with the dollars obtained from sales 90 days later. In this exposure we can anticipate the exact amount of the foreign currency and the precise date in the future when the transaction converting one currency into another will take place; hence, the name *transaction* or *conversion exposure*. The cash flows measured by transaction exposure may involve known future commitments that are not shown on the end-of-period balance sheet—for example, an agreement to pay a supplier within 30 days after a delivery of raw materials 6 months from now.

A foreign subsidiary which is financed in the local currency and which operates only in its domestic markets has a potential transaction exposure in only one instance—namely, the remittance of dividends to the parent. It is only in this case that a foreign exchange transaction is required. Although the subsidiary has many cash flows in its daily operations, none of these other flows involves a foreign exchange transaction.

Many business people argue that transaction exposure is the only relevant type of exposure. In this view, self-contained foreign subsidiaries that do not intend to pay dividends in the foreseeable future are not exposed to foreign exchange risk until the time when dividends start to be declared. However, the narrowness of the transaction concept of exposure to exchange risk can be seen by considering what happens to stock prices when a recession affects the economy. At such times, stock prices usually decline even for those companies which maintain a stable dividend. Although no change in the cash flow between a company and its stockholders may take place, the market penalizes the price of the stock. The market, in fact, is saying that under the new economic conditions the *value* of the company is less than before. By analogy, it can be argued that when the currency of a foreign country where a subsidiary is located depreciates, the *value* of that subsidiary to its owners who are located in another country decreases, regardless of the pattern of profit repatriation from the subsidiary.

An exposure measure should focus on the potential changes in overall value of the firm—that is, on all future cash flows, and not only on those cash flows that involve an exchange transaction. But, although the identification of cash flows involved in transaction exposure is relatively straightforward, the same cannot be said about the overall cash flows determining the value of the firm. As a result, we have two major competing measures of value of foreign operations. One is the value of the firm as measured according to accepted accounting principles; the other is the economic value to the parent company of the cash flows expected in the future in the foreign operation.

Accounting Exposure

The accounting value or book value of a firm is measured by the equity account—that is, the net of assets and liabilities—in the balance sheet. However, when measuring the book value of a foreign subsidiary, we must translate the value of foreign assets and liabilities into the currency unit of the parent and we must select an exchange rate to make such *translation*. For each account we have to choose either the *current exchange rate* on the date of the statement or the *historical exchange rate* prevailing at the time when the asset or liability was acquired.

If we follow accounting conventions to measure the value of foreign operations, then the amount of exposure to exchange risk in a foreign unit is measured by the *net of the accounts translated at current exchange rates*. If all accounts are translated at current exchange rates, then the amount exposed to exchange risk is equal to the capital account. If all accounts are translated at historical exchange rates there is no exposure to exchange risk.

Suppose Bongo Corporation, a U.S. company, has a South American subsidiary, Bongo Latino, which carries on manufacturing and distribution activities in Latin America. The *forecast* balance sheet of Bongo Latino for the end of next year is presented in Exhibit 10.1.[1] At

---

[1]The use of a forecast balance sheet incorporates future profits in this type of measurement of exposure to exchange risk.

EXHIBIT 10.1   Bongo Latino: Forecast Balance Sheet for End of Period

Assets		Liabilities and Equity	
Cash and securities	P 40	Accounts payable	P 60
Receivables	80	Taxes payable	20
Inventory	80		
		Total current liabilities	P 80
Total current assets	P200		
Net plant and equipment	100	Long-term debt	120
		Equity	100
Total assets	P300	Total liabilities and equity	P300

the time, the peso is worth $1.00. But the management of Bongo Corporation foresees that a 10% depreciation of the peso is very likely in the coming year. At the end of that year, what would be the loss from translating the depreciated peso investment of Bongo Corporation in Bongo Latino?

If the peso depreciates, any account which is translated at the exchange rate expected for the end of the year would be translated at an exchange rate of PO.90/$, and would be worth 10% less at the end of the next accounting period than it is worth today. For example, the cash and securities account translated at today's exchange rate of P1.00/$ is worth $40; if we translate it at the expected exchange rate of PO.90/$, it is worth $36. That is, 10% of the account ($4) is lost because of the 10% devaluation of the peso. However, any account which is translated at the historical exchange rate of P1.00/$ would maintain its accounting value in dollar terms.

There is general agreement among financial analysts that financial accounts (cash, receivables, and payables) should be translated at current exchange rates. If the proceeds from these accounts were exchanged into dollars, this would have to be done at current exchange rates and their dollar value would decrease with a depreciation of the foreign currency. However, the argument is not so clear with respect to the other accounts which have a longer time horizon and which traditionally are reported at the historical prices or rates at which they were originated. These other accounts are inventory, plant and equipment, and long-term debt.

The basis for most accounting concepts is cost; therefore, the historic cost based on the historic exchange rate for many of the other balance sheet accounts may be considered relevant. The depreciated book value of the plant may have little relationship to the current market value. Thus, if the value in local currency does not match market value, why should one worry about whether the translation rate used for converting its historic book value to dollars is the current one? After all, since the depreciation charges are simply a method to expense the original (historic) cost over a period of time, in this logic there is no point in translating the plant value at the current rate.

Let us now consider inventory. If inventory is thought of as historically produced goods not yet sold, or as goods in process, why should the dollar value be adjusted? If they are destined for sale in the Latin economy, then the price may not change with the peso depreciation, so their future value will likely be less in dollar terms. On the other hand, if they are for export, the peso depreciation may make the goods more competitive. Hence, total revenues in pesos might actually be higher in the future so that translating the inventory account at the current peso exchange rate would yield too severe a decrease in value. Similarly, if we retain a historic cost basis for inventory, then the historic cost in dollars should not be changed simply because of fluctuations in the value of the peso.

A similar conflict develops for long-term debt. Some people would argue that it should not be considered on a current exchange rate basis. These accountants would argue that the future payment of the liability is many years away, perhaps after other currency revaluations. The value of long-term debt is not adjusted to reflect market changes in interest rates, so why should it reflect changes in exchange rates? Furthermore, long-term liabilities often were incurred to purchase fixed assets; if the plant and equipment valuation is not lowered because of the currency depreciation, then the funds supporting it should not be. Other students of the subject argue that long-term debt should be translated at current exchange rates; the gain to the parent from financing its subsidiary in a depreciated currency occurs when the currency depreciates, regardless of when the debt is paid.

The combination of the alternative treatments of the controversial accounts produces four different methods of measuring exposure to exchange risk in accounting terms. The first method includes current accounts only and is usually called the *current/noncurrent method* (also referred to as *net current asset* or *net working capital method*). The *monetary/nonmonetary method* excludes inventory but includes the long-term debt. The *net financial asset method* includes all current accounts as well as the long-term debt. Finally, the *all-accounts method* translates all accounts at current rates.

The exposure for Bongo Latino under each method is presented in Exhibit 10.2. When there is a blank, the account is not included in the determination of net exposure. The final exposure is the sum of the positive and negative figures. Under the current/noncurrent method, the exposure is P120, equal to $120 at the initial exchange rate. This means that a 10% devaluation of the peso would result in a $12 translation exchange loss to the parent. Conversely, a 10% appreciation of the peso would result in a $12 exchange gain to the parent. Under the

EXHIBIT 10.2   Bongo Latino: Accounting Exposure to Exchange Risk under Alternative Translation Methods

		TRANSLATION METHOD			
	Current/ Noncurrent	Monetary/ Nonmonetary	Net Financial Assets	All-Accounts
Current assets, except inventory	P120	P120	P120	P120	P120
Inventory	80	80		80	80
Plant and equipment	100				100
Current liabilities	(80)	(80)	(80)	(80)	(80)
Long-term liabilities	(120)		(120)	(120)	(120)
Net exposure		P120	(P 80)	0	P100

monetary/nonmonetary method of calculating exposure, there would be an $8 gain from a 10% peso depreciation, for the firm owes $80 more in the now cheaper currency than it has in cash and other current assets. But there would be an $8 loss if the peso appreciates by 10%. There is no net exposure under the net financial assets method, and there is a positive exposure of P100 under the all-accounts method.

These methods, as well as variants of them, are in use in different countries around the world. Some countries use one method exclusively, while others use a variety of them, depending on the company. In the United States, all of the methods of translation described here, plus variations, were acceptable prior to January 1976. Since then, the Accounting Standards Board has issued two statements establishing the proper translation method. The first such statement was the highly debated Financial Accounting Standard No. 8 (FAS 8), issued in December 1975. In December 1981, FAS 8 was superseded by FAS 52. In FAS 52 all the balance sheet accounts are effectively translated at the exchange rate prevailing at the date of the balance sheet (the all-accounts method).

Most of the accounts in the income statement are translated in all methods at the average exchange rate prevailing during the report period. The major exception to this approach is the charge for depreciation. Depreciation is translated at historical rates in all the translation methods except for the all-accounts method, in which it is translated at the average exchange rate for the period.

The gain or loss derived from translating the income statement is already incorporated in the exposure measure based on the balance sheet, as long as the date of the balance sheet follows the period covered by the income statement. Alternatively, one could measure separately the book value exposure on the date of the initial balance sheet and then compute the exposure involved in profits to be generated in the succeeding accounting period.

In principle, any accounting gain or loss resulting from the translation process can be reported in one of three different manners:

1. Charge them against a reserve account in the balance sheet and do not report them in the income statement.
2. Report them in the income statement as an extraordinary item.
3. Report them in the income statement as part of operating income.

FAS 52 follows the first approach.[2] This is in contrast to the controversial FAS 8, which treated these exchange gains and losses as part of ordinary income, and in contrast to the *clean surplus theory* traditionally advocated by U.S. accountants.

Economic Exposure

Economic value is based on future cash flows discounted to a present value.[3] Conceptually, this is very difficult from the accounting value discussed previously. The gain or loss from economic exposure to exchange risk of Bongo Latino can be seen as the difference between its *dollar* (the parent's unit) net present value before and after the envisaged exchange fluctuations. Thus, the original dollar net present value may be computed using the following formula:

$$\$NPVo = \frac{\text{Original peso cash flow}_1 \times XRo_1}{(1+r)} + \frac{\text{Original peso cash flow}_2 \times XRo_2}{(1+r)^2} + \cdots$$

$$+ \frac{\text{Original peso cash flow}_n \times XRo_n}{(1+r)^n}$$

---

[2]For the application of FAS 52 to a numerical example, see Chapter 11.

[3]For forerunners of this concept, see Fredrikson, who argues that the relative expected exchange rate at the time of completion of a transaction should be forecast and used in the income statement, rather than the exchange rate in effect at the end of the year for, say, receivables with a foreign exchange loss charged on the financial statement. (See E. Bruce Fredrikson, "On the Measurement of Foreign Income," *Journal of Accounting Research*, Autumn, 1968, pp. 208–221.) A related break with accounting convention is given in Heckerman who notes that the value of the firm depends on the discounted value of future cash flows. Changing price levels for the parent and the subsidiary economies and the changing exchange rate affect this discounted value; he compares the adjustments to the balance sheet under this approach with normal accounting standards. (See Donald Heckerman, "The Exchange Risks of Foreign Operations," *Journal of Business*, January 1972, pp. 42–48.)

where XRo denotes the series of exchange rates between the peso and the dollar originally envisaged.

If a depreciation in the peso is now foreseen, there will be changes in both the peso cash flows and the exchange rates used to convert those flows into dollars. The new dollar net present value can then be computed by adjusting the terms in the preceding formula as follows:

$$\$NPVa = \frac{\begin{array}{c}\text{Adjusted}\\\text{peso}\\\text{cash flow}_1\end{array} \times XRa_1}{(1+r)} + \frac{\begin{array}{c}\text{Adjusted}\\\text{peso}\\\text{cash flow}_2\end{array} \times XRa_2}{(1+r)^2} + \cdots$$

$$+ \frac{\begin{array}{c}\text{Adjusted}\\\text{peso}\\\text{cash flow}_n\end{array} \times X\,Ra_n}{(1+r)^n}$$

where XRa denotes the new exchange rates after the peso depreciation. The gain or loss resulting from the peso depreciation and the adjustments in operations is then the difference between the original dollar net present value ($NPVo) and the adjusted dollar net present value ($NPVa).

If the peso cash flows adjust to compensate for any fluctuation in exchange rates, then the dollar net present value of Bongo Latino remains constant—that is, there is no exposure to exchange risk in economic terms. Thus, we can define economic exposure to exchange risk in a given currency as *the amount of cash flows in a currency which will not change proportionally to counteract a devaluation in that currency.*

As an illustration, we will assume cash flows in Bongo Latino for only 1 year in the amount of P100, equal to $100 at the initial exchange rate of P1/$. We can see the economic exposure to exchange risk of Bongo Latino under two alternative situations: (1) when the peso cash flows adjust for 100% of the devaluation; and (2) when the peso cash flows adjust for only 40% of the devaluation. The peso economic exposure is represented by the amount of cash flows that do *not* adjust to the devaluation. In the first case 0% of cash flows do *not* adjust to the devaluation, and in the second case 60% of cash flows do *not* adjust to the devaluation. Given the original peso cash flows of P100, the peso economic exposure to exchange risk is zero in the first case and P60 in the second case. Exhibit 10.3 presents the effects of two alternative devaluations of the peso, given the two possible adjustments of the peso cash flows.

EXHIBIT 10.3   Bongo Latino: Effects of Peso Devaluation under Two Alternative Economic Exposures to Exchange Risk

Percentage Adjustment in Cash Flows	Peso Economic Exposure[a]	%Δ XR	%Δ CF	New XR	New CF P[b]	New CF $[c]	$ Exchange Loss[d]
100%	0	10%	10%	0.90	110	99	−1
100%	0	20%	20%	0.80	120	96	−4
40%	60	10%	4%	0.90	104	93.6	−6.4
40%	60	20%	8%	0.80	108	86.4	−13.6

$$^a \left(\begin{array}{c} \text{Original} \\ \text{peso} \\ \text{cash flows} \end{array} \right) - \left(\begin{array}{c} \text{Percentage} \\ \text{adjustment} \\ \text{in cash flows} \end{array} \right) \times \left(\begin{array}{c} \text{Original} \\ \text{peso} \\ \text{cash flows} \end{array} \right)$$

$$^b \left(\begin{array}{c} \text{Original} \\ \text{peso} \\ \text{cash flows} \end{array} \right) + \left(\begin{array}{c} \text{Percentage} \\ \text{adjustment} \\ \text{in cash flows} \end{array} \right) \times \%\Delta XR \times \left(\begin{array}{c} \text{Original} \\ \text{peso} \\ \text{cash flows} \end{array} \right)$$

^{c}(New peso cash flows)(New XR)

^{d}\$100 original dollar value of peso cash flow less the new dollar value of this cash flow.

Even when the peso cash flows adjust by the same percentage as the percentage of the devaluation, there is a small exchange loss due to the impact of the devaluation on the *increase* in local currency cash flows. In the case of a 10% devaluation, the $1 of exchange loss is equal to 10% of the increase in peso cash flows of P10; and the exchange loss of $4 is equivalent to the 20% devaluation effect on the increase in cash flows of P20. The exchange loss when the peso flows adjust by only 40% of the devaluation can be seen as the impact of the devaluation on the peso economic exposure, P60, plus the impact of the devaluation on the increase in cash flows. The $6.4 exchange loss is composed of 10% loss on the economic exposure of P60 ($6) plus 10% of the increase in cash flows of P4 ($0.4). The $13.6 exchange loss is the result of 20% loss on the economic exposure of P60 ($12) plus 20% loss on the increase in cash flows of P8 ($1.6).

For any one period, we can define economic exposure more accurately as follows:

$$\begin{array}{c} \text{Peso} \\ \text{economic} \\ \text{exposure} \end{array} = \left(\begin{array}{c} \text{Original} \\ \text{peso} \\ \text{cash} \\ \text{flows} \end{array} \right) \left(1 - \begin{array}{c} \text{Percentage} \\ \text{adjustment} \\ \text{in cash} \\ \text{flows} \end{array} + \begin{array}{c} \text{Expected} \\ \text{change in} \\ \text{peso} \\ \text{cash} \\ \text{flows} \end{array} \right) \left(\begin{array}{c} \text{Expected} \\ \text{percentage} \\ \text{change in} \\ \text{exchange} \\ \text{rate} \end{array} \right)$$

An alternative approach is to consider how long it will take for the foreign firm to recover from the losses inflicted by a devaluation. The cash flows during the time period until the profits of that firm can revert to the dollar equivalent of profits at the predevaluation rate is the amount of economic exposure in that operation. If it is not expected that it will ever recover from the devaluation, then the total economic exposure is the foreign profits received in perpetuity—the whole value of the foreign firm.[4]

The analysis of the economic exposure of a foreign operation also should segregate the *operating cash flows* from the *financing cash flows*. These cash flows can be analyzed first assuming a given level of investment and capital structure; but if changes in the investment and capital structures are envisaged in the future, then the effects of these changes on any cash flow should be incorporated explicitly in the analysis.

Operating Cash Flows. Consider the present value of the subsidiary in the country that has just devalued its currency. The future operating cash flows in that currency may be more or less following the devaluation. In particular, the operating cash flows in local currency after the devaluation will depend on the following three major factors:

1. The export component of sales and the responsiveness of export sales to the lowered effective price after the devaluation
2. The effect of the devaluation on national income and the response of sales to changes in national income
3. The effect of the devaluation on domestic inflation and the ability of the company to realize increases in sales price and control the impact of inflation on costs

With lower export prices now possible, export sales may increase and the expected profits of the firm for the coming years may be over and above the profits expected before the devaluation. Similarly, if the devaluation increases domestic income, then the volume of local sales may increase enough to compensate for the effects of the devaluation on revenue per unit. Finally, if the devaluation has the usual effect of increasing local inflation, then we can expect to increase selling prices and, depending on the nature of costs, net profits. Of course, if price controls are imposed after the devaluation, price increases would not be possible, at least immediately. The new economic value of the firm will be the result of the combined interaction of the new economic conditions and management's reactions to these conditions.

In this presentation, we have assumed a given level of investments. When changes in the investment level are envisaged, the economic exposure to exchange risk will be affected by the pattern of cash

---

[4]For an alternative computation using balance sheet data and aggregate country data, see Christine R. Hekman, "Measuring Foreign Exchange Exposure: A Practical Theory and Its Application," *Financial Analysts Journal*, September-October 1983, pp. 59–65.

flows associated with the change in the investment level itself, as well as its eventual impact on future operating cash flows.

During the period when plant and equipment are being acquired and working capital is being increased, there will be net cash outflows associated with the new project. In the case of Bongo Latino the out-flows associated with the acquisition of land and the payment of labor are likely to be in pesos; the other outflows may be in pesos or another currency, depending on the location of the source of equipment and raw material. After the project becomes operational, if the additional sales and necessary inputs are denor..inated in pesos, there will be ad-ditional operating cash flows in pesos for the life of the project. The economic exposure to exchange risk of these additional cash flows may or may not be the same as the exposure of the earlier project. These new flows may also affect the capability of cash flows generated by ear-lier investments to adjust after a fluctuation in the value of the peso. (For example, after an increase in production levels it may be more dif-ficult to increase selling prices in response to a devaluation of the peso.) In case of a liquidation of foreign investments, there will be an increase in inflows as the operation winds down, and a permanent re-duction in operating cash flows thereafter.

An assessment of the ability of a foreign operation to adapt to fluc-tuations in exchange rates and the associated changes in the economy can be obtained from the analysis of past history. We want to see how the firm's sales and operating profits, and therefore costs, have per-formed relative to the local economic variables and in terms of the par-ent's currency. Measuring the performance of the operation relative to the local economy provides an index of how management is coping with local conditions;[5] measuring performance in terms of the parent's home currency provides an index of the variable of ultimate importance to the parent company. We will want to analyze the performance of lo-cal sales and net operating profits relative to the industry and national income, both in nominal terms (including inflation) and in real terms (excluding inflation); and then measure the performance of sales and net operating profits both in terms of the local currency and the par-ent's currency.

These historical relationships may not be valid in the future. In any case, they should be discussed with management in charge of op-erations, who have a better understanding of the current competitive environment of the firm. Herein lies one of the benefits of analyzing exposure to exchange risks in these terms: It forces operating personnel to plan for fluctuations in exchange rates.

---

[5]This topic is discussed at greater length in Chapter 11.

Financing Cash Flows. To illustrate the impact of alternative financing schemes on the overall economic exposure to exchange risk of Bongo Latino, we will assume the annual income statement and flow of funds statement presented in Exhibit 10.4. The income statement shows annual operating profits of P50 and net profits of P20. The difference between operating profits and net profits is the charge for interest expense in the amount of P30 (a 25% interest rate on the debt of P120). The flow of funds statement implies a stable level of investment and a constant capital structure. Depreciation charges are equal to new investment, and new loans equal debt repayment.

To simplify the analysis, we will assume that the operating profits of Bongo Latino are not exposed to exchange risk—that is, price adjustments are possible to compensate for the impact of any devaluation on the dollar value of operating profits. Initially we will assume also that the debt carries a fixed interest rate which applies also to the portion of the debt refinanced annually.

If the P120 debt of Bongo Latino is denominated in pesos, then the peso financing cash flows after the devaluation will remain constant; however, their dollar value will decrease. The peso financing flows are exposed to exchange risk when valued in dollar terms. Given our assumption of no exchange exposure in operating flows, there will be an increase in operating *peso* cash flows after the devaluation. Since the peso financing flows will remain constant, there will be an increase in peso net profits. If the initial capital structure is kept constant, these additional profits will be available for distribution to the owners. The devaluation increases the amount of dollar cash flows available to the parent. There is a net increase in the economic value of Bongo Latino equal to the present value of the financing flows times the percentage of the devaluation, received *in perpetuity*. In this situation the eco-

EXHIBIT 10.4 Bongo Latino: Annual Income Statement and Flow of Funds Statement

Annual Income Statement		Annual Flow of Funds	
Sales	P600	*Sources of Funds*	
Less cost of goods sold	535	Operations	P50
Gross profit	65	Depreciation	10
Selling and administrative		New loans	10
expenses	5	Total sources of funds	70
Depreciation	10	*Uses of Funds*	
Operating profit	50		
Interest expense	30	New investments	10
Foreign exchange gain/loss	—	Debt repayment	10
Net profits	P20	Dividend payments	50
		Total uses of funds	P70

nomic exposure of Bongo Latino to exchange risk is equal to the annual financing outflows in perpetuity.

If the debt of Bongo Latino is denominated in a currency other than pesos (say, dollars), then the peso financing cash flows after a devaluation of the peso will increase. More pesos will be required to meet the repayment of principal and the interest on the existing debt. However, at the same time, fewer dollars will be required to refinance the existing debt and maintain the given capital structure in pesos. With a 6-year debt, the annual repayments of $20, which initially required P20, now require P22. The payment of interest, which originally required P30, now requires P33. This represents an annual exchange loss of P5, which over 6 years will amount to a total loss of P30. However, given that we wish to maintain the initial capital structure in pesos, every year we will have to refinance only $18 to replace the initial $20 repaid in that year. After 6 years, the dollar debt will be $108, which at the new exchange rate will equal P120—the same as the initial amount of debt in pesos. During the first 6 years after the devaluation there will be P5 fewer funds available in profits for dividend payments. There will be a decrease in the economic value of Bongo Latino equal to the present value of the financing flows times the percentage of the devaluation, *for 6 years*. The economic exposure of Bongo Latino to exchange risk in this case is equal to the annual financing outflows for 6 years.

The removal of the assumption of a constant capital structure produces changes in financing cash flows while the capital structure is being modified, as well as a different pattern of financing cash flows afterward. An increase in the proportion of debt in the capitalization produces an increase in inflows of funds exposed to exchange risk during the years when the increase takes place. Assuming a constant level of operations, these additional funds would be available for liquidating equity capital. At the point when the debt structure stabilizes at a new level, the remittances of funds to the equity holders and the exchange exposure would revert to the initial P20 in dividends, less the additional interest expense on the higher debt; however, this dividend payment will be made now on a lower capital base. The increased leverage increases returns per dollar of investment; however, it also increases the amount of financial risk in this operation.

A decrease in the proportion of debt in the capital structure produces an increase in net peso outflows exposed to exchange risk during the years when the decrease takes place. Assuming a constant level of operations, the source of the funds used to reduce the amount of debt in the capital structure must be profits that otherwise would have been available to pay dividends to the parent company. When the capital structure stabilizes at the lower proportion of the debt, the payments of dividends exposed to exchange risk will return to the initial P20, plus the savings in interest expense. The returns per dollar of equity will have decreased, but so will the financial risk.

If the interest rate on the debt is not fixed, one should consider changes in interest rates resulting from a fluctuation in exchange rates. When the peso devalues against the dollar, changes in interest rates are more likely in the peso debt than in the dollar debt; however, both may change. If the direction of these changes in interest rates can be anticipated, they should be taken into account in the analysis of the economic exposure by modifying the proportion of the original financing cash flows we expect to adjust to a devaluation of the peso. This is particularly important in the case of a highly leveraged operation.

COVERING EXPOSURE TO EXCHANGE RISK IN DIRECT INVESTMENT

The value of foreign direct investment, in principle, can be covered through transactions in the forward exchange market and the money market, using the same tools we have discussed earlier. However, the implications of using these covers are somewhat different when they are applied to the exchange risk generated by the *value* of foreign operations. In addition, the foreign firm can manage operations in order to engineer a cover similar to the one produced by money market operations. We now discuss these two approaches to eliminating exchange risk.[6]

Covering Operations in Financial Markets

Consider a U.S. company that has a subsidiary in the United Kingdom. The company contemplates a *net positive economic exposure* in sterling in the amount of £200,000. For simplicity, ignore the distribu-

---

[6]Technically there is a difference between covering and hedging operations. *Covering* implies the protection of an identifiable and quantifiable *cash flow* in the exchange markets that could give rise to a foreign exchange loss in the *conversion* from one currency to another—for example, proceeds from export sales or dividends to be received in a foreign currency. Covering involves a self-liquidating transaction. *Hedging*, on the other hand, refers to the protection of the value of *assets* located in foreign countries and their financing. That is, hedging attempts to protect the value of future profits generated in foreign currencies although no foreign exchange transaction may be involved. In practice, the two terms—*covering* and *hedging*—are used interchangeably. See Paul Einzig, *A Textbook on Foreign Exchange* (London: Macmillan, 1966).

tion of this exposure through time and assume it matures in 1 year, with no dividends or other exchange transaction envisaged—that is, there is no transaction exposure. The company faces a potential loss in *value* in case of a sterling depreciation.

In order to understand better the mechanics of hedging an economic exposure, we will express this exposure in terms of explicit cash flows assumed to be available for distribution to stockholders as potential dividends. At an exchange rate of $2.50/£ we have the cash flows shown in the following table:

	CASH FLOWS 1 YEAR LATER	
	Sterling	Dollars
Net exposure	+200,000	
Dollar value equivalent which could be available for dividend distribution		-500,000

If sterling depreciates against the dollar, fewer dollars will be available for possible distribution to stockholders 1 year later. Effectively, the company has a net exchange position, long in sterling and short in dollars.

This formulation of the exposure problem points to the conceptual similarities and differences between exposed *value* and exposed *transactions*. In both there is a net exchange position. However, in value exposure only one of the cash flows—the sterling inflow—will materialize. The distribution of dollar dividends to stockholders is used only as an analytical device to value sterling flows in dollar terms—the parent's currency.

To eliminate the uncertainty about the exchange rate at which the sterling exposure will be valued in dollar terms, we can follow the procedures used earlier for covering an exchange position. We can lock in an exchange rate in advance to make such valuation as if the sterling flows were indeed to be converted into dollars. We have to generate cash flows in each currency to offset the ones producing the exchange position. In this example the hedging transaction must involve an outflow in sterling (to offset the inflow generated by the exposure) and an inflow in dollars (assumed to be needed for distribution to stockholders).

Assume the following rates prevail in the market:

Foreign Exchange Market	
Spot rate	$2.50/£
1-year forward rate	$2.45/£
Money Market	
1-year dollar	7%
1-year sterling	9%

The 1-year pound is trading at a 2% per annum discount against the dollar and interest rate parity holds. There is no incentive for covered-interest arbitrage. The company's exposure by currency, after the hedging operation, would appear as indicated in the next table.

	CASH FLOWS 1 YEAR LATER	
	Sterling	Dollars
Net exposure	+200,000	
Dollar value equivalent which could be available for dividend distribution		−500,000
Hedging transaction	−200,000	+490,000

In the forward market the covering transaction will be carried out by selling pounds against dollars for 1-year delivery at the forward rate of $2.45/£. The transactions that will occur 1 year later, under alternative spot rates prevailing then, are presented in the following two tables.

Transactions Associated with Depreciation of Sterling to $2.35/£	
Loss on valuation of net asset position	
£200,000 × $0.15/£ depreciation	$(30,000)
Gain on liquidation of forward contract	
Buy spot at $2.35/£, deliver at contract price of	
$2.45/£ (gain/£ = $0.10) £200,000 × $0.10/£ gain	20,000
Net gain (cost)	$(10,000)

Transactions Associated with Appreciation of Sterling to $2.60/£	
Gain on valuation of net asset position	
£200,000 × $0.10/£ appreciation	$ 20,000
Loss on liquidation of forward contract	
Buy spot at $2.60/£, deliver at contract price of	
$2.45/£ (loss/£ = $0.15) £200,000 × $0.15/£ loss	(30,000)
Net gain (cost)	$(10,000)

Regardless of whether the pound appreciates or depreciates in the spot market, the net of valuing the exposure and closing the forward contract is a loss of $10,000. This loss represents 2% of $500,000, the original dollar value of the sterling exposure, and it corresponds to the 2% discount on the forward pound relative to the initial spot rate. The forward contract locked in an exchange rate at which to value the sterling exposure. The cost of $10,000 in terms of today's spot rate ensures that if the pound depreciates below $2.45/£ the company is not hurt. However, should the pound actually appreciate to $2.60/£, a gain is foregone.

If the money market is used to hedge the exposure, the steps to be followed are:

1. Borrow £200,000 at 9% for 1 year.[7]
2. Convert the borrowing proceeds into dollars at the current spot rate, $2.50/£.
3. Invest the converted dollars at 7% for 1 year.

Again, a cost of 2% is being locked in to insure against a potentially greater loss if sterling depreciates by more than 2%.

Whether the money market or the forward market is used to hedge net exposure, there will be an exchange transaction involved at the end—a real cash flow. However, the £200,000 of net exposure is not available (unlike the exporter's collection of a trade receivable) for settling the hedging transaction. The sterling accounts receivable and payable producing the economic exposure are not expected to be liquidated for this purpose. On the other hand, the gain or loss from closing the forward contract is a real gain or loss in cash. If the exposure figure does not correctly measure the concept it intends to measure, then the company will be trading real cash flow gains or losses for paper ones. Herein lies the aversion of many companies to hedge ac-

---

[7]To cover a £200,000 exposure in 1 year, initially we have to borrow less than £200,000. The accumulation of interest will bring the total to £200,000 by the end of the year.

counting and economic exposures, preferring to hedge only conversion exposures.

Adjustments in Operations

The cash flows generated through covering transactions in the financial markets can be engineered through operations. In effect, these adjustments in operations are similar to disguised money market hedges. In the previous example, in which we were covering a net positive exposure in sterling, the adjustments in operations would be geared to generate outflows in sterling and inflows in dollars. These adjustments in operations can be made through transactions with third parties, or through intercompany transactions.

Operations with Third Parties.   Given an unwanted net positive exposure, the goal of these adjustments would be to generate cash in the exposed currency which can then be converted into the desired currency. Thus, local suppliers' terms of credit may be stretched and local customers' receivables reduced if at all possible. Either transaction would increase cash balancs in the foreign currency which can be converted into another currency. A conscious effort to reduce temporarily the level of sales or the size of operations may be the second line of attack. Alternatively, sales may be invoiced in a harder currency. However, these measures are likely to encounter very strong opposition from the people in the operating line.

The profits lost on the foregone sales are a clear cost of these approaches. Similarly, denominating export sales in hard currencies might be accomplished only at the expense of a reduction in price, since the buyer also has foreign exchange considerations to take into account. This decrease in price might neutralize and even decrease the net effect of billing in a hard currency. On the liability side, extending the terms on which suppliers are paid may be accomplished only by foregoing discounts for prompt payment and by facing in the future higher prices and less service from the supplier.

Intercompany Accounts.   When there are several subsidiaries in the same parent's orbit, intercompany accounts can often be used to great advantage. While the subsidiary in the devaluation-prone country may attempt to remit funds to the parent in the form of dividends or royalties (or withhold these payments in the case of an upvaluation-prone currency), this route is usually restricted to some degree by the local authorities. However, payment of accounts payable (even when they are intercompany accounts) will usually be allowed.

The change in the level of intercompany accounts is only a device to accomplish an exposure objective. Given a positive exposure and a certain level of intercompany accounts receivable and payable, the desired objectives will be accomplished if:

1. Subsidiaries in devaluation-prone countries pay their intercompany accounts payable as soon as possible and delay collecting their intercompany accounts receivable for as long as possible.
2. Subsidiaries in upvaluation-prone countries delay paying their intercompany accounts payable as long as possible and collect their intercompany accounts receivable as soon as possible.

In the case of the subsidiary in a devaluation-prone country, the company is effectively removing cash from the country when the subsidiary pays its intercompany payables in advance. The company also is reducing the entry of additional resources into that currency by delaying the collection of funds from sister subsidiaries. The opposite is accomplished with the suggestions regarding the subsidiary in the upvaluation-prone currency.

Although the logic behind these procedures is relatively simple, confusion often arises when the subject is discussed. There are two major sources of puzzlement. One source is the fact that at any point in time the net of consolidated intercompany accounts is zero. The intercompany account receivable of one subsidiary is the account payable of another. When the two given subsidiaries are consolidated into one reporting unit, the receivable of the first subsidiary cancels the payable of the other. However, this misses the point that the manipulation of the size of these intercompany accounts is only a tool to move resources from one currency into another. The statement about the impact of consolidation of intercompany accounts at one point in time is correct. However, if one can affect the level of these intercompany accounts before the exchange fluctuation takes place, one is effectively redeploying resources. Payables of a subsidiary in a weak currency can be reduced only by remitting funds which are then converted to a harder currency.

The second source of confusion in the use of intercompany accounts originates in the role of currency denomination. Actually, the currency of denomination determines only the tax effect of foreign exchange gains and losses after the revaluation takes place. Consider two subsidiaries that trade with one another. One subsidiary is in Germany; the other is in France. Assume that the German subsidiary sells products to the French one. The German subsidiary has an account receivable from the French subsidiary and the French subsidiary has an account payable to the German subsidiary. Now examine the impact of an appreciation of the German mark relative to the French franc when payment is made under alternative billing currencies. If the bill is issued in marks, then at the time of payment the French subsidiary will have a foreign exchange loss; it will have to generate more French francs than originally anticipated to pay the mark debt. In this case nothing happens to the German subsidiary. If the bill is invoiced in terms of French francs, then there is no foreign exchange effect on the French subsidiary when the payment is made. However, the German subsidiary now receives fewer marks than anticipated at the exchange rates prevailing at the time of the sale. The German subsidiary experiences a foreign exchange loss. Thus, regardless of the currency used in the denomination of intercompany trade, one of the units will have a foreign exchange loss if the payment to the German subsidiary (with the stronger currency) is not made before the appreciation of the mark. If such a loss must be accepted, for example, because of government controls on remittances from France into Germany, the choice of a specific currency for invoicing is immaterial if the tax rate is the same in the two countries. If that is not the case, then one will want the foreign exchange loss to fall in the country with the higher tax rate in order to reap the higher tax shelter benefit from the loss.

We have suggested that in the case of an upvaluation-prone currency, debts to third parties in that currency should be decreased while intercompany accounts payable of the subsidiary operating in the country of that currency should be increased. Both are debts of the subsidiary in the upvaluation-prone country. Why decrease one type of debt and increase the other? Both approaches increase net inflows in that currency. If asset levels are maintained constant, and if the reduction of payables to third parties is accompanied by an increase in financing in a weaker currency, then we eliminate an outflow and increase *net* inflows in the upvaluation-prone currency. By increasing the intercompany payables, the upvaluation-prone subsidiary can finance an increase in the resources that will augment future inflows in the relatively harder currency.

The cost of leads and lags in payments of intercompany transactions can be assessed only by making clear who is the final holder of the merchandise (including cash) and who is providing the financing. Once these facts are established, one can proceed to evaluate the interest expense involved, the net effective cost of the debt, and the returns obtained by the holders of the merchandise. When the merchandise is a financial asset, the return is easy to measure; it is simply the effective interest rate in the market. When the merchandise is goods, then one has to consider inventory carrying costs as well as profit margins.

Finally, in evaluating the cost of these operating adjustments to compensate foreign exchange risk, one must consider the factor of time. If these measures are necessary for a very short period because the change in currency values is imminent, then they might be worthwhile even if the net cost is very high in terms of annual interest rates. One would be paying a very high cost for a small period of time, while the devaluation impact would last much longer. On the other hand, a protracted use of these techniques is likely to be very costly.

SUMMARY

There are three measures of exposure to exchange risk: transaction exposure, accounting exposure, and economic exposure. *Transaction exposure* involves the cash flows requiring conversion in the exchange markets. *Accounting exposure* is a measure of net assets in the balance sheet translated at current exchange rates. *Economic exposure* measures the impact of exchange fluctuations on *all* operational cash flows regardless of whether they require exchange transactions.

In measures of accounting exposure, definitions of which accounts are translated at current rates and which are translated at historic or other rates are highly varied. Some of the variations are the current/noncurrent method (current assets less current liabilities), the monetary/nonmonetary method (current assets except inventory less current and long-term liabilities), and the net financial asset method (current assets less current and long-term liabilities). Under FAS 52, in the United States all accounts are translated at current rates and exchange gains and losses are direct charges to the equity account. In other nations, gains and losses may be charged through the income statement, or they may be segmented as a reserve liability account with reduction in the equity account but no adjustment in the asset and liability accounts.

The actual economic exposure of the firm may be very different from the accounting exposure, depending on whether the present value of the future cash flow is increased or decreased as a result of revaluations. In responding to any measure of exposure used for accounting purposes, a company manager induces real (economic) gains or losses in place of the accounting ones, depending on what happens to the underlying currencies.

Firms may reduce exposure by adjusting the exposed accounts through business operations with customers, suppliers, or other members of the same corporate family.

QUESTIONS

1. MNC Corp. will have a net liability position in Switzerland in the amount of 160 million Swiss francs (approximately $80 million).

Exchange Rates	
Spot rate—day 1	$0.50
Expected future spot rate	0.54
1-year forward	0.52
Interest Rates—1 Year	
U. S. dollar	10.00%
Swiss franc	4.50%

(a) What is the premium or discount in the forward Swiss franc?

(b) What would be the consequences of the Swiss net liability position if the forecast changes in the spot rate take place? What are the choices that MNC Corp. has to hedge its liability position in Swiss francs?

(c) Determine the cost of each of these alternatives if the actual spot rate at the end of the period is as shown in the table below:

	Case A	Case B	Case C
Spot rate—day 360	$0.50	$0.52	$0.55

(d) What course of action would you advise MNC Corp. to take?

2. Give a quick definition of exposure that applies regardless of the accounting method used by the company. What are some of the different accounting exposure measurements? Which do you think is most realistic? Would your statement hold for all corporations or would it be specific to particular types of business? To particular countries?

3. Why might accounting exposure differ from economic exposure? Do you believe there exists a difference for most corporations? Why or why not?

4. Consolidated Corporation instructed its subsidiary in Devaluland to remit funds to the parent as soon as possible when a new devaluation was likely. This action was completed, and the parent was surprised to see that there was still a large foreign exchange loss on the funds, even though they were owned by the parent. How could this happen? Who should be held accountable?

5. What options are open to reduce exposure in a devaluation-prone subsidiary? How might each of these options affect the business and the management incentives of the subsidiary?

6. How can a firm which covered itself completely in the forward market, based on its expected balance sheet as of the end of the period, still have a foreign exchange loss to report?

BIBLIOGRAPHY

Adler, Michael, and Bernard Dumas, "International Portfolio Choice and Corporation Finance: A Synthesis," *Journal of Finance*, June 1983, pp. 925–984

Aliber, Robert Z., *Exchange Risk and Corporate International Finance*. New York: Wiley, Halsted Press, 1978.

Ankrom, Robert K., "Top-Level Approach to the Foreign Exchange Problem," *Harvard Business Review*, July–Aug. 1974, pp. 79–90.

Antl, Boris, and Richard Ensor, eds., *Management of Foreign Exchange Risk*, 2d ed. London: Euromoney Publications, 1982.

Barnett, John S., "Corporate Foreign Exposure Strategy Formulations," *Columbia Journal of World Business*, Winter 1976, pp. 87–97.

Christofides, N., R. D. Hewins, and G. R. Salkin, "Graph Theoretic Approaches to Foreign Exchange Operations," *Journal of Financial and Quantitative Analysis*, Sept. 1979, pp. 481–500.

Dufey, Gunter, and Ian H. Giddy, "International Financial Planning: The Use of Market-Based Forecasts," *California Management Review*, Fall 1978, pp. 69–81.

Eaker, Mark R., "Denomination Decision for Multinational Transactions," *Financial Management*, Autumn 1980, pp. 23–29.

Eaker, Mark R., and Dwight M. Grant, "Optimal Hedging of Uncertain Foreign Exchange Exposure." Working paper, Edwin L. Cox School of Business, Southern Methodist University, 1981.

Einzig, Paul, *A Textbook on Foreign Exchange*. London: Macmillan, 1966.

Enthoven, Adolf J. H., "International Management Accounting: A Challenge for Accountants," *Management Accounting*, Sept. 1980, pp. 25–32.

Everett, Robert M., Abraham M. George, and Aryeh Blumberg, "Appraising Currency Strengths and Weaknesses: An Operational Model for Calculating Parity Exchange Rates," *Journal of International Business Studies*, Fall 1980, pp. 80–91.

Fredrikson, E. Bruce, "On the Measurement of Foreign Income," *Journal of Accounting Research*, Autumn 1968, pp. 208–21.

George, Abraham, "Cash Flow versus Accounting Exposures to Currency Risk," *California Management Review*, Summer 1978, pp. 50–54.

Giddy, Ian H., "Exchange Risk: Whose View?" *Financial Management*, Summer 1977, pp. 23–33.

Gray, S. J., "The Impact of International Accounting Differences from a Security-Analysis Perspective: Some European Evidence," *Journal of Accounting Research*, Spring 1980, pp. 64–76.

Heckerman, Donald, "The Exchange Risks of Foreign Operations," *Journal of Business*, Jan. 1972, pp. 42–48.

Heywood, John, *Foreign Exchange and the Corporate Treasurer*, p. 59. London: A. & C. Black, Ltd., 1979.

Jacque, L. L., "Management of Foreign Exchange Risk," *Journal of International Business Studies*, Spring/Summer 1981, pp. 81–101.

Koenig, Peter, "Using a Captive to Cope with Currency Exposure," *Institutional Investor,* Nov. 1981, pp. 191–94.

Levich, Richard M., and Clas G. Wihlborg, eds., *Exchange Risk and Exposure: Current Developments in International Financial Management.* Lexington, Mass.: D. C. Heath and Co., 1980.

Logue, Dennis E., and George S. Oldfield, "Managing Foreign Assets when Foreign Exchange Markets Are Efficient," *Financial Management,* Summer 1977, pp. 16–22.

Olstein, Robert A., "Devaluation and Multinational Reporting," *Financial Analysts Journal,* Sept.–Oct. 1973, pp. 65ff.

Pleak, R. E., "An Analysis of the FASB's Treatment of Foreign Currency Translation," *Management Accounting,* Sept. 1977, pp. 29–32.

Prindl, Andreas R., *Foreign Exchange Risk.* New York: John Wiley and Sons, 1976.

Reier, Sharon, "Socal's Great Currency Debate," *Institutional Investor,* Jan. 1982, pp. 210–12.

Rodriguez, Rita M., "FASB No. 8: What Has It Done for Us?" *Financial Analysts Journal,* Mar.–Apr. 1977, pp. 40–48.

———, *Foreign Exchange Management in U.S. Multinationals.* Lexington, Mass.: D. C. Heath and Co., 1980.

———, "The Increasing Attraction of the SDR to Business Corporations," *Euromoney,* Dec. 1981, pp. 168–179.

Roll, Richard, and Bruno Solnik, "A Pure Foreign Exchange Asset Pricing Model," *Journal of International Economics,* May 1977, pp. 161–79.

Schoenfeld, Hanns-Martin, "International Accounting: Development, Issues, and Future Directions," *Journal of International Business Studies,* Fall 1981, pp. 83–100.

Shank, John K., Jesse F. Dillard, and Richard J. Murdock, *Assessing the Economic Impact of FASB No. 8.* New York: Financial Executives Research Foundation, 1979.

Shapiro, Alan C., "Defining Exchange Risk," *Journal of Business,* Jan. 1977, pp. 37–39.

Smith, Alan F., "Temporal Method: Temporary Mode?" *Management Accounting,* Feb. 1978, pp. 21–26.

Wihlborg, Clas, "Economics of Exposure Management of Foreign Subsidiaries of Multinational Corporations," *Journal of International Business Studies,* Winter 1980, pp. 9–18.

GIBSON
CORPORATION

"FEAST OR FAMINE, but always asking for money." That is how Arlene Benson, treasurer of Gibson Corp., summarized the relatively brief history of the company's British subsidiary from 1974 to mid-1979.

The early years, starting with the original investment in 1974, certainly had been years of famine. Gibson had barely managed to get organized to produce at some relatively acceptable level of efficiency when England's economic growth slowed in 1977. Being a new entrant in a highly cyclical industry (Gibson sold equipment to the shipping and mining industries), it was not until early 1978 that Gibson U.K. began to recover. Although by then Gibson U.K. had a well-run plant producing equipment which was highly regarded in the British market, the losses up to that point had been severe. Gibson U.K. had not even been able to take advantage of the tax incentives granted by the British government because of the plant's location in a developing region. Income statement summaries for Gibson U.K. are presented in Exhibit I.1.

By 1978 the nature of Gibson U.K.'s worries began to change substantially. At the national level, the British economy returned to a faster rate of economic growth and the rate of inflation diminished. More important for Gibson's market, the promises of North Sea oil began to ma-

EXHIBIT I.1 Gibson U.K.: Income Statements 1975–1979 (millions of pounds)

	1975	1976	1977	1978	1979 (est.)
Sales	24.0	50.0	42.8	62.6	74.4
Cost of goods sold, excluding depreciation	22.0	42.5	35.7	50.0	57.1
Selling, administrative, and general expenses	4.0	6.0	6.1	7.1	7.5
Depreciation expense	1.7	1.7	1.7	1.8	2.0
Interest expense	0.4	0.8	0.8	2.3	2.8
	28.1	51.0	44.3	61.2	69.4
Profits (losses) before taxes	(4.1)	(1.0)	(1.5)	1.4	5.0
Taxes	—	—	—	—	—
Profits after taxes	(4.1)	(1.0)	(1.5)	1.4	5.0

terialize. These forces, combined with a new sales policy initiated by the company in late 1977, generated a surprising sales growth in 1978. So unexpected was the magnitude of this sales increase that it produced a new concern in the company. If sales continued to grow at the pace of 1978, production would soon outstrip the plant's optimum productive capacity level. After that point, additional increases in production would still be possible, but at increasing unit costs. So, by early 1979, Gibson U.K. began to plan for additional investments in its plant and equipment.

At Gibson Corporation the good news from Gibson U.K. was received with mixed feelings. They surely liked to see the sales growth in the British subsidiary. However, the plans for expansion presented new problems for the parent company. The early bad years, together with the financing of the new sales policy, had left the British subsidiary badly undercapitalized. Gibson U.K. would find it very difficult to obtain additional loans from the British banks under any reasonable terms—never mind the limits on borrowings that the Bank of England imposed on foreign-owned companies. Balance sheet summaries for Gibson U.K. are presented in Exhibit I.2.

If the British subsidiary could not obtain funds for the expansion

EXHIBIT I.2 Gibson U.K.: Balance Sheet Statements, 1975–1979 *(millions of pounds)*

	1975	1976	1977	1978	1979 (est.)
Assets					
Cash	4.5	0.5	3.8	1.5	1.2
Accounts receivable	2.5	5.0	4.0	18.0	24.4
Inventory	15.4	25.5	20.4	28.9	33.3
Other current assets	0.2	0.5	0.4	0.6	0.7
Total current assets	22.6	31.5	28.6	49.0	59.6
Plant and equipment	13.7	18.0	19.0	19.1	19.1
Less depreciation	1.7	3.4	5.1	6.9	8.9
Net plant and equipment	12.0	14.6	13.9	12.2	10.2
Total assets	34.6	46.1	42.5	61.2	69.8
Liabilities and Equity					
Accounts payable	5.5	8.2	6.9	9.7	10.9
Other payables	0.7	1.5	2.1	4.3	5.1
Short-term debt	0.1	1.4	0.5	13.3	15.3
Total current liabilities	6.3	11.1	9.5	27.3	31.3
Long-term debt	8.5	8.0	7.5	7.0	6.6
Total liabilities	14.8	19.1	17.0	34.3	37.9
Common stock capital	23.9	32.1	32.1	32.1	32.1
Retained earnings	(4.1)	(5.1)	(6.6)	(5.2)	(0.2)
Total equity	19.8	27.0	25.5	26.9	31.9
Total liabilities and equity	34.6	46.1	42.5	61.2	69.8

on its own, there was only one alternative available to finance the expansion: the parent company would have to provide the needed funds.

The fear of sending good money after bad money was not so large anymore, as it had been when Gibson U.K. had asked for help at the peak of its problems in 1976. However, the memories of having invested in the British subsidiary when the pound was at $2.35 in 1974, only to see it come down to $1.70 by 1977, were still very vivid in the minds of Gibson's senior management. In spite of the pound recovery in more recent years, at a value of $2.16 in June 1979, it was still below the rate prevailing at the time of the original investment.

It was with all these considerations in mind that Arlene Benson had approached Gibson's major bank in the United States, the Wabash National Bank, to ask for some financing proposals that would meet the company's needs in the United Kingdom. Conversations had taken place in early 1979 when Carlos Ruiz, a loan officer with the bank, had suggested something called a "preference share financing scheme." At the time, Mrs. Benson thought this proposal was interesting, but too complicated. However, as the months passed and the pressures to proceed with the new investment mounted, Mrs. Benson decided to talk with Mr. Ruiz again about his proposal. So far, the only other alternative financing source which suggested itself was to use the line of credit outstanding to borrow Eurodollars under a revolving term credit agreement Gibson Corporation had with the Wabash Bank.

In response to Mrs. Benson's request, Mr. Ruiz sent the letter presented in Exhibit I.3. Selected economic data for the United Kingdom are presented in Exhibit I.4.

EXHIBIT I.3   Gibson Corporation: Bank Proposal for the Preference Share Financing Scheme

---

June 24, 1979

Mrs. Arlene Benson
Gibson Corp.

Dear Arlene:

Pursuant to conversations we had, I am pleased to review for you the major points of the "preference share financing scheme" and its applicability to Gibson Corp.

I. *Objectives*
    The basic objectives of the scheme for Gibson would be:
    A. To increase the capital base of Gibson's U.K. subsidiary for Bank of England purposes, thereby allowing expansion of their plant capacity
    B. To increase sterling borrowing capabilities for the U.K. subsidiary

EXHIBIT I.3 *(Continued)*

     C.   To accomplish A and B above with a minimum of translation and transaction exposure to fluctuations in foreign exchange rates

II. *Description of the "preference share financing scheme"*
   - A. Gibson Corp. would apply to the Bank of England to borrow X amount of domestic sterling for a given period of generally 5 to 7 years (N.B.: Please refer to Section IV of this letter for explanation of the Bank of England permission and general terms of the sterling loan.)
   - B. Upon receipt of the Bank of England's permission, Gibson Corp. would borrow the funds and use them to purchase X amount of preference shares from Gibson U.K.
   - C. Gibson U.K. will use the funds it receives to reduce its sterling short-term borrowings by X amount, temporarily, and/or to increase its plant capacity.
   - D. Gibson U.K. will accumulate additional earnings through the reduction of its interest expense as a result of replacing its existing sterling borrowings with preference shares and also as a result of limiting future sterling borrowings with the use of preference shares.
   - E. At the end of X period, Gibson U.K. will redeem the preference shares from Gibson Corp., which in turn will utilize the proceeds it receives from Gibson U.K. to retire the sterling loan of X amount.

III. *Benefits*
   - A. Gibson U.K. will reduce its interest expense and thereby increase its net profits which are remittable in the form of dividends to Gibson Corp.
   - B. Gibson Corp. will borrow domestic sterling on a fully-hedged basis to make a capital contribution to its U.K. subsidiary, although interest payments may not be covered.
   - C. Gibson Corp. can use the interest paid on its domestic sterling loan as a tax deduction on its U.S. tax returns.
   - D. The capital position of Gibson U.K. will be improved and, as a result, Gibson U.K. could normally expect to increase its access to the short-term sterling borrowing market.
   - E. The end result of this operation will be a reduction in the exposure of Gibson to the pound sterling.

IV. *Bank of England Permission*
As you know, the Bank of England Exchange Control Regulations generally prohibit foreign companies access to the domestic sterling loan market and generally limit the use of domestic sterling borrowings by nonresident-controlled U.K. companies. However, the Bank of England appears to be much more receptive to allowing exceptions to this general rule on a case-by-case basis in the present economic climate in the United Kingdom, particularly in view of the future elimination of controls which Mrs. Thatcher's government has promised.

    Gibson Corp. and your U.K. subsidiary would have to obtain Bank of England approval to enter into this form of financing. The Bank of England considers each case on its own merits and I believe that you could make a very strong case for being allowed to enter into such a fi-

EXHIBIT I.3 *(Continued)*

nancing. I think that you should pitch your approach to the Bank of England along the following lines:

1. The major purpose of this borrowing is to expand your plant's capacity in the United Kingdom. This represents new investment.

2. One result of the expansion of your plant's capacity will be additional employment. I would think you would have to give the Bank of England some concrete ideas of how many new jobs you would expect to create.

3. As your new plant is located in a development area, this new employment would be created in an area where the government is most interested in reducing unemployment.

4. In addition to representing new investment and new employment, this project is import-saving. If you were to decide not to make this investment, you would begin to supply a portion of this machinery from the United States, which would result in an adverse effect on the U.K. balance of payments.

5. Your major customer is a nationalized industry. The increase in the machinery you supply them will result in more efficient, and therefore more profitable, operations.

6. If some export potential could also be developed as a result of this plant expansion, it would be very helpful to your case with the Bank of England. Based upon our conversations, I am led to believe that this may not be possible. However, I would urge you to review your plans carefully to see if such potential does exist.

7. I would not dwell on your idea of increasing your repatriations to the U.S. parent because I believe that the Bank of England would consider that a fairly important negative. Under the Bank of England's Exchange Control Regulations, a company is allowed to remit dividends upon application to the Bank of England, and their approval is readily given as long as the U.K. subsidiary can meet all its sterling liabilities. This could be handled in the normal manner at the time that it occurs.

In arranging the domestic sterling loan to Gibson Corp. which will be used to purchase the preference shares, the terms should be set on such a basis that the U.K. subsidiary's earnings can easily provide retirement of the preference shares to coincide with the loan's amortization schedule. A simple form of sinking fund can be arranged whereby the U.K. subsidiary places on deposit with a bank on an interest-bearing basis a preagreed amount of sterling which will be used to retire the preference shares. Obviously, if the earnings of the U.K. subsidiary are insufficient to retire the preference shares held by Gibson Corp. at par, the completely hedged nature of this financing proposal is defeated. Depending upon your overall corporate exposure to sterling, this may or may not be of importance.

I have talked to my associates in London to see what terms are now possible for sterling loans in order to give you some idea of what we could expect in establishing a financing scheme such as this. In general, the

EXHIBIT I.3 *(Continued)*

medium-term sterling market is looking at floating-rate loans for 5 to 7 years. It becomes much more difficult to arrange a financing for anything over 7 years. The interest rate would float at 1½% or 1¾% over the interbank rate for domestic sterling—that is, over domestic sterling LIBOR. For a 5-year loan, it would be possible to arrange repayment in a single installment at maturity. For 7 years, I would think you could expect a grace period ranging between 3½ years and 4½ years, followed by equal semiannual repayment installments. The main consideration from a bank's point of view in structuring such a loan is that it is done in a manner that coincides with the profit projections of the U.K. subsidiary, which must ultimately earn the sterling to be used in retiring the debt. Obviously, if you can establish such a financing with either a bank or a small group of banks to whom you are already close, it will make it much easier and also should result in a lower interest cost to you than if it were syndicated among a general group of banks.

One final point I should mention is the lack of applicability of Regulation M of the Federal Reserve Bank. In general, Regulation M states that any U.S. bank whose offshore branch lends funds to a U.S. corporation must keep a reserve requirement with the Federal Reserve which is currently 4% of the outstanding loan. The scheme I am outlining here involves just such a loan—that is, a London branch of a U.S. bank lending to a U.S. corporation, Gibson Corp. However, we have sought a clarification ruling on this point from the Federal Reserve Bank. They have indicated to us that in this particular "preference share financing scheme" as I have outlined it here, the loan is not subject to the reserve requirements of Regulation M. Therefore, Gibson would not incur the additional cost of the Federal Reserve Bank's reserve requirement.

You mentioned that you may well be in London in July. If you are, I would encourage you to call on our London branch, which would handle this financing if you should decide to proceed. I know you would enjoy meeting them and would find them most helpful and informative. Once your plans have firmed, please let me know and I will be delighted to arrange an appointment.

After you have had a chance to review this letter, I would be pleased to discuss any points or questions with you. We are most anxious to work with you on this proposal. I do hope that it is sufficiently attractive for you to proceed with it.

With very best regards,

Yours sincerely,

Carlos Ruiz
Vice-president

CR:mle

EXHIBIT I.4 Gibson Corporation: Economic Data for the United Kingdom, 1975–1979

	1975	1976	1977	1978	Jan.–June 1979
Exchange rate (U.S. dollars per pound, end of period)	2.02	1.70	1.91	2.03	2.16
Treasury Bill rate (percent, period average)	10.18	11.12	7.68	8.51	11.75
Domestic bank deposit rates, 3 months (percent, end of period)	10.50	14.13	6.37	12.25	13.75
Commercial bank lending rates to prime borrowers (percent, end of period)					
Domestic pounds (overdraft)	12.00	15.00	9.00	14.00	15.50
Eurodollars (3 months)	6.69	5.50	7.56	12.06	10.87
Eurocurrency deposit bid rates, 3 months[a] (percent, end of period)					
Sterling	11.00	16.12	6.62	12.62	14.00
Dollars	5.81	5.00	7.19	11.69	10.50
Domestic corporate bond yields (percent, end of period)	14.90	15.76	11.88	13.53	13.00
Industrial share prices (1975 = 100, period average)	100.0	119.8	153.6	173.0	200.0
Prices, industrial output (1975 = 100, period average)	100.0	117.3	140.5	153.3	165.0
Industrial production (1975 = 100, period average)	100.0	102.2	106.0	109.9	112.0
Gross fixed capital formation (billions of pounds)	20.54	23.60	25.91	29.22	14.9
Gross domestic product, 1975 prices (billions of pounds)	103.95	107.54	108.84	112.38	54.86
Trade balance (billions of pounds)	−2.88	−1.65	0.75	1.79	−0.88

[a]Offer rates are generally 0.125% above bid rates.

SOURCES: International Monetary Fund, *International Financial Statistics*, May 1980, pp. 398–401; and Morgan Guaranty Trust Company, *World Financial Markets*, July 1979.

11

Financial Control in the Multinational Enterprise

IN OUR DISCUSSION of management of exposure to exchange risk we saw how the measurement of exposure depends on the principles used to define it. Accounting principles produce one result; economic principles produce another. Although it is clear that economic principles produce a superior definition of value (at least theoretically), still we must rely on financial reports to assess economic value. However, financial statements are prepared according to "generally accepted accounting principles" that are not always generally accepted by economists; thus, in the first part of this chapter we will see how financial statements are affected by the monetary variations of inflation and exchange rate fluctuations.[1]

If we want operating management to respond to inflation and exchange fluctuations with economically sound decisions, we need a reporting system which properly takes these factors into account. To the extent that traditional financial statements fail to do this, we will want to develop alternative systems which measure management performance along these lines. In the second part of this chapter we suggest how to take these considerations into account in a proper management control system.

---

[1]The appendix to this chapter includes a section on accounting for inflation.

The chapter ends with a brief analysis of the alternatives available to organize the finance function within a multinational enterprise.

THE IMPACT OF INFLATION AND EXCHANGE FLUCTUATIONS ON FINANCIAL STATEMENTS

To show the impact of monetary phenomena on financial statements we will compare budget figures in which neither inflation nor exchange fluctuations are anticipated with actual figures after these phenomena have occurred. For the sake of simplicity, assume that the budget is met in volume terms—for example, number of units sold and produced. Any discrepancy between budget and actual figures is due to monetary phenomena—inflation and exchange fluctuations—and the fashion in which their effects are reported.

The company used in the example manufactures one unit per month. This unit is sold the following month. Thus, in a year it sells twelve units and manufactures twelve units. At the end of the year the company has one unit in inventory which was manufactured during the last month of the year and which will be sold during the first month of the following year. Inflation and exchange fluctuations proceed at an even rate throughout the year.

The Impact of Inflation

Exhibit 11.1 shows the impact of various rates of inflation on the major accounts in the income statement and the balance sheet. The last three columns show the actual results under 10%, 20%, and 30% annual inflation rates.[2]

As an illustration, we will follow the results of the case with a total annual inflation of 20%, or 1.67% per month. The unit sold the first month is sold at 1.67% over the budgeted price; the unit sold the second month is at 3.34% over budgeted price; and so on until the unit sold at the end of the twelfth month carries a price of 20% over the budgeted price. Thus, annual sales increase to 1,663, a 10% increase over the budget figure of 1,512, as the result of price increases to match the inflation rate. However, the cost of goods sold increases by only 8%, from a budget of 1,440 to the actual 1,561. The reported cost of goods sold is based on historical costs. The unit sold each month is manufactured in the preceding month at a cost lower than the one prevailing during the month when the sale occurs. For example, the cost of the first unit sold is the cost of inventory before inflation, 120. Be-

---

[2]Since we assume one unit is sold every month and that inflation proceeds at an even rate throughout the year, the average annual inflation rates reflected on sales are 5%, 10%, and 15%, respectively. This calculation of average inflation ignores the effects of monthly compounding; however, this simplification facilitates the presentation.

EXHIBIT 11.1 Impact of Inflation on Financial Statements When Budget Is Met in Terms of Units Sold (in local currency)

	Initial	Budget	Actual With Annual Inflation Rate of: 10%	20%	30%
			INCOME STATEMENT		
Sales[a]		1,512	1,588	1,663	1,739
Cost of goods sold[b]		1,440	1,500	1,561	1,622
Gross margin		72	88	102	117
Depreciation		40	40	40	40
Operating profits		32	48	62	77
Interest expense		14	14	14	14
Profits before taxes		18	34	48	63
Taxes		9	17	24	32
Profits after taxes		9	17	24	31
			BALANCE SHEET		
Assets					
Cash	0	58	66	73	80
Accounts receivable	160	160	176	192	207
Inventory[c]	120	120	132	144	156
	280	338	374	409	443
Plant and equipment	220	220	220	220	220
Less depreciation	—	(40)	(40)	(40)	(40)
	500	518	554	589	623
Liabilities Plus Equity					
Accounts payable	200	200	220	240	260
7% notes payable	200	200	200	200	200
Taxes payable	—	9	17	25	32
	400	409	437	465	492
Capital stock	100	100	100	100	100
Retained earnings	—	9	17	24	31
	100	109	117	124	131
	500	518	554	589	623

[a]Actual sales = (Budget sales) $\left(1 + \dfrac{\text{Inflation}}{2}\right)$

[b]Actual cost of goods sold = $\left(\begin{array}{c}\text{Initial}\\\text{inventory}\end{array}\right) + \left(\begin{array}{c}\text{Budget}\\\text{cost of}\\\text{goods sold}\end{array} - \begin{array}{c}\text{Initial}\\\text{inventory}\end{array}\right)\left[1 + \left(\dfrac{\text{Inflation}}{2}\right)\left(\dfrac{11}{12}\right)\right]$

[c]Actual inventory = $\left(\begin{array}{c}\text{Initial}\\\text{inventory}\end{array}\right)(1 + \text{Inflation})$

cause of the discrepancy between the rate at which reported sales and cost of goods sold inflate, reported gross margin increases by much more than 10%. In this example, the gross margin increases by 42% from 72 to 102.

Since depreciation charges are based on historical costs, the actual figure for this account in actual outcome is the same as in the budget, 40. Interest expenses remain constant because in the example it is assumed that incremental financing is obtained only from accounts payable, a non–interest-bearing debt.

The combination of higher prices in sales and the use of historical costs in other accounts makes reported profits before taxes almost three times as large as the budgeted figure. Unfortunately, the government will tax the incremental profits—50% in this example. Still, the actual profits after taxes in the case of a 20% inflation rate will be more than two and one-half times the profits after taxes budgeted in the absence of inflation.

Standard accounting practices used in the preparation of these financial statements make reported profits after taxes increase at a rate faster than inflation. The higher the inflation rate, the higher the rate by which reported profits will exceed budgeted profits. With budgeted profits of 9, a 10% inflation rate raises these profits to 17, (an 89% increase over actual) a 20% inflation rate to 24, (a 167% increase over actual) and a 30% inflation rate to 31 (a 244% increase over actual).

The figures in the actual balance sheets reflect the effects of inflation depending on the date when assets were acquired or liabilities incurred. Those assets acquired before inflation began are reported at cost figures which do not reflect current prices. This is the case for fixed assets. Accounts receivable and payable, on the other hand, reflect the higher prices affecting cost of inputs and products sold. These prices, however, are the ones prevailing at the time of the transactions. They are not current prices, which in the example are assumed to be higher.

A quick comparison between the actual reported and the budget figures will bring happiness when examining the income statement and dismay when looking at the balance sheet. However, according to our assumptions, the manager produced and sold the exact number of units expected in the budget. All the changes in these accounts are due solely to the increasing level of prices during the period and to the accounting practices followed to report them.

The Impact of Exchange Fluctuations

Exchange fluctuations affect financial statements in two ways. One effect takes place in the case of actual exchange transactions—for example, the payment for imports denominated in a foreign currency.

The other effect occurs in the process of translating financial statements expressed in a currency different from the one used for consolidation purposes.

The *transaction effect* of exchange fluctuations appears in the financial statements in a manner similar to a change in prices of sales or costs of goods sold. However, the impact of exchange transactions on net profits tends to be larger than the impact of inflation if the exchange fluctuation affects only revenues or costs, but not both simultaneously. For example, if export revenues are realized in a currency that appreciates, there will be a comparable increase in revenues. Given constant costs in the domestic currency, net profits will increase by a substantial multiple. On the other hand, if the appreciating currency affects costs but not revenues, a substantial net loss will occur if selling prices are not adjusted to reflect the increase in costs. See Exhibit 11.2.

Assuming a self-contained foreign operation without any imports or exports, the *translation effect* of exchange fluctuations appears whenever the financial statements of the foreign operation must be expressed in the currency of the parent company after exchange fluctuations between the two relevant currencies.

The procedure to translate financial statements in the United States is regulated by the financial profession. Since 1982, these statements are translated according to the rules established by Financial

EXHIBIT 11.2 Impact of Exchange Fluctuations on Export Revenues and Import Costs When Prices and Quantities Remain Constant

	Budget	REVENUE CURRENCY APPRECIATES		COST CURRENCY APPRECIATES	
		10%	20%	10%	20%
Sales	1,512	1,588[a]	1,663[a]	1,512	1,512
Cost of goods sold	1,440	1,440	1,440	1,500[b]	1,561[b]
Gross margin	72	148	223	12	(49)
Depreciation	40	40	40	40	40
Operating profits	32	108	183	(28)	(89)
Interest expense	14	14	14	14	14
Profits before taxes	18	94	169	(42)	(103)
Taxes	9	47	84	—	—
Profits after taxes	9	47	85	(42)	(103)

[a] Actual sales = (Budget sales) $\left(1 + \dfrac{\text{Appreciation}}{2}\right)$

[b] Actual cost of goods sold = $\left(\begin{array}{l}\text{Initial}\\ \text{inventory}\end{array}\right) + \left(\begin{array}{l}\text{Budget}\\ \text{cost of}\\ \text{goods sold}\end{array} - \begin{array}{l}\text{Initial}\\ \text{inventory}\end{array}\right)\left[1 + \left(\dfrac{\text{Appreciation}}{2}\right)\left(\dfrac{11}{12}\right)\right]$

Statement No. 52 of the Financial Accounting Standards Board. Briefly, according to this statement the accounts in the income statement are translated at average exchange rates for the period and the accounts in the balance sheet are translated at the exchange rates at the end of the reporting period. Exchange gains and losses derived from the translation of the balance sheet that are not incorporated in the value of translated profits are reported in a separate account within the equity section of the balance sheet.[3]

To illustrate the impact of exchange fluctuations on translation of financial reports, assume that each of the previous examples reflecting different rates of inflation represents a separate foreign subsidiary. In Exhibit 11.3 we compare the figures reported for 10%, 20%, and 30% rates of domestic inflation with different rates of depreciation and appreciation of the local currency against the U.S. dollar.

When the local currency depreciates against the dollar, the translation of sales and cost of goods sold into dollars tends to reduce the impact of local inflation on these figures. However, even when the rate of depreciation of the local currency is equal to the rate of inflation in that currency, the gross margin expressed in dollars is higher than the budget figure. (Cases A, B, and C in Exhibit 11.3.) The factor behind this result is that although the translation exchange rate applies to the current reporting year, the cost of goods sold in the local currency reflects a lag of one month in production costs, and therefore a lag in inflation rate. A similar effect can be seen in the figures for depreciation. Although the dollar figures reflect the depreciation of the currency for that year, the local-currency depreciation charge reflects historical costs in that currency and ignores the effect of inflation. The use of historical cost figures in local-currency accounting in cases A through C in Exhibit 11.3 means that operating profits and profits after taxes measured in dollars are substantially higher than the budget figures. This is the case even though budget is met in terms of units and the rate of inflation equals the rate of currency depreciation—purchasing power parity holds. Of course, when the currency depreciation is less than the rate of inflation (as in case D) or the currency actually appreciates in spite of the local inflation (case E), reported profits after taxes show a much greater improvement over budget.

In the balance sheet, assets and liabilities are translated at the exchange rate prevailing at the end of the period. The capital account is composed of the initial capital stock plus retained earnings. Since in our example there were no retained earnings at the beginning of the period, at the end of the period retained earnings are equal to the prof-

---

[3]Financial Accounting Standards Board, "Statement of Financial Accounting Standards No. 52," (Stamford, Connecticut: October 1981). See also the appendix to this chapter.

EXHIBIT 11.3 Combined Impact of Inflation and Exchange Fluctuations on Financial Statements When Budget is Met in Terms of Units Sold[a]

		ACTUAL WITH ANNUAL INFLATION AND LC EXCHANGE FLUCTUATION OF:									
	Budget	A: Inflation, 10%; Depreciation, 10%		B: Inflation, 20%; Depreciation, 20%		C: Inflation, 30%; Depreciation, 30%		D: Inflation, 30%; Depreciation, 10%		E: Inflation, 10%; Appreciation, 10%	
		LC	$	LC	$	LC	$	LC	$	LC	$
Income Statement											
Sales	1,512	1,588	1,512	1,663	1,512	1,739	1,512	1,739	1,656	1,588	1,667
Cost of goods sold	1,440	1,500	1,429	1,561	1,419	1,622	1,410	1,622	1,545	1,500	1,575
Gross margin	72	88	83	102	93	117	102	117	111	88	92
Depreciation	40	40	38	40	36	40	35	40	38	40	42
Operating profits	32	48	45	62	57	77	67	77	73	48	50
Interest expense	14	14	13	14	13	14	12	14	13	14	15
Profits before taxes	18	34	32	48	44	63	55	63	60	34	35
Taxes	9	17	16	24	22	32	28	32	30	17	18
Profits after taxes	9	17	16	24	22	31	27	31	30	17	17
Balance Sheet											
Total assets	518	554	504	589	491	623	479	623	566	554	609
Less total liabilities	409	437	397	465	388	492	378	492	447	437	481
Total ending equity	109	117	107	124	103	131	101	131	119	117	128
Capital stock	100	100	100	100	100	100	100	100	100	100	100
Retained earnings	9	17	16	24	22	31	27	31	30	17	17
			116		122		127		130		117
Equity adjustment for translation	—		(9)		(19)		(26)		(11)		11
	109	117	107	124	103	131	101	131	119	117	128

[a]LC = Local currency figures from Exhibit 11.1.
$ = Dollar values in the income statement are translated at the *average* exchange rate for the year. In the balance sheet, assets and liabilities are translated at the exchange rate at the *end of the period*. For example, with a 20% depreciation of the local currency, the income statement is translated at LC1.10/$, and the assets and liabilities accounts in the balance sheet are translated at LC1.20/$; the equity account is translated as the sum of the original value of the capital stock, plus the translated value of profits, plus an adjustment made to reflect the exchange gain or loss incorporated throughout the year into these two accounts. (For specific example showing the computation of this adjustment, refer to the accompanying text.)

its for the period. In these examples, assets minus liabilities (net assets) do not equal capital stock plus retained earnings expressed in dollars. This discrepancy results from the translation effect and requires an adjustment to the equity account. In cases A through D this adjustment is negative and in case E it is positive. The negative adjustment for the 20% inflation with 20% depreciation is analyzed in the accompanying table.

Loss in dollar value of net assets existing at the beginning of the year, LC100	
LC100 at initial rate of LC1/$	$100
LC100 at ending rate of LC1.20/$	83
Loss in value	$ 17
Loss in dollar value of profit of LC24	
LC24 at initial rate of LC1/$	$ 24
LC24 at average rate of LC1.10/$	22
Loss in value	$ 2
Net adjustment to equity account for translation purposes	$ 19

A MANAGEMENT CONTROL SYSTEM TO COPE WITH INFLATION AND EXCHANGE FLUCTUATIONS

A large portion of any control system is based on first establishing standards of performance and then comparing actual performance with the standards. Researchers have found that the two most widely used standards are rate of return and performance relative to the budget.[4] Both of these measures are based on the traditional financial statements—namely, income statement, balance sheet, and cash flow statement.

A simple management system that compares budget with actual figures can produce very misleading results. As we showed before, in an inflationary environment profits are overstated and balance sheet accounts appear out of control. Exchange fluctuations may correct part of these distortions if the exchange movements tend to compensate for inflation; however, one would hardly ever see a complete compensation

---

[4]See Robert N. Anthony, John Dearden, and Richard F. Vancil, *Management Control Systems*, rev. ed., Homewood, Illinois: Richard D. Irwin, 1972. Similar results were found by Sidney M. Robbins and Robert B. Stobaugh, *Money in the Multinational Enterprise*, Chapter 8, Basic Books, Inc., New York, 1973. They also found that as the size of the company increased, the emphasis on budgets for evaluation purposes also increased.

and the translation process can actually introduce additional distortions.

There are two main approaches to deal with the distortions introduced by inflation and exchange fluctuations:

1. Update the budget figures to include monetary developments; or
2. Segregate the impact of monetary developments from the actual figures.

In both approaches the budget and actual figures are compared on the same basis, with or without the monetary changes. This eliminates some of the possible misinterpretations. However, the philosophies behind the two approaches are very different. Updating the budget figures for inflation and exchange fluctuations assumes that these factors are outside the control of management and, therefore, should be left out of the evaluation process. On the other hand, segregating the impact of these factors from the actual figures allows for a measure of how management has responded to changes in the environment. We advocate the use of the second approach.

Objectives of a Management Control System

It is generally well accepted that a good management control system should accomplish the following objectives:

1. Motivate line managers to make decisions that are optimal for the company as a whole
2. Provide information that helps to evaluate the quality of management decisions[5]

Control systems which are based on financial statements prepared according to traditional accounting practices can defeat their purpose. Good decisions require the availability of relevant figures. Historical prices and exchange rates can give the wrong signals for decisions such as pricing, purchase of materials, and so forth. They can motivate managers to make decisions which will appear to show a good performance in the reports but which are detrimental to the future of the business— for example, to continue using inefficient equipment because the existing equipment shows a low depreciation charge according to historical costs.

---

[5]Robert N. Anthony, John Dearden, and Richard F. Vancil, *Management Control Systems*, rev. ed., Homewood, Illinois: Richard D. Irwin, 1972.

In addition to providing figures that are not always relevant for making decisions, the use of traditional financial statements as the basis of a control system can be faulted with two violations of general management principles. These principles are:

1. Managers should be held responsible only for variables that they can control.
2. All managers should be evaluated on the same basis.

In can be argued that inflation and exchange fluctuations are factors over which management has no control and, therefore, should be excluded from evaluation. Also, managers in overseas units can be perceived to be at a disadvantage relative to the domestic units, which do not have to deal in foreign exchange.

The consideration of these last two factors raises a conflict between fairness and motivation. The objective of these management principles is equity. On the other hand, the manager should be encouraged to respond to changes in the specific environment. Although the management process may be simpler in a stable situation than under inflationary conditions, a manager operating under the latter conditions should be expected to reflect the increasing prices in the decisions taken. A satisfactory management control system must provide a compromise between the objectives of fairness and motivation.

This tradeoff between equity and motivation can be seen in terms of the level in the profit and loss statement at which local management is held responsible. This produces at least five different possibilities:

1. Operating profits measured in local currency
2. Operating profits measured in the parent's currency
3. Profits after taxes measured in local currency
4. Profits after taxes measured in the parent's currency
5. Profits after taxes and after balance sheet translation measured in the parent's currency

The differences among these levels involve the decision of whether local management should be held responsible for four different areas: (1) the translation impact of exchange fluctuations on operations; (2) the effects of financing decisions; (3) the impact of exchange fluctuations on translation of financing costs; and (4) the impact of exchange fluctuations on the translation of the balance sheet.

Management must judge which is the most appropriate level to evaluate local performance. Part of this judgment will rely on the organization of the finance function. Depending on whether or not this is the responsibility of local management, one would use operating profits or profits after taxes as the yardstick. The decision between figures measured in the local currency or in the parent's currency is more debatable. Basically it becomes a philosophical question of whether we want local management to think like the management of other local operations, or like the U.S. shareholders would want them to think.

Regardless of the evaluation target chosen, we will want to analyze separately each item in the financial statements and to segregate the impact of inflation and exchange fluctuations contained in those statements as well as the effects that have been ignored by the statements. In the following presentation we deal first with operating profits, and then consider the desirability of including the results of the finance function in the evaluation of local management.

Evaluation of Operating Profits

The impacts of inflation and exchange fluctuations on operating cash flows can be divided into three major types:

1. The effects of higher prices and exchange fluctuations on sales
2. The cash flows, in addition to those measured by historical costs and exchange rates, required to replace inventory and fixed assets
3. The additional working capital required under the new monetary conditions

If we adjust the operating profits reported in the financial statements by these effects, we obtain a measure of operating profits after maintaining productive capacity. We can adjust operating profits first for the effects of domestic inflation and exchange transactions. Then, if we want to express adjusted operating profits in dollar terms, we can translate all the necessary figures.

Exhibit 11.4 presents the computation of adjusted operating profits for the examples discussed earlier. In the local currency columns, exchange fluctuations are reflected only to the extent that exports and/ or imports are denominated in a currency different from the one used to make the calculations. Also, to the extent that fixed assets must be replaced from sources outside the country, their current cost and depreciation charges would be affected by exchange fluctuations. Since we assumed self-contained units in our examples, exchange fluctuations do not affect the local currency figures.

Exhibit 11.4 begins with the figure for reported operating profits, which is then adjusted for the current cost of replacing inventory and fixed assets. Inventory must be replaced at the higher costs prevailing at the end of the period. By using historical costs in computing the cost

EXHIBIT 11.4 Adjustment of Reported Operating Profits to Reflect the Effects of Inflation and Exchange Fluctuations

	A: Inflation, 10%; Depreciation, 10%		B: Inflation, 20%; Depreciation, 20%		C: Inflation, 30%; Depreciation, 30%		D: Inflation, 30%; Depreciation, 10%		E: Inflation, 10%; Appreciation, 10%	
	LC	$	LC	$	LC	$	LC	$	LC	$
Reported operating profits[a]	48	45	62	57	77	67	77	73	48	50
Adjustments to reflect current costs										
Undercharge in cost of goods sold relative to current cost	12	11	24	20	36	28	36	28	12	13
Undercharge in depreciation of fixed assets relative to current cost	4	4	8	7	12	9	12	11	4	4
	16	15	32	27	48	37	48	39	16	17
Adjustment to reflect changes in working capital requirements[b] Additional needs for cash plus change in accounts payable	−4	−4	−8	−7	−12	−10	−12	−10	−4	−4
Total adjustments to reported operating profits	12	11	24	20	36	27	36	29	12	13
Operating profits after adjustments to maintain productive capacity	36	34	38	37	41	40	41	44	36	37
Budget operating profits	32	32	32	32	32	32	32	32	32	32
Variance	+4	+2	+6	+5	+9	+8	+9	+11	+4	+5
Variance excluding working capital	0	−2	−2	−2	−3	−2	−3	+1	0	+1

[a] For reported operating profits, see Exhibit 11.3.
[b] Dollar values for the adjustment figures are the local currency values translated at the exchange rate prevailing at the end of the period.

of sales, insufficient allowance for replacement of inventory at current costs was made. The additional cost of replacement not measured in cost of goods sold in these examples is 12, 24, or 36, depending on the annual inflation rate. (The initial unit in the inventory had a cost of 120.)

Additional funds are also necessary to replace plant and equipment at current costs. In the balance sheet this account is measured in terms of historical costs and the annual charge for depreciation is calculated accordingly. Assuming that the replacement cost has increased by the same percentage as the rate of inflation, the initial depreciation charge of 40 must be increased to reflect the additional cash that would be required to replace the fixed assets. The additional amount of cash required to replace fixed assets is 4, 8, or 12, depending on the inflation rate.[6]

To the extent that inflation and exchange fluctuations affect the requirement for working capital, this fact should be taken into account in the computation of adjusted operating profits. If a larger amount of net working capital must be maintained to continue sales at the inflated level, then this increment is not available to be distributed in the form of dividends. This higher level of working capital is necessary to maintain productive capacity. Notice that part of the change in working capital requirements has already been accounted for in the form of current cost of inventory. The remaining accounts in working capital to be considered are monetary accounts: cash, accounts receivable, and accounts payable. Thus, the additional level of cash which must be kept for transaction purposes as well as the additional funds which are tied up in accounts receivable constitute funds that are not available for distribution. On the other hand, an increase in accounts payable eases the need for parent's funds to be maintained in working capital.

For the sake of simplicity, we assume in this example that the need for cash for transaction purposes does not change with inflation. However, accounts receivable and accounts payable are allowed to increase in proportion to the inflation rate. In these examples it is assumed that the number of days' worth of sales and purchases in accounts receivable and payable is maintained. Since accounts payable are larger than accounts receivable initially, the net impact of inflation in these accounts is to release working capital. Usually a higher level of inflation requires additional working capital. In these examples inflation actually contributes funds in the amount of 4, 8, or 12, depend-

---

[6]This treatment is the simplest one, but as the next paragraph on working capital might suggest, one could adjust depreciation in a lump sum for the total change in the fixed asset's value beyond 1 year's depreciation. This question is related to the inflation accounting issues discussed in the appendix to this chapter.

ing on the inflation rate. (The initial balance in monetary accounts is 40 in net liabilities.)

The use of historical costs in reported profits hides the real economic impact of inflation. The fixed nature of the charges based on historical costs accounts for the greater negative impact of inflation as the inflation rate increases. To add insult to injury, taxes must be paid on profits generated simply because historical cost figures are used!

The translation of these adjustments into dollars at the exchange rates prevailing at the end of the period provides the dollar value of adjustments necessary to maintain the productive capacity of the given unit. If new dollar investments had to be made to bring the productive capacity to the initial level, the dollar adjustment figures provide the amounts that would be required.

If we exclude the funds generated by the increase in accounts payable, the adjusted operating profit figures are all approximately equal to the budget figures. If we include the funds produced by the additional accounts payable, the adjusted operating profit figures are higher than budget. The criterion for whether to include the working capital adjustment should be the permanence of this change. If it can be seen as a permanent economy in the relative amount of equity funds required in the business (because suppliers are providing the financing), it should be included. On the other hand, if the initial capital structure was more representative of what a long-term relationship should be, then the working capital adjustment provides a constant incentive for the operating manager to economize on working capital as much as possible.

The use of adjusted profit figures pinpoints the specific changes triggered by increasing prices and induces the manager to react to them. Since the various impacts can be disaggregated, the manager can then be evaluated on the degree of success with which each factor has been controlled.

Exhibit 11.5 disaggregates the impact of higher prices and exchange rates on operations. The amount of price increase incorporated in reported sales can be estimated by comparing reported sales with a figure for sales estimated at preinflation prices. By comparing the costs of operations expressed in terms of current costs with what these costs would have been in the absence of price increases, we can compute the impact of higher prices on costs. The inflationary component in accounts payable and receivable can be determined by comparing the reported net change in these accounts with what these changes would have been in the absence of price increases.

We can think of the decisions on which management is evaluated in terms of the degree of the manager's discretionary power in controlling the impact of monetary conditions. We classify these decisions into three major groups:

GROUP I. Decisions where the manager has the most control

1. Pricing
2. Credit policy

GROUP II. Decisions where the degree of control is only moderate

1. Inventory levels
2. Productivity
3. Alternative sources of materials

GROUP III. Decisions where the manager has the least control

1. Cost of fixed assets
2. Technology

Of course, this ranking only shows relations. These relations may show different degrees of control at different times. Also, the longer the planning horizon, the greater the control the manager has on these decisions—for example, using alternative sources of materials.

With this ranking of how much control the manager has over monetary variables, we can look again at Exhibit 11.5, where the impact of inflation is measured in terms of different variables. The objective now is to segregate the impact of general conditions from the decisions of the manager.

For sales, we are interested in two variables: pricing policy and quantity sold relative to budget. The amount of revenues from the price increases is shown in Exhibit 11.5 as the difference between reported sales and sales computed at preinflation prices. In these examples, prices were increased approximately by the same percentage as overall inflation rate. Next, compare the revenue figure at preinflation prices with the budget. In this fashion, we have a measure of success in increasing both prices and quantity sold. In these examples, it was assumed that the manager met the budget in terms of quantity, so the only difference between budget and reported profits is due to increased prices.

A similar analysis can be performed for the major costs of production. The reported costs measured in terms of current costs can be compared with what these costs would have been in the absence of various increases. This latter figure then can be compared with the budget fig-

EXHIBIT 11.5 Analysis of Variance in Profits

	A: Inflation, 10%; Depreciation, 10%		B: Inflation, 20%; Depreciation, 20%		C: Inflation, 30%; Depreciation, 30%		D: Inflation, 30%; Depreciation, 10%		E: Inflation, 10%; Appreciation, 10%	
	LC	$	LC	$	LC	$	LC	$	LC	$
Sales										
Reported sales[a]	1,588	1,512	1,663	1,512	1,739	1,512	1,739	1,656	1,588	1,667
Revenues at preinflation prices	1,512	1,512	1,512	1,512	1,512	1,512	1,512	1,512	1,512	1,512
Revenue increases due to price changes	76	0	151	0	227	0	227	144	76	155
Percentage price increase over preinflation	5.03%	0%	9.99%	0%	15.01%	0%	15.01%	9.52%	5.03%	10.25%
Cost of Goods Sold										
Reported cost of goods sold[a]	1,500	1,429	1,561	1,419	1,622	1,410	1,622	1,545	1,500	1,575
Costs at preinflation prices	1,440	1,440	1,440	1,440	1,440	1,440	1,440	1,440	1,440	1,440
Reported cost increase due to price changes	60	(11)	121	(21)	182	(30)	182	105	60	135
Additional funds required to maintain inventory	12	11	24	20	36	28	36	28	12	13
Total cost increases due to price changes	72	0	145	(1)	218	(2)	218	77	72	122
Percentage cost increase over preinflation	5.00%	—	10.07%	—	15.13%	—	15.13%	5.34%	5.00%	8.47%
Depreciation										
Reported depreciation[a]	40	38	40	36	40	35	40	38	40	42
Charge at preinflation price	40	40	40	40	40	40	40	40	40	40
Reported charge increase	0	(2)	0	(4)	0	(5)	0	(2)	0	2
Additional charge to reflect current costs	4	4	8	7	12	9	12	11	4	4
Total fixed asset cost increase	4	2	8	3	12	4	12	9	4	6

Percentage cost increase over preinflation	10.00%	5.00%	20.00%	7.50%	30.00%	10.00%	30.00%	22.50%	10.00%	15.00%
Changes in Working Capital										
Reported accounts payable[a]	220	200	240	200	260	200	260	236	220	242
Payables at preinflation costs	200	200	200	200	200	200	200	200	200	200
Change in payables	20	0	40	0	60	0	60	36	20	42
Reported accounts receivable[a]	176	160	192	160	207	160	207	188	176	194
Receivables at preinflation prices	160	160	160	160	160	160	160	160	160	160
Change in receivables	16	0	32	0	47	0	47	28	16	34
Net changes in working capital	+4	0	+8	0	+13	0	+13	+8	+4	+8
Net changes in LC working capital translated into $		+4		+7		+10		+12		+4
Taxes										
Reported taxes[a]	17	16	24	22	32	28	32	30	17	18
Taxes on preinflation income	9	9	9	9	9	9	9	9	9	9
Tax increase due to price changes	8	7	15	13	23	19	23	21	8	9
Percentage tax increase over preinflation	88.89%	77.78%	166.67%	144.44%	255.55%	211.11%	255.55%	233.33%	88.89%	100.00%
Total Variances excluding Taxes										
Additional revenues	+76	0	+151	0	+227	0	+227	+144	+76	+155
Cost of goods sold	−72	0	−145	−1	−218	−2	−218	+77	−72	+122
Depreciation	−4	−2	−8	−3	−12	−4	−12	−9	−4	−6
Variance in operating profits	0	−2	−2	−4	−3	−6	−3	+212	0	+271
Additional working capital	+4	+4	+8	+7	+13	+10	+13	+12	+4	+4
Variance in operating profits plus working capital	+4	+2	+6	+3	+10	+4	+10	+224	+4	+275

[a]Sources for reported figures are Exhibits 11.1 and 11.3.

349

ures. Thus, the actual increases in the cost of resources and the efficiencies achieved by the manager can be measured. Again, because we assumed that the manager met the budget in volume terms, the differences between budget and current costs is caused only by cost increases.

For both sales and cost of goods sold, the response of management to inflationary conditions can also be measured by comparing the various increases realized in both revenues and costs with the average increases that prevailed in the markets where the manager operates. Success in raising selling prices higher than the prevailing market without affecting the quantity sold is to be praised. A similar success can be attributed to increases in the company's specific costs which are lower than those experienced in the company's input markets in general.

Finally, it seems that the manager should be given credit for whatever improvement can be realized in the amount of net working capital required under the new conditions. The number of days' worth of purchases and sales involved in accounts payable and receivable should be examined. An increase in the former and a decrease in the latter would release working capital, an outcome to be encouraged. In the example, the days' worth of credit on both accounts remains constant. Thus, the release of working capital on these grounds is caused totally by external price and/or cost changes.

To the extent that allowance was made for inflation in the budget figures, the revised figures need to adjust only for the difference between the inflation rate originally planned and the one actually realized. This can add another dimension to the control system, as management is asked to face the problems created by inflation in advance during the budget procedure. This will sharpen management's perception of the impact of the inflationary process.

ORGANIZATION AND CONTROL OF THE FINANCE FUNCTION

So far the focus of this chapter has been on control of operations of the multinational enterprise, excluding financing decisions. Although our measure of distributable profits was based on the bottom line of the income statement, no assessment of the financing decisions was made. In fact, there are two major approaches to the finance function from the point of view of control:

1. The local manager is given the responsibility for all financing decisions and he or she is evaluated in terms of the bottom line of the income statement; or

2. The responsibility for financing decisions is placed at the parent company level and the local manager is evaluated only in terms of operating profits.

A compromise between these two approaches also is found where the parent company or a regional office works in an advisory capacity while the local manager has the full responsibility for the final decision.

The advantages and disadvantages of each of these approaches can be traced to the general pros and cons of centralization versus decentralization. An analysis of this issue is outside the scope of this book and can be found in most introductory texts on organization theory. However, some insights into this particular decision can be gained by reviewing the dimensions of finance decisions and some of the gains to be realized from centralization, at least for reporting purposes. These decisions have been studied in detail in earlier chapters, so we limit ourselves here to a brief presentation.

Financing

To the extent that some units in the system are net generators of funds while others are net users of funds, a centralized system can channel funds from where they are not needed to where they are needed without having to resort to financial intermediaries who will want to be compensated for the service. Also, when intercompany trade exists, a centralized system can serve as a clearinghouse for intercompany payments without requiring an actual cash transfer through the banking system. Cash transfers take time during which the firm is not compensated for the service.

Finally, the large size of a parent company may be required to obtain access to some international markets from which smaller subsidiaries would be barred or would obtain less favorable terms than the parent company. On the other hand, no centralized office in New York or Zurich may aspire to have an intimate knowledge of all the local financial markets around the world.

Exchange Exposure Management

With affiliates dealing in several currencies the only hope of obtaining an accurate picture of the aggregate exposure of the business to exchange fluctuations is through a centralized reporting system such as the one suggested in Chapter 7. Such a report would eliminate the need for many hedging transactions since for any given currency the net receivable position of one unit may compensate the net liability position for another. The alternative of having each unit covering the exposure independently would serve only to generate income for exchange traders.

A compromise between decentralized decision-making and centralized exposure management exercised by some corporations is based on having the parent company operate as a bank to the rest of the company. Any manager wishing to cover his or her exchange position can obtain forward contracts from the treasury office of the parent company at current market prices. This guarantees an exchange rate for the financial reporting of the manager. Then, it is up to the parent company to decide whether to obtain a forward exchange contract from a commercial bank. If the exchange position of the specific manager is compensated by the position of another operating unit, the parent company will see no need to acquire an exchange contract. Indeed, if the two operating positions neutralize one another, the acquisition of a forward contract would actually create an exchange position where none existed before.

Tax Management

There are as many tax authorities as countries in the world. A summary of some of the philosophies of taxation is presented in Appendix 2 to Chapter 13. In addition, an understanding of specific laws requires highly specialized skills. Thus, it is impossible to delegate this responsibility totally to operating management, which may be conversant with local tax regulations but which could not be expected to be aware of conditions in other countries or of the tax position of the consolidated company.

SUMMARY

Inflation increases nominal profits and exchange rate fluctuations add further to a corporate officer's difficulty in evaluating the performance of company divisions in nations other than the parent's home country. After indicating the variety of distortions created by inflation and exchange rate fluctuations, we suggest a restatement of the traditional income statement to show the specific effect of local country inflation on sales, cost of goods sold (inventory), depreciation (fixed assets), and working capital requirements. The resulting balance is distributable profits, and one can state this figure in the home country currency after evaluating the earlier figures against budget forecasts. Depending on the firm, the local manager may have sharply different abilities to control various aspects of the business, ranging from relatively great control over pricing strategy to relatively small influence over the cost of fixed assets, for example.

This system provides useful information in evaluating the local managers and operates to motivate the managers to behave in an optimal way from the parent's standpoint. It is offered as a reasonable compromise between the nonintersecting requirements of both complete fairness and effective motivation.

Confronting the ultimate philosophical issue of centralized versus decentralized management helps determine the parent company's policy regarding local managers' financing and exposure management responsibilities. One compromise between total local responsibility and total centralized operation is the creation of a parent bank from which the local manager can borrow or lend idle cash to cover exposed positions at market rates. The centralized treasury office nets the local positions from the various subsidiaries that it has financed, and then decides whether to offset the resulting cash or foreign exchange position itself in the real marketplace.

APPENDIX

COMPARATIVE ACCOUNTING PRACTICES

There are many differences among the accounting conventions used in various lands to prepare financial statements. In addition, the problems of high inflation rates and unstable exchange rates cast doubt on the validity of financial statements prepared according to traditional accounting principles that ignore the impact of these monetary phenomena. This appendix addresses these two issues. In the first section, we review some of the most important areas of discrepancy among accounting principles used in different countries. In the second section, we discuss the proposals advanced to measure the impact of monetary changes.

DIFFERENCES IN INTERNATIONAL ACCOUNTING STANDARDS

Although this text is not primarily concerned with accounting differences among countries, any financial analyst must assure comparability of reports from firms in different lands. The difficulty is that two firms may both have financial statements which have an auditor's statement that the reports were prepared "in conformity with generally accepted accounting principles applied . . . consistently." Yet the principles may be very different in the two lands. In reviewing and comparing statements from different firms, the reader must confirm that:

1. All the relevant data are present from which one can judge the results of the firm;
2. The standards are consistent across firms and within a given firm over the years; and
3. The principles of accounting are acceptable to the analyst.

Varying principles which might not be acceptable include practices on consolidation, definition of income, and price level adjustments for inflation.[1] These inconsistencies must be resolved in order to compare firms.

Some of the differences among various nations relate to the function of the auditor. In some cases the auditor is concerned with certifying statements that are in compliance with a body of principles and standards. In other nations the auditor merely agrees to management's statement that the reported figures conform with some governmental rules; the statements may have little to do with economic reality or previous financial statements of the firm. Firms in some nations have only one set of published statements (in contrast to the sharply different income statements often prepared for taxation purposes in the United States); thus, the managers have to resolve a conflict between high earnings for the public (or simply "fair" earnings) and low earnings to reduce taxability. Given a desire to minimize taxes, firms often report just sufficient profits to pay dividends that seem "reasonable," with the remainder of the earnings reduced by various reserves.

Perhaps the largest difference between the U.S. and non-U.S. systems derives from the basic issue of *disclosure*. Secrecy of operations is almost a watchword among many international corporate officers. For example, in 1966 the huge Swiss pharmaceutical house, F. Hoffman-LaRoche, published a statement that showed record profits of SwF39.7 million. There were no sales figures, no asset figures, and no cost comments. The board of directors noted that the results were an improvement over previous years. "Sales and earnings have increased in approximately equal proportions. . . . The volume of investment was again large and will hardly diminish in the foreseeable future." The report was sent only to shareholders; all other requests were denied.

---

[1]See the discussion by Gordon Shillinglaw, "International Comparability of Accounts," *Accounting*, Feb. 1966; or, Edgar Barrett, et al., "Japan: Some Background for Security Analysts," Parts 1 and 2, *Financial Analysts Journal*, Jan./Feb. and March/April 1974, for examples.

Such secrecy is related to the reserve of businessmen, the reluctance to alert tax authorities and labor unions, and other causes. One could speculate that the reluctance often is based on a disinclination to alert competitors to the size of the firm's operations. Sometimes management itself does not know what the consolidated profits and losses are, or it knows and does not like to reveal the results. This process of extreme secrecy viewed from the American shareholder's standpoint is diminishing with time and greater demand from shareholders in all lands for information about the corporate holdings. The case presented above is extreme, but discrepancies in disclosure compared to U.S. standards remain very large.

Other critics of non-U.S. financial statements have said that the critical problem is *consolidation.* Many of the foreign statements are not consolidated, or consolidation is optional from subsidiary to subsidiary. The foreign firm may mark up goods sold to unconsolidated sales subsidiaries in order to realize a high reported income for the parent (or at least some income!). The unconsolidated sales subsidiary, inventorying goods at inflated prices, may not be able to sell the goods at all, or at least not be able to sell them to recover cost. The first big Japanese bankruptcy in the economic success of that nation after World War II came in the mid-1960s when the Sanyo Special Steel Company, with capital of only $22 million, went bankrupt after "adjustments" showed the accumulated losses totaled over $222 million. Yet, these losses had been hidden in part by the unconsolidated subsidiary device. Because of a recent standard change, about 600 of the largest Japanese firms must now publish consolidated statements, thus eliminating many of the abuses of past years. However, many of the firms seem to be reducing direct firm ownership in the subsidiary to under 50%, hence avoiding the regulation.

The translation of foreign accounts varies internationally, and the impact can be seen in the United States before 1971. Prior to that date U.S. firms could consolidate subsidiaries in which the firm had more than a 50% interest, but ownership of less than 50% could be reported by using the equity method or the cost method. Under the equity approach, the pro rata inclusion of profits and losses of the subsidiary is included in the parent's income statement each year (hence, it is often referred to as "one-line consolidation"). Under the cost method, the initial investment of the firm in the subsidiary is retained as the value of the investment. Dividends as received are the income.

In 1966 the accounting regulations in effect in the United States required that domestic subsidiaries be included on either a consolidated basis or an equity basis, but foreign subsidiaries were excluded from this regulation. As a result, by 1970 the American corporations treated foreign subsidiaries in a wide range of ways. IBM and others consolidated all foreign subsidiaries. Some firms used the equity or the cost method exclusively. Many firms used a mixture of cost and equity, translating subsidiaries in relatively risk-free areas on an equity basis and others on a cost basis.[2] The current requirement is consolidation for more than 50% ownership, equity consolidation for more than 20% ownership, and dividends as received for 20% or less ownership.

A third major problem relates to the creation of *reserves*, secret or not. These reserves are charges against income in a particular year, and they mean that the definition of income is highly variable from year to year within a given firm and across firms in a given year. Generally, the goal is level income over time, with high reserves created in good years and vice versa. The reserves have a variety of purposes. Many of the definitions parallel the previous practice in the United States, where the term denoted any number of different accounts. Thus, reserves may be contra-accounts to reduce the value of a wasting asset, such as a reserve for depreciation. They may represent a contingency payment or future liability, such as a legal settlement or future costs for employee health insurance programs. They may be segmented retained earnings, sometimes earmarked for a particular project by vote of the shareholders or the board of directors ("reserve for future expansion"), or may be general ("free reserves") in the form of the American pattern of retained earnings. Finally, the reserves may be from special government tax programs, such as the British investment program of some years ago in which extremely rapid write-offs of some assets would be permitted when a certain portion of earnings were segmented as reserves for future construction outlays.

Another problem area relates to *depreciation* and the *revaluation process*. In periods of high inflation, many firms feel forced to revalue assets, as discussed below. Yet this process, which is often most dramatic in its effect on inventory and fixed asset values, can have sharp effects on the income statement through large depreciation charges or through great increases in the net worth of the company. Hence, the application of the depreciation schedule from year to year on a given asset as well as the process of revaluation of assets will often alter the income statement from what a U.S. reader would expect. Furthermore, the nature of the disclosure in footnotes on non-U.S. statements often masks the changes that have been made. The assumptions on which the charges are based are often unstated.

Another major difference is the concept of *retained earnings* or *earned surplus*. To the American shareholder in recent years, *clean* surplus is an accepted fact. It means that adjustments to the retained earn-

---

[2]Exceptions to the rule requiring equity or full consolidation for over 50% ownership occurred when the investor could not have "significant influence" over the policies of the subsidiary and when the subsidiary was operating under particular exchange controls.

ings or surplus account are made only through the income statement: There is no charge directly to the retained earnings account. Yet, from a review of many foreign financial statements, charges deemed not to be related to operations or not related to the current period's operations are often charged directly to the earned surplus account without the intermediary appearance in the income statement. Hence, the retained earnings account is sharply different from the American corporation's account under the same name.

Asset valuation is also a major issue. Thus, many U.S. firms use the LIFO method to value inventory; but most other nations forbid that convention. Also, the U.S. tax and financial reporting life for many fixed assets is fairly long compared to the rapid write-offs permitted firms in other lands. Finally, goodwill for some mergers must now be capitalized and amortized over no more than 40 years with no tax deductions in the United States. In contrast, other nations following different accounting conventions ignore the goodwill aspects of mergers altogether.

Whether the market of investors perceives the "true" earnings of firms operating under various conventions is a matter of intellectual faith and empirical analysis; the earnings as reported are different, however.

Treatments of tax liabilities, stock dividends, and other accounts also differ from nation to nation, but the preceding comments highlight some of the major difficulties. The form of presentation of financial statements also may differ greatly, since firms may use different conventions in reporting income compared to the U.S. form. However, the reader can often interpret the figures to recast them roughly in the form of the U.S. income statement. The greater difficulty, however, is in the valuation process by which the accounts were determined, as noted above. Accounting firms periodically brief their clients and publish small booklets that outline some of the more pervasive differences in accounting statements.[3]

Some of the variations in international accounting may be removed as a result of the International Accounting Standards Committee formed in 1973. This committee has representatives from twenty-two nations that are pledged to adopt the standards agreed upon. Although most western European nations are included, two significant nonmembers are Switzerland and Italy.

The first standard adopted required disclosure of significant accounting policies, a disclosure of changes in accounting standards in which the change had material effect, and the inclusion of comparable

---

[3]For example, see the *Guide to Foreign Financial Statements*, published annually by Price Waterhouse, New York.

figures for the prior period in all financial statements. Although these standards were not changes for U.S. practitioners, they represented a change for several nations. The next two standards dealt with inventory valuations and the rules for consolidation. Other standards scheduled for adoption deal with depreciation policies, the translation of foreign accounts, inflation accounting, and research and development outlays.

ACCOUNTING FOR INFLATION

The distortions that inflation and exchange fluctuations can cause on traditional financial statements have generated a multiplicity of proposals to measure the impact of these monetary problems. The major strands of thought in these proposals can be classified into two groups:

1. Proposals in favor of using constant purchasing power values
2. Proposals in favor of using current values[4]

Each of these sets of proposals departs from traditional accounting practices in a different manner. Actually, in the purchasing power proposals all the traditional principles are retained except for a change in the unit of measurement. Instead of using money as the unit of account, these proposals use units of current purchasing power calculated using a general price index such as the GNP deflator. The current-value proposals, on the other hand, depart from one of the basic principles of accounting—namely, the use of historical costs. Current-value methods of accounting measure assets on the basis of their *current value*, not historical costs. However, these methods retain units of money as the unit of account.[5]

The differences between these two systems of accounting for inflation can be seen best by contrasting their treatment of valuation of various assets and liabilities, and their implicit definition of profits. A summary of the practices in each system is presented in Exhibit 11.1A.

---

[4]The approach recommended by current-value accounting is the one used in the text in Chapter 11 to estimate the economic impact of inflation on operations.

[5]For a comprehensive examination of these proposals, see *Inflation Accounting*, Report of the Inflation Accounting Committee, Chairman F.E.P. Sandilands, presented to Parliament in September, 1975, London, Great Britain. This report favors the adoption of current-value accounting.

EXHIBIT 11.1A   Treatment of the Impact of Inflation on Various Accounts under Alternative Accounting Systems

	Purchasing-Power Systems	Current-Value Systems
Monetary assets	Gives rise to monetary loss for the decline in purchasing power since initially received. The monetary loss is reported in the income statement.	No change.
Liabilities	Gives rise to monetary gain for the decline in purchasing power since debt was contracted. The monetary gain is reported in the income statement.	No change.
Nonmonetary assets	Increases to reflect cost in terms of current purchasing power units. Equity figure increases in the same amount.	Increases to measure *value* to the business. Increase is charged to *reserve* account.
Revenues	Restated in terms of units of current purchasing power.	No change.
Cost of goods sold	Restated in terms of units of current purchasing power.	Increases to measure *value* to business at time of sale. Adjustment is shown as part of *operating* profits.
Depreciation	Increases to reflect change in purchasing-power units worth of cost consumed during the reporting period.	Increases to measure *value* to business consumed during the reporting period. Adjustment is shown as part of *operating* profits.
Operating profits	Restated revenues less restated cost of goods sold and depreciation, less monetary gains or losses.	Revenues less current value cost of goods sold and depreciation. No monetary gains or losses.

Valuation of Assets and Liabilities

Monetary Assets and Liabilities.   Purchasing-power proposals measure monetary assets in terms of units of current purchasing power. As inflation proceeds the purchasing power of these monetary assets decreases. Thus, monetary assets held at the beginning or acquired during the accounting period are worth less at the end of the period. Purchasing-power accounting identifies this monetary loss as part of operating profits and reports it in the income statement. Likewise, liabilities already outstanding at the beginning of the period or contracted some time between then and the end of the period are worth less. This gives rise to a monetary gain which is considered part of operating profits and is reported in the income statement in purchasing-power accounting.

Current-value systems, on the other hand, use money as the unit of measurement. Therefore, they do not identify any change in the value of monetary assets and liabilities. In terms of current value, $100 of marketable securities or debt are worth exactly $100 today regardless of when they were first acquired and the change in the general level of prices since then. In this system there are no monetary gains or losses to be recognized from holding monetary assets or liabilities during an inflationary period. Units of money measure the amount of funds which the monetary assets would fetch if they were redeemed today, or the amount of funds required to liquidate a liability.

Nonmonetary Assets. In the valuation of nonmonetary assets such as plant and equipment the use of purchasing-power units adjusts cost figures to reflect the change in purchasing power. Inflation increases the cost of equipment. However, the adjustment made for purchasing power reflects only the general increase in price levels, and not the specific increase in the cost of the given piece of equipment. By contrast, current-value accounting abandons the concept of historical cost expressed in whatever unit, and reports instead the *current value* of these assets. Alternatives used to estimate current value include replacement cost, net present value of the asset, and resale price. In practice, replacement cost is the method used most often by the advocates of this system of accounting.[6]

Measure of Profits

In the income statement, the thrust of the purchasing-power proposals is to restate all the accounts in terms of units of current purchasing power. However, the traditional valuation basis—for example, historical costs—is maintained. Basically, all the accounts are inflated to reflect the higher prices prevailing at the end of the period in the overall economy. Thus, the depreciation charge is increased by the overall rate of inflation.

Operating profit in the purchasing-power system is a restatement of sales and various costs of doing business in terms of dollars of the same purchasing power, regardless of when the transaction took place. The problems of mixing sales for, say, March measured in dollars with

---

[6]Replacement cost is also the method required by the Securities and Exchange Commission in the United States. Replacement cost figures for the balance sheet must be shown in footnotes to statements to shareholders. See Accounting Series Release No. 190, March 23, 1976.

a purchasing power for that month with cost figures expressed in dollars for, say, December is avoided by expressing all the figures in terms of dollars of the same purchasing power: the purchasing power at the end of the period.

In a current-value system the revenue figure is not altered. But cost of goods sold now reflects the value of the merchandise to the business at the time it was sold instead of historical costs. If a replacement cost system is used, the figure for cost of goods sold is the cost of replacing the inventory involved in the sale. Depreciation is the portion of the current value of the assets estimated to have been consumed during the reporting period. To reflect the higher costs, current-value systems adjust the traditional operating profit figure by a "cost of sales adjustment." This adjustment measures the difference between historical costs used in the traditional statements and current costs—the cost of replacing inventory and fixed assets—valued at the time sales took place. This adjustment is a separate entry in the income statement. This treatment is in contrast to the purchasing-power systems where the adjustments for changes in purchasing power are mixed with the traditional value for each account.

The implications of using a different unit of account in each system can be seen in what is included in the definition of profits. Current-value systems of valuation consider operating profits, after adjustments for current costs, as the relevant measure of profits for the period. Purchasing-power systems go one step further to compute operating profits. Monetary gains and losses derived from holding monetary assets and liabilities throughout the period are added to operating income to obtain operating profits for the period, all expressed in current purchasing power units.

Profit measures are an attempt to assess the gains or losses accruing to capital. Thus, the different profit concept in each of the two systems can be traced to their definition of capital. In purchasing-power systems the capital invested is measured by the equity account at the beginning of the period, the difference between assets and liabilities at that point. As the purchasing power of initial assets and liabilities changes, so does the purchasing power of capital. So, profits are the contribution to the equity account after the equity investment is updated to reflect its current purchasing power.

In a current-value system of accounting, capital is defined as productive capacity. Profits are the amount of funds which could be distributed after maintaining the productive capacity of assets. Since the monetary gains and losses derived from holding monetary assets and liabilities in an inflationary period are not gains or losses in terms of cash, they are not considered profit. In principle, the profit figure computed under this accounting system is available for distribution without impairing the productive capacity of the business. The additional charges over historical costs required to replenish the productive capacity of the business are included in the "cost of sales adjustment."

Under both systems most of the changes in value of nonmonetary assets are reflected directly in the equity account. Under purchasing-power proposals, assuming there has not been any change in the physical inventory of nonmonetary assets, the change in value in terms of purchasing power units is included in the adjustment of the additional equity for the change in purchasing power. For example, if there was a change in purchasing power of 10% during the period, both the value of plant and equipment and the equity account would be increased by the same amount—10% of the cost of plant and equipment. However, transactions in these assets during the reporting period, purchases and sales of nonmonetary assets, will be reported as part of monetary gains and losses. The value of the receipts and disbursements is adjusted for the change in purchasing power within the period.

In current-value accounting, all the changes in value in nonmonetary items are segregated within the equity account. Revaluation reserves measure the gains and losses from changes in the current value of nonmonetary assets. Proponents of this accounting system recommend that movements in these reserve accounts be identified separately, not mixed with other portions of the equity account.

Foreign Operations

When the reporting system involves units with operations in other countries, each of these sets of proposals suggests a different treatment. In a system of constant purchasing-power units, the relevant price level is the one in the country of the parent company, presumably the stockholders' home. The value of foreign operations is first translated from foreign currency into the parent's currency following the accepted principles of translation in this system. After the accounts are translated, they are adjusted for changes in the purchasing power of the parent's currency following the guidelines discussed earlier.

For proponents of current-value accounting, the relevant inflation rate is the one affecting the value of the assets to the business, given that the assets are located abroad. For example, what is the replacement cost, given that the asset is to be used in the specific country? Because of its location, the asset may be replaced from sources located in the same country, or it may be imported. Once the value of the assets is determined on this basis, then its equivalent value in terms of the parent's currency can be found by applying current exchange rates.

Inflation Accounting
in the United States

In 1983, the U.S. accounting profession finally specified the treatment of inflationary effects on the financial statements of U.S. firms. Statement 70 of the Financial Accounting Standards Board (FAS 70) requires U.S. corporations to show two supplemental income statements, in addition to the traditional statement based on historical costs. The first adjusts historical cost items (such as depreciable assets and some inventory) for the effects of *general inflation* using the Consumer Price Index (CPI) since the acquisition of these assets. Depreciation charges and cost of goods sold are recomputed based on the adjusted "cost" of these items to arrive at a new earnings figure. The second income statement adjusts these items by a *current cost* index reflecting the *specific price changes* over time in those assets. Equipment prices for the corporations have generally risen faster than the CPI, although it is difficult to adjust accurately for technological change. (Alternatively, firms may simply show adjustments to earnings based on historical costs for these two methods of inflation allowance.)

There are two other major adjustments regarding the balance sheets of firms in inflationary times which are also required. However, the changed values are shown in the equity accounts directly and are *not* entered in any restatement of income. The first concerns adjustments for the net monetary position of the firm and reflects whether the firm is in a net long or short position in monetary items. The second adjustment reflects the holding of assets which have risen in value in inflationary times.

FAS 70 allows companies to report current cost information for their foreign operations using either the U.S. price index or general price indices related to the foreign currencies. In this manner, the requirements for inflation adjustments in supplemental statements for reporting standards and the requirements of foreign currency adjustments for non-U.S. operations are linked.

QUESTIONS

1. "You characters in New York have all the expensive forecasting services of your big banks to tell you what is going to happen to interest rates and the peso. How am I supposed to know what to do sitting here in Mexico City?" (Mexican local manager). Comment.

2. "I know Latin American countries have relatively high inflation versus Germany, but if you look at the exchange rate, we always seem to

receive less, even allowing for the changing parities. Budget is never met. What is wrong?" (Berlin multinational president). Comment.

3.   "I am willing to evaluate the Indonesian subsidiary in their local currency, but I do not understand why they keep needing more money. Inflation always seems to drive up profits, but why can they not finance themselves? All we do is ship in more francs every 6 months. Something is wrong." (French multinational financial vice-president). Comment.

4.   "If only I had a British parent instead of a Swiss parent, I would look a lot smarter. That is really absurd." (Brazilian local manager). Comment.

BIBLIOGRAPHY

"Accountants Off Balance," *Economist*, Aug. 7, 1982, p. 18.

Anthony, Robert N., John Dearden, and Richard F. Vancil, *Management Control Systems*, rev. ed. Homewood, Ill.: Richard D. Irwin, 1972.

Arpan, Jeffrey S., and Lee H. Radebaugh, *International Accounting and Multinational Enterprises*. Boston: Warren, Gorham and Lamont, 1981.

Barrett, M. Edgar, and Jean-Louis Roy, "Financial Reporting Practices in France," *Financial Analysts Journal*, Jan.–Feb. 1976, pp. 39–49.

Benston, George J., "Public (U.S.) Compared to Private (U.K.) Regulation of Corporate Financial Disclosure," *Accounting Review*, July 1976, pp. 483–98.

Berg, Kenneth, et al., eds., *Readings in International Accounting*. Boston, Mass.: Houghton Mifflin Company, 1969.

Choi, Frederick D. S., and Gerhard G. Mueller, *An Introduction to Multinational Accounting*. Englewood Cliffs, N.J.: Prentice-Hall, Inc., 1978.

Cowen, Scott S., Lawrence C. Phillips, and Linda Stillabower, "Multinational Transfer Pricing," *Management Accounting*, Jan. 1979, pp. 17–21.

Cummings, Joseph P., and William L. Rogers, "Developments in International Accounting," *CPA Journal*, May 1978, pp. 15–19.

Davidson, Sidney, Clyde P. Stickney, and Roman L. Weil, *Inflation Accounting: A Guide for the Accountant and Financial Analyst*. New York: McGraw-Hill Book Company, 1976.

Feldman, Stewart A., and LeRoy J. Herbert, "The International Accounting Standards Committee," *CPA Journal*, Jan. 1977, pp. 17–21.

Financial Accounting Standards Board, "Statement of Financial Accounting Standards No. 52." Stamford, Connecticut, Oct. 1981.

Hole, Roderick C., and Michael A. Alkier, "German Financial Statements," *Management Accounting*, July 1974, pp. 28–34.

International Practice Executive Committee, *Professional Accounting in 30 Countries*. New York: American Institute of Certified Public Accountants, 1975.

Lessard, Donald R., and Peter L'Orange, "Currency Changes and Management Control: Resolving the Centralization/Decentralization Dilemma," *Accounting Review*, July 1977, pp. 628–37.

Madison, Roland L., "Responsibility Accounting and Transfer Pricing: Approach with Caution," *Management Accounting*, Jan. 1979. pp. 25–29.

Malmstrom, Duane, "Accommodating Exchange Rate Fluctuations in Intercompany Pricing and Invoicing," *Management Accounting*, Sept. 1977, pp. 24–28.

Merville, Larry J., and J. William Petty, "Transfer Pricing for the Multinational Firm," *Accounting Review*, Oct. 1978, pp. 935–51.

Miller, Elwood L., *Accounting Problems of Multinational Enterprises*, Lexington, Massachusetts: Lexington Books, 1979.

Robbins, Sidney M., and Robert B. Stobaugh, *Money in the Multinational Enterprise*, Ch. 8. New York: Basic Books, Inc., 1973.

Tang, Roger L. W., C. K. Walter, and Robert H. Haymond, "Transfer Pricing—Japanese vs. American Style," *Management Accounting*, Jan. 1979, pp. 12–16.

Treuherz, R. M., "Reevaluating ROI for Foreign Operations," *Financial Executive*, May 1968, pp. 64–71.

Tse, Paul S., "Evaluating Performance in Multinationals," *Management Accounting*, June 1979, pp. 21–25.

Willey, Russell W., *Foreign Exchange: The Accounting of Economics and Control*. Wilmington, Delaware: Nopoly Press, 1977.

Woo, John C. H., "Accounting for Inflation: Some International Models," *Management Accounting*, Feb. 1978, pp. 37–43.

Wyman, Harold E., "Analysis of Gains or Losses from Foreign Monetary Items: An Application of Purchasing Power Parity Concepts," *Accounting Review*, July 1976, pp. 545–58.

MARWICK HOME PRODUCTS, INC., ITALY

ON DECEMBER 23, 1978, Ms. Jane Rosenthal, treasurer of the International Division of Marwick Home Products (MHP), had 8 days left to reach a decision regarding the company's exposure in liras. Ms. Rosenthal's position was summarized in the following quote:

> For the 70 years that MHP has been operating in the international market, our policy has been to keep our exposure to foreign exchange risks at a minimum. To a large extent, we have accomplished this by financing our subsidiaries with funds raised in the countries where they are located. There are times, however, when borrowing in foreign markets is not sufficient to protect us against currency devaluations. In these cases, other means have to be used—some of which can be very expensive if our judgment proves to be wrong. In the past few years this problem has been magnified by the system of fluctuating exchange rates which has prevailed among major currencies. In these fluctuations, the formerly stable U.S. dollar often has depreciated against many other currencies.
>
> Because of credit and currency restrictions, in the case of the lira, we found the size of our exposure in this currency at the end of 1977 to be too high. In addition, based on past performance, we thought the possibility of a depreciation of the lira vis-à-vis the dollar during 1978 was significant. So we decided to hedge this risk by selling 1-year forward liras at a discount. The year has now gone by and, contrary to predictions, the lira has actually appreciated against the dollar. We now have to go to the spot market to buy liras at a high price to deliver on the forward contract which is coming due in a few days.
>
> The problem we face now is roughly similar to what we faced last year. The decision to hedge our exposure in liras at that time has proved to be expensive, but it is not clear to me that we should not take the same course of action now. Last August Italy unveiled a new economic plan developed in conjunction with the International Monetary Fund (the IMF), but I believe that the inherent instability of the Italian system will cause a depreciation of the lira against the dollar in 1979.

If the forward market route to hedging the lira exposure were used again, the options appeared to be: (1) sell liras forward for delivery in 1 year or a shorter period; (2) leave the lira exposure uncovered throughout the next year; and (3) do nothing now, but if the risks of a lira devaluation increase, then sell liras forward at that time. A publication issued by one of Marwick's banks in the United States the previous trading day listed the rates shown in the accompanying table.[1]

| | | EUROCURRENCY INTEREST RATES | |
	Exchange Rates	U.S. Dollar	Lira
Spot	Lit838.93/$		
1-month	Lit841.75/$	11.5000%	14.500%
3-month	Lit845.31/$	11.9375%	14.625%
6-month	Lit851.79/$	12.3750%	15.000%
12-month	Lit866.55/$	12.0625%	n.a.

MANAGEMENT OF THE FOREIGN EXCHANGE POSITION

Since January 1976, MHP's measure of exposure to exchange risk for internal management purposes had been the net of current assets minus all liabilities. This represented a combination of the exposure measure used for translating foreign financial statements into dollars for external reports and an adjustment for the value of inventories.

The exposure definition used for translating financial statements at the time was Statement No. 8 of the U.S. Financial Accounting Standards Board, FAS 8. In most cases this statement excluded inventory from among the current assets translated at current exchange rates. However, in cases of large devaluations of foreign currencies, MHP had often found that to comply with FAS 8 it also had to include inventory among the assets exposed to the effects of the devaluation. Taking into account the particular treatment of the inventory account for translation purposes, and also being convinced that it made more sense to include inventory than not to include it among the exposed assets, MHP defined exposure to exchange risk as the net of current assets minus all liabilities—or FAS 8 plus inventory.

---

[1]Source: Harris Bank, *Weekly Review, International Money Markets and Foreign Exchange Rates*, Dec. 22, 1978. The exchange rates are bid rates for liras and the Eurocurrency rates are bid rates for the respective currencies. All rates are closing rates in London. Discrepancies between interest differentials and forward discounts on the lira are due to differences in the timing of the last transaction recorded for the day.

Management of the exposure to exchange risk was conducted through policies and decisions affecting both cash balances and sources of financing for the subsidiaries. Thus, it was MHP policy to keep the cash account at a minimum consistent with cash payments in the subsidiary. When sizable amounts of cash were left in the accounts of the subsidiary because of an impending payment, this cash was invested in short-term securities in the local country's currency until payment was due. Under no condition was the subsidiary allowed to invest these funds in another country or currency. To the extent that there was some question about the possibility of a depreciation of the subsidiary's local currency, remittances from the subsidiary to the parent company were covered in the foward market. To the extent that an appreciation of the local currency was possible, an attempt was made to delay these remittances as long as possible.

The source of debt financing was determined through regular computations for each subsidiary of the cost of borrowing in local markets compared with the alternative of financing from headquarters. The after-tax interest costs in the local market were compared with the cost of money after taxes to the parent plus the exchange losses or gains under this second course of action.

The comparisons of the cost of alternative sources of financing often had led to selecting the local source of funds. Before 1971 this conclusion was usually supported by the belief that any change in most foreign currencies would be a devaluation against the dollar. Thus, high interest rates in local currencies were expected to be more than offset by the devaluation of those currencies against the dollar. After 1971, the successive depreciations of the dollar shattered this general belief, and the earlier notion of relative certainty about exchange market moves was replaced by a high feeling of uncertainty as to future developments in currency parities. However, in spite of the changes in the perceived world, financial decisions at MHP continued to rely heavily on foreign local markets. In the face of uncertainty, a wish to reduce the typical positive exchange exposure in a currency led again to favoring local currency over dollar borrowings.

Exhibit J.1 shows a measure of success for this financing policy for the company as a whole. Columns 1 and 2 report, respectively, the total level of loans in local currency and the actual interest cost incurred on those local-currency loans. Because those loans were in local currency, exchange losses were avoided on average. The magnitude of the losses avoided is shown in column 3. If, instead of raising these funds in the local markets, MHP had raised them in dollars, the interest costs would have been as reported in column 4. The positive numbers in column 5 indicate the net savings realized by using local sources of funds.

EXHIBIT J.1 Marwick Home Products, Inc.:: Overall Company Net Reduction in Exchange Losses Due to Local-Currency Loans *(thousands of dollars)*

Period	TOTAL LOANS IN LOCAL CURRENCY (1)	INTEREST COST ON LOCAL LOANS (NET)[a] (2)	EXCHANGE LOSS REDUCTION DUE TO LOANS[b] (3)	COST OF DOLLARS TO REPLACE LOCAL LOANS (NET)[c] (4)	NET REDUCTION (3) + (4) − (2) (5)
1/1/48–12/31/52	61,800	1,415	1,582	927	1,094
1/1/53–12/31/57	135,733	4,126	4,561	2,036	2,471
1/1/58–12/31/62	205,933	7,414	8,134	3,089	3,809
1/1/63–12/31/67	223,671	8,701	2,080	5,368	(1,253)
1/1/68–12/31/72	265,360	10,747	4,140	9,022	2,415
1/1/73–12/31/77	287,180	15,852	(689)	11,774	(4,767)
Total	1,179,677	48,255	19,808	32,216	3,769
1/1/78–12/15/78	63,486	3,225	(1,270)	3,733	(762)
Total 31 years	1,243,163	51,480	18,538	35,949	3,007

[a]Actual local interest paid net after taxes: 2.29% for 1948–52, 3.04% for 1953–57, 3.60% for 1958–62, 3.89% for 1963–67, 4.05% for 1968–72, 5.52% for 1973–77, 5.08% for 1978.

[b]Total of loans in local currency times average appreciation/depreciation: 2.56% for 1948–52, 3.36% for 1953–57, 3.95% for 1958–62, 0.93% for 1963–67, 1.56% for 1968–72, (0.24%) for 1973–77, (2.00%) for 1978.

[c]Alternative cost of funds after taxes if dollars had been used instead of local currency: 1.5% for 1948–62, 2.4% for 1963–67, 3.4% for 1968–72, 4.1% for 1973–77, 5.8% for 1978.

THE ITALIAN SITUATION

The Italian subsidiary manufactured and distributed most of the products developed by the parent company. These consisted of soap, deodorants, toothpaste, hair spray, detergents, window cleaners, and plastic bags, among others. The subsidiary's largest market was in industrialized northern Italy. However, some of the more basic products (such as soap) also sold well in the rest of Italy.

Lately, the subsidiary's growth in Italy was similar to the pattern of the company's growth in the United States; although not exceptional, it was commensurate with the growth in the local economy. Exhibits J.2–J.4 present the financial statements of Marwick-Italy for the preceding 5 years.

A review of the Italian economy and the stability of the lira at the time produced a mixed picture. First on the positive side was the impact of recent exchange rate movements. Since early 1976, when Italy abandoned the European snake completely and devalued the lira by 31.2% against the U.S. dollar, the lira had followed the middle road—appreciating against the dollar while depreciating against major European currencies. Because Italy pays for most of its imports in dollars and exports mostly to its neighbors in Europe, the post-1976 exchange rate movements had helped to create a surplus in the Italian balance of trade and to reduce greatly its level of external debt. Also, much of the remaining external debt had been refinanced as Italian banks borrowed at very favorable rates to retire older debts carrying higher interest rates. The inflation rate, while still high at 12.1% for 1978, was at its lowest level in years. Finally, the agreement between the Christian

EXHIBIT J.2 Marwick-Italy: Income Statements, January 1 to December 31, 1974–1978
(millions of liras)

	1974	1975	1976	1977	1978
Net sales	48,006	51,153	67,596	76,033	91,171
Cost of sales	29,209	32,567	42,225	48,244	59,191
Gross profit	18,797	18,586	25,371	27,789	31,980
Operating expenses					
Marketing	10,359	13,025	14,800	16,401	18,368
General and administrative	3,852	4,115	5,006	5,112	6,672
Net interest	117	135	166	462	623
Total operating expenses	14,328	17,275	19,972	21,975	25,663
Income before taxes	4,469	1,311	5,399	5,814	6,317
Provision for taxes	2,139	602	2,526	2,678	2,950
Net income	2,330	709	2,873	3,136	3,367
Dividends declared	1,137	550	1,211	1,737	2,056

EXHIBIT J.3 Marwick-Italy: Balance Sheets as of December 31, 1974–1978 *(millions of liras)*

	1974	1975	1976	1977	1978
			ASSETS		
Current assets					
Cash	3,120	1,172	3,918	2,293	3,753
Receivables (trade)	6,424	8,187	6,902	8,493	9,958
Intercompany accounts	323	406	357	357	417
Inventory	11,319	13,746	11,195	12,834	14,105
Prepayments	1,272	1,150	1,333	1,515	1,439
Total current assets	22,458	24,661	23,705	25,492	29,672
Net fixed assets	8,737	9,543	11,678	12,858	14,288
Investment in nonconsolidated subsidiaries	178	243	415	525	771
Total assets	31,373	34,447	35,798	38,875	44,731
			LIABILITIES AND EQUITY		
Current liabilities					
Bank notes and loans	2,236	4,154	2,653	4,313	4,041
Accounts payable (trade)	3,214	4,021	3,326	3,575	4,761
Intercompany accounts	287	412	300	312	337
Miscellaneous	2,332	2,554	3,180	3,086	3,525
Accrued taxes	1,454	1,420	2,290	1,584	1,405
Total current liabilities	9,523	12,561	11,749	12,870	14,069
Noncurrent liabilities					
Deferred taxes	1,122	487	1,651	2,035	2,194
Other deferred liabilities	2,719	3,231	2,568	2,741	5,928
Total noncurrent liabilities	3,841	3,718	4,219	4,776	8,122
Shareholders' equity					
Issued capital	1,734	1,727	1,722	1,733	1,719
Earned surplus	2,124	2,001	2,052	2,090	1,947
Retained earnings	14,151	14,440	16,056	17,406	18,874
Total shareholders' equity	18,009	18,168	19,830	21,229	22,540
Total liabilities and equity	31,373	34,447	35,798	38,875	44,731

Democrat party and the Communist party had increased political stability.

On the minus side were the unrest among the rank and file of the big union confederations and the high level of unemployment. Measures taken to curb inflation also had limited economic growth. Although the pressures for an expansionary monetary policy to stimulate economic growth were considerable, the inflation problem was still substantial. Such practices as the *scala mobile*—an automatic adjustment of wages and pensions every 4 months based on a price index— counteracted government attempts to control inflation. Further complicating matters were the so-called *autonomi,* small extremist unions not in the big confederations. Time and again they had shown their strength through work stoppages in key areas (such as transportation), which had paralyzed Italy's economy. Regardless of their political philosophy, all these militant unions were determined to increase their

EXHIBIT J.4 Marwick-Italy: Sources and Uses of Funds Statements, January 1 to December 31, 1974–1978 *(millions of liras)*

	1974	1975	1976	1977	1978
Sources of Working Capital				•	
Current operations					
Net income	2,330	709	2,873	3,136	3,367
Depreciation expense	219	238	242	272	307
Working capital from operations	2,549	947	3,115	3,408	3,674
Other sources					
Deferred taxes	122	(635)	1,164	384	3,159
Other deferred liabilities	312	512	(663)	173	187
Total new working capital	2,983	824	3,616	3,965	7,020
Uses of Working Capital					
Change in net fixed assets	416	1,044	2,377	1,452	1,737
Increases in investment in subsidiaries	104	65	172	110	246
Declaration of dividends	1,137	550	1,211	1,737	2,056
Total uses of working capital	1,657	1,659	3,760	3,299	4,039
Net increase (decrease) in working capital	1,326	(835)	(144)	666	2,981
Changes in Working Capital Composition					
Changes in short-term debt	327	1,918	(1,501)	1,660	(272)
Changes in accounts payable					
Trade	201	807	(695)	249	1,186
Intercompany	(13)	125	(112)	12	25
Changes in miscellaneous liabilities	(52)	222	626	(94)	439
Changes in accrued taxes	33	(34)	870	(706)	(179)
Less: Changes in accounts receivable					
Trade	632	1,763	(1,285)	1,591	1,465
Intercompany	41	83	(49)	0	60
Changes in inventory	312	2,427	(2,551)	1,639	1,271
Changes in prepayments	54	(122)	183	182	(76)
	(543)	(1,113)	2,890	(2,291)	(1,521)
Less change in cash	783	(1,948)	2,746	(1,625)	1,460
	(1,326)	835	144	(666)	(2,981)

members' paychecks. In the government sector the deficit was approaching the size of the U.S. deficit, although Italy's GNP was only about one-ninth of the United States' GNP. Companies' attempts to modernize their plants to increase productivity had run into difficulties in the capital markets: It was claimed often that government borrowings were crowding out private interests. In fact, many industries now looked to the government to help them.

Basic economic data for Italy are displayed in Exhibit J.5.

EXHIBIT J.5 Marwick-Italy: Economic Data

	1974	1975	1976	1977	1978	1978 First Quarter	Second Quarter	Third Quarter	Fourth Quarter
Exchange Rate									
(liras per $, end of period)	649.43	683.55	875.00	871.55	829.75	852.50	854.55	828.50	829.75
Interest, Prices, Production				*[% or Index Numbers (1975 = 100)]*					
Discount rate (end of period)	8.00	6.00	15.00	11.50	10.50	11.50	11.50	10.50	10.50
Govt. bond yield (long-term)	9.87	11.54	13.08	14.62	13.70	14.08	13.80	13.43	13.47
Share prices	134.7	100.0	82.4	66.5	67.4	60.8	61.7	70.0	76.9
Wholesale prices	92.2	100.0	123.8	144.3	156.4	151.5	155.7	157.8	161.4
Wages (contractual)	78.1	100.0	120.9	154.3	179.3	170.2	175.7	182.4	188.8
Industrial production, seas adt.	110.1	100.0	112.4	113.6	115.9	114.5	113.6	114.1	121.1
Industrial employment	99.9	100.0	98.6	99.6	98.6	98.4	98.1	100.0	98.1
Government Finance			*Billions of Liras; Year Ending December 31*						
Deficit (−) or surplus	−8,961	−16,523	−14,707	−22,531	−34,090	−10,683	−5,769	−5,964	−11,674
Financing: Net borrowing (liras)	8,940	16,487	14,666	22,454	33,630	10,643	5,641	5,910	11,436
Net borrowing (foreign currency)	3	9	2	28	311	16	95	10	190
National Accounts		*Billions of Liras: Quarterly Data Seasonally Adjusted at Annual Rates*							
Gross domestic product	110,719	125,378	156,657	190,083	222,369	208,000	216,964	225,672	238,840
Gross domestic product (1975 prices)	130,110	125,378	132,740	135,259	138,738	136,840	137,420	138,369	142,325
Balance of Payments				*Millions of SDRs*					
Trade balance	−7,075	−956	−3,671	−122	2,318	150	862	501	805
Current account	−6,679	−465	−2,463	2,098	5,076	315	1,424	1,992	1,345
Basic balance	−5,640	313	−2,199	2,964	6,142	356	1,716	2,261	1,809
Total change in reserves	770	2,504	−1,973	−5,318	−2,945	415	−1,869	−617	−874
Conversion rates: liras per SDR	782.1	792.7	960.9	1,030.2	1,062.5	1,052.0	1,057.6	1,059.5	1,080.7

SOURCE: International Monetary Fund, *International Financial Statistics* and *Balance of Payments Statistics*, various issues.

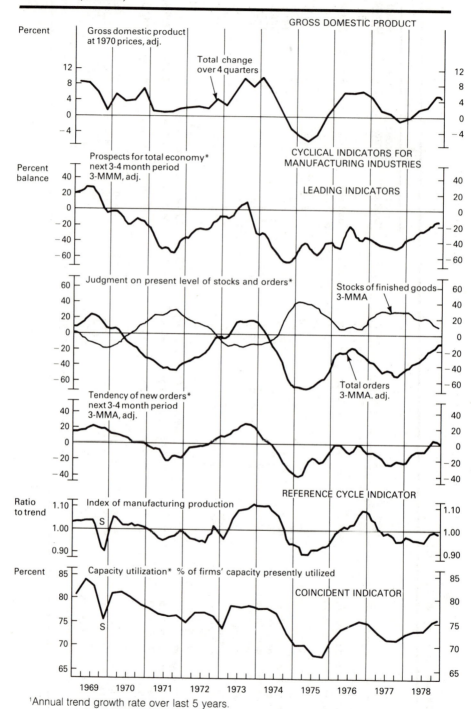

¹Annual trend growth rate over last 5 years.

SOURCE: Institute Nazionale per io Delia Congiuntura.

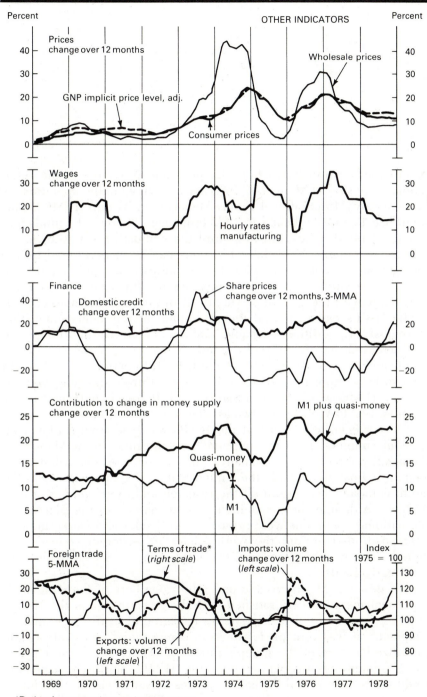

OTHER INDICATORS

Prices
change over 12 months

Wholesale prices

GNP implicit price level, adj.

Consumer prices

Wages
change over 12 months

Hourly rates
manufacturing

Finance

Share prices
change over 12 months, 3-MMA

Domestic credit
change over 12 months

Contribution to change in money supply
change over 12 months

M1 plus quasi-money

Quasi-money

M1

Foreign trade
5-MMA

Terms of trade*
(*right scale*)

Imports: volume
change over 12 months
(*left scale*)

Index
1975 = 100

Exports: volume
change over 12 months
(*left scale*)

1969 1970 1971 1972 1973 1974 1975 1976 1977 1978

*Ratio of export prices to import prices.
**N-NMA = N-Month Moving Average

SOURCE: *OECD Main Economic Indicators*, Dec. 1980, pp. 52–53.

MANUCRAFT,
INC. (A)

IN MID-1981, Armin Bernschot, vice-president in charge of the International Division of Manucraft, Inc., began reviewing the operations of the company's International Funds Management Group (IFMG). This group had been established in 1977 to manage Manucraft's funds outside the United States and to control the company's exposure to exchange risk. Before 1977 these functions had been performed by the finance managers of the individual subsidiaries under policy guidance from the treasury office at the company's headquarters in San Francisco. However, the growth of Manucraft in international markets during the 1970s had increased the magnitude of this management job enormously. In addition, exchange rate fluctuations during this period had increased the difficulty of the task. Thus, in 1977 the IFMG was established as a separate entity within the International Division. In order to have more immediate access to the European exchange markets, the IFMG was located in Switzerland. Its personnel comprised a manager, Guido Wehrli, and two assistants.

The special attention that the IFMG received from senior management stemmed from the importance of its function at Manucraft. Manucraft was a cash-rich company. A major source of this cash was the company's business outside the United States. The major user was the parent company, which did all the research and development of new products. Although they contained several manufacturing plants, the international operations were primarily a vast sales and marketing network positioned around the world. Sales to customers outside the United States were approaching 50% of the company's worldwide sales in the early 1980s.

In general, Mr. Bernschot and other members of the company's senior management were satisfied with the performance of the IFMG. However, given senior management's background in research and development, it was difficult for them to comprehend and evaluate the specialized nature of the group's functions. There was almost a fear that if something was wrong with the IFMG, senior management would not notice it until the consequences became painfully obvious.[1]

---

[1] One of the sources of concern to senior management, the group's trading activity, was described in the case titled "IFMG's Daily Trading Operations," in Chapter 7.

On paper, the operations of the IFMG appeared to be tightly controlled. Still, in spite of this control system, Mr. Bernschot was not certain that the IFMG was achieving the objectives set for the group or even whether these objectives made any sense. Further, he was not sure that the policies imposed on the group were appropriate for this type of operation, or consistent with its objectives. Were these objectives optimal? Was there anything dangerous in this operation? Could anything be improved?

THE OPERATIONS OF THE IFMG

Objectives

The objectives of the IFMG had been explicitly defined when the IFMG was created. These objectives were: (1) to protect the company against exchange losses on monetary assets and liabilities; and (2) to maximize earnings on funds held by the IFMG. However, management had specifically stated that from these two objectives the primary one was the protection of the dollar value of monetary assets and liabilities—the balance sheet accounts translated at current exchange rates according to the accounting rules applicable at the time.[2] Fluctuations in exchange rates affected the dollar book values of these accounts, and these changes in value had to be included in the income statement of the parent company as exchange losses or gains. When the amounts of such gains or losses were significant, they also had to be disclosed in a separate line in the published financial statements.

Acceptance of Exposures

Although avoiding exchange losses had top priority, it was recognized that there were trading profits to be made in certain cases if all exposures were not systematically covered—that is, profits could be made from anticipating exchange market moves or changes in interest rate differentials. Hence, the IFMG was allowed to decide, within lim-

---

[2]See Financial Accounting Standards Board, Statement No. 8, usually referred to as FAS 8. Although Manucraft expected this translation rule to be changed in the near future (an exposure draft issued by the Board with a new translation method was in circulation at the time), there was sufficient uncertainty as to what this new method would be, and when the change in method would become effective, that Manucraft decided to continue using FAS 8 as its basic definition of exposure until the Financial Accounting Standards Board finally pronounced what the new accounting principles were to be.

its set by corporate management, whether to cover an exposure either totally, or in part, or not at all.

In theory, the exposure limits allowed to the IFMG were set by corporate management. However, in practice, it was the manager of the IFMG, Mr. Guido Wehrli, who set the limits. Changes in limits were always reported to, and often discussed with, senior management. But these changes had always been initiated by the IFMG.

The exposure limits were set for each currency separately and were determined by many factors. According to Mr. Wehrli, these factors included: (1) whether a given currency was appreciating or depreciating against the U.S. dollar and the confidence in the duration of the trend; (2) the existence of previous exchange gains in a currency, which could be used to offset possible future losses or whether losses had been realized already; and (3) the size of the initial exposure in a currency, before hedging. Generally, if a currency was expected to appreciate, limits were increased for that currency; when losses were realized, however, limits were reduced without regard to expectations. In any case, the overall size of the exposure limits in each currency was constrained to a magnitude considered easy to liquidate should the need arise.

Hedging Undesirable Exposures

Once the maximum exposure desired in a currency was determined, any excess over this maximum had to be hedged. From the earlier days of IFMG a general policy had emerged in which any exposure covered was hedged in the money market using commercial bank deposits and borrowings. No forward contracts were used in the hedging operation. Exchange losses sustained on several forward exchange contracts in 1977 had tainted this hedging tool as "speculative" in the eyes of the senior management.

Given Manucraft's net asset position in most currencies, the hedging operations then consisted of borrowing the foreign currency, converting it to U.S. dollars, and investing the dollar proceeds. The cost of this hedging operation was the rate of interest paid on the borrowed funds less the rate of interest earned on the dollar investment. The manager of the IFMG always tried to obtain interbank rates for these hedging transactions, but this was not always possible. When interbank rates could not be obtained, the IFMG had to deal at the corporate rates available to prime borrowers. (Corporate management limited the size of the account that Manucraft could maintain with any one bank. This factor limited the profitability which some banks saw in the Manucraft account and therefore the rates at which these banks were willing to deal with Manucraft.)

Maturity of Borrowings and Investments

The maturity of borrowings and investments conducted for hedging purposes had an upper bound of 6 months set by corporate policy. Behind this policy was the need for the IFMG to remit cash to the parent at the parent's request without much advance notice. Although the average size of the pool of funds managed by the IFMG was fairly constant, the average turnover period was very short and the IFMG felt it should be able to meet any cash demand without loss on its investment. However, this position restricted the IFMG's ability to maximize interest income.

Given the 6-month constraint, the maturity decision for borrowings was then based on the fact that, traditionally, shorter maturities carry a lower interest rate than longer-term maturities. This consideration had led to borrowings with an average maturity of about 2 months. For investments, expected interest rates were compared to current interest rates. If interest rates were expected to rise, as had been the case recently, the tactic was to invest in very short maturities. This had led to an investment portfolio with maturities of less than 60 days. If interest rates were expected to decline, longer-maturity investments were investigated.

Tax Management

The management of the tax implications of IFMG operations was straightforward. All of the IFMG operations were performed and booked in Switzerland and taxed accordingly. The depreciation of the U.S. dollar against the Swiss franc in the 1970s had meant large losses for tax purposes in Switzerland. However, the strengthening of the U.S. dollar since mid-1980 had reversed the tax losses.

Intercompany Accounts Management

The IFMG was at the apex of a highly centralized international financial system in Manucraft. A large amount of intercompany trade gave rise to equally large amounts of intercompany billings and cash transfers. In Manucraft's cash management system, the manufacturing units transferred to the IFMG the accounts receivable owed to them by the marketing subsidiaries. This gave the IFMG control of funds to be received in the near future. The IFMG then paid interest to the marketing subsidiaries on prepayments and charged interest to them for delays in payment. The IFMG could direct a subsidiary either to advance or to delay payments in order to take advantage of local rates not accessible to outsiders such as the IFMG. However, in practice this was rarely done.

The currency denomination of the receivables transferred from the manufacturing units to the IFMG was the currency of the country where the buyer was located. However, 40% of the cost content of goods sold outside the United States was composed of materials that the European manufacturing plants purchased from the parent company.

This sophisticated system of intercompany funds management was restricted to Manucraft's foreign operations. The IFMG did not have any control over the parent company's flow of funds.

CONTROL OF IFMG OPERATIONS

The IFMG submitted weekly reports to senior management. These reports included the following: (1) cash balances by currency; (2) cash balances by subsidiary; (3) net monetary assets by currency; (4) conversion gains and losses; (5) net exchange gains and losses; (6) cash and borrowings by banking group; and (7) forecast net monetary assets by currency. Sample forms of this weekly report are presented in Exhibits K.1–K.7. Much of the information reported weekly was summarized and submitted monthly by telex. Finally, the manager of the IFMG made presentations to a supervisory committee on a semiannual basis.

EXHIBIT K.1   Manucraft (A):   Weekly Report—Cash Balances by Currency as of Dec. 30, 19xx
              (in thousand dollars)

Currency	Cash	Average Interest Rate	Borrowings	Average Interest Rate	Net Cash
U.S. dollar	86,048	17.2	—	—	86,048
French franc	4,412	12.9	26,052	11.4	(21,640)
German mark	4,372	9.2	11,296	13.0	(6,924)
Italian lira	2,892	17.5	3,990	17.9	(1,098)
Japanese yen	12,108	9.9	16,434	10.4	(4,326)
Pound sterling	27,206	16.7	—	—	27,206
Swiss franc	12,308	6.0	—	—	12,308
Others	13,648	5.0	41,450	16.6	(27,802)
Total	162,994	11.8	99,222	13.9	63,772
Month-to-date (equal weights)		11.9		14.1	

EXHIBIT K.2 Manucraft (A): Weekly Report—Cash Balances by Subsidiary as of Dec. 30, 19xx *(in thousand dollars)*

Subsidiary	Cash	Borrowings	Net Cash	Past Week Interest Income	Past Week Interest Expense	Past Week Net Interest Income
France	72	7,630	(7,558)	—	15.0	(15.0)
Germany	3,994	—	3,994	4.0	—	4.0
Italy	2,094	—	2,094	6.0	—	6.0
Japan	13,488	—	13,488	17.3	—	17.3
Switzerland	106,322	85,888	20,434	170.0	199.2	(29.2)
United Kingdom	19,454	—	19,454	53.2	—	53.2
Others	17,570	5,704	11,866	42.0	56.3	(14.3)
Total	162,994	99,222	63,772	292.5	270.5	22.0
Month-to-date				1,856.9	1,762.3	94.6

EXHIBIT K.3 Manucraft (A): Weekly Report—Net Monetary Assets by Currency *(in thousand dollars)*

Currency	End of November 19xx	Subsidiary Operations	IFMG Actions	As of December 19xx	Retranslated at Current Rate	Translation Gain or (Loss) Before Tax
U.S. dollar	133,496	(23,098)	(1,880)	108,518	108,518	—
Yen	10,454	5,600	(2,790)	13,264	13,264	—
Sterling	(480)	248	5,270	5,038	4,794	(244)
German mark	9,180	11,200	(12,854)	7,526	7,100	(426)
Swiss franc	10,224	(6,400)	3,406	7,230	6,644	(586)
French franc	(9,108)	8,000	2,636	1,528	1,482	(46)
Lira	584	1,100	—	1,684	1,676	(8)
Others	(3,118)	9,580	6,062	12,524	12,366	(158)
Total	151,232	6,230	(150)	157,312	155,844	(1,468)

EXHIBIT K.4 Manucraft (A): Weekly Report—Conversion Gains (Losses) for the Month of December 19xx *(in thousand dollars)*

TYPE OF TRANSACTION		Amounts Involved During the Period	Conversion Gain or (Loss)
Currency Bought	Currency Sold		
U.S. dollar	German mark	6,914	(239.4)
German mark	U.S. dollar	5,304	195.6
Sterling	U.S. dollar	5,272	102.6
U.S. dollar	Japanese yen	8,860	98.0
Japanese yen	U.S. dollar	6,166	(22.2)
Swiss franc	U.S. dollar	3,212	139.6
U.S. dollar	Swiss franc	3,744	(108.4)
French franc	Swiss franc	1,650	(39.8)
French franc	U.S. dollar	1,650	23.2
Others	Others	32,268	0.8
		75,040	150.0

EXHIBIT K.5 Manucraft (A): Weekly Report—Net Exchange Gains and Losses by Subsidiary *(in thousand dollars)*

Subsidiary	Conversion Results Since End November	Translation Results Basis December 30	Total Exchange Gain or (Loss) Before Tax	Tax Effects Conversions Results	Tax Effects Translation Results	Total Tax Effects	Net Exchange Gain or (Loss)
France	2	(192)	(190)	—	8	8	(182)
Germany	(10)	248	238	4	32	36	274
Italy	—	(4)	(4)	—	(2)	(2)	(6)
Japan							
Switzerland	232	(868)	(636)	(88)	(604)	(692)	(1,328)
United Kingdom	410	172+260	842	(212)	108	(104)	738
Manucraft Corp.	(394)	(444)	(838)	82	82	82	(756)
Others	(90)	(380)	(470)	44	36	80	(390)
Total	150	(1,208)	(1,058)	(252)	(340)	(592)	(1,650)

EXHIBIT K.6 Manucraft (A): Weekly Report—Cash and Borrowings by Banking Group as of Dec. 30, 19xx *(in thousand dollars)*

	CASH, MARKETABLE SECURITIES			BORROWINGS			
Banking Group	Maturities 0–60 days	Maturities 61 days or more	Total	Maturities 0–60 days	Maturities 61 days or more	Total	Total Net Exposure
A	12,290	4,000	16,290	28,272	—	28,272	(11,982)
B	17,274	7,000	24,274	22,186	—	22,186	2,088
C	30,696	824	31,520	6,152	3,090	9,242	22,278
D	3,694	—	3,694	—	—	—	3,694
E	10,530	3,000	13,530	7,450	6,652	14,102	(572)
F	9,058	—	9,058	—	—	—	9,058
G	4,762	—	4,762	—	—	—	4,762
Others	47,042	12,824	59,866	19,238	6,182	25,420	34,446
Total	135,346	27,648	162,994	83,298	15,924	99,222	63,772

EXHIBIT K.7   Manucraft (A):   Weekly Report—Forecast Monetary Assets by Currency
(in thousand dollars)

Currency	Exposure as of Dec. 30, 19xx	Forecast of Exposure Generation by Operations for Dec. 30, 19xx to Jan. 30, 19xx	Exposure Forecast for Jan. 30, 19xx
Yen	13,264	3,000	16,264
Sterling	5,038	2,000	7,038
German mark	7,526	6,000	13,526
Swiss franc	7,230	6,000	13,230
French franc	1,528	5,600	7,128
Lira	1,684	1,400	3,084
Others	12,524	24,000	36,524

12

Financial Policy in the Multinational Enterprise

WHEN WE DISCUSSED cash management problems and the financing of international trade we noted how we could provide the required financing and reduce the exchange risk simultaneously. We also showed how financing options have exchange risk implications, and how exchange risk decisions have financing implications. The fact is that the problem of financing a business and managing its exchange risk are so intimately related that they must be handled simultaneously in a coherent financial policy.

At the center of financial policy in a multinational enterprise must be the stance of management toward exchange risk. The cost of the raw material of financial decisions—money—is defined in terms of interest rate and exchange risk. All financing decisions affect the exposure of the business to exchange risk and they should be made within the framework of an overall exchange risk policy. Of course, the disposition of exchange risk remaining after financing decisions must be governed by the same policy.

The posture of management toward exchange risk in a given company depends on two major factors. One element is management's perception of the degree of efficiency in the financial markets. The other factor is management's evaluation of the impact of exchange rate fluctuations on the business. We now explore the types of financial policies that are consistent with alternative types of financial markets and present a framework for analyzing the decisions taken under alternative policies.

MARKET EFFICIENCY AND FINANCIAL POLICY

The aspect of market efficiency of greatest interest to management trying to decide upon a financial policy is that market's ability to incorporate all available information into the observed market prices. To the extent that a market succeeds in doing this, market prices will contain the best available forecast about future rates. At one extreme, the financial officer may think that he or she is unable to generate forecasts that are consistently superior to the market's forecast, regardless of how inaccurate these forecasts are; alternatively, the financial officer may feel capable of generating forecasts that are consistently superior to those of the market.

Efficient Financial Markets

In these markets all the available information is promptly acted upon and reflected in the observed market rates. As the many operators in the market try to take advantage of the change in expectations that any new information conveys, market rates fluctuate to incorporate this information. Under these conditions, the *expected* cost of borrowing in one currency or another one is the same; and the *expected* value of any exchange position is the same whether covered or not covered. In terms of *expected* values over the long term, the financial officer should be indifferent between choosing one financial policy or a different one—their *expected* costs would be the same.

However, over the short term, some financial policies can provide more certainty than others. Raising funds in the same currency as the one that will be available to repay the debt locks in the cost of the debt and reduces exposure to exchange risk. Covering the exposure to exchange risk remaining in that currency locks in an exchange rate at which foreign currency may be converted into the base currency. Over the long term (after we take into account the variability in interest rates available to refinance the debt and in forward rates available to renew the exposure cover), the expected cost of this financial policy would be the same as the cost of alternative policies. However, over the period encompassed by the known cost of the debt and forward cover, we will have reduced uncertainty about the amount of funds that will be available in the base currency.

On the other hand, as we begin to expand the time horizon of a financial policy of locking in financial rates, another risk begins to increase—namely, we are increasingly less able to anticipate the level and variability of the operating cash flows generated by the business. A policy of long-term debt may find us with borrowed funds that the business does not need; a policy of long-term forward contracts may find us with contracts covering exposures which never developed and which now produce a net exchange position. Thus, the elimination of financial uncertainty through long-term financial rates is limited by our ability to predict operating cash flows with any degree of certainty. The maximum reduction in uncertainty is achieved by matching the maturity of the debt and the forward contracts with the maturity of the operating cash flows they finance and protect against exchange risk.

In efficient financial markets the costs associated with the policy of short-term risk minimization are produced by institutional factors. On the borrowing side, even if the interbank interest differentials are unbiased estimates of future exchange rate fluctuations, the credit premium that the borrower pays in each currency may vary because of factors such as banking regulations. If in order to minimize exchange exposure, the company must pay a higher credit premium in one currency than in another, this additional premium is a cost of the strategy. In the exchange markets the spread between bid and ask price is often larger for forward rates than for spot rates. If we leave a positive exchange exposure open, the foreign currency will be sold eventually in the spot market; if we cover the exposure, we sell the currency in the forward market. Although over the long term the forward rate may be an unbiased predictor of future spot rates, in this situation a policy of always covering exposures in the forward market will cost more than leaving the exposures open, due to the premium paid to purchase the base currency in the forward market instead of the spot market.

The financial manager will want to ask whether fixing the financing costs at a known interest rate and eliminating exchange risk over the following year is worth paying X amount. Even if the financial manager truly believes in the efficiency of financial markets, paying ½% or 1% to lock a financing cost over the short term may not appear inordinate. That percentage is comparable to many of the fees paid to commercial banks in regular short-term transactions, such as discounting of export bills.

In the efficient market we have assumed in this section, it will also make sense to analyze the financing needs and exposures of the business in terms of their effects on a portfolio of currencies. Applying to currencies the concepts of portfolio theory developed in the context of the stock market, we can see the risk or variability of a currency value as having two components. One component is the so-called *systematic risk*, which is determined by the fluctuations in overall economic activity. The other component is the so-called *unsystematic risk*, which is specific to the conditions in the given currency. Systematic risk cannot be diversified in a portfolio; however, unsystematic risk can be diversified.

Taking into account the risk characteristics of each currency, we can build a series or *frontier of efficient portfolios* which minimizes risk for the given return or maximizes return for the given amount of risk (refer to the PP' curve in Exhibit 12.1). If we introduce a *market line* which at zero exchange risk produces the return in the home currency and which has a slope tangent to the frontier of efficient portfolios, we can define a *market portfolio* at that point of tangency (point X in Exhibit 12.1). In that portfolio the currencies whose returns are more positively correlated with the returns of the market portfolio have a smaller representation than currencies with less positive, or negative, correlation with the market.

The definition of the market portfolio also provides an instrument for choosing the proportion of the market portfolio and the home currency in the overall portfolio of the firm. The final return-exchange risk position of the firm will lie on the market line and have a specific combination of the market portfolio of currencies and the home currency. Given that the firm generates operating cash flows in the currencies in

EXHIBIT 12.1   Efficient Portfolios and Market Portfolio for Currencies

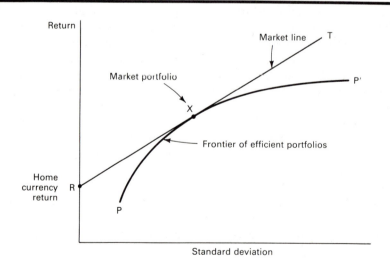

which it does business, to obtain the market portfolio we will borrow currencies in which the operating cash flows generate a proportion of funds higher than the one recommended by the market portfolio, and invest in the currencies in which the firm generates a proportion of cash flows lower than in the market portfolio. Once the market portfolio is obtained through this process, additional financing needs will be met by borrowing funds in different currencies in the proportions of these currencies in the market portfolio. If management prefers an exposure to exchange risk lower than the one offered by the market portfolio, it can reach such position by selling the currencies in the market portfolio against the home currency and moving along the segment RX of the market line (Exhibit 12.1). In the portion XT of the market line, the company will borrow base currency to finance foreign operations.[1]

In order to apply this portfolio approach to exposure management and financing decisions, we must have a matrix of variances and covariances among all the relevant currencies so we can define the optimum currency market portfolio. In addition, the application of this theory requires that this matrix remain constant over the relevant period and that the distribution of interest rates and exchange rates be normally distributed.[2]

Inefficient Financial Markets

If the analyst believes that his or her judgment or access to information is superior to the market's, then the analyst's expected cost of borrowing will be different in each currency and exchange exposures will have a different value, depending on whether they are covered or not. The final policy will depend on an evaluation of the tradeoff between the reduction in uncertainty accomplished by financial policies designed to minimize exchange risk, and the additional costs in terms of expected currency rates which such a strategy involves.

As an illustration, assume the following situation:

Market Rates
Interest rates: Currency A = 8%; currency B = 13%
Forward rates: Currency A carries a forward premium
                        Currency B carries a forward discount } of 5%.

Implied currency forecast: Currency A will appreciate by 5% against currency B.
Analyst's Currency Forecast   Currency A will appreciate by 2% against currency B.

---

[1]A mathematical explanation of these concepts is presented in the discussion of capital budgeting within the capital asset pricing model, in Chapter 16.

[2]This approach to exposure management is utilized in John H. Makin, "Portfolio Theory and the Problem of Foreign Exchange Risk," *Journal of Finance*, May 1978, pp. 517–534.

There is a discrepancy between market rates and the financial analyst's forecast. From the analyst's perspective, the market rates overvalue currency A and undervalue currency B. In purely speculative terms, the analyst would expect to profit from selling currency A and buying currency B at current market rates.

With currency A as the base currency, the effective cost of funds expected by the analyst is 8% for currency A and 11% for currency B. The market expects the cost of both currencies to be 8%. A cost-minimization strategy, given the analyst's forecast, dictates borrowing all the needed funds in currency A and no borrowings in currency B. An exchange risk-minimization strategy dictates borrowing both currency A and currency B in the amounts required for financing in each currency. In this decision, the relevant tradeoff is between the increased stability of net returns (after financing charges) achieved by borrowing currency B and the expected additional 3% cost of borrowing in that currency (the 5% depreciation of currency B expected by the market less the 2% depreciation expected by the analyst).

In this scenario the analyst would want to cover any positive exchange exposure in currency A and any negative exchange exposure in currency B. Covering a positive exposure in currency A (negative in currency B) can be done at 5% in the analyst's favor. It is necessary to sell currency A at a forward premium of 5% and buy currency B at a 5% forward discount. The 5% premium on currency A (discount on currency B) locks in an exchange rate which is superior to the spot rate the analyst expects at the end of the period—a 2% appreciation of currency A (depreciation of currency B).

The covering of negative exchange exposures in currency A and positive exposures in currency B has a real economic cost in the analyst's view. To cover these exposures it is required to buy currency A in the forward market at a 5% premium and sell currency B at a 5% discount. This locks in an exchange rate which is inferior to the one the analyst expects to prevail in the market at the end of the period. Leaving these exposures open, the analyst expects to pay only 2% in exchange cost at the end of the period, as compared to the 5% that can be locked in with the forward rate. The analyst's decision involves a tradeoff between the increased short-term certainty gained with a covered position and the economic cost of 3% for obtaining that certainty.

A financial policy designed to articulate the desire to constrain both exchange risk and financing costs in inefficient financial markets is to limit the exposure acceptable in each currency. Limits could be set in terms of a given percentage of operating profits; for example, the exposure in any currency may not exceed an amount such that if the maximum likely depreciation of that currency takes place, the exchange loss will not exceed a given percentage of operating profits generated in that currency.[3] Under this policy, financing needs will be met in the currencies available to meet the repayment of the debt until the exposure is brought down to the desired limit. If the financing needs are met and the exposure in a currency is still above the acceptable limit, then forward contracts will be used to bring the exposure in that currency within that limit. If the exposure limit in a currency is reached before all the financing needs are met, the remaining financing will be made in the currency with the lowest expected cost.

An alternative policy, which should produce similar results, involves meeting financing needs in the lowest-cost currency and then covering exchange risk in the various currencies to bring the exposures within acceptable limits. To the extent that the amount of forward cover is less than or equal to the amount of financing in a currency, the forward cover in fact reverses the financing decision from borrowing in the low-cost currency to borrowing in the currencies in which the exposures originally appeared. The net cost of this financing is the interest rate in the low-cost currency plus the forward premium or discount of the currency borrowed against the currency with the original exposure. This should be equal to the cost of borrowing the currency in which the original exposure occurs. On the basis of transaction costs, we would consider this double-transaction approach to borrowing in a currency to be inferior to borrowing directly in that currency. However, market inefficiencies in some currencies (such as credit market controls) can make the cost of the interest rate in a foreign currency plus a forward cover to be less than the interest rate alone in that currency.

RISK ANALYSIS OF ALTERNATIVE FINANCIAL POLICIES

We have specified the characteristics of financial markets and developed financial policies consistent with that specification. If we are not so sure about the efficiency of financial markets we will want to evaluate each financial policy according to the results it may produce under alternative market scenarios without committing to any financial policy over the long term.

---

[3]The exposure limit in one currency will be determined by solving for "Acceptable exposure" in the following equation:

$$\text{Exchange loss} = \text{Acceptable exposure} \times \text{Maximum likely devaluation}$$

Although a large variety of financial policies could be specified, we will concentrate here on three specific policies:

1. *Aggressive.* Make the best possible estimate of currency changes and act to minimize the cost of financing. Hedge exchange exposures only when the hedging cost is less than the expected change in currency rates.
2. *Zero-exposure.* Borrow in the currencies in which funds will be generated. Cover any remaining exposures.
3. *Do-nothing.* Finance in the currencies which minimize exposure. Do not cover any remaining exposure.

Steps in the Analysis

In applying this analytical approach, we can follow this sequence of steps:

1. Choose a financial policy. Determine which transactions will answer the three basic problems of the financial officer under that policy:
   (a) In which currencies should excess funds be invested?
   (b) In which currencies should funds be raised to meet financing requirements?
   (c) After questions (a) and (b) are answered, is there anything else to be done to achieve the desired foreign exchange exposure?
2. Establish the returns and costs of the financial transactions initiated under step 1 with a variety of scenarios. For each scenario, disaggregate the costs and returns of financial transactions into three major components:
   (a) Incremental financing
   (b) Remaining exchange exposure
   (c) Hedging undesirable exchange exposures
3. Repeat the analysis presented under steps 1 and 2 for alternative policies.
4. Select a decision criterion or criteria (for example, maximize expected value).
5. Evaluate the impact of each financial policy under alternative rate scenarios.
   (a) How do the policies compare under alternative decision criteria?
   (b) What is the probability of each rate scenario?
   (c) What probabilities of a given rate scenario will render a financial policy unacceptable?

Application of the Analysis

The Initial Data. To analyze the implications of alternative financial policies, we need three major sets of data:

1. The financial needs and exposure positions of the business in different currencies
2. Market interest rates and exchange rates
3. Distribution of future exchange rates at the end of the planning period

As an example, we will consider a U.S. multinational company with three subsidiaries—one located in the United Kingdom, one in the Netherlands, and one in France. These subsidiaries are self-contained within their respective countries. They manufacture their own products and sell them within their country in prices denominated in their national currencies. Exhibit 12.2 presents balance sheet data and a statement of sources and uses of funds for each of the foreign subsidiaries.

The two subsidiaries located in the United Kingdom and in France need temporary financing. The subsidiary in the Netherlands will generate excess funds during the year. Excluding the exchange implications of the financing decision, the accounting exposure in each of the three currencies measured according to FAS 52 is equal to total assets. It is estimated that 100% of the operating profits are exposed to exchange risk in the first year. Necessary adjustments to compensate for an exchange fluctuation can be made thereafter. Thus, the exposure to exchange risk measured in economic terms is equal to operating profits in the first year and there is no exposure thereafter. Since subsidiaries are self-contained within their respective countries and no dividends are planned, there is no transaction exchange exposure in any currency. After we take into account the financing decisions, the increase in borrowings may decrease the exposures measured according to any of the definitions. For the sake of simplicity we will eliminate the possibility of wrong forecasts for operations of the business and proceed as if they were known with certainty.

The other two sets of data needed to evaluate alternative financial policies are the market rates available at the time of the decision and the alternative scenarios of expected exchange rates which will determine the effective interest rates during the period. The upper section of Exhibit 12.3 presents the actual interest rates and exchange rates. The figures for actual rates show that interest rate parity holds in the Euromarkets. In these markets the forward premium or discount of each currency against the dollar approximates the interest rate differential between the two currencies.

The lower sections of Exhibit 12.3 present three different scenarios about developments in exchange rates. Each different assumption about future exchange rates defines a different set of effective interest rates, which are computed here as the algebraic sum of the actual nom-

EXHIBIT 12.2 Actual and Projected Financial Statements by Subsidiary *(in U.S. dollar equivalents at initial exchange rates)*

BALANCE SHEETS TODAY

United Kingdom		Netherlands		France	
Cash 45		Cash 10		Cash 2	
A/R 100		A/R 75		A/R 50	
Inv. 50		Inv. 75		Inv. 50	
P+E 100	Equity 295	P+E 20	Equity 180	P+E 5	Equity 107
295	295	180	180	107	107

FORECAST BALANCE SHEETS 1 YEAR LATER

United Kingdom		Netherlands		France	
Cash 45		Cash 30		Cash 2	
A/R 160	Borrow-	A/R 75		A/R 75	Borrow-
Inv. 90	ings 70	Inv. 75		Inv. 95	ings 50
P+E 100	Equity 325	P+E 20	Equity 200	P+E 5	Equity 127
395	395	200	200	177	177

FORECAST SOURCES AND USES OF FUNDS

	United Kingdom	Netherlands	France
Sources			
Operating profits	30	20	20
Required financing	70	—	50
	100	20	70
Uses			
↑ A/R	60	0	25
↑ Inventories	40	0	45
↑ Cash	0	20	0
	100	20	70

SUMMARY OF FORECAST FLOW OF FUNDS

Excess cash to be invested	Netherlands	20
Funds to be raised	United Kingdom	70
	France	50

EXCHANGE EXPOSURES (EXCLUDING FINANCING)

	Pound sterling	Dutch guilder	French franc
Accounting exposure (FAS 52)	+395	+200	+177
Economic exposure	+30	+20	+20
Transaction exposure	0	0	0

inal interest rate at the beginning of the period and the anticipated exchange rate fluctuation in the given currency.[4] In this example the number of possible exchange rate scenarios has been reduced to the following three:

1. The *most-likely* outcome (the scenario which the decision-maker holds with the highest probability)

---

[4]This method ignores the impact of exchange rate fluctuations on interest payments.

EXHIBIT 12.3   Actual and Anticipated Market Rate Scenarios

	US$	Pound sterling (£)	Dutch guilder (Hfl)	French franc (FF)
ACTUAL FOREIGN EXCHANGE AND MONEY MARKET RATES				
Spot rates		$2.3820/£	Hfl2.6275/$	FF4.6925/$
Forward 1-year rates		$3.3025/£	Hfl2.6095/$	FF4.9525/$
Forward premium (discount) against US $		−3.3%	+0.7%	−5.5%
Interest rates (1- year)				
Euromarket	12.5%	16.5%	11.7%	17.5%
Domestic	9.0%	14.0%	12.5%	14.0%
ANTICIPATED EXCHANGE RATE SCENARIOS AND EFFECTIVE INTEREST RATES				
Most-Likely Scenario				
Spot rates 1 year later		$2.20/£	Hfl2.50/$	FF4.80/$
Forecast % revaluation		−7.6%	+4.8%	−2.3%
Effective interest rates				
Euromarket	12.5%	8.9% (16.5 − 7.6)	16.5% (11.7 + 4.8)	15.2% (17.5 − 2.3)
Domestic	9.0%	6.4% (14.0 − 7.6)	17.3% (12.5 + 4.8)	11.7% (14.0 − 2.3)
No-Change Scenario				
Spot rates 1 year later—same as actual market rates				
Effective interest rates—same as actual market rates				
Opposite-to-Likely Scenario				
Spot rates 1 year later		$2.50/£	Hfl2.65/$	FF4.60/$
Forecast % revaluation		+5.0%	−0.9%	+2.0%
Effective interest rates				
Euromarket	12.5%	21.5% (16.5 + 5.0)	10.8% (11.7 − 0.9)	19.5% (17.5 + 2.0)
Domestic	9.0%	19.0% (14.0 + 5.0)	11.6% (12.5 − 0.9)	16.0% (14.0 + 2.0)

2. *No-change* from the current spot rates
3. Outcomes *opposite-to* the *most-likely* scenario anticipated

Since there is a simplifying assumption of a 1-year planning horizon, only the spot rates at the end of the period are needed. Interest
rates and forward rates for multiple horizons would be relevant if the
firm's manager were thinking in terms of sequential financing.

It should be noticed that if the probability distributions of future
exchange rates are normal, then the *most-likely scenario* anticipated in
this example differs from the one imbedded in current rates. In every
case the forecast spot rate is different from the current forward rate.
With normal distributions of future spot rates this would imply the
manager's belief in his or her ability to make forecasts which are superior to those made by the market, presumably because of market
inefficiencies. On the other hand, if the probability distributions of fu-

ture spot rates are not normal, the outcome which the manager expects with the highest probability (the distribution's mode) is typically not the same as the expected value or average reflected in market rates.

As we will show later, in order to reach a final decision we will have to assign probabilities to each of these market scenarios. The probability assignments will reveal the shape of the distributions envisaged by the decision-maker. Also, in a more comprehensive application of risk analysis, the various scenarios would each include a complete set of probability distributions. However, the analysis of a limited number of possibilities is considerably simpler and in many cases may be sufficient to identify the major implications of alternative strategies.

Implications of Alternative Financial Policies. The next step involves an assessment of the costs and returns of each financial policy under each rate scenario formulated previously. As we have suggested, it is useful to separate the implications of each of the components of the financial decision into: (1) financing itself; (2) residual exposure; and (3) hedging of the residual exposure. In principle, management may have a different attitude toward exchange risk involved in financing and exchange risk in the value of the subsidiary. Evaluation of a financing policy along these lines facilitates the development of alternative policies which management may eventually consider to be superior. For example, although management initially may have preferred eliminating all exchange risks, the evaluation of the implications of this policy under the expected market scenario may lead to revising this policy into eliminating exchange risks only in the financing decision.

In the *aggressive policy* the objectives of the financial officer are to invest funds at the highest effective rate expected by the manager and to borrow at the lowest effective rate expected. To choose the expected rate the manager will base his or her decisions on the rates anticipated under the most-likely rate scenario. In our example this means that the domestic pound at a 6.4% cost will be chosen as the source of all funds. If external markets must be used because of exchange controls in the United Kingdom, then Eurosterling will be chosen at an expected cost of 8.9%. This cost compares favorably with the cost of Euroguilders (at 16.5%) and the cost of Eurofrancs (at 15.2%). On the other hand, the domestic guilder provides the best expected return for excess funds (17.3%). If the domestic guilder is not accessible, then the Euroguilder provides the next best return.

If we constrain the problem so that domestic markets can be used only by local subsidiaries, the aggressive policy solves the problem of incremental financing in each subsidiary as follows:

United Kingdom:	− $70	Raise funds in domestic pounds.
Netherlands:	+ $20	Invest the funds in the domestic guilder market.
France:	− $50	Raise funds in Eurosterling.

The costs expected to result from these financing transactions, measured in terms of U.S. dollars, are presented in the upper panel of Exhibit 12.4. If the most-likely outcome indeed takes place, the total financing costs will be $5.47. However, if either of the other two alternative rate scenarios materializes, the financing costs will be higher— $15.55 in the no-change scenario and $21.73 in the opposite-to-likely scenario. Ignoring interest payments, the financing decisions affect the company's exposures to exchange risk as indicated in the accompanying table.

	£	Hfl	FF
Accounting exposure (FAS 52)			
Before financing	+ $395	+ $200	+ $177
Financing	− 120	—	—
After financing	+ $275	+ $200	+ $177
Economic exposure			
Before financing	+ $30	+ $20	+ $20
Financing	− 120	—	—
After financing	− $90	+ $20	+ $20
Transaction exposure			
Before financing	0	0	0
Financing	− $50	—	+ $50
After financing	− $50	0	+ $50

For accounting and economic exposures the financing decisions tend to produce negative or less positive exposures in pounds, and leave the exposures in guilders and francs as they were before financing. For transaction exposures the financing decisions create an exchange position, short in pounds and long in francs, due to the pound financing of the French operation. If we take into account the payment of interest, the exposures would tend to be more negative in pounds and more positive in guilders (the interest earned in the investment); however, to simplify the analysis we will ignore the impact of interest.

In practice, the financial manager will want to observe the effects of exchange exposure according to the various definitions, particularly in cases as the pound in this example in which we have a positive

EXHIBIT 12.4 Costs and Returns of Different Financial Policies under Alternative Rate Scenarios *(in U.S. dollar equivalents at initial exchange rates)*

	SCENARIO		
	Most-Likely	No-Change	Opposite-to-Likely
AGGRESSIVE POLICY			
Incremental Financing			
Borrow $70 in domestic £	−$70 × 6.4% = −$4.48	−$70 × 14.0% = −$9.80	−$70 × 19.0% = −$13.30
Invest $20 in domestic Hfl	+$20 × 17.3% = +$3.46	+$20 × 12.5% = +$2.50	+$20 × 11.6% = +$2.32
Borrow $50 in Euro-£	−$50 × 8.9% = −$4.45	−$50 × 16.5% = −$8.25	−$50 × 21.5% = −$10.75
Total cost (−) or return	−$5.47	−$15.55	−$21.73
Residual Economic Exposure			
£	−$90 × −7.6% = +$6.84	−$90 × 0 = 0	−$90 × +5.0% = −$4.50
Hfl	+$20 × +4.8% = +$0.96	+$20 × 0 = 0	+$20 × −0.9% = −$0.18
FF	+$20 × −2.3% = −$0.46	+$20 × 0 = 0	+$20 × +2.0% = +$0.40
Total cost (−) or return	+$7.34	0	−$4.28
Hedging	0	0	0
Total policy cost (−) or return	+$1.87	−$15.55	−$26.01
ZERO-EXPOSURE POLICY			
Incremental Financing			
Borrow $70 in domestic £	−$70 × 6.4% = −$4.48	−$70 × 14.0% = −$9.80	−$70 × 19.0% = −$13.30
Invest $20 in domestic Hfl	+$20 × 17.3% = +$3.46	+$20 × 12.5% = +$2.50	+$20 × 11.6% = +$2.32
Borrow $50 in domestic FF	−$50 × 11.7% = −$5.85	−$50 × 14.0% = −$7.00	−$50 × 16.0% = −$8.00
Total cost (−) or return	−$6.87	−$14.30	−$18.98
Residual Economic Exposure			
Must be eliminated			
Hedging			
£	−$40 × −3.3% = +$1.32	−$40 × −3.3% = +$1.32	−$40 × −3.3% = +$1.32
Hfl	+$20 × +0.7% = +$0.14	+$20 × +0.7% = +$0.14	+$20 × +0.7% = +$0.14
FF	−$30 × −5.5% = +$1.65	−$30 × −5.5% = +$1.65	−$30 × −5.5% = +$1.65
Total cost (−) or return	+$3.11	+$3.11	+$3.11
Total policy cost (−) or return	−$3.76	−$11.19	−$15.87

Exhibit 12.4 (Continued)

DO-NOTHING POLICY

Incremental Financing

Same decisions as in zero-exposure policy	-$6.87	-$14.30	-$18.98

Residual Economic Exposure

£	-$40 × -7.6% =	+$3.04	-$40 × 0 =	0	-$40 × +5.0% =	-$ 2.00
Hfl	+$20 × +4.8% =	+$0.96	+$20 × 0 =	0	+$20 × -0.9% =	-$ 0.18
FF	-$30 × -2.3% =	+$0.69	-$30 × 0 =	0	-$30 × +2.0% =	-$ 0.60
Total cost (−) or return		+$4.69		0		-$ 2.78

Hedging

	0	0	0

Total policy cost (−) or return	-$2.18	-$14.30	-$21.76

399

exposure when measured in accounting terms and a negative exposure when measured in economic terms. Here, we will proceed with our analysis using only economic exposure. Exhibit 12.4 shows the exchange gains and losses that would be obtained from the residual economic exposure, after financing, under the three rate scenarios envisaged in this analysis. With the most-likely scenario there would be an exchange gain of $7.34; with no change in exchange rates there would not be any exchange gain or loss; and under the opposite-to-likely scenario there would be an exchange loss of $4.28.

The next question is whether any of the remaining exposures should be covered in the exchange markets. With the aggressive policy based on the most-likely scenario, sterling is considered overvalued in the market, and the guilder and the franc are considered undervalued in the market. This means that only positive exposures in sterling and negative exposures in guilders and francs would be covered. Only in these instances would the current forward rate available in the market be more favorable than the spot rates we expect for the end of the period. Since we have a negative exposure in sterling and positive exposures in guilders and francs, the aggressive policy in this case would indicate leaving these exposures uncovered.[5]

It is at this point that the financial manager will want to analyze exchange exposures according to alternative measures. Even though the previous nonhedging decisions are consistent with minimizing financing costs and adopting exposures to exchange risk which are con-

---

[5]An alternative hedging policy which is more aggressive than the one described here would involve trying to generate exchange gains, at least to compensate the exchange losses anticipated from the residual exposure. Of course, this could be extended even more to generate exchange gains, subject only to a maximum limit on acceptable exposure. Limiting ourselves to the expected exchange loss of $0.46 in the franc position, we could generate a position short in sterling and long in guilders that we expect will compensate for this loss. Sterling was chosen for the short position because in this currency we expect a depreciation much larger than the depreciation anticipated by market rates; the long position in guilders is justified by the large appreciation we expect in that currency relative to the market's expectations. To determine the amount of the position required, taking into account the impact of exchange fluctuations on interest, we can use the following formula:

$$\text{Amount of position} = \frac{\text{Expected loss}}{(1 + R_I)(1 + \text{Reval}) - (1 + R_B)(1 - \text{Reval}_B) - 1}$$

where

R_I = Nominal interest rate on currency of investment
R_B = Nominal interest rate on currency borrowed
Reval = Percentage revaluation

Thus,

$$\text{Amount of position} = \frac{0.46}{(1 + 0.117)(1 + 0.048) - (1 + 0.165)(1 - 0.076) - 1} = 0.369$$

sistent with the company's *economic* exposure to exchange risk and the manager's forecast about rates, the manager may want to limit other variables and reverse the previous decisions. A typical situation is provided by the relatively large positive *accounting* exposures to exchange risk in our example. In case of a devaluation of any of those currencies, there would be a reported exchange loss larger than the one calculated following the measurement of exposure in economic terms. Thus, regardless of the economics of the decision, the manager may wish to limit the accounting exposure in such a way that the maximum exchange loss reported in the financial statements does not exceed a certain amount. To achieve this end those currencies will be sold forward in the exchange market.

Ignoring the possibility of engaging in "uneconomic" behavior, we can calculate the total cost of the aggressive financial policy under the three rate scenarios provided here. This total is composed of the cost of meeting the incremental financing needs plus the exchange gains and losses resulting from the remaining exchange exposures. Under the most-likely rate scenario there is a net gain of $1.87; under the no-change scenario there is a net cost of $15.55; and under the opposite-to-likely scenario there is a net loss of $26.01.

The costs and returns of the other two policies are also presented in Exhibit 12.4. Under the zero-exposure policy all the financing needs are met in the currency that will be available to repay the debt or that will be needed later on. The domestic or the Euromarket for each currency is used, depending on which one offers the better rate. In the example, this means borrowing in the domestic sterling and franc markets, and investing in the domestic guilder market. Any remaining exposure is covered in the forward market to eliminate all exchange risks. Under the do-nothing policy the incremental financing needs are met in a fashion that minimizes exposure to exchange risk. This provides the same decisions for financing as the zero-exposure policy. However, under the do-nothing policy any remaining exchange exposure is not covered regardless of market rates and expectations.

Selection of a Financial Policy. Using the preceding figures, we can now compare the total costs and returns of the three financial policies under each of the scenarios. With the most-likely scenario the aggressive policy produces the highest return ($1.87); the other two policies produce a net cost. Under both the no-change and the opposite-to-likely scenarios the lowest costs are obtained with the zero-exposure policy.

The next step is to choose one of the financial policies according to a desired criterion. Here the important variables are management's attitude toward *risk* and the *size* of the funds involved. Thus, management might be willing to gamble on a 50–50 proposition if the sum is $1. The same odds and the same gamble would not be so appealing if the amount involved is $1 million. The principle applies to the corporation as well as to the individual.

Among the criteria that management may use is the selection of the strategy with the highest *expected value* (least cost). To use this expected value decision rule, we need to assign probabilities to each scenario. For example, assign 0.6 to the most-likely alternative, 0.3 to no-change, and 0.1 to the opposite-to-likely scenario. With these probabilities, one can compute the expected value for each policy. Under the aggressive policy, the expected return is

$$0.6 \times (\$1.87) + 0.3 \times (\$15.55) + 0.1 \times (-\$26.01) = -\$6.14$$

Similarly, the expected values for the zero-exposure policy and the do-nothing policy are $-\$7.20$ and $-\$7.77$, respectively. Using expected value as the decision criterion, we would choose the aggressive financing policy.

With expected value as a criterion, another approach is to search for the break-even point at which there must be a "greater-than-$x\%$" expectation for the most-likely scenario for the aggressive policy to dominate, and below which $x\%$ the aggressive policy is no longer dominant. Thus, if the ratio of the probability of no-change scenario to the probability of opposite-to-likely scenario remains at 3 to 1, the strategy which would eventually come to dominate is the zero-exposure strategy. Thus, we can combine these two scenarios into one and solve algebraically for the probability (P) of the most-likely scenario below which the aggressive policy is no longer dominant and the zero-exposure policy comes to dominate. For this purpose we have the following system of simultaneous equations:

Expected value of zero-exposure policy:

$$P \begin{pmatrix} \text{Outcome} \\ \text{of zero-exposure policy} \\ \text{under most-likely} \\ \text{scenario} \end{pmatrix} + (1 - P) \begin{pmatrix} \text{Weighted outcome of} \\ \text{zero-exposure policy} \\ \text{under no-change and} \\ \text{opposite-to-likely} \\ \text{scenarios} \end{pmatrix}$$

Expected value of aggressive policy:

$$P \begin{pmatrix} \text{Outcome} \\ \text{of aggressive policy} \\ \text{under most-likely} \\ \text{scenario} \end{pmatrix} + (1 - P) \begin{pmatrix} \text{Weighted outcome of} \\ \text{aggressive policy under} \\ \text{no-change and} \\ \text{opposite-to-likely} \\ \text{scenarios} \end{pmatrix}$$

Using the results for each of the policies under alternative outcomes, and maintaining the ratio of probabilities of no-change to opposite-to-likely constant at 3 to 1, we can calculate the weighted values. Thus, the weighted outcome of the zero-exposure policy under no-change and opposite-to-likely is

$$\frac{3 \times (-\$11.19) + (-\$15.87)}{4} = -\$12.36$$

and the weighted outcome of "aggressive" under no-change and opposite-to-likely is

$$\frac{3 \times (-\$15.55) + (-\$26.01)}{4} = -\$18.16$$

Substituting in the simultaneous equations, we get:

$$P(-\$3.76) + (1 - P)(-\$12.36)$$
$$P(+\$1.87) + (1 - P)(-\$18.16)$$

These two equations are equal at the break-even point, P. Solving, we get $P = 0.507$. Below this probability of the most-likely outcome, the zero-exposure policy is superior on an expected value basis. In addition to this break-even analysis, management may want to examine other specific sets of probabilities, and review how the tradeoffs vary under alternative policies and different probability assessments.[6]

For the reasons indicated on the preceding $1 versus $1 million gamble, expected value may not be the main criterion. Management might not be willing to live with even a 0.1 probability of a $26.01 loss, which would be possible given an opposite-to-likely outcome under the aggressive strategy. It may be that such a loss would not be tolerated, rendering the expected value of this strategy unimportant.

The analysis of expected values for each policy can be tempered by considering an alternative selection criterion—namely, the range of possible outcomes under each policy. This range is largest for the aggressive policy (in which the outcomes range between +$1.87 and −$26.01) and lowest for the zero-exposure policy (with a range from −$3.76 to −$15.87). If we try to minimize the variability of possible outcomes, we would choose the zero-exposure policy in this case. This measure of variability could be based also on comparison of the standard deviations for each policy.

The final selection of a financial policy will be heavily affected by

---

[6]For further discussion of risk analysis, see Chapter 15.

management's degree of risk aversion. Generally, it is accepted that as risk increases, management requires more than a proportional increase in return or cost reduction. Generally, financial literature measures financial risk in terms of standard deviations. However, the risk aversion of management is likely to be biased in a fashion that a negative deviation is feared much more than a positive deviation of the same magnitude is welcomed. To the extent that this is true, the choice of a financial policy will be heavily influenced by the magnitude and probability of the extreme values the policy can produce—particularly the extreme "bad" outcomes.

Also, we should notice that although we merged interest income and expenses, and exchange gains and losses in the computation of the cost or return of a given financial policy, management appears to treat them differently in practice. Generally, exchange losses are given a greater significance than interest expense of the same magnitude. The financial practice of isolating exchange gains and losses may be responsible for this. It appears that interest expenses are seen as the normal part of doing business, while exchange gains and losses are not considered part of the regular business, but rather the product of "speculation."

SUMMARY

In the first part of this chapter we examined the implications of having efficient financial markets for financial management. In such markets the *expected* costs or returns of alternative policies are the same. However, the manager's risk preferences over the short term, as well as the ability to forecast the firm's cash flows into the future will favor some financial policies over the others. Finally, in efficient markets a portfolio approach to financial management would be possible. The resulting policy would combine the exposure derived from investing in the market portfolio with borrowing or lending in the home currency.

Under the assumption of imperfect financial markets we evaluated three popular exchange policies for dealing with the financial problems that the multinational enterprise faces. Based on effective interest costs from various financing sources, the raising and deployment of funds were assigned a net cost or profit. Then a charge for gains or losses on remaining exposure to exchange risk was inserted. Finally, a charge for hedging certain unacceptable exposure positions was included where what was unacceptable varied depending on the exchange policy under evaluation. The sum of the costs or returns associated with each of these components produced the total cost or return of the specific exchange policy for each outcome in the exchange markets. Implicitly, the sum of these components assumed that $1 of exchange loss is equivalent to $1 of interest cost. In fact, the utility of exchange losses may be different from that of interest. The aggressive strategy was selected from among three strategies examined as the one that minimized the expected cost of the finance function, given assigned probabilities for different eventual states in the foreign exchange markets.

This example has dealt mainly with the short-term financial planning of the international firm, analogous to working capital management in traditional domestic corporation finance. It is useful to contrast this situation with operations in a single domestic environment in which there are generally no problems in providing financing for a given subsidiary if the parent (or the consolidated firm) has surplus cash. When facing international financing, there are limits on the mobility of funds. There are tariff rules which alter the pricing structure that can be used to move funds from subsidiary to subsidiary. There are differential tax considerations. There are absolute limits on the removal of profits and/or cash transfers between firms. There are local borrowing limits. There are exposure complexities. All of these represent restrictions that simply do not apply in the totally domestic operation. Note that even if the consolidated international firm were in total balance, external transactions for the sake of local tax and tariff considerations and the exposure situation would still be required in many cases. There are some parallels in domestic conglomerates, where lenders to a given subsidiary and the decentralized incentive system for local managers influence cash transfers within the family, but these situations are not as constraining as most international examples.

In the preceding example we also followed a preestablished sequence of financial problems. We first solved the problem of providing incremental financing, then evaluated the impact of the residual exposure to exchange risk measured in economic terms, and finally decided whether or not to cover that exposure. An alternative sequence could result in different results, given that the actions under the alternative strategies would be changed. For example, if instead of the sequence used in the preceding example, the initial decision were based on creating a zero exposure in certain currencies, after which funds could be raised or deployed within a subset of the approved (that is, nondevaluation-prone) currencies, then the cost or return results would differ in some cases. In other situations there could be restrictions on quantities of funds that can be invested or borrowed in certain currencies by particular subsidiaries. These outer limits could be built into the analysis, if necessary.

The issue of intercompany transactions among sister companies was avoided, forcing each subsidiary to operate in the open markets without access to the domestic markets of other subsidiaries' national economies. In fact, this assumption could be eased in many organizational settings. The complexity of the analysis would be increased, together with problems of incentives and organizational rewards to the various subsidiary managers whose interests in a given situation would often conflict. The arm's-length guideline is a good operational rule for these transactions. The difficulty arises in dividing any extra savings one subsidiary realizes from having access to the domestic market of another subsidiary. Thus, the transfer price problem encountered in many firms (when one division sells a good to another division, and each division manager seeks a price which will maximize the division's profits) is encountered here as well.

Had the initial balance sheets included some debt for these three subsidiaries, then the firm would also have had the option of changing some of its debt exposure. This could have been done either by changing the currency of the debt or borrowing funds in another currency which then would be converted to the same currency as the existing debt. Either of these options might have been used under the zero-exposure strategy or under possible interpretations of the aggressive strategy. The all-equity assumption in the initial balance sheets is used here for simplicity. If there had been existing debt and the firm was unwilling or unable to make changes in the currency or to borrow additional amounts for conversion to an asset which would offset the existing debt in that currency, then the all-equity assumption is still valid for considering incremental costs and revenues of various strategies under various outcomes.

Ultimately, the computer models suggested here would permit evaluation of a number of alternative strategies considered by management. In addition, mathematical formulations under certainty could optimize strategies given certain cost and revenue functions together with limits on the amount of funds which may be channeled around the firm. These formulations can be run under different expectations about the effective interest cost figures (pivoting on what happens to the various currencies involved), and management can see how the optimum strategy alters with various scenarios. Each formulation provides an optimum under a given scenario. Management could then evaluate each optimum for its return under the alternative scenarios. An expected value weighting system or a complex utility formulation could be introduced to aid management in finding a reasonable strategy for dealing with its currency environment.

Of course, when the one-period model is replaced with a multi-period analysis, the computational difficulties are vastly increased. More serious than the mathematical programming, computer programming, and computer capacity problems are the difficulties in forecasting (1) subsidiary funds flow, (2) currency effective interest rates, and (3) currency spot and forward rates for many periods of varied lengths many years into the future. Although the use of more sophisticated analyses will increase in future years, the practicality of the forecasting is a serious obstacle.

Various mathematical approaches to handling foreign exchange exposure management have been considered for over 15 years. However, Carter and Rodriguez (1978) found that most managers of larger firms (an average of $2 billion in 1976 sales, with about one-third of earnings and assets outside the United States) were aware of the models but were not using them. Of these forty firms, approximately half the international financial officers used computer models. Most of these models, however, were data-gathering and compilation models that permitted "what-if" analysis of alternative outcomes and strategies. None involved mathematical programming. Typically, the models were offered by vendors such as banks as part of a package of international financial services. The managers generally felt that understanding the models was of value because it was a form of training for themselves. They also wanted the vendor for currency forecasts. However, they did not trust the models' tax and other routines, and they felt that if one had reasonable forecasts for rates, it was easy to know what actions to take without recourse to the programming models. In addition, a major complaint was the mass of data required to operate the models and the difficulties of updating inputs to the models. Most managers did not expect increased use of optimization models in the future, although one observed, "Everybody wants a security blanket, and a witch doctor can sell them even if the medicine is no good."

Part Two has reviewed the instruments of foreign trade financing, evaluating the costs of funding as well as the difficulties surrounding the definition of foreign exchange exposure. We have also discussed approaches to controlling and evaluating the local manager. This last chapter has offered a relatively simple approach for combining costs associated with particular exchange policies, evaluating those costs for several popular strategies under alternative outcomes of the world.

Part Three will turn to the problems associated with capital budgeting in the broader sense, analyzing the returns from projects in various nations over a longer period.

QUESTIONS

1. How does a strategy for dealing with foreign exchange risk differ from an outcome?

2. Why might a foreign exchange manager reject a strategy even though he or she concedes it is optimal on an expected value basis?

3. Why may there be different interest rates in the local and the Euro-markets of a given currency? How can a multinational corporation take advantage of these differentials?

4. One multinational firm has a policy of making each subsidiary within a given currency area responsible for its foreign exchange losses. What are some of the costs of this strategy? How would you decide upon a better strategy? What example would you suggest as a more desirable policy for the firm?

5. "I don't care what happens to the currency vis-à-vis our parent's currency. My job is to make a profit here." If the head of your subsidiary in a country with a devaluation-prone currency had this reaction, how would you deal with it?

BIBLIOGRAPHY*

Carter, E. Eugene, and Rita M. Rodriguez, "Foreign Exchange Models: What 40 U.S. Multinationals Think," *Euromoney,* Mar. 1978, pp. 95–111.

Feskoe, Gaffney, "Reducing Currency Risks in a Volatile Foreign Exchange Market," *Management Accounting,* Sept. 1980, pp. 19–24.

Fieleke, Norman S., "Foreign-Currency Positioning by U.S. Firms: Some New Evidence," *Review of Economics and Statistics,* Feb. 1981, pp. 35–42.

Folks, William R., Jr., "The Optimal Level of Forward Exchange Transactions," *Journal of Financial and Quantitative Analysis,* Jan. 1973, pp. 105–110.

Heckerman, Donald, "The Exchange Risk of Foreign Operations," *Journal of Business,* Jan. 1972, pp. 42–48.

Hoyt, Newton H., Jr., "The Management of Currency Exchange Risk by the Singer Company," *Financial Management,* Spring 1972, pp. 13–20.

Jucker, James V., and Clovis deFaro, "The Selection of International Borrowing Sources," *Journal of Financial and Quantitative Analysis,* Sept. 1975, pp. 381–407.

Lietaer, Bernard A., *Financial Management of Foreign Exchange Risk: An Operational Technique to Reduce Risk.* Cambridge, Mass.: MIT Press, 1971.

Makin, John H., "Portfolio Theory and the Problem of Foreign Exchange Risk," *Journal of Finance,* May 1978, pp. 517–34.

Rodriguez, Rita M., "Management of Foreign Exchange Risk in U.S. Multinationals," *Sloan Management Review,* Spring 1978, pp. 31–49.

———, *Foreign Exchange Management in U.S. Multinationals.* Lexington, Mass.: D. C. Heath and Company, 1980.

---

*See also the Bibliography to Chapter 11.

Rutenberg, David P., "Maneuvering Liquid Assets in a Multinational Company," *Management Science,* June 1970, pp. B671–B684.

Schwab, Bernard, and Peter Lusztig, "Apportioning Foreign Exchange Risk through the Use of Third Currencies: Some Questions on Efficiency," *Financial Management,* Autumn 1978, pp. 25–30.

Schydlowsky, Daniel, foreign exchange model described in Sidney Robbins and Robert Stobaugh, *Money in the Multinational Enterprise.* New York: Basic Books, Inc., 1973.

Shapiro, Alan C., "International Cash Management—The Determination of Multicurrency Cash Balances," *Journal of Financial and Quantitative Analysis,* Dec. 1976, pp. 893–900.

————, and David P. Rutenberg, "When to Hedge against Devaluation," *Management Science,* Aug. 1974, pp. 1514–20.

MANUCRAFT, INC. (B)

ARMIN BERNSCHOT'S INTERNAL review of the operations of the International Funds Management Group (IFMG) appeared to be going nowhere when he decided to engage the services of an external financial consultant.

Most of the final report submitted by this consultant evaluated each of the practices followed by the IFMG, given Manucraft's objectives. However, the report section that intrigued Mr. Bernschot the most was a final section in which the current IFMG objectives actually were challenged. It suggested that the objectives of the IFMG be stated in terms of a basket of currencies instead of the U.S. dollar.

Following is the section of the consultant's report where this topic was discussed.

A CURRENCY MARKET BASKET

In the present statement of objectives for the IFMG, exposure to exchange risk is measured in terms of nominal U.S. dollars, the currency in which Manucraft reports its earnings. These dollars are not adjusted for changes in value caused by inflation in the United States.[1] The risk in this strategy is that if the market underestimates the rate of inflation in the dollar, then the interest rate received on outstanding balances will not compensate the investor for the loss in purchasing power of the liquid funds entrusted to the company.

An alternative objective for the IFMG would take into account the limitations of using nominal dollars as the base currency and it would incorporate the risks in predicting monetary relationships. *This would be accomplished by defining the objective of the IFMG as maintaining the value of funds in terms of a basket of currencies.* This strategy utilizes diversification to manage monetary risk. As exchange rate fluc-

---

[1] Except for supplementary financial information on the impact of inflation on the company published under the requirements of Financial Accounting Standards Board, Statement No. 33.

tuations and relative inflation rates reflected in interest rates are underestimated in some currencies and overestimated in others, diversification among currency holdings can be used as a means to reduce this
risk to the firm.

The emphasis of the currency basket concept is on stability, not
necessarily on superior returns. On the other hand, to the extent that
the relationships between interest rate differentials and future exchange rate developments may be anticipated, this would produce a
superior return in addition to greater stability compared with the current policy.

In setting the composition of a basket of currencies and ignoring
speculation per se, there are three factors that should be considered:

1. ***Planned cash needs of Manucraft.*** The major development affecting the
   cash management function in the next 5 years would be Manucraft's investment program. The relative shares of this program decided for the
   United States and other countries would affect the composition of the
   market basket.

   Another demand for dollar cash outflows would be the dividend
   payments to shareholders. Both a U.S. investment program and the dividend policy would point to a currency basket with a relatively high component of U.S. dollars.

2. ***Manucraft's sources of revenues.*** A multinational company provides a
   channel for investors to purchase income diversification among the various currencies in which the multinational operates. To the extent that
   foreign equity markets are accessible to the investor only with high transaction costs, the multinational company may furnish the most efficient
   means of diversification among currencies available to the stockholder.
   However, if the value of foreign investments is converted into the home
   currency through financial hedging policies, stockholders are deprived of
   this diversification effect.

   In order to take into account the monetary diversification which the
   firm can provide for its stockholders, the currencies generated by the
   company's international operations would have an *increasing* representation in the proposed basket of currencies.

3. ***Evaluation of market rates.*** In particular, this would mean evaluation of
   interest rate differentials relative to anticipated inflation rates and exchange rate movements over the medium term of, say, 3 to 5 years. Currencies which are estimated to carry an interest rate higher than warranted by the anticipated exchange depreciation will have a greater
   weight in the basket than those for which the relationship is forecast to
   be in the opposite direction. (Implicitly, this factor is partially taken into
   account under the present system of changes in exposure limits. However, this is done only in a very limited fashion and for relatively short
   periods of time.)

Under the alternative objectives suggested here, the IFMG would
manage funds in terms of a basket of currencies instead of using the
U.S. dollar as the only base currency. To accommodate the new objec-

tives, the current policy of setting limits would have to be altered. The new policy would establish a range of weights permissible for any given currency. For example, the policy may say that German marks would represent 20% of the total funds exposed on average. However, the range could be allowed to fluctuate between 15% and 25% of the total. With total funds in the amount of $100 million, this would mean an exposure in marks which on average would be $20 million, but which could vary between $15 and $25 million over a 3- to 5-year period.

In setting the average level and the band over which the exposure limit for any specific currency could fluctuate, it would be useful to differentiate according to the time horizon involved in the decision:

1. *Long-term (5 to 10 years).* With this time horizon the major consideration would be the specific cash needs of Manucraft in different currencies. These include sources of supply, investment programs, and so forth. In general, the factors discussed previously in the context of setting objectives would be relevant here.

2. *Medium-term (3 to 5 years).* Analysis of relative inflation rates and interest differentials would be the basis for establishing the range of limits accepted for each currency over this period of time.

3. *Short-term (1 month).* The analysis setting these limits would be based on the same considerations as for the medium term—namely, inflation rates relative to interest rates. However, the acceptable range of the band would be much narrower.

For example, long-term considerations may dictate that 20% of the portfolio should be maintained in yen. Again, with a portfolio in the amount of $100 million, this would represent yen holdings in the amount of $20 million, on average. In the medium term it could be acceptable to have the range of limits fluctuate 50% around the average level. This would produce a range of specific limits between $10 million and $30 million. However, changes within this range would occur only slowly and in relatively small magnitudes—for example, every 6 months and in amounts of $3 to $5 million. The function of this limit is not to respond to the latest move in the market but to a forecast of the relationship between relative interest rates and expected exchange rates. This forecast should not be affected drastically by immediate market events, unless these events affect longer-term variables.

Once the medium-term objective is set, the range of acceptable fluctuations within 1 month would be perhaps only 10% of the average amount accepted. With a specific limit of $20 million set on the basis of long-term and medium-term considerations, the IFMG would have to maintain its holdings of yen between $18 and $22 million in this example, if it started the month at $20 million. Over several months, of course, the starting figure would drift up or down, but within the medium- and long-term limits.

This design would make the changes in limits much more rigid than it seems to be at the present time. Under the present system, with a set limit of $15 million, the exposure in yen could conceivably fluctuate between a net borrowed position of $15 million and a net asset position of $15 million—a total range of $30 million—from one day to the next. Under the proposed system the monthly counterpart would be only $4 million.

In the proposed system the limits would have a different function from the one they perform now. In the current system, limits are a concept used to safeguard Manucraft from short-term trading mistakes. In this proposed system, the limits would be a device to accomplish objectives of diversification and profit-taking over a much longer period of time.

Notice that if the average portfolio selected for long-term purposes under the alternative objectives had about 60% in dollars and 40% in other currencies, then the basket of currencies would not differ drastically from the composition of the IFMG portfolio allowed by the limits only recently (see Exhibits K.1 and K.3 of Chapter 11). In fact, the net effect of the new objectives in this situation would be to restrict the range of fluctuations made possible with the present system of limits.

FARMATEL S.A.,
1979

THE CUMULATIVE IMPACT of the industrial and financial developments of recent years was coming to a head at Farmatel by the end of 1979. As budgets for the following year began to be formalized, it was becoming increasingly clear to Mr. de Chomereau, treasurer of the company, that only a small portion of the anticipated financial needs could be met from Farmatel's traditional sources.

Farmatel was a family-owned French company selling pharmaceutical and chemical products worldwide. Although the pharmaceutical part of the business had exhibited a fairly stable rate of growth, the chemical portion had been severely affected by the huge increases in oil prices in recent years. To cope with this situation, most of the company's subsidiaries had increased substantially their accounts payable to the parent company, and even larger increases were forecasted for 1980. To make matters worse, these increased demands on the parent's financial resources coincided with the introduction by a competitor company in France of a new drug that was expected to take a substantial amount of sales away from Farmatel. Fortunately, Farmatel's research and development department expected to have in the market a new product by 1981 that would easily recover the lost sales.

COMPANY BACKGROUND AND ORGANIZATION

Farmatel's greatest strength traditionally had been in the area of research and development. Patents protected a high profit margin and the sales growth had been substantial. In the last 5 years, sales for the company as a whole had increased threefold, profits had doubled, and expenditures on research and development had quadrupled. The financing of this growth had been accomplished largely from retained earnings. In 1979 the combined total debt was less than 30% of the total of liabilities plus equity. Total sales in 1979 were FF3,960 million, of which foreign subsidiaries accounted for FF2,318 million (see Exhibit L.1).

414

EXHIBIT L.1 Farmatel S.A., 1979: France—Unconsolidated Income Statements, Balance Sheets, and Changes in Financial Position Statements, 1977–1980 *(millions of francs)*

Income Statement

	1977	1978	1979	1980 (Forecast)
Revenue				
Sales[a]: Domestic	896	993	1,067	1,048
Foreign	384	467	575	670
Interest income	17	19	22	24
Royalties received	40	54	70	84
Dividends received	20	24	30	39
Total revenue	1,357	1,557	1,764	1,865
Cost of goods sold	891	936	1,100	1,227
Gross profit	466	621	664	638
Operating expenses	286	331	384	436
Interest expense	24	26	45	62
Foreign exchange loss (gain)	2	2	7	10
Taxes	77	131	114	65
Net profit (:s)	77	131	114	65
Dividends paid	70	88	106	112

Balance Sheet

	1977	1978	1979	1980 (Forecast)
Assets				
Net fixed assets	256	287	299	304
Long-term assets and equity investment in subsidiaries	209	240	257	273
Inventory	142	146	178	187
Accounts receivable				
Intercompany	96	97	137	184
Other	149	161	178	179
Cash	14	11	6	5
Total assets	866	942	1,055	1,132
Liabilities and equity				
Common stock	325	325	325	325
Retained earnings	184	227	235	188
Long-term debt	195	201	211	206
Short-term debt	52	74	148	253
Accounts payable	110	115	136	160
Total liabilities and equity	866	942	1,055	1,132

Changes in Financial Position

	1977	1978	1979	1980 (Forecast)
Sources of working capital				
Current operations				
Net income	77.0	131.0	114.0	65.0
Depreciation expense	12.8	14.4	15.0	15.2
Working capital from operations	89.8	145.4	129.0	80.2
Other sources				
Long-term debt	8.2	14.5	22.2	4.6
Total new working capital	98.0	159.9	151.2	84.8
Uses of working capital				
Increase in long-term assets and equity investment in subsidiaries	20.5	31.0	17.0	16.0
Purchase of fixed assets	16.4	45.4	27.0	20.2
Reduction of long-term debt	5.1	8.5	12.2	9.6
Declaration of dividends	70.0	88.0	106.0	112.0
Total uses of working capital	112.0	172.9	162.2	157.8
Net increase (decrease) in working capital	(14.0)	(13.0)	(11.0)	(73.0)
Changes in working capital composition				
Increase in short-term debt	9.0	22.0	74.0	105.0[b]
Increase in accounts payable	6.5	5.0	21.0	24.0
Less: Increase in accounts receivable				
Intercompany	(3.0)	1.0	40.0	47.0
Other	6.0	12.0	17.0	1.0
Increase in inventory	2.0	4.0	32.0	9.0
	10.5	1.0	6.0	72.0
Less change in cash	(3.5)	(3.0)	(5.0)	(1.0)
	14.0	13.0	11.0	73.0

[a] Sales of foreign subsidiaries not included in this statement were FF1,332 in 1977; FF1,784 in 1978; FF2,318 in 1979; and FF2,803 were forecast for 1980.
[b] Required balancing amount.

The firm's fast growth had led to relative disorder in organization. In spite of confusing lines of responsibility, three major parts could be identified in the company: the parent operating and holding company, the French subsidiaries, and the foreign subsidiaries.

The Operating and Holding Company.   Within the operating and holding parent company there were three product divisions: pharmaceuticals, petrochemicals, and miscellaneous. Each of these divisions was organized on a functional basis. Among these functional departments, the managers of sales, manufacturing, and research and development reported directly to Farmatel's president.

The French Subsidiaries.   These subsidiaries were in the same product lines as the parent company. In addition, Farminter, an independent French subsidiary, operated as a sort of international division for Farmatel. In general, the French subsidiaries reported directly to the top management of Farmatel, but they communicated widely with the corresponding product divisions of the operating and holding company; for example, subsidiaries in the petrochemical business communicated directly with Farmatel's petrochemical product division. Their financial autonomy was variable. Some of them had a fairly independent borrowing policy. Others (especially laboratories) were heavily dependent on Farmatel funds.

The Foreign Subsidiaries.   The international operations of Farmatel were organized in an intricate fashion. Direct exports were channeled through Farminter. This subsidiary was the link between the product divisions of Farmatel and the exporting French subsidiaries on one hand, and the foreign clients on the other. In addition, to have better access to some markets, Farmatel had created several wholly-owned sales subsidiaries in these markets. Some of these sales subsidiaries (including the Brazilian one) had then established limited manufacturing or packaging operations because of tariff problems, patent necessity, or governmental pressures.

Because of the perceived need for increased coordination with the foreign subsidiaries, the product divisions at Farmatel bypassed Farminter and communicated directly with the individual managers of the foreign subsidiaries. In this relationship the sales departments of the French units were responsible for product quality, delivery dates, selling prices, and the terms of sale extended to the foreign subsidiaries. The product divisions tried to have the foreign subsidiaries absorb a regular and growing volume of production since the divisions were evaluated mainly in terms of sales growth. A smooth pattern of sales growth also contributed to the good relationships between the sales and manufacturing departments which appreciated having a steady flow in production.

The nature of the relationship between Farmatel and the foreign subsidiaries depended also on the size and nature of these subsidiaries. Three kinds of subsidiaries could be distinguished:

1. *Export sales subsidiaries* sold Farmatel finished products. These were mainly in Europe and Japan.

2. *Captive manufacturing subsidiaries* bought active principles from Farmatel and transformed these basic materials into specialty products. Most of these subsidiaries were in Latin America and the Far East.

3. *Integrated subsidiaries* bought bulk chemicals outside the group and transformed them into finished products. Among these, the subsidiaries in the United States and the United Kingdom also had their own research and development facility.

Subsidiaries in the third group were often large in size. They were relatively autonomous with general managers who regarded Farmatel more as an associate than as a parent company. These managers reported directly to Farmatel's president. Other subsidiaries generally reported to Farminter's president, although the largest ones were directly supervised by Farmatel's president. However, even those subsidiaries reporting to Farminter's president retained a right of appeal to Farmatel.

THE CONTROL SYSTEM

In general, control of the subsidiaries was exerted mostly through informal discussions between the parent company and the subsidiaries whose management was given a high degree of autonomy. The formalized part of the control system consisted of the subsidiaries submitting to the parent company a series of reports and financial statements for the current period and their forecast for 1 year ahead. These reports were: monthly sales forecasts, income statements, investment budgets, and balance sheets.

The foreign subsidiaries submitted these reports to Farminter who, in turn, used these figures to forecast the sales to foreign subsidiaries to be made by each of the French subsidiaries. These forecasts were also used by the manufacturing departments to schedule production. Farminter computed the accounting variance between actual and budgeted figures each month and indicated corrective actions to small subsidiaries. However, the focus of Farminter's analysis was mainly on commercial variables, especially sales volume.

The budget evaluation process was very simple with little feedback from headquarters to the subsidiaries during the budgeting phase. In fact, the subsidiaries' budget was not discussed much at headquarters as long as sales and profits showed an increase over the previous year's performance. A partial explanation for this behavior was the fact that no one at Farminter or Farmatel was particularly competent in international finance and accounting. The impact on the subsidiaries of different financial policies and accounting principles, of local environmental variables, or of variables such as currency parity changes was rarely considered.

The managers of the large subsidiaries reporting to the president sent the same kind of financial information as the small ones. However, their sales were less carefully monitored because they had no direct impact on the sales or manufacturing operations of the parent company. Their forecasts were accepted without discussion as long as profitability and sales were growing.

FINANCIAL POLICIES

There was a major dichotomy between the financial policies used by the larger subsidiaries and the policies used by the smaller ones at Farmatel.

Big, integrated subsidiaries were financially independent of the parent company. The managers of these subsidiaries tried not to depend on the parent company for their financing needs in order to avoid giving Farmatel any leverage over them. Their high profitability and the relatively low payout to Farmatel allowed them to finance their expansion from retained earnings. When external financing was necessary, they dealt with local banks with whom they had developed banking relationships over a long time. This was especially true of the United Kingdom subsidiary, controlled by Farmatel since 1946.

The smaller subsidiaries, who bought finished products or raw materials from the parent company, were much more dependent on Farmatel. An important part of their financing came from Farmatel's accounts receivable. When they had additional financial needs, they asked Farmatel for a lengthening of their credit terms or for a loan. In these cases the decision taken by Farminter and the sales departments was generally positive.

Some conflicts had arisen in the past about devaluation losses. Subsidiaries having an important volume of accounts payable to Farmatel were severely hit when a devaluation in the local currency suddenly increased the local currency value of these accounts. As a result, some had asked to be invoiced in local currency, and this change was accepted. In other cases the burden of the devaluation had been split on a 50–50 basis between Farmatel and the subsidiary.

At the parent level, the tasks of Mr. de Chomereau, Farmatel's treasurer, consisted mostly in managing the cash position and the short- and medium-term financing of the parent company. Mr. Boutrolles, the financial vice-president, was responsible for determining the long-term financial policy of Farmatel. This policy included financial structure, availability of funds for major investment projects, and dividend payment.

THE FINANCIAL SITUATION
AT THE END OF 1979

At the end of 1979 the smaller subsidiaries' lengthening in the maturity of their accounts payable to Farmatel was imposing a heavy financial strain on Farmatel. The parent company also was experiencing increases in its levels of inventories and accounts receivable from third parties. Domestic sales were forecast to increase slightly in 1980 and, because of governmental restrictions, it was going to be difficult to obtain additional short-term loans in France.

Taking the delicate present financial situation of Farmatel as a stimulus, Mr. de Chomereau had tried to demonstrate to Mr. Boutrolles that the financial autonomy of the subsidiaries was detrimental to the group's interest. He pointed out that the salespeople were not always acting in the best interest of the company by granting the subsidiaries very favorable financial terms. Mr. de Chomereau had asked Mr. Boutrolles whether some form of financial coordination between different units of the group would not be an improvement over the present situation. Mr. Boutrolles' reaction had been relatively cold. He explained to Mr. de Chomereau that the task of the financial department was already complicated enough, and that to advise Farminter's sales department on such matters would make this task even more complex. Furthermore, nobody in the finance department had experience and competence in the area of international financial management. Mr. Boutrolles stated that the subsidiaries were growing fast and profitably and that it would be unwise to disturb such a satisfactory situation.

Mr. de Chomereau was annoyed by this answer. He was sure that a more centralized management of the finances of the subsidiaries would ease the current financial problems of the parent company and improve the overall performance of the foreign operations. Data on three selected subsidiaries and their countries are presented in Exhibits L.2–L.5.

Given the seriousness of the financial situation, Mr. de Chomer-eau thought he also should begin considering the possibility of some Eurocurrency financing for 1980. A bank publication listed the London interbank offered rates (LIBOR) for Eurocurrencies given in the accompanying table.

	U.S. dollar	Pound sterling	French franc	German mark	Italian lira	Swiss franc	Japanese yen
3 months	14.94	16.62	14.12	8.88	19.00	5.50	8.25
12 months	13.06	15.00	13.75	8.19	18.00	5.25	7.62

Farmatel S.A., U.K. United Kingdom—Income Statements, Balance Sheets, and Changes in Financial Position Statements, 1977–1980 (millions of pounds)

Income Statement

	1977	1978	1979	1980 (Forecast)
Sales	32.10	36.93	42.74	45.33
Cost of goods sold	23.40	26.02	29.97	32.61
Gross profit	8.70	10.91	12.77	12.72
Operating expenses	5.05	5.73	6.71	7.32
Interest expense	.25	.30	.42	.38
Foreign exchange loss (gain)	.03	(.03)	.11	.12
Royalties	1.00	1.15	1.28	1.32
Taxes	.95	1.50	1.70	1.43
Net profit (loss)	1.42	2.26	2.55	2.15
Dividends paid	.70	1.63	1.47	1.02

Balance Sheet

	1977	1978	1979	1980 (Forecast)
Assets				
Net fixed assets	4.80	4.85	4.89	4.96
Inventory	3.63	4.11	4.81	5.40
Accounts receivable				
Farmatel subsidiaries	1.53	1.74	2.14	2.66
Other	3.52	4.34	5.37	5.65
Cash	.52	.22	.18	.19
Total assets	14.00	15.26	17.39	18.86
Liabilities and equity				
Equity	8.29	8.92	10.00	11.13
Long-term debt	2.48	2.48	2.43	2.38
Short-term debt	.38	.57	1.10	1.18
Accounts payable	2.85	3.29	3.86	4.17
Total liabilities and equity	14.00	15.26	17.39	18.86

Changes in Financial Position

	1977	1978	1979	1980 (Forecast)
Sources of working capital				
Current operations				
Net income	1.42	2.26	2.55	2.15
Depreciation expense	.53	.54	.54	.55
Working capital from operations	1.95	2.80	3.09	2.70
Other sources				
Sale of fixed assets	.10	.12	.30	.03
Long-term debt	3.50	.25		
Total new working capital	5.55	3.17	3.39	2.73
Uses of working capital				
Purchase of fixed assets	1.28	.71	.88	.65
Reduction of long-term debt	1.25	.25	.05	.05
Declaration of dividends	.70	1.63	1.47	1.02
Total uses of working capital	3.23	2.59	2.40	1.72
Net increase (decrease) in working capital	2.32	.58	.99	1.01
Changes in working capital composition				
Increase in short-term debt	(.89)	.19	.53	.08
Increase in accounts payable	(.07)	.44	.57	.31
Less: Increase in accounts receivable				
Farmatel subsidiaries	.21	.21	.40	.52
Other	.42	.82	1.03	.28
Increase in inventory	.38	.48	.70	.59
	(1.97)	(.88)	(1.03)	(1.00)
	.35	(.30)	(.04)	.01
Less change in cash	(2.32)	(.58)	(.99)	(1.01)

EXHIBIT L.3 Farmatel S.A., 1979: Italy—Income Statements, Balance Sheets, and Changes in Financial Position Statements, 1977–1980 *(millions of liras)*

	1977	1978	1979	1980 (Forecast)
Income Statement				
Sales	1,302	1,526	1,850	2,189
Cost of goods sold	963	1,083	1,265	1,494
Gross profit	339	443	585	695
Operating expenses	264	312	381	453
Interest expense	9	10	16	18
Foreign exchange loss (gain)	3	6	6	6
Royalties	38	44	54	64
Taxes	10	27	49	59
Net profit (loss)	15	44	79	95
Dividends	6	13	38	49
Balance Sheet				
Assets				
Net fixed assets	145	148	151	157
Inventory	165	183	211	248
Accounts receivable	270	303	396	478
Cash	12	25	17	18
Total assets	592	659	775	901
Liabilities and Equity				
Equity	301	332	373	419
Long-term debt	51	53	54	57
Short-term debt	13	23	33	41
Accounts payable (Farmatel)	227	251	315	384
Total liabilities and equity	592	659	775	901

	1977	1978	1979	1980 (Forecast)
Changes in Financial Position				
Sources of working capital				
Current operations				
Net income	15	44	79	95
Depreciation expense	7	7	8	8
Working capital from operations	22	51	87	103
Other sources				
Sale of fixed assets	1	2	4	5
Long-term debt	5	10	15	10
Total new working capital	28	63	106	118
Uses of working capital				
Purchase of fixed assets	13	12	15	19
Reduction of long-term debt	3	8	14	7
Declaration of dividends	6	13	38	49
Total uses of working capital	22	33	67	75
Net increase (decrease) in working capital	6	30	39	43
Changes in working capital composition				
Increase in short-term debt	5	10	10	8
Increase in accounts payable (Farmatel)	3	24	64	69
Less: Increase in accounts receivable	6	33	93	82
Increase in inventory	12	18	28	37
	(10)	(17)	(47)	(42)
Less change in cash	(4)	13	(8)	1
	(6)	(30)	(39)	(43)

EXHIBIT L.4 Farmatel S.A., 1979: Brazil—Income Statements, Balance Sheets, and Changes in Financial Position Statements, 1977–1980| (millions of cruzeiros)

	1977	1978	1979	1980 (Forecast)
Income Statement				
Sales	1,260	1,840	2,944	5,005
Cost of goods sold	869	1,195	1,876	3,447
Gross profit	391	645	1,068	1,558
Operating expenses	263	405	634	1,004
Interest expense	41	67	122	163
Foreign exchange loss (gain)	23	43	101	270
Royalties	13	25	55	69
Taxes	12	32	47	16
Net profit (loss)	39	73	109	36
Balance Sheet				
Assets				
Net fixed assets	58	60	70	70
Inventory	144	198	332	536
Accounts receivable	333	507	830	1,414
Cash	23	21	25	2
Total assets	558	786	1,257	2,022
Liabilities and Equity				
Equity	204	277	386	422
Long-term debt				
Farmatel	75	95	110	130
Other	22	25	30	32
Short-term debt	47	70	161	225
Accounts payable				
Farmatel	190	291	524	1,117
Others	20	28	46	96
Total liabilities and equity	558	786	1,257	2,022

	1977	1978	1979	1980 (Forecast)
Changes in Financial Position				
Sources of working capital				
Current operations				
Net income	39	73	109	36
Depreciation expense	6	6	7	7
Working capital from operations	45	79	116	43
Other sources				
Sale of fixed assets	3	5	3	5
Long-term debt	18	33	35	40
Total new working capital	66	117	154	88
Uses of working capital				
Purchase of fixed assets	11	13	20	12
Reduction of long-term debt	5	10	15	18
Total uses of working capital	16	23	35	30
Net increase (decrease) in working capital	50	94	119	58
Changes in working capital composition				
Increase in short-term debt	17	23	91	64
Increase in accounts payable				
Farmatel	31	101	233	593
Others	5	8	18	50
Less: Increase in accounts receivable	78	174	323	584
Increase in inventory	21	54	134	204
	(46)	(96)	(115)	(81)
	4	(2)	4	(23)
Less change in cash	(50)	(94)	(119)	(58)

EXHIBIT L.5 Farmatel S.A., 1979: Economic Data for Selected Countries[a]

	1977	1978	1979
France			
Nominal GNP (billions of francs)	1,887.1	2,147.8	2,451.1
Gross domestic product (billions of francs)	1,880.5	2,133.5	2,430.6
GDP, 1975 prices (billions of francs)	1,570.4	1,626.7	1,678.3
Industrial production, 1975 = 100	100	111	117
Wholesale price index, 1975 = 100	113.4	118.3	134.0
Prime rate (percent per annum)	11.35	10.95	13.65
Average exchange rate ($/FF)	.2035	.2216	.2350
Exchange rate ($/FF) spot	.2126	.2385	.2488
3-month forward	.2093	.2394	.2490
Premium (discount) against $ (percent per annum)	(6.21)	(1.51)	0.32
United Kingdom			
Nominal GNP (billions of pounds)	142.57	163.89	188.33
Gross domestic product (billions of pounds)	142.37	163.07	188.18
GDP, 1975 prices (billions of pounds)	109.41	113.28	114.27
Industrial production, 1975 = 100	106.0	109.8	112.6
Wholesale price index, 1975 = 100	140.5	153.3	172.0
Prime rate (percent per annum)	8.00	13.50	18.00
Average exchange rate (FF/£)	8.5763	8.6623	9.0263
Exchange rate (FF/£) spot	9.0217	8.5409	8.9807
3-month forward	9.1768	8.4896	8.9265
Premium (discount) of FF against £ (percent per annum)	6.88	(2.40)	(2.41)
Italy			
Nominal GNP (billions of lira)	189,663	222,232	269,241
Gross domestic product (billions of lira)	190,083	222,369	268,868
GDP, 1975 prices (billions of lira)	135,259	138,738	145,615
Industrial production, 1975 = 100	113.6	115.9	123.5
Wholesale price index, 1975 = 100	144.3	156.4	180.7
Prime rate (percent per annum)	16.00	15.00	19.50
Average exchange rate (lira/FF)	179.57	188.06	195.25
Exchange rate (lira/FF) spot	185.19	197.93	200.12
3-month forward	186.71	200.00	203.02
Premium (discount) against FF	3.28	4.18	5.80
Brazil			
Nominal GNP (billions of cruzeiros)	2,281.2	3,343.9	5,358.4
Gross domestic product (billions of cruzeiros)	2,321.4	3,410.0	5,511.7
GDP, 1975 prices (billions of cruzeiros)	1,151.2	1,220.6	1,298.7
Industrial production, 1975 = 100	204.1	280.8	437.8
Wholesale price index, 1975 = 100			
Prime rate (percent per annum)	52.05	61.70	57.00
Average exchange rate (cruzeiros/FF)	2.878	4.004	6.332
Exchange rate (cruzeiros/FF) spot	3.411	5.004	10.581

CHAPTER

13

Measuring Returns From International Projects

IN THE FOLLOWING chapters we will discuss the capital budgeting decision in the multinational company largely in terms of the traditional financial variables. However, the clothing in which risk and return emerge in an investment project is varied, particularly in foreign direct investment. Thus, we will begin the discussion of capital budgeting with a review of the factors that lead companies to invest abroad.

Having decided to contemplate investment in a foreign project, the raw material of the analysis then becomes the *expected cash flows* attendant to the project. Although reported profits are used as a standard for many evaluations of management, most expenses (such as payment for materials and wages) are paid from cash, not earnings, and the computation of accounting earnings is affected by many factors which do not include cash (such as depreciation charges). The determination of the cash flows associated with an international project presents difficulties similar to those encountered in a domestic project. However, the international setting usually is much more complex than the domestic one and a manager must consider additional factors peculiar to multinational operations. In this chapter we will see how some of these special factors affect the evaluation of a project's cash flows.

WHY INVEST ABROAD?

The explanations offered for foreign direct investment fall into two major groups. One set of theories points to specific factors by which a foreign investment can increase the return or reduce the total risk of a company in a competitive environment.[1] The other theories emphasize market characteristics as the major triggering force behind direct investment.

Direct Investment to Increase Returns or Reduce Risks

Comparative advantage, the classical explanation for international trade, can be also a major factor behind foreign investment. This basic concept of economics suggests that, in terms of the value of total output for the society, each productive asset is most effective if used in those tasks for which its relative advantage over other alternatives is greatest.

As an example, assume that there are two countries, A and B, each with 100 labor weeks of time available at equal labor rates. A product can be produced in either nation, but it must have two processes completed for the finished version. The units per process for each nation are shown in the accompanying table.

| | UNITS PRODUCED PER WEEK | |
	Process X	Process Y
Country A	10	5
Country B	6	2

Comparative advantage suggests that each nation's workers should be used where they have the largest relative advantage or smallest relative disadvantage. In this example, country A is more efficient in terms of units per week for both processes X and Y. This fact relates to *absolute efficiency.* However, its *relative efficiency* is greater for process Y, since the ratio $\frac{5}{2}$ is greater than $\frac{10}{6}$. Over 100 weeks, a policy of completing as many units as possible of process Y in country A would result in production of 500 units. Those units are then treated with proc-

---

[1] A review of the major economic elements that may contribute to direct foreign investment decision is found in Richard E. Caves, "International Corporations: The Industrial Economics of Foreign Investment," *Economica,* February 1971, pp. 1–27.

ess X in country B, using a total of 83.3 weeks. The remaining 16.7 weeks of unused time in country B are used to produce an additional 25½ finished units—completing both process X and process Y for these extra units. The total finished production from both nations is then 525½. Given the problem as defined, this is the maximum output possible.[2]

Translated to international corporate operations, the course of comparative advantage may be related to labor skills or unit costs, to transportation expenses for reaching the total market, and to capital markets, for example. In spite of much rhetoric about cheap foreign labor and its effect on American jobs, there are several aspects to the issue of relative labor costs and unit costs. These unit costs are a function of wage rates and capital (machinery and human training), which affect labor productivity. The wage rates paid in many countries appear low when compared with the wages paid in the United States. This fact alone is likely to make these other countries more attractive as an investment site for the multinational company when the goods to be produced require a large amount of labor. However, when the goods to be produced require a considerable amount of capital investment relative to labor, then the lower wages play a less important role in the final decision. On the other hand, other factors (such as the skill of the labor force) may make investing in high-wage countries more desirable.

When there are limited economies of scale in producing a product that has relatively high transportation costs, the firm may favor establishment of several plants around the world. The selection of investment sites in this case will try to minimize transportation costs to customers and to lower total unit costs. Countries selected would minimize average miles per unit delivered. In addition, special economies in transportation favoring one country over another may exist if there are differential geographic elements such as navigable waterways or mountainous terrain without railroads.

In the capital markets, freedom of transactions among currencies means that rates adjusted for risk should reach equilibrium. However, limitations on capital export and import can produce rate differentials among different countries' capital markets. For example, when the local government commits public policy toward encouragement of a particular enterprise, then special tax concessions and other arrangements

---

[2]A strategy of completing all process X in country A would provide 1,000 units, but this is beyond the capacity of country B for process Y since the maximum in process Y from country B at 2 units per week is 200 units in 100 weeks. Thus, country A would complete process X on these 200 units and complete both process X and process Y on an additional 266.7 units in the remaining 80 labor weeks, for a total finished production of 466.7 units. If one were to produce finished products separately in each country (the "no-trade" situation in international exchange, for example), then country A could produce 333.3 units and country B could produce 150 units, for a total of 483.3 units.

mean that, even if the capital markets were in equilibrium, the special arrangements may offer attractive financing incentives for the multinational corporation. On the other hand, the large multinational companies with access to major capital markets possess an advantage. Such access permits a lower discount rate when evaluating projects, placing the firm at an advantage over the domestic corporation in many nations which do not have such a capital market.[3]

Economic incentives for international operations may result simply from binding *operational constraints*. Independently of comparative advantage, certain raw materials may be available only in a few countries. Proximity to those supplies may force a location of manufacturing operations in some of those countries. Government policies may force production operations in their countries in order to sell in those countries. Finally, the local government may tie availability of the resource (bauxite, nickel, and so on) to the establishment of a local plant beyond the scope required by the firm's operation.

Taxation is another basic economic incentive to location decisions. Because management is charged with the responsibility of maximizing shareholder's returns in the long run, lower corporate taxes in particular areas of the world become important. The form of tax benefit differs. The absolute rate of taxes on profits may be low. The definition of taxable income may be more advantageous to the firm in some nations than in others; for example, the United Kingdom has periodically allowed free depreciation on some assets in particular industries, permitting firms to take as much depreciation as desired in a given year to offset all profits until the asset is fully depreciated. Finally, some nations may have very low taxes on dividend income or a very low withholding tax applied to dividend or interest payments outside the nation. Such an arrangement encourages the multinational firm to use this land as a base for a financing subsidiary which receives dividends from operating subsidiaries and remits payments to other firms in the same corporate family. These issues and the basic rules of U.S. taxation of international income are addressed in Appendix 2 to this chapter.

One economic motivation often linked to the acceptance of a good investment is *financial diversification,* or spreading the firm's risk throughout a wider range than any one nation will permit. By diversifying over basic markets, products, regions, and governments, the firm hopes to avoid dependence on the outcome of a single unique investment. This is the same intent as that which compels an investor to allocate a securities portfolio over many stocks.

---

[3]Robert Aliber, "A Theory of Direct Foreign Investment," in Charles Kindleberger, ed., *The International Corporation: A Symposium* (Cambridge, Mass.: MIT Press, 1970), pp. 17–34.

Market Characteristics and Direct Investment

As we will show subsequently, decisions arising from market considerations also can be expressed in terms of their impact on the return and risk of the company. However, the emphasis of these explanations is not in measuring return and risk, but on markets—although the results may not be incompatible.

In one major analysis of the decision of U.S. firms to invest abroad, the National Industrial Conference Board survey [see Polk, et al. (1966)] found that the main criterion dominating the decision was a concern for markets.[4] The companies usually referred also to some goal of return on investment, but the measurement of this return was very simple and was often expressed as a percentage of sales. Leading U.S. consumer goods firms especially were oriented in this manner. Such a strategy is not inconsistent with the economic goals noted earlier: Loss of markets may be the loss of a financial return, and the decision to invest abroad is made either to prevent economic losses or to profit from opportunities that are available in other lands.

Similarly, market dominance may be a reasonable companion to profitability under some circumstances. Gale presents a cross-sectional regression analysis based on 106 companies for which he evaluated the impact of market share, firm size, and concentration as explanatory variables for rate of return. Defining rate of return as net income on book equity over a 5-year period (1963–1967) and adjusting for leverage of different firms, he confirmed his hypotheses that positive relationships between market share and profitability were greater for: (1) high concentration industries, (2) moderate growth industries versus rapid growth industries, (3) relatively large firms versus smaller firms, and (4) large firms in high concentration industries with relatively moderate growth versus all other firms. He notes that "the findings of this study would seem to confirm our belief that interaction effects . . . play an important role in the determination of firm and industry performance." Thus, his conclusion is consistent with the strategy of a firm's seeking

---

[4]Other National Industrial Conference Board researchers confirm this motivation. Spitaller reviews various quantitative studies of both long-term portfolio capital and foreign direct investment. He concludes that the decision to invest abroad is primarily affected by the size of the foreign market, but he notes that the results are also consistent with the argument for differential rates of return. However, because of the aggregative nature of the data by which other researchers supported the importance of differential rates of return, Spitaller suggests that the other researchers did not consider the "unity of the investment decision of the international firm. This unity implies that the foreign investment decisions of a firm are interdependent." Hence, the broader strategy issue also appears in this conclusion. (See Erich Spitaller, "A Survey of Recent Quantitative Studies of Long-Term Capital Movements," *IMF Staff Papers*, March 1971, pp. 189–217.)

access to particular markets in the expectation of greater long-run profitability from obtaining a dominant market share.[5]

A subset of this emphasis on the market strategy has often been referred to in the context of the *product life cycle*. As presented by Vernon, the product life cycle suggests that the corporation will be forced to seek untapped markets because of increasingly broad penetration of a market and company's incremental investment. Thus, the product life cycle approach is a dynamic oligopoly theory, in which declining margins in one land induce the firm to go abroad. It will initially export, and then follow this policy with full manufacturing abroad as the export market is threatened by competition.[6]

Aharoni found that the decision process of major corporations to invest in Israel was dominated by a combination of the product life cycle and the absorption of organizational uncertainty as projects filtered upward. The absorption of organizational uncertainty, observed in many firms by various researchers, is the filtering process by which successive individuals in the decision-making process condense and delete risk elements associated with a project or decision. This study reinforces the blending of financial and economic factors with organizational and behavioral characteristics in the foreign investment decision process.[7] We will have more to say about organization behavior in Chapter 17.

Hymer found the decision for foreign investment motivated by one or more forms of *monopolistic advantage*.[8] The monopoly forms which give the firm an advantage abroad include technology, capital markets access, sourcing leads, management, or some other variable.

An *oligopolistic market structure* also can be associated with a decision to invest abroad. If there is limited product differentiation, economies of scale, and a small number of sellers, then an oligopolistic market structure induces a "follow the leader" strategy among the competitors. To prevent one member from dominating local or world markets, the other members of the industry are compelled to match one company's expansion lead. Often, this is simply a "me, too" attitude. However, this attitude can also be rationalized as the result of an effective reduction in the risk that management perceives in the investment.

---

[5]Bradley T. Gale, "Market Share and Rate of Return," *Review of Economics and Statistics*, December 1972, pp. 412–423.

[6]Raymond Vernon, "International Investment and International Trade in the Product Life Cycle," *Quarterly Journal of Economics*, May 1966, pp. 190–207.

[7]Yair Aharoni, *The Foreign Investment Decision Process* (Boston, Mass.: Graduate School of Business Administration, Harvard University, 1966).

[8]Stephen Hymer, "The International Operations of National Firms: A Study of Direct Investment," unpublished doctoral dissertation, Massachusetts Institute of Technology, Cambridge, Mass., 1960.

An investment that once appeared extremely risky because of the large number of unknowns involved could be perceived by the firm as less risky if a major competitor is investing in that area. In other cases the reaction is part of a well-conceived strategy based on industry economics in which the competitors believe the cost structure and economies of scale in marketing, production, sourcing, and so on, would permit one member to dominate if that firm could seize a large enough total market share.[9]

As an example of the explanations for foreign direct investment given by management we list here the reasons mentioned by top officers of General Electric:[10] (1) to stabilize markets rather than engage in cutthroat competition; (2) to diversify holdings; (3) to enforce patents; (4) to meet national feelings; and (5) to increase U.S. exports.

CASH FLOW DETERMINATION

The factors that provide the incentives for a foreign direct investment ultimately must be evaluated in terms of the cash flows they will produce. The multinational setting in which this analysis must be made often complicates the usual problems encountered in the traditional capital budgeting problem. We now discuss some of these difficulties.

Joint Projects

Revenues from any proposed project must be reviewed carefully if the firm has the ability to realize some of the revenues *independent* of this project. For example, there is no problem if a truck manufacturer has decided to establish a car manufacturing plant in another country. On the other hand, the proposed investment in the other country often will affect the operations of other units in the system of the multinational firm through vertical integration (such as a mining operation in Bolivia for a U.S. metal firm or a sales subsidiary in France for an Italian car manufacturer). The investment also may be a duplicate of the parent operation in major respects through horizontal combinations (such as a typewriter manufacturer creating a manufacturing and distribution outlet in another land).

---

[9]For a detailed analysis of the impact of oligopolistic markets on the multinational enterprise, see F. T. Knickerbocker, *Oligopolistic Reaction and Multinational Enterprise* (Boston, Mass.: Division of Research, Harvard Business School, 1973).

[10]Mira Wilkins, *The Maturing of Multinational Enterprise: American Business Abroad from 1914 to 1970* (Cambridge, Mass.: Harvard University Press, 1974), p. 68.

⌈When such joint effects exist, the firm evaluates the project by aggregating total demand for the product. Then, the executives ask themselves, "How much extra business can we create from this foreign operation? For that portion of the business which is 'taken' from an existing operation, what are the savings involved?"

For example, the ability to compete more effectively in the Brazilian home furnishings market might suggest to Frigidaire that the firm locate a refrigerator manufacturing plant there. This plant will have some sales generated from a new market, some sales taken from other competitors who are already there, and some sales which are substitutions of Frigidaire products that are currently imported. The first two components of sales are clearly incremental revenue. The last component, substitution of Frigidaire-Brazil refrigerators for Frigidaire-World refrigerators, may have differential benefits because of different costs of production and importation. However, unless cost savings are present, these sales are not relevant to the project. In the typical case the loss of the sales and profits to Frigidaire-World is a net cost that should be charged to the project.

Economies of Scale

When there are substantial production economies of scale, individual small projects should be charged for the additional costs involved in the diseconomies of not using a centralized manufacturing policy. Thus, while Honeywell manufactures computers in many nations, its major models tend to be manufactured in one location and shipped throughout the world. Clearly, management perceives total shipping costs of Honeywell's large 3500s to be less than the costs associated with diseconomies from small unit production if the machines were manufactured in more than one location.

Supervisory Fees and Royalties

⌈Parents often require *supervisory fees* and *royalty payments* from their subsidiaries as means of remitting funds from foreign projects. In evaluating the cash flows of a project and the cash flows to the parent, several cautionary notes must be considered in relation to a supervisory fee. First, for the *project,* the relevant cash flow is the after-tax cost of what a real payment for the supervision on patent use would be worth in an arm's-length transaction. An arbitrarily high fee, created to permit remission of the funds from the project to the parent, has no relevance in evaluating the worth of the project per se if it is an accounting or political expediency designed for currency remission. Second, for the parent evaluating the cash flow to itself from this project, the supervisory and royalty inflows after subtracting any incremental costs simply constitute one more cash return. On the other hand, taxing and business authorities in the host country may question the propriety of this arrangement unless both sides initially recognize and accept it as a device to permit cash remissions.

Tie-In Sales

A variant of the supervisory or royalty fee is the *tie-in sale*, in which the subsidiary must buy certain items from the parent. Sometimes this purchase represents an implicit royalty; other times, it is simply a device to ensure quality control and/or a low cost to all manufacturing facilities on an integrated, companywide basis (the "economy of scale" argument for a component of the final product, for example). The conclusion on how to treat this item is the same as for the supervisory fee. It is the value of the product at an arm's-length level for the project.

Inflation and Currency Fluctuations

Years ago the concern with the impact of inflation and currency fluctuations on cash flows of a project used to be restricted to investments in developing countries. Developed countries had low rates of inflation and relatively stable currencies. In recent years, however, the high rates of inflation in all the economically developed world and the instability of exchange rates have brought these concerns to the evaluation of all investments.[11]

In analyzing the impact of inflation on the cash flows of a project, we must consider the effects of inflation-increased wages and general operating costs as well as the ability to pass on cost increases in the form of higher prices. The market for the finished product may permit price increases exceeding the net cost increases, or allowable price increases may be less than cost increases. However, in the absence of a monetary correction policy (as in Brazil), the taxation assumptions are important. The problem is that depreciation is usually based on historical cost. The increase in earning power of an asset caused by the inflationary effects on the currency is taxed heavily. Thus, part of the cur-

---

[11]Inflation and exchange rate fluctuations also affect the discount rate used to evaluate projects. This issue is discussed in Chapter 14.

rency erosion might be recovered by higher selling prices. Yet this recovery is accomplished by higher profits, which are taxed using the original cost basis of depreciation. A similar situation appears with the evaluation of the terminal value of the project. This value will be increased by inflation; however, part of this increase will be taxed away.

Different aspects of a project are likely to be affected by different rates of inflation. Labor costs may increase at an expected rate of 5% per year and raw materials at 4%; many of the fixed costs of the firm (such as depreciation or amortization of research and development costs), may not change if replacement of fixed assets is not contemplated in the near future. Accordingly, the rate of price increase needed to sustain standard profits over the short term usually will be much less than the inflation rate associated with many of the costs; the costs apply to a fraction of the revenues, whereas the sales price increase applies to all the revenues.

Inflation in another economy poses additional problems in the evaluation of a project because of the potential effect of inflation on the *currency exchange rates.* With a relatively high inflation rate and goods whose quantity demanded is sensitive to price changes, the country must eventually devalue its currency. A country's relatively high inflation makes its goods less competitive in the world market and forces the country's balance of payments into continuous deficits. The country loses reserves and faces eventual depreciation of its currency. However, over the short term, relative rates of inflation and exchange depreciations often differ. In addition, the inflation rate relevant to exchange rate fluctuations is an *average* of the inflation rates that prevail in different sectors of the economy. The specific investment project will be exposed to only a portion of the various sectors in the economy.

Value of Equipment Contribution

When manufacturing is involved in a project, the contribution of used equipment from the parent can be a central item. The equipment may cost $100,000 new, have a depreciated book value for tax purposes of $40,000 to the parent, and have a fair used market value in the project's host country of $60,000.[12] Transferring the equipment to the project at any price above $40,000 forces the parent to incur either a capital

---

[12]Except for import duties and shipping charges, the used market price in the host country and the parent's home country should be the same. In the absence of this identity, the relevant price would be the *higher* charge, assuming the parent would operate to maximize its own return from the sale of used equipment. From the *project's* standpoint, the relevant price is the *lower* one. That is, the parent manager could sell the equipment at the higher price, taking a profit. In a second transaction, the project manager then could buy similar equipment at a lower price.

gains tax or ordinary income tax on recapture of depreciation, depending on the situation and the interpretation. On the other hand, transferring at any price below $60,000 means that there is an implicit investment or subsidy in the project by the parent in the amount by which the nominal value differs from $60,000.

The *value* of the equipment to the project may be taken as the fair market price in the host country ($60,000). However, the cost of the equipment to the parent is the present book value ($40,000), plus shipping expenses, plus any tax payment due because of the difference between the book value and the market value in the foreign country. Assume shipping costs paid by the parent are $5,000. This cost implies a $15,000 difference between the book value of the equipment adjusted for transportation costs ($45,000) and the local market value ($60,000). This $15,000 would be treated as excess depreciation subject to recapture by the taxing authorities in the parent's country. Using a 50% tax rate, the parent company would owe the tax authorities $7,500. Thus, the cost of the investment to the parent is $52,500, composed of the $40,000 book value plus the $5,000 shipping costs plus $7,500 for incremental taxes. Since the host country accepted the value of the equipment at $60,000 as part of the investment, the parent company is making a profit of $7,500 ($60,000 − $52,500), which is part of the investment in the new project.

Because the economics of equipment typically are intertwined with production, it may be difficult for the parent to look at a project in this light. However, the incremental cash flow associated with the project investment is the focus of the analysis, and the relevant price to the project is the fair market price ($60,000).

The parent can help the project in another way which eliminates the problem of the taxes imputed to the parent by depreciation recapture on a $60,000 sale. If tax authorities in the two countries permit it, the parent may be able to claim a transfer of the equipment to the project at $40,000 in value (hence, incurring no tax by selling at book value), whereas the local taxing authorities may permit a higher valuation (for example, $80,000) for purposes of depreciation and/or investment by the parent. A higher value for depreciation purposes permits the project to shelter more of its income from profitable operations from local taxes. A larger base for investment also increases the parent's claim on profits (as a percentage of investment) or loan repayments (in the event much of the investment is called a "loan"). This transaction often is illegal because taxing authorities may require a common basis for valuation.[13]

---

[13]In the National Industrial Conference Board study cited earlier in the text, one of every eight companies interviewed said they contributed machinery to their foreign subsidiaries, usually to Latin American countries and less frequently to European subsidiaries.

These considerations may be relevant even when the equipment contributed by the parent is new. This is particularly the case when the parent company is the manufacturer of the equipment and when the specialized nature of the equipment does not allow for a readily available market price. In this case the host country may challenge the true value of the equipment and the home country may question the allocation of revenues between profits and costs.

Taxation of Income

The cash flows available from a project are affected by the taxes paid to the governments involved. Although there is little merit in learning the details of current international taxation agreements (because tax laws, treaties, and enforcement practices change over time), one must be aware of the basic concepts that determine the general philosophy of taxation affecting a project.[14] We now examine some of these concepts.

It is generally accepted that *equity* dictates that persons in similar situations should pay similar taxes. However, the definition of "similar situations" is largely affected by some of the concepts to be discussed briefly here.

Foreign income can be taxed on a cash basis or on an accrual basis. On a *cash basis,* foreign income is taxable when it is received in the form of cash for dividends, royalties, and so forth. On an *accrual basis,* income is taxed according to the period in which sales and associated costs are incurred and the *right* to receive cash is confirmed. The actual cash receipts and expenditures may not have taken place or may have taken place several accounting periods before. Given the complexities associated with accrual systems, there is a tendency for countries to tax foreign income on a cash basis instead of on an accrual basis. However, the result also is a function of how the taxable entity is defined.

A broader definition of the *corporate entity* reduces the merits of this argument with respect to the multinational. Thus, if Shell is not just a corporation in the Netherlands, but is in fact a worldwide citizen, then taxes should be due on that worldwide income. Sometimes a broad entity concept is desired by the parent for tax purposes; the use of a branch for foreign operations makes it possible for the U.S. corporation to consolidate branch losses in earlier years, offsetting taxable

---

[14]Information about tax arrangements of a particular country can be furnished by local governmental, financial, and legal sources. In addition, popular business chronicles in many industrialized countries often feature the latest "tax haven." A summary of some tax issues and a bibliography are contained in Appendix 2 of this chapter.

profits in other operations. At other times, the parent prefers a separate subsidiary in another land, especially when such an arrangement delays or avoids imposition of taxes by the parent's home country. This avoidance is especially valuable when the firm wishes to transfer funds from one nation to another. If the home land taxes profits only when these profits are remitted home, then a "tax-haven" subsidiary which receives funds from a foreign operating subsidiary can reinvest these funds in some other land. Had this intermediate corporation not existed, the withdrawal of profits from the operating subsidiary would have created a tax liability in the home country, reducing the amount that could be reinvested in the other land.

Once the entity is broadened to include operations in other lands, then there is a jurisdictional question. The policy among nations has been to recognize the injustice of *dual taxation* upon the same entity. Country X will tax the operations of Zebracorp in its land and perhaps impose withholding taxes on dividends remitted to the home nation. The home land may permit Zebracorp to receive partial or total credit for the taxes paid to country X. Typical choices involve the option either (1) to deduct the taxes paid to country X from gross income taxable at home, or (2) to compute the taxes that would have been due at home had all income been received there and then to deduct the taxes paid in country X from the home country tax liability. Normally, Zebracorp will prefer the latter course, in which there is a full credit against the home country's taxes for the taxes previously paid, as opposed to a simple deduction against taxable income.

Many nations also operate on the basis of special *tax treaties* which further adjust the amounts that may be paid or withheld in those countries. In these situations the subsidiary may not even have to file a tax return in country X if the operations are carefully kept within well-defined guidelines. For example, the United States presently has special tax treaties with more than twenty nations which permit this nonfiling.

Finally, tax laws are influenced by *special policies* that are designed to achieve certain goals. The country may wish to sponsor particular types of development by granting major income tax concessions such as lower rates, a moratorium on taxes, or rebates. To meet competition from other nations, taxes may be deferred or reduced on trading companies or export financing corporations. As an example of special governmental tax incentives for exports, Ireland eliminates all corporate income taxes until 1990 on firms' profits from export sales. Since Ireland is a member of the European Economic Community, which provides free trade benefits to firms operating in the EEC nations, this benefit is substantial. Alternatively, special taxes may be imposed which force companies to repatriate earnings in consideration of the parent country's balance of payments.

Remission of Funds

For the *project*, the relevant cash inflow is the return from operations after adjustment for local corporate taxes. From the *parent's* view, however, the crucial variable is the remission of funds to the parent treasury in New York or London. Accordingly, from this point of view the cash flows are related to (1) the investment; (2) the supervisory payments net of the costs to provide the supervision; (3) royalties, interest, and dividend remission; and (4) loan principal and equity return.

In the 1966 study by the National Industrial Conference Board, corporation managers noted that the key factor in a country's remittance policy was the *possibility* of remittance, whether or not the managers had expectations of large remittances. The European countries' record of liberal policy on remittance was in their favor, although some experienced executives feared that recent restrictions might recur. Some managers attempted to negotiate formal agreements on withdrawals, although this approach typically applied to earnings and not to capital. Managers of newer companies favored parent loans rather than equity to a greater degree than managers of experienced multinationals, although the risk for long-term loans is similar to that of equity. Managers of the newer firms assumed these "loans" were more easily retrievable, while others felt that easy availability of equity from the parent was a poor motivator for the local manager when compared to a loan obligation with fixed principal repayment. Companies with an "international" appearance were not as concerned about remission as the "nationals with international operations." Some managers viewed earnings on a flexible approach, looking at each land individually. Others regarded the cash generated by earnings as a pool that should be remitted to a tax haven for the reasons noted earlier.

EVALUATING INTERNATIONAL CASH FLOWS: AN EXAMPLE

As an illustration of the concepts discussed in the preceding section, we will analyze a specific investment case: Zebracorp's proposed project in Palma.

Selecting Relevant Operating Cash Flows

First we will assume that there are no restrictions on cash flow repatriations and that the exchange rates are expected to remain constant.

Zebracorp currently exports 5,000 units per month to country X at a price of $2.00 per unit. The variable cost of producing these units and delivering them to Palma, the capital and major distribution point of the country, is $1.00 per unit. The Minister of Development has approached Zebracorp with a proposal that, instead of exporting to country X, the firm install a small manufacturing operation in Palma that would cost $300,000. In return for an increase in tariffs against other firms, Zebracorp will agree to sell its product at $1.80, to buy certain raw materials from local suppliers, and to use local managers. The total costs of local labor and materials will be $0.50 per unit. The sale price and the prices paid locally will be fixed in local currency for 5 years. After that period Zebracorp will turn over the investment to a local investor for the sum of $1.00. Under this proposed arrangement Zebracorp believes it can sell about 10,000 units per month. Other materials can be purchased from the parent at $0.30 per unit, and the parent will receive a direct contribution to overhead after variable costs of $0.10 per unit sold. There is a 5-year straight-line depreciation of the $300,000 of equipment. Taxes are 50% of profits in country X and the parent country also has a 50% tax rate with direct credit for country X's taxes.

Should Zebracorp accept the Minister's proposal? We begin by looking at the cash flows in Exhibit 13.1. The rate of return on the proposed project, after taking into account the revenues foregone from the current export sales, is only 3.3%.[15]

After this analysis, the company decides to reject the project. The Minister then hints that Alphacorp, a major competitor, is probably interested in the proposal. Does this fact change the decision? If Zebracorp executives believe the Minister's assertion, then they must accept a probable loss in sales of the 5,000 units presently sold. Hence, the relevant cash flow in this case is the basic cash flow of the project, $96,000 per year for 5 years, and the rate of return is now 18% (see Exhibit 13.1).

Cash Flows to Parent versus Cash Flows to Project

Suppose the Minister of Development, upon hearing of Zebracorp's intentions not to invest in Palma, then notes that it would be appropriate if all the cash from the project were left on deposit locally, at no interest. At the end of the 5-year period the accumulated cash may be remitted to the parent.[16] What is the rate of return of the project to

---

[15]For those readers unfamiliar with discounting and the calculation of the rate of return, a brief summary of these concepts may be found in Appendix 1 to this chapter. Tables of present values of 1 unit of a currency received in a future period at different discount rates are shown at the end of this book.

[16]Note that the restriction is expressed in terms of *cash*, not profits. In this example, the amount of cash available from the project is higher than profits by the amount of the depreciation. In a project with indefinite life, the restriction is likely to be expressed in terms of profits.

EXHIBIT 13.1 Palma Project: Initial Proposal

Cash Flow Generated By Project		
Revenues = 10,000 × $1.80	$18,000	per month
Variable costs = 10,000 × $0.80	−8,000	per month
Operating profit per month	$10,000	per month
Operating revenues per year		$120,000
Depreciation ($300,000/5)[a]		−60,000
Profit for tax purposes		$ 60,000
Local taxes at 50%		−30,000
Profit after taxes		30,000
Depreciation[a]		+60,000
Net annual cash flow in country X		$90,000
Yearly profit on materials sold by parent		
(12 × 10,000 × $0.10 less 50% of total for taxes)		6,000
Net cash flow to parent with full repatriation		$96,000
Cash Flow Foregone On Exports		
Revenues = 5,000 × $2	$10,000	per month
Variable costs = 5,000 × $1	−5,000	per month
Extra profits	$ 5,000	per month
Extra taxes at 50%	−2,500	per month
Extra cash flow per month	$ 2,500	per month
Extra cash flow per year which is foregone		−30,000
Net incremental cash flow		$66,000
Rate Of Return		
$66,000 return per year, for 5 years, on a $300,000		
investment		3.3%
Ignoring foregone export sales, $96,000 return per		
year, for 5 years, on a $300,000 investment		18.0%

[a]Depreciation is a noncash expense, subtracted to compute taxable income, then added back to compute cash flow.

Zebracorp? If the funds are blocked until later years, the only cash flow to the parent during earlier years relates to the profits in the materials produced—$6,000 per year. In the fifth year the parent would receive $450,000 accumulated in cash. From the point of view of cash flows available to the parent, the rate of return is 10.2% (see Exhibit 13.2).[17]

If the example is altered to allow for a deterioration in the exchange rate of the local currency vis-à-vis the parent country's cur-

[17]Notice that we separate the operating cash flows generated by the project and the alternative *channels* by which that cash may be remitted. When government does not dictate a specific channel, tariff and tax considerations may dictate different approaches.

EXHIBIT 13.2 Palma Project: Cash Flows and Rate of Return to Project and to Parent When Cash is Not Repatriated Until Fifth Year and Exchange Rates Are Constant

	CASH FLOWS TO:	
	Project	Parent
Investment	$300,000	$300,000
Cash flow per year (5 years)	96,000	6,000
Terminal cash flow (5th year)	0	450,000
Rate of return	18.0%	10.2%

rency, then the results change again, regardless of whether the analysis is computed in terms of local currency (the cruzeiro) or parent currency (the U.S. dollar). Suppose the expected deterioration is 5% per year after the first year, with an initial exchange rate of Cr10/$.

The value of the raw material profits will deteriorate if the prices of raw materials purchased from the parent are fixed in cruzeiros. The relevant cash flow to the parent is *dollar cash flow* above the manufacturing cost. With constant costs of operation, the profit margin will shrink. The example included payment of $0.30 per unit, equal to Cr3.00 at the initial exchange rate of Cr10/$, and variable profits of $0.10 before tax. By the fifth year the cruzeiros will have deteriorated by 20%, and the value of the payment at that point is only 80% of $0.30, or $0.24. Hence, assuming production costs continue to be $0.20 per unit, the unit cash flow contributed is $0.04. Thus, after a 20% decline in exchange rates, the actual margin has declined 60% from $0.10 per unit to $0.04 per unit.[18]

The unit profit to the parent from selling raw materials after allowance for the 5% annual deterioration in the cruzeiro is presented in the upper part of Exhibit 13.3. Adding to these figures the dollar value of the local operating cash flows, we can compute the dollar value to Zebracorp of the project's cash flow—even though portions of the flow are not remitted to the parent. This produces a rate of return of 13.8%. However, in terms of cash flows actually received by the parent, only the proceeds from the raw material purchases are received during the earlier years. Assuming the funds are blocked until the fifth year, the operating cash flows are not received by the parent until then, after a total depreciation of the cruzeiro of 20%. Under these conditions, Exhibit 13.3 shows that the rate of return to the parent, in contrast to the project as a whole, is only 5.4%.

Alternatively, the manager may wish to value the return of Zebra-

---

[18]As a general formula in any simple inflationary evaluation, if x is the percentage change in gross revenues per unit and y is the initial profit margin, then the percentage decrease or increase in profits (z) is (x/y) times 100. Using the example, $x = -20\%$, $y = 33\frac{1}{3}\%$, and $z = (-20\%/33\frac{1}{3}\%) \times 100 = -60\%$.

EXHIBIT 13.3 Palma Project: Cash Flows and Rate of Return to Project, Measured in U.S. Dollars, When Cruzeiro Depreciates and Cash Is Not Repatriated Until Fifth Year

	Year 1	Year 2	Year 3	Year 4	Year 5
			CASH FLOWS TO PROJECT		
Cash flow to parent from sale of raw materials					
Unit payment	$ 0.30	$ 0.285	$0.2708	$0.2572	$ 0.2444
Cost	(0.20)	(0.20)	(0.20)	(0.20)	(0.20)
Unit profit[a]	$ 0.10	$ 0.085	$0.0708	$0.0572	$ 0.0444
Yearly cash flows[b]	$ 6,000	$ 5,100	$ 4,248	$ 3,432	$ 2,661
Local operating cash flows	90,000	85,500	81,225	77,164	73,306
Total cash flows	$96,000	$90,600	$85,473	$80,596	$ 75,967

Dollar return on $300,000 investment = 13.8%

CASH FLOWS TO PARENT

Cash flow to parent from sale of raw materials[b]	$ 6,000	$ 5,100	$ 4,248	$ 3,432	$ 2,661
Terminal cash flow[c]	—	—	—	—	366,528
Total	$ 6,000	$ 5,100	$ 4,248	$ 3,432	$369,189

Dollar return on $300,000 investment = 5.4%

[a]The rough approach in the text ignored the effects of compounding. Thus, the 5% is applied to a smaller base each year, leaving $0.044 per unit in year 5, rather than the $0.040 mentioned in the text.

[b]Equal to unit profit, times 120,000 units, less 50% tax.

[c]Equal to [$90,000 × 5 years × (0.95)^4]

corp in terms of local currency, the cruzeiro. Since the payments for new materials were assumed to be made in cruzeiros, the local currency values and the associated investment and cash flows create roughly the same value as the return calculated earlier for a constant exchange rate, 18.0%. However, the flows must be adjusted for the decline in profits to the parent associated with the depreciation of the cruzeiro. The cruzeiro value of those raw material profits will be lower than under no depreciation of the local currency against the parent's currency. As a result, the rate of return should be slightly lower. The local investment is Cr3,000,000 (assuming an initial exchange rate of Cr10/$), local income is Cr900,000 per year, and the firm generates cruzeiro income for the parent as noted in Exhibit 13.4. The adjusted rate of return is 17.5%.

Thus, depending on the currency used to measure cash flows, and on whether one considers total project cash flows or only the cash flows received by the parent, there are sharply divergent returns associated

EXHIBIT 13.4 Palma Project: Cash Flow and Rate of Return to Project, Measured in Cruzeiros, When Cruzeiro Depreciates

	Year 1	Year 2	Year 3	Year 4	Year 5
Cash flow to parent from sale of raw materials					
In U.S. dollars[a]	$6,000	$5,100	$4,248	$3,432	$2,661
Exchange rate	Cr10/$	Cr10.5/$	Cr11.03/$	Cr11.58/$	Cr12.16/$
In cruzieros	Cr60,000	Cr53,550	Cr46,834	Cr39,730	Cr32,345
Local operating cash flows	900,000	900,000	900,000	900,000	900,000
Total	Cr960,000	Cr953,550	Cr946,834	Cr939,730	Cr932,345

Cruzeiro return on CR3,000,000 investment = 17.5%

[a]From Exhibit 13.3.

with this simple investment. A summary of the rates of return computed is presented in Exhibit 13.5.

From the point of view of the parent company, there are two major problems. First, the currency is blocked. The parent has substantial cash flows from the project which remain idle because of restrictions of the host country's government. Second, in terms of the currency invested by the parent, the loss in dollar purchasing power of the local currency is substantial.

These problems are acute in this case of a 5-year investment horizon. However, very often the investment by the parent company has a much longer time horizon, in which case the impact of initial controls on repatriation of cash and changes in the relative value of currencies may be evened out over the long run, if local prices are allowed to change. If the parent intends to continue expanding a profitable local operation, then a repatriation restriction is irrelevant to the evaluation of the project. The expansion of the operation would require that profits be retained and reinvested in the project anyway, instead of being

EXHIBIT 13.5 Palma Project: Comparative Rates of Return

	With Cruzeiro Depreciation	Constant Cruzeiro/Dollar Rate
Returns to total project		
Measured in local currency (Cr)	17.5%	18.0%
Measured in U.S. dollars	13.8%	18.0%
Returns to parent in U.S. dollars with profit repatriation blocked until fifth year	5.4%	10.2%

remitted to the parent company. Even if the project does not require any reinvestment, the blocked funds could be invested temporarily in a short-term project in the country or invested in the bonds of the local government or local industry and provide a positive rate of return. This issue is now addressed.

REINVESTMENT OF A PROJECT'S CASH FLOWS

We have evaluated the Palma project in terms of the internal rate of return of the specific project. The computation of internal rates of return assumes implicitly that all the cash flows generated by the project can be *reinvested* at the calculated rate of return. This may or may not be true in the specific project.

From the standpoint of the parent, which requires funds for other projects, or the project where there are currencies blocked by the host country, management needs to focus on the reinvestment rate for the specific project. In many cases reinvestment will be in the project itself. However, the rate of return on these reinvestments may not be the same as for the original project. If the reinvestment rate is dictated by a host country blocking repatriation, then the rate obtained from reinvestment probably will be below the one obtained in the original project. A reasonable approach to take into account reinvestment rates is the use of the *terminal rate of return* (TROR). This approach is also useful in any situation in which there are unequal project lives.[19]

The TROR requires the analyst to state the reinvestment rate for cash flows from a project. The reinvestment rate assumed to compute the TROR may be the firm's cost of capital[20] or it may be a lower rate based on investment of the idle cash in short-term securities. It may change over time, reflecting alternative reinvestment rate assumptions. Whatever the rate, the cash throw-offs from a project are compounded *forward* to some horizon point in the computation of TROR. The initial investment is compared to this summed horizon value (the sum of each year's cash flows compounded forward to the same point). Then the internal rate of return which will equate the investment to that compounded horizon value is computed.

---

[19]Again, readers who wish to review discounting are referred to Appendix 1 in this chapter. A more detailed discussion of the terminal rate of return can be found in Carter, *Portfolio Aspects of Corporate Capital Budgeting* (Lexington, Mass.: D. C. Heath and Company, 1974), pp. 31–38. The concept of the Terminal Rate of Return is related to the duration concepts which are increasingly part of the financial institution literature. For examples and explanations, see Walter J. Woerheide, "Measuring the Interest Rate Risk Exposure of Savings and Loans," Chapter 3 in *The Savings and Loan Industry: Current Problems and Possible Solutions*, Westport, Connecticut: Greenwood Press, 1984.

[20]In this case the terminal rate of return will produce the same ranking of projects as when the cash flows are discounted at the company's cost of capital.

Algebraically, assume that the reinvestment rate is r'. Each period's cash flow, Y_i, is compounded forward to the horizon, n, at this rate. The TROR (r_T) is the rate of return equating the initial investment, Y_0 (<0), and the sum of compounded horizon values to 0. Thus,

$$0 = Y_0 + \frac{Y_1(1 + r')^{n-1}}{(1 + r_T)^1} + \frac{Y_2(1 + r')^{n-2}}{(1 + r_T)^2} + \cdots + \frac{Y_n}{(1 + r_T)^n}$$

$$= Y_0 + \sum_{i=1}^{n} \frac{Y_i(1 + r')^{n-i}}{(1 + r_T)^n}$$

Assume Zebracorp considers another \$300,000 project in country Y with a stable currency and similar returns of \$96,000 per year for 5 years. The taxation policy is the same, but none of the return is related to purchases of parts from the parent. Hence, all of the \$96,000 is generated by the project in country Y. If free repatriation is assumed, then the rate of return to the parent is the discount rate which equates a \$300,000 investment with \$96,000 per year for 5 years, or 18.0% as calculated in Exhibit 13.1.

If currency repatriation is blocked and cash must be kept idle, the rate of return must be based on a \$300,000 investment and \$480,000 (equal to $5 \times \$96,000$) received at the end of the fifth year. The return is then 9.9%.

Finally, assuming the money can be reinvested locally at 5% after taxes, we may compute a terminal rate of return. This is the return for which a \$300,000 investment will provide the amount received after 5 years from the project's operating cash flows and reinvestment cash flows. The calculation is shown in the accompanying table.

\$96,000 first year invested for 4 years at 5% compounded	\$116,689
\$96,000 second year invested for 3 years at 5% compounded	111,132
\$96,000 third year invested for 2 years at 5% compounded	105,840
\$96,000 fourth year invested for 1 year at 5% compounded	100,800
\$96,000 fifth year received at the end of the year	96,000
Total at end of fifth year	\$530,461
Terminal rate of return on a \$300,000 investment	12.1%

The *net terminal value* (NTV) is computed in similar fashion except that the investment is compounded forward at some opportunity (reinvestment) rate and subtracted from the compounded value of the accumulated operating cash flows. However, when the discount rate is related to the cost of capital, this decision rule will provide the same accept or reject signal as a normal net present value evaluation. In the case of the project with low reinvestment rates the results may differ.

In evaluating a single project, a manager may need to make various assumptions for projects located in different countries as well as study a given project under alternative hypotheses about repatriation and reinvestment. Consider how the relative rankings of the projects vary (1) when there is free repatriation, (2) when the currency is blocked, and (3) when the currency is blocked but with a reinvestment assumption. A sample of such calculations is shown in Exhibit 13.6. The outlay for each of three projects is held constant at $1,000, the horizon period is 5 years, and the reinvestment rate is 10%.

Although these examples are simplified to provide level cash flows in most cases and changing parity rates are ignored, observe that the pattern of reinvestment affects the results and that depending on the assumptions made regarding repatriation and reinvestment, the return to the parent from an investment will vary sharply.[21] In particular, notice the following:

1. Under a simple rate of return calculation, the project with a very short life and high flows in early years is favored.
2. When the currencies are blocked, all project returns decline. The declines are especially sharp for projects B and C where the blocking period relative to the productive life of the investments is large.

EXHIBIT 13.6   Rate of Return and Project Rankings Under Alternative Measures of Returns[a]

	PROJECT		
	A	B	C
Cash Flows			
Outlay	($1,000)	($1,000)	($1,000)
Year 1	0	700	400
Year 2	200	700	400
Year 3	300	0	400
Year 4	400	0	400
Year 5	800	0	0
Total inflows	$1,700	$1,400	$1,600
Terminal value of inflows at 10%	$1,869	$1,957	$1,042
Rate of return (Cash received yearly, reinvested at rate of return)	14%	(25%)	22%
Rate of return (Blocked until year 5, no reinvestment)	(11%)	7%	10%
Terminal rate of return (Blocked until year 5, reinvested at 10%)	13%	14%	(15%)

[a]The preferred choices are circled. Figures are rounded to the nearest whole percentage.

[21]The zeros in later years for projects B and C are for ease of calculation. They can be replaced with small values and the earlier flows adjusted to provide similar rankings.

3. Under TROR, a reversal of project rankings is obtained. A project that was never dominant under the other two evaluations becomes the most desired project.

Because the terminal rate of return calculations eliminate one of the main objections to the rate of return analysis (that is, in the latter calculation the reinvestment rate is the same as the project's rate of return),[22] and because the rate of return can be more appealing to corporate executives than net present value (even though the latter is technically superior) this measure will be included in future examples in this text.

SUMMARY

A variety of theories emphasize different factors in corporate investment decisions beyond the simple goals cited in normative financial theory. In the international environment, considerations such as comparative advantage, taxation policy, operational constraints or incentives relating to resources, the basic profit opportunities of a foreign investment, diversification strategies, and a strategy to limit losses are economic variables that may influence a decision to invest abroad.

Several descriptive studies of the motivation of firms abroad note the importance of market share and growth opportunities coupled with uncertainty absorption created by multiple layers of management. The product life cycle, in which maturation of the markets at home induces the corporation to move abroad, is consistent with the motivation found in some studies.

Among the difficulties encountered in measuring the cash flows in a foreign project, we discussed the problems presented when there are substantial interdependencies or joint effects with the parent sponsor of the project. These interdependencies include vertical and horizontal combinations, alternative cost and revenue assumptions for the finished products, and economies of scale in production or distribution. The use of royalties or supervisory fees as they affect the return also must be considered.

In looking at inflation and its effects upon cash flows, we stressed that an inflationary environment may result in different rates of increase for various cost components, and indeed the general rate of in-

---

[22]For example, create a cash flow and compute the rate of return. Delay receipt of $1.00 from one year's cash flow to a later year and compound it at the rate of return of the project. This action will provide a new cash flow which has the same rate of return as that of the original project. Hence, the implicit worth of the earlier receipt is the rate of return; that is, the implied opportunity cost of the funds is independent of the firm's cost of capital.

crease in the price of the product may be higher or lower than some general economywide inflation index. Inflation will also have differing effects upon the value of the firm's assets and upon the effective corporate tax rate, depending on what adjustments are made to the income statement in determining taxable income for cost items such as depreciation. Finally, currency parities may adjust only imprecisely to different national inflation levels across countries.

Another important problem in the estimation of the cash flows in a foreign project is the impact on the value of investment when there is a contribution of equipment from the parent. A brief introduction to the major concepts of taxation argued that the enlarged concept of the corporate entity has increasingly made governments believe that corporations in their land should pay taxes on profits earned anywhere in the world with some adjustment for local taxes paid in other lands. In response, a major motivation for tax havens has been to avoid the taxes on funds removed from one foreign subsidiary to be invested in another foreign subsidiary. Finally, there are special national or supranational policies designed to encourage foreign trade or to protect a balance of payments position.

The issue of the *remission* of funds and the concern of companies for the return of cash to the parent has been raised but not resolved. This concern led to the discussion of whose cash flows are relevant— the parent's or the project's. This issue will return later, but there are sharply divergent returns depending on the numeraire selected for evaluating the cash flows and on the cash flows received by the project versus the parent.

In evaluating the returns, we used the familiar concepts of rate of return and net present value. These standards were supplemented by the *terminal rate of return*, which permits an explicit consideration of the reinvestment rate for projects. This assumption is especially important when there are blocked funds that cannot be removed from a host country until a later period. The returns of a project vary depending on which standard of evaluation is considered. Tables of present values of one unit of a currency received at various periods and at different discount rates are shown in the Appendix to this book.

QUESTIONS

1. What factors make the cash flows from a project create different values for the parent and for the subsidiary which undertakes the project?

2. How does the terminal rate of return differ from the rate of return? How would you use it in a project which has revaluations (appreciation or depreciation) likely for the local currency against the parent's currency? Does it make a difference if the funds are blocked or remitted?

3. "I don't worry about anticipating currency changes; all I care about is the absolute level of inflation. I just reduce the value of the funds by that amount to get the equivalent in German marks." (German corporate executive). Do you agree with this analysis?

4. How would you attempt to cope with the political risks in a country when the government has a record of rapid changes in personnel?

5. "They claim we exploit them since we demand a 1-year payout on all projects. But, you know, we have had so many things nationalized in Latin America in the last 30 years with all these revolving governments that a short life is all we can fairly anticipate. Now, one country may feel we exploit them if they do not have nationalization in a given decade, but we have to look at our portfolio of returns from all the nations over many years. So we have no choice." Comment.

BIBLIOGRAPHY

Aharoni, Yair, *The Foreign Investment Decision Process.* Boston: Graduate School of Business Administration, Harvard University, 1966.

Aliber, Robert, "A Theory of Direct Foreign Investment," in *The International Corporation: A Symposium,* Charles Kindleberger, ed., pp. 17–34. Cambridge, Mass.: MIT Press, 1970.

Boadway, Robin, "A Note on the Treatment of Foreign Exchange in Project Evaluation," *Economica,* Nov. 1978, pp. 391–98.

Bruno, Catherine J., and Mark R. Eaker, "Further Evaluation of Financing Costs for Multinational Subsidiaries." Working paper. Dallas, Texas: Edwin L. Cox School of Business, Southern Methodist University, 1981.

Carter, E. Eugene. *Portfolio Aspects of Corporate Capital Budgeting.* Lexington, Mass.: D.C. Heath and Company, 1974.

Carter, William Gilbert, "National Support of International Ventures," *Columbia Journal of World Business,* Sept.–Oct. 1972, pp. 6–12.

Caves, Richard E., "International Corporations: The Industrial Economics of Foreign Investment," *Economica,* Feb. 1971, pp. 1–27.

Davidson, William H., "The Location of Foreign Direct Investment Activity: Country Characteristics and Experience Effects," *Journal of International Business Studies,* Fall 1980, pp. 9–22.

Foster, Earl M., "The Impact of Inflation on Capital Budgeting Decisions," *Quarterly Review of Economics and Business,* Autumn 1970, pp. 19–24.

Gale, Bradley T., "Market Share and Rate of Return," *Review of Economics and Statistics,* Dec. 1972, pp. 412–23.

Hackett, John T., "The Multinational Corporation and Worldwide Inflation," *Financial Executive,* Feb. 1975, pp. 64–73.

Hymer, Stephen, *The International Operations of National Firms: A Study of Direct Investment.* Unpublished doctoral dissertation, Massachusetts Institute of Technology, 1960.

Labys, Walter C., "International Commodity Markets, Models, and Forecasts," *Columbia Journal of World Business,* Winter 1976, pp. 36–45.

Lessard, Donald R., "Transfer Prices, Taxes, and Financial Markets: Implications of Internal Financial Transfers within the Multinational Firm," in *Proceedings of the New York University Conference on Economic Issues of Multinational Firms,* Robert G. Hawkins, ed. New York: JAI Press, 1977.

Mikesell, Raymond F., et al., *Foreign Investment in the Petroleum and Mineral Industries.* Baltimore. Johns Hopkins Press, 1971.

Olstein, Robert A., and Thorton L. O'Glove, "Devaluation and Multinational Reporting," *Financial Analysts Journal,* Sept.–Oct. 1973, pp. 65–84.

Polk, Judd, et al., *U.S. Production Abroad and the Balance of Payments.* New York: National Industrial Conference Board, 1966.

Remmers, H. L., "A Note on Foreign Borrowing Costs," *Journal of International Business Studies,* Fall 1980, pp. 123–34.

Spitaller, Erich, "A Survey of Recent Quantitative Studies of Long-Term Capital Movements," *International Monetary Fund Staff Papers,* Mar. 1971, pp. 189–217.

Vernon, Raymond, "International Investment and International Trade in the Product Life Cycle," *Quarterly Journal of Economics,* May 1966, pp. 190–207.

Wilkins, Mira, *The Maturing of Multinational Enterprise: American Business Abroad from 1914 to 1970.* Cambridge, Mass.: Harvard University Press, 1974.

Discounting Techniques to Evaluate Cash Flows: Net Present Value and Internal Rate of Return

ONCE THE CASH flows are determined for a project, we need a means to evaluate these cash flows considering the time value of money. *Net present value* and the *internal rate of return* are two means by which to discount cash flows.

Suppose one has X dollars (e.g., $10) and the discount rate is r (e.g., 10%). At the end of 1 year the value Y_1 of the holding is:

$$Y_1 = X(1+r) \qquad Y_1 = \$10(1+0.10) = \$11.00$$

At the end of 2 years:

$$Y_2 = Y_1(1+r) = X(1+r)^2 \qquad Y_2 = \$10(1+0.10)^2 = \$12.10$$

Y_2 represents the *terminal value* of investment X at the end of the second year compounded annually at the rate r. One can reverse the procedure. Given Y_2 dollars at the end of 2 years and the rate of discount r, then X, the amount of money equivalent to Y_2 dollars 2 years hence, can be found.

$$X = \frac{Y_2}{(1+r)^2} \qquad X = \frac{\$12.10}{(1+0.10)^2} = \$10$$

and X is the *present value* of Y_2.

In capital budgeting, one estimates the Y values (yearly net cash flows) for the investment. A discount rate is selected which is the opportunity cost of funds to the firm (the cost of capital), r. Then X, the *net present value (NPV)* of the stream of cash flows, can be computed. This stream includes the initial investment, Y_0, which is negative, and the other $Y_i s$ which may be negative or positive.

$$X = Y_0 + \frac{Y_1}{(1 + r)} + \frac{Y_2}{(1 + r)^2} + \ldots + \frac{Y_n}{(1 + r)^n}$$

If the net present value is positive ($X > 0$), then the investment is considered desirable because it covers the cost of funds to the firm.

The rate of return *(ROR)* is also called the *discounted rate of return, internal rate of return,* or *return on investment.* The ROR is the rate at which the future cash flows can be discounted to equal the investment. It is obtained by using the same equation, but a slightly different analysis. Instead of assigning a discount rate r, the equation is solved for that rate for which the net present value of the stream of cash flows of an investment equals 0. That is,

$$0 = Y_0 + \frac{Y_1}{(1 + r)} + \frac{Y_2}{(1 + r)^2} + \ldots + \frac{Y_n}{(1 + r)^n}$$

where Y_0 is negative, representing the cash investment by the firm in the project.

These two standards will not always rank projects in the same way. Further, it is possible for a project to have more than one internal rate of return. One difficult assumption is that the project cash flows evaluated under a ROR calculation are presumed to continue to earn at that rate when reinvested. However, in evaluating single projects in the international setting, a general adjustment is useful which eliminates the limitations of some of the assumptions contained in these two models. This adjustment, the *terminal rate of return,* was discussed in Chapter 13.

International Taxation

2

ONE OF THE most complex aspects of international business is the area of international taxation. Understanding the rules surrounding domestic treatment of foreign income is the first difficulty. That obligation is compounded by the need for a thorough understanding of tax policies in the other nations that are potential bases for operations. The written code and the practical effect of the rules force most firms to rely extensively on local legal and tax representatives to explain the alternatives for business organization, dividend policy, capital structure, and so on. Several references are included in this appendix for the reader who desires more background information on the taxing policies in many nations. The excellent bibliography of international tax sources by Owens and Hovemeyer includes a detailed breakdown of publications concerning taxes in many specific nations.[1]

THE PHILOSOPHY OF TAXATION

Nations have a variety of reasons for enacting any particular tax. Sometimes taxation is for social reasons: to punish particular behavior, to en-

---

[1]Elisabeth A. Owens and Gretchen A. Hovemeyer, eds. *Bibliography on Taxation of Foreign Operations and Foreigners* (Cambridge, Mass.: International Tax Program, Harvard Law School, 1976).

courage other actions, or to redistribute income. Sometimes taxation is enforceability: A customs duty with an honest customs service and one port makes that tax more operational than some income taxes. Sometimes taxation is related to an international pattern, and reciprocity or comparable incentive policies dictate a particular code.

Many European nations have used a value-added tax (VAT) as a major source of revenue. Tax analysts consider this a national sales tax as opposed to an income tax. The tax is applied to the value of a product at each point in manufacture and is based on the selling price of the good. Each firm can credit against the tax the amount of VAT passed onto it by other suppliers and manufacturers. The advantage of the tax is that it encourages honesty. It is based on revenues, not profits; and since deductions from the applied tax must be supported, each manager in the chain is encouraged to seek accurate figures from the suppliers. VAT can be adjusted or forgiven to stimulate or discourage export sales, thus responding to balance of payments or domestic inflation problems. The problem with VAT is that there is a possibility of misallocation of resources, since VAT is a sales tax instead of an income tax. However, most nations that adopted a VAT have used it to replace an existing sales (turnover) tax. Some critics argue that the immediate imposition of such a tax causes an increase in inflation, but this charge can be blunted where governments pursue effective fiscal and monetary policies. VAT also is criticized for being a regressive tax, borne with regard to consumption rather than income. Most nations would like to rely on an income tax for individuals and corporations since it can be shown with minimal assumptions that an income tax on profits will reduce total output less than a sales tax or gross turnover tax will.

One major issue is *equity*. Most taxing authorities believe that people who have comparable incomes should pay the same tax and people who have different incomes should pay different taxes. When applied to personal income, this philosophy usually results in a variety of deductions from income for various minimum expenditures that are considered appropriate. There often is an allowance for extraordinary expenses that may occur, such as large medical bills. In the international scene this policy means that a corporation doing business abroad should pay taxes somewhere, regardless of its multinational status. The firm should be taxed on all income regardless of where earned, but there should be offsets for income taxes which different jurisdictions may impose. The basic concern, however, is that taxes should be paid on income as earned, and the taxation system should be equitable, however difficult that term is to define.[2]

Equity is a difficult issue when comparing tax rates on personal income in various countries. First, incomes have to be adjusted for *comparable purchasing power,* and the bundle of goods for a standard of living is related to the starting point. An Englishman who requires Jacob's water biscuits daily will find the cost of living substantially higher in Italy than a comparable Italian would face. Second, the tax rates have to be compared both *internally* and *externally.* British executives are quick to note high British taxes. For example, investment income can be taxed at 98% (with an asset tax which in some cases runs the total tax over 100%). The marginal tax on a $21,000 family income is 60% compared to 25% in the United States. On the other hand, an internal U.K. standard would have an argument for a progressive income tax by noting that less than one in twenty British taxpayers has an income above $8,600 per year. Furthermore, the British executive is far more able than a U.S. counterpart to have "perks," such as automobiles, paid for by his or her firm.[3] Third, the definition of taxable income and the existence of other taxes also must be considered. As an example, Swiss state and federal taxes on an income of SwF100,000 in 1979 were 5% and 17%, respectively. However, the Canton of Zurich added another tax of 25.5%. In addition, for all tax purposes, the Swiss code includes imputed rent for owner-occupied homes, further increasing the tax burden.[4] Variations in wealth taxes, capital gain taxes, and

---

[2]In terms of "double dipping," sometimes the taxing authorities are quite happy as long as only one taxpayer under their jurisdiction claims a deduction, such as depreciation, on a given asset. However, to the extent that another entity claims a different deduction for another taxing authority, this is tolerated. Thus, in the large asset area such as ships, aircraft, and the like, a number of arrangements have been created involving a British bank's purchase of an asset which is then immediately deducted in full against other revenues for British Inland Revenue purposes. Immediately, however, the bank offers a long-term lease to the ultimate American user of the asset, with a market-value purchase option at the end of the lease. For U.S. Internal Revenue Service purposes, this action taints the arrangement as a lease, meaning that the U.S. firm cannot treat payments as a lease deduction, but must regard the arrangement as a purchase with bank financing. However, such a tax treatment then allows the U.S. firm to deduct the investment tax credit, depreciation, and interest, as it would under any purchased asset which secures debt. (See "Two Bites at the Cherry," *Economist*, Apr. 18, 1981, p. 66.)

[3]Most countries of Western Europe have permitted revisions of various business accounts since World War II for tax purposes to adjust for inflation. Most of these adjustments have involved a single index applied to depreciable assets, although some countries included other accounts such as land and inventory. Countries such as Austria, France, and Italy provided annual adjustments if inflation exceeded a certain level; most other countries had a single adjustment to these accounts. Often smaller businesses did not take advantage of these optional adjustments, for typically a one-time tax was imposed on the step-up in basis, which ranged from ½% to 10%. The Scandinavian countries, Canada, the United Kingdom, and the United States have not permitted such adjustments, but instead have relied on changes in their codes involving accelerated depreciation, special investment credits, and the like to offset inflation. See George E. Lent, "Adjusting Taxable Profits for Inflation: The Foreign Experience," in Henry J. Aaron, *Inflation and the Income Tax* (Washington, D.C.: Brookings Institution, 1976), pp. 195–213, for more discussion of this adjustment for inflation within nations.

[4]See the letter from Niklaus Outhy, *Economist*, Feb. 24, 1979, p. 8.

death duties further complicate the analysis of tax burdens across nations.

A second issue in taxation is the *social or economic goals* that are encouraged or discouraged by the tax policy. Much of the concern over the U.S. tax policy relates to the loss or creation of jobs for U.S. workers. Various studies exist on U.S. exports and investment abroad and their effect on the balance of payments, the first level of jobs, and the ultimate level of jobs according to various assumptions of what the U.S. government would do in the absence of such jobs. Worldwide, one would expect that free trade would result in greater total output, but the total level of employment and the allocation of that employment *among* nations and among skill levels within nations are at the center of the controversy. No firm statement can be made, for the research tools necessary to understand this subject are not sufficiently refined and the data are not always available. A brief exchange of two proponents of different views is contained in the references to this appendix as part of the U.S. Congressional hearings on taxation of foreign income.

NATIONAL CORPORATE TAXATION POLICIES

Whatever the issues of philosophy, when the corporation faces the corporate tax scheme in a particular nation, there are special factors to be considered.

First, *taxes may be absolutely low* on corporate profits. The lands noted for especially hospitable taxes include Switzerland, Liechtenstein, Luxembourg, Panama, the Netherlands Antilles (Curação), the Bahamas, and Bermuda. Withholding taxes on intercorporate dividends are typically nonexistent in these nations, unlike some major industrial lands where high corporate tax rates and dividend withholding rates restrict the ability to move intercorporate funds about. Exhibit 13.1A summarizes some of these effective tax rates.

Second, the *definitions of taxable income* may be highly divergent among various nations. For example, constructive receipt is important. One nation may deem profits to be taxable as received on a cash basis whereas another nation would treat the same profits as taxable as earned on an accrual basis. One nation may provide greater latitude on the creation of reserves, permitting an offset of taxable revenues by these allocations for future contingencies. Some countries may give full credit for taxes on the income paid in other countries or have no tax on intercorporate dividends or earnings. Especially rapid depreciation or depletion arrangements also affect the definition of taxable income.

Third, *tax treaties* with other nations may influence the total taxation bill of the parent corporation. The United States has tax treaties with more than 30 nations, primarily with members of the European Economic Community and other industrialized nations. As a result, special allowance for avoiding withholding on dividends and interest paid by firms to nationals of the involved countries, special tax reductions on intercorporate dividends, and the like contribute to a simplification of the regulations which will affect any firm. The effects of some of these treaties are suggested in Exhibit 13.1A, for the normal withholding on dividends from corporations in most of those nations would be 30%–40%.

The ability to use low-tax countries solely as tax havens is limited. Many industrialized countries such as the United States are increasingly cautious about the definition of income and where it is held. Often, income is taxed regardless of remission, as emphasized in the 1962 U.S. tax reform measures. In addition, some of these countries, especially smaller developing nations, resent the label of a tax haven while at the same time desiring the economic contributions of major corporate investment. These lands are turning to industrialization, to the development of tourism, or to other tangible assets as an alternative to the tax haven option. Although pleased to provide help to corporations desiring to avoid the export controls imposed by their home countries, these nations believe their appeal simply as a tax-reducing location is not desirable. Other countries revel in their tax status; the Cayman Islands even has an official Tax Haven Committee to boost its image of low taxes.

The complexities of a particular tax code are too involved for any person but the specialist. However, as an aid to understanding the possible patterns in taxation for foreign income, the remainder of this appendix will outline some of the major issues in U.S. taxation of foreign source income. It is based in part on Michael J. McIntyre's *United States Taxation of Foreign Income with Special Emphasis on Private Investments in Developing Countries.*[5]

U.S. TAXATION OF INTERNATIONAL INCOME OF CORPORATIONS—BACKGROUND

The U.S. taxing authorities focus upon the *status* of the taxpayer (resident or citizen versus all others) and the *source* of the income. Citizens and residents generally are taxed on worldwide income, but with a

---

[5]Cambridge, Mass.: International Law Program, Harvard Law School, 1975.

EXHIBIT 13.1A Foreign Taxes on Subsidiaries of U.S. Corporations

Country	Statutory Corporate Income Tax Rate	Withholding Tax on Dividends to U.S. Parent	Maximum Foreign Net Tax on Earnings Remitted to the United States	Withholding Tax on Interest to U.S. Parent	Withholding Tax on Patent and Royalty Payments
Europe					
Belgium	48%	15%	55.8%	15%	0
Denmark	37%	5%[a]	40.2%	0%	0
France	50%	5%[a]	52.5%	10%	5%
Germany	46–63%[b]	15%[c]	54.1%	0%	0%
Greece	44%	38%	65.3%	43.4%	0%
Ireland	45%	35%	64.3%	35%	0%
Italy	36%[d]	5%[a]	39.2%	15%	0%
Netherlands	48%	5%[a]	50.6%	0%	0%
Norway	23–51%[e]	5%[a]	26.9%	15%	15%
Spain	36%	16.5%	46.6%	24%	15.4%
Sweden	56%[f]	5%[a]	58.2%	0%	0%
Switzerland	~10%[g]	15%	23.5%	5%	0%
United Kingdom	52%	15%[h]	~56.2%	0%	0%
The Americas					
Argentina	33%	17.5%	44.7%	11.25%	18%
Brazil	30%	25%	47.5%	25%	25%
Canada	40%[i]	15%	49.0%	15%	15%
Colombia	40%	20%	52.0%	0%	47.2%
Mexico	42%[j]	20%	53.6%		
Venezuela	42%[k]	15%	57.5%	42%[k]	42%[k]
Others					
Australia	46%	15%	54.1%	0%	20%
Japan	30–40%[e]	10%[a]	37.0%	10%	10%
South Africa	43%	15%	51.6%	10%	12.9%

[a] The withholding rates for these countries are all 15% except when a firm is owned almost completely by the U.S. parent, e.g., 90% or more in most cases. Some cases require a lower percentage of ownership, such as the Netherlands (25%), Norway (50%), and Sweden (50%).

[b] The effective German corporate tax rate on distributed profits (e.g., dividends) is about 46% and the effective corporate tax rate on undistributed profits is about 63%. These taxes are made up of a deductible municipal income tax averaging 15%, and federal taxes of 36% on distributed profits and 56% on undistributed profits.

cThe rate increases to 25% if the recipient owns at least 10% of the equity and reinvests more than 7½% of the dividends received.

dIncludes net effect of deductible local income taxes of about 14.7% gross.

eFirst figure is tax on distributed income; second figure is tax on undistributed income. "Maximum foreign net tax" column calculations assume all profits are distributed.

fIncludes net effect of local income taxes averaging 26% which are deductible from income taxable at the 40% national rate.

gThe federal income tax rate varies from 3.63% to 9.8% depending on the ratio of profits to net worth. In addition to the federal tax, each canton imposes its own income tax. The cantonal rates vary from 5% to 40%.

hThe U.S. U.K. Income Tax Treaty has been renegotiated. The treaty entitles a U.S. shareholder to a refund from the U.K. Inland Revenue of a portion of the advance corporation tax payable by the U.K. corporation when paying a dividend, less a withholding tax on the sum of the dividend and the refund.

Example:

	U.S. Corporation owning 10% or more of U.K. Corporation
Dividend paid	$65,000
Refund of advance corporation tax	17,500
	82,500
Less:	
Withholding tax @5%	4,125
Total received	$78,375

The proposed new treaty, which has been ratified by the British Parliament will be effective from various dates, some predating ratification.

iManufacturing profits. On other corporate profits, tax is 46%. Province taxes which vary from 0% to 7% are not included.

jThe Mexican corporate tax begins at 6% and reaches 42% on all income over $66,000.

kThe Venezuelan corporate tax rate on businesses not involved in the exploitation of minerals or hydrocarbons is 15% of income up to $23,000 progressing to 50% of income over $6,512,000.

SOURCE: Based on *Foreign and U.S. Corporate Income and Withholding Tax Rates*, Ernst and Ernst, New York, 1978, and J. Peter Gaskins, "Taxation of Foreign Source Income," *Financial Analysts Journal*, Sept.-Oct. 1973, p. 57. Many of these figures are based on tax treaties between the U.S. and the country listed. In some cases, the rates may not apply to a specific corporation.

credit for income taxes paid to other jurisdictions. For example, as an administrative expedient for U.S. citizens working abroad, the 1981 Economy Recovery Tax Act allows these citizens to exclude $95,000 of foreign income from U.S. taxes annually after 1985. Nonresidents are generally taxed only on their U.S. income. There are special rules to limit tax avoidance. A corporation's status is determined by incorporation and not by nationality or residence of shareholders. Corporations incorporated in the United States are U.S. corporations; all others are foreign corporations, even though all the shares may be owned by a U.S. corporation or citizens.

If *less than* 50% of the gross income of a *foreign* corporation is from conduct of a trade or business in the United States, then all its dividend and interest payments are considered foreign source income to the recipient, and special calculations may apply as noted below. Dividends paid by a *U.S. corporation* are considered foreign source income to the recipient only if *80% or more* of that corporation's gross income is from foreign sources. Special rulings apply for mineral companies and other firms in particular industries.

TAX POLICIES—AN OVERVIEW

The basic guideline within the tax system is that the United States claims jurisdiction over *all income* of its citizens and residents *wherever earned*. There is a credit for the income taxes paid to other nations, ranging up to the level of taxes that would have been paid had that income been earned in the United States. Alternatively, these foreign taxes may be deducted from taxable income. Furthermore, the foreign corporation often has deferral of taxes on its income from foreign sources until the income is remitted as dividends. On the other hand, whereas a U.S. firm can exclude from its taxable income 100% of dividends from a U.S. company in which it owns 80% or more of the stock, and 85% of the dividends otherwise, there is no exclusion of dividend income received by a U.S. corporation from a foreign corporation. There is no Investment Tax Credit or Asset Depreciation Ranging (ADR) treatment accorded a foreign corporation when its income is computed for tax credits applicable to the owning U.S. parent corporation. As noted later, it is very difficult to determine income in the international context. While about one-fifth of all U.S. corporate profits is earned abroad and the U.S. taxes paid on foreign profits are about 5%, the timing of the profits, their definition, and the tax rates applicable to them are highly debatable. None of this foreign definition seemed particularly important when foreign earnings were a small part of the U.S. firm's total earnings, but now the issue is vital given the basic guideline of full U.S. jurisdiction over all income. The variations in taxation arise from issues such as *how* the income is earned, *where* it is earned, and how the earning business is *structured*.

SECTION 162

Since 1958 this section of the U.S. Internal Revenue Code has denied tax deductions for payments made to foreign government officials or employees in the form of bribes. The source and amount of any illegal income must be declared and the tax must be paid. The U.S. Code has similar provisions for domestic bribes. Under the 1982 Tax Equity and Fiscal Responsibility Act (TEFRA), however, a "bribe" to secure foreign business may be deducted for U.S. tax purposes as long as it is a legal payment in the foreign country and also is not illegal under the U.S. Foreign Corrupt Practices Act. Other nations follow different patterns; foreign bribes are deductible as business expenses under British Inland Revenue regulations.

Under Sections 884 and 888 as revised in 1976, a firm participating in an international boycott in order to do business in another foreign country loses the foreign tax credit, the Domestic International Sales Corporation (DISC) tax benefits, and a deferral of tax on earned income on any boycott income. Income resulting from illegal payments is treated as a new class of Subpart F income (see below) to shareholders of controlled foreign corporations. Such income is considered to be immediately distributed and taxable, whether or not the corporation makes such a distribution.

SECTION 482

A part of the U.S. Internal Revenue Code that has continuing impact on the decisions of individuals and firms is only one sentence in length. However, Section 482 permits the Treasury to allocate income and expenses among firms that are owned or controlled by the same interests if such an allocation is necessary to prohibit an evasion of taxes or to reflect income clearly. Tax credits and allowances also may be apportioned among firms which are not organized or incorporated in the United States. The key in application is the value realized in an arm's-length transaction (that is, a fair price between an informed and willing buyer and seller). This value is difficult for courts to determine. Various safe harbors are available, and the purpose of the enforcement is only to affect U.S. tax liabilities; hence, according to enforcement officials, it is not designed as a general harassment of multinationals. Once the IRS makes an allocation under Section 482, however, the burden of proof is on the taxpayer to show that both the allocation method and the result of the allocation are arbitrary. The IRS provides detailed rules on how to allocate income among related parties in the most common situations.

SECTION 861

Allocation of expenses among subsidiaries is always a problem, especially when there is a clear joint product and when taxes are involved. For example, in 1974 the Internal Revenue Service made a well-publicized attack on the allocation of corporatewide research and development (R&D) under Section 861. Even though the outlays were made in the United States, the IRS argued that many of the benefits accrued to foreign operations. Hence, it wished to have more of the cost of research and development allocated to foreign operations. The effect of such an allocation is to reduce foreign income (and taxes that were usually credited against the U.S. tax liability) while increasing U.S. taxable income.

Revisions in the Code now mean that firms that have large amounts of interest, research and development, and general administrative costs will find themselves eligible for fewer foreign tax credits. Usually, firms have tried to allocate as much of these expenses to the high tax environment as possible, and typically this has meant charging the U.S. (parent) corporation with most of these expenses. The foreign subsidiaries were charged only with the marginal costs for their operations. In 1977 IRS rulings elaborated on how they would expect proration to take place. A brief explanation of these rulings and an exercise are included with the questions at the end of this appendix.

Under the 1981 Economic Recovery Tax Act, firms were allowed to allocate their U.S. research and development activities entirely to U.S. operations for two tax years after August 13, 1981. This action represented a deliberate policy change, and was designed to subsidize the R&D activities of U.S. corporations.

SECTION 882

A foreign corporation carrying on business in the United States is taxed at the U.S. rate on business profits. This provision of the Code is designed to prevent the creation of foreign subsidiaries by U.S. corporations to carry on various business activities in this country. It is also consistent with the policy of taxing the receipt of income from all activities carried on in this country.

TAX CREDITS (SECTIONS 901, 902, AND SO ON)

Although there is the possibility of treating foreign taxes as a deduction from income, most corporations will elect to take the foreign income taxes as a direct credit against their U.S. tax liability. Only income taxes or in-lieu income taxes are eligible for credit. The indirect credit rules generally apply only to corporations, and for the credit to be applicable, the U.S. corporate parent (P) must have 10% or more of the stock of the foreign corporation (S1). The credit is applicable only in the year in which the dividends are received by P.

There is also a pyramid effect, since P can credit foreign income taxes paid by a subsidiary (S2) owned by S1 and by another subsidiary (S3) owned by S2. This three-tier rule relates to receipt of dividends by P. Each participant (P, S1, and S2) must own at least 10% of the stock in the next firm. Furthermore, P must have at least 5% direct or indirect ownership of the corporation that paid the tax for it to be creditable. Thus, P, owning 50% of S1 which owned 25% of S2 which in turn owned 15% of S3, would be able to take credit for taxes paid by S1 (50% beneficial ownership) and S2 ($0.5 \times 0.25 = 12\frac{1}{2}\%$ beneficial ownership) but not for S3 ($0.5 \times 0.25 \times 0.15 =$ less than 5%) even though each firm in the chain owned at least 10% of the next lower firm.

The basic procedure is to *gross up* the dividends received in the United States to taxable income prior to the payment of a portion of the foreign income and dividend withholding taxes. The ratio of the dividends declared by the foreign subsidiary to foreign profit after tax is a multiplier added to the income taxes paid in the foreign land. To this product is added any withholding taxes on dividends imposed by the foreign land, and the sum of these two items is the maximum total tax credit for that year. Thus, dividends received are increased by some portion of foreign income and dividend withholding taxes, and the U.S. tax is computed as if that figure were entirely U.S. corporate operating income. Against the calculated tax liability is then credited some of the foreign tax payments, reducing the payment to the Internal Revenue Service. See the calculations for subsidiaries A and B in the exercises following this appendix.

There is generally an *overall* limitation that lumps all foreign source income together. The ratio of that income to total taxable income (foreign and domestic) times the applicable U.S. tax rate provides the maximum credit. This calculation is done to assure that the total tax credits do not exceed what would have been paid in the United States had the entire income been from domestic sources. This calculation is beneficial to firms for which high tax payments in some countries would yield larger credits than could be used. Credits from these countries may then be combined with those from other lands where the tax rates might be lower to give the total credit. For example, assume that the domestic tax rate is 50% and that P has local taxable income of $100 in A and $100 in B. Local taxes are $60 in A and $30 in B and the balance is remitted to P as dividends with no withholding. Then the maximum credit against U.S. taxes would be 50% of $200, or $100, and all $90 of the tax payments could be credited against the U.S. tax liability. This is the "grossing up" process, for the U.S. income is increased to the level before the foreign taxes, and then the U.S. tax calculation is based on that higher level. If the calculations were on a *per country* basis, there would be a full credit for the 30% liability paid in B, but only $50 from the A tax payments would be creditable since the U.S. taxes on that income would have totaled only $50.[6]

Note that the limitation on credit is based on the U.S. tax rate applied to the foreign source income as defined by the U.S. Tax Code. Thus, the foreign tax rate may be less than the U.S. rate, but an allowance for deductions that the foreign government did not permit (hence lowering U.S. calculated taxable income) can mean that not all the foreign taxes are creditable even though they were applied at a nominally lower rate. For example, a $30 foreign tax on $100 of foreign income seems fully creditable if the balance was remitted as a dividend. If the additional deductions of expenses reduce the income to only $50, then a 50% U.S. tax rate means a maximum credit of only $25. Furthermore, investment in the stock of the parent or a loan to the parent by a controlled foreign corporation is also now included as a dividend payment for tax purposes in order to prevent tax avoidance through remission of profits by this investment or loan. There is a 2-year carry back and a 5-year carry forward for credits in the event of excess credits in any year.

LIMITATIONS ON DEFERRALS

Foreign operations of U.S. corporations are taxable as the income is earned. As noted, a foreign corporation that is completely owned by a U.S. parent may defer U.S. taxes on its foreign source income (as defined above) until remission of dividends to the parent. Because of

---

[6]Formerly, firms could calucate tax liabilities on a per country basis, which was useful when losses in one country would use up possible tax credits from other countries on an overall calculation.

abuses, the 1962 tax reform program limited deferral in a number of cases largely related to so-called Subpart F income (Sections 951–964). Essentially, a tax is payable on undistributed base company income (defined below) of controlled foreign corporations. This income is treated as a constructive dividend even though the foreign corporation has not remitted the funds to the shareholders. The taxes are imposed on the shareholders of controlled foreign corporations. The definition of control is largely based on the number of shareholders, nationality, and the percentage of ownership. The tax applies only to certain companies (more than 50% of ownership is by U.S. persons where "person" can be a corporation) and only to certain shareholders (more than 10% interest) where applicable. In making the determination of whether more than 50% of the voting control is by U.S. persons, only shareholders with 10% or more of the stock are counted in this figure. Thus, even though more than 50% of the stock might be owned by U.S. citizens or residents, if a sufficient number of these persons have less than 10%, the firm would not be a U.S.-controlled foreign corporation. As an extreme example, eleven U.S. shareholders each owning 9% of the stock would not have a controlled foreign corporation.

Base company income generally can be described as income from operations carried on by a foreign subsidiary for tax minimization purposes. Base company income includes foreign personal holding company income[7] (which mainly deals with income from various investments), base company sales income, and base company services income. Foreign base company sales income includes income from the sale of goods produced and sold outside the country of incorporation and the net income from property which is either bought from or sold to a related person (that is, a parent or another subsidiary) or sold on behalf of a related person. See McIntyre for a detailed definition of income in these categories.[8] Subsidiary D in the exercises shows the tax treatment for this corporation.

For many purposes, some of the advantages of deferral can still be realized in the area of sales income through use of a domestic international sales corporation (DISC) which is described below. Another interesting exclusion from this foreign base company income is income from sales or services performed in the country of incorporation. Thus,

---

[7]Foreign personal holding company income restrictions are designed to prevent individuals from using the tax deferral provisions to avoid taxes on dividends, interest, and capital gains from various transactions. A *controlled* foreign personal holding company is a firm in which more than 50% of the ownership is by five or fewer U.S. citizens or permanent residents and in which 60% or more of the gross income in the first year and 50% or more in subsequent years is foreign personal holding company income. This income is automatically base company income to a controlled foreign corporation even though it is *not* a foreign personal holding company.

[8]*United States Taxation of Foreign Income with Special Emphasis on Private Investments in Developing Countries*, cited earlier.

if the firm were to incorporate a subsidiary in every nation in which it does business, then the foreign base company income rules would not apply to those sales. In addition, if less than 10% of the gross income of a foreign-controlled corporation were base company income, then none of the income would be so considered. (If more than 90% of the gross income were base company income, then all the income would be so treated. Between these two points the income would be prorated and base company income would be taxable whether or not distributed.) If the foreign-controlled corporation were to pay taxes of at least 90% of the U.S. level on the income or make a substantial dividend distribution to its shareholders, or a minimum combination of foreign taxes and dividend distribution existed, there would be no special tax. Financial income (dividends, interest, and capital gains) from less developed countries and shipping income from operations of vessels or aircraft in foreign trade are excluded if earnings are reinvested in shipping activities. Several of these provisions are direct consequences of the 1975 Tax Reduction Act.[9]

Most firms operate with branches in the earlier years of foreign operations when losses are expected since the losses of branches can be consolidated with the U.S. parent. However, the 1976 Tax Reform Act permits the Internal Revenue Service to recover taxes on foreign losses which offset U.S. profits if the foreign operations later produce profits on which taxes are otherwise deferred.

DOMESTIC INTERNATIONAL SALES CORPORATIONS (SECTIONS 991–994)

These special U.S. corporations were permitted by 1971 legislation designed to encourage export sales by U.S. firms. Essentially, the firms can defer tax on 42.5% of their *gain* in export earnings. The shareholders of a DISC are treated as if they have received the remaining 57.5% of the income (whether or not the earnings were distributed) and are taxable as individuals or corporations on that income. The DISC itself is not taxable. The shareholders are entitled to the foreign tax credit for foreign taxes on a DISC. In addition to certain restrictions on the asset

---

[9]Special provisions of the 1975 Tax Reduction Act were designed to restrict the use of foreign tax credits (instead of deductions) for royalties paid to foreign governments by international oil companies. Specifically, the Act denies credits if two conditions occur: the price on which the taxes are based is not the market price (i.e., if artificial "posted" prices are used for tax levies) and the oil company has no "economic interest" in the oil (i.e., if it does not own the oil). However, there is substantial question about the meaning of "economic interest" and the impact of this provision is unclear. Various other provisions also tightened the foreign credit benefits for the international oil companies. Subsequent 1983 IRS regulations reduced these restrictions.

base, the main requirement for DISC treatment under the Code is that 95% of the gross income must be from export activities.

A major benefit of the DISC legislation is the encoded "safe harbors" which specify how profits can be determined for a DISC. A "safe harbor" means there is no IRS challenge if the figures are accurate. Under Section 482, as noted, the amount of income could be a source of dispute since the major activity of a DISC is likely to be reselling of purchased manufactured goods from its parent to export customers. However, the legislation creating DISCs permitted the taxable income to be the greater of (a) 4% of total export receipts plus 10% of the DISC's promotion expenses, (b) 50% of the combined income of both the selling firm (the parent in most cases) and the DISC plus 10% of the DISC's promotion expenses, or (c) the actual taxable income under normal Section 482 accounting standards.

Under the 1976 Tax Reform Act, DISC tax benefits are now available for the gain in average annual export profits over a 1972–1975 base period. The export profit base level is 67% of the annual average export profit in the 1972–1975 period. Tax on half the profit over that base level is deferred. The base on which the moving average is calculated will move forward one year each year after 1980. New exporters or exporters with foreign profits of less than $100,000 will not have any DISC restriction because their base will be considered zero until 1980. Exported military products are eligible for half the normal DISC benefit.[10]

The 1982 Tax Equity and Fiscal Responsibility Act introduced a corporate minimum tax, which essentially provides that the corporation pays the greater of its tax liability under the normal regulations or its tax liability computed as 15% of net taxable income less $50,000, plus various preference items. One of these preference items is income from a DISC. Hence, the value of the DISC provisions is reduced for a few corporations which are subject to the minimum tax.

Responding to criticisms from the General Agreement on Tariffs and Trade which charged that the DISC arrangement was illegal under the agreements, the Reagan administration proposed adjustments in the program in 1983. The adjustments involved terminating the DISC program and replacing it with a requirement for a foreign operation to which sales would be made at market rates. This subsidiary could then claim special tax treatment on its income. The net effect, based on fiscal 1984 data, would increase the subsidy to the export earnings of American firms from $1.1 billion to $1.3 billion.

---

[10]Prior to 1980 a U.S. corporation whose entire operations were carried on outside the United States but in the Western Hemisphere with 90% of its gross income from active conduct of a trade or business and with 95% of its gross income from outside the United States could be taxed under a special arrangement as a Western Hemisphere Trading Corporation (WHTC), providing an effective tax rate of as low as 34%.

POSSESSIONS CORPORATIONS (SECTION 936)

There are special provisions made for corporations carrying on business in U.S. possessions such as the Canal Zone, Guam, American Samoa, and others. Puerto Rico is also eligible for special treatment under its commonwealth status. To be treated as a possessions corporation, 65% of the gross income must be from the active conduct of a trade or business in a possession. The possessions corporation is then given the option to receive a special tax credit equal to the U.S. tax on its income from active conduct of a business in the possession. Any income tax paid to a foreign or possession government by a corporation electing this treatment is neither deductible nor creditable against U.S. taxes. However, dividends from a possessions corporation are eligible for the 85% or 100% corporate dividend exclusion by a receiving corporation.

For example, under the 1976 Tax Reform Act, U.S. corporations were allowed to repatriate profits from their Puerto Rican subsidiaries at any time free of additional U.S. taxes. Previously, U.S. firms had either reinvested their subsidiaries' profits in Puerto Rico, or at least outside the United States, since the only way profits earned in the Commonwealth could be remitted tax-free to the U.S. corporate parent was by ending the Puerto Rican corporation. However, the new benefit was somewhat offset by the Puerto Rican government's imposition of a new 10% tax on profits sent from the country.

The issues related to cost allocation and R&D expenses, discussed earlier in terms of Sections 482 and 861, repeatedly resulted in litigation regarding possessions corporations, particularly in Puerto Rico. The favorable tax treatment of Puerto Rican source income plainly encouraged firm managers to shift as much net income to the Commonwealth as possible. To simplify matters, the 1982 TEFRA created several methods for allocating costs on different product lines which had substantial value added from Puerto Rican operations. As long as 60% of the total labor and 25% of the value added to the raw materials in a product occurred in the Commonwealth, the simplest method allowed a 50–50 division of the total income from a product jointly manufactured and sold in the United States and Puerto Rico.

CAPITAL GAINS

Gains from the sale of stock in a foreign-controlled corporation are normally taxed at ordinary income tax rates. Gains from a less developed country (LDC) corporation are sometimes eligible for the favorable 30% corporate capital gains tax rate if the ownership has been for at least 10 years, at least on the portion of the gain in value attributed to operations prior to 1976.[11]

EXCHANGE GAINS AND LOSSES

The tax treatment of foreign exchange gains and losses is a grey area. Most of the rules involve case law, and the rulings have been contradictory. Part of the question involves *when* a transaction takes place. When there are parent loans to a subsidiary, does the loss from repayment in an upvalued currency occur when the subsidiary repays the parent, when the parent repays the loan to the bank, pro rata with repayment, or when? The other major part of the question involves whether the loss is a *capital* loss or an ordinary loss. One critic has noted that the choices open to the corporation managers on how to translate their foreign operations really permit them to play a "heads-I-win, tails-you-lose" game with the Treasury. Furthermore, as Musgrave notes, the managers may use different methods for various subsidiaries operating abroad.[12]

Branch operations are consolidated into the U.S. parent's return under two methods. Under a *net worth* method, the balance sheet is valued with the current accounts at year-end (current) rates and the remainder of the accounts at the historic rates. Thus, a loss on a short-term loan that must be repaid 1 month after the close of the tax year in an appreciated currency will be realized in this period even though there is no payment until the next year. Under the *net income* method, funds remitted during the year to the parent are valued at the rate in effect at the time of remission; unremitted income is valued at the year-end rate. Exchange gains and losses are shown only as included in net income, which usually occurs when repayment is made. Usually a *two-transaction* approach is required. Thus, if goods are purchased and paid for after an upvaluation of the remitting currency, there is a loss on the payment of the account payable, and there is a separate adjustment later if the inventory proves to be worth more than its cost basis in the parent currency.

---

[11]To encourage investment and sales to so-called less developed countries (LDCs), special tax provisions have been permitted for firms doing business in those lands. Essentially, LDCs include all countries with the exception of most of Western Europe, Australia, Canada, Japan, New Zealand, South Africa, the Soviet bloc, and China. An LDC corporation is a firm involved in active trade or business which has 80% of its gross income from LDC sources and 80% of its assets involved in its trade or business in an LDC. The firm need not be incorporated in an LDC, but it cannot be incorporated in the United States.

[12]Peggy B. Musgrave, "Exchange Rate Aspects in Taxation of Foreign Income," *National Tax Journal*, Volume 28, 1975, pp. 404–13.

WITHHOLDING TAXES

If there is a desire to avoid withholding on payments of dividends and interest to investors and debtholders in other lands, the use of various foreign finance subsidiaries becomes important. For example, Rosenberg and Singer show how to create such a subsidiary depending on where the funds are used and where the investors or lenders are.[13] Under U.S. regulations, an "80–20" corporation will be free from a requirement to collect withholding on interest payments. This firm can meet that requirement as long as *less* than 20% of its gross income is from the United States, from which the 80–20 name is derived. Dividends or interest payments to this finance subsidiary from overseas subsidiaries would be subject to various withholding provisions in those countries depending on their tax treaties (or lack thereof) with the United States and with each other. These payments are excluded from U.S. taxes assuming consolidated returns are filed and the income of the foreign subsidiaries is included with the U.S. parent; other treatments possible include the 85% and 100% exclusions in some cases.

On the other hand, if the firm wanted to borrow funds from its finance subsidiary for operations in this country, then technically there should be withholding of taxes on interest payments since 50% or more of the financial subsidiary income would be related to the conduct of a trade or business in the United States (that is, all interest receipts would be from the operating parent). Withholding can be avoided here by creating the financial subsidiary in the Netherlands Antilles, for example, where the treaty provisions with the United States specifically omit withholding on interest payments by that finance subsidiary to foreign shareholders even if all the subsidiary's income is from a U.S. source. When there is a split need for funds, the authors advocate 80–20 corporations in both the United States and the Virgin Islands, with the former used for lending to the foreign subsidiaries and the latter for lending to the U.S. operations.

Much of the need for the 80–20 corporation has disappeared with two changes in the U.S. tax law. First, withholding on dividends and interest payments to non-U.S. residents has been eliminated. Second, the Securities and Exchange Commission (SEC) now permits direct offerings of Eurobonds by American corporations as long as there is a specific statement that they are not to be sold in the United States. Previously, managers often used 80–20 corporations to avoid filing a prospectus with the United States SEC in connection with major offerings of securities to non-U.S. residents.

---

[13]Herbert C. Rosenberg and Stuart R. Singer, "Selecting an International Finance Subsidiary: A Review of Available Methods," *Journal of Taxation*, May 1969, pp. 296–98.

TAX CHANGES—A PROBLEM OF ANALYSIS

Many tax bills have been introduced to change the foreign tax credit system, permitting only deductions for foreign taxes rather than a credit. Other bills have been suggested to avoid the deferral or postponement of taxes, taxing foreign income as earned rather than as remitted. Probably the most aggressively pursued target of some tax reformers is the whole less developed country area. In 1975 the holding company option, in which LDC income could continue to receive special tax benefits through several layers of corporate parents, was eliminated.

Most of these enacted and proposed reforms have sought to place foreign income of the U.S. corporation on the same basis as domestic income and to treat foreign income taxes the same as U.S. states' corporate income taxes. However, there is a curious asymmetry in most of the reformers' logic, aside from the policy and balance of payments implications of their arguments. If parity is the goal, then the foreign operations of U.S. corporations should be allowed the same benefits as domestic corporations: ADR on depreciable assets; the Investment Tax Credit of 10%; elimination of taxes on intercompany dividend income when there is consolidation for tax purposes, or elimination of income taxes on 85% of intercompany dividend income when there is no consolidation; Subchapter S corporations (permitting partnership treatment of corporate profits for certain corporations which continue to have the benefits of limited liability); and DISC treatment of income from third-country export sales by the foreign operations.

With the changes of taxing foreign income as earned, eliminating the foreign tax credit, and eliminating special LDC treatment, initial total world tax collections would increase by $900 million per year. Adding these changes which place the foreign corporation of a U.S. parent on the same footing as a domestic counterpart, then the total tax collection would *decrease* by over $1,600 million, based on a 1976 U.S. Department of Commerce staff study for the House Ways and Means Committee.

Horst provides another set of figures for the change in domestic and foreign direct investment resulting from an end to deferral of foreign income and repeal of the foreign tax credit for U.S. multinationals.[14] Firms were assumed to deduct foreign income taxes prior to computing U.S. tax liability. He completed the analysis under situations in which the existing debt/equity structure remained as it was (Case 1 in Exhibit 13.2A) and in which the foreign subsidiary substituted debt for

[14]Thomas Horst, "American Taxation of Multinational Firms," *American Economic Review*, June 1977, pp. 376–89. See also T. Itagaki, "Systems of Taxation of Multinational Firms under Exchange Risk," *Southern Economic Journal*, Jan. 1982, pp. 708–23.

EXHIBIT 13.2A   Estimated Impact of Repealing Deferral and the Foreign Tax Credit and Allowing Only a Deduction for Foreign Taxes Paid: On New Domestic and Foreign Investment, New Funds Advanced to Subsidiaries, Consolidated After-Tax Income, and Domestic and Foreign Taxes Paid by U.S. Manufacturers, 1974

	Initial Value	CASE 1 (INITIAL PARAMETERS)		CASE 2 (RELIANCE ON DEBT)	
		Absolute Change	Percentage Change	Absolute Change	Percentage Change
Domestic investment	36,400	9,291	25.5	3,970	10.9
Foreign investment	18,300	− 10,283	− 56.2	− 4,997	− 27.3
New funds for subsidiary	2,710	− 15,725	− 580.3	− 8,060	− 297.4
Consolidated after-tax income	15,149	− 2,974	− 19.6	− 3,107	− 20.5
U.S. taxes paid	6,005	3,028	50.4	2,953	49.2
Foreign taxes paid	5,001	− 504	− 10.1	− 144	− 2.9

SOURCE: Thomas Horst, "American Taxation of Multinational Firms," *American Economic Review*, June 1977, p. 386.

all its equity, a desirable practice since the interest on foreign debt would reduce total-system taxes (Case 2). Although this change could cause firms to move investment from foreign operations to domestic operations, based on his initial parameters, the total world investment by these firms would decline by over $1 billion. However, the U.S. tax liability would increase initially by about $3 billion under either Case 1 or Case 2.

Future revisions are likely in the Code, but the form of the revisions is most uncertain. For reasons noted at the start of this appendix, the position of most observers varies considerably depending on what they use as an initial reference point of equity and how they can approach that position from the existing state of the Code.

EXERCISES ON TAXATION OF FOREIGN INCOME

ASSUMPTIONS

A. Parent corporation is subject to a 50% tax rate.
B. U.S. corporation owns the following:
    Subsidiary A: Fully-owned foreign subsidiary located in Europe in a developed country
               B: Fully-owned foreign subsidiary located in Europe in a developed country
               C: 5% ownership in foreign subsidiary located in Europe in a developed country
               D: Fully-owned "foreign controlled corporation" in Europe
C. Total earnings, taxation, and dividends of each subsidiary are as indicated in the following table:

	A	B	C	D
	(million dollars)			
Earnings before taxes	$100	$100	$100	$100
Income taxes	65	65	45	50
Profit after taxes	35	35	55	50
Dividends declared	35	20	30	0
Withholding tax	3	2	3	0

QUESTIONS

1. What are the taxes payable to the U.S. government?

Subsidiary A

Dividends received		$ 32
Gross up:		
Direct credit (withholding tax)	3	
Indirect credit		
(proportion of income taxes)		
(35/35) × 65	65	68
(proportion is based on profits *after* taxes)		
Taxable income		$100
U.S. taxes	50	
Less tax credits	(68)	
Excess tax credit	$ 18	

Subsidiary B

Dividends received		$ 18
Gross up:		
Direct credit (withholding tax)	2	
Indirect credit (income tax)		
(20/35) × 65	37	39
Taxable income		$ 57
U.S. taxes	28.5	
Less tax credits	(39.0)	
Excess tax credit	$ 10.5	

Subsidiary C

Dividends received		$ 1.35
Gross up:		
Direct credit	0.15	
Indirect (not available, ownership is less than 10%)	0	0.15
Taxable income		$ 1.50
U.S. taxes	0.75	
Less tax credit	(0.15)	
Taxes due	$ 0.60	

Subsidiary D

Dividends received		$ 0
Undistributed earnings		50
Gross up:		
Indirect credit (income tax)		
(50/50) × 50		50
Taxable income		$100
U.S. taxes	50	
Less tax credit	(50)	
No taxes due	$ 0	

(foreign and U.S. tax rates are the same)

2. How much credit for foreign taxes can be claimed this year? How much excess tax credit can be carried forward to future years?

There is a total tax credit of $157.15 million from a direct calculation ($68 + 39 + 0.15 + 50) plus another $0.60 million carry-over credit from the other subsidiaries to subsidiary C. The credit carry forward, or excess tax credit is $27.9 million ($18 + 10.5 − 0.60).

3. If the taxes included as income taxes in the European subsidiaries were mostly value-added taxes, would you modify your computations?

Value-added taxes are not considered income taxes by the United States. Therefore, the indirect credit for income tax will be lost in the given computations. In addition to value-added taxes, excise, franchise, and property taxes do not qualify as a general rule.

4. What would be the considerations to change these operations from foreign subsidiaries to U.S. branches?

(a) Foreign corporations lose the right of consolidation for tax purposes (except for some 100%-owned Mexican and Canadian subsidiaries). As a consequence, taxes on dividends must be paid.

(b) Branch form gives greater exposure of the U.S. parent's affairs to foreign officials.

(c) Domestic form maximizes the tax deductibility of foreign operating losses. Losses can be spread over 9 years.

(d) Domestic form preserves the statutory depletion allowances and development costs available to taxpayer in the natural resource extraction business.

(e) Domestic form gives some freedom from the Code's regulations against tax avoidance. For example, Section 367 requires an advance ruling from the Revenue Service in order to qualify a formation, division, or reorganization of a foreign corporation or liquidation of a foreign subsidiary for nonrecognition of gain.

(f) Repatriation of earnings from a branch or U.S. subsidiary is often not subject to withholding taxes as are dividends.

(g) Foreign firm makes possible deferment of U.S. tax payment until dividends are paid. This allows for planning of tax credits.

5. Unless a taxpayer can show that the loan was for a specific property, the *interest expense* must be allocated to various classes of gross income (assume U.S. and foreign). There are two methods of allocation: One method is based on *assets*. Here the interest expense is apportioned based on either the tax book value or the fair market value of the assets. Interest is apportioned to various operations in the same ratio that the assets in various operations bear to the total of all assets. Under the *gross income* method of allocating interest expense, the interest is apportioned on the basis of gross income from different operations (revenue minus operating expenses) if the allocation is at *least* 50% of the amount allocated to each source under the asset method. If the 50% test is *not* met, the 50% proportion is assigned to the category in question and the balance is assigned to the other category of operations. Thus, the rule is to allocate the lower amount to foreign source income computed under the asset method or the gross income method, but at least 50% of the amount is allocated by the asset method.

Research and development expenditures are allocated to various product categories based on the Standard Industrial Classification (SIC) Code. Then, a proration between domestic and foreign sales is made, unless the R&D is undertaken only for one government's legal requirements and the benefits of the R&D do not accrue to other operations (for example, animal tests for the U.S. Food and Drug Administration in order to sell a drug in the United States). *Within* each product classification, the R&D is allocated either by a sales method or a gross income method. Under the *sales method,* the manager first may allocate 30% of the R&D expense to the area where at least 30% of the R&D was performed (assume the United States). The balance is allocated on the proportion of gross sales from each source to total sales. The 30% *exclusive apportionment* may be increased if the taxpayer can show either limited application or long-delayed application of the product elsewhere.[1] Under the *gross income* method, the allocation is based on the ratio of a source's gross income to total gross income for the firm, as long as the allocation of R&D is not less than 50% of the amount allocated under the sales method. If it is, then the taxpayer may allocate 50% of the amount calculated under the sales method to the lower source and the balance to the other source.

Consider the following problem: X, a domestic corporation, manufactures and distributes electric motors, a product within SIC Major Group 35. Y, its wholly-owned foreign subsidiary, sells these motors abroad. During 1979 X had $200,000 in interest expense and spent $80,000 on research and development in the United States. Sales and gross income for the two firms are shown in the following table:

	X	Y	Total
Sales	$ 9,000,000	$4,000,000	$13,000,000
Gross income	4,000,000	1,000,000*	5,000,000
Asset values (average of beginning and ending book values, ignore market value)	30,000,000	8,000,000	38,000,000

*Includes a $450,000 dividend plus a gross up of $550,000 in foreign taxes on the local operation's $1,000,000 net income.

---

[1]If the taxpayer can show that the R&D will not have benefit for many years outside the United States, then the present value of that benefit using a 10% discount rate can be used in place of the exclusive apportionment figure as a U.S. expense.

Assume a tax rate of 50% and a foreign tax credit as shown in subsidiary A. What are the tax allocations for the firm for interest and R&D? What are the final tax payments of the firm? If no allocation were required, how would the tax payments appear? What excess tax credits exist under allocation and nonallocation?

TAXATION REFERENCES

Arthur Andersen and Company, *Tax and Trade Guides*. Separate booklets, New York, various dates.

Commerce Clearing House, *Common Market Reporter*. Two vols., loose-leaf, Chicago, Ill., various dates.

Commerce Clearing House, *World Tax Series*. Chicago, Ill., various issues.

Coopers and Lybrand, *International Tax Summaries*. Loose-leaf, New York, various dates.

Feld, Alan L., *Tax Policy and Corporate Concentration*. Lexington, Mass.: Lexington Books, 1982.

Fialka, John J., "Corporate Tax Haven in Netherlands Antilles Is Bracing for a Disaster," *Wall Street Journal*, Oct. 11, 1982, p. 1.

Fuerbringer, Jonathan, "U.S. Drive on Tax Havens," *New York Times*, Sept. 3, 1982, p. D-3.

Harriss, C. Lowell, "Value-Added Taxation," *Columbia Journal of World Business*, July–Aug. 1971, pp. 78–86.

Haskins and Sells, *International Tax and Business Service*. Two vols., loose-leaf, New York.

Hellawell, Robert, *United States Taxation and Developing Countries*. New York: Columbia University Press, 1980.

Horst, Thomas, "American Taxation of Multinational Firms," *American Economic Review*, June 1977, pp. 376–89.

Howard, Fred, "Overview of International Taxation," *Columbia Journal of World Business*, Summer 1975, pp. 5–11.

Hufbauer, G. C., and D. Foster, "U.S. Taxation of the Undistributed Income of Controlled Foreign Corporations." Washington, D.C.: Office of International Tax Affairs, Department of the Treasury, April 1976.

———— , **and J. R. Nunns,** "Tax Payments and Tax Expenditures on International Investment and Employment," *Columbia Journal of World Business*, Summer 1975, pp. 12–20.

International Bureau of Fiscal Documentation, *Guides to European Taxation*. Three vols., looseleaf; and *Supplementary Service to European Taxation*. Loose-leaf. Amsterdam, Holland.

Itagaki, T., "Systems of Taxation of Multinational Firms under Exchange Risk," *Southern Economic Journal*, Jan. 1982, pp. 708–23.

Krause, Lawrence, and Kenneth Dam, "Economic Effects of Taxing Foreign Source Income," *Federal Tax Treatment of Foreign Income*. Washington, D.C.: Brookings Institution, 1964.

Lent, George E., "Adjusting Taxable Profits for Inflation: The Foreign Experience," in Henry J. Aaron, *Inflation and the Income Tax*, pp. 195–213. Washington, D.C.: Brookings Institution, 1976.

McIntyre, Michael J., *United States Taxation of Foreign Income with Special Emphasis on Private Investments in Developing Countries*. Cambridge, Mass.: International Law Program, Harvard Law School, 1975. This is a revision of Arie Kopelman, *United States Income Taxation of Private Investments in Developing Countries*. New York: United Nations Secretariat, 1970.

Musgrave, Peggy B., "Exchange Rates Aspects in the Taxation of Foreign Income," *National Tax Journal*, Vol. 28, 1975, pp. 404–13.

――― , "The OEDC Model Tax Treaty: Problems and Prospects," *Columbia Journal of World Business*, Summer 1975, pp. 29–39.

Owens, Elisabeth A., and Gretchen A. Hovemeyer, eds., *Bibliography of Taxation of Foreign Operations and Foreigners*. Cambridge, Mass.: Harvard Law School, 1976.

Paules, Edward P., "A Guide through the Tax Maze," *Euromoney*, Oct. 1980, pp. 252–60.

Polk, Raemon M., "Financial and Tax Aspects of Planning for Foreign Currency Exchange Rate Fluctuations," *Taxes*, Mar. 1978, pp. 131–42.

Prentice-Hall, Inc., *Tax Ideas—Tax Transaction Guide*. Two vols., loose-leaf, Englewood Cliffs, N.J., various dates.

Price Waterhouse and Company, Information Guide Series. Separate booklets, New York, various dates.

Sale, Timothy J., "Tax Planning Tools for the Multinational Corporation," *Management Accounting*, June 1979, pp. 37–41.

Sato, Mitsuo, and Richard M. Bird, "International Aspects of the Taxation of Corporations and Shareholders," *International Monetary Fund Staff Papers*, Washington, D.C., 1976.

Schmitz, Marvin N., "Taxation of Foreign Exchange Gains and Losses," *Management Accounting*, July 1976, pp. 49–51.

Stein, Herbert, et al., *Proposals to Modify the Taxation of U.S. Citizens Working Abroad*. Washington, D.C.: American Enterprise Institute for Public Policy Research, 1981.

Stone, Lawrence M., "United States Tax Policy toward Foreign Earnings of Multinational Corporations," *The George Washington Law Review*, Vol. 42, 1974, pp. 557–67.

Tanzi, Vito, *Inflation and the Personal Income Tax: An International Perspective*. Cambridge, England: Cambridge University Press, 1980.

U.S. Congress, Committee on Ways and Means, *General Panel Discussion on Taxation of Foreign Income*. Exchange of letters between Professor Peggy Musgrave and Professor Robert Stobaugh, Feb. 1973, pp. 1881–86.

ALPHA S.A.

ALPHA S.A. was a company manufacturing dresses in country A. With its current plant valued at $10,000,000, Alpha could produce 120,000 dresses a year. It was expected that this plant would last for 10 more years. Labor and raw materials were $5.00 per dress, and last year Alpha sold 100,000 dresses at $30 each. The firm was entirely equity financed, with additional net working capital (beyond payable financing provided by suppliers) of $100,000. The income statement for this year was forecast as shown in the accompanying table.

Sales ($30 × 100,000)	$3,000,000
Labor and raw material ($5 × 100,000)	500,000
Depreciation ($10,000,000 ÷ 10)	1,000,000
Profit before taxes	$1,500,000
Income taxes (40%)	600,000
Net profits after taxes	$ 900,000

Señorita Damon, the dress designer, believed she had discovered a new market for her dresses in country B. She thought that, although such sophisticated dresses appealed to Latin taste, nothing of this type was being produced in country B. Thus, she believed she could sell 10,000 dresses annually, for at least the next 5 years, at a selling price of $25. This price was specified in terms of country A's currency, and she thought there was no foreign exchange risk involved.

Señorita Damon planned to receive a commission of 20% of sales. Sales terms were planned to be net-60 days against an export draft. A commercial bank in country A appeared willing to discount these export bills at 12% per annum. The export sales would require an investment of $100,000 initially for working capital.

Country B had a 30% tax on income. The income tax rate in country A was 40%. Country A allowed tax payments made to foreign countries to be deducted before computing taxable income in country A.

QUESTIONS

1. If Alpha's owners require a rate of return of 20%, should they accept Srta. Damon's proposal?

2. An alternative proposal would meet a potential requirement of country B's government for manufacture of the dresses in country B. With local manufacture, it was thought that up to 80,000 dresses a year could be sold in country B. In this case, Srta. Damon would not receive any sales commission, but it would be necessary to make an investment of $10,000,000 in plant, plus $100,000 for working capital, in country B. The labor, materials, and export draft costs for this investment would be the same per dress as estimated in the export proposal in question 1. If these sales of 80,000 dresses per year could be sustained for 10 years, would you approve this investment?

3. Evaluate the investment in country B, under the same conditions as in question 2, but with the following new assumptions: Now, country B is offering a direct subsidy in the form of a contribution in cash for 40% of the initial capital. In addition, country B is willing to reduce income taxes to 15%. In country A the tax rate on foreign income— not on local income—has also been reduced to 20% on the gross foreign income before foreign taxes. However, foreign taxes may then be taken as a credit against the tax liability to country A, although the tax liability may not be reduced below 0. (The depreciation charge for $10,000,000 for 10 years will be allowed by both countries.)

14

The Acceptance Criteria for International Projects

THE PREVIOUS CHAPTER outlined how a manager determines the relevant cash flows in international investments. The manager also needs to consider the return that should be demanded for a single project. First there are the traditional corporate finance precepts on the cost of capital as the relevant hurdle rate. But we must also assess what adjustment, if any, must be made to take into account the fact that the project is located in a foreign land. As we will see, the nature of the adjustments depends on the type of capital market we envisage.

After reviewing the theory on cost of capital and its applicability to international projects we will return to a topic we discussed earlier: Which cash flows are the relevant ones—those to the parent or those to the project? We propose an eclectic view. Finally, we consider the use of return on equity as an alternative hurdle rate.

COST OF CAPITAL: THE BASIC THEORY

Investors in financial assets are the source of funds for the business that invests in real assets. The investors in financial assets expect certain return after assessing the risks of the firm; therefore, for the firm to fulfill the investors' expectations, their funds must be used in projects that have a risk-return profile consistent with the investors' expectations. If we assume, for the sake of simplicity, that the firm has only one project, then the minimum rate of return the project must yield is the cost of the funds used to finance it—its *cost of capital.*

A project or a firm can be financed in many ways; however, some ways are better than others. Some combinations of sources of funds produce a total cost of capital lower than other combinations. This combination of the sources of funds used to finance the firm is called the *capital structure* of the firm. The optimum capital structure for a firm is that one which minimizes the total cost of funds for that firm. To find the optimum capital structure we have to know the risks of the firm and the returns it expects to generate. With this information we can search for the optimum capital structure at which point the cost of funds will be the lowest.

The risks of a firm fall into two major groups: (1) the risks derived from the investment projects themselves—the *business risk;* and (2) the risks derived from how the firm is financed—the *financial risk.* To illustrate, we can say that the purchase of an established department store in a growing metropolitan area has less business risk than the decision to invest in a new imaginative computer system in a foreign country. For a company with any given business risk, the financial risk increases with the amount of debt, or senior securities, in the capital structure. The higher the proportion of the firm's cash flow committed to the payment of interest and principal, the higher the probability that the firm may default on its obligations. Thus, for a firm with a given business risk we can see how the returns expected by the financial investors will change as we increase the financial risk—that is, as we include more debt in the firm's capital structure.

The return expected by lenders is the payment of interest, plus the devolution of the principal of the loan. Under normal conditions, this means that the cost of debt to the firm is the cost of interest payments, after taxes. This interest cost is bound to be lower than the cost of equity because lenders have priority claim in liquidation, as well as first claim on earnings each period. However, as the amount of debt in a firm increases, the risk of default increases, and so does the cost of debt.

Although the computation of the return expected by equity holders is the subject of substantial controversy in financial theory, there is agreement that equity requires a return higher than debt because equity investors face the full risks related to the swings in the operations of the business, as well as the risks associated with the presence of debt. The returns to equity holders are a residual after lenders have been paid. As a greater amount of debt, or any senior security, is added to the capital structure, common equity holders require a higher return. As the proportion of debt increases, the financial risk of equity holders increases since the probabilities of financial insolvency increase.

Exhibit 14.1 shows a graphic representation of the total cost of the firm's capital and its components as a function of the proportion of debt in the capital structure of the firm. The cost of capital (k_0) is a weighted average of the cost of debt (k_d) and the cost of equity (k_e). Algebraically, the cost of capital is defined as follows:

$$k_0 = \frac{D}{D + E} k_d + \frac{E}{D + E} k_e$$

where D and E denote the amounts of debt and equity, respectively. As we increase the proportion of debt in the capital structure, the cost of capital initially declines as the relatively cheaper debt is substituted for the more expensive equity. At some point the steadily increasing equity cost, combined with the increasing cost of debt, will cause the cost

EXHIBIT 14.1   Cost of Capital and Capital Structure

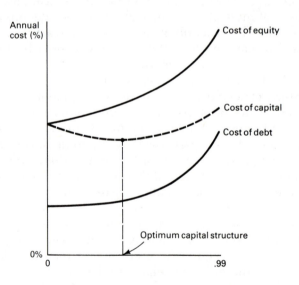

Proportion of debt-to-total assets
(Debt divided by debt-plus-equity)

of capital to flatten and then to rise. There is a continuing controversy over whether there is a unique debt-to-equity ratio, or a range of ratios at which the cost of capital is the lowest. The lowest point (or points) in the cost of capital curve defines the *optimum capital structure* and the *lowest cost of funds* for the firm.

The most famous critics of this traditional model, Modigliani and Miller, would suggest that the only benefit of debt financing is the tax deductibility of the interest. However, later versions of their theory would still have the cost of capital curve turning upward at some point as the risk of financial insolvency increases.[1]

THE COST OF CAPITAL AS THE REQUIRED RATE OF RETURN

Having identified a cost of capital for the firm with a given business risk and optimal capital structure, we must realize that the optimal capital structure is a long-term concept which may not apply in any given year or in the financing package used that year, and that the business risk for the firm is an average of the business risks of all its projects. These facts must be taken into account when using the cost of capital figure as the minimum rate of return that a project must be expected to yield.

The Long-Term Capital Structure

The job of the financial manager is to choose the best capital structure for the firm in the long run and then to time the issues of debt, equity, and preferred stock to minimize the company's cost of capital over time. There are periods in the markets when a debt or equity issue is relatively favorable; therefore, the financial officer should seek to avoid the periods of highest cost for issuing these securities. Expectations may change, of course. In the last few years, many firms that refused to issue debt at an interest cost of 12% were rapidly seeking funds 18 months later at 12½%. The difference was that the 12% rate appeared at a time of rising rates which eventually reached over 15% for seasoned corporate debt issues. When the market turned down to "only" 12½%, many managers were happy to have these lower rates.

---

[1]For those readers interested in the assumptions behind this analysis and for additional references, see an introductory text such as Weston and Brigham, *Managerial Finance*, 5th ed. (Hinsdale, Ill.: Dryden Press, 1975) or Van Horne, *Financial Management and Policy*, 6th ed. (Englewood Cliffs, N.J.: Prentice-Hall, Inc., 1983). In particular, see Van Horne, Ch. 9, for a discussion of the Modigliani and Miller position.

The 12½% rate became more reasonable once the higher rates had been seen.

For the evaluation of specific projects, this approach means that the financial manager must focus on the long-term capital structure and cost of capital for a project with the given risk characteristics. Otherwise, the executive would be tempted to commit the error of evaluating capital projects on the basis of the particular financial alternative considered at a point in time. Thus, if the company is issuing debt with an after-tax cost of 4%, it might use a discount rate of 4% in evaluating projects. Some years later, an exceedingly high debt ratio induced by following this policy over time would force an equity issue. Assume that the manager believes equity costs to be 15%. The implication is that the projects being evaluated that year should meet a 15% hurdle rate. The motivation of a divisional manager would be to submit all the low-return projects in debt financing years, saving the higher-return projects for equity financing years and/or urging a competing division manager to meet the equity hurdle rate.

The conclusion is that the firm should decide on an optimum capital structure for the whole firm and for its component subunits over time. The cost of funds figures associated with these capital structures are used as the hurdle rates each year, regardless of the particular financing which is undertaken that year. Although the conclusion is obvious to most practicing financial executives, its subtlety is often missed when evaluating major projects or proposals which have particular mortgage debt attached to them. In most cases a lender considers the overall capability of a business and not just the security of a mortgage on a proposed new building. Similarly, the presence of a mortgage on a building may in turn affect the potential availability of debt from other lenders. Hence, to give the new building the benefit of all the debt (resulting in a lower hurdle rate for the new building as a project) ignores the effect of reduced debt availability for the remainder of the corporation.

The Business Risk Specific to the Project

When a firm engages in multiple projects with different business risks, the firm's cost of capital is related to the return and risk of all of its investments. The firm's cost of capital is similar to a weighted average of the costs of capital for each of the projects in which the firm operates. This implies that when evaluating a specific project we should try to approximate the cost of capital that would correspond to that project, instead of using the cost of capital for the firm as a whole. In this approach, riskier projects will have a higher cost of capital than less risky ones. When the parent company is a passive holding company, the cost of capital of the components can be computed as separate entities by looking at how the market evaluates publicly traded competitors of those subunits. If a market for those subunits does not exist, the needed information can be obtained from discussions with lenders and investors in those entities.

In an efficient market, the investor in financial assets would be able to concoct optimal portfolios to take advantage of the benefits of diversification. Therefore, the cost of capital of specific units should take into account the contribution that this unit makes to a well-diversified portfolio—the so-called *market portfolio*—even if the firm's portfolio of projects is different from that market portfolio. The contribution of a project to the diversification of the portfolio depends on the correlation between the project's returns and the returns of the portfolio. A project whose returns are poorly correlated with the portfolio contributes more to the diversification of that portfolio than a project whose returns fluctuate together with those of the market.[2] Thus, the minimum rate of return required from a project usually will be lower when the project is considered as a possible component of a portfolio, than when the project is considered in isolation.

In inefficient markets in which investors in financial assets cannot have access to specific projects except through the specific firm, and in which capital markets are segmented, the firm may have access to a lower cost of capital to finance projects, than the cost of capital that any project in isolation would have. In this case a strategic decision must be made as to whether the benefit from the imperfection to which the firm (but not the project) has access should be passed on to the specific project in the form of a lower hurdle rate.[3]

COST OF CAPITAL FOR A FOREIGN PROJECT

The Case of Efficient Markets

In efficient markets, the cost of capital chosen to discount the returns from a project with a given risk is intrinsically the same whether the project is located in the home country or abroad. However, the cost of capital figure should correspond to the cost of capital in the currency

---

[2]For a more detailed description of the computation of the market portfolio and the effects of diversification in general see Chapter 16.

[3]Whatever the intellectual justification, higher hurdle rates are used for riskier projects. In Fremgen's survey, 54% of the 179 respondents indicated their firms used higher discount rates when evaluating riskier projects. See James M. Fremgen, "Capital Budgeting Practices: A Survey." *Management Accounting*, May 1973, pp. 19–25.

used to measure the returns from the project. Both the returns and the cost of funds should be expressed in the same unit of account, or currency. In an efficient market the investor in financial assets would have access to the project in the foreign country as well as in the home country, and if both have the same risk (including an adjustment for country risk), then the investor would demand the same return. However, the same return for both projects may be consistent with demanding a 22% return in terms of dollars and a 35% return in terms of pesos, if the investor expects a depreciation of the peso against the dollar of 13%.

As we have seen earlier, in efficient markets the fluctuations in exchange rates anticipated by the market are incorporated in the observed exchange rates. In equilibrium, a firm that expects to generate pesos in the future would be indifferent between financing its operations in pesos or, say, dollars. If the interest rate in pesos is 24% and the interest rate in dollars is 11%, we can say the market expects a depreciation of the peso (appreciation of the dollar) of 13%. In terms of pesos, the cost of both pesos and dollars is 24%: the cost of pesos is the interest rate of 24%, while the cost of dollars is the dollar interest rate, 11%, plus the expected appreciation of 13%. In terms of dollars, the cost of both pesos and dollars is 11%: the cost of pesos is the interest rate of 24% less the expected depreciation of 13%, while the cost of dollars is the interest rate of 11%.

Equity holders can also express their returns in terms of any currency. The rate of return required in any one currency would depend on the basic rate required for undertaking the given amount of risk, plus the exchange rate fluctuation expected in the future. Continuing the previous example, we see that if the equity holders in the specific company require a return of 30% measured in dollars, then they would require a return of 43% if this return were in pesos—that is, the 30% required in dollars, plus the 13% depreciation expected for the peso against the dollar.

According to the formula for the cost of capital presented earlier, a project that had an optimal capital structure of 40% debt and 60% equity would have the following cost of capital:

MEASURED IN DOLLARS

$$\$k_0 = 0.40(11\%) + 0.60(30\%) = 22.4\%$$

MEASURED IN PESOS

$$Pk_0 = 0.40(24\%) + 0.60(43\%) = 35.4\%$$

The difference between the cost of capital measured in dollars, 22.4%, and the cost of capital measured in pesos, 35.4%, is the rate of depreciation of the peso against the dollar expected in the future, 13%.[4]

Particularly when evaluating projects located in foreign countries, the issue of how to take inflation into account becomes very important. It is often suggested that this (usually higher) rate of inflation expected in the foreign country should be incorporated in the cost of capital or discount rate used to evaluate that project. However, as a general rule, inflation that is widely expected is built into the cost of debt and equity in the country with the given inflation. Hence, the weighted cost of capital measured in that currency already reflects such anticipated price changes—and so should the forecast cash flows for projects being evaluated in that country. Unless the manager has superior forecasting ability, it is unrealistic to add a further increase to the discount rate derived from the cost of capital to adjust for inflation.

If we choose to evaluate the project in terms of the home currency, say dollars, then the differential inflation rate will be reflected first in the estimate of higher future cash flows in the foreign currency, and then penalized by a higher depreciation rate when the cash flows are expressed in dollars. As an example, assume that the cash flows of a 1-year project in the absence of inflation would be P100; with inflation of 13% it would be P113. If the original exchange rate was P1/$, then purchasing power parity would indicate that the exchange rate at the end of the period would be P1.13/$. Using the peso expected cash flow and cost of capital we obtain the following present value:[5]

$$\frac{P113}{(1+0.3831)} = 81.70$$

---

[4] A more precise presentation of the relationship between the dollar and the peso cost of funds, with a 13% expected depreciation of the peso against the dollar will have the cost of funds in pesos equal to:

$$\text{Peso cost of funds} = \text{Dollar cost of funds } (1+0.13) + 13$$

This produces the following figures for the various peso costs of funds:

$$\text{Peso cost of debt} = 11\%(1+0.13)+13\% = 25.43\%$$
$$\text{Peso cost of equity} = 30\%(1+0.13)+13\% = 46.90\%$$
$$\text{Peso cost of capital} = 22.4\%(1+0.13)+13\% = 38.31\%$$

Alternatively,

$$\text{Peso cost of capital} = 0.40(25.43\%)+0.60(46.90\%) = 38.31\%$$

[5] This formulation uses the more accurate calculation of the peso cost of capital shown in footnote 4.

If we convert the peso cash flows into dollars at the exchange rate expected to prevail at the end of the period and use the dollar cost of capital figure, we obtain the same present value:

$$\frac{\$100}{(1 + 0.2240)} = 81.70$$

Fundamentally, using the local weighted cost of capital in evaluating projects is beneficial because if properly computed, that cost accounts for much of the inflationary pressures. This viewpoint prevents the foreign corporation with a domestic cost of capital of (say) 12% from concluding that it would be much better off in country X where almost any project earns 20%. This behavior is prevented simply by forcing the multinational corporation to reflect that much of the earnings in country X are inflationary, and the local cost of capital would probably be at least 15%.

To avoid the difficulties involved in measuring the impact of inflation on the evaluation of projects, many companies completely ignore inflation. This is done on the assumption that the rate of inflation in sectors where the project will operate is the same as for the economy as a whole. We think this assumption is incorrect in many instances. Inflation rates in the economic sectors in which the project will operate often are different from the average for the economy as a whole. However, the overall rate of inflation in the economy is the one that investors will consider in trying to maintain the purchasing power of their money. To incorporate the impact of inflation correctly, the cash flows should reflect the rate of inflation specific to the project, while the cost of capital reflects the overall inflation rate expected in the economy. The impact of inflation on both cash flow figures and the cost of capital should be considered separately and explicitly.[6]

---

[6]Foster presents a model relating inflation rates to net present value, allowing for three differential inflation rates. These are changes in general price levels (adjusting the discount rate), increases in some revenues because of the ability to pass on higher costs, and increases in variable costs. He notes that the general rate of inflation may differ from the revenue or cost increases. In the case of costs, labor market imperfections or considerations of capital intensive options may allow a lower rate of increase in costs. For revenues, the question is the elasticity of revenues with the general price increases. This elasticity reflects the ability to pass along general price increases. Foster also introduces the capital costs for fixed-debt obligations and adjusts for taxes in his formula. A fixed-debt formula relies on an "imbedded" debt cost, and does not ensure that the capital structure remains in balance. This particular version of Foster's formula forces a unique matching of projects and debt which is not always practically or theoretically desirable. See Earl M. Foster, "The Impact of Inflation on Capital Budgeting Decisions," *Quarterly Review of Economics and Business*, Autumn 1970, pp. 19–24.

The Case of Inefficient Markets

The financial markets of most countries are better described as inefficient than as efficient. Many situations can contribute to the market failure which creates an inefficient market, possibly resulting in inappropriate prices and returns in particular markets. An investment may be extraordinarily large, or its returns may be so far in the future that the lack of information on which returns can be estimated is a serious impediment to pricing. There may be other information failures: investors in other nations, whether corporate or individual, may simply not know about a project. Hence, the returns to someone present in the economy may be extraordinarily large because other investors are not bidding for the project. There may be barriers to capital movement: nations attempt to restrict the corporate and individual citizens in movements of funds out of the country from time to time. Other nations restrict capital inflows, in an effort to protect their own infant industries (or powerful ruling class) or for nonmarket issues such as an avoidance of "foreign" domination. Finally, investors and societies alike may perceive noneconomic factors in the sense of irrational or discriminatory actions. Foreign investors may know that the fact that they invest in a project makes nationalization more likely by a host government; hence, the foreign investor's return is lower than a domestic investor's return in an expected value sense. This outcome is related to the adverse selection concern in economics, in which a party to the activity has knowledge of characteristics that are known to affect the outcome, but that are not known or controllable by another party. Finally, currency parities do not interact in perfect symmetry reflecting divergent trends in inflation in various economies. Short-term and long-term capital flows from various motivations as well as the presence of international economic impact from the United Nations and the International Monetary Fund judgments, themselves colored with political considerations, affect currency parities as well.

There are segmented capital markets, there is disequilibrium in the markets, and there are special financing arrangements unique to many projects depending on their location. When these imperfections in the capital market do exist, the determination of the lowest cost of capital is not possible theoretically. However, the manager still must find a hurdle rate by which to accept or reject projects in foreign countries. An approximation to the cost of capital under those imperfect conditions must be found. The way that local investors react to similar projects will provide some guidance in this endeavor, although this reaction is not necessarily a theoretically optimal decision rule.

Thus, one returns to the basic conclusion that the relevant starting cost of capital for business and financial risk should be based on what the subsidiary would have to earn operating in its own environment. Bearing in mind currency and political risks and possible imperfections in the capital markets which permit lower capital costs of the parent to be passed through, one can consider whether this investment is desirable from the standpoint of the parent.

In particular, there are two factors that may account for the different cost of capital for a foreign project than for a domestic project with the same total risk. These factors are the proclivities of different countries to have overall different capital structures and the ability of financial markets to assess information not contained in reported financial statements.

Country Differences in Capital Structures. The local capital structures may differ sharply from the capital structure for a similar firm in the home country. For example, the debt load afforded most Japanese firms is grossly above the comparable debt load of an American firm in the same industry. Exhibit 14.2 shows tabulations of debt ratios in different nations. In part, this additional debt is because of the involvement of the government of Japan on both sides. The government-owned Bank of Japan provides debt via commercial banks to major industries on the government's favored list. Lenders know that the government is committed to protecting business. Hence, the risk of bankruptcy is reduced given the government commitment to preserve the major corporation as an economic force in Japan and throughout the world.

The local capital structure considerations may provide a lower capital cost in some cases than the parent's home country would permit. Typically, the local capital structure will provide a higher cost to the project if the home country is an industrialized nation and the local country is a less developed land.[7]

The Effects of Consolidated Financial Statements. In the context of a cost of capital analysis, if the consolidated risk position of the firm is changed by the addition of a major subsidiary in a high-risk area, then the minimum expected return to shareholders and to lenders should be increased. However, this conclusion is based on the awareness of lend-

---

[7]From their survey, Stonehill and Nathanson found that 64% of the respondents who used a cost of capital concept did *not* vary it for foreign investments. In terms of income, the largest group counted cash flow plus retained earnings as "income." See Arthur Stonehill and Leonard Nathanson, "Capital Budgeting and the Multinational Corporation," *California Management Review,* Summer 1968, pp. 39–54.

EXHIBIT 14.2 Debt Ratios in Selected Industries and Countries, 1966–1967[a]

	Alcoholic Beverages	Automobiles	Chemicals	Electrical	Foods	Iron and Steel	Nonferrous Metals	Paper	Textiles	Total
Benelux	45.7	—	44.6	37.5	56.2	50.0	59.2	35.9	54.2	47.9
France	35.8	36.0	34.3	59.1	24.7	33.7	55.0	35.5	20.9	37.2
West Germany	59.2	55.1	54.8	67.5	42.5	63.8	68.1	71.8	44.9	58.6
Italy	64.9	77.3	68.2	73.6	66.4	77.9	67.5	—	66.6	70.3
Japan	60.9	70.3	73.2	71.1	78.3	74.5	74.5	77.7	72.2	72.5
Sweden	—	76.4	45.6	60.1	46.8	70.0	68.7	60.7	—	61.2
Switzerland	—	—	59.7	50.8	29.2	—	26.3	—	—	41.5
United Kingdom	43.8	56.5	38.7	46.9	47.6	44.9	41.7	46.6	42.4	45.5
United States	31.1	39.2	43.3	50.3	34.2	35.8	36.7	33.9	44.2	38.7
Total	48.8	58.7	51.4	57.4	47.3	56.3	55.3	51.7	49.4	

[a]The numbers in the matrix represent average total debt as a percentage of total assets based on book value. Each company is weighted equally; that is, the individual company debt ratios are summed and divided by the number of companies in each sample.

SOURCE: Stonehill, Arthur, and Thomas Stitzel, "Financial Structure and the Multinational Corporation," *California Management Review,* Fall 1969, pp. 91–96. U.S. corporations are the ten largest in each industry (four only for automobiles), ranked by 1965 sales and reported in *Moody's Industrial Manual* (New York: Moody's Investor Service, Inc., June 1966). Japanese corporations are the largest publicly owned corporations in each industry as reported in *Kaisha Shikiho* (Quarterly Reports on Corporations) (Tokyo: Toyo Keizai Shinpo Sha, July 1967). European corporations are all the publicly owned corporations reported in *Beerman's Financial Yearbook of Europe* (London: R. Beerman Publishers, 1967).

491

ers and this awareness seems to be affected at times by the degree of disclosure in financial reports.

For example, throughout the period when lease payments of U.S. companies had to be reported only as a footnote to the financial statements, many advocates of leasing emphasized that leasing expanded the debt capacity of the firm. This argument was based largely on the assumption that the lenders did not adjust for the lease commitments, which were every bit as mandatory for the going concern as debt payments. Since at the time lease payments did not have to be shown in the body of the balance sheet, leasing was referred to as "off-balance sheet financing." In fact, many lenders acknowledged that they adjusted for lease commitments; yet the adjustments made were often cursory if they existed at all, and they differed from analyst to analyst within the same lending institution. (Since 1977 new capital lease payments of U.S. companies must be capitalized and reported in the main body of the balance sheet.)

The apparent myopia of investors in the leasing example and other cases can be attributed, at least in part, to reporting standards that did not require the consolidation of subsidiaries' financial statements. Disclosure of the combined income generated by subsidiaries and the combined total assets and leverage of the system was not required in these cases.

Currently, the U.S. rules for consolidation of financial statements of subsidiaries depend on the percentage ownership of the parent of the subsidiary. The requirements range from declaring only dividends (that is, a one-line income item—dividends from subsidiaries), to a pro rata inclusion of profits and losses, to a full merging of the balance sheets and income statements with a minority interest shown where the subsidiary is not 100% owned. Ownership of less than 50% does not require consolidation of the balance sheet and the subsidiary's leverage—that is, off-balance sheet financing is possible. See Exhibit 14.3.

EXHIBIT 14.3   U.S. Rules for Consolidation of Financial Statements

Percentage of Beneficial Ownership by Parent in Subsidiary	Consolidation for Financial Reporting Purposes
0–19%	Dividends as received
20–49%	Pro rata inclusions of profits and losses
50–100%	Full consolidation[a]

[a]Consolidation may be avoided in the case of some majority-owned foreign operations if the parent can convince its auditors that it does not have control of the subsidiary or there are substantial restrictions on the repatriation of cash.

CASH FLOWS TO PARENT VERSUS CASH
FLOWS TO PROJECT

In Chapter 13 we saw how we obtain very different internal rates of return depending on whether we use cash flows to the parent or cash flows to the project. We will now reexamine this issue under the light of cost of capital theory. At the most basic level, the ultimate return and risk considerations should be for the parent company's stockholders. Hence, dollar remittances to the U.S. parent and a return consistent with the risk of operating the foreign subsidiary are appropriate for this example. However, two general issues complicate this view.

First, the investors in the parent are increasingly from a world-wide family. If the shareholder group wants only U.S. investments, the impact of their nationality on the external portfolio is not significant. However, these non-U.S. investors may want a worldwide purchasing power return; therefore, their concern is a currency basket weighted in some way with the dollar only one part of the contents. In addition, just as many U.S. shareholders have increasingly emphasized a variety of noneconomic issues (such as South African operations, minority employment, and the environment), so, too, many of these non-U.S. shareholders demand increasing concern by the company management for the firm's operations worldwide, especially in the shareholders' lands.

Second, and more directly, many companies in the true multinational tradition accept their role as worldwide investors. Hence, the fact that funds are blocked in removal from country X is about as relevant as knowing that a plant in California is not readily marketable. The fact that assets are restricted in a nation on a temporary or a long-term basis is merely an additional inconvenience for the U.S. corporation, just as a low-skill labor force, poor commuter facilities, bad railroad connections, or limited banking associations may be part of operating in some parts of the United States. Obviously, blocked funds are more serious than weak communications or nonmarketable plants in California, but the difference is one of degree, not substance. The immobility of assets and the restrictions on business practice are facts of corporate life not unique to operations in particular countries.

Hence, to the extent that the corporation views itself as a true multinational, the effect of restrictions on repatriation may not be severe. If the firm anticipates continued investment in a country which is in a growing market, the restriction is not even an issue to be addressed in a "good-citizen or bad-citizen" framework. Rather, the commitment is made for long-term continuing investments in the country and the restriction on repatriation is generally irrelevant.

In most cases the firm will verify that the project return and the parent return are both agreeable. However, these are but two goals, and the firm will probably have a number of other goals or constraints of a financial nature, plus nonfinancial standards. Among the financial considerations beyond the return of the project and the return to the parent are liquidity, reported earnings, and alternative uses of cash.

In terms of company liquidity, even if the returns are satisfactory, the parent may have stringent needs for cash in particular years which a given international project cannot meet. Hence, this constraint may be binding.

The consolidation standards may mean that the huge reported losses in the early years of a project will be too large to be acceptable to the current managers, who fear adverse shareholders' reaction. Alternatively, relatively high reported earnings may be linked to a need for cash remissions if the parent wishes to maintain a particular dividend payout ratio of (say) 40% of reported earnings. Hence, the reported earnings may relate directly to the liquidity issue.

If the parent plans to invest the funds in the local country, then the project return and reinvestment rate may dominate. At the other extreme, reinvestments outside the local country mean the parent return in the parent currency will prevail. Hence, a multinational may emphasize different return standards for various nations depending on how a given project fits the corporation's portfolio of projects now and in the future.

Thus, return and risk are but two financial aspects of international investments, and other financial values operate as constraints. In extreme cases these and other values may become dominant goals.

THE COST OF EQUITY AS A HURDLE RATE

An alternative to the concept of the average cost of capital is the concept of return to equity, one of the components of the total cost of capital. This approach can be particularly useful when special financing arrangements are attached to the specific project. However, in order for this approach to lead to correct conclusions we must specify the financing sources throughout the entire life of the project.

An example of a situation in which management usually concentrates its analysis on the return to equity is the shipping industry. In this case the yard that manufactures the ship traditionally supplies a substantial amount of the total funds required, secured only by the ship. The return to the equity holders is a function of the ship's cost, the revenues and operating expenses, and the timing of the particular financing scheme offered by a given shipyard. This last item is often a source of erroneous conclusions. Holding the cost, revenue, and operating cost assumptions constant, it is obvious that the shorter-loan (faster payback) option will have a lower return to equity in normal settings. Essentially, the cheaper debt financing will be paid off sooner, meaning that the ship will be financed increasingly by larger portions of equity over its life. Without debt on which to lever the return to equity in later years, the return to equity will be lower than otherwise would be the case. The analysis is valid, however, only if one assumes that no other financing is available in later years. One can argue that short-term financing might be used in later years to replace some or all of that debt. Alternatively, one needs to consider if the low-debt balance sheet afforded by the rapid repayment of debt under the shorter-lived debt option would not permit more debt from other lenders for financing additional projects.

In some situations the particular financing may be dominated uniquely and completely by the particular project at hand. Special joint ventures or subsidiaries in which the parent firm offers no guarantees may be regarded as unique projects with their own costs of capital. For example, Freeport Minerals traditionally operates in this manner. Nationalization of its huge Cuban nickel plant caused the parent to lose its equity in the subsidiary and several banks to lose huge amounts of loans to the project secured by that plant. However, the effect on the other lenders to Freeport and the rest of Freeport's operations was minimal. This case is probably atypical. The corporation will often fulfill a moral obligation (perhaps induced by enlightened self-interest in assuring itself a welcome for future financing options) to pay off liabilities of legally separate entities. This behavior was seen when American Express repaid debts of its legally separate warehousing subsidiary in the wake of the salad oil scandal.[8]

Confusing the cost of capital with the cost of equity can lead to a fallacious analysis; the pyramidal structure which can result is presented in Exhibit 14.4. Advocates of this position say the following: "We shall invest in that project in country X, and we know our parent has a cost of capital of (say) 12%. Accordingly, we shall borrow as much local money as possible and then invest the balance ourselves. As long as we can earn our 12%, we are in fine shape."

What is the fallacy of this argument? We will ignore major risk considerations and differential inflation rates, and assume the proposed project is comparable to other projects of the firm. Assume that the parent and all subsidiaries are able to obtain 50% debt and 50% equity

---

[8]See Norman C. Miller, *The Great Salad Oil Swindle*, Baltimore, Maryland: Penguin Books, 1966.

EXHIBIT 14.4 Pyramidal Corporate Structure (M-million)

```
Holding Corp.
$2M Debt at 4%    ⎫
  2M Equity at 20% ⎬  12% Cost of capital
                   ⎭
            Subsidiary 1
            $4M Debt at 4%    ⎫
              4M Equity at 12% ⎬  8% Cost of capital
                               ⎭
                    Subsidiary 2
                    $8M Debt at 4%   ⎫
                      8M Equity at 8% ⎬  6% Cost of capital
                                      ⎭
Consolidated
Debt     $30M
Equity     2M                 Subsidiary 3
                              $16M Debt at 4%    ⎫
                                16M Equity at 6% ⎬ 5% Cost of capital
                                                 ⎭
```

with debt carrying a consistent cost of 4% after tax. Call the parent a holding company and let two of the subsidiaries act as holding companies. That is, they do nothing but invest their capital (raised by debt and equity issues) in the equity of other firms. Although in this example they have invested directly in only one other firm, in the typical pyramiding situation the units invest in a variety of firms. An analysis of the conclusions drawn from Exhibit 14.4 may suggest why such "diversification" is used.

Consider the final operating company, subsidiary 3. The lender to this firm is content, assuming the $16 million in debt is reasonably secured by real assets. The lenders to the other firms are not concerned, for the firms have only a 0.5 debt-to-total-capitalization ratio. However, if these lenders go beyond the simplest of analyses, they see that their ultimate real assets for security are downstream. Furthermore, the lender to subsidiary 3 would have first claim on the assets under normal circumstances. To take the first case, consider the lender to Holding Corporation. When this lender considers the consolidated statement, it is apparent that the real "firm" has $30 million in debt and only $2 million in equity. This lender's $2 million of debt stands behind an additional $28 million of debt, and all of the indebtedness is secured by the $32 million of assets of subsidiary 3. (For kindness' sake in this example, assume that the assets of subsidiary 3 do exist and are reasonably valued, a situation that does not always occur.)

This exaggerated situation points out the fallacy of merely charging the subsidiary with the cost of capital of the parent when that investment is really equity. In fact, the subsidiary should be charged with the appropriate cost of equity for going into *that* business in *that* land. Typically, this charge for equity will be higher than the parent's cost of capital. Accordingly, the cost of funds to the usual subsidiary will be increased.

SUMMARY

This chapter reviewed the corporate financial theory on the *cost of capital* and the impact of business and financial risk on the return to shareholders. The use of *different discount rates* for projects of varying degrees of risk was suggested as plausible, providing that discount rates were based on what firms active in that type of project would require as a capital structure in the open market or on what is reasonable based on the general riskiness of the project.

In a fully efficient international capital market, the cost of capital for projects of similar risk would be invariant with regard to location or currency. Furthermore, in an asset pricing framework, well-diversified international investors would pay nothing for a multinational firm's raw diversification. Likewise, currency parities over time would reflect differential national economic inflation trends, and hence the currency of revenue and cost determination would be of no interest to the managers. Inefficient markets involve some form of *market failure*, such as projects of extraordinary size, lags in information to firms or investors, an immobility of capital either because of capital export or import restrictions, an extraordinarily long life for a project, or the fact that currency parities are influenced by many factors other than relative national inflation. Moreover, foreign firms and investors may perceive many noneconomic and nonmarket factors that will appear with their participation in some project, under the idea of adverse selection.

After noting the alternative means by which managers may evaluate the risk of a project, we considered once again the issue of *whose returns* are to be considered. The tradition of concern with the welfare of shareholders is blunted by two considerations. First, many shareholders are not citizens of the parent country, especially in the case of a U.S. parent. Second, a socially responsible corporation committed to a given region or area as a true multinational may not be preoccupied with bringing funds home. Special considerations aside, the returns in the national currency of the parent corporation are generally the dominant index of worth, even with allowance for liquidity, earnings per share, and other items.

Focusing only on the *return to equity* may be appropriate when the project is truly freestanding, as is the case with project financing. Both the lenders to the project and the firm's general creditors must recognize that the project will not receive extra financing from the parent should extremely bad outcomes imply total loss to the parent unless it supplies more funds.

We examined the fallacy of *pyramiding*, in which the local capital structure is used in conjunction with a low cost of equity from the parent-investor to justify a very low discount rate for a project in a foreign land. The appropriate discount rate for a project in another nation is generally no less than the discount rate implied by domestic financing of that project using domestic capital sources if available. The divergence of capital structures from nation to nation was noted.

QUESTIONS

1. "If the parent's cost of capital is 15%, its equity investment in a subsidiary only needs to be charged to the subsidiary at 15%." Why or why not?

2. "Regardless of the interest rate, we always borrow in a cheap currency with a likely devaluation, since that minimizes our financing costs." Give an example in which this strategy would fail. Do you think it is a good rule of thumb?

3. What data would you desire in order to evaluate the risk of a project in a particular country? Why would one corporation find a given level of risk acceptable while another one might reject it? Does this indicate the irrationality of corporate management?

4. With worldwide operations, IBM has about 300 American nationals working for it outside the United States. Do you think this policy is a good one? What firms could use it more profitably than other firms, or do you believe it makes sense for all firms?

BIBLIOGRAPHY

Booth, Laurence D., "Capital Budgeting Frameworks for the Multinational Corporation," *Journal of International Business Studies*, Fall 1982, pp. 113–23.

Carter, E. Eugene, *Portfolio Aspects of Corporate Capital Budgeting*. Lexington, Mass.: D.C. Heath and Company, 1974.

Chenery, H. B., "Comparative Advantage and Development Policy," *American Economic Review*, Mar. 1961, pp. 18–51.

Foster, Earl M., "The Impact of Inflation on Capital Budgeting Decisions," *Quarterly Review of Economics and Business*, Autumn 1970, pp. 19–24.

Fremgen, James M., "Capital Budgeting Practices: A Survey," *Management Accounting*, May 1973, pp. 19–25.

Hackett, John T., "The Multinational Corporation and Worldwide Inflation," *Financial Executive*, Feb. 1975, pp. 64–73.

Hymer, Stephen, "The Efficiency (Contradictions) of Multinational Corporations," *American Economic Review*, May 1970, pp. 441–48.

Johnson, H. G., "A Theoretical Model of Economic Nationalism in New and Developing States," *Political Science Quarterly*, June 1965, pp. 169–85.

Malkoff, Alan R., "Foreign Acquisition Analysis: A Suggested Approach," *Management Accounting*, June 1979, pp. 32–36.

Polk, Judd, et al., *U.S. Production Abroad and the Balance of Payments*. New York: National Industrial Conference Board, 1966.

Severn, Alan K., and David R. Meinster, "The Use of Multicurrency Financing by the Financial Manager," *Financial Management*, Winter 1978, pp. 45–53.

Stonehill, Arthur, and Leonard Nathanson, "Capital Budgeting and the Multinational Corporation," *California Management Review*, Summer 1968, pp. 39–54.

CHAOLANDIA'S SUPER-WIDGETS

IN EARLY 1984 the manager of Aggressive Enterprises in Chaolandia submitted the super-widgets project for approval by the parent company. Chaolandia was a developing country and Aggressive Enterprises operated there in the form of a locally-incorporated subsidiary.

Product. Super-widgets. Aggressive Enterprises had been manufacturing widgets in Chaolandia. The new project would allow the country to produce more powerful widgets, super-widgets.

Investment Requirements. It was estimated that 250,000 Chaolandia pesos (CP) would be required for plant and equipment. There was no parent investment for working capital. However, CP75,000 of the CP250,000 required for plant and equipment could be provided by the parent out of obsolete equipment it maintained in its warehouse. Chaolandia's government was agreeable to this transfer. The government also agreed to a 5-year, straight-line depreciation method for the CP250,000 of plant and equipment.

Project Life. Although the market for super-widgets was expected to continue expanding for at least the next 20 years, Chaolandia's government insisted on making arrangements for the purchase of the company by the government after 5 years. At that time, the government proposed to purchase the super-widget plant for CP450,000.

Demand. At a price of CP550 per unit, the demand for super-widgets was estimated as indicated in the following table:

	Domestic	Exports
	(units)	
1985	125	40
1986	200	100
1987	225	125
1988	250	175
1989	250	175

The domestic demand was considered to be completely price inelastic. That is, for the likely prices in the future, the quantity demanded appeared to be independent of the price charged. However, this was not the case with exports. Export demand was considered to be more responsive to price changes. It was thought that for each 1% increase in prices, the export quantity demanded decreased by 0.3%. The growth in export quantity anticipated in the table represented the expected penetration of the export market at the initial price of $200. The export figures did not take into account any possible change in export prices. Chaolandia's exports could affect the sales of some of the other divisions of Aggressive Enterprises. However, this impact was expected to be nominal at least during the first 5 years of the project.

Prices. The engineers had estimated that an initial price of CP550 was appropriate, given the competition. However, historical inflation in the country made it possible to count on an annual 23% increase in prices. The CP550 for 1985 already incorporated the rate of inflation between 1984 and 1985.

Variable Costs. Variable costs were estimated by the engineering department as shown in the following table:

Raw material	
Domestic	CP130 per unit
Imported	85 per unit
Labor	40 per unit

Domestic costs were expected to increase at an annual rate of 27% because of inflation in the industry and labor contracts. Import prices were subject to fluctuations in the exchange rate. Cost estimates for 1985 already incorporated the rate of inflation between 1984 and 1985.

Fixed Costs. The estimates of fixed costs are provided in the following table:

Supervisory fees to the parent	CP25,000 annually
Selling and administrative expenses	20,000 annually
Depreciation	50,000 annually

The supervisory fees had been approved by Chaolandia's government and were to remain fixed for the 5-year life of the project. In fact, these fees were a form of royalty and did not involve additional expenditures at home. Selling and administrative expenses were subject to a 25% inflation rate per annum. Depreciation was to be based on a straight-line method, as approved by Chaolandia's government.

Exchange Rates. The economics department of Aggressive Enterprises had forecast the exchange rates listed in the next table.

	CP per $
1984	2.75
1985	2.75
1986	3.25
1987	3.25
1988	3.50
1989	3.50

Taxes. Taxes were as follows:

Chaolandia's taxes	15% income tax, with no loss carry forward 30% withholding tax on dividends
Parent country taxes	On income: 45%, allowing tax credit for taxes paid abroad On capital gains: 40%

Remittances. There was no control on repatriation of earnings. It was expected that all the profits after taxes would be remitted to the parent company.

Cost of Capital Applicable to Chaolandia. This cost was estimated at 35%. The production of super-widgets in Chaolandia was not expected to alter the risk profile of Aggressive Enterprises.

1. Would you accept the project?
2. What assumptions do you consider to be critical in your analysis? Use Exhibits M.1 and M.2 for your projections.
3. How would you analyze the project if earnings repatriation were prohibited during the initial 4 years of the project?
4. How would you analyze the project if Aggressive Enterprises intended to continue operating Super-widgets for the next 20 years (that is, the government would not purchase it at the end of the fifth year) and a control in earnings repatriation existed? Assume earnings repatriation at the present time is limited to 12% of annual earnings.
5. Chaolandia's government and financial institutions have offered several alternatives to finance the project. These alternatives include several degrees of leverage with local funds. However, these local funds are much

more expensive than the rate Aggressive Enterprises pays in the home country. How would you analyze the project if an independent financial package had to be created for its financing, and the relevant question became: What is the return on equity of Aggressive Enterprises?

EXHIBIT M.1 Chaolandia's Super-Widgets: Pro Forma Statement (in Chaolandia pesos)

	1985	1986	1987	1988	1989
Revenues					
Sales (units)					
1. Domestic					
2. Exports					
3. Total					
4. Price per unit					
5. Gross revenue					
Expenses					
Raw material (per unit)					
6. Domestic					
7. Imports					
8. Labor (per unit)					
9. Total variable costs per unit					
10. Number of units					
11. Total variable costs					
12. Supervisory fees					
13. Selling and administrative					
14. Depreciation					
15. Total expenses					
16. Profit before taxes					
17. Local taxes (15%)					
18. Profit after taxes					
19. Withholding taxes (30%)					

EXHIBIT M.2   Chaolandia's Super-Widgets: Cash Flow Analysis (in parent country dollars)

	1984	1985	1986	1987	1988	1989
Exchange Rate:						
Cash Inflows						
1. Profit after taxes						
2. Depreciation						
3. Supervisory fee						
4. Terminal value						
5. Total cash inflows						
Cash Outflows						
6. Initial investment						
7. Chaolandia withholding taxes						
8. Parent country taxes on:						
9. Dividends						
10. Fees						
11. Capital gains (40%)						
12. Total cash outflows						
13. Net cash flows						
14. Discount factors at 35%						
15. Discounted flows						
16. Net present value						

15

Risk
Evaluation
in Foreign
Investments

IN THIS CHAPTER we will discuss the major types of risk encountered in foreign projects. Each of these risks has been mentioned in the context of the determination of the cash flows relevant to a project and the estimation of the cost of funds for that project. Here we will discuss them more formally as factors affecting the probability distribution of the returns of a project.

In the first part of the chapter we review briefly the nature of the business and financial risks affecting a foreign project. The risks due to the possible acts of a sovereign government, the so-called political risks, are discussed in greater detail. Then we introduce the methods available to measure and analyze the total risk in a project. The chapter concludes with an extended example in which a project's risks are analyzed from different vantage points using a computer simulation model.

ECONOMIC RISKS

Business and *financial risks* are the risks normally evaluated in the domestic capital budgeting problems. The risks introduced by *inflationary conditions* affect any domestic project; the risks of *exchange rate fluctuations* are particular to international projects.

Business risk relates to the probability of different operating cash flows in a particular line of business, but independent of the political risk of the country. The probability that a given number of units will be sold at the given selling price summarizes the concepts involved in business risk. Thus, cyclical businesses (capital goods industries such as steel, for example) have a higher business risk than noncyclical businesses. New businesses in an industry generally have higher risk than established firms because of the extra risk attendant to choice of location and development of an effective organization. Finally, independently of political considerations, an investment in any industry which is relatively young in a country is riskier than a similar investment in another country where that industry has reached its mature stage.

The main tools available to reduce business risk are long-term sales contracts fixing prices with buyers of the firm's products and with suppliers to the firm. These contracts can lock in a gross revenue per unit for the life of the contracts. However, quantities sold usually remain within much broader boundaries in these contracts and contribute to the business risk of the firm. In addition, these long-term contracts may have to be renegotiated in cases of extreme changes in economic conditions.

Financial risk refers to the variability of returns introduced by the specific way in which the project or the firm is financed. As a greater amount of debt or preferred stock is added to the capital structure, the probability that the firm will not be able to meet payment of interest and principal on the debt (and any required dividend on the preferred stock) in a given period increases—the risks of the financial investors in the firm increase. This will be reflected in a higher required rate of return by these investors, particularly the equity holders who have a claim on returns only after more senior investors such as lenders have been paid.

The business risk associated with a firm and an industry will have some influence on the capital structure. Even the best established firms in a high-risk industry are unlikely to have the same proportion of debt at a cheap price as a firm in a low-risk industry with many marketable current assets, for example. In addition to these industry characteristics, there are different financial policies followed by corporate officers. Some firms may have relatively high debt (that is, added financial risk) while others in the same industry and with an equally seasoned business have a more conservative structure, perhaps with no debt. Also, as shown in Chapter 14 the same industry may be leveraged to different degrees depending on the specific country and the local financial institutions, including government supports.

The uncertainty created by financial risk can be reduced somewhat by having long-term debt with redemption features and having ample lines of credit outstanding. The uncertainty as to the specific cost of funds can be minimized by tailoring the maturity of interest rates to the time horizon within which selling prices can be adjusted to reflect changes in the cost of funds.

Superimposed on the traditional business and financial risks, an international project has risks introduced by the instability of monetary conditions (inflation risk and exchange risk). Even when we are fairly certain that a project will sell a given number of units at a specified price—a project with low business risk—we may be uncertain as to the net cash flows we will obtain from these sales after we take into account inflation and currency fluctuations.

As we described in the discussion of economic exposure to exchange risk, the ability of a firm to increase prices depends on the demand for the product, the competitive environment of the firm, and government regulation of prices at the time.[1] The impact of inflationary conditions on the local cost of funds depends on the local market's efficiency as well as the market's ability to anticipate future rates of inflation. If a project cannot adjust immediately to changes in prices and exchange rates, the return obtained from this project will depend on the magnitudes of these changes and the degree of response of which the project is capable.

The minimization of these monetary risks involves entering into long-term contracts in which allowances are made for these fluctuations. For example, a manager might make sales prices adjustable according to domestic inflation or fluctuations in the value of the domestic currency. In particular, adjusting local prices according to exchange fluctuations effectively changes the currency denomination of the sale from the local currency to the other currency in the exchange rate used as reference.

POLITICAL RISKS

Political risks involve the vulnerability of the returns of a project to the political acts of a sovereign government. Although currency devaluations and monetary policies are also government acts that affect the returns obtained from a project, political risk usually refers to those acts which contest the ownership of the project by a foreigner. In particular, we will refer to the *blockage of funds* and *expropriation*.

---

[1]See the section titled "Economic Exposure" in Chapter 10.

Blockage of Funds

A common problem associated with political risk is a temporary *block on the currency*. Black market operations, whatever moral attitude the corporation may hold toward them, are usually not available for the relatively large and highly visible transactions associated with a corporation from a major developed nation attempting to terminate its operations in a small developing land. Ownership may continue, but there is simply no way to remove funds from the country. This situation confronted many Indians in the wake of General Amin's actions in Uganda in 1972–1974. Some of them felt they still owned their businesses, and nothing the Ugandan government did directly contradicted this premise. The Indians, many of whom were Ugandan citizens, operated from Kenya after widespread racial violence against them in Uganda, yet they had no means by which they might remove funds from their Ugandan operations.

There are brokers of varying degrees of reputability and legality who engage in the trading of blocked accounts. The most obvious way to eliminate blockages in such countries as Greece, Turkey, and the Soviet Union is to arrange swaps between two corporations, each lending to the other in the land where its own funds are restricted.[2] In other times, a parent may charge a high rate of interest on loans to a subsidiary in a country that blocks currency repatriation.

War and revolution also add great uncertainty to the eventual repatriation of funds. Even after the Russian Revolution, Exxon (then Jersey Standard) continued to invest. The Russians seized the firm's $160,000 investment in Azerbaijan in 1920. Exxon invested another $8.8 million over the next 5 years, confident that the investment was still theirs. Sometimes, executives who are overly enthusiastic about a business environment ignore both political liberties and international relationships. Many American executives rejoiced in Nazi Germany. Henry Ford continued to invest. Thomas Watson of IBM liked the environment for business. Corn Products president George Moffett said it was less onerous than the New Deal: "In Germany . . . there is no uncertainty, no political caprice, and no nonsense. You reach an agreement with the government and it sticks. You have a problem and you go to the government and get a clear, immediate answer, whereas in America you may spend weeks trying to find out where you stand with the New Deal and then just as you seem to have reached an understanding there is an overnight change in policy . . . "[3] These comments

---

[2]See Chapters 8 and 9.

[3]Mira Wilkins, *The Maturing of Multinational Enterprise: American Business Abroad from 1914 to 1970* (Cambridge, Mass.: Harvard University Press, 1974), p. 188.

may refer more to the New Deal (with complaints that are familiar to-day when business executives deal with the Soviet bloc countries), but the attitude toward Germany was startling. Poor forecasting and an in-sensitivity to the environment for many German citizens are not unique to American corporate presidents. Ultimately, most American assets in Germany that were not destroyed in the war were returned, even though remissions were blocked and the assets could not be sold for exchangeable currency during the war. A similar sequestering occurred for U.S. assets of foreign nationals whose countries were occupied by the Nazis, even before the United States declared war on Germany.

Note that these blocks have generally been interpreted as public policy applicable to many firms. There may also be specific limitations on transfers from a particular firm. As we subsequently define the area of expropriation, this limitation may be more appropriately considered as the host country's involvement in the operation of the individual firm.

These repatriation blocks can be evaluated using the *terminal rate of return* to discount the blocked funds, with and without a reinvest-ment assumption.[4] When the risk of blocked funds is substantial, the effect of such block on the return of a project will be significant and should be considered explicitly.

The two instruments used most often to minimize the risk of blocked funds in a project are the payment of supervisory fees and roy-alties by the project, and the naming of the parent's equity contribution in the project as a loan. The payment of fees and royalties and the re-payment of debt are considered to be required by the conditions of the investment and the financing agreement. Accordingly, these payments are expected to have a better chance of approval by the local govern-ment than dividend repatriation.

When local governments complain about excessive amounts of parent loans to the subsidiary, these loans are sometimes converted to direct loans against inventory and accounts receivable. Although this policy reduces the security for the local senior lenders, it does give the parent a legitimate basis for lending. A disadvantage of this strategy is that with a growing business the inventories and accounts receivable are likely to expand. This expansion requires a greater fund commit-ment by the parent at a time when a withdrawal may be desired. How-ever, the growing business may be in a better position to substitute lo-cal debt for parent debt at this point.

In terms of the total debt on the consolidated corporate balance sheet, intercompany loans are eliminated. Thus, the effect on the debt-to-equity ratio of the consolidated firm is nil. However, from the stand-

---

[4]For a discussion of the terminal rate of return see Chapter 13.

point of the debt-bearing capacity of the local firm, local lenders may be more skeptical of a parent's high debt obligation. Placing the parent's debt in a subordinated position dispels this local concern.

From the standpoint of taxes, the U.S. parent with a favorable outcome of a project may expect to reduce most of the investment by tax-free loan repayments and then pay a capital gains tax on the sale of the small equity investment in the firm if and when that sale is made. However, Section 482 of the 1962 Revenue Act places the burden of proof on the parent to show that these are bona fide loans. The Internal Revenue Service can argue that much of the loan principal being remitted is a dividend payment, and as such is subject to tax.

Remitting royalties and supervisory fees *may* also be more advantageous than remitting dividends for tax reasons. These payments usually are considered deductible business expenses for local country taxes. Even when they are not deductible, the local country may tax these remissions at a lower rate than dividends because there is a *dividend withholding tax* in addition to the *corporate tax*. Hence, the payment may be exposed to lower total taxes than the straight dividend from corporate profits. However, the United States taxes the income from royalties and supervisory fees in full, whereas dividends received can be given credit for some taxes paid locally.[5]

Today, many local authorities recognize the legitimate concern of parents about remission. On the other hand, they are also concerned about the development of their own nations. Accordingly, the typical investment contract for a major project will specify the capital structure of the firm and will limit supervisory fees or royalties to (say) 5% of gross revenues.

Expropriation

From the standpoint of the *corporation*, we define *expropriation* broadly, with pure nationalization of ownership and complete involvement in the operation by the national government being a relatively infrequent, extreme example. Generally, *expropriation* refers to an increased and substantial operating involvement by the host government that causes a downward revision to the initial understanding in the parent corporation's management role and cash flows from the operation.

---

[5]A readable and comprehensive summary of the impact of various channels by which multinational firms may transfer resources among units is contained in Donald R. Lessard, "Transfer Prices, Taxes, and Financial Markets: Implications of Internal Financial Transfers within the Multinational Firm," *Proceedings of the New York University Conference on Economic Issues of Multinational Firms*, edited by Robert G. Hawkins (New York: JAI Press, 1977).

What is expropriated is the owner's right to operate fully the corporation.

The risk and expected value of particular situations may be very hard to assess. For example, even at the extreme of nationalization, the risk may range from complete uncertainty to a high probability of a takeover. Even given a takeover, there may be substantial variation in the possible compensation, ranging from nothing to market value paid immediately. In addition, assessing the probabilities tends to be very difficult and highly subjective. Nevertheless, the following comments are offered to cope with broadly defined expropriation. When the situation warrants, the corporation's officers will consider the worst-case assumption, calculating the maximum loss if expropriation occurs in various years.[6] Additional approaches to the problem may be found in many of the references cited in the bibliography.

The more direct political risk is expropriation. This may be gradual, with increasing demands for participation by locals or by the host government in the profits and ownership of the business. Initially, it may take the form of a high sales tax or the right to buy into the equity of the firm at some price. Often the price is extremely low and related to the book value of the firm. Later, formal plans for takeover may include a 5-year phasing of nationals into key operating positions. The more dramatic course is a pure takeover, as, for example, the American copper operations in Chile or the international petroleum corporations in Libya. In its extreme form, expropriation can be a 1-hour affair in which military forces with heavy armaments surround the offices and the corporate managers are given 30 minutes to evaluate the situation. They are provided with transportation to the airfield where a DC-3 removes them from the land after an unusual avoidance of baggage clearance and customs formalities.

The firm may employ a variety of techniques to alter the probabilities of expropriation, no matter what the transition in governments might bring. One way of categorizing actions designed to lessen the probabilities or the effect of expropriation is shown in Exhibit 15.1. First, there are influences on the government in a positive vein. Second, there are negative inducements for the government to avoid expropriation. Finally, there are outside options which sometimes alter the probabilities, but more often they alter the effect.

---

[6]The possibility of a war between the host and parent governments further aggravates the situation. On the other hand, the American subsidiaries of the German I. G. Farben produced chemicals for the Allied war effort while General Motor's German subsidiaries manufactured trucks for the Wehrmacht in World War II. (See *The New York Times,* Mar. 13, 1974, p. 36.) During World War I, the Germans dealt very carefully with the U.S. assets impounded in Germany, for they had far *more* assets in the United States. Most of the units continued to operate autonomously, even though the sequestered assets could not be sold and their earnings could not be remitted to the German owners.

EXHIBIT 15.1   Coping with Political Risk

Positive Approaches		Negative Approaches
Prior negotiation of controls and operating contracts		License or patent restrictions under international agreements
Prior agreement for sale	Direct	Control of external raw materials
Joint venture with government or local private sector		Control of transportation to (external) markets
		Control of downstream processing
Use of locals in management		Control of external markets
Joint venture with local banks		
Equity participation by middle class	Indirect	
Local sourcing		
Local retail outlets		

External Approaches to Minimize Loss

International insurance or investment
   guarantees
Thinly capitalized firms:
   Local financing
   External financing secured only by
     the local operation

The positive approaches involve indicating to the host government the firm's interest in the nation on a longer-term basis. Careful negotiation may result in contracts addressing the firm's obligation to employ locals and to accommodate various control agreements relating to management, profitability, and investment.[7] Perhaps the agreements provide for eventual termination of the foreign ownership. There can be a joint venture with local private partners or the host government, either now or in later years, with arrangements made for the government to have a long-run minority or majority position. Such contracts indicate the firm's commitment to meet the government in achieving political, developmental, and financial goals for the project. Indirectly, the firm can provide for reinforcing the government's nonfinancial goals by sourcing capital equipment and operating supplies locally; by using locals for unskilled, skilled, and managerial roles; and by spreading equity throughout the local citizenry.

The last policy is usually operated in the form of substantial investments by a few big banks controlled by the wealthier citizens of the country. An alternative approach, somewhat limited in the absence of a well-developed equity market, is to encourage investment by as

---

[7]Sometimes national employees do not identify as fully with the country as expected. The late president of National Cash Register, Stanley C. Allyn, told of the NCR office in the path of the Wehrmacht as it rumbled into Paris. One tank swerved from the column and headed for the office. Out jumped a pistol-bearing German soldier who hammered on the door. Meeting the local French official, he remarked, "I'm from the Berlin office. Sorry I can't stay long, but I was wondering: Did you make quota last year?" See Mira Wilkins, *The Maturing of Multinational Enterprise: American Business Abroad from 1914 to 1970* (Cambridge, Mass.: Harvard University Press, 1974).

many of the middle class as possible. The disadvantages of this indirect pressure on the government are the costs of handling small investors (many of whom may be relatively unsophisticated financially) coupled with stockholder resentment created when a dividend is not passed. The indirect pressure on the government, of course, is that nationalization or other forms of political involvement in the management of the firm force the government to contend not only with workers who may be unhappy under government operation (as in the Chilean copper case), but also with a wide range of investors who either lose their investment or anticipate poor results from increased government involvement. Hence, the joint venture or involvement of local middle-class equity participation may be a direct way of responding to a government's goals, but it also may be an indirect way of forcing the government to reckon with higher domestic costs from an expropriation move. However, the local government may prefer the multinational which brings in all the hard currency needed for the project instead of absorbing local funds.

Among the negative approaches to limiting the risk of expropriation is the restriction of inputs or outputs. By having the local venture provide only one step in the process (such as processing basic raw materials or selling imported goods manufactured elsewhere), nationalization of the operation prevents the government from retaining a viable business. Where there is a sizable producing operation which depends on external markets, control of those external markets, of the transportation to those markets, or of intervening processing required to provide the final good to those markets all constrict the government.

For example, oil-producing countries in the Middle East were limited in their abilities to nationalize local oil operations when most of the downstream refining capacity and market outlets were controlled by their foreign partners (the international oil companies) who presumably would not be pleased by an expropriation. To the extent that the international oil companies could supply their refineries from other sources and no other refineries were available (the situation prevailing in the late 1950s and 1960s), the ability of the Mideast nations to profit from expropriation was reduced. In later periods, it was the limited availability to the oil companies of alternative economic sources of crude oil which increased the Mideast nations' position—even though most of the tanker fleets were either owned or under long-term charter to the oil companies. The benefit of nationalization to the oil-producing nations, of course, was greater influence in the whole production process from crude oil to consumer petroleum products.

Control of transportation, the situation of United Fruit (now United Brands) vis-à-vis various small Latin countries (known in former days as "banana republics" for their main United Fruit product), prevented those nations from nationalizing plantations. Put simply, the bananas would rot before alternative transportation could be developed, and unless all these nations acted in concert, the effect on United Fruit from one nationalization would have been relatively insignificant.[8]

A corporation which controls critical international licenses or patents has influence on the government, for operating illegally without these licenses brings sanctions upon the nation. Many Western nations and companies have been reluctant to invest in the Eastern bloc for many years because of Soviet indifference to international copyright and patent agreements.

Finally, as suggested in Exhibit 15.1, the company has outside options to minimize, if not the risk, at least the cost of an expropriation. Private carriers in the United States issue many political risk policies, since government guarantees and insurance are not as extensive as many managers prefer. As an example, in recent years, a firm would pay about 15% of face amount for a 3-year contract termination policy in a high-risk country versus about 4% for a low-risk country. Worldwide in 1980, firms paid $700 million in political risk insurance premiums, with about $500 million to government agencies. In the United States, firms paid about $100 million in premiums, with approximately $40 million paid to the private carriers.[9] Investment guarantees from OPIC (the Overseas Private Investment Corporation) and other sources mean that any expropriation can be recovered to some degree. The determination of value may be very different for the corporation (which views the operation as a going concern) and the insurance agency (which may view it at book value). Also, there are limits on the types of risks that can be covered.[10] Such insurance programs have a negative effect on the host governments, for inhospitable investment environments are well noted by these insurance organizations and are transmitted to potential investors who inquire about insurance and risks. Such insurance may eventually be developed through the United Nations or regional insurance banks, for the collective benefits to most developing countries would seem to be considerable.

Another strategy followed by many investors in unstable environments is to pay whatever price is required for local financing or for unguaranteed outside financing supported by the local investment. In the event of nationalization, the corporation negates any debt obligation,

---

[8]The merits of concerted action were learned well in the Middle East by the Organization of Petroleum Exporting Countries.

[9]See "Insuring Against Risk Abroad," *Business Week*, Sept. 14, 1981, pp. 59ff.

[10]For example, OPIC features inconvertibility insurance which allows a company to protect against freezes in currencies, by law or simply by a foreign government's refusal to issue foreign exchange upon application for remission. Typically the U.S. firm requests payment from OPIC when a government has refused exchange for 60 days after application from the firm; OPIC pays based on an exchange rate 30–60 days prior to the claim, and the contracts with OPIC can run for 20 years. See Richard Stern, "Insurance for Third World Currency Inconvertibility Protection," *Harvard Business Review*, May/June 1982, pp. 62–63.

leaving the local lenders to fight with the local government about repayment. Alternatively, as occurred in the Freeport Cuban nickel operation, the major banks can be left to argue with the new government while the corporation goes on its way (home).[11] This strategy also reduces the foreign exchange loss from currency devaluations in the host country (assuming the loans are denominated in the local currency), and serves as a motivational device for the local manager, who can be told that the capital costs are dictated by that environment and not by simple parent policy.

However, the cost of this insurance must be considered. In some situations the interest rate differential exceeds any reasonable expectation for currency realignment. A high local interest rate may compensate in part for the lender's reluctance to leave money in the local currency which is likely to depreciate. Beyond this level, the rate charged may reflect the scarcity of the capital markets and the deliberate monetary policy of the host country attempting to encourage the inflow of foreign exchange. Hence, the cost of the insurance is the differential over the life of the loan for local financing as opposed to alternative external financing proposals.

As an example, if currency rates are stable and there are no major inflationary effects, then borrowing locally at 20% instead of externally at 10% means the borrower pays a 10% yearly premium on the amount borrowed to avoid expropriation risk on that part of the investment, or to protect against the unlikely event of a devaluation of the local currency. If the plant is expropriated, that loan is never repaid to the local sources. Of course, the expropriating government may make some token payment, and that payment will be given to the local lenders.

Finally, bribes are also possible as a form of insurance against expropriation. The Organization for Economic Cooperation and Development (OECD) members adopted a voluntary code of behavior in June 1977, stating that firms should not make contributions to seekers

---

[11]These examples, of course, actually reverse the conventional corporate finance evaluation where additional debt *increases* the financial risk to the equity holders. In these situations, local debt or unguaranteed debt permits the equity holders both to improve their return because of the leverage and to have less risk from expropriation. On the other hand, the higher debt burden increases the risk that inability to meet debt payments will force loss of equity in the business. In many cases, however, the increased risk of insolvency in no way compares with the benefit of avoiding substantial losses from expropriation.

As suggested in Question 4 in Appendix 2 to Chapter 13, American firms generally do not receive the standard deduction for tax purposes of a loss from a foreign operation which they would receive from a domestic operation. Since they are taxed on earnings as distributed, the loss is not recognized until the operation is ended. Thus, there is an unusual effect from large external debt in a hard currency for a subsidiary in a high-inflation economy, such as was the position with many corporations possessing dollar-denominated debt in their Mexican businesses in 1983. The severe deterioration of the peso meant that equity typically suffered a sharp loss, given the dollar-denominated debt. Yet, if the firm was an American subsidiary, no U.S. tax savings could be generated. The one specific exception to this pattern of U.S. tax effects on foreign income is in the case of Canadian and Mexican subsidiaries that are 100% owned. Under Section 1504 of the Code, the returns can be consolidated with the U.S. parent for tax purposes by election.

of political office or pay bribes unless legally permitted. This code of behavior also suggested disclosure of sales and profits by geographic area and urged firms not to exploit any dominant market positions. The impact of these strictures remains to be seen, but it is likely to be negligible. As with codes of ethics for U.S. congressmen, the problem is *enforcement*, not *standards*, and there is no legal implication of the OECD code unless each member nation passes legislation along these lines. Even then, enforcement is hampered unless there is an exchange of information and other cooperation among the nations. It is also useful to draw a distinction between bribes and extortion. Money changes hands, but the question is who initiates the exchange (if anyone knows). Years ago Guatemalan dictators regularly gave large land holdings to various army generals to ensure their continued support. The generals had no use for the land and neither did anyone else. However, they were able to sell it at high prices to United Fruit, who feared their displeasure. This tale, of course, is not unique in time, place, or corporation.

Public Policy and the Economics of the Firm

This discussion of political risk points to the essential conflict between the developing nation's government—concerned with the growth of the country's economy and the welfare of its people—and the multinational corporation—preoccupied with earning a fair return on the shareholder's investment consistent with general corporate responsibility and a justifiable level of risk.

On the one hand, the firm may segment proposed investments based on risk and rate of return. Classically, the firm will demand a higher return where there is greater risk, whether that risk be economic or political. Accordingly, limitations on the firm's freedom to repatriate funds, the imposition of blocked or semiblocked currency restrictions, and the polite inquiry by the potential host country's negotiators about eventual sharing of the ownership of the proposed venture with the local government or other nationals all cause the assessment of the project's risk to increase.

On the other hand, the local country is interested in a partner that will improve the country itself. The corporation is expected to bring in not only hard currency but also a new business that will produce a good product at a fair price with suitable employment policies. It is only natural that the local negotiators will take strong interest in the intentions of the firm. They may understandably impose safeguards to prevent the rapacious devouring of the resources of the land by a corporate octopus whose single goal is to remove as much profit as rapidly as possible.

Thus, the firm wants stability and a hospitable environment, and it is willing to continue investment in the country given that environment. The host country, concerned about the nature of some corporations, wants an enduring commitment not only to profits but also to a reasonable corporate citizenship in terms of pricing, employment, and proper corporate demeanor. Worries on the part of the firm cause it to inquire about repatriation agreements. Worries on the part of the local negotiators cause them to seek plans for substantial national representation on the board, or for restrictions on the pace at which the firm can remit its profits. However, these issues, once raised, reinforce the concerns of the firm's envoys about nationalization or expropriation, at the most serious level; or minority voting blocks and repatriation restrictions at the least obnoxious level.

Hence, the cycle begins, and the cobweb created by this action and reaction, followed by intensified action and intensified reaction, creates not only ill will but also very rigid contracts. The result is the situation viewed today: The local countries resent major corporations (often American) that have high returns from foreign operations which are remitted rapidly. The American corporation, in turn, worries about the increasing risks from longer-term investments in nations where political instability and currency shocks are a yearly (if not monthly) fact of life. Stated simply, worries about risk induce greater profiteering, usually translated into "high returns remitted rapidly." This action, in turn, supports the local countries' contention that the multinationals are tempted to bleed their lands for a larger corporate goal of maximizing profits.

Finally, even in the absence of the risk-generating cycle described previously, there is a basic conflict for the multinational company desiring to be a good local citizen (whether from local economic self-interest or survival, or from the view of responsible business practice) and its need to use global transfers of skills and resources which form the basis for the multinational firm. As an example, there are difficulties imposed on local fiscal and monetary policy of a given nation-state by the existence of the multinational firm, since there is no multinational fiscal and monetary authority.

THE EVALUATION OF RISK

Measuring Total Risk in a Project

In addition to identifying the business and financial risk, inflation and currency risk, and exchange and expropriation risks, it is necessary to determine the composite risk that is present in a project. After looking at historical information about the type of business in general and the profitability of business in that country in particular, the firm's managers form judgments about the probable performance of a project in that country.

Management's judgment about a project must be based first on estimates of the distribution of possible outcomes of a project's major components: sales, market share, advertising costs, wage rates, and so on. Then, the relationships among crucial variables must be established; for example, if market share increases by 8% in year 4, the increase in sales will have an expected value of $3 million and a standard deviation of $50,000. Finally, management must estimate the impact of all the assumptions on the dispersion of the various criteria used to evaluate the project: internal rate of return, terminal rate of return, earnings per share, sales growth, and the like. This can be done most effectively with the aid of a computer and a simulation program.[12]

If the criterion is the internal rate of return, and the company is considering project A and project B as two mutually exclusive alternatives, their distributions of returns might be as shown in Exhibit 15.2. Notice the greater risk in project B. Although project B has a higher rate of return than project A, one management might prefer project B, arguing that a higher risk is fully justified by the return, and another management might prefer the safer (but lower) return of project A.

In addition, risk analysis may reveal to the manager that some projects are not what they seem at first. Thus, in comparing the rate of return or net present value of two projects on the basis of the most likely single value (mode) for *each* of the many underlying variables, a manager might find one project has the higher value with certainty. However, on the basis of a complete simulation, the executive might learn that the other project has a higher mode for rate of return or net present value because of the form and interactions of the underlying distributions which must be combined.

Finally, risk analysis and simulation may be used as part of sensitivity analyses which enable one to explore the effect of shifts in any or all of the underlying variables.

Risky Projects in Capital Budgeting

To calculate net present values with risky projects one has two options. One option is the one discussed in Chapter 14, in which we chose a discount rate consistent with the capital structure which would

---

[12]Simulation involves repeated chance trials using calculations from a random number generator adjusted to provide various probability distributions.

EXHIBIT 15.2   Cumulative Rate of Return Distributions for Two Projects

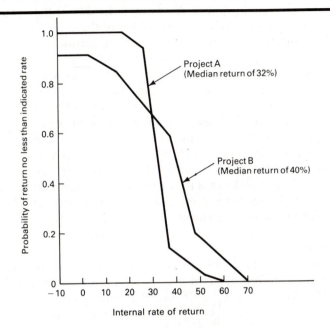

be appropriate for a project with that risk profile, considering the industry, the country, and the risk attitude of management. This leads to what is called a *risk-adjusted discount rate*. The other option to incorporate risk explicitly in the evaluation of a project is to analyze the risk characteristics of the returns of the project or to adjust the returns of the project to compensate for the relative amount of risk.[13]

To take into account the shapes of the distributions of returns we can calculate the standard deviation and variance for these distributions.[14] From these measures of dispersion, we can impute requirements for the required return. This can be done by computing the *coef-*

---

[13]For a discussion of risk analysis and simulation techniques, see E. Eugene Carter, *Portfolio Aspects of Corporate Capital Budgeting* (Lexington, Mass.: D. C. Heath and Company, 1974), Chapters 2 and 3.

[14]Variance in algebraic terms is computed as follows: Let
- Y_i be a return in category i,
- P_i be the probability of category i occurring,
- $\bar{Y}$ be the average of all Y_i values, weighted by the probability of Y_i occurring

$$(\bar{Y} = \sum_{i=1}^{N} P_i Y_i = P_1 Y_1 + P_2 Y_2 + \cdots + P_N Y_N)$$

Then the variance is equal to

$$\sum_{i=1}^{N} P_i (Y_i - \bar{Y})^2$$

ficient of variation, which is defined as the ratio of the standard deviation of the distribution to the expected value of that distribution.

In Exhibit 15.3 the standard deviation of the rate of return of project C is 10% and the expected terminal rate of return is 20%. Then, the coefficient of variation of the terminal rate of return in this project is 0.5. When this project is compared with project D, we find that both projects have the same coefficient of variation. Project D has a standard deviation of 6% and an average rate of return of 12%, yielding a coefficient of variation of 0.5. However, project E, with a much higher terminal rate of return than the previous two projects, 25%, but a very high standard deviation of return of 15%, would have a coefficient of variation of 0.6, making it less desirable than the other two projects.

The problem with the coefficient of variation measure is that management's attitude toward risk is not necessarily uniform with regard to the ratio. For example, in Exhibit 15.3, management is not likely to be indifferent between projects C and D, although they have the same coefficient of variation.

An equally good measure to incorporate risk explicitly in the analysis of returns is to require a project to have a return minus the standard deviation (or some constant times the standard deviation) that is at least, say, 10%. Alternatively, management may focus simply on the probability of a loss. If the probability of a loss is greater than $N\%$, no return will be sufficiently high to invest. Another standard is to say that when the return is reduced by a constant times the probability of a loss, the resulting figure must be greater than, say, 10%. All these rules are only armchair standards for coping with risk and depend on the risk aversion of management.[15]

Risk aversion is a measure of one's disinclination to take risks. Risk aversion can be expressed by index numbers that measure the willingness of an individual to gamble in given situations. If one assumes that most individuals prefer less risk to more risk for a given level of expected return, then one can see how the level of risk an individual is willing to accept in exchange for a potentially higher expected return changes with income or with wealth.

---

[15]Conrath found that executives analyzed projects consistent with a decision rule that P(loss) < 10% and E(Return) = 30% + 3 × P(loss). (David W. Conrath, "From Statistical Decision Theory to Practice: Some Problems with the Transition," *Management Science,* Apr. 1973, pp. 873–83.) Alderfer and Bierman found that subjects in a gambling situation consistently had a strong aversion to loss and preferred an alternative with a lower mean and higher variance but with a lower probability of loss to another alternative with a higher mean, lower variance, and higher probability of loss. (Clayton T. Alderfer and Harold Bierman, Jr., "Choices with Risk beyond the Mean and Variance," *Journal of Business,* July 1970, pp. 341–53.) From a field study of eight firms, Mao concluded that the negative semivariance (the variance of outcomes below the mean) was a far better measure of risk than variance. (James C. T. Mao, "Survey of Capital Budgeting: Theory and Practice," *Journal of Finance,* May 1970, pp. 349–60.)

EXHIBIT 15.3 Average, Standard Deviation, and Coefficient of Variation for the Return Distributions of Three Projects

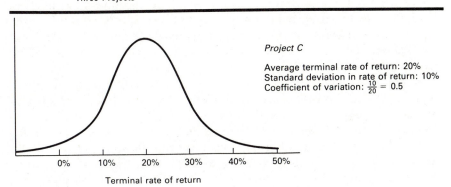

Project C

Average terminal rate of return: 20%
Standard deviation in rate of return: 10%
Coefficient of variation: $\frac{10}{20} = 0.5$

Terminal rate of return

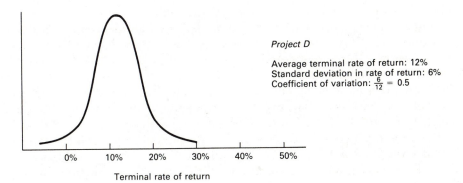

Project D

Average terminal rate of return: 12%
Standard deviation in rate of return: 6%
Coefficient of variation: $\frac{6}{12} = 0.5$

Terminal rate of return

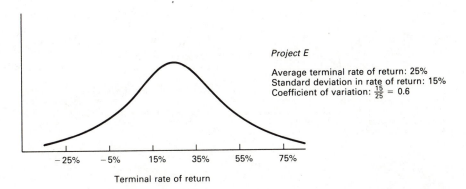

Project E

Average terminal rate of return: 25%
Standard deviation in rate of return: 15%
Coefficient of variation: $\frac{15}{25} = 0.6$

Terminal rate of return

To replace the dependency on variance and its inadequacy as a measure of risk, one may substitute a more formal approach of charging each period's cash flow with the cost of reducing risk in that period. This adjusted cash flow then may be included in computing the adjusted terminal rate of return after this insurance premium has been included. This approach parallels the idea of a *certainty equivalent* that has been discussed in business decisions by Raiffa and others.[16]

A rational and consistent decision-maker will be indifferent between some certain value and a distribution of uncertain returns. For example, one may choose to accept $0.50 rather than a gamble with equal probabilities of $0 and $1.00. Depending on whether one is risk-averse or risk-prone, one might accept (for example) $0.45 or $0.55, respectively, rather than accept the gamble. Similarly, one can generalize this concept to (1) uncertain payments at some future time period and (2) a distribution of outcomes more detailed than the two possibilities ($0 or $1) shown here. In analyzing a capital budgeting project or a portfolio, the manager must obtain a distribution of cash flows that may be expected in each year. Then, he or she must decide what payments would be acceptable with certainty in place of that uncertain cash flow in that year. This certainty equivalent value is then discounted at the risk-free rate (U.S. government bonds, for example) because this risk of the project has been considered already.[17]

Apart from management specification problems, the disadvantage of this approach is the large difficulty in dealing with a portfolio of projects.[18] The certainty equivalent of a portfolio distribution in the nth year is *not* the sum of the certainty equivalents of the projects within that portfolio unless the projects, individually and collectively, are so small as to warrant the assumption of a linear utility function for the manager over that interval.

---

[16]See Howard Raiffa, *Decision Analysis: Introductory Lectures on Choices Under Uncertainty* (Reading, Mass.: Addison-Wesley, 1968).

[17]In making this decision operationally, several simplifications can be employed which distort the results somewhat from the theoretical values. Thus, one may assume a_i, a coefficient for transforming the expected value of the cash flows in year Y_i to the certainty equivalent $a_i Y_i$. Under this simplification, the net present value of the certainty equivalents of an N-year project with cost of capital r is:

$$\sum_{i=1}^{N} \frac{a_i Y_i}{(1+r)^i} \qquad (0 \le a_i \le 1)$$

Essentially, the selection of a_i is designed to compensate for the parameters of the cash flow distribution other than the expected value.

[18]For a discussion of risk measures in a portfolio see Chapter 16.

RISK ANALYSIS SIMULATION:
AN EXTENDED EXAMPLE

To illustrate these concepts we will examine a specific case history: Freeport Mineral's investment in the Greenvale nickel project in Australia.[19] Given the relative political stability of Australia, the risks of this project are economic ones. We will examine the implications of various types of business risks associated with the mine development and operation, and the financial risks associated with the alternative financing packages available at the beginning of the case. Both of these risks are also affected by currency fluctuations. The risk analysis will be based on a computer simulation model developed for this purpose.

Background

Originally a major sulphur producer, Freeport Minerals decided in 1970 to diversify its operations in the wake of a breakdown in what had been an extremely profitable oligopolistic sulphur market. In 1966 the firm received 85% of its income from sulphur. By 1968, with sulphur prices at $40 per ton, there was evidence that a large number of entrants into the market had depressed prices. By 1970 sulphur sold for $20 per ton. Accordingly, Freeport decided to begin operating in other mineral areas and hoped to derive only 15% of its income from sulphur by 1975.

The nickel industry was dominated by International Nickel (INCO), whose operations were mainly in the United States and Canada. Freeport also was interested in nickel and had several proftable ventures in this field. One of the opportunities which became available was the Greenvale proposal in Australia. This project would cost approximately $264 million to develop, based on 1971 cost estimates. This amount included $111 million for a nickel processing plant, $45 million for a special railway, and $15 million for the mine development. The remaining outlays were allocated for preoperating expenses (including interest during the construction period), inflation, and working capital.

The basic project was expected to produce revenues of $72.2 million per year for 20 years based on anticipated ore reserves, a price of $1.35 per pound for nickel, and yearly production of about 22,300 tons

---

[19]This case was prepared entirely from public sources, and Freeport's management was not consulted.

of nickel, plus a small amount of cobalt. Given figures for operating costs consistent with the company's knowledge and confirmed by the experience of other firms in Australia, Freeport constructed a forecasted income statement for the project. Using accelerated depreciation, depletion standards consistent with Australian tax policies, and a tax rate of 38%, the projections of the Greenvale project are as shown in Exhibit 15.4.

The following two major financing options were under consideration:

1. A loan for $135 million in U.S. dollars at 8%, payable in level installments of principal over a 10-year life period commencing at the end of 1975. This would be from a group of major insurance companies.

2. A yen loan of $160 million at 6% with eighteen annual level principal payments commencing at the end of 1975. This offer was from one of the major customers of the nickel, a Japanese business association (*zaibatsu*). Although this loan would require concessions from the pricing base and would be accompanied by a long-term contract, the management of Freeport thought the loan was a generous one.

When these financing options were considered, the resulting financial cash flows were as shown in Exhibit 15.4. Freeport was uncertain where the cash throw-offs would be reinvested. If the money were brought to the United States, additional taxes would have to be paid. However, by adjusting the ownership of the firm among various other corporate interests, U.S. taxes on the profits could be avoided until the funds were returned to the United States.

Sources of Risk in the Project

Construction Costs. The firm would commit $264 million for the project, but there was some chance that the cost might be considerably higher. The project already included $43.4 million for cost escalations and contingencies. In the event all of these funds were not needed, they would be returned prior to initial production. In the event other funds were required, they would be paid at an early point in the development of the project as the increased construction costs or plant difficulties appeared. Basically, management was confident that the construction costs would be between $205 and $325 million.

Production. Although the firm was confident of the mineral reserves, a major uncertainty related to the year when the production would be on stream, partially because the project would utilize a new technology to extract the nickel. Accordingly, there was a possibility that only partial production would begin in 1975, perhaps at 80% of the

EXHIBIT 15.4 Freeport Minerals Greenvale Project: Income Statement, Cash Flow Statement, and Measures of Return (*millions of U.S. dollars*)

INCOME STATEMENT

	1975	1976	1977	1978	1979	1980	1981	1982	1983	1984	1985	1986	1987	1988	1989	1990	1991	1992
Revenues	$72.2	$72.2	$72.2	$72.2	$72.2	$72.2	$72.2	$72.2	$72.2	$72.2	$72.2	$72.2	$72.2	$72.2	$72.2	$72.2	$72.2	$72.2
Less total operating costs	36.1	36.1	36.1	36.1	36.1	36.1	36.1	36.1	36.1	36.1	36.1	36.1	36.1	36.1	36.1	36.1	36.1	36.1
Less interest (8% U.S. loan, 10 years)	10.8	9.7	8.6	7.6	6.5	5.4	4.3	3.2	2.2	1.1								
Profit before taxes	25.3	26.4	27.5	28.5	29.6	30.7	31.8	32.9	33.9	35.0	40.5	40.5	40.5	40.5	40.5	49.2	49.2	49.2
Taxes	0	10.0	10.5	10.8	11.2	11.7	12.1	12.5	12.9	13.3	15.8	15.8	15.8	15.8	15.8	19.1	19.1	19.1
Net profit	25.3	16.4	17.0	17.7	18.4	19.0	19.7	20.4	21.0	21.7	24.7	24.7	24.7	24.7	24.7	30.1	30.1	30.1

FINANCIAL AND OPERATING CASH FLOWS

	1975	1976	1977	1978	1979	1980	1981	1982	1983	1984	1985	1986	1987	1988	1989	1990	1991	1992
Net profit	$25.3	$16.4	$17.0	$17.7	$18.4	$19.0	$19.7	$20.4	$21.0	$21.7	$24.7	$24.7	$24.7	$24.7	$24.7	$30.1	$30.1	$30.1
Depreciation	14.2	14.2	14.2	14.2	14.2	14.2	14.2	14.2	14.2	14.2	9.8	9.8	9.8	9.8	9.8	1.1	1.1	1.1
Tax savings (accelerated depreciation for tax purposes)	3.0	1.9	1.0	.2	(.7)	(.7)	(.7)	(.7)	(.7)	(.7)	(.3)	(.3)	(.3)	(.3)	(.3)	—	—	—
After-tax interest[a]	10.8	6.0	5.3	4.7	4.0	3.3	2.7	2.0	1.4	.7								
Operating cash flow	53.3	38.5	37.5	36.8	35.9	35.8	35.9	35.9	35.9	35.9	34.2	34.2	34.2	34.2	34.2	31.2	31.2	31.2
Principal and after-tax interest (8% U.S. loan, 10 years)	24.3	19.5	18.8	18.2	17.5	16.8	16.2	15.5	14.9	14.2								
Equity cash flow (U.S. loan)	29.0	19.0	18.7	18.6	18.4	19.0	19.7	20.4	21.0	21.7	34.2	34.2	34.2	34.2	34.2	31.2	31.2	31.2
Principal and after-tax interest (6% Japanese loan, 18 years)	14.9	14.5	14.2	13.9	13.5	13.2	12.9	12.5	12.2	11.9	11.5	11.2	10.9	10.6	10.2	9.9	9.6	9.2
Equity cash flow (Japanese loan)	38.4	24.0	23.3	22.9	22.4	22.6	23.0	23.4	23.7	24.0	22.7	23.0	23.3	23.6	24.0	21.3	21.6	22.0

MEASURES OF RETURN

	Operating Cash Flow	Equity Cash Flow $135 million, 8% U.S. Loan, 10 years	Equity Cash Flow $160 million, 6% Japanese Loan, 18 years
Rate of return[b]	11.0%	14.4%	19.9%
Terminal rate of return (10% reinvestment rate)	10.7%	12.1%	16.5%
Net present value at 10%	$18.9	$49.6	$80.9

a Because of start-up expenses, projections assume there are no savings to tax-deductibility of interest in 1975, and no taxes are payable in that year.
b All return calculations assume average investment is made 2 years before initial operating cash inflows.

planned level. Final production would certainly increase from the starting point to the full level over 4 years.

Mineral Content.   There was some small doubt about the richness of the mineral deposits. This quality figure might deviate somewhat from the expected nickel content, although the range was probably not much more than ±10%.

Market Price.   From other analysis, the management believed that the starting market price was likely to be higher than the estimated $1.35. This price might grow from the time of the initial investment by about 5% to 6% per year based on forecasts of the world's economy. Because nickel was a key commercial ingredient, world industrial activity was a barometer of nickel demand. When this price increase was related to world industrial production, the growth rate was tempered by a possibility that additional nickel production would enter the market and decrease prices.

Operating Costs.   The possible escalation in labor rates and materials costs during the life of the plant was expected to be related to the strength of the Australian economy, which itself was linked to world industrial production. Operating costs were expected to increase by slightly less than the price of world nickel, subject to the performance of the Australian economy.

Currency Fluctuations.   Although the loans were firm commitments subject to the company's meeting various financial tests each year, Freeport management was concerned about the exchange rates of the loan currencies available. Specifically, the U.S. dollar might deteriorate over time while the yen might appreciate. For its financing analysis, management decided to assume both that the dollar might depreciate and appreciate relative to other currencies. Since the revenues were always denominated in dollars, this factor would have little influence on the profile of the project, except for the operating costs which would be paid in Australian dollars. On the other hand, a continuing appreciation of the Japanese yen over the life of the project could prove costly. Management felt that the yen might well appreciate by an average of 2% per year for the next 8 to 10 years, but was not willing to forecast beyond that. Furthermore, it was hard to anticipate the yearly links in appreciation of the yen; lower than average appreciation in one year might simply be a temporary delay offset by a higher appreciation in a later year. Basically, they believed that the yen was likely to remain strong vis-à-vis the dollar for at least 10 years. They felt that the basic interest rate differential of 2% on the yen loan against the dollar loan reflected the assessment of lenders as well.

For the immediate future, however, there was a much higher probability of a sharp yen appreciation, perhaps by as much as 10% within a year or so. In addition, one economist in the firm was convinced that this action could be a chain, resulting in a high probability of an additional 10% appreciation in a few years.

Evaluation of the Project's Risks

A risk analysis combines these uncertainties and the interrelationships into a computer model. Using these relationships and a random number sampling function within the model, we can present the financial results showing these risk elements. When combined with the accounting relationships for income statements, balance sheets, and discounted cash flow, the results are useful to management in evaluating the possible risk associated with a project. The inputs used for the Freeport model are given in Exhibit 15.5.

Exhibit 15.6 presents the results of the simulation analysis performed under the assumptions described. Distributions of rates of return are presented for operating cash flows and for returns on equity. The returns on operating cash flows have been calculated under two assumptions: (1) The cash generated by the project is reinvested at the same rate as the rate for the project, producing the internal rate of return; and (2) the cash generated by the project is reinvested at 10%, a measure of the terminal rate of return. The returns on equity are calculated under the two alternative sources of financing: U.S. dollars at 8% and yen at 6%. The returns on equity are also calculated under the two assumptions about reinvestment rates.

The rate of return on operating cash flows shows a tighter distribution when the 10% terminal rate of return is assumed than when the cash generated by the project is reinvested at the same rate as the project. This is because the average internal rate of return on operating cash flows, ignoring the terminal rate of return, is well above 10%. Simulation outcomes in which the operating cash flow rate of return is below 10%, had such outcomes been present, would have been improved by the assumption of a 10% reinvestment rate. Initial rates of return above 10% are reduced by the assumption of a 10% reinvestment rate.

The rate of return to equity shows a much wider range of possible returns under the yen financing than under the U.S. dollar financing. Therefore, each possible outcome has a lower frequency under the yen financing than under the dollar financing. In both sources of financing,

EXHIBIT 15.5 Freeport Minerals Greenvale Project: Simulation Variables and Assumptions

Random Variable	Symbol	Frequency	Distribution of Random Variable	Range of Random Variable	Calculation
Construction	A	1st year	Poisson	Mean = .4	$A = 205 + [120 \times (X)]$ X = Random variable
Production	B	1st year	Uniform	.7 to 1.0	B = Random variable Year 1 $B(1) = B \times$ expected value 2 $B(2) = (B + ((B-1)/4)) \times$ Expected value 3 $B(3) = (B + ((B-1)/2)) \times$ Expected value 4 $B(4) = (B + 3 \times ((B-1)/4)) \times$ Expected value 5–18 $B(5)$ through $B(18) =$ Expected value
Mineral content	C	1st year	Normal	Mean = 1 Standard deviation = .05	$C = X$ X = Random variable
Price	D	Annual	Normal	Mean = 1.06 Standard deviation = .03	$D(Y) = D(Y-1) \times (X)$ X = Random variable Y = Year
Operating costs	E	Annual	Uniform	.95 to 1.00	$E(Y) = E(Y-1) \times (X_1) \times (X_2)$ X_1 = Random variable from price index, X X_2 = Random variable .95 to 1.00 Y = Year
Yen appreciation	F	Annual	Normal	Mean = 1.02 Standard deviation = .002	

Appreciation	Probability in Year 1	Probability of Year 3 Appreciation[a]	
		0%	10%
0%	.50	.50	.50
10%	.50	.25	.75

[a]Given that appreciation in year 1 on the columns to the left has occurred from year 4 onward, a normal distribution with a mean of 2% and a standard deviation of .2% is assumed to reflect the probabilities of appreciation in any year.

528

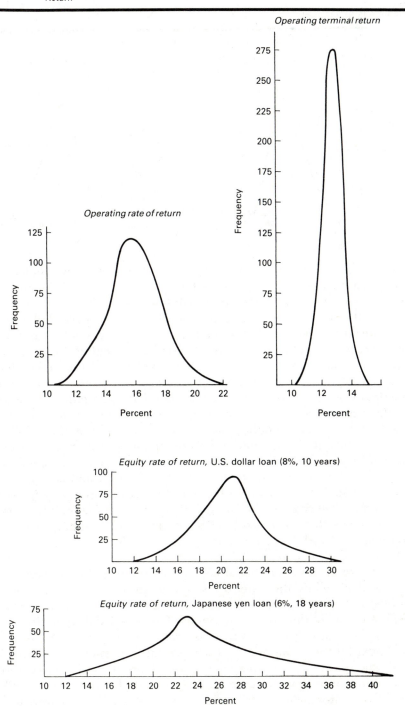

EXHIBIT 15.6 *(Continued)*

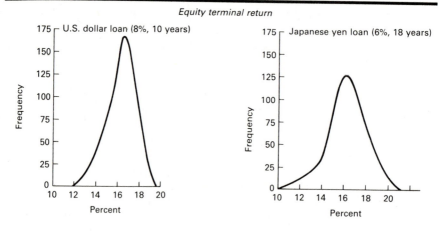

Equity terminal return

the spread of returns to equity is narrowed considerably when the assumption of a reinvestment rate of 10% is incorporated, for the same reason as in the case of operating cash flows.

Is the lower average return to equity shown on the dollar financing caused by the short life of the loan (10 years versus the 18-year life of the project and the 18-year yen loan)? In evaluating this issue, management must consider the alternatives available at the end of the 10 years or available in steps beginning after a few years of mineral production. Looking at the conventional debt coverage ratios, we see that in the earliest years the average coverage on the yen loan is significantly better than the dollar loan, as shown in Exhibit 15.7. However, if the debt/capitalization rate is considered and reinvestment opportunities are ignored, the firm appears more conservatively financed under the dollar option because the loan is lower initially and is repaid more rapidly. This table also shows the adjusted returns to equity *if the dollar loan is converted to 18 years,* with all the other assumptions maintained. From this basic result, one sees again the inappropriate nature of the short-lived debt assumption if dollar refinancing options or the 18-year dollar loan are available.

There are two additional advantages retained by the yen loan in this analysis when the criterion is equity rate of return. First, the *loan is larger,* and with no other financing available, the capital structure is different under the two assumptions. Given a fixed operating return above the cost of debt, leverage assures that the return to equity will be larger for the greater-debt situation if the debt rates are similar. Second, the appreciation of the yen averages more than 2% per year for 10 years, meaning that the cost of the yen loan for those years will be slightly greater than the 6% nominal rate plus 2%. However, in later

EXHIBIT 15.7 Freeport Minerals Greenvale Project: Impact of Alternative Financing Plans on Debt Ratios and on Return to Equity

	DEBT SERVICE COVERAGE RATIOS[a]			DEBT/ CAPITALIZATION		
	Outcomes Under Certainty					
	1975	1980	1986	1975	1980	1986
$135M U.S. dollar loan (10 years)	2.3	3.2	—	.51	.25	0
$160M Japanese yen loan (18 years)	2.7	3.1	6.6	.61	.44	.24
$135M U.S. dollar loan (18 years)	3.6	4.0	7.3	.51	.37	.20

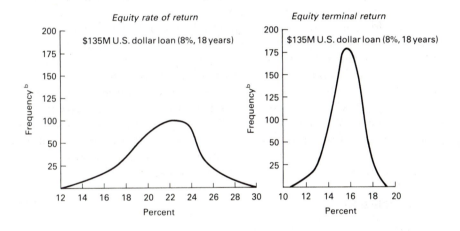

[a]Debt service coverage ratio is net income after tax plus interest divided by the sum of loan principal repayment plus interest. An alternative definition, giving results slightly different from those here, is net operating income after tax divided by principal repayment plus after-tax interest.

[b]Frequency is per 1,000 simulation trials.

years (years 11 through 18), this appreciation is not present, consistent with the expectations of Freeport management discussed earlier. Hence, the *average rate of the yen loan is lower* than the U.S. dollar loan for the full 18 years.

For the return on equity to be the same as the one assumed in the computation of the long-term cost of capital, the capital structure, once selected, must remain in balance over the entire life of the project. Thus, in any period, the cash flow from a project must (1) pay the returns on debt and equity and (2) retire debt and equity in the *exact* proportion as the initial capital structure. Over time, the return to all components will be as indicated in the capital structure discussion. However, when there are different debt repayment schedules or no additional refinancing options available, then the applicability of a particular debt repayment schedule to the analysis will alter the return to equity. An analyst needs to examine carefully whether the assumption of a proportional capital structure over the life of a project is warranted. If not, the infusion of subsequent debt issues is relevant.

In this case Freeport management needs to review its expected financing options for the next 5 to 10 years. If these choices are sufficiently uncertain or costly, then payment of a higher rate for a long-term loan may be warranted; a long-term loan that matches the life of the project serves to keep the capital structure in balance. Hence, it may be regarded as a form of insurance against financial risk. In the event the Japanese loan were not available, then the company might be willing to pay (say) 9% for a U.S. dollar 18-year loan, for example.

In addition to this consideration, Freeport needs to review the dispersion in returns it wishes to tolerate. The dispersion of possible outcomes for the rate of return and the terminal return to *equity* is *greater* under the Japanese loan than under either the 10-year or 18-year U.S. proposals, as would be expected given the appreciation uncertainties. Whether management wishes to live with this dispersion is a question Freeport has to resolve. There is also the dispersion of *operating* returns. Freeport management must review the dispersion and returns relative to other corporate opportunities that are available, as well as the dispersion from existing operations.

Conclusion

This approach to evaluating uncertainty provides additional information to Freeport management on the distribution of returns from its project. There may be an analysis of other variables (for example, first-year earnings per share contribution or expected cash flow for each year). From these basic computations, management may wish to complete *sensitivity analyses* on the variables which are random. This may include the investigation of a faster growth in expected value of nickel prices or the impact of a greater dispersion of construction costs on the returns. *Other variables could be randomized* and the impact of their uncertainty on the returns could be calculated. Most important, the possibilities of *more sophisticated financing arrangements* could be studied, such as sequencing of different loans or the sharing of equity participation.

The Greenvale project is not necessarily unwise as an investment. The use of computer risk analysis simulation merely permits a greater awareness of the uncertainties surrounding the project than otherwise would be available. This uncertainty may dictate contingency planning for certain outcomes and may suggest that certain financing strategies are more sensible than others.

Freeport management needs to consider not only the Greenvale project, but also the impact of other nickel projects as well as the other operations of the corporation. From the parent's viewpoint, the variance in returns from Greenvale is one input to the variance in the corporation's return. That corporate variance is a function of the interrelationships among the various projects in which the parent has invested. Portfolio considerations will be analyzed in Chapter 16.

SUMMARY

We reviewed the standard considerations of *business* and *financial risk* which appear in the discussions of capital structure in a course on domestic corporate finance. Business operations inherently possess different types of risk, and the addition of debt to a firm's structure adds financial risk to the return to equity. We also noted the presence of uncertainty in regard to divergent inflation patterns and the movement of currency parities over time, adding further risk to a foreign operation.

In the area of political risk, *blockage* of repatriations can be considered ex ante in the context of a *terminal rate of return* calculation. Various forms of convertibility insurance as well as parent activities such as denoting part of the contribution to the subsidiary as debt (whose principal must be repaid) or requiring the subsidiary to make royalty or supervisory fee payments to the parent are useful. From the standpoint of complete expropriation of the operation, we trichotomized the available options. In the positive sense, long-term agreements regarding a turnover of the operation and basic control, the selection of a joint venture mode of organization, local sourcing of materials, massive local employment, and local investment are ways to minimize a host government's interference. In a more negative sense, a parent's control of markets through licenses, transportation, or other items effectively can preclude the operation of some ventures without the cooperation of the parent corporation. Finally, outside factors which can mitigate the effect of nationalization include insurance programs, project financing (with local or external debt which cannot involve the rest of the firm's operations), and outright bribes.

The problem of insecure corporations confronting worried governments of developing countries was addressed. Each is concerned about undesirable actions of the other; yet each protective reaction by one reinforces the anxiety felt by the other. Supranational insurance schemes were suggested as one means to stop this cycle of mutual action and reaction.

We illustrated how various standard methods for coping with risk in a capital budgeting framework can be employed. These methods include risk-adjusted discount rates, indices of dispersion (the coefficient of variation), and certainty equivalents. Risk analysis simulation was also offered as a method for considering the influence of various types of risk upon a project return.

An extended example involving Freeport Minerals was presented. Using risk analysis and some basic capital structure insights, we offered an illustration of how the firm's management might consider the riskiness of a proposed Australian nickel project.

BIBLIOGRAPHY

Aharoni, Yair, *The Foreign Investment Decision Process.* Boston: Graduate School of Business Administration, Harvard University, 1966.

Bhattacharya, Anindya K., *Foreign Trade and International Development.* Lexington, Mass.: D.C. Heath and Company, 1976.

Carter, E. Eugene, *Portfolio Aspects of Corporate Capital Budgeting.* Lexington, Mass.: D.C. Heath and Company, 1974.

Caves, Richard E., "International Corporations: The Industrial Economics of Foreign Investment," *Economica,* Feb. 1971, pp. 1–27.

Dunning, John H., ed., *Economic Analysis and the Multinational Enterprise.* London: Allen and Unwin, 1974.

Hawkins, R. G., N. Mintz, and M. Provissiero, "Government Takeovers of U.S. Foreign Affiliates," *Journal of International Business Studies,* Spring 1976, pp. 3–16.

Hoskins, Colin G., "Capital Budgeting Decision Rules for Risky Projects Derived from a Capital Market Model Based on Semivariance," *The Engineering Economist,* Mar. 1978, pp. 211–22.

Hymer, Stephen, "The Efficiency (Contradictions) of Multinational Corporations," *American Economic Review,* May 1970, pp. 441–48.

———, "The International Operations of National Firms: A Study of Direct Investment." Doctoral dissertation, Massachusetts Institute of Technology (1960). Cambridge, Mass.: MIT Press, 1976.

Kelly, Marie Wicks, *Foreign Investment Evaluation Practices of U.S. Multinational Corporations.* Ann Arbor, Michigan: UMI Research Press, 1981.

Knickerbocker, F. T., *Oligopolistic Reaction and Multinational Enterprise.* Boston: Graduate School of Business Administration, Harvard University, 1973.

Kobrin, Stephen J., "The Environmental Determinants of Foreign Direct Investment: An Ex Post Empirical Analysis," *Journal of International Business Studies,* Fall 1976, pp. 29–42.

———, "When Does Political Instability Result in Increased Investment Risk?" *Columbia Journal of World Business,* Fall 1978, pp. 113–22.

———, "Political Risk: A Review and Reconsideration," *Journal of International Business Studies,* Spring 1979, pp. 67–80.

Meeker, Guy B., "Face-Out Joint Venture: Can It Work for Latin America?" *Inter-American Economic Affairs,* Spring 1971, pp. 25–42.

Mikesell, Raymond F., et al., *Foreign Investment in the Petroleum and Mineral Industries.* Baltimore, Md.: Johns Hopkins Press, 1971.

Oblak, David J., and Roy J. Helm, Jr., "Survey and Analysis of Capital Budgeting·Methods Used by Multinationals," *Financial Management,* Winter 1980, pp. 37–41.

Peville, James P., "Why Not Project Financing?" *Management Accounting,* Oct. 1978, pp. 13–22.

Polk, Judd, et al., *U.S. Production Abroad and the Balance of Payments.* New York: National Industrial Conference Board, 1966.

Robock, Stefan H., "Political Risk: Identification and Assessment," *Columbia Journal of World Business,* July–Aug. 1971, pp. 6–20.

Scaperlanda, Anthony E., and Laurence J. Mauer, "The Determinants of U.S. Direct Investment in the EEC," *American Economic Review,* Sept. 1969, pp. 558–68.

Sokoloff, Georges and Francoise Lemoine, *China and the U.S.S.R.: Limits to Trade with the West.* Totowa, New Jersey: Allanheld, Osmun, 1982.

Spitaller, Erich, "A Survey of Recent Quantitative Studies of Long-Term Capital Movements," *International Monetary Fund Staff Papers,* Mar. 1971, pp. 189–217.

Stoever, William A., *Renegotiations in International Business Transactions.* Lexington, Mass.: Lexington Books, 1981.

Stonehill, Arthur, et al., "Financial Goals and Debt Ratio Determinants: A Survey of Practice in Five Countries," *Financial Management,* Autumn 1975, pp. 27–41.

Tomlinson, James W., *The Joint Venture Process in International Business.* Cambridge, Mass.: MIT Press, 1970.

Truitt, J. Frederick, "Expropriation of Foreign Investment: Summary of the Post–World War II Experience of American and British Investors in the Less Developed Countries," *Journal of International Business Studies,* Fall 1970, pp. 21–34.

Wynant, Larry, "Project Financing for Extractive Ventures," *Management Accounting,* Oct. 1978, pp. 29–35.

THE WORTHINGTON BOTTLING COMPANY

HERBERT JOHNSON HAD recently been appointed treasurer of the International Division of the Worthington Bottling Company. He was the first person to occupy that position in the company. Until then, the finance function of the International Division had been managed directly from Corporate Treasury.

Mr. Johnson's first task was to develop a comprehensive policy for financing Worthington's foreign investments. Worthington already had numerous investments around the world. However, each one had been treated as an isolated case by Corporate Treasury. At the time, this approach had been necessary because of the limited experience of the company in foreign markets. However, the heterogeneous character of the foreign operations that had resulted now suggested the need for some general policies. In fact, the creation of the position of treasurer for the International Division already was a response to this need.

HISTORICAL BACKGROUND

The Foreign Investment Decision

Ten years earlier the senior management of Worthington Bottling had decided to diversify the company along country lines instead of product lines. As managers of a relatively small bottling company, they felt they knew how to make bottling equipment. They were not so sure they could be equally successful in other types of packaging (a line of diversification suggested by their investment bank) or operating in unrelated industries (a popular mode of diversification at the time).

In the same cautious manner, senior management had decided that foreign investments would take the form of joint ventures with local partners. Several factors suggested this approach. First, a bottling company needed a product to bottle. Given the large bulk of most bottled items relative to their value, shipping bottled products across country borders was usually not economical. Therefore, there was a need to have a good knowledge of the local market. A local partner could contribute this knowledge more easily than market research conducted by Worthington's management or an independent consulting firm. In addition to knowledge, a strong local partner could supply local business contacts in the industrial field as well as in the financial community.

Another major factor influencing the decision to seek the joint venture route was the treatment of these investments for financial reporting in the United States. Joint ventures in which the American company has less than 49% of the equity are consolidated in the United States under the equity method. A full consolidation of the balance sheet, showing the leverage of the foreign company, is not required. This factor led to Worthington management's decision to restrict foreign investments to minority ownership of no more than 49%, except when unavoidable.

Finally, the low profile that a joint venture afforded the foreign investor in the local market was appealing to Worthington's senior management. Having had no other experience in foreign countries, they shuddered at the idea of being involved in the local politics of nationalism. Worthington's management had even considered insuring their foreign investments with the U.S. Office of Private Investment Corporation, but they had found the insurance premiums to be very expensive.

Management also thought that entry into the European market could be made only through acquisition of an existing company. By the time Worthington had decided to operate in other countries in the 1970s, the European market for the bottling industry was nearly saturated with the existing companies. Acquiring existing companies did not appear as attractive as starting a new company that would use Worthington's bottling technique and equipment. Therefore, senior management chose to ignore the highly industrialized countries in their search for foreign investment outlets.

To choose among developing countries, they first developed evaluation techniques. The objective of these techniques was to select a number of developing countries where the state of industrial development was relatively high, the rate of economic growth relatively rapid, and the market size relatively large. These factors, together with a measure of political stability, were considered essential prerequisites for the success of a bottling company. There was no point in spending time analyzing projects in countries where the market would not justify the economical use of Worthington's bottling technology.

After developing a preliminary list of potentially acceptable countries, the process of generating specific projects became highly informal. Conversations with investment bankers, travel to the specific countries, talks with governmental agencies, and just sheer accident produced contacts with potential local partners.

The local partners in these countries often had a common characteristic. They were members of a local group of industrial and financial
companies—similar to the so-called Japanese *zaibatsu*. In each country
one could find between three and five such groups, with the membership in each group defined along family lines. Among these partners
some wanted to place as much equity investment as possible and others wanted to have as much debt as possible, depending on their liquidity and alternative investments available. The final structure of the
project could be heavily influenced by the investment preferences of
these partners.

The evaluation of the project by Worthington's management
aimed at optimizing the total income stream to the parent company—
that is, dollars received in the United States. Dollars were received by
Worthington under three different categories: profits from the sale of
equipment (in some projects this factor had been enough to recover
most of the investment), license fees, and dividends.

Projects were evaluated in terms of their internal rate of return on
Worthington's cash investment, ignoring unrepatriated income and domestic division overhead. The impact of the project on financial reports
was also considered; however, this factor was of secondary importance.
Worthington's management insisted that projects had to be justified on
a cash basis. The internal rate of return of these projects in the past had
been over 30%, in contrast to the 12% obtained from new investments
in the United States.

Worthington's equity contribution had always been made in the
form of cash. As a mature company in a mature industry in the United
States, Worthington did not have any liquidity problem. In fact, given
the small size of each of these projects in isolation, and even in combination, foreign investment at Worthington had proceeded without
any cash constraint.

At the time Mr. Johnson was reviewing the foreign operations of
Worthington, the company had some forty joint ventures around the
world, mostly in Latin America. All of them could be considered small
relative to the parent company, although the ventures themselves were
often important factors in their respective local markets.

Financial Policy

There were four major considerations the corporate treasurer kept
in mind when structuring the financing of the joint ventures:

1. Emphasis on debt over equity
2. Minimization of the impact of devaluations of foreign currencies against
   the U.S. dollar

3. Generation of financial ratios that were in conformity with local practices
4. Insistence in not granting guarantees from Worthington Bottling to the lenders

The emphasis on debt over equity was consistent with Worthington's cautious approach to foreign investment. The more leverage the joint venture could obtain, the less the investment which ultimately would be required from Worthington. This emphasis on debt over equity had raised the possibility of making Worthington's investment in the joint ventures in the form of debt instead of equity. An important advantage of investing in this form was considered to be the lesser governmental control on interest and principal repayments than on dividend payments. Debt also made it possible to repatriate the whole investment. Equity investments were usually subject to maintaining a minimum of paid-in capital. In spite of these alleged advantages of investment in the form of debt, Worthington had found it difficult to negotiate this point with the local partners. With only rare exceptions, Worthington did not have any long-term loans to any of the joint ventures.

The objective of minimizing the impact of devaluation of foreign currencies against the U.S. dollar made Worthington denominate the sales of equipment and the license fees in dollars, instead of the local currencies. This concern also introduced a preference for debt denominated in the local currency, which could help hedge the exposures derived from the investment in assets. The desirability for local debt, in turn, made it important to maintain financial ratios that were consistent with those prevailing in the local market.

The goal of no guarantees from the Worthington Company to lenders had been a source of some debate with the partners. At times, better terms could have been obtained from lenders if Worthington had been willing to provide a guarantee. However, the corporate treasurer argued that guarantees did affect the credit rating of the company and the indentures on specific borrowings. Also, there was a question of whether U.S. tax law could consider these guarantees as a capital contribution. But perhaps the most important factor in the corporate treasurer's mind was the belief that a Worthington guarantee could convey the wrong message to the local partner, who might then leave the financial responsibility for the joint venture in Worthington's hands instead of sharing this responsibility.

Once a joint venture was formed, the management agreement called for the Worthington Company to appoint the financial manager for the operation as well as some key operating personnel. But once the manager in charge of finance was appointed, the day-to-day financial management was conducted totally by the local management. Thus, short-term borrowings were the total responsibility of local management and Worthington's management provided only annual revisions. Long-term borrowings did require advance consent from Worthington.

Worthington's corporate treasurer tried to maintain a 50% dividend payout in each of the foreign investments—the same payout as Worthington's. However, this policy did not always work. Local needs and the needs of the partners came to bear on the dividend decision and the 50% payout was more the exception than the rule. However, in the aggregate, the foreign ventures came close to contributing 50% of their profits in dividends.

Consistent with the delegation of the financial management to the foreign units, foreign exchange management was also left in the hands of the local financial officer. In fact, the local management was evaluated in terms of profits measured in dollars. Of course, this was a point that often was difficult to explain to the local partners who were not very interested in the value of their profits measured in terms of a foreign currency—U.S. dollars. Thus, Corporate Treasury still felt responsible for watching the translation exposure of these foreign operations. Finally, management of exposure in transactions in different currencies was left totally to the local management. These exposures were often (but not always) hedged, depending on the cost of the hedge.

HERBERT JOHNSON'S FACTS

The general comments Mr. Johnson received from the corporate treasurer and senior management amounted to a very conservative foreign investment strategy designed to minimize the amount of investment and to maximize the amount of cash received by Worthington: Invest as little equity from Worthington as possible and obtain as high a debt-to-equity ratio as possible. When the debt was denominated in local currency, this strategy also helped to minimize foreign exchange exposure and political risks. Although it seemed to be a cohesive strategy, the only inconsistency appeared to be the fact that Worthington could obtain such a high rate of return in foreign investments—often triple the one obtained in domestic investments. If foreign investments were so profitable, why not follow exactly the opposite strategy: Maximize the amount of investment in the form of 100%-owned companies with very little leverage?

The cohesiveness that these general principles appeared to possess disappeared when Mr. Johnson began examining the actual data for the subsidiaries. Exhibit N.1 shows such data for a selected number of subsidiaries. All of the standard financial ratios ranged widely when the different subsidiaries were compared. If the general preferences of

EXHIBIT N.1   The Worthington Bottling Company: Financial Data for Subsidiaries in Different Countries

	Colombia	Mexico	Venezuela	Brazil	Hong Kong	Saudi Arabia	Kuwait
Subsidiary Data							
Capital structure							
Accounts payable	3%	8%	7%	12%	—%	5%	8%
Short-term notes	10	11	17	20	—	40	21
Long-term debt	47	9	28	17	24	37	51
Partner's equity	20	30	29	30	—	11	14
Worthington's equity	20	42	19	21	76	7	6
	100%	100%	100%	100%	100%	100%	100%
Debt-to-equity ratio (debt defined as short-term plus long-term debt)	1.42	0.28	0.94	0.72	0.32	4.28	3.60
Dollars-to-local currency debt ratio (debt defined as short-term plus long-term debt)	4.2	0.53	1.62	0.86	0.00	0.00	0.00
Interest rates							
Short-term notes: local currency	31%	18%	9%	52%	—	9%	8%
Long-term notes							
Local currency	—	—	—	—	—	0%	4%
Dollars	11%	11%	11%	11%	—	—	—
Country Data							
(Average over period of operation in country)							
Interest rate on term debt	32%	23%	12%	50%	8%	7%	10%
Dividend repatriation allowed	20%	unlimited	20%	unlimited	unlimited	unlimited	unlimited
WPI inflation rate (per annum % change)	24%	20%	10%	40%	8%	16%	7%
Devaluation (−) or upvaluation (+) rate (per annum % change)	− 10%	− 14%	− 1%	− 44%	—	+ 2%	+ 2%
Currency trading status	controlled	free	free	controlled	free	free	free
Dividend withholding tax rate	20%	20%	20%	25%	0%	0%	0%
Local income tax rate	?	40%	42%	30%	18%	tax holiday	no tax
Traditional debt-to-equity ratio	1.1 or higher	1.1 or higher	1.1 or higher	1.1 or higher	?	?	1.5 or higher

EXHIBIT N.2 The Worthington Bottling Company: Decisions Involved in Choosing a Financial Structure

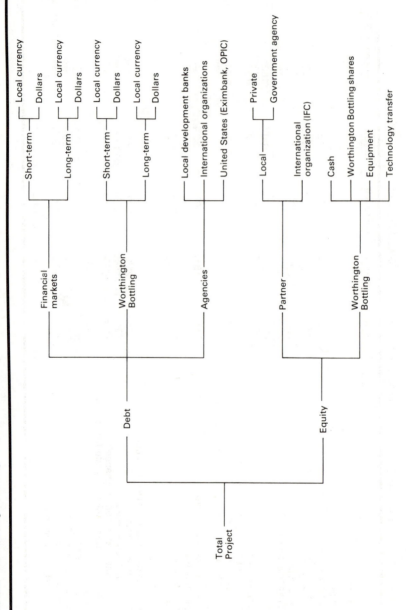

Worthington's management had remained constant, only two major factors could explain the vast dissimilarities among these companies: differences in local financial market conditions and differences in partners' preferences.

In an effort to find some rationale for the financial structures of Worthington's foreign joint ventures, and also to provide a general framework for future policymaking, Mr. Johnson developed the diagram presented in Exhibit N.2. In this diagram he tried to present the major choices to be made in arriving at a final financial structure for a foreign operation.

STEINBECK
CORPORATION

IN EARLY 1982, after months of negotiations, a firm proposal for a joint venture between Steinbeck and the People's Republic of China was beginning to emerge. The joint venture was to assemble electronic parts in China.

Steinbeck's interest in this joint venture in China could be traced to two major factors: (1) a strategy initiated in 1971 for fast growth into foreign markets and for vertical integration; and (2) the constant need to reduce the major cost component of its products—namely, labor. The joint venture in China offered access to inexpensive labor and, possibly, an entry into a new market that could expand rapidly in the future.

Steinbeck Corporation was founded in 1920 to manufacture electronic components sold to radio manufacturers. In the late 1940s, the firm entered the television parts market. However, for its first 50 years, Steinbeck remained a small domestic company. It was not until 1971, after a large influx of capital and management, that the company began manufacturing final products (such as television receivers) and began moving aggressively in international markets. By 1981, Steinbeck's international operations included the Far East, Latin America, and Europe. Most of these operations included both manufacturing and marketing. Some activities involved fully-owned subsidiaries, while others were joint ventures. The income from these operations represented more than half the increase in Steinbeck's net income from $1.3 million in 1976 to $2.0 million in 1981. Exhibit 0.1 presents Steinbeck's financial statements for 1981.

As John Goldenberg, vice-president of international operations, sat to analyze the joint venture proposal in China, he was excited with the challenge of being one of the first Western companies to consider investing in China since the creation of the People's Republic. On the other hand, he was concerned with the additional risks that such a venture would involve. These risks appeared particularly significant when he considered the alternatives of expanding existing operations in Taiwan, where the costs would be higher, but the risks better understood.

EXHIBIT 0.1 Steinbeck Corporation: Parent Company Financial Statements for 1981 *(in thousands of U.S. dollars)*

BALANCE SHEET ASSETS

Current assets		
Cash and marketable securities	500	
Accounts receivable	6,000	
Inventories	3,000	
Total current assets		9,500
Investment in subsidiaries		1,000
Property, plant, and equipment		
Buildings (net of depreciation)	4,000	
Equipment (net of depreciation)	6,000	10,000
Other assets		500
Total assets		21,000

LIABILITIES AND EQUITY

Current liabilities		
Accounts payable	4,000	
Accrued taxes	1,000	
Total current liabilities		5,000
Long-term debt		3,000
Common stock		10,500
Retained earnings		2,500
Total liabilities and equity		21,000

INCOME STATEMENT

Sales	80,000
Cost of goods sold	50,000
Gross margin	30,000
Administrative and selling expenses	24,500
Depreciation	1,000
Interest expense	500
Operating profit	4,000
Income taxes (.46 of profits)	1,840
Profit after tax	2,160
Extraordinary income (loss) of Latin American facility	(160)
Net income	2,000

THE JOINT VENTURE PROPOSAL

The partners in the joint venture would be Steinbeck Corporation and Wang Industries, a company owned by the Chinese State Industrial Service. For purposes of profit distribution, Steinbeck would be deemed to own 49% of the joint venture and Wang Industries 51% for the first 10 years of the venture. At that point, Steinbeck's 49% share of the joint venture would be transferred to the Chinese government.

Responsibilities of the Partners

In the initial investment, Steinbeck would be responsible for building and equipping the manufacturing plant according to specified technology at an estimated cost of $1.2 million. About $1 million of the total construction cost was represented by equipment to be bought in the United States and exported to China. The remaining $200,000 represented construction materials and labor to be acquired in China. Wang Industries would provide the plant site.

In the management of operations, Steinbeck would be responsible for purchasing the materials used to manufacture the final parts to be produced by the joint venture and for training the Chinese employees. Wang Industries would arrange for the availability of labor and utilities.

The Chinese law on joint ventures specified that problems between the partners should be settled through consultation among them and that the management of the joint venture should be based on the principles of equality, mutual benefit, and friendly cooperation. Wang Industries appeared willing to assure Steinbeck that no major decision would be taken without Steinbeck's consent.

Output and Sales

Steinbeck would commit to the purchase of the entire output expected to be produced by the plant during the first 10 years—200,000 units. The price of these units would be fixed at yuan 174.2 per unit. This price was $100 at the current exchange rate of yuan 1.7417 per U.S. dollar. However, if Steinbeck were to pay in U.S. dollars, then a discount would be available and the price of the part would be fixed at $90 for 1982, escalating at 12% per year in U.S. dollars. If the actual rate of production of the plant varied from the projected annual rate of 20,000 units, then the duration of the sale contract would be shortened or lengthened so that Steinbeck would be obliged to purchase only a total of 200,000 units from the company.

Termination Agreement

China's joint venture law of 1979 required that a foreigner's share in the ownership of a joint venture company be transferred to the government within a specified period of time determined according to the type of technology contributed by the foreign partner. In general, light industry firms such as Steinbeck were expected to be given a term of

10 to 15 years; heavy industry was expected to be allowed 25 years. However, depending on the viability of the company, the partners to the joint venture could, with the approval of the Foreign Investment Commission, delay or advance the date of termination initially established.

The quantity and price at which Steinbeck might purchase output from the factory after the transfer of its share of ownership in the company to the Chinese government would have to be negotiated in the future.

Management

The chairman of the board of directors would be appointed by the Chinese partner. Steinbeck would designate one or two vice-chairmen. In addition, Steinbeck would contribute the personnel needed to train the Chinese workers and staff all major positions during the first 3 years of operations. During this period, Chinese deputies would be trained to assume these posts after the initial 3 years.

Joint Venture Contract

No firm contract had been drawn with Steinbeck. However, Goldenberg was mindful of the advice provided by several experts on Chinese joint ventures. It had been suggested more than once that everything from the financing of the enterprise, profits, and taxes, to the cost of labor, materials, and the selling price of the output should be included in the contract. For example, although the Chinese agreed to provide the labor for this project, labor still had to be treated as an expense in the annual income statement for the joint venture. In essence, joint venture agreements were new to the Chinese, and there was no established code of laws governing them.

CASH FLOWS ASSOCIATED WITH THE JOINT VENTURE

Expenses

Expenses, to a large extent, would be contractual. Any discrepancy between the figures eventually accepted in the contract and the actual figures would be absorbed by the partner responsible for that cost.

Training Costs. A U.S. technician would be sent to China to train the 200 workers to be employed in the factory. The cost of this technician was estimated at $20,000. After the initial training, it was expected that Chinese foremen would be able to train other new employees. However, Steinbeck would also send a technician every year for 1 week to monitor the training procedure at an estimated cost of $3,000 per year.

Labor, Land, and Utilities. Wang Industries was planning to charge $60,000 annually for the 200 workers employed in the company and $120,000 for the use of land and utilities. These charges would be adjusted according to the local inflation rate—15% per annum recently.

Parts. The current market price of the parts to be imported into China to manufacture the final component was $30. These parts would be bought in the United States and one could expect their price to increase with the rate of U.S. inflation—12% recently.

Supervisory Fees. Two technical managers would be sent from the United States. Their salaries would be based on U.S. salaries and payable in U.S. dollars. Wang Industries was willing to accept a charge of $90,000 a year for the two technicians, whose salaries would be indexed to the U.S. inflation rate.

Depreciation. The Chinese were expected to agree to the straight-line depreciation of $1 million of the investment over 10 years. These depreciation-generated cash flows could be repatriated annually in full to Steinbeck, the partner providing funds for the depreciable equipment.

Technical Fees. The use of Steinbeck's patented technology would be compensated by the joint venture paying 2% of sales per annum, payable in U.S. dollars. Given the estimated output of 20,000 units per year at a sales price of $100, the technical fee would amount to $40,000 annually.

Chinese Income Tax. Under Chinese law, the tax rate on profits would be 30%, plus a municipal surtax of 3%. However, in the first profit-making year, a joint venture scheduled to operate for 10 years or more would be exempt from income taxes. It would be allowed a 50% tax reduction in the second and third years. For companies that introduced high technology, the total tax exemption of the first year of profitable operations could be extended to the second and third years. Although the law did not specify what constituted high technology,

Goldenberg thought that Steinbeck's technology would qualify for this treatment.

Revenues to Steinbeck

Joint Venture Sales.   The output to be bought by Steinbeck from the joint venture was expected to be sold, half to Steinbeck's subsidiary in Hong Kong and half to other television set manufacturers in the Pacific. Steinbeck's subsidiary in Hong Kong manufactured television sets which were sold in Malaysia, Indonesia, New Zealand, and in the United States, with the latter accounting for 50% of the sales of this subsidiary. The manufacturers to whom the other parts were expected to be sold were located primarily in Hong Kong and Singapore. The current market price for the parts to be produced by the joint venture was $110. In the past, the price of these electronic components had increased together with the local rates of inflation—about 18% in the recent past. Goldenberg believed that contracts with these other manufacturers would be easy to obtain and that the contract could be negotiated in U.S. dollars. However, these contracts had not been negotiated. Moreover, Goldenberg wondered if it was reasonable to assume that price increases in the future would be as high as those in the past, for current component prices were near U.S. prices for the identical items.

Technical Fees.   These fees were as specified in the expenses of the joint venture.

Withholding Taxes.   Remittance of profits were subject to a 10% dividend withholding tax on the remittances. However, if a foreign company reinvested its share of profits in China for at least 5 years, it would be entitled to a 40% refund of its share of income taxes on the joint venture. At the time of the analysis Steinbeck was not considering this reinvestment alternative, but instead planned to repatriate the maximum funds possible each year.

U.S. Income Taxes.   Steinbeck's effective tax rate in the United States was 46%. It was expected that the U.S. Internal Revenue Service would allow a tax credit to Steinbeck for the income and withholding taxes paid to the Chinese government including the municipal surtax collected by the central government. This was the treatment generally accorded by the IRS to income and withholding taxes paid to foreign governments. However, there had not been a ruling regarding taxes paid to the People's Republic of China.

Financing

Financing of the investment needed by the joint venture would be arranged by Steinbeck on its own account with international banks. Financing from Chinese sources was impossible since the Chinese Central Bank constrained lending to foreigners and even encouraged the local partners in joint ventures to finance their share through foreign bank loans. Financing of the joint venture on its own account was unlikely to be considered by any foreign bank.

The following financing alternatives appeared to be available for Steinbeck to generate a $900,000 loan, assuming Steinbeck contributed $300,000 in equity as well:

1. Finance in the United States at a fixed rate of 16% for 5 years. Installment payments would be due annually in the amount of $180,000 plus interest.
2. Finance in the United States at a fixed rate of 14% for 10 years. Installment payments would be $90,000 per annum plus interest.
3. Borrow in the Asian dollar market at 2% above the 6-month Asian interbank offered rate (AIBOR) for 5 years. Installment payments would be $180,000 per annum. The current 6-month AIBOR was 13%, so the interest rate payable by Steinbeck for the first 6 months would be 15% per annum.

ECONOMIC AND POLITICAL ENVIRONMENT
IN CHINA

The main attraction of the China joint venture for Steinbeck was the availability of cheap land and inexpensive labor. In contrast to the annual average of $3,000 per worker charged by Wang Industries in China, similar workers earned $6,000 in Taiwan and $15,000 in the United States. Already, many companies based in Hong Kong were negotiating joint ventures in China in order to take advantage of the lower costs there. But uncertainties did exist as to the productivity of labor, given the inability to control or provide incentives to workers and the lack of management and accounting systems. On the other hand, after operating in several culturally different countries, Goldenberg had found it relatively easy to train labor to manufacture electronic parts to meet international quality standards.

The other attraction of a business operation in China to Steinbeck was China's potential as a new market for electronic parts and products once the venture was underway and productive. At the time there was no law prohibiting the sale to the Chinese of the final product manufactured by a joint venture with a foreign partner. In fact, marketing departments in many U.S. companies saw major opportunities for market expansion in China. However, this market was not likely to materialize for some time.

On one hand, Goldenberg saw the potential for future growth within China, where labor was abundant and cheap. On the other hand, his experience and knowledge of foreign operations in China was limited. As of yet, there had been only minor American business investments in China. The facts which did exist showed that the investor had to make a significant commitment in executive time, effort, and expense. China faced the classic problems of an emerging economy: underdevelopment of transport and communications, shortage of qualified technicians and research workers, exhaustion of agricultural land, erratic weather conditions, and lack of investment capital.

However, the big unknown in this joint venture was the Chinese political attitude toward Western business. It was only since 1978 that China had taken a strong stance in promoting joint ventures with foreigners and expanding foreign trade. As a result, the China International Trust and Investment Corporation (CITIC) was created to attract foreign investment and technology. At the time, the State Council was the supreme authority over foreign trade. Both the Ministry of Finance and the Ministry of Foreign Trade were under its control and supervision. The government had set up the Foreign Investment Control Commission in August 1979 to scrutinize and approve all joint venture agreements. Since then, authority had shifted from the central government to the local provinces in order to encourage them to deal directly with foreign investors. However, decentralization had created some confusion because of the lack of overall policy guidelines and inconsistency in the types of agreements.

Considering the political and cultural changes that had occurred in China over the last century and especially in the last 20 years, it was evident that the country was in a state of flux, prone to rapid political changes. Although the Chinese government clearly announced that the capital of a foreigner in a joint venture would not be confiscated or expropriated, the political history of China since the creation of the People's Republic gave grounds for concern. China could be ruled by a different regime in 5 years. The advanced age of most Chinese leaders and the existence of a whole generation of bureaucrats trained during the anti-Western periods of the Cultural Revolution and the Gang of Four were not reasons for optimism.[1]

---

[1] A more detailed description on the political and economic environment in the People's Republic of China is presented in the note following this case, "Background Note on the People's Republic of China."

THE TAIWAN ALTERNATIVE

Since 1974, Steinbeck had been manufacturing electronic components in Taiwan, capturing the benefits of cheap labor and high productivity in addition to a friendly government policy that encouraged foreign investment. The plant in Taiwan was in an industrial zone where multinational corporations could invest and be exempt from Taiwanese taxes. Also, Taiwan had a capital market, in which Steinbeck could potentially obtain funds for expansion at an interest cost of approximately 18%. Whenever possible, Steinbeck preferred its subsidiaries or joint ventures to finance their own operations rather than to use loans from the parent company. However, as Taiwan itself had developed over the last 20 years, its own electronics firms competed with Steinbeck both for export sales and for the supply of labor and land.

As a result of the development of Taiwan, the cost of an expansion comparable in size to the venture proposed in China at the time would amount to $3 million for the factory and equipment. Further, the average assembly worker in Taiwan earned $6,000 per annum. These costs were in contrast to the $1,200,000 investment in the People's Republic of China for plant and equipment plus start-up outlays, and a $3,000 annual labor cost per worker. However, if Steinbeck were to answer its increased production needs by expanding in Taiwan, additional training of the labor force would not be necessary. The Taiwanese people had been very successful in learning quickly the assembly work involved in electronic parts. Furthermore, the quality of the parts produced had quickly equalled American standards in the industry.

BACKGROUND NOTE ON THE PEOPLE'S REPUBLIC OF CHINA*

IN ORDER TO understand better the state of affairs involving the establishment of joint ventures in China, a brief review of recent Chinese history relating to the development of foreign trade policies is in order. Western understanding of China's policy formulation processes is often superficial and speculative, especially when attempting to correlate domestic policies to foreign trade policies. What is known must be extracted from studies geared toward the disciplines of economics and political science and pieced together.

THE COUNTRY

As a separate entity, China takes on the trappings of a potential superpower. With the sheer magnitude of the numbers presented with respect to its resources, China ranks with the United States and the Soviet Union in total production of a number of resources. It ranks second only to the United States in total grain production, ranking in the top six of all the major grains, eleventh in total known oil reserves, and fourth in total energy production. China's GNP has increased steadily since the economic recovery program was initiated following the Sino-Soviet split, and has kept pace with the average world growth rate, with the major increases due primarily to the expanding industrialization.

In spite of these impressive figures, on a per capita basis, China ranks with the underdeveloped nations; its extremely large population reduces the large total figures to relatively low per capita figures. For example, although China ranks second only to the United States in total grain output, its population is 4.6 times that of the United States. This large population makes China a net grain importer.

---

*This note was prepared by Greg Johnson, Research Assistant, under the supervision of Professor Rita M. Rodriguez.

Although China ranks fourth in the world in terms of total land area, approximately two-thirds of the land is not arable, being too arid, too mountainous, or too high in elevation to be used to any agricultural advantage. In the past decade, through improved techniques and technology, the land that is arable has had an increased production between 30% and 40%. But with the little remaining land that can be utilized, the continuing infringement of an expanding industrial economy, and an increasing population, the agricultural aspect of the Chinese economy looks grim. See Exhibit O.2.

EXHIBIT O.2 Background Note on China: Population and Land—
China and Other Countries

POPULATION, 1976

China	852,133,000
India	610,077,000
Soviet Union	256,674,000
United States	215,118,000
Indonesia	139,616,000
Japan	112,768,000
Brazil	109,181,000
Bangladesh	80,558,000
Nigeria	64,750,000
West Germany	61,513,000
Italy	56,169,000
United Kingdom	55,928,000
France	52,915,000

GEOGRAPHIC SIZE (square kilometers)

Soviet Union	22,402,200
Canada	9,976,139
China	9,596,961
United States	9,363,123
Brazil	8,511,965
Australia	7,686,848
India	3,287,590
Argentina	2,766,889
Sudan	2,505,813
Algeria	2,381,741
Zaire	2,345,509
Greenland	2,175,600

AGRICULTURAL LAND AREA (million square kilometers)

Soviet Union	5,999.8
Australia	4,793.5
United States	4,413.0
China	2,873.0
India	1,770.6
Argentina	1,378.3
Brazil	1,267.3
Mexico	1,029.1

SOURCE: Kaplan et al., *Encyclopedia of China Today* (Fair Lawn, N.J.: Eurasia Press, 1979).

ECONOMIC AND POLITICAL PHILOSOPHIES

In 1949 Mao created a Communist totalitarian regime in China whose basic ideologies were futuristic and highly goal-oriented. The period from 1949 to 1953 was a time of consolidation, reconstruction, and reform aimed at transforming China from a subsistence agricultural economy that was weak and technologically backward into a powerful and independent industrial state.

By 1953, when Mao's regime had stabilized, it began to end its long period of isolationism by joining the Communist bloc and forming a military alliance with the Soviet Union, thereby compensating for its own lack of world political experience, allies, and military weaponry. The period from 1953 to 1957 represented both the height of Soviet influence in Chinese development strategy and the beginning of China's disenchantment with Soviet models. The First Five-Year Plan under Soviet influence was based on the assumption that China's development would embody unambiguous priorities, stressing the growth of heavy industry over light industry and industry over agriculture. Its basic characteristics were (1) an emphasis on investment in the development of heavy industry; (2) the continued transformation of agriculture, based on large-scale state farms; and (3) concentration of major economic activity in those areas of the country where skills and resources were most abundant. These policies had the net effect of reducing the rural agricultural labor base, creating massive unemployment and social unrest in the urban areas, decreasing agricultural output, and decreasing the land-to-population ratio.

In 1958 China began its Great Leap Forward (GLF), a program meant to use both modern and old-fashioned technology, marginal as well as central sources of raw materials, skilled and unskilled labor, large and small scale, urban and rural industry to achieve its goals. Due to the decentralization of control and the relaxing of previous operative restrictions and control mechanisms, overall production was continuing to grow, but at a highly uneven pace that was creating serious and growing imbalances, waste, and confusion. To add to this increasing chaos, the Sino-Soviet disputes came to a climax with a total Soviet recall of all technical and aid personnel from China, with most industrial projects disrupted or disbanded.

The period from 1960 to 1965 was another period of readjustment and recovery. Although it was agreed to place "agriculture first, with industry as the leading factor" to renew the tenet of self-reliance, there was bitter disagreement between ever-widening political factions as to the relationship between revolution and modernization. The two lines of political thought were the moderate Liuist philosophies and the post-GLF Maoists, whose conflicts, debates, and dissension raged until 1966.

In 1965, the Great Proletarian Cultural Revolution began in the intellectual and university student circles, but soon spread to become, in 1966, a larger cultural upheaval aimed at most major policies that had developed since the Great Leap Forward. It was at this point that self-reliance philosophies reached their peak as all vestiges of bourgeois influence were openly attacked and the main theories stressed political purification and egalitarianism. As the political unrest intensified, masses of Red Guards and factions of workers were forming various alliances which were often backed or manipulated by factions that had developed within the Communist party. One of the anti-Mao groups was supposedly backed by Liu Shao-ch'i, who subsequently became the target of Red Guard attacks and was eventually removed from all political positions. As the chaos continued, Mao finally issued a direct order to form united-front organizations to "grasp revolution and promote production" to minimize the effects on the economy. Unlike the Great Leap Forward, the only major economic repercussions were the work stoppages and production halts brought about by revolutionary activity. In 1969, Lin Piao was named as Mao's heir and the Party was given power over all government organs.

As the Great Proletarian Cultural Revolution wound down, 1970 saw the beginnings of a resumption of central planning and production. Although the "Revolution" was over, there still remained a substantial amount of political factionalism, as a number of the older cadre of the Party had been purged and newer, younger members had been recruited and/or promoted. This created an "Old Guard versus Young Turks" face-off in the battle for reorganization.

The early 1970s also saw an attempted revitalization of trade based on two factors: the increased availability of capital due to massive defense budget cuts and the feasibility of sizable foreign exchange earnings from petroleum exports. A new long-term program was also initiated to place agriculture on firm productive footing, with the goal of increasing food production by 30% to reduce dependence on imports. The period from 1972 to 1974 saw a new policy thrust as $500 million was allocated for the purchase of industrial plants from Japan, Western Europe, and the United States, and increased support was given to rural agricultural growth.

With the 1971 ouster of Lin Piao completed, an anti-Lin campaign began in 1973 which attacked the economic improvement methods then employed as being against Party and revolution policy. This campaign continued until Chou En Lai stated in 1975 that the newest economic policy placed modernization at its core in a two-stage process:

(1) to achieve an independent and comprehensive industrialization base by 1980, and (2) to advance to the front ranks in world power in agriculture, industry, defense, science, and technology.

In January 1976 Chou En Lai died and a new wave of political factionalism arose as power struggles began. As a result, Mao named Hua Kuo Feng (a relative "outsider") as acting premier. In September 1976, Mao died and Hua was named as chairman of the Communist party. Shortly after these proceedings the Gang of Four were arrested for "attempts to overthrow the government." This was seen as a victory for those who sought to pursue the policies of Mao in an intelligent and rational manner over those who wished only to gain power and had no interest in China's economic and social problems. By this time the political arena had quieted down and in 1977 Hua was renamed as premier and officially declared the Cultural Revolution as ended. He reinstated Deng Xiao-p'ing to the Politburo and as chairman of the Party in 1978.

Although Hua was premier, the major political philosophies seemed to be those of Deng Xiao-p'ing and were rooted in the basic philosophies of the Cultural Revolution, for which he had been purged in the late 1960s. These philosophies were based on placing sole priority on economic development to the detriment of the social and political goals of Mao. By this time Deng had staffed key economic agencies with his allies, but this did not prevent another campaign against Deng in 1979 for his radical departures from the old Maoist theories. In anticipation of this occurring, Deng had developed a foreign policy designed to put the opposition in a "no retreat" situation in the event of his fall from power. His policy included five basic tactics: (1) quick monetary incentives for workers to generate enthusiasm; (2) long-term economic commitments with foreigners with which his successors would have to cope; (3) an unexpected candor about standards of living in other nations designed to stimulate rising expectations at home; (4) a campaign of investments, purges, rehabilitations, and other measures designed to make huge bureaucracies responsive to his far-reaching demands; and (5) massive reinterpretations of Maoist thought to coincide with his philosophies. Deng's assault on the Maoist system was a failure. China could not absorb or pay for the massive industrial and technological imports; vastly underdeveloped transportation, fuel, and power facilities were not capable of providing the necessary support; and urban unemployment rose drastically as youths delegated to rural agricultural sectors returned to the cities in attempts to benefit from industrial work incentives.

With the failure of Deng's program some of his colleagues designed a program that was more ambitiously reformist than some of the younger Maoists would have produced, but it was still within the basic political orthodoxy and it was adopted in 1979. This new program was a scaled-down version to be implemented over a 3-year period and was to rectify sectoral imbalances in the economy, strengthen enterprise management, increase the use of material incentives, and upgrade production performance in existing plants. There was also to be a shift in investment priorities away from heavy industry toward agriculture and light industry. At this time the Communist party put forth and demanded adherence to the "four principles": support for the socialist path; the dictatorship of the proletariat; rule by the Communist party; and the sanctity of Marxist-Leninist and Mao Tse-Tung thought.

In 1981, Premier Zhao attacked what many foreign business executives see as a major problem in doing business with China—the extremely tangled and tortoiselike bureaucracy which was formed as a method for opposing factions to slow down proceedings—and adopted measures to clear out the multiechelon departments, superfluous hands, and deputy and nominal chiefs. Zhao also stated that although the current restructuring program, begun in 1979, would still take another 5 years, the economy would grow slowly and growth would accelerate into a new period of economic vitalization by the 1990s. Also, he stated that the country sought to improve its financial and economic situation by emphasizing a higher standard of living.

However, if China's commitment to modernization is to continue, the country must generate enough economic progress to prove its worth, and to do so it must overcome great obstacles.

FOREIGN TRADE POLICIES AND SELF-RELIANCE

Self-Reliance

Any study of Chinese foreign trade policy formulation should include an explanation of the Chinese concept of self-reliance—the concept of relying as much as possible on its own resources while making external sources ancillary. The concept evolved through decades of painful experience, beginning in the mid-nineteenth century and aggravated by the split with Moscow in the late 1950s. Self-reliance can be envisioned as China's response to a long history of political and economic humiliations suffered at the hands of foreign powers. From the beginning of the People's Republic of China, Mao's basic philosophy was that of relying mainly on the country's own resources. The concept of self-reliance requires the formulation of policies that "minimize strategic and financial dependence on foreign countries" and "maximize utilization of domestic resources, the largest of which is manpower." Although Mao had allowed for a flexible interpretation of this philosophy, as illustrated by the massive reliance on Soviet financial and industrial support in the 1950s, self-reliance dictated that trade and imports supplement rather than substitute for indigenous development. In the 1960s Deng Xiao-p'ing stated that developing countries must keep hold of their natural resources and shake off foreign control to develop their natural economies. This idea was intensified by the international ostracism and isolation from the Western world following the Sino-Soviet split.

In 1972 the flexibility of Mao's basic self-reliance philosophies was tested in the reformulation of trade policies. The foreign policy of the People's Republic of China had been minimal (in fact, nearly nonexistent) for more than a decade. At this point key decisions were made to accelerate the pace of development through increased imports to facilitate rapid development of the domestic economy, although these decisions met with some internal dissent by opposing factions.

In 1981, Premier Zhao discarded the old Maoist tenet that China should strive for self-sufficiency and declared that the country should instead boldly advance in the world market, increase exports, and step up economic links with foreign countries. He even went so far as to suggest the exportation of surplus laborers.

Foreign Trade Policy

To understand China's foreign trade policy, it is necessary to be familiar with its prevalent domestic policies, for one is a reflection of the other. In the past, when a traditional Maoist was in the political forefront, the emphasis was on self-reliance and internal control; when a moderate was in charge, more emphasis was placed on foreign trade. With the advent of modernization it became necessary to deal with foreigners, which led to debate and political dissension.

In the mid-1960s the Chinese were contemplating the expansion of foreign trade beyond that which was absolutely necessary for survival, but the Cultural Revolution, with its emphasis on self-reliance and egalitarianism, put a halt to any moves in that direction. It was not until the 1970s that any moves were made toward the resumption of foreign trade on the part of the Chinese. The first moves toward international involvement came when the People's Republic of China succeeded in its attempts to have Taiwan expelled from the United Nations and itself seated instead.

Before normal relations could be resumed with the United States certain concessions had to be made by the United States. The issues at hand were: (1) the recognition by the United States of Taiwan as a part of mainland China; (2) the cessation of patrols by the Seventh Fleet through the Taiwan Strait; and (3) the withdrawal of all U.S. troops from Taiwan. During his 1972 trip to Peking, President Nixon agreed to all of the demands; in fact, he had ordered the cessation of Seventh Fleet patrols in 1969. As for the other two demands, the recognition of China over Taiwan was one of simple logistics (choosing 800 million over 12 million) and the withdrawal of troops was more symbolic than anything else, as the actual defenders of Taiwan were spread out on American bases and aircraft carriers throughout the Pacific. It was also in keeping with the Nixon doctrine, which made it the responsibility of the governments of America's allies in Asia to contribute more toward their own defense. Despite the concessions made by Nixon and their acceptance by the Chinese, foreign trade is only now beginning to take shape.

The implications of the policy of expanding and liberalizing foreign trade will not benefit all Western businesses equally. Many American firms, holding what they thought were legitimate contracts (from Deng's overzealous policies), ended up holding "letters of intent" and were forced either to give up hope or to sit and wait. The policy also limited imports of entire plants and consumer goods and expanded the importation of technology and manufacturing processes. Strict standards were also imposed to prevent the importation of plants for which adequate supplies of power and raw materials did not exist.

On the exportation side, Peking will push exports (textiles, light manufactured goods, and an increasing supply of machinery equipment) to expand exchange holdings, with coal and oil exports added in the late 1980s. To reduce further the depletion of scarce foreign exchange resources, China will try to initiate barter trade, coproduction and processing, product paybacks, and joint equity ventures.

Another factor affecting China's attempt to expand foreign trade is the actual financing of new ventures. In the past, on the domestic front, China has operated as one large corporation with the State receiving all profits, absorbing losses, and giving financial aid in the form of grants. With this system there were no incentives to cut costs or increase profits. Due to the increase in foreign trade, China has been planning, with the assistance of the World Bank, a subsidiary to its People's Construction Bank, which would initiate loans to companies on an individual-ownership basis and expect repayment with interest.

On the international level the Chinese are unhappy about prevailing high interest rates and are waiting for them to recede. A previous offer of $2 billion in U.S. Export-Import Bank funds, presented by the Carter administration, still holds, and China has signed for its first Export-Import loan of $57 million at a 12% rate.

As of 1978, there were numerous foreign projects in progress, including a number of U.S. projects in various stages of development (see Exhibits O.3 and O.4). A summary of China's political and economic history from 1949 to 1979 is provided in Exhibit O.5.

EXHIBIT 0.3 Background Note on China: U.S.-China Foreign Trade Projects (1978)

Company	Project	Estimated Value
Intercontinental Hotels	Five or six 1,000-room hotels	$500 million
Hyatt International	10,000-room hotel chain	$800 million
Prestige Sportswear and Oxford Industries	Machinery	$100,000
Coastal States Gas	Import Chinese crude oil	$50 million
Boeing	Three 747s	$150 million
Kaiser Engineers	Develop iron ore mines	Unknown
Sperry Rand	Computers	$6 million
International Business Machines	Model 138 computer	Unknown
Continental-Ensco Co.	Seven oil-drilling rigs	$40 million
Pennzoil, Mobil, Union, Exxon, and Phillips	Oil and energy development	$5 billion
Ford Motor Co.	700 light- and heavy-duty trucks, parts and tools	Unknown
Bethlehem Steel	Ore-processing plants	$100 million
U.S. Steel	Iron ore plant	Unknown
Coca-Cola (exclusive)	Plant and equipment	$2 million
La Choy	Canning plants	Unknown

SOCIAL FACTORS

The major social factors facing the Chinese during their economic expansion deal mainly with rising social inequality and population distribution. During the brief association with the Soviets, Mao realized that the Soviet method of industrialization was to build up urban centers at the expense of the rural sectors. Mao saw this as a potential source of peasant dissension and fought for the rapid collectivization of agriculture. With rapid industrialization China is faced with a work force geared toward labor-intensive methods. More efficient industrial methods would utilize fewer workers, thereby increasing an already high urban unemployment rate. With a lack of concern for labor efficiency serving as a deterrent to technological advancement, higher wages for industrial workers are offered as incentives. With limited access to job availability, workers in rural agricultural sectors are abandoning their lower-paying jobs and seeking the higher-paying jobs in the cities. The inevitable consequence will be growing social inequality. The heart of the program is the idea of rewarding the most productive workers and increasing the gap between them and those who contribute less to rapid economic growth, mainly the rural agricultural workers. Those who benefit the least will provide the impetus for eventual social backlash against modernization.

Another aspect of this growing social problem is the concept known as the "iron rice bowl." The family whose head works for a large-scale, state-owned enterprise will most likely live in enterprise housing, attend movies at enterprise auditoriums, send the children to

EXHIBIT 0.4 Background Note on China: U.S.-China Foreign Trade, 1950–1976 *(in millions of 1976 U.S. dollars.)*

Year	Total Turnover	Exports	Imports	Balance	Year	Total Turnover	Exports	Imports	Balance
1950	1,210	620	590	30	1964	3,220	1,750	1,470	280
1951	1,900	780	1,120	−340	1965	3,880	2,035	1,845	190
1952	1,890	875	1,015	−140	1966	4,245	2,210	2,035	175
1953	2,295	1,040	1,255	−215	1967	3,895	1,945	1,950	−5
1954	2,350	1,060	1,290	−230	1968	3,765	1,945	1,820	125
1955	3,035	1,375	1,660	−285	1969	3,860	2,030	1,830	200
1956	3,120	1,635	1,485	150	1970	4,290	2,050	2,240	−190
1957	3,055	1,615	1,440	175	1971	4,720	2,415	2,305	110
1958	3,765	1,940	1,825	115	1972	5,920	3,085	2,835	250
1959	4,290	2,230	2,060	170	1973	9,870	4,895	4,975	−80
1960	3,990	1,960	2,030	−70	1974	13,950	6,570	7,380	−810
1961	3,015	1,525	1,490	35	1975	14,315	6,930	7,385	−455
1962	2,675	1,525	1,150	375	1976	13,200	7,000	6,200	800
1963	2,770	1,570	1,200	370					

SOURCE: Kaplan et al. *Encyclopedia of China Today* (Fair Lawn, N.J.: Eurasia Press, 1979).

EXHIBIT 0.5 Background Note on China: Political and Economic Chronology, 1949 to 1979

Year And Period	GNP (billion 1973 US dollars)	GNP Per Capita	Population (millions)	Steel Output (millions of metric tons)	Industrial Production (1957 = 100)	Crude Oil Output (millions of metric tons)	Total Grain Output (million tons)	Political Leaders (Chairman CCP) (Premier)
1949–1952 Rehabilitation								
1949	$ 40	$ 74	N.A.	0.16	20	N.A.	108.1	Mao Tse-Tung Chou En Lai
1950	49	89	—	0.16	27	—	124.7	
1951	56	101	—	0.90	38	—	135.0	
1952	67	117	—	1.35	48	500	154.4	
1953–1957 First Five-Year Plan								
1953	71	122	N.A.	1.77	61	N.A.	156.9	
1954	75	125	588	2.22	70	—	160.4	
1955	82	134	601	2.85	73	—	174.8	
1956	88	141	614	4.46	88	—	182.5	
1957	94	147	627	5.35	100	1,400	185.0	
1958–1960 Great Leap Forward								
1958	113	172	642	11.08	145	—	200.0	Liu Shao ch'i Chou En Lai
1959	107	160	655	13.35	177	—	165.0	
1960	106	155	667	18.67	184	—	150.0	
1961–1965 Readjustment and Recovery								
1961	82	118	679	8.00	108	—	162.0	
1962	93	133	692	8.00	114	6,800	174.0	
1963	103	144	705	9.00	137	—	183.0	
1964	117	160	718	10.80	163	—	200.0	
1965	134	179	732	12.50	199	10,000	200.0	
1966–1969 Great Proletarian Cultural Revolution								
1966	145	190	746	15.00	231	—	215.0	Liu Shao-ch'i Chou En Lai
1967	141	180	759	12.00	202	—	230.0	
1968	142	178	773	14.00	222	—	215.0	
1969	157	192	787	16.00	265	—	220.0	
1970–1979 Resumption of Regular Planning								
1970	179	214	801	17.80	313	22,000	240.0	Lin Piao Chou En Lai
1971	190	222	815	21.00	341	—	246.0	
1972	197	225	828	23.00	371	—	240.0	
1973	217	241	842	25.50	416	—	250.0	
1974	223	243	855	23.80	432	65,000	265.0	
1975	254	—	869	—	502	80,000	270.0	Deng Xiao-p'ing Hua Kuo Feng
1976	—	—	883	—	—	—	275.0	
1977	—	—	896	—	—	95,000	—	
1978	—	—	909	—	—	—	—	
1979	—	—	922	—	—	—	—	

enterprise schools, utilize enterprise health facilities, and expect at least one of the children to replace his or her parent upon the latter's retirement. Two aspects of labor policy are basic to this system: (1) For broad social reasons, enterprises hire more workers than they need; and (2) once hired, a person is never fired. The extreme Maoists claim that this humane approach to employment is what truly distinguishes China and makes it superior to capitalist countries. The problem arises in the fact that, although it has important social benefits, it creates inefficiency, and foreign firms contemplating joint ventures in China will want the authority to fire inefficient workers. One Chinese internal proposal for compensation was to reward efficient workers with shorter hours for the same pay rather than fire inefficient workers.

At present, a minor social problem created by modernization is the danger of being corrupted by what Premier Zhao referred to as the bourgeois way of life. Speculation, smuggling, tax evasion, embezzlement, and bribery are already reported in some areas.

*

BIBLIOGRAPHY

"China is Planning Bank to Finance Capital Projects," *Wall Street Journal,* Nov. 2, 1981, p. 29.

"China's Trade with Industrial Nations, Especially North America, Surged in 1980," *Wall Street Journal,* Nov. 12, 1981, p. 29.

Ching, Frank, "U.S. Speeds Up Exports to China of Technology," *Wall Street Journal,* Nov. 19, 1981, p. 32.

————, "China Adds Ideology Rifts to Old Woes as It Moves to Boost Foreign Trade," *Wall Street Journal,* Nov. 24, 1981, p. 28.

————, "China's Premier Upbeat about Economy but Says Revamping to Take 5 More Years," *Wall Street Journal,* Dec. 1, 1981, p. 26.

————, "China Expects Economic Gains to Speed in 1990s," *Wall Street Journal,* Dec. 2, 1981, p. 28.

Copper, John Franklin, *China's Global Role.* Palo Alto, Cal.: Hoover Institution Press, 1980.

Fenwick, Ann, "Chinese Foreign Trade Policy and the Campaign against Deng Xiao-ping." In *China's Quest for Independence: Policy Evolution in the 1970s,* ed. Thomas Fingar. Boulder, Col.: Westview Press, 1980.

Hinton, Harold C., ed. *The People's Republic of China: A Handbook.* Boulder, Col.: Westview Press, 1979.

Hsiung, James C., and Samuel S. Kim, eds. *China in the Global Community.* New York: Praeger Press, 1980.

Kaplan, Frederic M., Julian M. Sobin, and Steven Andors, *Encyclopedia of China Today.* Fair Lawn, N.J.: Eurasia Press, 1979.

Lieberthal, Kenneth, "China: The Politics behind the New Economics," *Fortune,* Dec. 31, 1979, pp. 44–50.

Nee, Victor, "The Political and Social Bases of China's Four Modernizations," *Columbia Journal of World Business,* Summer (1979), pp. 23ff.

"Top Peking Official Concedes that China Has Economic Ills," *Wall Street Journal,* Nov. 17, 1981, p. 30.

Portfolio Considerations in the Multinational Capital Budgeting Process

IN OUR DISCUSSIONS of project risk and the cost of capital, we have mentioned that we should take into account not only the project under consideration, but also its relationship to other projects in the firm and to the investment opportunities of stockholders. The firm can be seen as a portfolio of projects; stockholders have access to diversification through other securities in the market.

The financial theory of portfolios has been developed mostly in the context of equities in efficient capital markets. The applicability of this theory to foreign capital markets has been tested and the results are still inconclusive. However, the theory provides a useful framework for incorporating the effects of diversification in the process of project evaluation. We will review this theory very briefly, describing only its major components. This provides two major contributions to the capital budgeting process: (1) the evaluation of projects in the form of alternative portfolios of these projects; and (2) the measurement of the cost of equity for the project, taking into account the relationship between the project and the market of securities available to stockholders.

Since growth and diversification often take the form of acquisitions, Appendix 1 to this chapter presents a summary of antitrust legislation. Appendix 2 surveys the studies regarding portfolio diversification with an international securities universe.

THEORY OF FINANCIAL DIVERSIFICATION

The Basic Theory

There are three major developments in the financial theory related to portfolios and diversification. Each of these developments builds upon the preceding ones and can be accepted independently of later ones. We now summarize these theories.

Markowitz' Concept of Efficient Portfolios.[1] This framework suggests that the risk-averse investor can diversify over a security universe by selecting those securities which provide portfolios with maximum expected return for a given variability in that return; or, alternatively, seek portfolios which have minimum variability for a given level of expected return. There is a family or *frontier of efficient portfolios* tracing a curve with each portfolio having greater expected return and greater variance or lower expected return and lower variance than any of its neighbors (see Exhibit 16.1). The investor can select the desired portfolio from among this group according to the desired risk-return tradeoff. The portfolios on this frontier are efficient portfolios; all other

EXHIBIT 16.1   Efficient Portfolios and the Optimum Portfolio When a Risk-Free Asset Exists

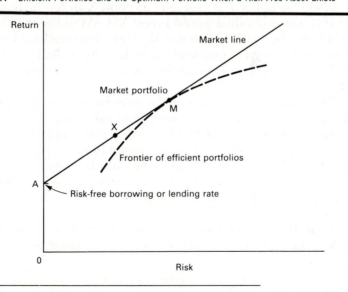

---

[1]Harry Markowitz, *Portfolio Selection: Efficient Diversification of Investments* (New York: John Wiley and Sons, 1959).

portfolios are either inefficient (offering lower expected returns for the same variability, for example) or infeasible (having greater expected returns and the same variability), since by definition the efficient set of portfolios has maximum return for a given variability.

Tobin's Separation Theorem.[2]   If borrowing and lending opportunities are available, it may be possible for the investor to move to a position of greater utility based on one of the efficient portfolios and suitable amounts of borrowed or loaned funds—hence, the Tobin term *separability*. The decision on the optimum portfolio and the decision on how much to borrow can be made independently; the borrowing or lending strategy still utilizes one of the efficient portfolios in the final decision.

Lintner-Mossim-Sharp Market Portfolio.[3]   By introducing the possibility of borrowing or lending at a *risk-free* rate, there is only one portfolio—the *market portfolio*—which is compatible with achieving the maximum utility for all market participants. Following the separation theorem, individual participants achieve their preferred risk-return tradeoff by borrowing or lending at the market's risk-free rate, in conjunction with their investment in the market portfolio. All possible risk-return tradeoffs in the market lie on a *market line*, which represents combinations of borrowing or lending at the risk-free rate and investing in the market portfolio. For example, at point X in the market line in Exhibit 16.1, the individual would invest XM/AM in the risk-free asset and AX/AM on the market portfolio M. This identification of a unique market portfolio has great implications for how individual securities are priced. These implications are spelled out in what is known as the *capital asset pricing model*.

These models for investment decision have been tested empirically in the U.S. security market with reasonably good results. In addition, extensions of the analysis in a slightly different framework have been used to evaluate performance of mutual funds ex post by comparing them to a market portfolio combined with borrowing and lending options open to a naive investor. The investor buys a well-diversified market portfolio and then borrows or lends to move to a suitable composite asset position.

As these theories have been extended to the international securities market, the empirical researchers have often faced severe difficul-

---

[2]James Tobin, "Liquidity Preference as Behavior Toward Risk," *Review of Economic Studies*, February 1958, pp. 65–86.

[3]Students with no background in investments or corporate finance are advised to review the introductory materials in any corporate or investment finance text prior to these sections, which are of a very summary nature.

ties and lack of conformity to an integrated world-security market. Particularly, the identification of a world-market portfolio requires the existence of efficient markets in every country and the freedom for the investor to move from investments in one country to investments in another. Only under these assumptions could a unique world-market portfolio be identified and reached. A summary of the research on international capital markets, containing tests of whether these markets are segmented or integrated, is presented in Appendix 2 to this chapter. At best, the results are mixed.

Multinationals' Contribution to Diversification

If we substitute projects for securities in the preceding discussion, we can extend the analysis of security portfolios to capital budgeting.

Consistent with basic capital budgeting theory, higher returns can be obtained only by assuming higher risks. But because of the benefits of diversification, the portfolio that allows the firm to diversify results earns a surplus return. The total risk of the diversified firm is lower than the simple sum of the risks of the component projects on their own. In this sense, the corporation can achieve through diversification among projects the same results as the individual investor who diversifies among companies.

Whether the corporation can do better than the individual investor depends on the corporation's access to projects in which the individual cannot invest directly. If the corporation has an advantage over individuals in diversification skills, then the total risk of the corporation for the given level of expected return may be lower than what investors could obtain independently for that expected return. This would be the case because the lower risk is available only to investors in the diversified corporation and not to investors who carve their investments from among the company's projects.

The ability of the corporation to create special diversification opportunities is challenged on two grounds: (1) The cost of monitoring and coordinating the broadly diversified firm may exceed any potential benefits from the spreading of risk, and (2) some critics discount the existence of benefits from corporate diversificaton. They argue that the investor can adequately diversify (through investment in a mutual fund). If both criticisms are granted, the broadly diversified firm is economically inefficient, for there is a net cost of coordination that is not offset by any diversification benefits unrealizable by individual investors on their own!

For the multinational enterprise, in particular, one can argue that it is very likely that it can diversify more efficiently than individuals could. The multinational company has access to investments in countries whose capital markets could hardly be described as efficient. These companies also gather a mass of information about international opportunities in their lines of business that would be hard to duplicate by any financial investor. Finally, multinational companies can package projects in a fashion which financial investors could not do. For example, these companies can negotiate special tax and repatriation agreements with governments, enter in joint ventures with local partners, and engineer projects with components in different countries. Ultimately, the multinational firm can overcome some of the elements of market failure (noted in Chapter 15) that contribute to inefficient markets.

In the following two sections we will apply the concepts of portfolio theory to capital budgeting.

DEVELOPING EFFICIENT PORTFOLIOS OF PROJECTS

The condition that makes it possible to develop an efficient security portfolio—one which maximizes return for a given amount of risk or minimizes risk for a given amount of return—is the interdependency that exists among the variations in the returns of the component securities. Independently of market efficiency, if we are given a set of securities with a certain expected return and risk, we would be able to select combinations of securities that are superior to the others, because the portion of the risk of each security varies with the return in the other securities. Likewise, if such an interdependency exists among the projects the firm is contemplating, we should be able to select combinations of projects that are superior to the others.

Construction of a Portfolio of Projects

The measure of risk used by financial theory is the standard deviation or variance of the distribution of possible returns of a security. In our discussion of risk analysis we also used the standard deviation or variance of the project as a measure of the project's risk. But how does one compute the variance of a portfolio of projects?

Suppose that three projects are considered by Freeport Minerals. Each is a nickel plant, with one in each of two Australian states and one in Ghana. Each project has an expected return and standard deviation. Freeport wants to invest in two plants, but it is unsure of which two are preferred. The standard deviation of an investment in the two Australian plants may be very close to the sum of the plants' individual standard deviations; each of them shares most of the same risks with respect to the world nickel market, costs in Australia, the value of the U.S. dollar, inflation, and so on. They have high positive *correlation*.

On the other hand, the standard deviation in return on the same money invested in the Ghanian plant and either one of the Australian plants may be substantially less than the simple sum of the two projects' standard deviations. There is obvious diversification. Freeport has reason to hope that a labor strike or severe inflation or devaluation in one country, for example, would not necessarily follow in the other. It is true that both pairs of investments are subject to the same technological and world market conditions of nickel, but there is a benefit from spreading the risk geographically.

Finally, Freeport management might elect more diversification by investing in one Australian nickel plant and in a Peruvian zinc operation. There is then geographic diversification and product diversification.

These examples should present intuitive reasons for rejecting the sum of projects' standard deviations as a measure of portfolio risk. The standard deviation or variance of a project pays no heed to any other project. Accordingly, another statistical measure is required. Between each project and every other project, the *covariance* can be computed to provide a measure of their *joint* riskiness. Further, the variance of a portfolio of two or more projects can be found by combining the respective variances and covariances.

As an example, assume that the three mentioned projects have the mean, standard deviation, and covariance figures shown on the upper part of Exhibit 16.2. From these figures, we can compute the mean results and standard deviations for the four possible combinations of projects, as shown in the middle portion of the exhibit.

These calculations assume that there are equal dollar investments required in each investment. The mean portfolio return is

$$R = \sum_{i=1}^{n} a_i r_i$$

where i reflects the projects in the portfolio, a_i is the fraction of the budget invested in each project (and $\sum_{i=1}^{n} a_i = 1$), and r_i is the mean return of project i.

EXHIBIT 16.2   Projects and Portfolios of Projects: Returns and Standard Deviations

| | COMPONENT PROJECTS | | Zinc Mine |
| | Nickel Projects | | |
	Australia	Ghana	Peru
Mean return	0.20	0.25	0.20
Standard deviation	0.10	0.25	0.12

Covariances $\llcorner$———— 0.020 ————$\lrcorner$ $\llcorner$———— 0.006 ————$\lrcorner$
                             $\llcorner$———— 0.0024 ————$\lrcorner$

POSSIBLE PORTFOLIOS

A. Australian and Ghanaian Nickel Operations

Mean return $= 0.5(0.20) + 0.5(0.25) = 0.225$ or 22.5%

Standard deviation $= \sqrt{0.25(0.10)^2 + 0.25(0.25)^2 + 2(0.25)(0.020)}$
                     $= \sqrt{0.028125}$
                     $= 0.168$ or 16.8%

B. Australian Nickel Operation and Zinc Mine

Mean return $= 0.5(0.20) + 0.5(0.20) = 0.20$ or 20%

Standard deviation $= \sqrt{0.25(0.10)^2 + 0.25(0.12)^2 + 2(0.25)(0.0024)}$
                     $= \sqrt{0.0073}$
                     $= 0.085$ or 8.5%

C. Ghanaian Nickel Operation and Zinc Mine

Mean return $= 0.5(0.25) + 0.5(0.20) = 0.225$ or 22.5%

Standard deviation $= \sqrt{0.25(0.25)^2 + 0.25(0.12)^2 + 2(0.25)(0.006)}$
                     $= \sqrt{0.02223}$
                     $= 0.149$ or 14.9%

D. All Three Projects

Mean return $= 0.33(0.20) + 0.33(0.25) + 0.33(0.20) = 0.215$ or 21.5%

Standard deviation $= \sqrt{0.11(0.10)^2 + 0.11(0.25)^2 + 0.11(0.12)^2 + 2(0.11)(0.02)}$
                     $\qquad + 2(0.11)(0.006) + 2(0.11)(0.0024)$
                     $= \sqrt{0.015807}$
                     $= 0.126$ or 12.6%

SUMMARY

Portfolio	Mean Return	Standard Deviation	Coefficient of Variation
B. Australian nickel operation and zinc mine	20.0%	8.5%	0.42
D. All three projects	21.5%	12.6%	0.59
A. Australian and Ghanaian nickel operations	22.5%	16.8%	0.75
C. Ghanaian nickel operation and zinc mine	22.5%	14.9%	0.66

The standard deviation of the portfolio return is

$$S = \sqrt{\sum_{i=1}^{n} a_i^2 S_i^2 + \sum_{i=1}^{n} \sum_{j=1}^{n} a_i a_j S_{ij}} \qquad (i \neq j)$$

where S is the standard deviation of the portfolio, a_i and a_j are the fractions of the portfolio invested in projects i and j, S_i is the standard deviation of project i, and S_{ij} is the covariance between projects i and j. The covariance (S_{ij}) between projects is the correlation between projects i and j (ρ_{ij}) times the standard deviation of each project, or $\rho_{ij} \times S_i \times S_j$.

A summary of the results obtained for each of the four portfolios is shown on the bottom part of Exhibit 16.2. The efficient portfolios, in increasing order of returns, are portfolios B, D, and C. Portfolio A can be eliminated as being inferior to portfolio C—both portfolios yield a mean rate of return of 22.5%, but portfolio A has a higher standard deviation than portfolio C. The benefits of diversification can be seen by comparing portfolio B (which yields a mean return of 20%) with the nickel project in Australia or the zinc mine in Peru. Each of those projects yields the same mean return, but each has a higher standard deviation than the portfolio combining the two of them, portfolio B.

Other things constant, management would select one of the three efficient portfolios depending on their risk-return tradeoff. Conservative managements would probably opt for portfolio B, with a mean return of 20% and a standard deviation of 8.5%. The next alternative increases the mean return to only 21.5%, while the standard deviation increases to 12.6%. However, the final decision will depend on management's risk preferences, as well as other attributes of the projects that cannot be summarized effectively in terms of mean return and standard deviation.

The diversification effects achieved through the combination of projects can be computed for other criteria using the same procedures and formulas. These criteria may include terminal rate of return, net present value, earnings per share in a given year, growth rates in sales, and so on.[4]

Development of Data to Construct
a Portfolio of Projects

In the previous example we were given the data necessary to estimate the return and standard deviation of the possible portfolios of projects. We were given the mean and the standard deviation for each

---

[4]In some cases the formulas for combining these figures would be slightly different from the ones presented here. This will occur when one cannot use the basic rate of return equations which parallel the investment security example. See E. Eugene Carter, *Portfolio Aspects of Corporate Capital Budgeting* (Lexington, Mass.: D.C. Heath and Company, 1974), pp. 83–88, for an explanation of this difference.

of the three projects, together with the covariance between the possible pairs of projects. Now we show how to generate these data.

In our discussion of risk analysis we showed how to obtain means and standard deviations for a specific project by specifying the nature of the probability distributions of the different factors which affected the project. Using a computer simulation model we derived the resulting probability distribution for the project. To derive a covariance among projects we can follow the same simulation procedure, but now the resulting probability distribution will be for a combination of projects—that is, a portfolio.[5] We begin with the same data we had for one project, and provide these data for each of the projects we wish to consider in a portfolio. Then, we select the specific portfolio of projects we wish to consider.

In a joint simulation the outcome of each project is computed for a given trial—a sample of projects—and stored in relation to the outcome of all the other projects on that trial. Then the sampling process is reinitialized and the simulation is repeated. When projects are dependent on some common variable (such as GNP or growth in a particular area of the economy) this process assures a common value for those underlying factors. From the data it is possible to compute the mean, variance, and covariance of the projects on each criterion since the simulation trials store values of each project's outcome in conjunction with all other projects' outcomes on a given trial.

Given multiple goals of managers, a useful tool to complement this simulation model is an interactive computer model. Assume the manager is concerned about ten major criteria: sales, earnings per share, and cash flow for each of 3 years, and the net present value. By providing a range of computing options which enable the manager to see the results of various portfolio combinations, the model permits selection of the final portfolio in a rapid manner. Nothing in this model

---

[5]The most evasive measure on any standard to be evaluated is likely to be the estimate of covariance between projects. If correlation of returns among the projects is known, one can compute the covariance, and vice versa. There are two other ways of estimating the portfolio figures.

First, one may ask managers to specify correlation between projects. This task is difficult to accomplish even if the manager is thoroughly familiar with the concept. If it is possible in a given situation, such correlations can generate the covariance matrix. On the other hand, if the existing firm is huge in relation to any proposed project, the loss in accuracy in the variance of firm and project portfolio is nominal when the correlations between new projects are ignored. Rather, all that must be estimated is the correlation of each new project with the existing firm's asset base or some market standard.

A second approach is to use equivalent formulas which allow an estimate of the maximum variance in portfolio net present values from some compendium of project present value variances, ignoring the covariances between projects or between projects and the firm or "market."

Under either alternative, there is a nontrivial problem created given the possible combinations that can occur for a portfolio of projects. Thus, if one calculates all possible combinations of projects and analyzes the outcomes, the task is enormous. A portfolio of one to twenty potential projects would involve computing over one million combinations unless some simplifying rule is used.

would prevent using any of the mathematical programming formulations for starting portfolios. The manager would want to resimulate the final portfolio to obtain a detailed distribution of returns and outcomes.

As an example, there may have been a general decision made by the firm about the type of projects that are to be reviewed; the joint simulation is then completed. These variance-covariance data are inserted into the interactive model and the executive faces a computer terminal, provided with information such as shown in Exhibit 16.3. In this program, the executive has a number of filtering options available:

1.   The program may be used to determine **portfolio data**. It presents the capital outlay and the results on any of the criteria for any combination of projects legally allowed. The program would include interest cost for any debt used.

2.   *Confidence levels* (based on the assumption of a normal distribution for the specific criterion of interest) may be printed for the portfolios chosen by the executive. These confidence intervals are derived by using the standard deviations of the portfolio to compute 25%/75%, 10%/90%, 5%/95%, and 1%/99% ranges for the criteria required by the executive.

3.   *Comparison options* permit the executive to study the effectiveness of the proposed portfolio vis-à-vis the current operation in meeting various goals for future years. Based upon statistical compilations in the program, the executive could view the probability that earnings per share in the second year would be no less under the proposed portfolio than expected second-year earnings per share of the existing firm alone. These probabilities are explicitly presented for each of the ten criteria.

4.   *Portfolio-project comparisons* allow the executive to view how the proposed portfolio would be altered on each of the ten criteria by adding or deleting a particular project. The comparison indicates the amount by which the expected values and standard deviations of the portfolio would be changed by the addition or deletion of a project.

5.   *Mean search routines* permit the executive to seek altered values from the expected outcome of the portfolio on any criterion. When using this option, the manager may indicate the criterion and the number of proposals desired (N). The program will return the N projects with the greatest effect in increasing or decreasing the expected value under consideration. The program would review all projects, those currently in the proposed portfolio, or those currently out of the proposed portfolio, as requested. The manager's specification will depend upon whether the desire is to eliminate from the portfolio projects which have an unfavorable impact on a criterion (for example, a binding budget constraint and low earnings per share in the first year) or to add projects which would increase an outcome (for example, projects to boost sales in the second year).

6.   *Variance search routines* require the manager to input the same information as under the mean search routine. The program searches for those projects in and/or out of the current portfolio which must increase or decrease the variance on a given criterion.

EXHIBIT 16.3 Sample Questions on Interactive Computer Models Used to Select Portfolios of Projects

WHEN THE COMPUTER TYPES-OPTION?-PLEASE ANSWER WITH ONE OF THE RESPONSES
SHOWN BELOW

OPTION   DESCRIPTION

≡ ≡ ≡   ≡

Option	Description
NP	STARTS A NEW PORTFOLIO
PC	PORTFOLIO CONTENTS
EC	LIST PROJECT ENTRY COSTS
IP	LIST ILLEGAL PROJECT COMBINATIONS
A	ADD A NEW PROJECT TO YOUR PORTFOLIO
D	DELETE A PROJECT FROM YOUR PORTFOLIO
P	PORTFOLIO STATISTICS
SP	SHORT PORTFOLIO OUTPUT
C	COMBINE PROJECTS
MR	RANK PROJECTS BY MEAN VALUES
VR	RANK PROJECTS BY VARIABILITY (STD. DEV.)
END	STOPS PROGRAM

WHEN THE COMPUTER TYPES-CRITERION?-PLEASE ANSWER WITH ONE RESPONSE
SHOWN BELOW

CRITERION   DESCRIPTION

≡ ≡ ≡   ≡

Criterion	Description
S1	SALES IN YEAR 1
S2	SALES IN YEAR 2
S3	SALES IN YEAR 3
CF1	CASH FLOW IN YEAR 1
CF2	CASH FLOW IN YEAR 2
CF3	CASH FLOW IN YEAR 3
EPS1	EARNINGS PER SHARE IN YEAR 1
EPS2	EARNINGS PER SHARE IN YEAR 2
EPS3	EARNINGS PER SHARE IN YEAR 3
NPV	NET PRESENT VALUE

Naturally, it is not required to use these goals. The manager might favor these goals plus an average growth in earnings per share for the next 5 to 10 years, or plus a certain percentage of sales and earnings from major regions of the world or from major product lines.

Multiperiod decisions when the future portfolio opportunities are not known compound the problem. One option is to build in probable funds requirements and returns for future projects, penalizing the projects under current review if they do not generate sufficient cash flows in particular future periods. In addition, only by earmarking particular debt sources for unique opportunities can the viability of special financing options applicable only to given projects be included in such a model. The benefits of pooled resources providing better debt rates than the simple sum of the individual projects can be taken into account with the subsequent resimulation of the desirable portfolio after use of the interactive model.[6]

IMPLICATIONS OF A WORLD-MARKET PORTFOLIO FOR PROJECT EVALUATION

An alternative to evaluating the covariance between projects to obtain a portfolio that meets a suitable risk-return profile for the corporation is to obtain the discount rate appropriate for specific projects with given risk characteristics. This is the approach we followed in our discussion of the cost of capital as an investment hurdle rate. However, at that time we concentrated on the total risk of the firm and discussed only briefly the issue of possible security diversification by stockholders who can invest in a market portfolio and a risk-free asset. The ability of stockholders to diversify their investments reduces the total risk these individuals see in specific companies. When this fact is taken into account, the discount rate that the firm uses as an acceptance criterion must be modified accordingly. One model that incorporates these concepts is the *capital asset pricing model* (CAPM).

The prescriptions of the CAPM are based on the conclusion that, optimally, the investor will purchase combinations of the market portfolio and the risk-free asset. The line connecting these possible combinations is called the *market line*. This market line, shown in Exhibit 16.1, provides the tradeoffs between risk and return available to the investor.[7]

Briefly, the CAPM suggests that the relevant discount rate for a project is based on the covariance between that project and the *market portfolio*, which in our context would be a world-market portfolio (that is, some well-diversified, efficient portfolio that holds corporate project portfolios from around the world). This covariance is combined with estimates of the expected *market return* and the return from a *risk-free asset* to determine the required return for the project.

Given forecasts of the world-market return and variability, the risk-free rate, and the various projects' returns under different market

---

[6]These issues are discussed in detail in E. E. Carter, *Portfolio Aspects of Corporate Capital Budgeting.* (Lexington, Mass.: D. C. Heath and Company, 1974), Chapter 8.

[7]If one does not believe that the capital markets are efficient, then the market line traced as a ray from the risk-free rate will not necessarily be tangent at the market portfolio but would be tangent at some other point. However, the strategy outlined here is still open to a naive security or project investor: The investment is split between some broad market investment and a risk-free security.

outcomes, then the minimum required rate of return can be determined. If the project returns more than this minimum, it is a desirable investment.

Although derived from slightly different precepts, the capital asset pricing model approach parallels the beta analysis used in modern security portfolio selection. This analysis says that one can compare the return of a security (R_E) to the risk-free return (R_F) and the market return (R_M) through the following formulation:

$$(R_E - R_F) = \alpha + \beta(R_M - R_F)$$

Beta (β) is the measure of the volatility of the security or portfolio (that is, mutual fund) with respect to the market return. Beta is the covariance of the security with the market divided by the variance of the market return (σ_{EM}/σ_M^2). Alpha (α) is a measure of any excess return for the security above what is required, given its volatility. A negative value of alpha implies that the return of the security over the periods evaluated was not sufficient to compensate investors for its volatility.

For *project* evaluations, alpha is removed and one rearranges terms to solve for R_E, the required return on equity in the project. This gives the result that

$$R_E = \beta(R_M - R_F) + R_F \tag{1}$$

or, since $\beta = \dfrac{\sigma_{EM}}{\sigma_M^2}$,

$$R_E = \frac{\sigma_{EM}}{\sigma_M^2}(R_M - R_F) + R_F$$

$$= R_F\left(1 - \frac{\sigma_{EM}}{\sigma_M^2}\right) + R_M\frac{\sigma_{EM}}{\sigma_M^2}$$

The higher the covariance between the given security and the market portfolio, the higher the required return. At the extreme, a project which moves with the market does not contribute anything to the diversification of this market. The risk of such a project is equal to the market's risk, the so-called *systematic risk* which cannot be diversified. On the other hand, a project with very low covariance with the market portfolio will be required to yield a lower return because of its contribution to the diversification of the total portfolio. This type of risk is called *unsystematic risk*.

To determine the minimum rate of return acceptable in a project we follow the approach suggested earlier in the discussion of the cost of capital. The cost of equity, computed as shown in equation (1), is combined with the cost of debt in the proportions of debt (D) and equity (E) used in the capital structure adequate for the project as follows:

$$R_{\text{Project}} = R_E\left(\frac{E}{D + E}\right) + R_D\left(\frac{D}{D + E}\right)$$

where R_E is found using the covariance of the project and the market and an estimated beta.

Even if beta can be estimated from similar projects or the returns of similar firms in the market, if there is any leverage the observed beta will not be the same as the beta for a firm or project with different leverage. Then the manager must decide how to compute a cost of capital for a project with leverage which differs from the standard.

One approach is to compute first the beta for the equity in a no-debt project (β_E). Suppose that one uses the Modigliani-Miller argument that the only increase in value for a levered firm comes from the tax deductibility of debt interest. The value of this tax shield can be subtracted from the total market value of the levered firm's debt and equity, or the similar firm which represents the proposed project. In the case of perpetual debt, the cumulative value of the tax savings from the debt interest is the tax rate, T, of the firm times the value of the debt, D.

In other cases the present value of all the future interest payments after tax discounted at the pretax debt rate must be computed directly. These calculations provide the value of the firm under 100% equity financing once the increment in observed market value derived from the tax deductibility of interest is eliminated. Using historical data for the existing firm or project (or comparable firms), one could obtain data on the return in total value for the firm in each period.

For example, if the value, V, is the sum of equity and debt, and it is also equal to the value under all equity, V_A, plus the tax savings of perpetual debt (TD) by assumption, then the value of the all-equity firm is equal to the observed equity value plus $(1-T)D$, or

$$V = E + D = V_A + TD$$
$$V_A = E + (1 - T)D$$

The return in each period for the all-equity firm is the change in this total value plus the income, which is the dividend (Div) and interest income (C), divided by beginning value, or

$$\frac{V_{A_{t+1}}}{V_{A_t}} = \frac{E_{t+1} + Div + C + (1 - T)D_{t+1}}{E_t + (1 - T)D_t}$$

If this valuation is completed for each historical or hypothetical future period, its volatility can be evaluated in the capital asset pricing model shown in equation (1). This analysis provides the estimate of β_E, for by definition the value of the all-equity firm and its volatility coincide with the value of the equity and the volatility of TD. In other cases the present value of all the future interest payments after tax discounted at the pretax debt rate must be computed directly. These calculations provide the value of the firm under 100% equity.[8]

Again, assume the perpetual debt case and the Modigliani-Miller conclusion that the increment in value from leverage arises only from the tax deductibility of interest. Then the cost of capital, R_p, will be the cost of equity with no debt (using β_E, R_M, and R_F from the earlier estimates) times the product of one minus the tax rate times the proportion of debt in the firm or project:

$$R_P = [\beta_E(R_M - R_F) + R_F]\left[1 - (\text{Tax rate})\left(\frac{\text{Additional debt}}{\text{Value of no-debt project}}\right)\right]$$

This calculation assumes that the cost of debt, R_D, is the same as R_F and that there is perpetual debt. It also ignores the effect of bankruptcy on the value of the firm (that is, the value will increase up to 99% debt), but the assumption may not be unreasonable for acceptable levels of debt, especially if assets can be sold in bankruptcy at their market value. Also ignored is the common situation in which the bankruptcy of the firm depends on the total risk of all projects, not just one project. The usual assumptions of the CAPM (homogeneous expectations, no transaction costs, perfectly divisible securities, no taxes, fixed quantities of all assets, a sufficiently large number of investors so that all are price-takers, and no cost of information which is fully and immediately available to all investors) are sufficient for the one-period proofs to hold.

These assumptions may be violated in international markets. For example, manipulation is a regular feature of many foreign stock markets for several reasons. First, accounting standards throughout the world are usually lower than in the United States, so that data are not available or are not believable. Rumors can be started with little to refute them. Second, low (if any) margin requirements permit a small

---

[8]Alternatively, one can estimate β_E from the observed βs of the levered firm if leverage was constant for the entire period. In this case, the direct estimate of β_E is $\beta_E = \beta/[1 + (1 - T)D/E]$. See Mark E. Rubenstein, "A Mean-Variance Synthesis of Corporate Financial Theory," *Journal of Finance*, Mar. 1973, pp. 167–81.

amount of money to be leveraged by an operator. Finally, the size of the float of securities as well as the smaller size of many companies means that a small amount of money can move a large proportion of the company's average daily stock volume, permitting highly volatile price changes whose benefits accrue largely to the manipulators.[9]

The theoretical impact of this model is substantial. However, the determination of reasonable forecasts for the market return and the risk-free return in the future makes it difficult to apply in practical situations. Whatever the estimation problems in the risk-free return evaluation, the biggest question is: What is the market return? When it is in the international setting, is it the return in the home country's security market? If this figure is used as the estimate of the future market return, then the links between variability in that market return to future years and the equity returns of the projects under review must be determined when the appropriate debt load for the project is included.

The portfolio simulation approach outlined earlier produces covariances as a by-product of the individual project simulations in the portfolio process. These covariance estimates refer only to the projects that the firm is contemplating. It can be argued that, in most cases, these projects constitute only a subset of all the projects included in the market portfolio to which the investor has access. In this case the total risk of a portfolio of projects, although it makes allowance for covariances, would still contain a portion of risk which the investor could diversify away by investing in the market portfolio. However, to the extent that the corporation has access to special projects which are not available in the market portfolio, the analysis of the total risk of the special portfolio contributes new insights. Some of the risk of these special projects may be correlated with the market portfolio, but the remainder constitutes a unique source of diversification that only the specific corporation can contribute. Finally, the simulation approach makes it possible to incorporate into the analysis multiple goals (other than variance in returns) which management may believe relevant.

In practice, both types of analyses—the simulation approach and the CAPM framework—can complement one another.

---

[9]For example, see William M. Carley, "Foreign Stock Markets Often Do Very Little to Curb Manipulation," *Wall Street Journal*, Oct. 6, 1976, pp. 1ff.

A more colorful account of divergences in international security standards may be seen in "Investing in Japan: They Do Things Differently There" (*Economist*, Oct. 3, 1981, pp. 75–77). As an executive from a securities firm commented to the interviewer, "Anywhere else in the world I would have been put in prison for half of what I was doing 10 years ago. Things must be getting tighter here: today it's only a third." Other remarks in the article suggest that securities houses are routinely expected to drive up a firm's share price just prior to an equity offering, permitting the firm to raise more money. In addition, thugs regularly receive protection money from corporations in order to avoid disrupting the firm's annual meetings.

SUMMARY

This chapter reviewed the basic concepts of financial diversification, drawing upon the theoretical and empirical work carried out with regard to the U.S. equity markets over the last 30 years. From the original work by Markowitz, we sketched the evolution of additional measures for risk, moving from a security to a market context. We emphasized that risk and return must be related in terms of the selection of any optimum portfolio of investments ex ante.

In the international sense, multinational firms may be able to overcome some of the elements of the world economy which could lead to inefficient markets and market failure. Thus, for example, the multinational firms may have superior information or greater access to international capital markets, which make them efficient diversifiers for individual investors throughout the world, although there is a cost to management of large organizations. We suggested that portfolios may be created using the capital asset pricing framework, various interactive program concepts on a computer system, or involving optimization schemes from mathematical programming. In any case, we showed how a project's cost of equity can be adjusted for various degrees of proposed leverage, given historic market price observations of equity returns and a historic debt-to-equity ratio.

Appendix 1 to the chapter discusses the elements of U.S. antitrust policy affecting U.S. multinationals and notes various attempts to create global standards. Appendix 2 summarizes some of the literature on international security returns and risk.

1

Antitrust Legislation: Strategy and Stricture

ONE IMPORTANT FACTOR affecting the decision to invest in domestic markets or in foreign lands is antitrust legislation. The United States has played a leading role in the development and enforcement of this type of legislation. However, in recent years other nations and international agencies appear to be generating similar concerns.

Although antitrust case law evolves over time, in the United States after World War II a series of decisions and consent decrees left American business restricted in the manner of investing abroad. The Department of Justice sought to prohibit actions by American firms abroad through joint ventures or wholly-owned subsidiaries that would operate to the detriment of competition in the American market.

Cartels were a major target of the antitrust division of the Department of Justice. Although legitimate controls on patents and trademarks were allowed, joint venture agreements that restricted the ability of company A's subsidiary, company B (owned in conjunction with another subsidiary or an independent firm), to compete in company A's home territory were prohibited, as were restrictions on company B's selling in territories of other company A's subsidiaries. Company A might *restrict* company B's uses of patents or trademarks, but could not prohibit company B's *sales* activities.

Sometimes firms argued that the operations were part of the same large company, and there was no prohibition against divisional coordination in a corporation. In the American Timkin case, common control, patents, and policies did not change the fact that the subsidiaries had minority owners and legally were separate corporations subject to American restrictions on their activities.

Alcoa is famous in American antitrust law for both the domestic and the international aspects of the case. Essentially, Alcoa had a near monopoly of the American aluminum market, and a successful case of the antitrust division won a decision. The final judgment by Judge Learned Hand in district court (caused by the disqualification of too many Supreme Court justices because of prior interests) made clear that even if Alcoa had behaved in a simple competitive spirit and had not sought dominance, a monopoly per se was evil and could be broken up. (Judge Hand made clear that Alcoa was not so pure of spirit.) After the war, government aluminum plants were sold to other firms so that Alcoa's market dominance was reduced. Aluminum Limited of Canada was owned by many of the same shareholders, largely the Mellon and Davis families. Aluminium Limited made agreements with European firms to restrict imports to the United States. The firm had business headquarters in New York and its shareholders were mainly U.S. citizens. Judge Hand stressed that Aluminium Limited was guilty under U.S. antitrust law and declared that *any* corporation *anywhere substantially* affecting U.S. commerce could be challenged. In 1950 the Alcoa shareholders had to give up their ownership in one of the two companies.

Other firms were attacked for activities that the firm's managers argued were in pursuit of the 1918 Webb-Pomerene Law, which allowed U.S. exporters jointly to sell abroad. Many firms invested abroad under this law and argued that they were protected from antitrust prosecution. This argument was generally rejected.

Judge Wyzanski, in the Minnesota Mining case of 1950, found the firm guilty of antitrust violations, even though the firm argued that nationalistic feeling, exchange rate issues, exchange controls, and the like had caused the firm to sell in third country markets its British-subsidiary produced goods rather than American goods. In essence, Judge Wyzanski argued that the greater profitability of British production for the third market was no defense since the market could have been served at a profit from the United States. He implied that *branches* were acceptable but that separate corporations were vulnerable for restraints on activities completely outside the United States if those activities could rebound to American commerce.

Wilkins (1974) argues that in the long run, this period of strict antitrust enforcement probably helped American business, for firms were less willing to become involved in joint ventures with Americans or with Europeans who themselves had no interest in appearing in U.S.

courtrooms.[1] Accordingly, the American firms were more wary about going abroad. When they did go abroad, they approached it on their own and with determination. The American firms certainly learned that cartel-inducing agreements had to be avoided.

There are also concerns about antitrust enforcement by other nations. For example, the European Economic Community (EEC) under Articles 85 and 86 of the Treaty of Rome has restrictions on corporate practices and anticompetitive strictures that relate to the United States Sherman Act, Clayton Act, and Federal Trade Commission Act. However, several aspects of the Articles limit impact on the European firms:

1. Enterprises are broadly defined. In contrast to some of the U.S. cases noted above, European antitrust enforcement does not apply to practices between wholly-owned subsidiaries or between officers of the same company.

2. Only activities involving more than one nation are regulated. Although nominally U.S. antitrust activity applies to antitrust violations in interstate commerce, the U.S. Acts have broad impact; thus, the Clayton Act deals with acquisitions in "any line of commerce in any section of the country." Furthermore, officials can cite the impact of intrastate commerce upon interstate commerce.

3. Exemptions for "good" cartels are permitted upon application to the EEC Commission or upon qualification under one or more blanket agreements provided in the interests of rationalizing certain industries. Such encouragement toward cartelization is based upon a need for the smaller EEC companies in certain industries to reach certain minimum size in order for economies of scale to permit more effective competition with large corporations outside the EEC.

4. Small agreements or mergers are generally ignored completely. The U.S. Antitrust Division for its own efficiency will often ignore smaller cases, but they are still violations of the law and will be prosecuted as such on occasion.

5. Mergers themselves have rarely been challenged. The one case pursued by the EEC Commission involved Continental Can. The decision affirmed the right to challenge mergers, but it did not support the charge of monopolization. Some years ago the Commission circulated a proposal regarding prior notification of any merger (including joint ventures) between firms whose combined sales exceed $1 billion. The proposal has never been acted upon.[2]

---

[1]Mira Wilkins, *The Maturing of Multinational Enterprise: American Business Abroad from 1914 to 1970.* (Cambridge, Mass.: Harvard University Press, 1974), pp. 295–300.

[2]A lucid summary of many of the similarities and contrasts in U.S. and EEC antitrust law is given in Robert T. Jones, "Executive's Guide to Antitrust in Europe," *Harvard Business Review,* May–June 1976, pp. 106–18.

2

Empirical Research on Internationally Diversified Portfolios

THERE ARE VARIOUS articles reviewing the effects of diversification using international security and bond portfolios. Building on the basic Markowitz and Tobin framework, Grubel[1] showed the effects of diversification using market indices in eleven countries, arguing that U.S. investors could gain from such international diversification. Then, using indices of stock market performance for twenty-eight countries, Levy and Sarnat[2] evaluated the benefits of diversification across national borders using data from the 1951–1967 period. They found that investments in the U.S. and Japanese stocks would have been 50%–70% of optimal portfolios, largely because of the negative correlations during this period between the stock market indices in these two lands. Predictably, because of the high positive correlation of Western European countries and the U.S. stock market performance in the same period, investment in the securities of the European nations was small. Investments in developing countries were usually recommended in the final portfolio because of diversification effects, even though the standard deviation of investment returns in underdeveloped countries' securities was often very large.

Using ten nations and an evaluation of the arithmetic average of yields on long-term government bonds in those countries, Miller and

---

[1]Herbert G. Grubel, "Internationally Diversified Portfolios: Welfare Gains and Capital Flows," *American Economic Review*, Dec. 1968, pp. 1299–1314.

[2]Haim Levy and Marshall Sarnat, "International Diversification of Investment Portfolios," *American Economic Review*, Sept. 1970, pp. 668–75.

Whitman[3] similarly considered the benefits of diversification, although they ignored covariances between the returns on European and American securities. The separation theorem implies that choice between risky and riskless assets can be made independently, *not* that choices among two segregated portfolios of risky assets can be made independently, the pattern followed by Miller and Whitman.

Evaluating weekly, 1-month, and 2-month rates of return of industry subindices for securities traded in the United States, the United Kingdom, and West Germany from January 1, 1965, to June 30, 1967, Grubel and Fadner[4] found that positive correlation among various pairs of assets was an increasing function of holding period (implying that random short-run effects may cause lower correlations in those periods) but that average correlation levels were still greater for within-country comparisons than for between-country comparisons. For the period in which they evaluated the securities, they acknowledged that the currencies' exchange rates were stable. The instability of the more recent years might create even less correlation of between-country industry index comparisons, suggesting even greater benefits from the intercountry portfolio diversification, given that lower correlation improves the portfolio in a risk-return sense for a constant expected return.

Agmon[5] argues for a weak support of the one-market approach to the world security markets, although the author cautiously notes that his results are not inconsistent with a segmented market. A one-market view holds that arbitrage between national security markets is sufficient to create an equilibrium. Although the Agmon study has been criticized for having results that were not inconsistent with the segmented market hypothesis (which the author acknowledged) and for other statistical difficulties, the remaining problem which seems to plague most of the international studies is that the results obtained are not sufficient to prove or to disprove any case; they can be consistent with a number of different hypotheses about the structure of the international capital markets and their risk interdependence or risk independence.[6]

---

[3]Norman C. Miller and Marina v. N. Whitman, "A Mean-Variance Analysis of United States Long-Term Portfolio Foreign Investment," *Quarterly Journal of Economics*, May 1970, pp. 175–96.

[4]Herbert G. Grubel and Kenneth Fadner, "The Interdependence of International Equity Markets," *Journal of Finance*, Mar. 1971, pp. 89–94.

[5]Tamir Agmon, "The Relations among Equity Markets: A Study of Share Price Comovements in the United States, United Kingdom, Germany, and Japan," *Journal of Finance*, Sept. 1972, pp. 839–55.

[6]For a criticism of the Agmon paper, see Michael Adler and R. Hoersch, "The Relationship among Equity Markets: Comment," *Journal of Finance*, Sept. 1974, pp. 1311–17. Then see Bruno Solnik's further efforts in this regard ("The International Pricing of Risk: An Empirical Investigation of the World Capital Market Structures," *Journal of Finance*, May 1974, pp. 365–78) and the resulting criticism by Buckner Wallingford ("Discussion: The International Pricing of Risk," *Journal of Finance*, May 1974, pp. 392–95). Solnik notes the impact of the various national markets, but he argues that his results are consistent with an international capital asset pricing model which takes into account both national and international portfolios; see his "An International Market Model of Security Price Behavior," *Journal of Financial and Quantitative Analysis*, Sept. 1974, pp. 537–54.

Lessard presents results for sixteen major countries' market returns for recent years using monthly data of various periods.[7] The results are consistent with either segmented or integrated world markets. From his careful work, he concludes that U.S. investors lost little if they were not diversified across many countries because the U.S. market is such a large percentage of any world market measure. In the absence of severe barriers to international investment, most other investors, except for Canadians, endured greater risks for a given return ex post if they constrained themselves to a domestic portfolio rather than investing in a fully diversified world portfolio. In an equally-weighted-by-country world market index, a relatively low proportion of domestic variance in a national market index was explained by a world market factor. Individual *securities* typically had more of their variance explained by country factors than by industry elements using an equally weighted market index. Applying cluster analysis to weekly stock market indices data for twelve countries from 1963 to 1972, Panton, Lessig, and Joy found that these indices have substantial comovement and that the comovements persist over time.[8]

There are other problems with most of these studies. The first criticism is that a national index of security prices may not be an efficient portfolio from the standard risk return model of Tobin and Markowitz, although it may approach it. Second, the national index is only one portfolio, not the set of efficient (national) portfolios. Third, there is a question of whether inclusion of some of the securities of another nation would aid the diversification more than inclusion of the whole portfolio (that is, the index) of another nation's security universe. Fourth, any evaluation of portfolio diversification in terms of the random walk hypothesis must reckon with Solnik[9] and McDonald.[10] Among others, these authors note imperfections in the European stock market price behavior when analyzed on the same basis as the U.S. studies of the random walk model. Fifth, Solnik cogently argues that the nature of the available data and the quality of the tests that have been used are not sufficient to determine whether markets are completely segmented or integrated;[11] contrary to the Panton et al. study,

[7]Donald Lessard, "World, Country, and Industry Relationships in Equity Returns: Implications for Risk Reduction through International Diversification," *Financial Analysts Journal*, Jan.-Feb. 1976, pp. 32–38.

[8]Don B. Panton, V. Parker Lessig, and Maurice Joy, "Comovement of International Equity Markets: A Taxonomic Approach," *Journal of Financial and Quantitative Analysis*, Sept. 1976, pp. 415–32.

[9]Bruno Solnik, *European Capital Markets* (Lexington, Mass.: D.C. Heath/Lexington Books, 1973).

[10]John G. McDonald, "French Mutual Fund Performance: Evaluation of Internationally Diversified Portfolios," *Journal of Finance*, Dec. 1973, pp. 1161–80.

[11]Bruno Solnik, "Testing International Asset Pricing: Some Pessimistic Views," *Journal of Finance*, May 1977, pp. 503–12.

Solnik notes that there is often low covariance between national markets, which results in international benefits from diversification. Sixth, the question of what numeraire to use for the investor is unsettled; different currencies used as a standard, or different currency bundles, suggest very different conclusions about diversification of portfolios and the international pricing of securities in an efficient market view of the world.

QUESTIONS

1. What are the arguments for the existence of a corporation's ability to be an efficient diversifier? Do you believe the arguments?

2. Why does a joint simulation produce the covariances between projects?

3. Under what conditions is variance a bad measure of risk?

4. Why is the market line shown in Exhibit 16.1 linear? If the borrowing and lending rates were different, how would that change the analysis required for an investor's decision?

5. How can a firm obtain a reasonable estimate of the local cost of capital for a project? Why might a multinational corporation have an advantage over a local firm in terms of the cost of capital?

BIBLIOGRAPHY

Abrams, Richard K., and Donald V. Kimball, "U.S. Investment in Foreign Equity Markets," *Economic Review*, Federal Reserve Bank of Kansas City, Apr. 1981, pp. 17–30.

Adler, Michael, and R. Hoersch, "The Relationship among Equity Markets: Comment," *Journal of Finance*, Sept. 1974, pp. 1311–17.

Allan, Iain, "Return and Risk in International Capital Markets," *Columbia Journal of World Business*, Summer 1982, pp. 3–23.

Berstrom, Gary L., and Mark England-Markun, "International Country Selection Strategies," *Columbia Journal of World Business*, Summer 1982, pp. 42–45.

Brewer, H. L., "Investor Benefits from Corporate International Diversification," *Journal of Financial and Quantitative Analysis*, Mar. 1981, pp. 113–26.

Carter, E. Eugene, *Portfolio Aspects of Corporate Capital Budgeting*. Lexington, Mass.: D. C. Heath and Company, 1974.

Clark, Peter B., and Richard D. Hass, "The Portfolio Approach to Capital Movements: A Comment," *Journal of Political Economy*, May-June 1972, pp. 612–16.

Cohen, Kalman J., Walter L. Ness, Jr., Hitoshi Okuda, Robert A. Schwartz, and David K. Whitcomb, "The Determinants of Common Stock Returns Volatility: An International Comparison," *Journal of Finance*, May 1976 (Proceedings), pp. 733–51.

Gultekin, N. Bulent, "Stock Market Returns and Inflation: Evidence from Other Countries, *Journal of Finance*, March 1983, pp. 49–65.

Hilliard, Jimmy E., "The Relationship between Equity Indices on World Exchanges," *Journal of Finance*, Mar. 1979, pp. 103–14.

Hughes, John S., Dennis E. Logue, and Richard James Sweeney, "Corporate International Diversification and Market Assigned Measures of Risk and Diversification," *Journal of Financial and Quantitative Analysis*, Nov. 1975, pp. 617–37.

Ibbotson, Roger G., and Laurence B. Siegel, "The World Market Wealth Portfolio," *Journal of Portfolio Management*, Winter 1983, pp. 5–17.

Jones, Robert T., "Executives' Guide to Antitrust in Europe," *Harvard Business Review*, May-June 1976, pp. 106–18.

Kornbluth, Jonathan S. H., and Joseph D. Vinso, "Capital Structure and the Financing of the Multinational Corporation: A Fractional Multiobjective Approach," *Journal of Financial and Quantitative Analysis*, June 1982, pp. 147–78.

Lessard, Donald, "International Portfolio Diversification: A Multivariate Analysis for a Group of Latin American Countries," *Journal of Finance*, June 1973, pp. 619–33.

Maldonado, Rita, and Anthony Saunders, "International Portfolio Diversification and the Intertemporal Stability of International Stock Market Relationships, 1957–78," *Financial Management*, Autumn 1981, pp. 54–63.

Markowitz, Harry, *Portfolio Selection: Efficient Diversification of Investments.* New York: John Wiley and Sons, 1959.

Senchack, Andrew J., and William L. Beedles, "Is Indirect International Diversification Desirable?" *Journal of Portfolio Management*, Winter 1980, pp. 49–57.

Shawky, Hany A., and David A. Ricks, "Capital Budgeting for Multinational Firms: A Theoretical Analysis," *Southern Economic Journal*, Jan. 1981, pp. 703–13.

Shouse, Mary C., and Mary E. Martin Zellerbach, "The Theory and Price of International Index Funds," *Columbia Journal of World Business*, Summer 1982, pp. 46–52.

Solnik, Bruno, *European Capital Markets.* Lexington Mass.: D. C. Heath/Lexington Books, 1973.

Solnik, Bruno, and Bernard Noetzlin, "Optimal International Asset Allocation," *Journal of Portfolio Management*, Fall 1982, pp. 11–21.

Stehle, Richard, "An Empirical Test of the Alternative Hypotheses of National and International Pricing of Risky Assets," *Journal of Finance*, May 1977, pp. 493–502.

Stulz, Rene M., "A Model of International Asset Pricing," *Journal of Financial Economics*, Sept. 1981, pp. 383–406.

———, "On the Effects of Barriers to International Investment," *Journal of Finance*, Sept. 1981, pp. 923–34.

Subrahmanyam, Marti G., "On the Optimality of International Capital Market Integration," *Journal of Financial Economics*, Mar. 1975, pp. 3–28.

Tennison, Debbie C., "Insider Trading on World's Exchanges Gets Closer Scrutiny by Many Countries," *Wall Street Journal*, May 17, 1982, p. 32.

Tobin, James, "Liquidity Preference as Behavior toward Risk," *Review of Economic Studies*, Feb. 1958, pp. 65–86.

van Agtmael, Antoine W., and Vihang R. Errunza, "Foreign Portfolio Investment in Emerging Securities Markets," *Columbia Journal of World Business*, Summer 1982, pp. 58–63.

VonFurstenberg, George M., "Incentives for International Currency Diversification by U.S. Financial Investors," *International Monetary Fund Staff Papers*, Sept. 1981, pp. 477–94.

THE SMYTHE POWER COMPANY

Founded by William Morgan Smythe in 1910, the Smythe Power Company was a diversified manufacturer of large power-generating equipment, from hydroelectric turbines to steam generators to small nuclear reactors. The firm also produced a wide range of electric, gasoline, and diesel motors for automobiles, trucks and construction equipment, and the consumer market. The firm had been profitable except for the period from 1935 to 1939, and had diversified widely in Western Europe in the 1950s and to Latin America and Africa in the 1960s. The diversification effort had resulted in manufacturing and distribution facilities in many countries, as well as full selling efforts of the complete product line of generating equipment throughout most of the world.

On January 1, 1984, Smythe officially began using a new financial system which had two main objectives:

1. To centralize all financing decisions in the treasury department
2. To charge each foreign operation with a cost of capital which reflected local conditions

The treasury department had been working for some time to centralize funds management for the foreign operations. For the domestic operations the management of short-term investments and borrowings was centralized at the company headquarters in Oklahoma. Extending this centralized system to apply to the foreign subsidiaries appeared only logical. However, under the earlier system, in which operating managers for the foreign subsidiaries were responsible for profits after financing charges and taxes, these managers had reacted somewhat negatively to most of the financing policies that treasury had tried to enforce.

As to the computation of the cost of capital of foreign subsidiaries, management thought that the returns obtained in different countries should reflect the financial conditions of the country and be comparable to what Smythe could obtain from other alternative investments. However, the company's internal reporting system in existence before 1984, to the extent that it recognized explicitly that there was a cost involved in using the parent company's funds, did so by using the same cost of capital for all the foreign operations.

CENTRALIZATION OF FINANCING DECISIONS

Under the system in existence before 1984, the general manager of each subsidiary was responsible for the majority of financial decisions, including short-term borrowings and investments, foreign exchange exposure management, and capital structure. Dividend policy was more influenced by the parent company. However, even in this case, the local manager still had substantial leverage on the final decision on when the funds were actually transferred.

For all intents and purposes the performance of specific subsidiaries was judged in terms of income after tax (IAT) figures measured in dollar terms, and after exchange gains and losses associated with the translation of financial statements. The IAT figure was adjusted further to reflect the cost to the subsidiary of using the parent company's funds—a cost which was measured by the amount of total assets in the subsidiary and the cost of capital of the parent company in the United States. However, the focus for the evaluation of the performance of subsidiaries remained at the IAT level.

Under that system, decisions which led to higher IAT figures unfortunately were not always those which were the best for the company as a whole. For example, that system provided little incentive for local subsidiaries to pay dividends to the parent. If profits were paid out in the form of dividends, an alternative financing source had to be obtained. Funds had to be borrowed in the local markets to maintain the desired level of operations. But this financing source involved an expense (interest payments) which reduced the level of IAT. The use of internal funds did not affect IAT in that system.

Under the new system the treasury department would have major responsibility for the following: capital structure decisions, dividend policy, cash management, debt management, bank relations, foreign currency translation exposure, and foreign currency transaction exposure related to borrowings. The transfer of these responsibilities from general management to treasury was not as drastic as it first appeared. Every region in the world already had its own treasurer in the Smythe organization, and many countries also had a treasurer. These treasurers were to continue to report administratively to the managers of the region and good communication between general management and treasury was expected.

The treasury department already had centralized control of the management of the subsidiaries' accounts receivable. This had been accomplished a couple of years earlier, and made it possible to maintain common credit policies for all subsidiaries and an aggregate credit limit for every customer.

Senior management thought that the centralization of financing decisions in treasury would make it easier to reach decisions which were optimal for Smythe as a whole, instead of optimal for specific subsidiaries and suboptimal for the company as a whole. At the operational level this centralization was expected to allow for more efficient cash management programs (as all the liquid resources in the company were managed as a pool) and greater leverage with banks (as borrowing needs were also pooled).

It was also anticipated that the transfer of financing decisions from general management to treasury would improve the efficiency of general operations. The centralization of financing decisions would free general managers' time, which could then be concentrated solely on what they were best equipped to handle—namely, operations.

The financial statements of subsidiaries were to be adjusted to reflect this transfer of responsibility for financing decisions. Exhibits P.1 and P.2 present financial statements for a foreign subsidiary prepared under the old and the new financial systems and show the adjustments that were to be made under the new system. In the balance sheet, $908 in the cash and marketable securities accounts is removed from total assets in the new system. (The adjustments in the liabilities and equity sections are explained subsequently with the computation of the subsidiary's investment.) In the income statement, the following items are removed from the traditional statement: interest income ($67), interest expense ($971), and *translation* exchange gains and losses ($112). (Foreign exchange gains and losses from *transactions* remain in the subsidiary's income statement.)

Under the new system the results of operations in foreign subsidiaries would be measured substantially in the same manner as divisions of the parent company in the United States. Although managers of foreign operations were still responsible for IAT figures measured in U.S. dollars, under the new definition of IAT the effects of fluctuations in exchange rates on reported earnings were limited to the effects on sales and operating expenses. These effects were comparable to the concerns of domestic divisions involved in the export market. The effects of foreign exchange fluctuations on translation of the balance sheet were excluded from IAT.

As we will show in the next section, exchange considerations were reflected more or less indirectly in the computation of the local cost of capital; however, because of the fashion in which these computations were applied, foreign subsidiaries were now much more in-

EXHIBIT P.1 The Smythe Power Company: Subsidiary's Balance Sheet—Old and New Systems Compared

	OLD SYSTEM			NEW SYSTEM (In U.S. Dollars)	
	In Local Currency	Average Translation Rate	In U.S. Dollars	Adjustments	Total
Assets					
Cash and marketable securities	45,419	LC50.02/$	908	(908)	—
Receivables	207,479	49.99	4,150		4,150
Inventories	229,631	50.00	4,593		4,593
Progress billings	(169,279)	49.99	(3,386)		(3,386)
Other	15,010	50.03	300		300
Total current assets	328,260		6,565	(908)	5,657
Net Fixed Assets	98,930	13.92	7,107		7,107
Investments in affiliates	22,254	16.06	1,386		1,386
Total assets	449,444		15,058	(908)	14,150
Liabilities & Equity					
Current liabilities					
Excluding short-term debt	273,757	50.00	5,475		5,475
Financial investments					
Short- and long-term debt	112,345	50.00	2,247	(2,247)	—
Equity	63,342	8.63	7,336	1,339[a]	8,675[b]
Total financial investments	175,687		9,583	(908)	8,675
Total liabilities and equity	449,444		15,058	(908)	14,150

[a]Short-term and long-term debt of $2,247, less cash of $908.

[b]This is the dollar equivalent of the investment measured in local currency, LC130,268. In local currency, investment is equal to equity (LC63,342), plus short-term and long-term debt (LC112,345), less cash and marketable securities (LC45,419).

EXHIBIT P.2 The Smythe Power Company: Subsidiary's Income Statement—Old and New Systems Compared

	OLD SYSTEM			NEW SYSTEM (In U.S. Dollars)	
	In Local Currency	Average Translation Rate	In U.S. Dollars	Adjustments	Total
Net sales	548,892	LC69.44/$	7,904		7,904
Direct cost	266,992	69.46	3,844		3,844
Margin	281,900		4,060		4,060
Operating expenses	145,047	69.43	2,089		2,089
Depreciation	3,010	13.20	228		228
Operating profit	133,843		1,743		1,743
Interest income	4,623	69.00	67	(67)	—
Interest expense	(67,407)	69.42	(971)	971	—
Foreign exchange gains and losses					
Transaction	(15,708)	69.50	(226)	—	(226)
Translation			112	(112)	—
Income before taxes	55,351		725	792	1,517
Taxes	12,846		185	270	455
Income after taxes (IAT)	42,505		540	522	1,062
Capital charge: LC75,376, equal to 67.3% of average investment of LC112,000, translated at average exchange rate of LC69.45/$[a]				1,085	
Income after capital charge (IACC)					(23)

[a]Average investment is based on an investment of LC93,732 at the beginning of the period, and LC130,268 at the end of the period. See Exhibit P.1.

sulated from the short-term instability which had characterized the exchange markets in recent years.

CHARGE FOR LOCAL COST OF CAPITAL

Although interest income and expenses were now to be excluded from IAT, the IAT figures were to be adjusted by a charge for the use of capital. This adjustment generated what was called income after capital charge (IACC). This capital charge had two components: (1) the amount of investment in the subsidiary, and (2) the estimated local cost of capital.

Measuring Investment

The amount of investment in a foreign subsidiary was to be measured in terms of variables directly under the control of general management, excluding the financial variables for which treasury now had responsibility. Thus, investment was measured basically as the sum of debt (other than trade payables) plus the equity account in the balance sheet. Alternatively, investment could be measured as total assets in the balance sheet minus cash and minus trade payables.

As an illustration, in Exhibit P.1 the amount of investment in the subsidiary under the new system is LC130,268, equivalent to $8,675. In local currency, the amount of investment equals total assets of LC449,444, less cash of LC45,419, and less current liabilities other than short-term debt of LC273,757. One could arrive at the same figure for the amount of investment by adding book equity (LC63,342) to short-term and long-term debt (LC112,345) and subtracting cash (LC45,419). The amount of investment expressed in dollars, $8,675,is obtained following the same procedure, but using the various items after *each one* is translated into dollars at its specific translation exchange rate.

For any given period, the amount of investment used as the basis for the capital charge was an average of the amount of investment at the beginning and at the end of the period. At the bottom of Exhibit P.2, the investment base for the capital charge (LC112,000) is computed as the average of the investment calculated for the end of the period (LC130,268) and the figure given for the beginning of the period (LC93,732).

The cost of capital figure was applied first to the average investment figure expressed in local currency. Thus, in Exhibit P.2, the cost of capital of 67.3% is applied first to the average investment figure of LC112,000 to produce a charge of LC75,376. This figure is then translated into dollars at the average exchange rate for the period, LC69.45/$ in this case, to produce a final charge of $1,085.

Measuring Cost of Capital

The measure of local cost of capital was designed to reflect the fact that a good return in local currency should be very different for countries such as Argentina, on one hand, and Germany, on the other. Interest rates, exchange risk, inflation, and many of the other variables which determine financial return are very different from country to country, and different from the United States—the base used to compute cost of capital for all subsidiaries in the past.

More specifically, the local cost of capital was computed as follows:

A. *Local cost of debt* (k_d)

$$k_d = \text{Local cost of debt after taxes}$$

$$= \text{Local cost of debt } (1 - \text{tax rate})$$

where the local cost of debt would reflect the interest cost of debt expected for the following year in the particular country; in most countries this represented the cost for short-term debt. The tax rate reflected the statutory tax rate in the country, independently of the temporary tax status.

B. *Local cost of equity* (k_e)

$$k_e = \text{Smythe's expected return in the given country}$$

$$= \text{U.S. } k_e + (\text{Local inflation rate} - \text{U.S. inflation rate})$$

The cost of capital in the United States (U.S. k_e) was based on management's assessment of the return on equity necessary to generate the financial performance which a company like Smythe should produce for its stockholders.[1] The inflation rates were measured by the Consumer

---

[1]The cost of equity computed following this procedure fell within the range of figures obtained from more theoretical financial models such as the dividend yield-plus-growth models, or analysis of Smythe's systematic risk in the context of a capital asset pricing model framework.

Price Index, and were the rates expected to prevail in the year for which the cost of capital was being computed.

C. *Local cost of capital (k_o)*

$$k_0 = k_d \text{ (Percentage debt} + k_e \text{ (Percentage equity}$$
$$\text{in capital structure)} \qquad \text{in capital structure)}$$

where k_d and k_e were computed as discussed previously. The percentages of debt and equity in the capital structure in the given country were the values considered to be normal proportions of debt and equity in that country. In practice, most of the subsidiaries' capital structures were now close to these target figures. The use of the country as the focus for this computation followed the model used in the United States. The cost of capital charged to all of the parent's divisions in the United States was the same, regardless of their product line or type of activity.

As an illustration of the computation of the charge for local cost of capital, we can make the following assumptions:

- Expected local cost of debt: 100%
- Statutory local tax rate: 30%
- Expected U.S. cost of equity: 18.7%
- Expected local inflation rate: 107.9%
- Expected U.S. inflation rate: 11.7%
- Target percentage of debt in local capital structure: 50%
- Target percentage of equity in local capital structure: 50%

These figures represented expectations for the following year. Using the suggested formulation, we have:

$$k_d = 100(1 - 0.30) = 70 = 70\% \text{ p.a.}$$

$$k_e = 18.7 + (107.9 - 11.7) = 114.9 = 114.9\% \text{ p.a.}$$

$$k_0 = 70(0.50) + 114.9(0.50) = 92.45 = 92.45\% \text{ p.a.}$$

This cost of capital charge was to be applied throughout the year to the average investments of the subsidiary during the reporting period, which for internal purposes was 1 month. In cases, as in the example, where high local rates of inflation produced a very high local cost of capital figure, an adjustment had to be made to this figure before applying it to monthly statements. This adjustment scaled down the figure so that, after accounting for the effect of monthly compounding, at the end of the year it resulted in the cost of capital calculated on a per annum basis for that country. Thus, in Exhibit P.2, the cost of capital figure, adjusted for the effect of monthly compounding, is 67.3%.[2] This rate was applied to the average investment of the subsidiary during the period, LC112,000, and the resulting charge was translated into dollars at the average rate, as described earlier.

This new local cost of capital charged to each subsidiary was to be computed at budget time. The rate would not be altered throughout the year, regardless of the actual rates prevailing in the market and the actual sources of financing used.[3] Thus, although the cost of capital charge reflected differences in inflationary conditions and, therefore, exchange rate fluctuations in the local currency, the fashion in which the system was applied insulated the operating manager from fluctuations in these variables within the year.

Soon after the cost of capital figures began to be generated by treasury, the planning department at Smythe sought to use them to evaluate projects in different countries. For this use, however, the treasury department modified the numbers to reflect the appropriate time horizon.

The cost of capital just calculated had only a 1-year time horizon, which was considered to be appropriate for evaluating performance from year to year. However, for evaluating capital projects, a longer time horizon was used. Thus, for each country there were different cost of capital figures depending on the year in the future considered. The methodology for computing these numbers was the same as discussed in this section; however, the specific values for expected inflation differed with the particular year in the future. A manager wanting to evaluate the planned cash flows from a new project would discount the cash flows from each future year at a different rate.

---

[2] $0.673 = (\sqrt[12]{1.9245} - 1) \times 12$

[3] The actual figures for interest expense and interest income would appear in a special account for the treasury department. Analysis of this account would show any discrepancy between the estimates made for these figures and the actual ones. Treasury would also track other variables, such as translation exchange gains and losses, which affected the cost of capital. However, a complete reconciliation between the figures reported for financial accounting purposes and the cost of capital figures computed following the new methodology was conceptually impossible.

CHAPTER

17

Organizational Behavior, Business Strategy, and the Investment Decision

THROUGHOUT THIS WORK we have been given a specific project or group of projects to analyze and we have analyzed them primarily in terms of financial variables—particularly return and risk, as measured by the standard deviation of the expected return. However, the variables that generate these projects usually are not of a financial nature, at least directly. These other variables play an important role not only in determining which projects are actually brought up for financial analysis, but also they are often important determinants of the final decision.

Thus, before closing this work, we would like to put it in perspective by adding a brief discussion of two topics which are crucial and which provide the milieu in which the financial decisions analyzed in this text take place. One is the behavioral characteristics of the organizations that make the decisions of which projects to evaluate, which projects to accept, and which projects to reject. The other topic is the business strategy which any project must fit into and which often suggests those projects worthy of further analysis.

DECISION-MAKING IN A BUSINESS ORGANIZATION

One comprehensive structure developed to explain organizational decision-making is *A Behavioral Theory of the Firm* by Richard M.

Cyert and James G. March.[1] In their work, Cyert and March treat the
organization as a *coalition* of decision-making individuals. How these
individuals reach decisions within the organizational framework is
then described by relational concepts.

Elements in a Decision

Cyert and March find three major components in the decision
process: goals, expectations, and choice.

The *goals* in a decision are formed through formal and informal
bargaining among the participants, and these goals evolve through
time. A goal can be characterized by its dimension—the target of the
goal—and by its aspiration level—how far the goal is to be carried out.
The dimensions of the goal are highly influenced by the nature of the
changing membership in the coalition of individuals. For example,
the decision of a new president of General Motors (GM) to emphasize the production of small cars to offset the impact of imported
compacts shows the goal of offsetting foreign competition. The level of
aspiration may fluctuate from holding market share to eliminating foreign competition.

Expectations formed by the coalition members are a function of
the information gathered. Accordingly, changes in the system of sampling information, in the presentation of information to the firm, and in
the range of information available affect firm expectations. If the GM
president installed a new information system and received daily selling
data by model, instead of weekly reports 10 days after each week
ended, then the expectations of the firm (that is, its view of the automobile world) would probably be different at any given point in time
from what would otherwise be the case.

Cyert and March analyze *choice* as occurring in response to a
problem and affected by standard operating rules for coping with an
uncertain environment. They assume multiple and changing goals, and
the choice process is to obtain an "acceptable decision which meets
the minimum level for various goals." Thus, the GM president may
have seen a problem as "stop the erosion of GM world-market share by
foreign compacts." GM administration may have an alert system which
triggers the response—for example, any 10% decline in sales volume
maintained more than two quarters in a row. A general task force may
be assigned to review the situation and make recommendations (the
normal response to a volume decline). The recommendation may be for
a restyling of a certain body shell, even though all participants know
there may be other options that additional intensive study might reveal

---

[1]Richard M. Cyert and James G. March, *A Behavioral Theory of the Firm* (Englewood Cliffs,
N.J.: Prentice-Hall, Inc., 1963).

as a superior choice. However, this restyle recommendation is consistent with the time frame, certain cost structures, and no more than a certain level of production disruption.

Relational Concepts

There are four relational concepts which Cyert and March believe affect the decision framework:

1. *Quasi resolution of conflict* occurs because departmentalized rationality usually prevails over the single-mindedness of centralized decision-making. By having local rationality (in which subunits operate with subgoals), by using acceptable level-decision rules (minimum-or-better standards rather than maximization), and by the occurrence of sequential attention to goals at various tiers in the organization, potential conflict is reduced. Decisions are made to accommodate and to resolve disagreement among coalition members for the time being. In this approach, no formal or long-term conflict resolution is involved.

2. The *search* for problem solutions is influenced by the decision process in that search is motivated, simple-minded, and biased. A problem evokes a search process to find an acceptable-level solution. A solution is sought by seeking alternatives within the neighborhood of the problem itself and in the area of the most obvious alternative. If this procedure fails, the search process is broadened until an acceptable alternative is found.

3. *Organizational learning* is the process by which organizations adapt over time. Firms adapt in *goals* based on past performance, past expectations, and past performance of comparable organizations. There is adaptation in *attention rules*; coalition members learn to study parts of their environment and to ignore other information. Organizations adapt in *search rules*, for if a search is unsuccessful, the search rules themselves are altered until a solution is found.

4. *Uncertainty-avoidance* behavior is practiced by organizations that use short-run "fire-fighting techniques" to solve problems after they occur, rather than to anticipate them. Cyert and March argue that firms typically do not anticipate the future by seeking a maximum expected value or a minimum level of operations. Rather, they ignore the problem and focus on *short-run feedback* as a response to problems that develop. They seek a *negotiated environment* in which standard pricing policies for members of the industry, normal business practices, and other such phenomena allow the firm to reduce the uncertainty present in its competitive environment.

Capital Budgeting within the Organization

One can expand on the basic Cyert and March framework to see how it applies to the capital budgeting decision. We now report Carter's findings in this area.[2]

---

[2]E. Eugene Carter, "The Behavioral Theory of the Firm and Top-Level Corporate Decisions," *Administrative Science Quarterly*, December 1971, pp. 413–28.

Multiple Organizational Levels for Decisions. Within *A Behavioral Theory*, the emphasis upon unilevel or multilevel coalitions served to avoid a discussion of the influence that tiers of individuals have upon decision-making. For example, the final consensus is the result of highly filtered goals in which a participant received a somewhat ordered goal system from above, modified it according to his or her interests and biases, and transmitted it lower in the organization. *The requirement that decisions pass through many organizational levels itself influences the outcome of those decisions.* Whatever the goals of the board of GM, the interaction of engineers, marketeers, stylists, and so forth, will all affect the decision process as decisions move through the organization.

Bilateral Bargaining. Related to the multiple level consideration is the two-party (superior-subordinate) formation of expected project performance. The final expectations of the coalition are the result of *sequential* bargaining at *various levels* in the firm, rather than the result of a group consensus. The automobile engineer concedes a certain engine performance in the compact car in order to gain approval of the marketing department; together they recommend a particular model for production to the group vice-president for that automobile division.

Uncertainty and Goals. Goals found in a firm are related to the degree of uncertainty present in the firm's general environment and to the uncertainty present in a particular project's forecasts. In strategic decisions the firm may use a partial adjustment in goals to handle uncertainty. *The number of goals adjusts to accommodate the degree of uncertainty.* Thus, a simple goal of maximum rate of return may dominate a decision on which GM division would bring out a previously approved new model. On the other hand, a potential decision for GM to build a mass transit system in Seattle is likely to trigger many more issues as part of the discussion. How much does GM want to be in mass transit? What timetable is appropriate for this new venture? Will it detract from automotive and truck production?

Stimulus for Search. Many factors (in addition to a problem) generate search. Some of these stimuli might be:

1. The desire of an executive to meet a certain goal which is related to personal well-being.
2. A top executive's decision to have the firm enter a new area, even though profits and sales are satisfactory in the current field. For instance, if GM has an interest in mass transit, then the problem is less important than a general philosophy of management to diversify.
3. A change in managers. The new manager may have fundamentally different beliefs on what the firm should be doing.

4. Opportunity-oriented search. The fact that a business operates in certain economic, geographic, and industrial markets means that particular opportunities will occur. The nature of the business means that certain opportunities will come to management regardless of any search effort.

The Pollyanna-Nietzsche Effect. Managers may operate as if a *decision resolves all uncertainty* present in the data on which the decision was based. A "think-positive" mental attitude can be used to stimulate successful performance by the organizational participants. Thus, the new GM president could forget the uncertainty surrounding a task force's recommendation of a restyled model intended to lessen the foreign penetration of GM's world-market share. The president could act as if the project will stop these competitors.

Organizational Behavior in International Operations

From this discussion of *A Behavioral Theory of the Firm*, one can judge the impact of these concepts upon the international operations of the firm. For example, the impact of changes in the coalition members on the goals and choice process of the firm is important. England and Lee (1971) found that there were different priorities among Japanese, Korean, and American managers in the degree to which they pursued organizational harmony, growth versus earnings, and so on. The main maximization criteria for American managers were productivity, organizational efficiency, and profit maximization. For Japanese managers, the main criteria were productivity and organizational growth. Carter (1974) concluded that American managers were significantly less interested in cash flow as a decision criterion than European managers, but all managers tended to emphasize growth in earnings per share.[3] Thus, as the firm expands beyond its national borders, inclusion of other executives from different cultures will alter the decision criteria and the decision process.

Interviewing managers of eighty-seven firms in five countries across four industries, Stonehill et al. (1975) found that the main goal of corporate officers was to maximize corporate earnings in total (France, Japan, and the Netherlands) or on a per share basis (the United States). These authors suggested that national cultural factors and institutional restrictions (such as tax codes, lack of fully developed equity markets, restrictions on credit availability, income distribution, and accounting regulations) would continue to encourage managers'

---

[3]E. Eugene Carter, *Portfolio Aspects of Corporate Capital Budgeting* (Lexington, Mass.: D.C. Heath and Company, 1974), pp. 144–147.

concern with factors other than maximizing shareholders' wealth, the normative goal of most finance textbooks. Consistent with the Cyert and March concepts, the executives favored goals that enabled them to retain control and to have their enterprises prosper. These authors also found that the major determinant of debt ratios was financial risk (measured by fixed-charges coverage), rather than a national or industry factor of risk. This goal was only slightly more important than ensuring the availability of capital to the firm.

These factors diminish the impact of a financial evaluation based only on a rate of return criterion. These organizational realities are important and often have great effect on the type of projects evaluated and the standards applied. Financial evaluations are important for a final decision, for the financial results provide one basis for the decision. The arguments within the organization will be whether a project has a *reasonable* return, *given* the organizational and environmental constraints. The impact of organizational or behavioral characteristics of the firm on its standards and strategy is considerable. However, those organizational elements influence the nature of the financial evaluations; they do not negate them.

BUSINESS STRATEGY
AND THE INVESTMENT DECISION

Although this book emphasizes the *financial* considerations of investments, prior to such analysis must come resolution of the issue of the corporation's *strategy*. Also called the question of policy or corporate philosophy of operations, the topic concerns such issues as:

> "What is our primary expertise to be in 10 years?
>
> "Where do we want to operate by geographic region and by product line?"
>
> "Without changes in our operating policies and business lines, where will we be in 20 years?"

Thus, the heuristic the firm employs to reduce the number of projects subjected to detailed analysis is a screening process based on an answer to the question:

> "In terms of our corporate strategic plan, would this operation fit our future image of the firm?"

Only if there is an affirmative answer should the firm pursue a financial analysis of the project.

Within the area of traditional capital budgeting, most analysts recognize the presence in many projects of an option component. That is, a given project may produce knowledge, market position, or general skills which will permit the firm to invest in undefined and unquantified future projects at a later point. These projects, presumably desirable in a present value sense, represent the option component of the current project.

In fact, most firms concentrate their efforts in particular areas, and do not consider all feasible projects, but only projects which are in some way related to a more general conceptual model of what the firm is and intends to be. Thus, the *operational strategy* for seeking and for screening projects will depend on a series of heuristic decision rules for evaluating the general nature of projects, and for reducing the range of possible projects which are geographically or operationally related to existing operations; the range of the search is expanded only as current options are perceived as incapable of achieving the general goals of the firm.

In this part of the chapter, we shall review a possible set of screening devices—the organizing heuristics which might be used to reduce the raw number of projects. These heuristics are really measures for classifying projects on various attributes (for example, product type or country risk), using crude indices which are then combined. The most desirable global strategies are then selected for a more refined and detailed analysis, ultimately producing the general expansion strategy for the firm.

Many of the factors considered in the decision to invest abroad have been reviewed in the preceding chapters. Some of these factors were related to economic considerations, such as market structure. Other factors were related to the fashion in which business firms make decisions. In this section we attempt to unify these considerations into a simple framework that may be useful to the financial manager evaluating investment proposals. Only the skeleton of the analysis is given, but the specific details of any situation should be placed easily in this analytical construct. The approach consists of three steps:

1. Statement of alternative strategies according to specific criteria
2. Evaluation of each strategy in terms of risk and return
3. Selection of the strategy or combination of strategies that suits management's preferences and capabilities

Statement of Alternative Strategies

In order to limit the number of product and country combinations that a multinational company will consider, it can develop a series of criteria to select alternative strategies. These criteria could be designed by the managers who are acquainted with the characteristics that make a strategy worthy of further consideration. We will discuss three criteria: (1) product life cycle stage, (2) market characteristics, and (3) replacement versus expansionary projects.

Using *product life cycle stages* as a criterion, Stobaugh (1969) classifies countries according to market size, investment climate, availability of local resources, and distance to major producing centers. Products, in turn, are classified according to freight costs, economies of scale in production, and consumers' needs for the products. Under this scheme, a table is prepared containing an index number for each product in each country. The strategies implied by this table are usually based on expanding operations into those products and countries where the index numbers are high and where the competitors are not yet established.

One way of using *market characteristics* to select strategies would be to classify the products according to potential market growth and present market penetration. This decision rule will select products in those countries where a large market share is held or where promising growth exists. An alternative way to use market characteristics is to classify products according to income or price elasticity and to favor those countries where income levels are such that the product has the best chance to enjoy a large market.

A *replacement-expansion* approach to selecting potential strategies divides investments into those which represent replacement of old projects (for example, a plant to substitute a fully depreciated one) and those which involve an expansion. This latter group could be subdivided into projects which are expansions of old ideas and those which are entirely new ideas. Again, a table of index numbers could indicate relative desirability of projects.

The objective of the exercise of screening the company's products and the world according to certain criteria is to derive a list of strategies (combinations of products and countries) which management can evaluate. A composite index might be created by summing the weighted index scores of each country-product combination for all the tables. The index numbers of some of these combinations will further reduce the number of strategies that management considers. Hence, a reduced composite score for countries and products might suggest the family of strategies for final review.

Strategy Evaluation

Traditional financial theory evaluates projects along two dimensions: return and risk. In this context, risk has usually been measured by the size of the standard deviation of the return of the project before financing considerations.[4] Once management has decided upon a reduced number of strategies (combinations of products and countries) it wishes to consider further, it estimates the return and the risk associated with each of those strategies or combinations of strategies. Alternatively, if management does not wish to prepare a full risk evaluation for each broad strategy or potential product-country offering, it may attach a premium or discount to the return required from each strategy. Suppose the required return in traditional investments domestically is 15%. If the project is a new product in a less developed country (LDC), the required return may be raised to 26%. Once these adjustments are determined, they could be presented in the tabular form of Exhibit 17.1. For any given proposal, the adjustment to the required rate is taken from the table. For the example of the new product in an LDC, if it has low income elasticity of demand, high growth, a large market, and a stable government, then the premium is +4 +2 +3 +2, or 11% for a total required return of 26%.

This analysis assumes simple additive relationships for risk, although a correlation among various risks is presumed to exist. For example, in every case the premium requested for political instability is higher when the product has a low income elasticity or a low growth potential. The rationalization for this assignment of required premiums may be that management believes that, regardless of the overall political stability of the country, local authorities are more likely to interfere with the operations of a foreign-owned plant producing staple commodities with low income elasticity in a stagnant economy of low growth

EXHIBIT 17.1 Increases in Return Required to Adjust for Risk

		PRODUCT							
		NEW				OLD			
		Income Elasticity		Growth Potential		Income Elasticity		Growth Potential	
Country		High	Low	High	Low	High	Low	High	Low
Less Developed Countries									
Effective	Large	+2	+4	+2	+4	+1	+3	+1	+3
market size	Small	+4	+6	+4	+6	+3	+5	+3	+5
Political	High	+5	+8	+5	+8	+5	+7	+5	+7
instability	Low	+2	+3	+2	+3	+1	+2	+1	+2
Developed Countries									
Effective	Large	+1	+3	+1	+3	0	+1	0	+1
market size	Small	+2	+4	+2	+4	+1	+2	+1	+2
Local	High	+2	+4	+2	+4	+1	+2	+1	+2
competition	Low	+2	+3	+2	+3	0	+1	0	+1

---

[4]This measure of risk refers to *total risk*. Under the capital asset pricing model, the relevant risk is only that portion of total risk that is linked to the covariability of the asset with some market, as discussed in Chapter 16.

potential than with the operations of a plant producing a product with the opposite characteristics. This is a crude approach to the assessment of these premiums. More sophisticated mathematical approaches are easy to envision once the basic concept is accepted. The output of this analysis will be a quick screening of proposed strategies which can be used in the appraisal process for major product lines in different lands by a decentralized firm.

CORPORATE STRATEGY AND THE DECISION
TO INVEST ABROAD

The management of a company will decide which critical variables should be represented in the rows and columns of Exhibit 17.1. In any case, each combination of product and country could be described either by two variables, the expected return and its standard deviation, or by the premium figures in the table that reflect adjustments to desired return for risk.

Selection of a Strategy

The final step is for management to relate these choices to what they want the company to be in the future. In Exhibit 17.1 each entry was considered to be independent of every other entry when the evaluation was made. However, management may find it can reduce the average risk by combining some strategies. At this point, *constraints* imposed on the company as a whole must be brought to bear. One such constraint may be the percentage of earnings tolerated as subject to repatriation controls before the capitalization rate of the stock is penalized. Other constraints that management might want to introduce at this level are the availability of management resources and various qualitative considerations such as contribution to the development of other countries or of management itself.

Finally, an appropriate variable to be introduced at this point is *size*. Once management has decided upon the appropriate mix of products and countries for a certain budget size, the next step is to repeat the process for the next budget size. The outcome of this analysis might be the choice of a similar strategy with a comparable risk-return configuration. Alternatively, management might choose a strategy which produces a risk-return balance different from the previous budget size. Each of these strategies for each budget size can be plotted in a diagram as shown in Exhibit 17.2. A simplified final table of options described according to the risk-return characteristics could be completed as in Exhibit 17.3.

EXHIBIT 17.2   Risk-Return-Budget Size Evaluation

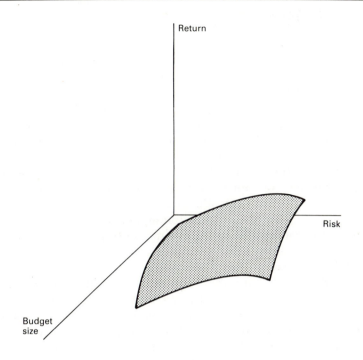

EXHIBIT 17.3   Comparative Budgets: Summary Results[a]

Country	BUDGET 1 Products $(1, \ldots, M)$			
Developed	$R^1_{11}\ \sigma^1_{11}$	$R^1_{12}\ \sigma^1_{12}$	$\cdots$	$R^1_{1M}\ \sigma^1_{1M}$
LDC	$R^1_{21}\ \sigma^1_{21}$	$R^1_{22}\ \sigma^1_{22}$	$\cdots$	$R^1_{2M}\ \sigma^1_{2M}$

Country	BUDGET 2 Products $(1, \ldots, M)$			
Developed	$R^2_{11}\ \sigma^2_{11}$	$R^2_{12}\ \sigma^2_{12}$	$\cdots$	$R^2_{1M}\ \sigma^2_{1M}$
LDC	$R^2_{21}\ \sigma^2_{21}$	$R^2_{22}\ \sigma^2_{22}$	$\cdots$	$R^2_{2M}\ \sigma^2_{2M}$

Country	BUDGET N Products $(1, \ldots, M)$			
Developed	$R^N_{11}\ \sigma^N_{11}$	$R^N_{12}\ \sigma^N_{12}$	$\cdots$	$R^N_{1M}\ \sigma^N_{1M}$
LDC	$R^N_{21}\ \sigma^N_{21}$	$R^N_{22}\ \sigma^N_{22}$	$\cdots$	$R^N_{2M}\ \sigma^N_{2M}$

[a] For R^k_{ij} and σ^k_{ij}, i is a Developed (1) or LDC (2) environment, j is a Product (1 through M), and k is a Budget level (1 through N).

SUMMARY

Certain organizational and behavioral theories discuss the motivation of managers in the corporate decision process, such as the goals-expectations-choice trichotomy of *A Behavioral Theory of the Firm*. This theory can be extended to the capital budgeting process to include such concepts as the impact of multiple levels on the decision process, the bilateral bargaining between the sponsor of the project and the managers responsible for its approval, the influence of uncertainty on the goals of the firm, the variety of motivations for the search process, and the impact of the Pollyanna-Nietzsche effect in which uncertainty is forgotten after a decision is made.

In suggesting an operational strategy for the firm to employ in its decision, we introduced an index evaluation of projects on various criteria. The index might include variables such as the income elasticity and growth potential of new or old products, the market size, the political risk, and so forth. An initial screening is based on the product life cycle, general market evaluations, financing strategies, or whether the investments are replacement or expansion proposals. The variations in these outcomes for various budget sizes are reviewed. When these screenings are completed, management can review the mean return and variability of return for the final sets of projects, considering them in more detail after this initial filtering process. Thus, the broadest strategy seeks screening rules which will preclude detailed analysis of many projects, yet include the most desirable projects, especially those which possess a large option component in the sense of providing benefits to the firm in the form of future possible projects derived as a result of investing in today's project.

QUESTIONS

1. Explain the product life cycle as applied to foreign investment decisions. How would you restate this cycle in terms of *A Behavioral Theory of the Firm* concepts?

2. How might an entrepreneur differ from a corporate manager in motivation to establish international operations? What does the lack of concentrated stock ownership in the hands of management suggest about the motivations of the corporate managers in U.S. firms?

3. "They have cheaper wage rates than we do. Therefore, they can undersell us in everything. We must have tariffs or quotas to limit the amount of foreign imports." What economic concepts are ignored in this objection?

4. How do relatively cheap capital in one nation and relatively cheap labor in another nation affect the allocation of industry between them? What does the international mobility of capital suggest for your conclusion?

5. The auto industry is often cited as an example of an oligopolistic industry. If true, what would this structure suggest for the international movements of the firms? Does this conclusion seem to occur?

BIBLIOGRAPHY

Aharoni, Yair, *The Foreign Investment Decision Process.* Boston, Mass.: Graduate School of Business Administration, Harvard University, 1966.

Banker, Pravin, "You're the Best Judge of Foreign Risks," *Harvard Business Review,* March-April, 1983, pp. 157–165.

Bhattacharya, Anindya K., *Foreign Trade and International Development.* Lexington, Mass.: D. C. Heath and Company, 1976.

Carter, E. Eugene, "The Behavioral Theory of the Firm and Top-Level Corporate Decisions," *Administrative Science Quarterly,* Dec. 1971, pp. 413–28.

———, *Portfolio Aspects of Corporate Capital Budgeting.* Lexington, Mass.: D. C. Heath and Company, 1974.

Caves, Richard E., "International Corporations: The Industrial Economics of Foreign Investment," *Economica,* Feb. 1971, pp. 1–27.

Daniels, John D., *Recent Foreign Direct Manufacturing Investment in the United States: An Interview Study of the Decision Process.* New York: Praeger Special Studies, Praeger Publishers, 1971.

England, George W., and Raymond Lee, "Organizational Goals and Expected Behavior among American, Japanese, and Korean Managers—A Comparative Study," *Academy of Management Journal,* Dec. 1971, pp. 425–38.

Fatemi, Nasrollah S., Gail W. Williams, and Thibaut DeSaint-Phalle, *Multinational Corporation,* 2nd ed. New York: A. S. Barnes and Co., 1976.

Gale, Bradley T., "Market Share and Rate of Return," *Review of Economics and Statistics,* Dec. 1972, pp. 412–23.

Hennart, Jean-Francois A., *Theory of Multinational Enterprise.* Ann Arbor, Michigan, University of Michigan Press, 1982.

Hymer, Stephen, "The Efficiency (Contradictions) of Multinational Corporations," *American Economic Review,* May 1970, pp. 441–48.

————, "The International Operations of National Firms: A Study of Direct Investment." Doctoral dissertation, Massachusetts Institute of Technology, Cambridge, Mass., 1960, published by MIT Press, Cambridge, Mass., 1976.

Knickerbocker, F. T., *Oligopolistic Reaction and Multinational Enterprise.* Boston, Mass.: Graduate School of Business Administration, Harvard University, 1973.

Kravis, Irving B., and Robert E. Lipsey, "The Location of Overseas Production and Production for Export by U.S. Multinational Firms," *Journal of International Economics,* May 1982, pp. 201–223.

Mazzolini, Renato, "Creating Europe's Multinationals: The International Merger Route," *Journal of Business,* Jan. 1975, pp. 39–51.

————, "Behavioral and Strategic Obstacles to European Transnational Concentration," *Columbia Journal of World Business,* Summer 1973, pp. 68–78.

Meeker, Guy B., "Face-Out Joint Venture: Can It Work for Latin America?" *Inter-American Economic Affairs,* Spring 1971, pp. 25–42.

Nehemkis, Peter, "Business Payoffs Abroad: Rhetoric and Reality," *California Management Review,* Winter 1975, pp. 5–20.

Polk, Judd, et al., *U.S. Production Abroad and the Balance of Payments.* New York: National Industrial Conference Board, 1966.

Root, Franklin R., *International Trade and Investment,* Part Four, 4th ed. Cincinnati, Ohio: South-Western Publishing Co., 1978.

Stobaugh, Robert, "Where in the World Should We Put That Plant?" *Harvard Business Review,* Jan.–Feb. 1969, pp. 129–36.

Stonehill, Arthur, et al., "Financial Goals and Debt Ratio Determination: A Survey of Practice in Five Countries," *Financial Management,* Autumn 1975, pp. 27–41.

Tsurumi, Yoshi, "Japan's Challenge to the U.S.: Industrial Policies and Corporate Strategies," *Columbia Journal of World Business,* Summer 1982, pp. 87–95.

Vernon, Raymond, "International Investment and International Trade in the Product Life Cycle," *Quarterly Journal of Economics,* May 1966, pp. 190–207.

————, ed., *The Product Life Cycle and International Trade.* Boston, Mass.: Division of Research, Harvard Business School, 1972.

Wells, Louis, "Text of a Product Cycle Model of International Trade: U.S. Exports of Consumer Durables," *Quarterly Journal of Economics,* Feb. 1969, pp. 152–62.

Wilkins, Mira, *The Maturing of Multinational Enterprise: American Business Abroad from 1914 to 1970.* Cambridge, Mass.: Harvard University Press, 1974.

Yoshihara, Kunio, *Sogo Shosha: The Vanguard of the Japanese Economy.* Oxford: Oxford University Press, 1982.

Glossary[1]

Acceptance. See *bankers' acceptance.*

Accommodating Accounts. In the balance of payments, those accounts that for analytical purposes can be considered triggered by the need to finance other transactions included in the balance of payments. Also called *compensating* or *financing accounts.*

Account Party. The party whose bank issues a letter of credit—usually the buyer.

Accounting Exposure. See *balance sheet exposure, transaction exchange gain or loss,* and *translation exchange gain or loss.*

Accrual System. Accounting system in which the returns and costs are reported when legally incurred rather than when the cash flow associated with the receipt or the payment materializes.

Advising Bank. A correspondent of an issuing bank that notifies the beneficiary of a letter of credit without adding its own engagement to that of the issuing bank.

---

[1]Some of these legal definitions are based on citations of Robert N. Corley and William J. Robert, *Principles of Business Law,* 11th ed. (Englewood Cliffs, N.J.: Prentice-Hall, Inc., 1979).

Agent. A person authorized to act for another (a principal). The term may apply to a person in the service of another, but in the strict sense an agent is one who stands in place of the principal. If A works for B as a secretary, he is a servant in the legal sense, but he may also be an agent. If A takes orders for B, he acts in place of B and is an agent.

Annuity. In law, a sum of money paid yearly to a person during his or her lifetime. It arises by a contract under which the recipient or another person deposits funds with the grantor. The grantor then returns a designated portion of the principal and interest in periodic payments upon the arrival of the beneficiary at a designated age. In general, an annuity is payment of a flat sum of money over a specific period of time.

Arbitrage. Transactions made to take advantage of temporary imperfections in the market. For example, if one could buy potatoes for 20¢/lb in one market and sell them for 25¢/lb in another, one could make a profit of 5¢/lb through arbitrage. An arbitrage transaction does not involve any risk. Because contracts are made, the returns derived from the transaction are known from the beginning, even though part of the transaction may take place in the future. Also see *space arbitrage* and *covered-interest arbitrage*.

Ask Price. The price at which a trader giving a quote is willing to sell a given item. Also called *offer price*.

Assignment. The transfer of a right, usually arising from a contract. Such rights are called "choses in action." A sells and assigns his or her contract right to purchase B's Plymouth convertible to C. A is an assignor. C is an assignee. The transfer is an assignment.

Autonomous Accounts. In the balance of payments, those accounts that for analytical purposes can be considered motivated purely by economic considerations rather than by the need to finance international transactions.

Bailment. The delivery of personal property (as opposed to real property) to another for a special purpose. Such delivery is made under a contract, either expressed or implied, that the property shall be redelivered to the bailor or placed at his or her disposal upon the completion of the special purpose. A loans B his horse. A places a watch with B for repair. A places her furniture in B's warehouse. A places her securities in B's bank safety deposit vault. In each case A is a bailor and B is a bailee.

Balance in Invisibles. In the balance of payments, the balance of the service accounts.

Balance of Indebtedness. Financial statement prepared for a given country summarizing the levels of assets and liabilities that the country has vis-à-vis the rest of the world. Also known as the *investment position* of the country.

Balance of Payments. Financial statement prepared for a given country summarizing the flow of goods, services, and funds between the residents of the country and the residents of the rest of the world during a certain period of time. The balance of payments is prepared by using the concept of double-entry bookkeeping, in which the total of debits equals the total of credits or the total sources of funds equal the total uses of funds.

Balance Sheet Exposure. Various forms of accounting exposure which differ as to which assets and liabilities are translated at historic rates (unexposed) and which accounts are translated at current rates (exposed). "Exposure" is the net balance sheet exposure of assets minus liabilities which are translated at current rates. See also *exposure to foreign exchange risk.*

Bankers' Acceptance. When a draft has been accepted by a bank, and the bank guarantees that payment will be made at some date in the future, that certified draft is called a bankers' acceptance. It may be traded freely among other parties, and the bank will pay the party that submits the draft to it at maturity.

Banking Day. That part of any day on which a bank is open to the public for carrying on substantially all of its banking functions. (Article 4 of the U.C.C.: Bank Deposits and Collections)

Basic Balance. In the balance of payments, the net balance of the flow in trade of goods and services, unilateral transfers, and long-term capital.

Bearer. The person in possession of an instrument, document of title, or security payable to bearer or indorsed in blank (with no name or order following the indorsement).

Beneficiary. The party in whose favor a letter of credit is issued—usually the seller.

Bid Price. The price at which a trader giving a quote is willing to purchase a given item.

Bill of Lading. A record of the shiping of goods from a transporter confirming the receipt of goods for shipment and means of transportation. The general term *bill of lading* is used for marine and surface transport. The term *airbill* is usually used for air shipments.

Blocked Funds. Funds which cannot be repatriated because the local monetary authorities forbid conversion into foreign exchange.

Bond. A promise under seal to pay money. The term is generally used to designate the promise made by a corporation, either public or private, to pay money to the bearer. Bonds also can be issued by governments. U.S. government bonds; Rock Island Railroad bonds.

Capital Account. In the balance of payments, the section that records the changes in financial assets and liabilities. The capital account is divided into two major sections: long-term flows and short-term flows.

Capital Structure. The combination of long-term debt and various types of equity in the financing of the firm.

Cash System. Accounting system in which only cash flows are reported, independent of when the obligations are contracted.

Cashier's Check. A bill of exchange drawn by the cashier of a bank, for the bank, upon the bank. The drawer bank cannot put a "stop order" against itself after the check is delivered or issued to the payee or holder.

Collateral. Security placed with a creditor to assure the performance of the obligator. If the obligation is satisfied, the collateral is returned by the creditor. A owes B $1,000. To secure the payment, A places with B a $5,000 certificate of stock in X Company. The $5,000 certificate is called *collateral*.

Collecting Bank. Any bank handling an item for collection except the payor bank. (Article 4 of the U.C.C.: Bank Deposits and Collections)

Commission. The sum of money, interest, brokerage, compensation, or allowance given to a factor or broker for carrying on the business of his or her principal.

Compensating Accounts. See *accommodating accounts*.

Condition. A clause in a contract that has the effect of investing or divesting the legal rights and duties of the parties to the contract. .

Confirming Bank. A correspondent bank that adds its own engagement to that of the issuing bank in a letter of credit guaranteeing that the credit will be honored by the issuer or a third bank.

Consignee. A person to whom a shipper directs a carrier to deliver goods, generally the buyer.

Consignment. The delivery, sending, or transferring of property ("goods, wares, and merchandise") into the possession of another, usually for the purpose of sale. Consignment may be a bailment or an agency for sale.

Consortia Bank. A more or less permanent group of banks whose objective is to provide joint financing to customers.

Convertible Eurobond. A Eurobond that can be converted into equity of the issuing company under prescribed conditions.

Convertibility. In foreign exchange, the ability to convert one currency into another.

Correspondent Bank. A bank that in its own country handles the business of a foreign bank. There are also domestic correspondents in different areas of the same country.

Cost of Capital. In corporate finance, the weighted rate of return expected by various parties financing the firm. The return that bondholders expect is the market interest rate on the debt. The return that equity holders expect is a function of dividends received and capital gains as the stock appreciates in value, adjusted for risk. The weights used to combine these rates of return are the proportions that each of these sources of funds contributes to the capitalization of the firm. The cost of capital traditionally is used as a hurdle rate that projects must yield as a minimum in order to be accepted by the firm.

Covenant.   A promise in writing. It is often used as a substitute for the word contract. There are covenants (promises) in deeds, leases, mortgages, and other instruments under seal and in unsealed instruments such as insurance policies and conditional sale contracts.

Covered-Interest Arbitrage.   A process of borrowing a currency, converting it into another currency where it is invested, and selling this other currency for future delivery against the initial currency. The profits in this transaction are derived from discrepancies between interest differentials and the percentage discounts or premiums among the currencies involved in the forward transaction.

Covering.   The generation of cash flows in a given currency in the money market or in the forward exchange market at predetermined rates with the purpose of matching the cash flows generated by operations in that currency. The purpose of covering is to make cash inflows equal cash outflows for the given currency for specified maturities. This produces a *square position*. Covering usually refers to trade transactions that produce a payable or a receivable in foreign exchange to be liquidated at a future date. The covering transaction eliminates the risk of fluctuations in foreign exchange rates during the intervening period. *Covering* and *hedging* are terms often used interchangeably. See also *hedging*.

Credit Entry in Balance of Payments.   The part of an international transaction that represents a source of funds or international purchasing power to the country reporting the balance of payments. A credit entry reflects a decrease in the holdings of foreign assets owned by local residents or an increase in the liabilities to foreigners owed by the residents of the reporting country.

Credit Tranche.   The amount that a member country of the International Monetary Fund can borrow from the fund over the gold tranche.

Cross Rate.   The calculation of a foreign exchange rate from two separate quotes that contain the same currency. For example, if one has the rate of French francs per U.S. dollar and the rate of German marks per U.S. dollar, one can then calculate the cross rate between French francs and German marks.

Current Account.   In the balance of payments, the section that records the trade in goods and services and the exchange of gifts among countries.

Customer.   As used in letters of credit, a customer is a buyer or other person who causes credit to be issued. The term also refers to a bank which procures issuance or confirmation on behalf of that bank's customer.

Debit Entry in Balance of Payments.   The part of an international transaction that represents a use of funds or international purchasing power to the country reporting the balance of payments. A debit entry reflects an increase in the holdings of foreign assets owned by local residents or a decrease in the liabilities owed to foreigners by the residents of the reporting country. Debit entries are usually preceded by minus signs in balance of payments tables.

Depository Bank. The first bank to which an item for collection is transferred, which may also be the payor bank.

Direct Investment. Purchase of a foreign financial asset in which substantial involvement in the management of the foreign operation is presumed. In practice, it is any equity holding that represents more than 10% ownership of the foreign firm.

Discount Rate. (1) In capital budgeting analysis, the rate which is applied to future cash flows to bring them to a present value. (2) In trade terms, the rate which is applied to a non–interest-bearing note which can be translated into a rate for early payment of the note. Thus, a note payable at face in 6 months might sell for 2% less than its face amount, implying an annual rate of 4%. (3) In foreign exchange markets, the difference between the forward and the spot rate.

Document of Title. This term includes bill of lading, dock warrant, dock receipt, warehouse receipt, order for the delivery of goods, and any other document which in the regular course of business or financing is treated as adequate evidence that the person in possession of it is entitled to receive, hold, and dispose of the document and the goods it covers.

Documentary Draft. A draft the honor of which is conditioned upon the presentation of a document or documents. *Document* means any paper including document of title, security, invoice, certificate, notice of default, and the like. Also referred to as a *documentary demand for payment.*

Draft. An order to pay. A check is one form of a draft.

Drawee Bank. The bank upon which a draft is drawn. Also called *paying bank.*

Edge Act Corporations. Financial institutions incorporated in the United States under the Edge Act. Edge Act corporations are owned by commercial banks and restrict their income mostly to foreign sources. The major advantage a commercial bank achieves in establishing an Edge Act corporation is to be able to conduct abroad some activities which are forbidden to U.S. banks.

Efficient Market. A market in which equilibrium conditions prevail, in which there are sufficiently large numbers of buyers and sellers to prohibit any incentive for arbitrage transactions, and in which the tradeoffs between return and risk are fully equilibrated.

Elasticity. Elasticity measures the degree of responsiveness in one variable to changes in another variable. For example, the price elasticity of exports might measure the degree of responsiveness in exports to changes in prices; the income elasticity of imports might measure the degree of responsiveness in imports to changes in income.

Eurobond. Bond underwritten by an international syndicate and sold mostly outside the country of the currency in which it is denominated.

Eurocurrency. Monies traded outside the countries where they are the domestic currencies. For example, Eurodollars are U.S. dollars traded outside the United States.

Exchange Rate. The price of one currency expressed in terms of another currency.

Exposure to Foreign Exchange Risk. The amount of a person's or business's holdings that is not denominated in the domestic currency and whose value will fluctuate if foreign exchange rates vary. Also see *balance sheet exposure.*

Financing Accounts. See *accommodating accounts.*

Fixed Currency. A currency whose official value relative to gold and other currencies is maintained by a central bank. The bank intervenes to buy and to sell the currency when it deviates from the official value.

Floating Currency. A currency whose exchange rate relative to those of other currencies is allowed to fluctuate more or less freely. "Dirty floating" occurs if the central bank intervenes to keep the currency from deviating outside the country's desired range.

Floating Lending Rate. A lending rate that is established at a fixed number of percentage points above a given rate, such as the London interbank offered rate (LIBOR), and which is renegotiated periodically, often every 6 months. Renegotiation occurs throughout the life of the loan.

Floating Policy. An insurance policy that covers a class of goods located in a particular place that the insured had on hand at the time the policy was issued, but which—at the time of loss—may not be the identical items that were on hand at the time the policy was issued. A fire policy covering the inventory of a hardware store is an example.

Foreign Bond. Bond sold outside the country of the borrower but in the country of the currency in which the bond is denominated. The bond is underwritten by local institutions and is issued under the regulations prevalent in that country.

Foreign Exchange. Currency other than the one used internally in a given country.

Forward Rate. Foreign exchange rate for currency to be delivered at a future date.

Gold Tranche. The amount that each member country of the International Monetary Fund contributes in the form of gold as part of its membership quota in the Fund. This amount can be borrowed readily by the contributing country.

Guarantor. One who by contract undertakes "to answer for the debt, default, and miscarriage of another." In general, a guarantor undertakes to pay if the principal debtor does not.

Hedging. The generation of a position in a given currency in the money market or in the forward exchange market at predetermined rates with the purpose of matching the net position generated in that currency with the net exposure position of the business operations as evidenced by balance sheets. The purpose of hedging is to make the net position at a given date equal zero. The accounts included in the exposed balance sheet items are determined according to accounting rules. When balance sheet items are translated into specific cash flows in the future which the firm wishes to protect against fluctuations in exchange rates, the hedging transaction becomes a covering transaction. *Covering* and *hedging* are terms often used interchangeably. Also see *covering*.

Income Elasticity. See *elasticity*.

Indemnify. Literally, to save from harm. Thus, one person agrees to protect another against loss.

Indexing. In some nations the practice of adjusting mortgage or other debt issues by some measure of inflation to preserve the purchasing power of the debt in constant monetary units. In Brazil, indexing is applied to wages, business accounts, and all debt issues, a broader scope than that of most nations using indexing.

Indorsement. Writing one's name upon paper for the purpose of transferring the title. When a payee of a negotiable instrument writes his or her name on the back of the instrument, he or she is indorsing the instrument.

Inflation. The overall rate of increase in prices of a package of goods and services in a given country. This rate of increase may differ among different economic sectors.

Intermediary Bank. A bank to which an item is transferred in the course of collection other than the depository or payor bank. (Article 4 of the U.C.C.: Bank Deposits and Collections)

Issuing Bank. The bank that issues a letter of credit—usually the buyer's bank.

Leads and Lags. The practice of quickly moving funds into a given currency (lead) or delaying the movement of funds into a given currency (lag) with the objective of benefiting from expected changes in exchange rates.

Letter of Credit. An agreement sent from one party (usually a bank) to another concerning funds which will be made available upon completion of some business transactions. Usually, a buyer sends a letter of credit to the seller of goods when they are not known to each other. Upon certification of shipment of the goods in question and submission of a draft, the local bank will arrange for funds to be made available to the exporter. It is established and regulated within the scope of Article 5 of the U.C.C.: Letters of Credit.

Liability. In its broadest sense, the word means any obligation one may be under by some rule of law. It includes debt, duty, and responsibility.

Locking in a Rate. In a foreign exchange market, establishing the exchange rates at which inflows and outflows of a currency will take place at a given future time.

Long Position. Situation occurring when anticipated inflows of a currency exceed the anticipated outflows of that currency over a given period of time.

Marginal. Incremental unit. Units usually refer to costs or revenues.

Merger. Two corporations are merged when one corporation continues in existence and the other loses its identity by absorption. *Merger* must be distinguished from *consolidation,* by which both corporations are dissolved and a new one created to take over the assets of the dissolved corporations.

Multiplier. In monetary economics, the factor by which an initial deposit could grow through multiple loans after the initial monetary deposit. The multiplier is defined as the reciprocal of the reserve requirement adjusted for leakages in the system.

Mutuality. A word used to describe the fact that every contract must be binding on both parties. Each party to the contract must be bound to the other party to do something by virtue of the legal duty created.

Negligence. The failure to do that which an ordinary, reasonable, prudent person would do, or the doing of some act which an ordinary, prudent person would not do. Reference must always be made to the situation, the circumstances, and the knowledge of the parties.

Negotiating Bank. A bank chosen by the beneficiary when a letter of credit allows negotiation.

Net Effective Interest Rate or Yield. The yield in a given currency adjusted for changes in the exchange rates.

Net Exchange Position. A net asset or liability position in a given currency. This is the term commonly used by exchange traders. Also called a *net long or short position*.

Net Exposure Position. See *balance sheet exposure.*

Net Present Value. The value in current dollars when future receipts and outlays are discounted at some rate.

Nominal Interest Rate. The interest rate specified to be paid on the face amount borrowed. In a bond the nominal rate is the coupon rate. The actual amount of funds borrowed may be more or less than the face amount, thus changing the net yield of the funds involved. See also *yield.*

Numeraire. The standard which is used for measurement. In international corporate finance this refers to the currency chosen by the firm as reference against which all other currency cash flows are measured.

Obligee. A creditor or promisee.

Obligor. A debtor or promisor.

Offer Price. The price at which a trader giving a quote is willing to sell a given item. Also called *ask price.*

Outright Forward Rate. Forward exchange rate expressed in terms of the amount of one currency required to buy a unit of another currency.

Par Value. Under the Bretton Woods system, the value of a currency measured in terms of gold or the U.S. dollar, which was maintained at a fixed rate relative to gold.

Paying Bank.   The bank on which a draft is drawn. Also called *drawee bank*.

Payor Bank.   A bank by which an item is payable as drawn or accepted. (Article 4 of the U.C.C.: Bank Deposits and Collections)

Pledge.   The deposit or placing of personal property as security for a debt or other obligation with a person called a *pledgee*. The pledgee has the implied power to sell the property if the debt is not paid. If the debt is paid, the right to possession returns to the pledgor.

Points.   In foreign exchange markets, the amount of premium or discount in the forward price from the spot price. A point is a unit of a decimal, usually the fourth place to the right of the decimal point. Which decimal place is implied varies from currency to currency.

Portfolio Investment.   Purchase of a foreign financial asset with the sole purpose of deriving the returns that the security provides without intervening in the management of the foreign operation.

Preferred Stock.   Stock that entitles the holder to dividends from earnings before the owners of common stock can receive dividends.

Presenting Bank.   Any bank presenting an item except a payor bank. (Article 4 of the U.C.C.: Bank Deposits and Collections)

Price Elasticity.   See *elasticity*.

Rate of Return.   In capital budgeting, that discount rate for which the cash inflows can be discounted to equal the discounted cash outflows, i.e., where the net present value is zero.

Reinsurance.   Under a contract of reinsurance, one insurance company agrees to indemnify another insurance company in whole or in part against risks which the first company has assumed.

Remitting Bank.   Any payor or intermediary bank remitting for an item. (Article 4 of the U.C.C.: Bank Deposits and Collections)

Reserve Accounts.   In the balance of payments, the accounts reflecting the changes in the amount of resources that the government of the country has at its disposal to settle international payments. These resources are composed of gold and foreign currency which is fully convertible into other currencies, such as the U.S. dollar.

Revolver.   A loan with floating rates where not only the rates but also the amounts (within the limits of a given line of credit) are renegotiated periodically.

Revolving Loan.   See *revolver*.

Risk Analysis.   Study of the various outcomes under different assumptions and under different probabilities that each of these outcomes will take place.

Safe Harbors.   Rules set in legislation which, if met, guarantee special (favorable) treatment to the party. Thus, a taxpayer who meets certain requirements may have a lower tax rate even though other taxpayers might conceivably win the favorable treatment as well when they did not meet the same requirements. Safe habors are sufficient, but not necessary, qualification.

Satisfaction. The release and discharge of a legal obligation. Satisfaction may be partial or full performance of the obligation. The word is used with *accord,* which means a promise to give a substituted performance for a contract obligation; satisfaction means the acceptance by the obligee of such performance.

SDRs. Special Drawing Rights. Money created by the International Monetary Fund with the approval of a large majority of member countries and distributed among all member countries. This paper money is used only in transactions among governments and between governments and the IMF.

Security. Security may be bonds, stocks, and other property placed by a debtor with a creditor, with power to sell if the debt is not paid. The plural of the term, *securities,* is used broadly to mean tangible items such as promissory notes, bonds, stocks, and other vendible obligations.

Settle. To pay in cash, by a clearing house settlement, in a charge or credit, by remittance, or as otherwise instructed. A settlement may be either provisional or final. (Article 4 of the U.C.C.: Banks Deposits and Collections)

Short Position. Situation in which anticipated outflows of a currency exceed the anticipated inflows of that currency over a given period of time.

Simulation. Analytical technique in which outcomes are estimated under alternative sets of assumptions.

Space Arbitrage. The purchase of a currency in a given market accompanied by a sale of that currency in another market where it commands a higher price.

Speculative Transaction. A transaction in which the eventual net return or cost is not known in advance. In international finance, the major sources of speculative risk occur when the transaction produces a net asset or liability position in a given currency and when the cash inflows and outflows in a given currency are not matched according to maturity.

Spot Rate. Foreign exchange rate for currency delivered within 2 days.

Spread. The difference between the bid and ask prices in a price quote.

Square Position. Position when the cash inflows match the cash outflows in a given currency for a certain date or period of time.

Swap Position. Position when a given currency is simultaneously purchased and sold, but the maturity of each of the transactions is different.

Swap Rate. Forward exchange rates expressed in terms of premiums or discounts from the spot rate.

Tax Haven. A country that imposes little or no tax or withholding on the profits from transactions carried on that country, especially on income from dividends and interest.

Terminal Rate of Return. Internal rate of return when the net cash flows produced by the project during its life are assumed to be reinvested at a predetermined rate of return.

Terms of Trade. The ratio of export prices to import prices. Export and import prices in this ratio are each aggregated and combined into a sum for which the total in a given year equals 1,000.

Transaction Exchange Gain or Loss. The increase (gain) or decrease (loss) in a cash flow because the cash flow was denominated in another currency and the exchange rate between the two currencies changed.

Translation Exchange Gain or Loss. The foreign exchange gain or loss associated with the conversion (for financial consolidation) of the balance sheet expressed in another currency into the numeraire currency. The gain or loss arises when the exchange rate between the two currencies fluctuates and exposed assets do not equal exposed liabilities.

Trust Receipt. A document establishing that the borrower holds certain goods in trust for the lender.

U.C.C. Uniform Commercial Code.

Unilateral Transfers. In the balance of payments, the accounts that measure gifts sent in and out of the reporting country.

Value Date. Date when funds are to be received or paid according to a contract.

Withholding Tax. A tax collected by the source originating the income, in contrast to one paid by the recipient of the income after the funds are received. For example, a withholding tax on interest payments to foreigners means that the tax proceeds are deducted from the interest payment made to the lender and collected by the borrower on behalf of the government.

Yield. The amount of funds involved in interest payments as a percentage of the amount lent or borrowed; the present market price of a security in the currency of the instrument.

Present
Value
Tables

TABLE A Present Value of $1

Years Hence	1%	2%	4%	6%	8%	10%	12%	14%	15%	16%	18%	20%	22%	24%	25%	26%	28%	30%	35%	40%	45%	50%
1	0.990	0.980	0.962	0.943	0.926	0.909	0.893	0.877	0.870	0.862	0.847	0.833	0.820	0.806	0.800	0.794	0.781	0.769	0.741	0.714	0.690	0.667
2	0.980	0.961	0.925	0.890	0.857	0.826	0.797	0.769	0.756	0.743	0.718	0.694	0.672	0.650	0.640	0.630	0.610	0.592	0.549	0.510	0.476	0.444
3	0.971	0.942	0.889	0.840	0.794	0.751	0.712	0.675	0.658	0.641	0.609	0.579	0.551	0.524	0.512	0.500	0.477	0.455	0.406	0.364	0.328	0.296
4	0.961	0.924	0.855	0.792	0.735	0.683	0.636	0.592	0.572	0.552	0.516	0.482	0.451	0.423	0.410	0.397	0.373	0.350	0.301	0.260	0.226	0.198
5	0.951	0.906	0.822	0.747	0.681	0.621	0.567	0.519	0.497	0.476	0.437	0.402	0.370	0.341	0.328	0.315	0.291	0.269	0.223	0.186	0.156	0.132
6	0.942	0.888	0.790	0.705	0.630	0.564	0.507	0.456	0.432	0.410	0.370	0.335	0.303	0.275	0.262	0.250	0.227	0.207	0.165	0.133	0.108	0.088
7	0.933	0.871	0.760	0.665	0.583	0.513	0.452	0.400	0.376	0.354	0.314	0.279	0.249	0.222	0.210	0.198	0.178	0.159	0.122	0.095	0.074	0.059
8	0.923	0.853	0.731	0.627	0.540	0.467	0.404	0.351	0.327	0.305	0.266	0.233	0.204	0.179	0.168	0.157	0.139	0.123	0.091	0.068	0.051	0.039
9	0.914	0.837	0.703	0.592	0.500	0.424	0.361	0.308	0.284	0.263	0.225	0.194	0.167	0.144	0.134	0.125	0.108	0.094	0.067	0.048	0.035	0.026
10	0.905	0.820	0.676	0.558	0.463	0.386	0.322	0.270	0.247	0.227	0.191	0.162	0.137	0.116	0.107	0.099	0.085	0.073	0.050	0.035	0.024	0.017
11	0.896	0.804	0.650	0.527	0.429	0.350	0.287	0.237	0.215	0.195	0.162	0.135	0.112	0.094	0.086	0.079	0.066	0.056	0.037	0.025	0.017	0.012
12	0.887	0.788	0.625	0.497	0.397	0.319	0.257	0.208	0.187	0.168	0.137	0.112	0.092	0.076	0.069	0.062	0.052	0.043	0.027	0.018	0.012	0.008
13	0.879	0.773	0.601	0.469	0.368	0.290	0.229	0.182	0.163	0.145	0.116	0.093	0.075	0.061	0.055	0.050	0.040	0.033	0.020	0.013	0.008	0.005
14	0.870	0.758	0.577	0.442	0.340	0.263	0.205	0.160	0.141	0.125	0.099	0.078	0.062	0.049	0.044	0.039	0.032	0.025	0.015	0.009	0.006	0.003
15	0.861	0.743	0.555	0.417	0.315	0.239	0.183	0.140	0.123	0.108	0.084	0.065	0.051	0.040	0.035	0.031	0.025	0.020	0.011	0.006	0.004	0.002
16	0.853	0.728	0.534	0.394	0.292	0.218	0.163	0.123	0.107	0.093	0.071	0.054	0.042	0.032	0.028	0.025	0.019	0.015	0.008	0.005	0.003	0.002
17	0.844	0.714	0.513	0.371	0.270	0.198	0.146	0.108	0.093	0.080	0.060	0.045	0.034	0.026	0.023	0.020	0.015	0.012	0.006	0.003	0.002	0.001
18	0.836	0.700	0.494	0.350	0.250	0.180	0.130	0.095	0.081	0.069	0.051	0.038	0.028	0.021	0.018	0.016	0.012	0.009	0.005	0.002	0.001	0.001
19	0.828	0.686	0.475	0.331	0.232	0.164	0.116	0.083	0.070	0.060	0.043	0.031	0.023	0.017	0.014	0.012	0.009	0.007	0.003	0.002	0.001	0.001
20	0.820	0.673	0.456	0.312	0.215	0.149	0.104	0.073	0.061	0.051	0.037	0.026	0.019	0.014	0.012	0.010	0.007	0.005	0.002	0.001	0.001	
21	0.811	0.660	0.439	0.294	0.199	0.135	0.093	0.064	0.053	0.044	0.031	0.022	0.015	0.011	0.009	0.008	0.006	0.004	0.002	0.001		
22	0.803	0.647	0.422	0.278	0.184	0.123	0.083	0.056	0.046	0.038	0.026	0.018	0.013	0.009	0.007	0.006	0.004	0.003	0.001	0.001		
23	0.795	0.634	0.406	0.262	0.170	0.112	0.074	0.049	0.040	0.033	0.022	0.015	0.010	0.007	0.006	0.005	0.003	0.002	0.001	0.001		
24	0.788	0.622	0.390	0.247	0.158	0.102	0.066	0.043	0.035	0.028	0.019	0.013	0.008	0.006	0.005	0.004	0.003	0.002	0.001	0.001		
25	0.780	0.610	0.375	0.233	0.146	0.092	0.059	0.038	0.030	0.024	0.016	0.010	0.007	0.005	0.004	0.003	0.002	0.001	0.001			
26	0.772	0.598	0.361	0.220	0.135	0.084	0.053	0.033	0.026	0.021	0.014	0.009	0.006	0.004	0.003	0.002	0.002	0.001				
27	0.764	0.586	0.347	0.207	0.125	0.076	0.047	0.029	0.023	0.018	0.011	0.007	0.005	0.003	0.002	0.002	0.001	0.001				
28	0.757	0.574	0.333	0.196	0.116	0.069	0.042	0.026	0.020	0.016	0.010	0.006	0.004	0.002	0.002	0.002	0.001	0.001				
29	0.749	0.563	0.321	0.185	0.107	0.063	0.037	0.022	0.017	0.014	0.008	0.005	0.003	0.002	0.002	0.001	0.001	0.001				
30	0.742	0.552	0.308	0.174	0.099	0.057	0.033	0.020	0.015	0.012	0.007	0.004	0.003	0.002	0.001	0.001	0.001	0.001				
40	0.672	0.453	0.208	0.097	0.046	0.022	0.011	0.005	0.004	0.003	0.001	0.001										
50	0.608	0.372	0.141	0.054	0.021	0.009	0.003	0.001	0.001	0.001												

SOURCE: By permission from Robert N. Anthony, *Management Accounting: Text and Cases*, rev. ed. Homewood, Ill.: Richard D. Irwin, Inc. 1960.

TABLE B Present Value of $1 Received Annually for N Years

Years (N)	1%	2%	4%	6%	8%	10%	12%	14%	15%	16%	18%	20%	22%	24%	25%	26%	28%	30%	35%	40%	45%	50%
1	0.990	0.980	0.962	0.943	0.926	0.909	0.893	0.877	0.870	0.862	0.847	0.833	0.820	0.806	0.800	0.794	0.781	0.769	0.741	0.714	0.690	0.667
2	1.970	1.942	1.886	1.833	1.783	1.736	1.690	1.647	1.626	1.605	1.566	1.528	1.492	1.457	1.440	1.424	1.392	1.361	1.289	1.224	1.165	1.111
3	2.941	2.884	2.775	2.673	2.577	2.487	2.402	2.322	2.283	2.246	2.174	2.106	2.042	1.981	1.952	1.923	1.868	1.816	1.696	1.589	1.493	1.407
4	3.902	3.808	3.630	3.465	3.312	3.170	3.037	2.914	2.855	2.798	2.690	2.589	2.494	2.404	2.362	2.320	2.241	2.166	1.997	1.849	1.720	1.605
5	4.853	4.713	4.452	4.212	3.993	3.791	3.605	3.433	3.352	3.274	3.127	2.991	2.864	2.745	2.689	2.635	2.532	2.436	2.220	2.035	1.876	1.737
6	5.795	5.601	5.242	4.917	4.623	4.355	4.111	3.889	3.784	3.685	3.498	3.326	3.167	3.020	2.951	2.885	2.759	2.643	2.385	2.168	1.983	1.824
7	6.728	6.472	6.002	5.582	5.206	4.868	4.564	4.288	4.160	4.039	3.812	3.605	3.416	3.242	3.161	3.083	2.937	2.802	2.508	2.263	2.057	1.883
8	7.652	7.325	6.733	6.210	5.747	5.336	4.968	4.639	4.487	4.344	4.078	3.837	3.619	3.421	3.329	3.241	3.076	2.925	2.598	2.331	2.108	1.922
9	8.566	8.162	7.436	6.802	6.247	5.759	5.328	4.946	4.772	4.607	4.303	4.031	3.786	3.566	3.463	3.366	3.184	3.019	2.665	2.379	2.144	1.948
10	9.471	8.983	8.111	7.360	6.710	6.145	5.650	5.216	5.019	4.833	4.494	4.192	3.923	3.682	3.571	3.465	3.269	3.092	2.715	2.414	2.168	1.965
11	10.368	9.787	8.760	7.887	7.139	6.495	5.937	5.453	5.234	5.029	4.656	4.327	4.035	3.776	3.656	3.544	3.335	3.147	2.752	2.438	2.185	1.977
12	11.255	10.575	9.385	8.384	7.536	6.814	6.194	5.660	5.421	5.197	4.793	4.439	4.127	3.851	3.725	3.606	3.387	3.190	2.779	2.456	2.196	1.985
13	12.134	11.343	9.986	8.853	7.904	7.103	6.424	5.842	5.583	5.342	4.910	4.533	4.203	3.912	3.780	3.656	3.427	3.223	2.799	2.468	2.204	1.990
14	13.004	12.106	10.563	9.295	8.244	7.367	6.628	6.002	5.724	5.468	5.008	4.611	4.265	3.962	3.824	3.695	3.459	3.249	2.814	2.477	2.210	1.993
15	13.865	12.849	11.118	9.712	8.559	7.606	6.811	6.142	5.847	5.575	5.092	4.675	4.315	4.001	3.859	3.726	3.483	3.268	2.825	2.484	2.214	1.995
16	14.718	13.678	11.652	10.106	8.851	7.824	6.974	6.265	5.954	5.669	5.162	4.730	4.357	4.033	3.887	3.751	3.503	3.283	2.834	2.489	2.216	1.997
17	15.562	14.292	12.166	10.477	9.122	8.022	7.120	6.373	6.047	5.749	5.222	4.775	4.391	4.059	3.910	3.771	3.518	3.295	2.840	2.492	2.218	1.998
18	16.398	14.992	12.659	10.828	9.372	8.201	7.250	6.467	6.128	5.818	5.273	4.812	4.419	4.080	3.928	3.786	3.529	3.304	2.844	2.494	2.219	1.999
19	17.226	15.678	13.134	11.158	9.604	8.365	7.366	6.550	6.198	5.877	5.316	4.844	4.442	4.097	3.942	3.799	3.539	3.311	2.848	2.496	2.220	1.999
20	18.046	16.351	13.590	11.470	9.818	8.514	7.469	6.623	6.259	5.929	5.353	4.870	4.460	4.110	3.954	3.808	3.546	3.316	2.850	2.497	2.221	1.999
21	18.857	17.011	14.029	11.764	10.017	8.649	7.562	6.687	6.312	5.973	5.384	4.891	4.476	4.121	3.963	3.816	3.551	3.320	2.852	2.498	2.221	2.000
22	19.660	17.658	14.451	12.042	10.201	8.772	7.645	6.743	6.359	6.011	5.410	4.909	4.488	4.130	3.970	3.822	3.556	3.323	2.853	2.498	2.222	2.000
23	20.456	18.292	14.857	12.303	10.371	8.883	7.718	6.792	6.399	6.044	5.432	4.925	4.499	4.137	3.976	3.827	3.559	3.325	2.854	2.499	2.222	2.000
24	21.243	18.914	15.247	12.550	10.529	8.985	7.784	6.836	6.434	6.073	5.451	4.937	4.507	4.143	3.981	3.831	3.562	3.327	2.855	2.499	2.222	2.000
25	22.023	19.523	15.622	12.783	10.675	9.077	7.843	6.873	6.464	6.097	5.467	4.948	4.514	4.147	3.985	3.834	3.564	3.329	2.856	2.499	2.222	2.000
26	22.795	20.121	15.983	13.003	10.810	9.161	7.896	6.906	6.491	6.118	5.480	4.956	4.520	4.151	3.988	3.837	3.566	3.330	2.856	2.500	2.222	2.000
27	23.560	20.707	16.330	13.211	10.935	9.237	7.943	6.935	6.514	6.136	5.492	4.964	4.524	4.154	3.990	3.839	3.567	3.331	2.856	2.500	2.222	2.000
28	24.316	21.281	16.663	13.406	11.051	9.307	7.984	6.961	6.534	6.152	5.502	4.970	4.528	4.157	3.992	3.840	3.568	3.331	2.857	2.500	2.222	2.000
29	25.066	21.844	16.984	13.591	11.158	9.370	8.022	6.983	6.551	6.166	5.510	4.975	4.531	4.159	3.994	3.841	3.569	3.332	2.857	2.500	2.222	2.000
30	25.808	22.396	17.292	13.765	11.258	9.427	8.055	7.003	6.566	6.177	5.517	4.979	4.534	4.160	3.995	3.842	3.569	3.332	2.857	2.500	2.222	2.000
40	32.835	27.355	19.793	15.046	11.925	9.779	8.244	7.105	6.642	6.234	5.548	4.997	4.544	4.166	3.999	3.846	3.571	3.333	2.857	2.500	2.222	2.000
50	39.196	31.424	21.482	15.702	12.234	9.915	8.304	7.133	6.661	6.246	5.554	4.999	4.545	4.167	4.000	3.846	3.571	3.333	2.857	2.500	2.222	2.000

SOURCE: Same as Table A.

Index